ALL IN ONE

CRCP

Crystal Reports®
Certified Professional

EXAM GUIDE

Annette Harper

McGraw-Hill/Osborne

New York • Chicago • San Francisco • Lisbon
London • Madrid • Mexico City • Milan • New Delhi
San Juan • Seoul • Singapore • Sydney • Toronto

McGraw-Hill/Osborne
2100 Powell Street, 10th Floor
Emeryville, California 94608
U.S.A.

To arrange bulk purchase discounts for sales promotions, premiums, or fund-raisers, please contact **McGraw-Hill**/Osborne at the above address. For information on translations or book distributors outside the U.S.A., please see the International Contact Information page immediately following the index of this book.

CRCP Crystal Reports® Certified Professional All-in-One Exam Guide

1234567890 DOC DOC 0198765

Book p/n 0-07-225785-7 and CD p/n 0-07-225786-5
parts of
ISBN 0-07-225784-9

Project Editor Leslie Tilley	**Indexer** Jack Lewis
Acquisitions Coordinator Jessica Wilson	**Composition** Apollo Publishing Services, Dick Schwartz
Technical Editors Keith Boyer, Clark Timmins	**Illustrator** Sue Albert, Kathleen Edwards, Melinda Lytle
Copy Editor Leslie Tilley	**Series Design** Peter F. Hancik
Proofreader Linda Medoff	

This book was composed with Corel VENTURA™ Publisher.

For their forbearance; I dedicate this book to
my husband, Chris, the workaholic, who understands;
and to my daughter, Katie, the Art History major,
who does not understand but puts up with me anyway.

ABOUT THE AUTHOR

Annette Harper has worked with Crystal Reports for more than nine years in many different capacities. After 18 years in the corporate world, she started Sage Link, LLC, a consulting firm specializing in Crystal Reports and Oracle. She is the author of *Crystal Reports 9 on Oracle* (2003), also published by McGraw-Hill/Osborne. Annette holds several industry certifications in addition to the CRCP, including the Oracle Certified Professional DBA designation (OCP), the Oracle Certified Associate PL/SQL Developer designation (OCA), and the Certified Novell Engineer designation (CNE).

Annette's e-mail address is annette@sage-link.com. She encourages readers to contact her with any comments or questions about the book.

About the Technical Editor

Keith Boyer is the founder and chief operating officer of Data Management Group, a consulting firm focusing on business intelligence and custom web-based systems. He has also served as CEO of LANtech Solutions, a technical networking firm providing telecommunications and client-server solutions to organizations in the mid-Atlantic region. Keith is a CRCP- and CECP-certified consultant, trainer, and developer, and holds a degree in Computer Science/Information Systems from Point Park University in Pittsburgh.

About LearnKey

LearnKey provides self-paced learning content and multimedia delivery solutions to enhance personal skills and business productivity. LearnKey claims the largest library of rich streaming-media training content that engages learners in dynamic media-rich instruction complete with video clips, audio, full motion graphics, and animated illustrations. LearnKey can be found on the Web at http://www.LearnKey.com.

CONTENTS AT A GLANCE

CONTENTS

ACKNOWLEDGMENTS

My heartfelt thanks go to Leslie Tilley, who did not seem to mind making the same corrections to my text in chapter after chapter and whose eagle eye spotted my many inconsistencies, poorly worded sentences, and occasional complete gibberish. Clark Timmins read an early version of the book and made many valuable comments that I am sure have added greatly to its quality and use as a study guide. Keith Boyer had the unenviable job of technical editor. Thanks for making me look good, Keith.

Thanks to everyone at McGraw-Hill/Osborne. Thank you for your patience, Tim. Jessica, thanks for keeping everything organized and for not keeping track of how many times I forgot to attach the attachment.

INTRODUCTION

There are many different domains within information technology, and as each grows and matures, certain skills, experience, and knowledge become recognized as necessary for a professional in that domain. Soon, a certification program is born. The existence of the Crystal Reports Certified Professional (CRCP) designation is an indication that report development has reached a level of both complexity and value that justifies the cost of testing and certifying skilled practitioners.

Prior to the creation of the publicly available CRCP program, only Crystal Decisions partners could be certified Crystal Reports developers. Now independent consultants and reporting specialists employed in any business can attain certification to advance their careers.

The CRCP Exams

The CRCP is an industry standard certification program, meaning that it is based on exams given at independent, monitored testing centers and does not *require* that you attend any particular vendor courses. To obtain the CRCP designation, you must pass three exams: RDCR200, RDCR300, and RDCR400. RDCR300 comes in three versions, one for each of the three available electives. The majority of the exam is the same across all three versions, with approximately 10 to 20 percent of the questions coming from the elective material.

NOTE The predecessor to the CRCP was the Authorized Crystal Engineer (ACE) program, which required you to take a course and a test, both via the Web. The ACE was available for Crystal Reports 8.5 and 9. The CRCP is specific to version 10 of Crystal Reports, although there is much overlap with previous versions.

As the CRCP program continues to evolve, it will be increasingly important for current and aspiring IT professionals to have resources available to assist them with further education and exam preparation. At the time of publication, all the exam objectives have been posted on the Business Objects training and certification web site, and the beta exam process has been completed. For the most up-to-date information on Crystal Reports certification, visit the Business Objects certification page.

Why Get Certified?

Why should you seek certification? There are two basic reasons for going through the certification process. One is to advance your career. The other is to advance your knowledge.

I hope that these goals are complementary. Some IT folks believe that certification means nothing—that it does not prove you are an expert—because it is not equivalent to years of experience. If you know the product already, they feel, you will learn nothing from certification study.

I agree that certification does not prove you are an expert, but it does prove that you have the basic foundation of knowledge in the areas being tested. This, plus experience, *may* make you an expert, or it may not. That depends on your inherent abilities. Certification is one objective measure that employers or clients can use to compare prospective employees or consultants. If you have years of experience and are not certified, an employer is apt to wonder why. They are likely to use certification as their first filter and go on to more subjective comparisons afterwards.

My personal experience over many different certification programs has been that I always learn something new, whether or not I was already very experienced with an application. Just as there is no substitute for the knowledge gained by actually working with a product, there is also no substitute for the knowledge gained by formal study. There are always multiple ways to solve any particular reporting problem. If you do not know your application inside out, you will not have access to *all* of those methods.

Taking the Exams

The exams are given at Pearson VUE testing centers in major cities worldwide (in English only). You can register at http://www.pearsonvue.com/crystal (you must create a Pearson VUE web account to register online). You can take the exams on any date and at any time that is available for the exam center that you select. The test numbers are RDCR200A, RDCR300A (SQL Commands elective), RDCR300B (Complex Formulas elective), RDCR300C (OLAP elective), and RDCR400. Each exam costs $150.

The CRCP Exam Information Guide states that the exams must be taken in order, first RDCR200A, then one of the RDCR300 exams, and finally RDCR400. After passing RDCR400, you are certified. You can use the designation and will receive an official certificate in the mail. There is currently no associated logo for you to use. Business Objects will verify that you are certified if requested to do so by potential and current employers, clients, or anyone else who needs such verification.

The exams are given on a computer. They are multiple-choice, with some questions having more than one correct response. You can mark questions for later review. You can return to any question and modify your response as long as you have not submitted the test. There is no penalty for guessing. (An unanswered question is the same as an incorrectly answered question.) You can add notes to questions. In fact, this is highly recommended if you find a question to be confusing. Thoroughly explain your response, and if you do not pass the exam, you can request that your comments be reviewed. After you submit the test, it will be graded, and you will be shown your score onscreen immediately. You will also receive a paper copy of your score report.

If you fail an exam, you can take it again later; there is no penalty except for the cost of the repeat tests. Unfortunately, the score report does not break down your score by topic, so you will not know which areas to concentrate on if you have to retake an exam.

When you arrive for your examination, you must show identification and sign in. You are not allowed to take anything with you into the examination room. (You will be given materials that you can write on during the exam, but these must be handed back when the exam is over. Nothing that you have written is used as part of the grading process; it is merely discarded.) There may be other people taking exams in the same room, but it is unlikely that they will be taking the same exam. You will be monitored during the exam, probably by video camera.

RDCR200A Exam

The Level 1 examination consists of 55 questions. The passing score is 65 percent (36 questions correct) and you have 90 minutes to complete the exam.

This exam covers basic report creation. No specific weightings are given by Business Objects for its list of objectives, but you should understand or be able to do the following:

- Know the Crystal Reports environment and basic menus and speed buttons
- Create a report by connecting to a data source, placing fields on the report, and creating groups, sorts, and summaries
- Format report objects and report sections
- Understand record selection formulas
- Understand the concept of saved data (saved with the report file and saved during the development process)
- Create lines and boxes
- Create text objects and embed fields in text objects
- Know the Crystal Reports special fields and what they represent
- Create a summary-only report with the grouping passed to the server
- Create basic formulas, including the use of Booleans, If-Then-Else structures, date computations, and string manipulations
- Apply conditional formatting using the Highlighting Expert or formatting formulas
- Create basic charts
- Know common report export formats
- Use and manage repository objects
- Create formulas that use built-in functions and operators, variables, and arrays
- Understand variable scopes
- Create and use report templates
- Create and use parameters and display parameter values on the report
- Create and format cross-tabs
- Create mailing label–type reports

- Create running totals using the Running Total Expert or regular formula fields
- Understand Crystal Reports' group sorting capabilities

If you have worked with Crystal Reports for six months to a year, you will have a good background for this exam. However, everyone is not exposed to every topic in their work environment. Review the exam objectives at the beginning of each chapter to determine where your strengths and weaknesses are, and concentrate on the sections that you need most.

RDCR300 Exam

The Level 2 examination consists of 55 questions. The passing score is 75 percent (41 questions correct) and you have 90 minutes to complete the exam. You must choose one of the three electives when registering for this exam.

This exam covers advanced report creation. You should understand or be able to do the following:

- Understand the report processing model and the related evaluation time functions
- Create linked, unlinked, and on-demand subreports and understand how subreports are processed
- Use shared variables to pass information from subreports to the main report
- Understand complex formula constructs, such as the loop control structures, dynamic arrays, and nesting functions
- Create and use custom functions
- Be very familiar with the Database Expert
- Create connections to data sources using ODBC or native drivers
- Understand the impact of structural changes in a report's data source
- Link tables and understand the different join types
- Push processing to the server using SQL Expressions in selection formulas
- Understand the effect of NULL values on formulas, including record selection formulas
- Use web resources and other utilities to research and solve report-related problems

Depending on which elective you selected, there will also be questions on additional topics.

SQL Commands Elective (RDCR300A)   If you choose the SQL Commands elective, your exam will have additional questions covering the creation and use of SQL Commands. You should understand or be able to do the following:

- Understand how SQL is used in Crystal Reports
- Create simple SELECT statements

- Know the difference between SQL Commands and database views or stored procedures
- Create and modify SQL Commands
- Create, modify, and use command parameters
- Understand how command parameters differ from regular report parameters
- Know the types of reporting problems that can be solved using SQL Commands

Complex Formulas Elective (RDCR300B)   If you choose the Complex Formulas elective, your exam will have additional questions covering several depreciation functions, interest computation functions, bond valuation functions, and yield computation functions. You should understand what each function requires as arguments and what it returns.

OLAP Elective (RDCR300C)   If you choose the OLAP elective, your exam will have additional questions covering the creation and use of OLAP grids. You should understand or be able to do the following:

- Understand basic OLAP terminology
- Connect to OLAP data sources
- Create and format an OLAP grid
- Use OLAP grid parameters
- Understand slices and pages
- Create a chart based on an OLAP grid
- Sort, filter, and hide elements of the OLAP grid
- Be familiar with the Calculation Expert
- Apply conditional formatting to elements of the OLAP grid

This exam covers more advanced topics than the Level 1 exam and so requires both a broader and deeper understanding of Crystal Reports capabilities. You might gain the necessary knowledge through a normal working experience, but it is more likely that study of the specific topics will be required. The result of this study will be not only a passing score but also new techniques to use in your own report development.

RDCR400 Exam
The Level 3 examination consists of 40 questions. The passing score is 80 percent (32 questions correct) and you have 90 minutes to complete the exam.

This exam differs significantly from the previous two, where the emphasis is on understanding and using the Crystal Reports application. This exam requires an understanding of the report development *process*, of which the actual report creation is just one step.

In addition, it covers the creation of Business Views, which are a feature of Crystal Enterprise. You should understand or be able to do the following:

- Know the seven steps that comprise the report development methodology used by Business Objects
- Understand the benefits of using a methodology
- Gather user requirements and differentiate between user, technical, and business requirements
- Create a report specification document
- Know ways in which reports can be documented
- Solve some common report design problems
- Know the architecture of Business Views, including all the component objects
- Understand the Business Views security model
- Create and modify each of the Business View component objects: Business Views, Business Elements, Data Foundations, Data Connections, and Dynamic Data Connections

The required passing score is very high for this exam, and the material covered is probably not familiar to a large number of report developers, so it is likely to be the most difficult exam. Understanding Business Views and the report development methodology can be accomplished via study and practice; however, a significant history of report development will be helpful for questions dealing with specific report design problems. The text supplies examples of common problems that you should work through to familiarize yourself with possible solutions.

About This Study Guide

There are no prerequisites for use of this study guide except a general knowledge of computer application use such as you might get from using Microsoft Office products. It is helpful if you have some knowledge of basic programming, the SQL language, and database structures. Any prior experience with Crystal Reports will be beneficial.

Organization

The book is organized into parts and chapters. Part I of the study guide covers installation and introduces Crystal Reports to new users. You should at least skim the first chapter to ensure that your installation meets the requirements for the book, but you may skip Chapters 2 and 3 if you are an experienced Crystal Reports developer. If you are new to Crystal Reports, read Chapters 2 and 3; they will give you a good introduction.

Parts II, III, and IV cover the Level 1, 2, and 3 exams, respectively. The last three chapters of Part III cover the three electives. Of those chapters you only need to read the one that corresponds to the elective you have chosen.

All the chapters in this book are organized similarly and consist of the following elements, although some chapters will not have all of them.

Discussion Sections   The bulk of the chapter content covers the material you need to know to pass the exams. However, in addition to pure exam coverage, the text describes other features and capabilities and discusses other topics useful to report developers. Within the descriptive sections, you will see Tips, Cautions, Notes, and Exam Tips. Tips contain hints that you may find useful when working with Crystal Reports. Cautions point out possible undesirable or unexpected results. Notes contain information that is especially important or that could be overlooked. Exam Tips highlight certain topics that are specifically queried on an exam.

Exercises   At the end of each major section of the text, you will find exercises. I strongly encourage you to work through each exercise. Doing the exercises and thinking about them will strengthen your understanding of the material. In addition, if you can immediately apply new knowledge to your own daily work, that will ensure you retain it.

Exercises may be reused in later chapters, so create a separate folder on your system for each chapter, and place the files you create in each chapter's exercises in the appropriate folder. A few exercises require files that are supplied on the accompanying CD. All such files are stored in the Study Guide Resources directory in the corresponding chapter folder.

TIP   Within each exercise, text that must be entered using the keyboard is shown in **boldface** type.

Quick Tips   Toward the end of each chapter, before the questions and answers, you will find a "Quick Tips" section. This section lists the important concepts covered in the chapter in brief bullet points. Use this section as a refresher.

Questions and Answers   The very last section of the chapters contains questions and answers. You should attempt to answer each question. Answers with explanations follow the list of questions. If you find yourself answering questions incorrectly, return to the corresponding part of the text and reread it.

Requirements

To use this study guide, you need the Crystal Reports 10 application. Installation is covered in Chapter 1. You will also need Internet access for downloading application updates and documentation and so you can explore the Business Objects support sites for Crystal Reports.

Crystal Reports 10 is available in four editions: Standard, Professional, Developer, and Advanced Developer. In addition, two language-customized versions are available: Crystal Reports for Java and Crystal Reports for .NET. The CRCP exams require exposure to several features that are not available in the Standard Edition, such as reporting from OLAP sources and familiarity with the repository. Therefore, the Professional version of

Crystal Reports 10 is the minimum required to use this study guide. The Developer Edition is used throughout the text, so if you are using the Professional Edition, some options may be covered that are not available to you. Any references to Crystal Reports in the text mean the Professional Edition or higher.

 NOTE The Professional, Developer, and Advanced Developer editions of Crystal Reports 10 ship with a five-concurrent-access user license of Crystal Enterprise Standard Edition for testing and development, so no separate purchase of Crystal Enterprise is required in order to complete the study guide exercises.

You can download a trial version of Crystal Reports to use with this study guide from the Business Objects web site. Go to the Crystal Reports 10 product page and click the Crystal Reports 10 Advanced Developer Evaluation Download link. You will be taken to the evaluation download page at http://www.businessobjects.com/products/reporting/crystalreports/eval10/eval_download.asp. You must be registered and logged in, and you will be required to fill out a short survey. You will then be allowed to download the software, and key codes will be sent to you via e-mail for installation.

Three separate files can be downloaded. Select the Crystal Reports 10 Developer Evaluation link, which downloads the CR10AdvDevEn.exe file, and the Crystal Enterprise 10 Professional link, which downloads the CE10EN.exe file. You do not need the Crystal Enterprise Embedded file.

PART I

Installation and Quick Start

1

Installing Crystal Reports 10 and Crystal Enterprise 10

In this chapter you will learn the steps needed to install Crystal Reports 10 and Crystal Enterprise 10 for use with this study guide:

- Installation preliminaries
- System requirements
- Installing Crystal Enterprise
- Installing Crystal Reports
- Installing DataDirect ODBC drivers
- Modifying an installation

An understanding of the installation process for Crystal Reports 10 or Crystal Enterprise 10 is not a CRCP exam objective; installation is covered here for practical reasons. You may work in an environment where both products are installed and configured for you. However, it is more likely that you will be doing the installation yourself or that you will be an evaluator of, contributor to, or tester of the installation. Or you may be installing the products in a private or test environment in order to follow along with the study guide exercises.

NOTE   Because installation is not covered on the CRCP exam, no Quick Tips or Questions are included in this chapter.

The installation and configuration of complex applications like Crystal Reports and Crystal Enterprise must be customized to fit your environment. In the real world you would research all the available options and choose those that meet your goals for the product. For example, you would install only the database drivers that are required for reporting from your particular data sources. This chapter will cover an installation that is sufficient for use with this study guide. If your existing installation includes all the necessary components, then you need not reinstall.

Crystal Reports installation options that are not required for use of this study guide are covered to help you make informed configuration decisions later. In addition, installation of Crystal Enterprise is required for some sections of the study guide in order to meet CRCP exam objectives that deal with the integration of Crystal Reports into the Crystal Enterprise environment, including the use of the Crystal Repository, publishing reports to Crystal Enterprise, and the use of Business Views. A simple Crystal Enterprise environment is created; advanced Crystal Enterprise options are not discussed.

Installation Preliminaries

Before installing Crystal Reports or Crystal Enterprise, you should visit the Business Objects support site and search for updated information and files.

Exercise 1.1: Searching for Up-to-Date Installation Information

1. Open a web browser and go to http://support.businessobjects.com/search.
2. Click the Advanced Search link, as shown here, to go to the Advanced Search page.

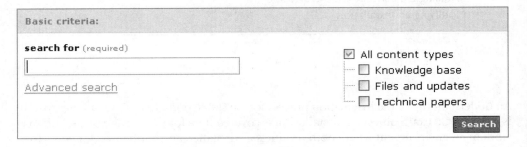

3. On the Advanced Search page, type the word **install** into the Search For box.
4. Check All Content Types.
5. In the Select Product drop-down box, select Crystal Reports.
6. In the Select Version box, select 10.
7. In the Select Language box, choose English. Your settings should look like Figure 1-1.
8. Click the Search button and the screen will display all technical support content for Crystal Reports 10 installations.

 NOTE Files for languages other than English may be displayed. The search engine does not currently filter languages correctly.

Browse the displayed files to determine if any are applicable to your situation. As of this writing there were several documents of interest, including

- cr10_Install_en.pdf, the installation chapter from the *Users Guide*

- cr_xtremelogo.zip, the Xtreme logo, which is not installed by default but is required for use with the XTREME sample schema
- cr10_release_en.zip, current release notes for Crystal Reports 10
- cr10_supported_platforms.pdf, a detailed list of currently supported platforms
- cr10_UserGde_en.zip, the *Crystal Reports Users Guide*

Now repeat the steps in Exercise 1.1 to search for Crystal Enterprise 10 installation documents. Current files of interest for installation are

- ce10_release_en.zip, release notes for Crystal Enterprise 10
- ce10_supported_platforms.pdf, the list of currently supported platforms
- ce10_install_en.pdf, the installation guide.

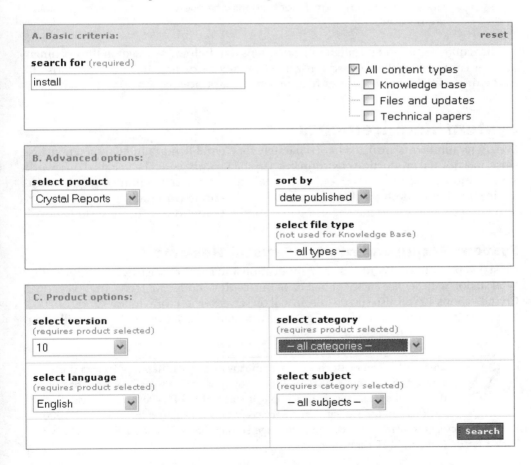

Figure 1-1   Searching for new installation information

Registered users of Crystal products should also visit the download center at http://www.businessobjects.com/products/downloadcenter to check for available downloads. Currently, the DataDirect ODBC drivers that are missing from the Crystal Reports 10 release files are available as InstallODBCDriversv10.zip. Other valuable additions may be posted there in the future.

Business Objects' Technical Support releases hot fixes for Crystal Reports and Crystal Enterprise each month. These can be found at http://support.businessobjects.com. In the drop-down box in the Self-Serve Support Shortcuts section, choose Download Monthly Hot Fixes, and then click Crystal Reports or Crystal Enterprise. Tech Support also occasionally releases service packs. Current service packs are available through the same site; choose Download Service Packs.

TIP If you sign up for automatic notification of hot fixes from the support site you will receive e-mail notifications when new hot fixes or service packs are released.

The requirements and installation instructions that follow are based on the documentation accompanying the released version of Crystal Reports 10 and Crystal Enterprise 10. At the time of this writing, no hot fixes or service packs for version 10 were available.

System Requirements

System requirements are listed here separately for Crystal Reports and Crystal Enterprise since, in a normal production environment, Crystal Reports would be installed on a workstation and Crystal Enterprise would be installed on a server. Combined requirements for installation of both products on a single stand-alone workstation-type system are also given for those who may be using that configuration for certification study.

System Requirements for Crystal Reports 10

Crystal Reports 10 is a Windows-only application and requires Microsoft Windows 2000 Workstation with Service Pack 3 or higher, or Microsoft Windows XP Home or Professional. Crystal Reports 10 will also successfully install on server versions of Windows 2000 or 2003. You must have administrator privileges on the system where Crystal Reports will be installed.

CAUTION The platforms.txt accompanying Crystal Reports 10 lists the supported operating systems. However, it may not always be up-to-date with the actual application. For example, it states that NT Workstation with Service Pack 6a can be used and that Service Pack 4 is required for Windows 2000. During an actual installation, I received a message stating that Windows 2000 with Service Pack 3 is adequate and NT cannot be used.

Hardware requirements for Crystal Reports 10 are a 450 MHz Pentium II processor, 128MB of RAM, and 350MB of available hard disk space. These are the *minimums*; a 600

MHz Pentium III processor and 256MB of RAM are recommended. In addition, if you are installing from CD, a CD-ROM drive is required.

System Requirements for Crystal Enterprise 10

System requirements for Crystal Enterprise 10 vary depending on the operating system environment. (You can view the list of supported platforms and requirements by locating the ce10_supported_platforms.pdf on the Business Objects technical support site.) Crystal Enterprise can be installed on Windows, Solaris, and AIX. Only the Windows installation will be covered in this guide. In addition, various components of Crystal Enterprise can be installed on different servers, but only stand-alone installation will be covered here.

Crystal Enterprise 10 can be installed on a Microsoft Windows Server 2000 with Service Pack 4 or on a Microsoft Windows Server 2003. For demonstration or study purposes, it can be installed on Windows 2000 Workstation with Service Pack 4 or Windows XP Professional. The stand-alone installation outlined in this chapter uses Windows XP Professional.

Crystal Enterprise requires a web server. Several web servers are supported, as shown in the Supported Platforms document. Since the installation covered in the following sections uses Windows XP Professional, Microsoft IIS 5.0 will be used as the web server.

Crystal Enterprise requires a database for storage of its administrative data and for the Crystal Repository. Several DBMSs are supported on Windows and UNIX. For demonstration purposes, the Microsoft Database Engine (MSDE) will be used. (However, the MSDE is not recommended for production use due to its limitations.)

Hardware requirements for Crystal Enterprise 10 on Windows include a 700 MHz Pentium III processor, 512MB of RAM, and 2GB of available hard disk space. For installation from CD, a CD-ROM drive is required.

System Requirements for
Combined Stand-Alone Installation

To create a stand-alone installation of Crystal Reports 10 and Crystal Enterprise 10 on a single system, you will need a 700 MHz Pentium III processor; 512MB of RAM; 2GB of free disk space; a CD-ROM drive; and Windows 2000 with Service Pack 4, Windows XP Professional, or Windows Server 2003.

Installing Crystal Enterprise

If you are installing Crystal Enterprise and Crystal Reports on the same machine, install Crystal Enterprise first. This sets up a file structure that encompasses both products, ensuring that the later installation of Crystal Reports will be trouble-free.

The installation instructions that follow assume a Windows XP Professional system with no web server, Crystal Reports products, or Crystal Enterprise products installed. It is also assumed that no versions of the MSDE or SQL Server exist on the installation machine. The installation for Windows 2000 is similar, although rebooting may be required.

If you wish to run multiple versions simultaneously, you *must* install the earlier version first. If you are installing upgrade versions and do not need to keep previous versions, but you wish to follow these instructions exactly, uninstall all Crystal products before proceeding. You will be prompted to insert the CD or other proof of ownership of the prior version during the install.

Verify System Requirements

Before starting the installation, verify that your system meets the requirements as described here.

Operating System

If you are not sure what operating system or service pack version is installed on your computer, right-click the My Computer icon on the Windows desktop, and choose Properties. You will see some system information on the General tab. For Windows XP, as seen in Figure 1-2, the operating system and service pack are in the upper left of the System Properties dialog box. Verify that you are using Windows 2000, Service Pack 4 or higher, or Windows XP Professional.

Hardware

In the same System Properties dialog box, you can verify the processor and RAM available. Verify that you have a 700 MHz Pentium III processor or higher and at least 512MB of RAM. To check available disk space, in Windows Explorer, right-click the drive letter

Figure 1-2
Verifying your
system properties

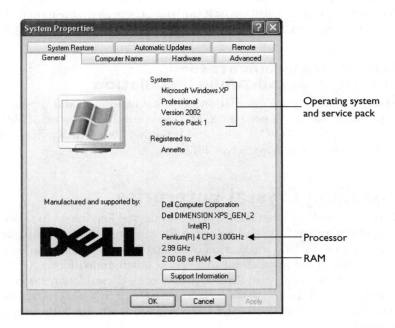

that you plan to use for the installation, and choose Properties. On the General tab, verify that the free space is at least 2GB, as shown here.

| | Used space: | 23,995,895,808 bytes | 22.3 GB |
| | Free space: | 95,969,812,480 bytes | 89.3 GB |

Installed Applications

To verify that no old versions of Crystal Reports or Crystal Enterprise are installed, go to Control Panel and choose Add or Remove Programs. Browse the list displayed to verify that no Crystal products are installed, as shown here. Note that the list is in alphabetical order.

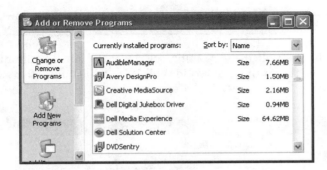

To verify that SQL Server or MSDE is not installed, go to Control Panel and open the Services window. You may need to choose Administrative Tools | Services. Verify that no entry for MSSQLSERVER appears in the list of services.

Installing IIS

Crystal Enterprise requires a web server. The following steps install IIS on a Windows XP Professional system. If you are using Windows 2000 some steps may vary.

Exercise 1.2: Installing IIS

1. Go to Control Panel and open Add or Remove Programs.
2. Click Add/Remove Windows Components.
3. Check the Internet Information Services (IIS) box, as shown in Figure 1-3. (If the box is already checked, then IIS is already installed and you can click Cancel.)
4. Click Next and wait for the installation to complete.
5. When the installation is complete, click Finish.
6. Close the Add or Remove Programs dialog box.

Figure 1-3

Using the
Windows
Components
Wizard to
install IIS

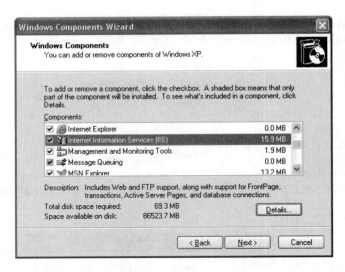

To verify that IIS is installed and running, select Control Panel | Administrative Tools | Services. You should see an entry for World Wide Web Publishing with a status of Started, as shown here.

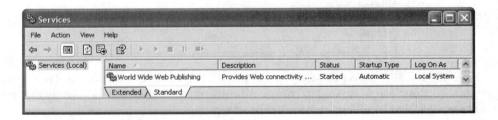

Crystal Enterprise Stand-Alone Installation

The following instructions create a stand-alone installation of Crystal Enterprise 10 on Windows XP Professional. If you are using a different operating system or installing with different options, your steps may vary.

 CAUTION You should be aware that the version of Crystal Enterprise that ships free with Crystal Reports Professional and higher editions is the Standard Edition. The Standard Edition of Crystal Enterprise lacks some features and functionality available in other editions.

Exercise 1.3: Installing Crystal Enterprise

1. If you purchased Crystal Enterprise via download, you have a file called CE10En.exe (for the English version). Execute this file to unpack the installation files and create a directory structure similar to that found on the installation CD. (If you have an installation CD, this step is not required.)

2. Execute the setup.exe file from the root of the file directory or the Crystal Enterprise CD.

3. The first page of the installation wizard will appear. Follow the instructions about closing other applications, and then click Next.

4. Select the radio button to accept the license agreement, and then click Next.

5. On the User Information page, enter your name, organization, and key code. Then click Next.

6. On the Directory Selection page, click Next to accept the default directory and path for Crystal Enterprise.

7. On the Install Type page, verify that New is selected, and click Next.

8. On the MSDE Security Configuration page, enter a password for the Administrator account. The name of the MSDE Administrator account is sa. Click Next.

9. On the Start Installation page, click Next to begin the install process. This is a lengthy process, but you can follow its progress on the screens that display.

10. Once the installation is complete, you will be asked to register your product. Follow the instructions to complete the registration, or choose to register later.

11. The installation will then complete and backup files will be removed. When the message "Crystal Enterprise 10 has been successfully installed" appears, clear the Launch Crystal Publishing Wizard check box, and then click Finish. (The Crystal Publishing Wizard allows you to publish existing reports to Crystal Enterprise.)

To verify that the Crystal Enterprise installation is complete and working, open a web browser and go to http://*computername*/crystal/enterprise10, entering the name of the computer where you installed Crystal Enterprise in place of *computername*. You should see a page similar to Figure 1-4.

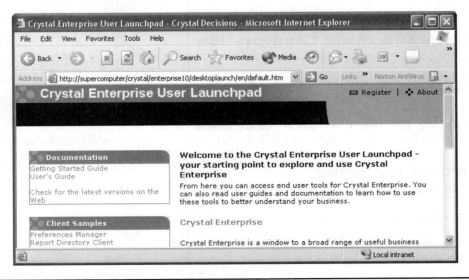

Figure 1-4   Verifying that Crystal Enterprise is ready for use

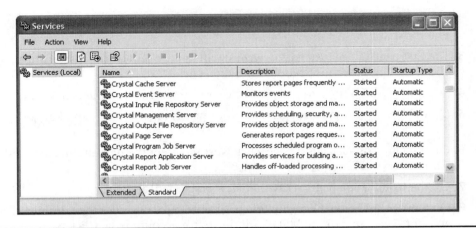

Figure 1-5 Checking that Crystal Enterprise services are running

You can also verify that the Crystal Enterprise services are running by selecting Control Panel | Administrative Tools | Services. You should see the services listed in Figure 1-5.

Scroll down in the Services dialog box to verify that the MSSQLSERVER service is also now installed and started. You will notice the SQL Server icon in the Taskbar's notification area after your next reboot.

> **NOTE** Installation of the MSDE causes SQL Server services to load. This is because the MSDE is simply a version of SQL Server that does not contain the full feature set.

Crystal Enterprise Configuration

There can be many complex steps involved in Crystal Enterprise configuration. For purposes of this study guide, you will simply change the Administrator's password and create a user account for yourself.

Changing the Administrator's Password

Since the administrator's password is initially blank, it is good practice to change it.

Exercise 1.4: Modifying the Crystal Enterprise Administrator's Password

1. Go to Start | Crystal Enterprise 10 | Crystal Enterprise User Launchpad.

2. From the Crystal Enterprise User Launchpad screen, click the Crystal Enterprise link.

3. Log on as Administrator with a blank password.

4. In the upper right-hand corner of the page, click the Preferences link.

5. On the Preferences page, in the upper right-hand corner, click the Change Password link.

6. Enter a new password in the New Password and Confirm New Password text boxes and click Submit.

7. Close the browser windows.

Creating a New Crystal Enterprise User Account

To create a new Crystal Enterprise user account for use with the study guide, complete Exercise 1.5.

Exercise 1.5: Creating a Crystal Enterprise User Account

1. Go to Start | Crystal Enterprise 10 | Crystal Enterprise Admin Launchpad.

2. From the Crystal Enterprise Admin Launchpad screen, click the Crystal Management Console link.

3. Log on as Administrator with the password you changed in the previous section.

4. On the Crystal Management Console page, click the Users link.

5. On the All Users page, click the New User button.

6. On the New User page, fill in an account name, full name, and e-mail address of your choice, as shown in Figure 1-6. Leave all other options set to their defaults, and click OK.

7. After the page refreshes, close the browser.

8. Go to Start | Crystal Enterprise 10 | Crystal Enterprise User Launchpad.

9. From the Crystal Enterprise User Launchpad screen click the Crystal Enterprise link.

10. Log in to the new user account with a blank password.

11. A screen will appear for you to use to change the blank password to something of your choice.

12. Close the browser.

You now have a Crystal Enterprise account to use as you work through the study guide. Along with the user account, a folder of the same name was created, and you were granted full control of that folder.

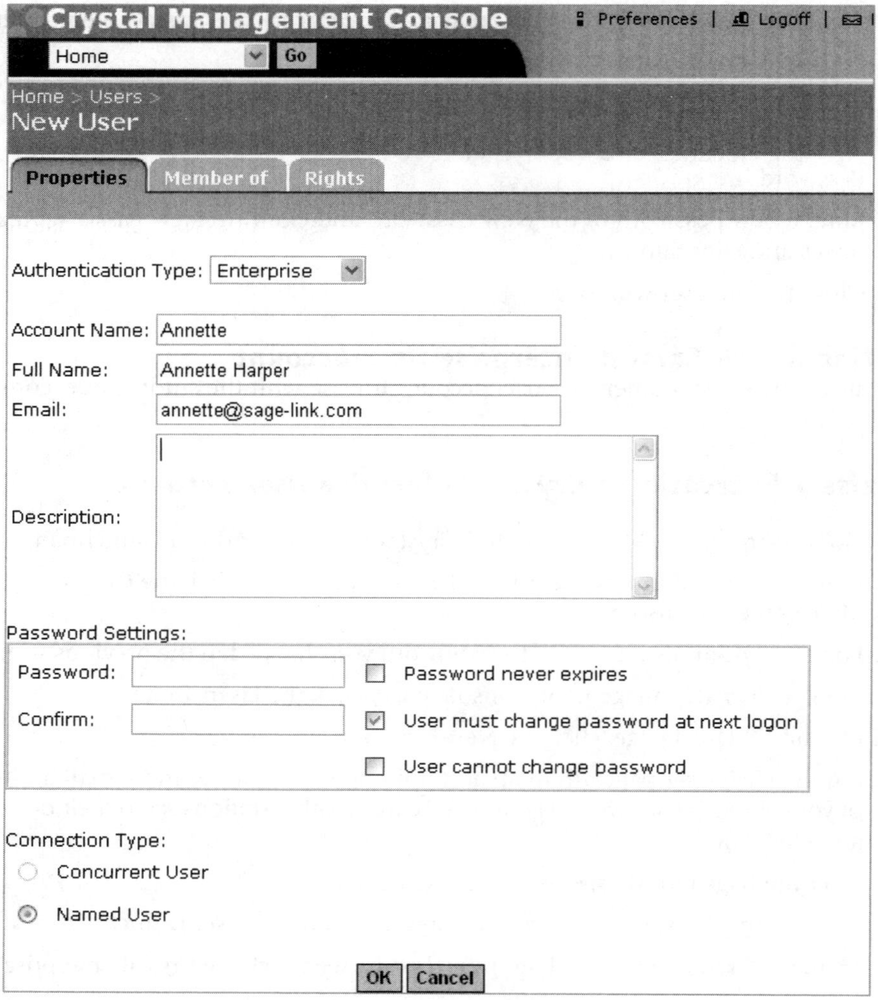

Figure 1-6   Creating a new Crystal Enterprise user

Optional Steps

The following steps copy important information from the installation CD to your system for easy access. Most of these documents have equivalent online help versions, but if you prefer to read the PDFs, follow these instructions.

1. Copy the Docs, Platforms, and Samples folders from the installation CD to C:\Program Files\Crystal Decisions\Enterprise 10 (or whatever directory you installed the program in). You will need to change the name of the Samples folder to Admin Samples, because a Samples folder already exists in the installation directory.

2. Right-click the Windows Start button, and select Explore All Users.

3. Expand the Programs node, and select the Crystal Enterprise 10 node.

4. Create a folder called Documentation in the Crystal Enterprise 10 folder.

5. With the Documentation folder selected, right-click in the right-hand pane, and choose New | Shortcut.

6. In the Create Shortcut wizard, browse to C:\Program Files\Crystal Decisions \Enterprise 10\docs\admin.pdf, and click Next.

7. Name the shortcut **Administrator's Guide,** and click Finish.

8. Repeat steps 5 through 7 for the other documents listed here.

File	Shortcut Name
Admin.pdf	Administrator's Guide
Business_view.pdf	Business View Administrator's Guide
Documentmap.pdf	Document Map
Getstarted.pdf	Getting Started Guide
Install.pdf	Installation Guide
License.pdf	License Agreement
Odbcref.pdf	DataDirect Connect for ODBC Reference
User.pdf	User's Guide
Whatsnew.pdf	What's New in Crystal Enterprise
Platforms.txt	Supported Platforms

Now when you go to Start | Programs | Crystal Enterprise 10 | Documentation, you will have quick links to these documents.

Install the Repository Samples

Repository sample objects are supplied but not installed with Crystal Enterprise 10. To install the sample objects into the repository, complete Exercise 1.6.

Exercise 1.6: Install the Repository Samples

1. Go to Start | Programs | Crystal Enterprise 10 | Business View Manager, and fill in the log-on information using either the default Administrator password of blank, if you have not reset it, or the new password.

2. Cancel the Welcome dialog box if it is displayed. Then go to the Tools menu and choose Install Repository Samples.

3. Pick English from the Install Repository Samples dialog box, and click OK.

4. Click Yes in the Override Existing Samples dialog box.

5. Wait for the installation to complete, and then click OK to complete the process and close the box.

6. Close Business View Manager.

A very simple installation of Crystal Enterprise 10 is now complete. For other options, please consult the documentation that accompanies Crystal Enterprise.

Installing Crystal Reports

The following instructions are for installing the Developer Edition of Crystal Reports 10 on Windows XP Professional. If you are using a different operating system, different edition, or installing with different options, your steps may vary. A custom installation is demonstrated in order to explain all the various options.

Exercise 1.7: Installing Crystal Reports

1. If you purchased Crystal Reports via download, you will have a file called CR10ProEn.exe (for the English version). Executing this file will unpack the installation files and create a directory structure similar to that found on the installation CD. (If you have an installation CD, this step is not required.)

2. Execute the setup.exe file from the root of the file directory or the Crystal Reports CD.

3. Read the instructions on the Welcome page about closing other applications, and click Next to continue.

4. Select the button to accept the license agreement, and click Next.

5. Enter your name, organization, and key code, and click Next.

6. On the Select Installation Type page, choose Custom. Accept the default destination folder or change it as needed, and then click Next.

7. The Select Features page will be displayed. On this page you can choose which features to install by clicking the down arrow next to the drive icons, as shown here. You can choose to have the feature installed immediately, installed the first time it is accessed, or made unavailable.

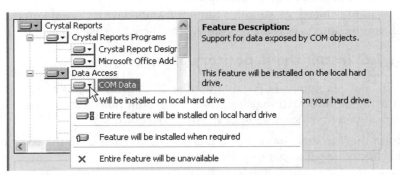

8. On the Select Features page, expand the Crystal Reports Programs node, as shown here. Two items are listed: The Crystal Reports Designer is the actual Crystal Reports

application and must be installed. The Microsoft Application Add-Ins are additions for Microsoft Access and Excel that allow Crystal Reports to function seamlessly inside those products. If you choose to install them, a Crystal Reports button will be added to Access and Excel to invoke the Crystal Reports designer and work with Access or Excel data.

9. Expand the Data Access node. This node lists all the possible data sources that Crystal Reports can be configured to use, as shown here. For this study guide, the Access option is required. Choose any other options that you need. See the Crystal Reports Developer's Help file for more information on each option.

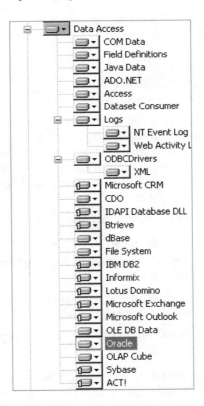

TIP The options listed on the Select Features install page may appear with different names or in different locations once the installation is complete and the Crystal Reports Database Expert is used to choose a report data source. In addition, there may be multiple data access options for any given data source. For example, Oracle data can be accessed natively via the Oracle Server option, via ODBC, or via OLE DB.

10. Expand the Export Support node. The Export Support node lists all the possible export destinations and formats that Crystal Reports can be configured to use, as shown here. Choose any soptions that you need. Some of the options are formats and some are destinations. See Chapter 11 for more information.

> Export Support
> Lotus Domino Mail
> Acrobat PDF Format
> Application Destination
> Character Separated Forma
> Crystal Reports Format
> Disk File Destination
> Excel Format
> HTML Format
> Lotus Notes Destination
> Microsoft Exchange Public F
> Microsoft Mail Destination
> ODBC Data Source Format
> Record Format (columns of
> Report Definition Format
> Rich Text Format
> Text Format
> Word for Windows Format
> XML Export

11. The Custom Charting feature installs additional charting capabilities. Select it if desired.

12. The Geographic Mapping feature adds the ability to create reports that display data via maps. Select the options you need.

13. There are two options under the Developer Components feature, .NET and Report Design Component. If you plan to incorporate Crystal Reports into .NET applications, select the .NET option. If you want to use Crystal Reports in Visual Basic applications or other applications that use ActiveX, install the Report Design Component.

14. Sample Reports are set to install by default. Click Next.

15. On the Start Installation page, click Next to begin the installation.

16. When the installation program is finished copying files, it will ask if you want to allow a system restart. Click Yes.

17. Your system will reboot, and Crystal Reports will resume the installation. Continue with registration or choose to register later.

18. When the message "Crystal Reports 10 has been successfully installed," appears, click Finish.

To verify that Crystal Reports has been installed, go to Start | Programs | Crystal Reports 10. In the Welcome to Crystal Reports dialog box, select the Open an Existing Report radio button. Then select More Files, and click OK. Select the C:\Program Files \Crystal Decisions\Crystal Reports 10\Samples\En\Reports\General Business\Employee Profile report, and click Open. You will be asked to log on to Crystal Enterprise. Log on as the user you created earlier. The report will open and you will see the first page of data displaying information for Justin Brid.

Optional Steps

The following steps copy important information from the installation CD to your system for easy access. Most of these documents have equivalent online help versions, but if you prefer to read the PDFs, follow these instructions.

1. Copy the Docs folder from the installation CD to C:\Program Files\Crystal Decisions\Crystal Reports 10, or the directory where you installed Crystal Reports.

2. Right-click the Start button, and select Explore All Users.

3. Expand the Programs node, and select the Crystal Reports 10 Tools node.

4. Create a folder called Documentation in the Crystal Reports 10 Tools folder.

5. With the Documentation folder selected, right-click in the right-hand pane, and choose New | Shortcut.

6. In the Create Shortcut wizard, browse to C:\Program Files\Crystal Decisions\ Crystal Reports 10\Docs\documentmap.pdf, and click Next.

7. Name the shortcut **Document Map**, and click Finish.

8. Repeat steps 5 through 7 for the other documents listed here.

File	Shortcut Name
Documentmap.pdf	Document Map
Install.pdf	Installation Guide
License.pdf	License Agreement
Platforms.txt	Supported Platforms
RUNTIME.txt	Runtime Software Definition
Techref.pdf	Technical Reference Guide
User.pdf	User's Guide
Whatsnew.pdf	What's New in Crystal Reports

Now if you go to Start | Programs | Crystal Reports 10 Tools | Documentation, you will have quick links to these documents.

Installing DataDirect ODBC Drivers

Licenses for several DataDirect ODBC drivers are included with Crystal Reports and Crystal Enterprise. These drivers have been installed with the program installations in previous versions. For version 10, the drivers were not available with the released software and need to be downloaded and installed separately. Crystal Reports is written to work with these ODBC drivers, and they may perform better than ODBC drivers from database vendors or other sources.

TIP   The DataDirect ODBC license is valid for use only in Crystal Reports. The DataDirect drivers cannot be used in any other environment or application unless you purchase them directly from the DataDirect.

Exercise 1.8: Installing DataDirect ODBC Drivers

1. If you have not previously downloaded the drivers, open a browser and go to http://www.businessobjects.com/products/downloadcenter. Click the I Accept link. The download file is the same for Crystal Reports and Crystal Enterprise, so click the Crystal Reports link. Click the Download DataDirect Drivers – All Languages – 8 MB link, and save the file to your disk.

2. Unzip the download file and look in the docs\En directory for the release notes. Read the release notes for up-to-date information concerning the drivers. This directory also contains an installation guide and ODBC reference.

3. You must have administrator privileges to install the ODBC drivers. If you need to log on as a different user, do so now.

4. Execute the setup.exe file from the root of the unzipped directory.

5. Choose English as the language.

6. Choose Next from the welcome screen.

7. On the Setup Type page, choose Custom, and click Next.

8. A list of the available drivers will be displayed, as shown in Figure 1-7.

9. Uncheck any drivers that you do not want to install. Click Next.

 TIP Drivers that contain "Wire Protocol" in their names do not require the installation of the related database's regular client software. For example, you do not need to install the Oracle client software to connect to Oracle databases using Oracle_Wire_Protocol_Driver.

Figure 1-7
Installing
DataDirect
ODBC drivers

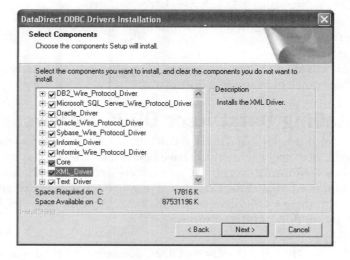

10. On the Start Copying Files page, click Next.

11. The installation program will stop some services while it copies files. You will then be asked if you want to restart the services. Click Yes.

12. Click Finish on the Complete page.

To verify that the drivers you selected were installed, go to Control Panel | Administrative Tools, open the Data Sources (ODBC) dialog box, and click the Drivers tab. You should see the drivers you installed, as shown in Figure 1-8. All the Crystal-licensed ODBC drivers have "CR" as the first two letters of their name.

Optional Steps

The following steps copy important information from the download directory to your system for easy access.

1. Copy the install_odbc.pdf and odbcref.pdf files from the directory InstallODBCDriversv10\docs\En folder to C:\Program Files\Crystal Decisions\ Crystal Reports 10\Docs or the directory where you installed Crystal Reports.

2. Right-click the Start button, and select Explore All Users.

3. Expand the Programs node, and select the Crystal Reports 10 Tools node.

4. With the Documentation folder selected, right-click in the right-hand pane, and choose New | Shortcut.

5. In the Create Shortcut wizard, browse to C:\Program Files\Crystal Decisions\ Crystal Reports 10\Docs\odbcref.pdf, and click Next.

6. Name the shortcut **DataDirect ODBC Reference Guide**, and click Finish.

Figure I-8
Verifying installed
ODBC drivers

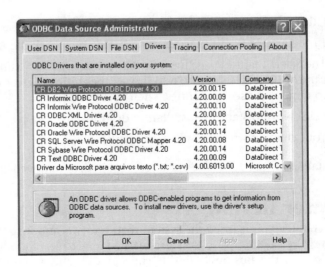

7. Repeat steps 5 through 7 for the other documents listed here.

File	Shortcut Name
odbcref.pdf	DataDirect ODBC Reference Guide
install_odbc.pdf	DataDirect ODBC Installation Guide

Now if you go to Start | Programs | Crystal Reports 10 Tools | Documentation, you will have quick links to these documents.

Modifying an Installation

Occasionally you may need to add or remove product options. For example, you may need to add a data access option that was not originally installed. This is easily accomplished using the Windows Installer. To modify an installation, use the following steps:

1. Go to Control Panel | Add or Remove Programs.

2. Select Crystal Reports 10, as shown here.

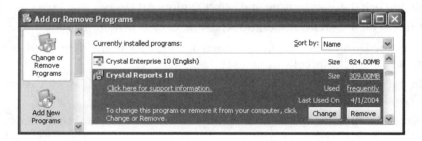

3. Click the Change button.

4. In the Add or Remove Application dialog box, click the Add/Remove button.

5. The Select Features page from the Crystal Reports 10 Setup will be displayed. You can check new features to add those capabilities or clear features' check boxes to remove those capabilities. Then click Next.

6. Click Next to start the installation or uninstall.

7. Your changes will be made. Click Finish.

Crystal Enterprise 10 can be modified, repaired, or removed using the same process.

Chapter Review

In this chapter, you learned the system requirements and install process for Crystal Reports and Crystal Enterprise. You also learned how to search for updated installation information on the Business Objects support web site, how to install the DataDirect drivers, and how to modify an installation of Crystal Reports or Crystal Enterprise.

Database Concepts and the XTREME Sample Data

Exam RDCR200 expects you to be able to define database concepts. This chapter describes

- Database concepts
- The XTREME sample data

The act of creating a report starts with finding the necessary data. That data is almost always stored in a database, and that database is almost always a relational database. Understanding the structure of relational databases is invaluable to a report developer.

EXAM TIP   Specific knowledge of the XTREME sample data is not a CRCP exam objective. It is included here because all examples and exercises in the text use it.

Database Concepts

A very loose definition of a database would be any collection of information. For example, a telephone book is a database: it is a collection of phone numbers. Your daughter's Good Charlotte CD is a database: it is a collection of songs. Your yellow sticky note with today's tasks on it is a database. However, as report writers we deal mainly with much more formalized databases.

All databases in professional use today grew out of the work of E. F. Codd at IBM in the 1970s. Dr. Codd produced the relational database theory that modern databases employ. In concert with the development of the relational database theory, a method for creating, manipulating, and utilizing the information stored in the database was created. This language became known as Structured Query Language or SQL (pronounced as either *ess-q-el* or *sequel.*)

Crystal Reports can use many different types of data sources, including your PC's filing system and event log, but we are mainly concerned with using data from applications that define themselves as relational database management systems (RDBMS). These come in two main flavors: desktop databases and SQL databases.

The distinction between the two types can be blurry, but desktop databases are usually intended primarily for use by one person at a time (though most have some multiuser capabilities), run on a personal PC or workstation, have proprietary query and manipulation languages (though they may also offer ODBC interfaces), lack a SQL engine, and lack the capability to service large amounts of data or a large number of users. Examples of desktop databases include Microsoft Access, Borland Paradox, and Microsoft FoxPro.

SQL databases are usually intended for use by many people simultaneously, run on servers, contain a SQL engine, and have much more extensive security capabilities than desktop databases. Examples of SQL databases include Oracle, SQL Server, Informix, IBM DB2, Interbase, and Sybase.

Both database types have many features in common. The following sections describe general database structures in a way that is meant to be useful and easy for beginning report writers to understand. It will not be highly theoretical, nor will it necessarily adhere to all the principles of relational database management. (This chapter covers database structures only; the SQL language is discussed in later chapters.)

TIP It is very important that you learn and understand the features that are specific to the database or databases that you work with most. The generic knowledge covered here is a starting point and will help you use Crystal Reports to create reports, but being able to take advantage of the unique strengths of a particular database will make you a much more valuable report writer.

Databases

A *relational database* is a collection of related tables. The physical structure of a database can vary widely between vendors. For example, an Access database is contained completely in one physical file, while an Oracle database may span many files and even be spread across multiple computers. The physical structure of the database is of little concern to the user, however, because once you are connected to them, the logical structure of all databases is similar—they all consist of tables with similar characteristics.

Tables

A *table* is a rectangular structure made up of columns and rows. The terms *columns* and *rows* are commonly used in SQL databases, but Crystal Reports calls the same structures *fields* and *records*. A table must be rectangular in the sense that each row must have the same number of fields and each field must exist in every row. An individual table commonly contains information about only one type of "thing," and each row represents an instance of that "thing." For example, a Product table contains information about products and nothing else; it does not contain any information about customers or vendors. Each record in the Product table contains information about one particular product and no other products. Note that relational database theory does not require there to be any inherent physical order of records in a table.

Records

A *record* is a collection of related fields. Records, or rows, usually contain one or more fields, or columns, that uniquely identify a particular record. For example, a product record might be made up of the fields Color, Weight, and Description. For this example to be useful, however, it would also need a unique identifier, so that you know which product it refers to. The addition of a Product ID field would tell you that this is the information for a particular product.

Fields

Fields are the smallest division in a database. A field contains a single bit of information: say a fact or an attribute of one entity. How the "single bit" is defined depends on the requirements of the application or applications that use the database.

 NOTE In some advanced databases, a field may not be the smallest division. For example, in an object-relational database a field may contain an entire object. However, Crystal Reports cannot interpret or use such complex data forms.

For example, consider a database that stores address information. The application that uses this database needs to create mailing labels, so a field called Address has been created that contains both the house number and street name. An example of the contents of Address might be "1234 Sunshine Street." Another application also needs address information, but it has a further requirement to ensure that the house number contains only numeric characters. Because this database must act on the house number separately from the street name, it includes two fields, House Number and Street; "1234" is stored in the House Number field and "Sunshine Street" is stored in the Street field.

Data Types

A field must have a *data type*. The data type defines the type of data that can be stored in the field. Crystal Reports uses the data types String, Number, Currency, Date, Time, Date and Time, Picture, and Memo. The underlying data source may have many more data types, but each is mapped to a Crystal type for reporting purposes.

String String fields hold sequences of characters. String fields have a defined length, and their contents may or may not extend to the entire length of the field. String fields are also called *text fields*. String fields can include regular alphabetic characters, numbers, spaces, and other special characters. The Address field just described is a string field.

Number Number fields hold only numeric characters and the decimal point. They can have decimal portions. Arithmetic can be performed on number fields.

NOTE Some fields that contain only numbers, such as a Zip Code field, are usually not defined as Number but as String. Since no arithmetic needs to be performed on such a field, it need not be defined as Number.

Currency   Currency is a special form of the Number data type. Currency fields are assumed to contain monetary numeric values, and Crystal Reports will automatically display a currency symbol for such fields. The underlying database may store these numbers and perform calculations on them in special ways to ensure that rounding errors in the cents position do not occur.

Date   The Date data type is used to create fields that contain dates. A date field will contain year, month, and day portions. Different databases store dates in different ways, but Crystal Reports treats them all similarly.

Time   The Time data type is assigned to fields that contain times. Crystal Reports will recognize hours, minutes, and seconds, but not fractional seconds, even if they exist in the underlying data. Very few databases have a separate Time data type.

Date and Time   Date and Time fields contain both date and time information stored together in one field.

Picture   A Picture field contains a graphic image to display. Crystal Reports recognizes metafile, bitmap, JPEG, TIFF, and PNG files.

Memo   Memo fields contain what most databases call binary large objects, or BLOBs. The most common example of a memo field is a large text field. These fields differ from String fields in that they can be much larger and can contain embedded formatting. Crystal Reports currently recognizes rich text format (RTF) and HTML formatting and can properly display memo fields containing such formatting.

Null
Fields of any data type can be null or empty. The concept of a null field value and its consequences will be discussed in more detail later, but for now understand that null means lacking a value; it is not equal to 0 for a number field. An empty string may or may not equate to null, depending on the implementation of the underlying database type.

Owner
Some databases have the concept of a *table owner* or *schema*. For databases that have this concept, it acts as a categorization or grouping mechanism within a database. All database structures such as tables have an owner or belong to a particular schema. A table belongs to one and only one owner or schema, and the owner name is prefixed to the table to distinguish it from other tables of the same name that belong to different schemas. For example, if Mary created a table called Product, it would exist in her schema, and would be available to other users as Mary.Product. If Joe also created a table called Product, it would exist in his schema and be available to other users as Joe.Product.

Report writers do not typically create database objects such as tables (though they may create views and stored procedures), so they tend to deal primarily with tables owned by other users or stored in schemas other than their own. Users typically have full privileges to the objects in their own schema, but must be specifically granted access to objects in other schemas. The schema name is usually the same as the user ID of the owner. However, in most large databases specific schemas are created to support specific applications, and so their names do not correspond to real people. For example, if the XTREME sample tables were created in Oracle, by the user Joe, they would probably be created in a schema called XTREME and not in the Joe schema. The Product table would be accessed as XTREME.Product.

Primary Keys

Most tables should and will have a *primary key* defined. The primary key is a field or combination of fields that uniquely identifies a row in the table. Since each record in a table should contain information about only one entity, a key is required to uniquely identify each row. The primary key is declared as part of the definition of the table, and the DBMS will not allow more than one row to have the same primary key.

As an example, suppose that we have a table of customers. The customer table contains fields for the customer's first name, last name, phone number, and address. What will uniquely identify one customer from another? In this case, it is probably the combination of the customer's last name and first name fields.

Using fields that have intrinsic meaning (such as last name) for primary keys is common practice, but what if two customers have the same last and first names? For that reason, database designers often create a special field to serve as the primary key, such as a Customer ID field. In that case, you would see the key field along with the other fields in Crystal Reports.

 TIP As a report writer, it is not usually your responsibility to decide what the primary key should be, but merely to determine what it is. But using Crystal Reports as your only tool, you cannot determine unequivocally the primary key for tables in most databases. There are many possible ways to obtain primary key and other database structure information. For some databases, such as Access, you can probably use database tools yourself to explore the structure. For others, you may need to request a data dictionary from the DBA in charge of the database.

Records in desktop databases may be stored physically in order by their primary key. Records in SQL databases are usually not stored in any particular order.

Foreign Keys and Linking

Earlier, we defined a database as a group of related tables. Relational databases may or may not have the primary relationships between tables defined as part of the table definitions, and therefore have them enforced by the database engine. Whether enforced or not, there will be logical relationships between some tables. If the relationships are defined (and enforced) within the database, then the database is said to have *referential integrity* for those relationships. A relationship exists where there is a logical connection from a field in one table to a field in another table. The connection is called a *link* and the fields are called *link fields*. If referential integrity constraints are defined, then the database engine will not allow values to be inserted into the link fields that would make the connection fail or leave orphaned records.

These relationships may take two general forms. One table may contain a field that is the primary key in a second table. For example, Figure 2-1 shows three tables from the XTREME sample database: a Supplier table that contains information about Suppliers, a Product Type table that contains information about product types, and a Product table that contains information about each product.

The Product table has as two of its fields the primary keys of the Supplier and Product Type tables. A logical relationship exists between the Supplier ID field in the Product table and the Supplier ID field in the Supplier table. Product and Supplier can be linked together using the Supplier ID field. This possible relationship has been defined in the database, as is indicated in the figure by the arrow that points from the Product table to the Supplier table. A similar relationship exists between the Product Type ID in the Product table and the Product Type ID in the Product Type table. In this form, the Supplier ID and Product Type ID fields in the Product table are called *foreign keys* because they point to a primary key field in another table. The foreign key fields are indicated in Figure 2-1 by the "FK" next to them.

Figure 2-1
Tables and their relationships

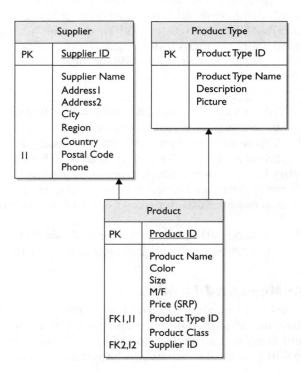

In this form, the tables that the arrows point to are often called *lookup tables,* because a matching record is looked up in that table using the foreign key value in the main table. This type of lookup is used when the entity in the main table can have only one instance of the foreign key field. In our example, a product can have only one supplier and only one product type.

The other general form is required for a many-to-many join. This form involves two related tables that have their relationship defined in a third table, as shown in Figure 2-2. The XTREME sample database contains an Orders table and a Product table. One order can contain many products, and one product can be part of many orders, so the Orders Detail table was created to define the many-to-many relationship. You can see that neither Product nor Orders contains a foreign key, but the Orders Detail table contains the primary keys of both tables and acts as a mapping between them. In this case, the Order ID field and the Product ID field in the Orders Detail table are both foreign keys pointing to the Orders and Product tables respectively, and combined they are also the primary key of the Orders Detail table. (Linking tables is discussed in more detail in Chapter 18.)

SQL

As mentioned previously, SQL is the language most often used to interact with large databases. (Desktop databases may have their own proprietary language and not use SQL.) SQL is used to create tables, populate them with data, and modify the data that already exists in them. SQL is also used to retrieve data from the database. The SQL SELECT command is used to return data from the database. A complete SELECT statement is commonly called a *query* and returns none, one, or many rows containing the fields requested.

Figure 2-2
A many-to-many link

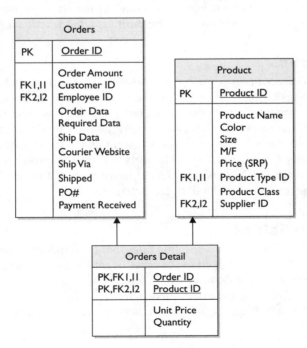

NOTE Crystal Reports can be thought of as a query-generation tool. Crystal Reports generates queries (SELECT statements) that fulfill the report requirements. However, Crystal Reports is much more than a query-generation tool, as it allows extensive manipulation and formatting of the returned data for presentation to the report user.

Views

Most databases have the capability to present alternative *views* of the data they contain to the user. A view can be thought of as a virtual table, although it does not exist as a physical structure containing data the way that a table does. A view is a query that is stored in the database. A view is the dataset that would be returned by the query that defines it, if the query were executed. Crystal Reports treats views identically to tables, reinforcing the virtual table concept, but the underlying database may treat a query on a view much differently than a query on a table.

Stored Procedures

Stored procedures are programs written in a proprietary database language, stored in the database, and executed by the DBMS on the database server. Stored procedures of a particular form can be used as datasets by Crystal Reports, much like tables and views. Stored procedures are typically created when extensive processing is required to produce the data needed by a report. If the processing is difficult or impossible to implement using standard SQL, a stored procedure may be used. The specific requirements for stored procedures that are usable with Crystal Reports vary depending on the database type. For more information, search for "stored procedures" on the Business Objects tech support web site.

Functions

Most DBMSs contain some system-defined functions, such as an absolute value function, various string-manipulation functions, and so on. In addition, users may create special-purpose functions that are stored in the database and usable in database queries. Report writers can use both built-in functions and user-defined functions in two areas of Crystal Reports. Database functions can be used in SQL Expression fields and in SQL Commands. In addition, Crystal Reports may translate some selection criteria to use database functions. (Don't worry, SQL Expressions, SQL Commands, and selection formulas will be discussed in detail in later chapters.)

System Tables

All SQL databases contain special tables that hold metadata and other system information. They are usually called *system tables* or *catalog tables*. These tables are maintained by the RDBMS itself and do not contain any application data. The system tables contain information about the database, such as lists of existing table names, field names, which fields are in which tables, and so on. Report writers rarely need to access the system tables to fulfill user requirements, but they may use the system tables to gather information about the database. It is possible to write reports based on system tables just as it is with regular user tables. For example, you can create a data dictionary report if you have the required privileges to read the system tables and understand their structure.

 TIP   Consult your database documentation for the structure of the system tables, and request SELECT privileges to your database's system tables. You can then create a Crystal Report that will always tell you the current structure of your database. This can be extremely useful if the data dictionary maintained by the DBA or other administrative staff is rarely updated.

Indexes

Indexes are database structures that are intended to speed up the retrieval of records. An in-depth discussion of indexing is beyond the scope of this book and is not required for the CRCP examinations. However, understanding which fields in your database are indexed can be important when optimizing a report. For some databases, Crystal Reports will indicate which fields are indexed; for others, it cannot. Consult a data dictionary to be sure.

Primary keys are always indexed, and foreign keys are usually indexed. Other fields may be indexed if they are used often for record selection. Index creation is usually the responsibility of the DBA or application developer, but that person should have a good understanding of the queries that will be used for reporting when they are developing their index strategy.

 CAUTION   Do not be overly quick to request new indexes. Proper indexing is a complex task, and the simple addition of new indexes may not have the desired effect. If you are designing a report that is not executing in an appropriate time frame, share the underlying SQL query with the DBA and request that he or she optimize the query. Having the entire query will allow the DBA to use the best method to obtain the desired result.

Database Security

All SQL databases and many desktop databases will have security controls that must be satisfied to gain access to the information stored in the database. The first level of security is the requirement of a user ID and password. Supplying these usually allows you to connect to a specific database, but it may not gain you access to any particular tables. For SQL databases, many different types of database privileges exist. The most important ones for a report writer are discussed here.

To be able to query records in tables, you must be granted the SELECT privilege. The SELECT privilege is granted for individual tables. To use stored procedures as datasets in Crystal Reports, you must be granted the EXECUTE privilege for the stored procedure. To use user-defined database functions, you must be granted the EXECUTE privilege for the functions. To use views as data sources, you must be granted the SELECT privilege for the view, but you do not need the SELECT privilege for the individual tables contained in the view. If your database has the concept of owners or schemas, you will have all database privileges for your own schema, but you must be granted rights specifically in other schemas.

XTREME Sample Data

Crystal Reports installs a sample Microsoft Access database called XTREME. The XTREME database will be used extensively throughout this book, so an overview of its structure is presented here.

The XTREME database contains data for the imaginary company, Xtreme Mountain Bikes. Xtreme Mountain Bikes sells mountain bikes and accessories. The database contains information about the company's employees, their customers, suppliers and products. In addition, several views exist to support particular reporting needs. Figure 2-3 shows a diagram of the XTREME database.

Figure 2-3 is a typical data model diagram. It has one box for each table and view in the database. Boxes with a white background are tables. Boxes with gray shading depict views. The name of the table or view is shown at the top. The field names are listed in the rows in the boxes, and if keys or indexes exist, the box is split vertically and they are shown in the left-hand column. "PK" denotes the primary key. If a primary key exists, it is shown in the first row or rows with a dividing line between it and the other fields. The field name of the primary key is underlined. Foreign keys are tagged with "FK" followed by a sequence number: FK1 for the first foreign key in a table, FK2 for the second foreign key in a table, and so on. Indexed fields are indicated by the letter "I" followed by a sequence number.

The Employee table contains one record for each employee of Xtreme Mountain Bikes. It has a generated key field called Employee ID. Employee contains fields for the personal information about employees, such as their name, phone number, birth date, and photo. In addition, it contains work-related information such as the employee's position, Social Security number, supervisor, and salary.

An additional item of note that may not be obvious from looking at the data model is that the Supervisor ID contained within each Employee record is the Employee ID of a different employee; it is the Employee ID of another Employee record. The Supervisor ID could actually be linked to the Employee ID, creating what is called a *recursive join*. The Reports To field is similar and can also be used to create a recursive join. Though the actual link is not defined in the database, and so no foreign key is indicated, the Supervisor ID and the Reports To field can be joined to the Employee ID in a SQL query.

NOTE   Links need not be defined in the database to be used in Crystal Reports. Crystal Reports will allow you to link any two fields that are of the same data type and length. However, it is likely that most of the links that you create in Crystal Reports will correspond to links defined in the database.

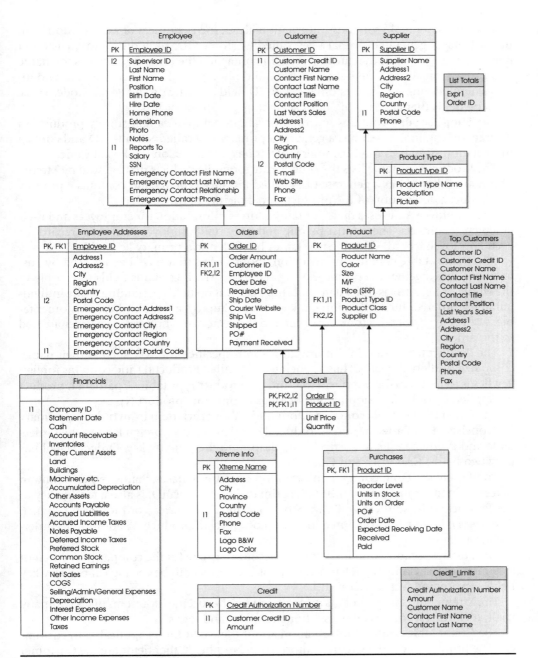

Figure 2-3   The XTREME data model

The Customer table contains information about the customers of Xtreme Mountain Bikes. It has a generated primary key called Customer ID. In addition to a customer name, it contains fields that are required for contacting the customer, such as the name of a contact, an address, an e-mail address, and phone numbers. Customer has two indexes defined: one on the Customer Credit ID field and one on the Postal Code. These must be fields that are used often for searching, grouping, or linking.

The Supplier table contains information about companies that supply products to Xtreme Mountain Bikes. It has a generated primary key called Supplier ID and contact information similar to the Customer table. It has one index on the Postal Code.

The Product Type table lists the general categories of products that are sold by Xtreme Mountain Bikes. It has a generated key called Product Type ID and contains a product type name, a description of the product, and a picture of the product.

The Employee Addresses table contains address information for employees and their emergency contacts. There must be one and only one Employee Addresses record for each Employee record, since the two tables have identical primary key fields.

The Orders table contains information about orders that have been placed by customers. It has a generated primary key called Order ID. It contains fields that apply to the whole order, such as order date and ship date, but no fields pertaining to the individual items ordered. It contains foreign keys to the Employee table and the Customer table, so the employee who took the order and the customer who made the order are tied to the order.

The Product table contains information about specific products, such as their name, color, size, and price. Product has a generated key called Product ID and contains foreign key fields to link it to the Supplier table and the Product Type table. A particular product is supplied by only one supplier and belongs to only one product type.

The Orders Detail table contains information about each item in an order. Its primary key consists of an Order ID and a Product ID, which are also foreign keys to the Orders table and Product table, respectively. In addition to the primary key, Orders Detail has only two fields, Unit Price and Quantity.

The Purchases table contains information about purchases that Xtreme Mountain Bikes has made from their suppliers. Its primary key, Product ID, is also a foreign key to the Product table, so there will always be only one Purchases record for each product. Purchases contains information about the stock level of products in addition to ordering information.

The Financials table contains aggregate accounting data for the company on different statement dates. Company ID and Statement Date appear to be the logical primary key fields but are not declared as such.

The Xtreme Info table contains information for the Xtreme Mountain Bikes company itself, including its name, address, phone number, and logos.

The Credit table contains information about the credit limits applicable to customers. The primary key is the Credit Authorization Number. Other fields are the Customer Credit ID that tells which customer the credit authorization is for and the amount field that gives the amount of credit that should be extended to the customer.

The views in the XTREME database were created to simplify particular reports. The Top Customers view contains customer information for customers who purchased over $50,000 worth of products from Xtreme Mountain Bikes in the previous year. The List Totals view computes the total order amount using the unit price and quantity from the Orders Detail table. The Credit_Limits view contains information about customer's credit limits and has a parameter to choose the limit desired. Views contained in most databases cannot have parameters. Since this view has a parameter, Crystal Reports will recognize it as a stored procedure rather than a view.

Data model diagrams created by different applications will vary in how they present the database structure. For example, Figure 2-4 is the Relationships display from the sample Access database. Note that not all the database tables are displayed by default, only those with defined relationships. A bold font is used to highlight the primary key fields. The links between tables lack arrows but they point directly to the linked fields. Data model diagrams created by other applications will display information in other ways.

Chapter Review

This chapter described general database concepts and the XTREME sample database in detail. The major structures of a database are tables, records, and fields. A database is made up of tables; tables are made up of records; and records are made up of fields.

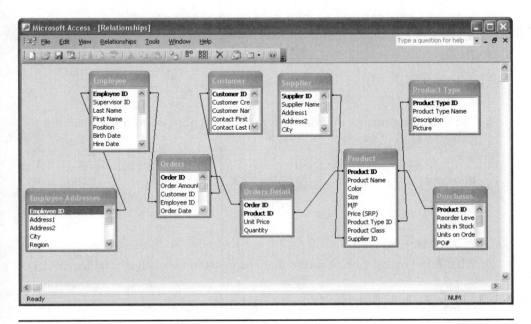

Figure 2-4   XTREME Access relationships

Fields hold a single fact. Records hold related fields for a single entity. Tables consist of multiple records, each representing a single entity. Tables can be linked to each other using similar fields from each table.

Quick Tips

- A database is a collection of tables and is used as a data source by Crystal Reports.
- A table contains multiple records, all having the same fields, where each record represents a different entity.
- A record is composed of fields that describe an entity.
- A field holds a single attribute of an entity.
- In a relational database, tables can be linked on similar fields.

 EXAM TIP   You need to know only very basic database concepts for the exam. Understand the following terms: *database, table, record, field, link,* and *relational database.*

Questions

1. The database structure that holds a single value is a
   a. table
   b. record
   c. field
   d. link
   e. database

2. The database structure that contains many collections of information about only one kind of object or entity is a
   a. table
   b. record
   c. field
   d. link
   e. database

3. What is the connection between identical fields in two different tables called?
   a. Table
   b. Record
   c. Field
   d. Link
   e. Database

4. The database structure that contains the attributes of one unique object or entity is a

   a. table

   b. record

   c. field

   d. link

   e. database

5. In a database (not necessarily in Crystal Reports), an empty or null numeric field is treated as if it contained the value zero.

   a. True

   b. False

6. The structure that corresponds to a data source in Crystal Reports is a

   a. table

   b. record

   c. field

   d. link

   e. database

The following questions can all be answered by referring to Figure 2-3. Note that no questions specifically concerning the XTREME database will be on the exam, but these questions will help to clarify database concepts for you.

7. How many tables are there in the XTREME database?

8. List the views in the XTREME database.

9. Which table has a compound primary key?

10. Which table has no primary key?

11. Which table has the fewest number of fields?

12. Which table is likely to have the most rows?

13. Which tables are linked to the Orders table?

14. Which two tables appear to have linkable fields, but have no link defined in the database?

Answers

1. **c.** A field is the smallest division in a database and holds a single fact or value.

2. **a.** A table contains many records, but those records all describe only one kind of object or entity.

3. **d.** The connection between two tables based on an identical field is called a *link*. Links may also be used to refer to the fields that are connected.

4. **b**. A record consists of a group of fields and contains information about only one entity or object.

5. **b**. A null numeric field is not treated as if it were equal to zero by most databases. Fields of any data type can be null and they are treated in a special manner and not as if they were blank or zero.

 CAUTION Crystal Reports has a configuration setting that, when set, treats null fields as zero.

6. **e**. A database is called a *data source* in the Crystal Reports development environment.

7. There are 12 tables in the XTREME database.

8. There are three views in the XTREME database: List Totals, Top Customers, and Credit_Limits.

9. The Orders Detail table is the only table with a compound primary key. Its primary key consists of the two fields Order ID and Product ID.

10. The Financials table has no primary key.

11. The Credit table has the fewest number of fields (three). The List Totals view has the fewest number of fields in a view.

12. By simply looking at the names of tables, you can make some guesses about their size. You would expect only a few employees, a few suppliers, and a limited number of products, but more customers. Hopefully, each customer places multiple orders and each order is for more than one product. Given this logic, you would expect the Orders Detail table to have the most records. The following are the record counts for each table.

Table Name	Record Count
Employee	15
Customer	269
Supplier	7
Product Type	8
Employee Addresses	15
Orders	2192
Product	115
Orders Detail	3684
Financials	4
Xtreme Info	1
Purchases	44
Credit	322

13. Employee, Customer, and Orders Detail are linked to the Orders table. Orders contains foreign keys to Employee and Customer, and Orders Detail contains a foreign key to Orders.

14. Customer and Credit both contain the Customer Credit ID. It would seem that they could be linked on this field, and Customer Credit ID in the Customer table would become a foreign key field. However, Customer Credit ID is not the primary key of the Customer table, so the link is not defined.

Quick Start Using the Report Wizards

In this chapter you will learn some Crystal Reports basics and create several reports using the report wizards:

- List report
- Grouped report
- Summary report
- Group Sorted report
- Chart report
- Filtered report
- Report formatted with a template
- Cross-tab report
- Mailing-label report
- OLAP report

This chapter is intended as a hands-on introduction to Crystal Reports for beginners, and although some exam objectives will be covered tangentially here, they are covered in more depth in subsequent chapters. If you are an experienced Crystal Reports user, you may skip this chapter.

NOTE   Because use of the report creation wizards is not an exam objective, no Quick Tips or Questions are included in this chapter.

As you work through the exercises in the chapter, do not be concerned if you initially feel somewhat confused. Though you may not understand everything that you are told to do, you are working with the application and gaining a base of knowledge that will be expanded upon in the rest of the book. The exercises are given systematically, and you should have no difficulty completing them. You will notice that there is much repetition across the exercises. This is not meant to bore you, but to simulate real life. Every report, no matter how complex or trivial, is started using the same steps.

Crystal Reports Basics

To complete the exercises, you need a very basic understanding of the Crystal Report environment. Crystal Reports is structured similarly to Microsoft Office applications, with a menu, toolbar, and work area. Many of the menu items are identical to Office applications such as File | Save, File | New, Help, and so on. If you are familiar with Office, you will have no difficulty navigating in Crystal Reports.

The file extension that Crystal Reports uses for its report files is .rpt. When you are requested to save the reports that you will create in the exercises, they will be saved as .rpt files by default.

When a report is opened in Crystal Reports, two tabs appear: Design and Preview. When you use the report wizards to create reports, they automatically open with the Preview pane displayed. In the Preview pane, you can scroll up and down on a single page using the scroll bars, or you can move from page to page using the page navigator that is displayed at the top right of the pane. The Design tab is discussed in detail in later chapters; you do not need to understand it now. Other tool and dialog boxes may open within the application. You will learn all about each of them in later chapters.

Sections

Report sections are mentioned in this chapter, but a detailed understanding of them is not required for completion of the exercises. Crystal Reports is a *banded* report generator. This means that it generates the report in bands across the page. The band where the individual record information is displayed is called the *detail section*. There will be at least one detail band for each record in the report when it is displayed.

Every Crystal Report also has four other bands: the report header section, report footer section, page header section, and page footer section. The report header band appears only once in any report, at the very beginning. Similarly, the report footer appears only at the very end of the report. The page header and page footer sections appear on every page of the report, at the top and bottom of the page. If a report has groups, then each group will have a group header section and group footer section. Any section can be split into multiple subsections, but only the default sections are used in this chapter.

Report Wizard Types

Crystal Reports has wizards that can assist you with report creation. When you open Crystal Reports, a welcome dialog box is displayed, as shown in Figure 3-1. To create a new report using a wizard, select that radio button and click OK. The Crystal Reports Gallery, shown in Figure 3-2, will then be displayed. The Gallery lists the available report wizard types, which currently include Standard, Cross-Tab, Mail Label, and OLAP.

NOTE If you have the display of the welcome dialog box turned off, you can get to the Gallery by choosing File | New.

Figure 3-1 Crystal Reports welcome dialog box

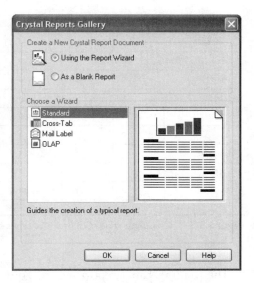

Figure 3-2 Crystal Reports Gallery

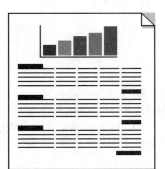

The Standard report wizard is the one used most often; it guides you through the creation of typical row-oriented reports. Most of the reports created in this chapter will use the Standard wizard.

The Cross-Tab report wizard guides you through the creation of a *cross-tab report*. A cross-tab report aggregates one or more fields by another field or fields. A cross-tab looks similar to a spreadsheet, but the fields in its main body of cells are always summarized in some way—typically summed or counted—based on the field values in the column and row headers. For example, if you wanted to know how many of each product type was sold by country, a cross-tab would be appropriate; an example is shown in Figure 3-3.

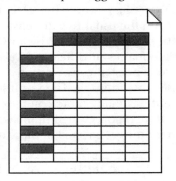

NOTE Cross-tabs can be added to any report. Use the Cross-Tab wizard only if the cross-tab will be the only content in the report.

	Argentina	Aruba	Australia	Austria	Bahamas	Banglades	Barbados	Belgium
Competition	0	2	4	10	0	0	0	17
Gloves	0	0	0	7	0	0	0	11
Helmets	0	0	4	10	0	0	0	25
Hybrid	2	0	0	0	0	0	0	22
Kids	0	0	0	1	0	0	0	10
Locks	0	0	1	12	0	3	0	5
Mountain	0	0	1	10	2	0	1	21
Saddles	0	0	3	8	0	0	0	4
Total	2	2	13	58	2	3	1	115

Figure 3-3   Cross-tab report of product types by country

The Mailing Label report wizard guides you through the creation of a report that prints labels. It will help you visualize the size of the label and format it as necessary to print in the proper multiples for the label type you choose.

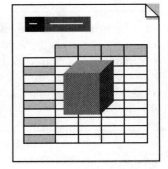

 NOTE   Any report can be formatted to create labels, but the ability to choose from standard Avery label types is available only in the Mail Label wizard.

The OLAP (online analytical processing) report wizard guides you through the creation of a report that uses an OLAP cube as a data source. An OLAP data source differs from the usual two-dimensional relational database table. OLAP data is data that has been presummarized by an OLAP engine and exists in a cube structure that contains summaries at different levels or hierarchies. The OLAP cube must already exist on a supported server for Crystal Reports to use it. The result looks like a cross-tab report but has many more complex and dynamic features. The OLAP report created in this chapter is very simple. OLAP reporting is covered in more detail in Chapter 23.

 NOTE   OLAP grids can be added to standard reports. Use the OLAP wizard if the OLAP grid will be the only content in the report.

Creating a List Report

A *list* is the simplest type of report. It is used when you want to display one or more fields from each record of one or more tables. To create a simple list report, only two steps are required. You must select the data source and the fields to display. Every report created with the Standard wizard starts as a list report, although it may have other features added.

> **NOTE**   The use of terms *list report, grouped report, summary report,* and so on in this chapter is intended to aid you in understanding the levels of complexity possible in reports. These terms should not be considered definitions and are not used on the CRCP exams.

Data Screen

The first thing you must do when creating any report is to choose the data you want the report to contain. The Crystal Reports wizards have a Data screen, shown in Figure 3-4, that makes this a simple process. On the Data screen, you simply choose the data source you want from the left-hand pane, Available Data Sources, and move it into the right-hand pane, the Selected Tables list, by using the arrow button or dragging it.

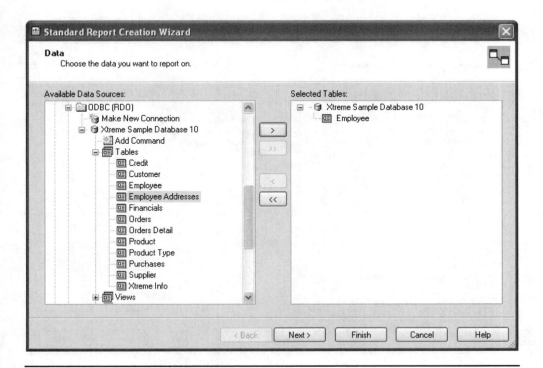

Figure 3-4   Selecting a data source

The application may prompt you for necessary connection information before completing the move. Connection information varies by database type. For the examples in this chapter, you will be using an ODBC connection to the XTREME sample database and you will be given the necessary steps for creating a connection when it is required.

 TIP Many screens in the Crystal Reports wizards have two lists of items with several buttons in between them. The buttons on each screen behave similarly. The single-arrow buttons act on the items in the lists that are highlighted (selected). The right-pointing arrow moves any highlighted items from the left-hand list to the right-hand list, and the left-pointing arrow does the reverse. The double arrows, when available, will move all the items from one list to the other.

Fields Screen

Once you have selected the data source, you will be presented with a Fields screen, as shown in Figure 3-5. On the Fields screen, you move the fields that you want in the report from the Available Fields list to the Fields to Display list by using the arrow buttons or dragging. Fields that are added to the report in the Fields screen will be displayed in the detail section of the report.

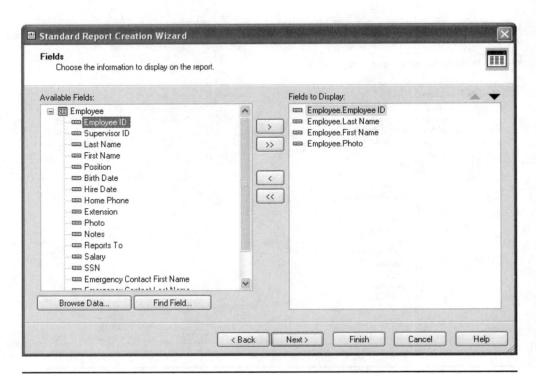

Figure 3-5 Selecting fields to include

TIP You can select more than one field using the SHIFT or CTRL key, just as you would in Windows Explorer. To select several fields that are in consecutive order, select the first one, hold down the SHIFT key, and then select the last one. All the fields in between will be highlighted and you can move them into the Fields to Display list by using the single-arrow button. To select multiple fields that are not in consecutive order, select the first one, and then hold the CTRL key while you click on the others.

Exercise 3.1: Creating an Employee List Report

1. Open Crystal Reports, choose Using the Report Wizard from the welcome dialog box, and click OK.

2. Select the Standard wizard and click OK.

3. Open the Create New Connection folder.

4. Scroll down until you see the ODBC (RDO) folder, and open it. An ODBC Data Source Selection dialog box will be displayed.

5. Scroll until you see Xtreme Sample Database 10 in the Data Source Name list. Select it as shown in Figure 3-6, and click Next.

Figure 3-6

Selecting the XTREME sample database

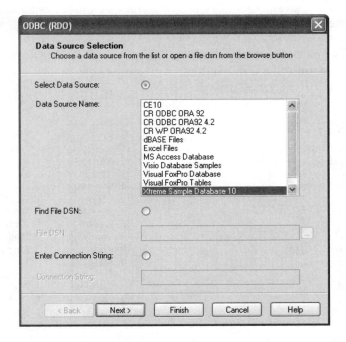

6. In the Connection Information dialog box, you can leave the User ID and Password boxes empty because no security is defined for the sample database. Click Finish. You will be returned to the Data screen, and there will be an entry for the Xtreme Sample Database 10 under the ODBC folder.

7. Open the Tables folder and select Employee. Click the single-arrow button to move the Employee table to the Selected Tables list, and click Next.

8. In the Fields screen, move Employee ID, First Name, and Last Name into Fields to Display.

9. Click Finish. The report will process, and you will see the list of employees in the Preview window, as shown in Figure 3-7.

10. You could now continue to modify the report, save it, print it, export it, and so on. For now, save it. Select File | Save. The Save As dialog box will open. Use the Create New Folder button to create a folder called **CRCP Exercises** in which to store your exercises. Then navigate to that folder, name the report **Exercise 3.1**, and save it.

 NOTE Crystal will create a temporary filename for you. The filenames that Crystal generates use the word *Report* followed by a number, so the name of this report is Report1.rpt until you change it. The first time you attempt to save a report, Crystal recognizes that it uses a temporary name and displays the Save As dialog box so that you can override the default name.

 11. Close the report by choosing File | Close or clicking the close button for the maximized report window.

Figure 3-7
Previewing the Employee list report

Employee ID	First Name	Last Name
1	Nancy	Davolio
2	Andrew	Fuller
3	Janet	Leverling
4	Margaret	Peacock
5	Steven	Buchanan
6	Michael	Suyama
7	Robert	King
8	Laura	Callahan
9	Anne	Dodsworth
10	Albert	Hellstern
11	Tim	Smith
12	Caroline	Patterson
13	Justin	Brid
14	Xavier	Martin
15	Laurent	Pereira

CAUTION If the report window is not maximized the close button for the individual report window and the close button for the Crystal Reports application are identical—both look like the button shown here. Do not click the close button for Crystal Reports or the entire application will close.

Creating a Grouped Report

A grouped report builds on a list report by adding a group. A group gathers together all the records that have the same value in a given field and adds a header and footer for the group. For example, if you group by the Country field, then all the records that have "USA" in that field will be listed together with a group header section for USA starting the group and a group footer section for USA ending the group. Groups are often used together with summaries at the group level; however, the simple example used in this section contains a group but no summary.

Grouping Screen

The Standard report wizard has a Grouping screen, shown in Figure 3-8. The Grouping screen is used to add groups to a report. Fields are moved from the Available Fields list to

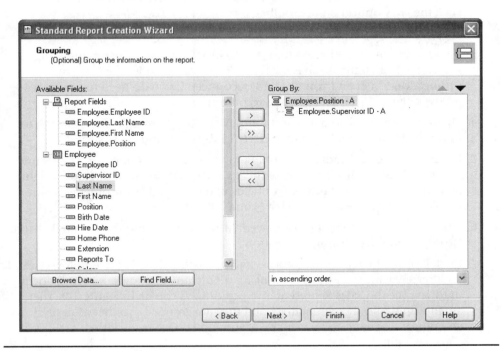

Figure 3-8 Selecting fields for grouping

the Group By list to create groups on those fields. More than one field may be added to the Group By list. If more than one field is added, the order of the fields in the list is important. The grouping hierarchy is shown visually in the Group By list, which creates a treelike structure to show which groups will be subordinate to other groups. You can change the order using the arrow buttons at the upper-right of the Group By list.

The Available Fields list contains a folder for Report Fields and one folder for each table used in the report. Fields that have already been added to the report in the Fields screen will appear under the Report Fields folder *and* under the table that they come from. Fields from any folder can be added to the Group By list; a field need not have been added to the report in the Fields screen to be used as a group field. If a field is added as a group by field, it will also become a report field, and it will be listed in the detail section of the report to the left of the other detail fields.

When you add a group, Crystal Reports automatically sorts the group instances. You can choose the sort order for each group by selecting the group and then choosing "in ascending order" or "in descending order" in the drop-down box immediately below the Group By list.

Exercise 3.2: Creating a Grouped Report

1. Open Crystal Reports, choose Using the Report Wizard from the welcome screen, and click OK. If Crystal Reports is already open, choose File | New, or click the New button on the toolbar.

2. Select the Standard wizard and click OK.

3. If you have not disconnected from the XTREME database since completing Exercise 3.1, then the database will still be available under the Current Connection folder and you need not reconnect. If you do need to reconnect, follow steps 3–6 in Exercise 3.1 to reconnect.

4. Open the Tables folder and select Employee. Click the single-arrow button to move the Employee table to the Selected Tables list, and click Next.

5. In the Fields screen, move Position, Employee ID, Last Name, and First Name into the Fields to Display list. Use the up and down arrows at the upper right of the list to change the position of fields in the list so that the order is Position, Employee ID, Last Name, and First Name. Click Next.

6. The Grouping screen will be displayed. Move Position into the Group By list to create an employee listing by position.

7. Click Finish. The report will process and you will see the list of employees in the Preview window. Most positions have only one employee, so scroll down until you see the Sales Representative position, as shown in Figure 3-9. There are multiple Sales Representatives and they are grouped together as desired. You will notice that a group header and group footer have been added automatically.

Sales Manager			
Sales Manager	5	Buchanan	Steven
Sales Manager			
Sales Representative			
Sales Representative	9	Dodsworth	Anne
Sales Representative	7	King	Robert
Sales Representative	6	Suyama	Michael
Sales Representative	4	Peacock	Margaret
Sales Representative	3	Leverling	Janet
Sales Representative	1	Davolio	Nancy
Sales Representative			
Vice President, Sales			
Vice President, Sales	2	Fuller	Andrew
Vice President, Sales			

Figure 3-9   Employees by position report

 NOTE   You may be wondering why you have been instructed to click Finish even though the Next button is still available. As soon as Crystal Reports has enough information to create a report, the Finish button becomes available and you may click it to end the wizard and generate the report. Each of the exercises in this chapter will take you further in the wizard until all the screens have been described.

8. You could now continue to modify the report, save it, print it, export it, and so on. For now, save it by choosing File | Save, put it in the CRCP Exercises folder, and save it as **Exercise 3.2**.

9. Close the report by choosing File | Close or clicking the close button for the report window.

Grouping is covered in detail in Chapter 7.

Creating a Summary Report

Summary is a term used in Crystal Reports for any type of aggregation, including summing, counting, and averaging, and for other measures that apply to a group of records, such as the maximum, minimum, variance, standard deviation, mode, and so on. Summaries are often created for groups, but they can apply to the entire report as well.

When you create a summary, Crystal Reports creates a new field called, logically enough, a summary field. Summary fields become report fields and can be used much like other report fields, except that they dynamically redefine themselves to apply to whatever group section that they are placed in. For example, if you create a summary field that contains the count of customers by country, this summary field will be put in the group footer for the country group by default. If you move this summary field into the group footer for a group that is grouped by region, it will change its definition and become the count of customers by region. Summary fields can be placed in group headers or footers or the report header or footer. When placed in either a group header or footer, the summary applies to the group. When placed in a report header or footer, the summary applies to the whole report. Summary fields cannot be placed in detail sections.

Summaries Screen

The Standard report wizard has a Summaries screen, as shown in Figure 3-10. The Summaries screen is used to add summary fields to groups on a report. Fields are moved from the Available Fields list to the Summarized Fields list to create summaries on those fields. More than one field may be added to the Summarized Fields list.

The grouping hierarchy created in the Grouping screen is displayed in the Summarized Fields list. You can create summary fields for any group in the list. Before moving a field from the Available Fields list to the Summarized Fields list, select the group that you want it to apply to in the Summarized Fields list. You can move the same field more than once, and so create different types of summaries based on the same field. For example, you can sum the order amount and average it.

You can also create the same summary type for different group levels. To create the same summary for different groups, just move the same field into different groups and choose the same summary operation. For example, if you want the sum of the order

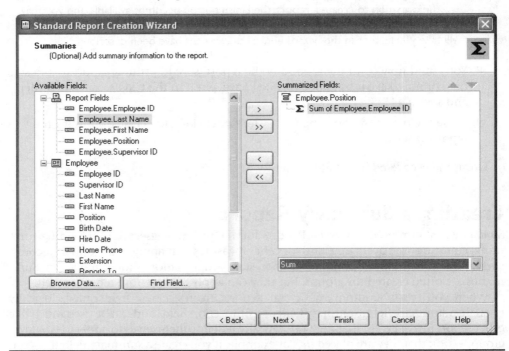

Figure 3-10   Selecting summary fields

amount by country and region, move the Order Amount field under the Country group and under the Region group.

Once you have moved the field, you can select it and then change the type of summary using the drop-down box below the Summarized Fields list. Many types of summaries can be created for numeric fields; other field types have fewer summary type options. For example, you cannot sum the first name field, but you can count it.

Exercise 3.3: Creating a Summary Report

1. Repeat steps 1–6 of Exercise 3.2, and then click Next. The Summaries screen will appear with a summary already added. Crystal Reports will add all numeric fields to the summary list automatically. Crystal Reports cannot differentiate between a numeric field that should be used for summarizing and a numeric field that is not appropriate for aggregation; it simply chooses to sum the Employee ID field because it is numeric.

2. Change the summary type to Count using the drop-down box below the Summarized Fields list.

3. Click Finish. The report will process and you will see the report in the Preview window. Most positions have only one employee, so scroll down until you see the Sales Representative position, as shown in Figure 3-11. The count of employees by position has been added to the group footer.

4. Save the report by choosing File | Save. Put it in the CRCP Exercises folder, and call it **Exercise 3.3**.

5. Close the report by choosing File | Close or clicking the close button for the report window.

Summarizing is covered in detail in Chapter 7.

Sales Manager			
Sales Manager	5	Buchanan	Steven
Sales Manager	**1**		
Sales Representative			
Sales Representative	9	Dodsworth	Anne
Sales Representative	7	King	Robert
Sales Representative	6	Suyama	Michael
Sales Representative	4	Peacock	Margaret
Sales Representative	3	Leverling	Janet
Sales Representative	1	Davolio	Nancy
Sales Representative	**6**		

Figure 3-11   Summary report

Creating a Group Sorted Report

Crystal Reports' group sorting capability is commonly called *Top-N* or *Bottom-N* reporting. A group sorted report is one where the groups on the report are displayed in order using some summary value for the group rather than the value in the group by field. For example, if you have a group by country and a summary field that is defined to be the total order amount by country, you could sort the groups such that the country having the largest total order amount is displayed first on the report, followed by the country with the second largest total order amount, and so on, instead of alphabetically by the country name.

Entire groups may be filtered out of the report if they are not in the top so-many groups or bottom so-many groups. For example, you could sort the country groups by total order amount, as just described, and stipulate that only the countries with the five highest total order amounts be displayed. Crystal Reports would then display only five countries and filter out all others. Crystal Reports can also use percentages for the sorting and filtering. For example, you could say that you want to display the groups that contribute the top 20% of the total order amount. Crystal would then sort the groups from largest total order amount to smallest and display only enough countries to obtain at least 20% of the grand total order amount.

Group Sorting Screen

The Standard report wizard has a Group Sorting screen, as shown in Figure 3-12. The Group Sorting screen in the Standard wizard is not full-featured and allows only the top

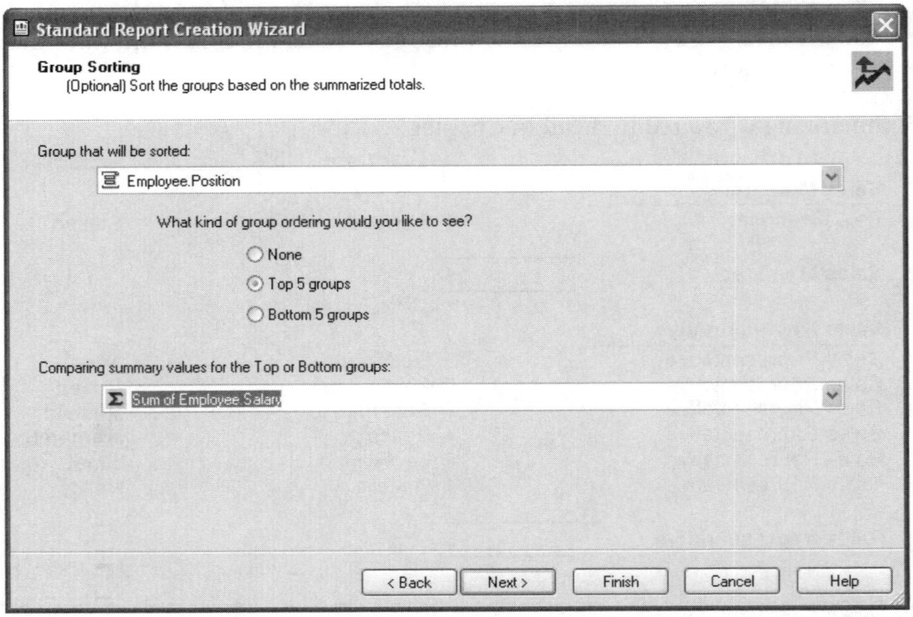

Figure 3-12   Setting up group sorting

five or bottom five groups. To do no group sorting, you must select the None option. For more flexibility, you can use the Group Sorting Expert that is covered in Chapter 13.

Exercise 3.4: Creating a Group Sorted Report

1. Repeat steps 1–6 of Exercise 3.2, and then click Next. The Summaries screen will appear with two summaries already added.

2. Change the summary type to Count for the Employee ID field using the drop-down box below the Summarized Fields list. Leave the summary for Salary as Sum. Your Summaries screen should look like Figure 3-13.

3. Click Next. The Group Sorting screen will appear. Select the radio button for Top 5 Groups. In the Comparing Summary Values drop-down box, choose the Sum of Employee.Salary option, as shown in Figure 3-12.

4. Click Finish. The report will process and you will see the report in the Preview window. Since the report was configured to return only the top five groups based on the total salary for the group, the Sales Representative position is listed first, as shown in Figure 3-14, followed by the next four highest groups.

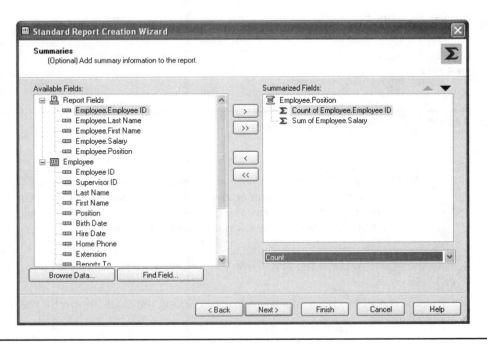

Figure 3-13 Editing summaries for group sorted report

Position	Employee ID	Last Name	First Name	Salary
Sales Representative				
Sales Representative	9	Dodsworth	Anne	$35,000.00
Sales Representative	7	King	Robert	$37,000.00
Sales Representative	6	Suyama	Michael	$30,000.00
Sales Representative	4	Peacock	Margaret	$35,000.00
Sales Representative	3	Leverling	Janet	$33,000.00
Sales Representative	1	Davolio	Nancy	$40,000.00
Sales Representative	**6**		**$210,000.00**	
Vice President, Sales				
Vice President, Sales	2	Fuller	Andrew	$90,000.00
Vice President, Sales	**1**		**$90,000.00**	
Marketing Director				
Marketing Director	13	Brid	Justin	$75,000.00
Marketing Director	**1**		**$75,000.00**	
Business Manager				
Business Manager	10	Hellstern	Albert	$60,000.00
Business Manager	**1**		**$60,000.00**	
Marketing Associate				
Marketing Associate	14	Martin	Xavier	$50,000.00
Marketing Associate	**1**		**$50,000.00**	
Grand Total:	**15**			**$668,000.00**

Figure 3-14   Group sorted report

NOTE   The grand totals for the count of employees and total salary are not the sums of the records shown on the report but the sums of all the records before the top five groups were selected. This is the result of the way that Crystal Reports processes data. It is discussed in Chapter 15.

5. Save the report by choosing File | Save. Put it in the CRCP Exercises folder, and call it **Exercise 3.4**.

6. Close the report by choosing File | Close or clicking the close button for the report window.

Creating a Report with a Chart

Crystal Reports allows you to add charts to reports. The charting options are extensive and are covered fully in Chapter 10, but this section offers a suggestion of the possibilities.

Chart Screen

The Standard report wizard includes a Chart screen, as shown in Figure 3-15, that allows you to easily add a chart to the report. The Chart screen is not full-featured, but it allows you to quickly add one simple chart to a report.

Exercise 3.5: Creating a Chart Report

1. Repeat steps 1–6 of Exercise 3.2, and then click Next. Click Next on the Summaries screen. The Group Sorting screen appears. Leave the radio button set for None.

2. Click Next. The Chart screen appears. Choose Pie chart and set the Show Summary drop-down box to Sum of Employee Salary. The title of the chart will automatically reflect your choices, although you can change it if desired.

3. Click Finish. The report will process and you will see the report in the Preview window. The chart will be added to the report header section and will look

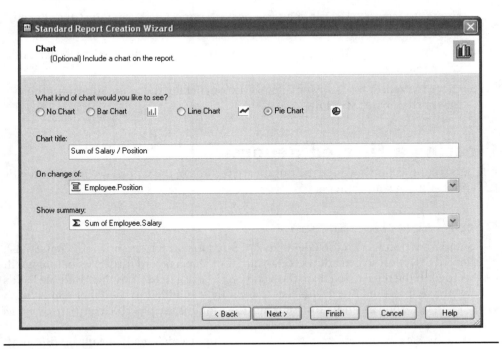

Figure 3-15   Adding a chart

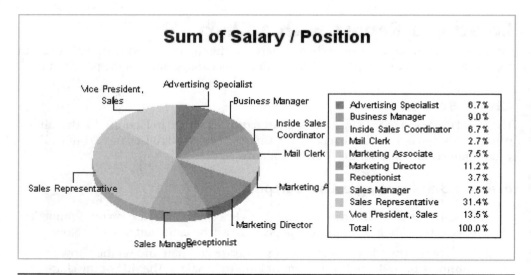

Figure 3-16   Chart report

similar to Figure 3-16. The chart can be further modified using the Chart Expert, which is described in Chapter 10.

4. Save the report by choosing File | Save. Put it in the CRCP Exercises folder, and call it **Exercise 3.5**.

5. Close the report by choosing File | Close or clicking the close button for the maximized report window.

Creating a Filtered Report

A filtered report is one in which the number of records in the report has been limited by the application of some criteria.

Record Selection Screen

The Standard report wizard includes a Record Selection screen, as shown in Figure 3-17. The Record Selection screen allows you to add tests that a record must pass before it will be included in the report. To create the test, you choose a field from the Available Fields list and move it to the Filter Fields list. Once a field is added to the Filter Fields list, a drop-down box appears under the list. This box contains the possible comparison types that can be used.

If you choose any option other than "is any value" (which really means no filtering), one or more other boxes will appear where you select the comparison value or values. You may add filters on more than one field. If you create multiple filters, they must all be

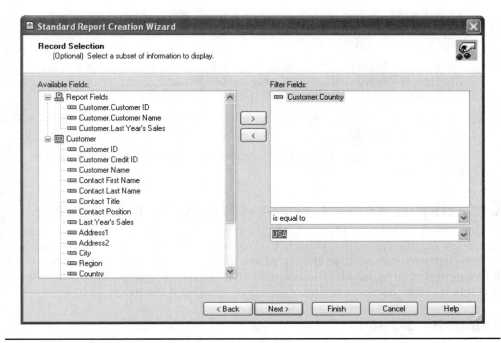

Figure 3-17 Selecting records to include in a report

true for a given record to be included on the report. The tests that you create are applied to every record in the table, and only those that pass it are displayed in the report.

NOTE Tests created using the Record Selection screen become the selection formula for the report. The Record Selection screen is sufficient for many types of reports, but the selection formula may be edited directly to create filters that are more complex. Record Selection is discussed in more detail in Chapter 6.

Exercise 3.6: Creating a Filtered Report

1. Repeat steps 1–5 of Exercise 3.2. The Grouping screen will be displayed; do not add any groups. Click Next.

NOTE Because you did not add any groups, the Summaries, Group Sorting, and Chart screens will not be displayed.

2. The Record Selection screen appears. Move Country to the Filter Fields list.

3. In the drop-down box, choose "is equal to."

4. In the second drop-down box choose "USA."

5. Click Finish. The report will process, and you will see the report in the Preview window. The report will contain only those customers whose country field contains "USA," as shown in Figure 3-18.

6. Save the report by choosing File | Save. Put it in the CRCP Exercises folder, and call it **Exercise 3.6**.

7. Close the report by choosing File | Close or clicking the close button for the report window.

Creating a Report Formatted with a Template

Crystal Reports has many different kinds of formatting options. A *report template* is a collection of specific formatting choices that can be applied to existing or new reports. Crystal Reports comes with several templates, and users can create their own as well. A template is just a regular RPT file whose formatting can be applied to another report. Any report can be used as a template. Template creation is covered in Chapter 9.

Template Screen

The Standard report wizard has a Template screen in which an existing template can be applied to the new report. The Template screen lists available templates, as shown in

Customer ID	Customer Name	Last Year's Sales	Country
1	City Cyclists	$20,045.27	USA
2	Pathfinders	$26,369.63	USA
3	Bike-A-Holics Anonymous	$4,500.00	USA
4	Psycho-Cycle	$52,809.11	USA
5	Sporting Wheels Inc.	$85,642.56	USA
6	Rockshocks for Jocks	$40,778.52	USA
7	Poser Cycles	$10,923.00	USA
8	Spokes 'N Wheels Ltd.	$25,521.31	USA
9	Trail Blazer's Place	$123,658.46	USA
10	Rowdy Rims Company	$30,131.46	USA
11	Clean Air Transportation Co.	$23,789.25	USA
12	Hooked on Helmets	$52,963.82	USA
13	C-Gate Cycle Shoppe	$29,618.11	USA
14	Alley Cat Cycles	$298,356.22	USA
15	The Bike Cellar	$30,938.67	USA
16	Hercules Mountain Bikes	$18,000.00	USA
17	Whistler Rentals	$68,000.00	USA
18	Bikes and Trikes	$12,000.00	USA
19	Changing Gears	$26,705.65	USA
20	Wheels and Stuff	$25,556.11	USA
21	Uni-Cycle	$52,428.13	USA
22	Crank Components	$8,030.11	USA
23	Corporate Cycle	$27,081.31	USA

Filtered report

Figure 3-18   Filtered report

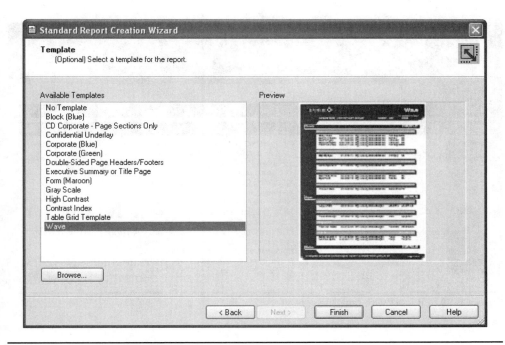

Figure 3-19   Previewing templates

Figure 3-19. You can choose one of the templates in the list or browse to choose any existing report file. A preview of the formatting appears in the Preview pane.

Exercise 3.7: Creating a Report from a Template

1. Open Crystal Reports, choose Using the Report Wizard from the welcome dialog box, and click OK. If Crystal Reports is already open, choose File | New, or click the New button on the toolbar.

2. Select the Standard wizard and click OK.

3. If you have not disconnected from the XTREME database since completing Exercise 3.6, you need not reconnect. If you do need to reconnect, follow steps 3–6 in Exercise 3.1.

4. Open the Tables folder and select Customer. Click the single-arrow button to move the Customer table to the Selected Tables list, and click Next.

5. In the Fields screen, move Country, Customer ID, Customer Name, and Last Year's Sales into the Fields to Display list. Click Next.

6. The Grouping screen will be displayed. Move Country to the Group By list. Click Next.

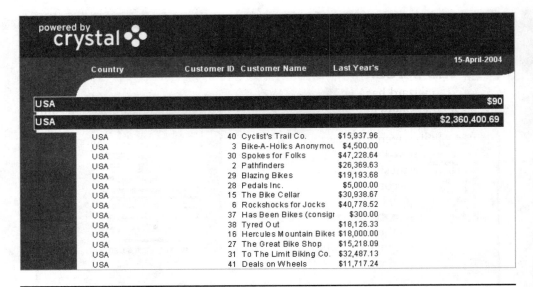

Figure 3-20   Report with template applied

7. In the Summaries screen, change the summary type for Customer ID to Count. Click Next.

8. In the Group Sorting screen, choose the top five of the groups based on the sum of Last Year's Sales. Click Next.

9. In the Chart screen, choose No Chart, and click Next.

10. In the Record Selection screen, do not add any filters; just click Next.

11. The Template screen will appear. You can browse and see the preview of different templates. Choose Wave.

12. Click Finish. The report will process and you will see the report in the Preview window. The formatting from the template will be applied, as shown in Figure 3-20.

13. Save the report by choosing File | Save. Put it in the CRCP Exercises folder, and call it **Exercise 3.7**.

14. Close the report by choosing File | Close or clicking the close button for the report window.

Creating a Cross-Tab Report

A Cross-Tab report is one that contains one or more cross-tabs. Cross-tabs are generally placed in the report header or footer or a group header or footer since they usually do some sort of aggregation at the whole report level or a group level. The Cross-Tab wizard creates one cross-tab and places it in the report header.

Cross-Tab Screen

The Cross-Tab wizard has many of the same screens as the Standard wizard. It has the same Data, Link, Chart, and Record Selection screens as the Standard wizard. Its unique screens are the Cross-Tab screen, and the Grid Style screen.

The Cross-Tab screen, shown in Figure 3-21, has an Available Fields list and a Cross-Tab panel. The Cross-Tab panel has three boxes: The Summary Fields box contains the field(s) that you want summarized in the cells of the cross-tab. The values in the fields of the Rows box will become the rows of the cross-tab report, and the values of the fields in the Columns box will become the columns of the cross-tab. Fields are moved from the Available Fields list to the other boxes by using the arrow buttons or dragging. Under the Summary Fields box there is a drop-down list used for choosing the type of summary desired. All summary types that are appropriate for the selected summary field are displayed in the box and you may choose one.

The Cross-Tab screen combines the operations that are performed by the Grouping and Summaries screens of the Standard wizard. In it you choose the fields that will be summarized, the type of summary, and two or more grouping fields. The differences are that no Fields screen is required, because no detail-level records will be displayed, and the groups are arranged in a cross-tab fashion rather than one under the other. For example,

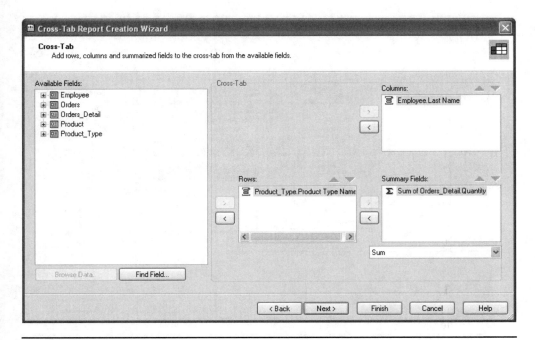

Figure 3-21   Setting up a cross-tab grid

in a standard report, you might have a group for Country and beneath that, a group for Product Type. Each country will be displayed, followed by each Product Type. In a cross-tab report, the Product Type groups will be listed multiple times, once under each country to which they apply. You can have a group by Country and a group across Product Type. In this case, the countries will be listed down the page in rows, and the product types will be listed across the page in the columns, with the appropriate summary showing in the intersection of the column and row.

Link Screen

The Link screen is displayed immediately after the Data screen in the Standard, Cross-Tab, and Mail Label wizards if more than one table is selected in the Data screen. (Linking has not been discussed yet because it is an advanced topic.) The Link screen is used to define the appropriate links between the chosen tables, as shown in Figure 3-22. Crystal Reports will create links for you automatically in most cases, and you need not understand it now. Linking is covered in Chapters 5 and 18.

Grid Style Screen

The Grid Style screen, shown in Figure 3-23, is used to apply optional formatting to a cross-tab report. If you like one of the predefined styles, you can use it to format your report. Otherwise, you can create custom formatting later, after finishing with the report wizard.

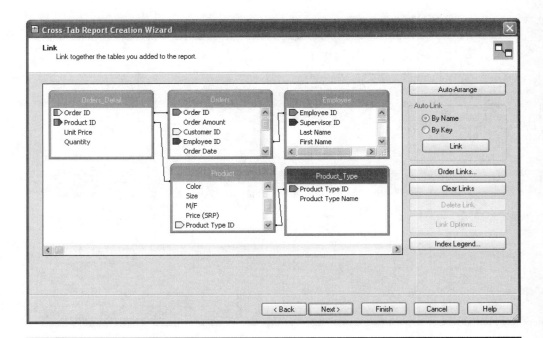

Figure 3-22   Defining links

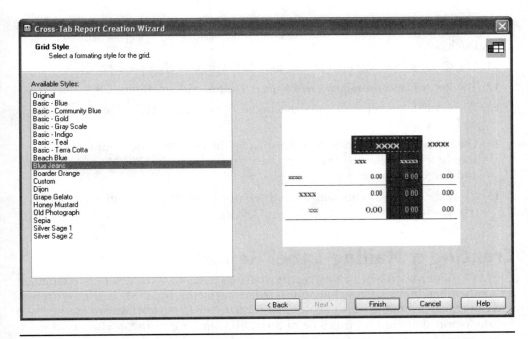

Figure 3-23   Selecting a grid style

Exercise 3.8: Creating a Cross-Tab Report

1. Open Crystal Reports, choose Using the Report Wizard from the welcome dialog box, and click OK. If Crystal Reports is already open, choose File | New, or click the New button on the toolbar.

2. Select the Cross-Tab wizard and click OK.

3. If you have not disconnected from the XTREME database since completing Exercise 3.7, then the database will still be available under the Current Connection folder and you need not reconnect. If you do need to reconnect, follow steps 3–6 in Exercise 3.1.

4. Open the Tables folder. Move the Order Details, Orders, Employee, Product, and Product Type tables to the Selected Tables list, and click Next.

5. The Link screen will appear. The links that Crystal Reports creates for you should be appropriate in this case. Your Link screen should look like Figure 3-22. Click Next.

6. The Cross-Tab screen will appear.

7. Move Orders_Detail.Quantity to the Summary Fields list.

8. Move Employee.Last Name to the Columns list.

9. Move Product_Type.Product Type Name to the Rows list.

10. Click Next.

11. The Chart screen will appear. Choose No Chart, and click Next.

12. The Record Selection screen will appear. Do not add any filters. Click Next.

13. The Grid Style screen will appear. Choose Blue Jeans, as shown in Figure 3-23, and click Finish.

14. The report will be processed and display in the Preview pane. Your report should look similar to Figure 3-24. Save the report in the CRCP Exercises folder, and name it **Exercise 3.8**.

15. Close the report by choosing File | Close or clicking the close button for the report window.

Creating a Mailing Label Report

The Mail Label wizard will create a report where each record is printed in a rectangular area rather than in rows. Crystal Reports is still using bands, but the bands are narrower and can repeat across the page in columnar format. The Mail Label wizard can be used for any report that requires this type of formatting and not only for label creation. It might be used to create postcards, name tags, and so on.

Label Screen

As with the Cross-Tab wizard, the Mail Label wizard has many of the same screens as the Standard wizard. It has the same Data, Link, Fields, and Record Selection screens, for example. Its unique screen is the Label screen shown, in Figure 3-25.

	Davolio	Dodsworth	King	Leverling	Peacock	Suyama	Total
Total	1,245	1,269	1,393	1,193	1,233	1,279	7,612.00
Competition	220	234	225	214	207	229	1,329.00
Gloves	180	223	195	179	210	165	1,152.00
Helmets	321	270	293	246	256	217	1,603.00
Hybrid	79	88	120	81	87	107	562.00
Kids	42	42	55	50	39	49	277.00
Locks	64	89	75	92	87	100	507.00
Mountain	245	196	302	213	221	301	1,478.00
Saddles	94	127	128	118	126	111	704.00

Figure 3-24   Cross-tab report

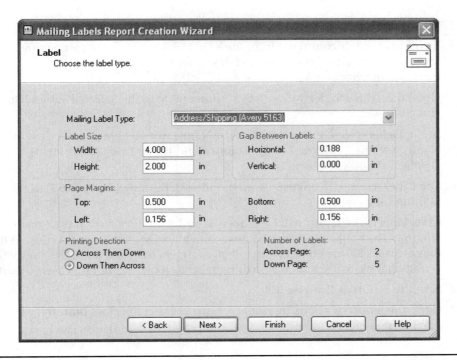

Figure 3-25 Selecting a label style

The Label screen has a Mailing Label Type drop-down box where you can choose from standard label sizes. Once you pick a label, the Label Size, Gap Between Labels, and Page Margins are filled in for you. If you need a custom size, you can choose User-Defined Label and fill in the other boxes yourself. You set the labels to print individual records across the page and then down, or down the page and then across.

TIP The Standard wizard and the Cross-Tab wizard help you to create reports that you could reproduce by starting with a blank report. The Mail Label wizard is somewhat different, because it is the only place where you can pick from standard Avery label types. You could create labels by starting with a blank report, but you would then need to know the exact size and locations of the labels for the product that you use—they would not be supplied for you.

Exercise 3.9: Creating a Mailing Label Report

1. Open Crystal Reports, choose Using the Report Wizard from the welcome dialog box, and click OK. If Crystal Reports is already open, choose File | New, or click the New button on the toolbar.

2. Select the Mail Label wizard and click OK.

3. If you have not disconnected from the XTREME database since completing Exercise 3.8, you need not reconnect. If you do need to reconnect, follow steps 3–6 in Exercise 3.1.

4. Open the Tables folder. Move the Customer table to the Selected Tables list, and click Next.

5. In the Fields screen, move Contact First Name, Contact Last Name, Customer Name, Address1, Address2, City, Country, and Postal Code to the Fields to Display list and click Next.

6. The Label screen will appear. Choose Address/Shipping (Avery 5163) as the Mailing Label Type.

7. Click Finish. The report will be processed and then displayed in the Preview window. The Mail Label wizard puts each field in a separate detail section so that they are stacked one on top of the other, as shown in Figure 3-26. Obviously that is not what we really want our mailing label to look like, but it is a good start.

8. Save this report as **Exercise 3.9**.

9. Close the report by choosing File | Close or clicking the close button for the maximized report window.

Chris	Heather
Christianson	Davis
City Cyclists	Rockshocks for Jocks
7464 South Kingsway	1984 Sydney Street
Suite 2006	Austin
Sterling Heights	USA
USA	78770
48358	
Christine	Alex
Manley	Smith
Pathfinders	Poser Cycles
410 Eighth Avenue	8194 Peter Avenue
DeKalb	Eden Prairie
USA	USA
60148	55360

Figure 3-26   Mailing label report

Creating an OLAP Report

An OLAP report is one that contains one or more OLAP grids based on OLAP cubes. An *OLAP cube* is a multidimensional data source that has summaries precomputed across its dimensions.

OLAP Data Screen

The OLAP Data screen is the first screen involved in choosing a data source for an OLAP grid. The OLAP Data screen has two buttons that are used to select a data source, the Select Cube and the Select CAR file buttons, as shown in Figure 3-27. The Select CAR file button is used to create a report based on a Crystal Analysis application. The Select Cube button is used to choose an OLAP cube from an OLAP data source.

Crystal OLAP Connection Browser Dialog Box

Clicking the Select Cube button opens the Crystal OLAP Connection Browser dialog box, as shown next. In the OLAP Connection Browser you pick the OLAP Connection

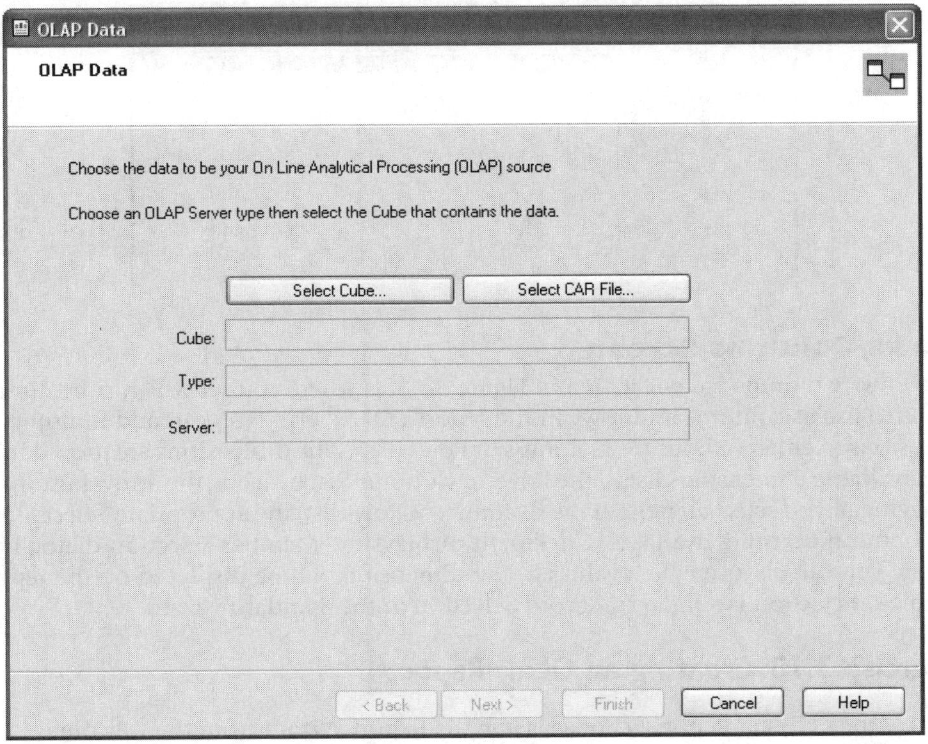

Figure 3-27   Choosing a data source for an OLAP grid

that you want to use for the OLAP grid. If the connection you want is not listed, click Add Server to create it.

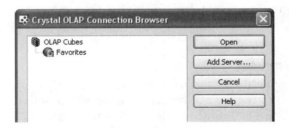

New Server Dialog Box

The New Server dialog box is used to add OLAP connections to the report. The New Server dialog box has a drop-down box where you choose the Server Type, as shown here. You must create a caption for every connection type. The entries required in the Server Options panel vary depending on the connection type.

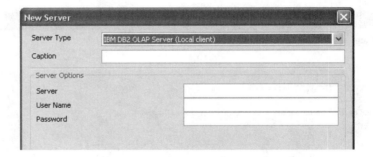

Rows/Columns Screen

The Rows/Columns screen, shown in Figure 3-28, is where you set which cube dimensions to use as columns and rows in the report's OLAP grid. You can add multiple dimensions to either or both the Columns or Rows list. Cube dimensions are moved from the Available Dimensions list to the Rows or Columns list by using the arrow buttons or dragging. If you select an item in the Columns or Rows list, the appropriate Select Members button becomes available. Clicking it displays the Member Selection dialog box, where you can choose which values of the dimension will be displayed on the report. Member Selection is similar to Record Selection in the Standard wizard.

Exercise 3.10: Creating an OLAP Report

1. Open Crystal Reports, choose Using the Report Wizard from the welcome dialog box, and click OK. If Crystal Reports is already open, choose File | New, or click the New button on the toolbar.

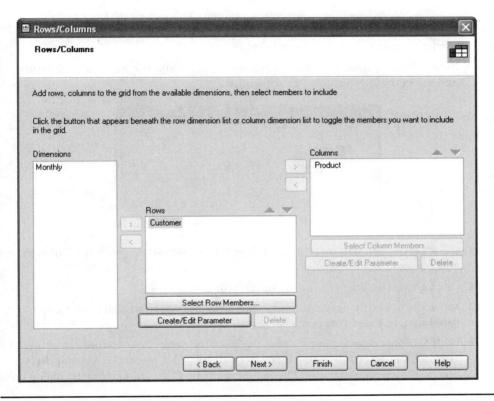

Figure 3-28   Selecting rows and/or columns

2. Select the OLAP wizard, and click OK.

3. The OLAP Data screen appears. Click the Select Cube button.

4. The Crystal OLAP Connection Browser dialog box appears. Click the Add Server button.

5. The New Server dialog box appears. For this report, set the Server Type to Holos HDC Cube (Local Client).

6. For the caption, enter **Exercise 3.10**.

7. In the Server Options panel for the HDC file, click the ellipsis button to browse to the sample HDC file. Browse to C:\Program Files\Crystal Decisions\Crystal Reports 10\Samples\En\Databases\Olap Data\Xtreme.hdc. (If you installed Crystal Reports to a nondefault location, the path may differ.) Click the Test Connection button to verify that your connection is good.

8. When you receive the "Connected Successfully" message, click OK.

9. Click OK to close the Add Server dialog box.

10. In the OLAP Connection Browser dialog box, expand the Exercise 3.10 server and select the Xtreme cube, as shown here.

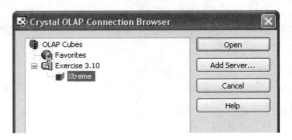

11. Click Open. You will be returned to the OLAP Data screen with the Cube, Type, and Server boxes filled in.

12. Click Next. The Rows/Columns screen will be displayed.

13. Move the Monthly dimension into the Rows list. Make sure that Monthly is listed first, before Customer.

14. With Monthly selected in the Rows list, click the Select Row Members button. The Member Selection dialog box will be displayed. Clear the Year Total check box, and then check Jan and Dec, as shown here. Click OK to close the dialog box.

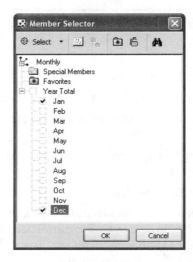

15. With Customer selected in the Rows list, click the Select Row Members button. The Member Selection dialog box will be displayed. Check USA, CA, and each company under CA, as shown here. Click OK to close the dialog box.

16. With Product selected in the Columns list, click the Select Column Members button. The Member Selection dialog box will be displayed. Uncheck All Products, and then check the three products that contain "Roadster," as shown here. Click OK to close the dialog box.

17. Click Finish. The report will be processed and displayed in the Preview window, as shown in Figure 3-29. (Your display will probably differ, as some reformatting was done to this figure in order to show the entire grid easily.)

			Roadster Jr BMX Saddle	Roadster Micro Mtn Saddle	Roadster Mini Mtn Saddle
Jan	USA				
	CA				
		Bike Shop from Mars			
		Changing Gears			
		Off the Mountaing Biking			
		Rowdy Rims Company			
		Sporting Wheels Inc.			
		Tyred Out			
Dec	USA		1,013.55	212.60	8,927.91
	CA				837.30
		Bike Shop from Mars			837.30
		Changing Gears			
		Off the Mountaing Biking			
		Rowdy Rims Company			
		Sporting Wheels Inc.			
		Tyred Out			

Figure 3-29   OLAP report

18. Save this report as **Exercise 3.10**.

19. Close the report by choosing File | Close or clicking the close button for the report window.

Chapter Review

This chapter gave you a quick look at Crystal Reports using the Report Wizards. Many different screens from the various wizards were described. Table 3-1 lists each screen with a short description of its purpose and an indicator of the order in which it appears in each wizard.

You have seen how easy it is to create many different types of reports. However, you may be thinking that the wizards are restrictive and you require more flexibility.

Screen	Purpose	Standard Wizard	Cross-Tab Wizard	Mail Label Wizard	OLAP Wizard
Data	Pick tables to use in the report.	1	1	1	
Link	Create links between the tables chosen. This screen appears only if more than one table is added to the report in the Data screen.	2	2	2	
Fields	Pick fields to display on the report.	3		3	
Grouping	Choose fields to group the report by. These may already have been added to the report or not.	4			
Summaries	Add summary fields. This screen is only displayed if groups have been added to the report.	5			
Group Sorting	Choose to display all groups or only the top five or bottom five on the report, sorted in order by some group summary field. This screen is only displayed if at least one summary field has been created.	6			
Cross-Tab	Choose the fields that will be used to create the cross-tab report.		3		
OLAP Data	Choose the OLAP cube to base the report on.				1
Rows/ Columns	Pick which dimensions to use as rows and columns. You can also filter the member list in this screen.				2
Slice/Page	Decide what to do with dimensions from the cube that were not used as rows or columns.				3
Style	Apply a formatting style to the OLAP grid.				4
Chart	Add a chart to the report. This screen is only displayed for the Standard wizard if a group summary field exists.	7	4		5
Label	Choose a label size and format from available standard formats, or create a custom format.			4	
Record Selection	Create filters to eliminate some rows from the report.	8	5	5	
Template	Choose a formatting template to apply to the report.	9			
Grid Style	Choose a style to apply to the grid.		6		

Table 3-1   Wizard Screens

The wizards should be thought of as only a starting point for any report. You can always add more complexity and your own formatting later. You can even create a report from scratch and not use the report wizards at all, as you will learn in Part II.

 TIP   Many professional report developers never use the report wizards, thinking that they do not need the help that the wizards supply. In my own experience, using the wizards helps me create the basics of a report much quicker than I could by starting with a blank report, and I usually use them to jump-start my report development.

PART II

Exam RDCR200, Basic Reporting

Exploring the Environment

Exam RDCR200 expects you to be able to
- Define the design environment
- Preview a report
- Save a report

In this chapter you will learn the following components of the design environment:
- Preview tab
- Design tab
- Menus
- Toolbars

Crystal Reports is similar to most Windows applications. It has menus, toolbars, dialog boxes, and a main work area where multiple application files can be opened simultaneously. For Crystal Reports, the application files are report files, files with an extension of .rpt. When a report file is open in Crystal Reports, two tabs appear at the top of the document window, a Design tab and a Preview tab, as you can see in Figure 4-1. The Preview tab will not appear until the report has been run or refreshed.

Design Tab

When the Design tab is selected, the Design window is displayed, as shown in Figure 4-1. The Design window displays the structure of the report; it acts as shorthand for giving instructions to the report engine about how you want the report to look. If you want a certain database field to be displayed on the report, then placing a field object for that field onto the Design window will instruct the report engine to retrieve that field from the database and display it at that relative location when the report is run. You can also apply formatting to the report object in the Design window, and it will be applied to the field when the report is run.

The Design window is analogous to a programming language: it is where you do the work of report creation. You can do report-design work in the Preview window as well, but the Design window is an abstract definition of the report that uses placeholders rather than actual data.

Tabs

Section boundaries

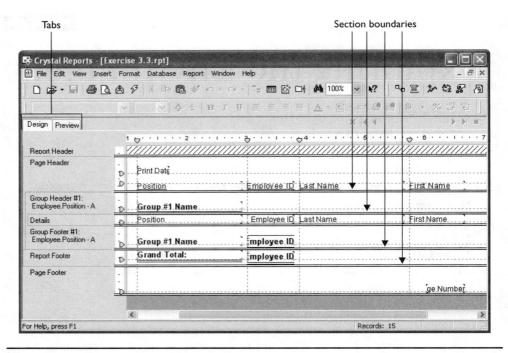

Figure 4-1 Viewing the document window

Report Objects

The largest area of the Design window represents the report page. Objects are placed on the page to add them to the report. Report objects appear as boxes or frames with only the corners drawn. The object name is displayed inside the box. As much formatting as possible is displayed for each object. For example, you will see underlining and boldface in Figure 4-1.

TIP To see more formatting, particularly for numeric fields, go to File | Options and clear the Show Field Names check box on the Layout tab. This will cause Crystal Reports to display strings of Xs for character fields and 5s for numeric fields instead of the field name. When displaying 5s, the format of numeric fields can also be shown.

Sections

The Design window is divided into sections by boundary lines (see Figure 4-1). Hovering the mouse pointer over a boundary will cause the mouse pointer icon to change to the symbol shown here. You can then hold down the left mouse button and drag the boundary line up or down to change the size of a section. Crystal will not let you decrease the size of a section if objects are in the way. You must first move or delete any objects that would be cut off by your boundary line movement and then move the boundary line.

Every report contains at least five sections: Report Header, Page Header, Details, Report Footer, and Page Footer, in that order. Any section may be *suppressed*, or forced to not display, but it will still exist in the Design window in the proper order. In the discussion that follows, the placement of the sections is described as they will appear in the final processed report; in the Design window, they simply follow one after the other.

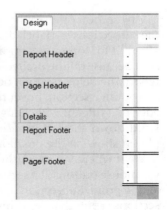

 EXAM TIP   Know the five default sections and their proper order.

The Report Header section is displayed only once, at the start of any report. It may be used to create a title page or to display a cross-tab or any other information that should be shown only once or applies to the entire report. It is always displayed before the first Page Header section. If the Report Header section is longer than one page, no page headers or page footers will be displayed until after the report header is completely displayed.

The Page Header section appears at the top of every page of the report except the page that contains the report header. It will appear after the report header if the two sections are on the same page or at the top of the next page if there is a page break between the two sections. The Page Header section is commonly used to display the report's title and column headers for the report fields. Place any objects in this section that you want to appear at the top of every page of the report.

The Details section will be repeated once for each record displayed on the report when the report is processed. (It appears only once on the Design window, as do all the sections.) The Details section usually contains the bulk of the report information.

The Report Footer section appears only once on the report, at the end. Unlike the Report Header, if the Report Footer section takes up more than one page, each of those pages will still display page headers and page footers. The Report Footer section is commonly used to display grand total summaries for the report, footnotes, and other comments. Place any information here that needs to be displayed only once on the report, at the end.

The Page Footer section appears at the bottom of each page after the report header has been fully displayed. It is commonly used to display the page number. Place any objects in the Page Footer section that you want to appear at the bottom of each page.

If groups are added to a report, then a group header and group footer for each group will be created. Reflecting the hierarchical nature of groups, the group headers and group footers are wrapped in layers around the Details section. The outermost group is labeled #1, the next group is #2, and so on.

When the report is run, one Group Header and Group Footer section will be created for each unique value contained in the group-by field. The detail records that contain that value will be grouped together, with a group header preceding them and a group footer following them.

Any section can be split into subsections. If a section is split, the subsections are labeled a, b, c, and so on. Sections are usually split for formatting purposes. The Details section might be split because all the desired data will not fit in one row on the report; the fields can then be placed on multiple rows.

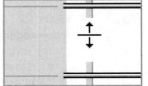

To split a section, hover the mouse pointer over the vertical edge of a ruler. It will change to the splitter icon, shown next. Hold down the left mouse button. A gray line will be displayed showing the position of the new section boundary. Move it where you want the split to occur and then release the mouse button. The section will be split into two sections at that point. Subsections can also be created by adding new sections rather than splitting existing sections.

In the Design window, section names can be set to abbreviations, called *short section names*, which require less space on the screen. The abbreviations are RH for Report Header, PH for Page Header, D for Details, RF for Report Footer, PF for Page Footer, GH for Group Header, and GF for Group Footer.

Rulers

The design window has both vertical and horizontal rulers. The ruler at the top of the design window displays the width of the report *between the margins*, in inches. The default settings are for a regular 8 1/2 × 11–inch page with the margins set at the default value for the currently selected printer. If the default for the printer is a left margin of 1/4 inch and a right margin of 1/4 inch, the ruler will show 8 full inches.

TIP   Keep in mind that the Design window displays only the page area between the margins. You do not need to leave extra white space at the sides for a margin but can place your objects close to either side. The actual page margin will display in the Preview window.

The vertical ruler in the Design window restarts for each section. The horizontal ruler is fixed and displays exactly where fields will be displayed horizontally on the page. However, the vertical ruler does not; it displays only where the field will be placed vertically *within a section*. It cannot display exactly where a field will be displayed vertically on the page, because until the report is generated the exact number and placement of the various sections is not known.

In either ruler, you may see small arrows. These arrows indicate the position of guidelines. You can select and move the arrows to move the guidelines. You will see the actual guidelines if you have chosen to display them; otherwise they will be invisible until you move the guideline arrow. Report objects can be attached to guidelines to assist with placement on the page.

Exercise 4.1: Exploring the Design Tab

1. Open the report that you created in Exercise 3.7. (Use File | Open and browse to find it, or choose it from the recently opened files list in the File menu.)

2. Click the Design tab and notice the difference in appearance from the Preview window.

3. Note the location of the Group Header and Group Footer sections.

4. Note how much of the report formatting is visually depicted, even in the Design window.

5. Increase the height of the Details section by selecting the bottom boundary line and dragging it down. Click the Preview tab and note how the detail rows now have space between them. Go back to the Design tab.

6. Count the number of sections in the report (11).

7. Split the Page Header d section. You should now have a Page Header e section.

8. Examine the rulers and any guidelines that are visible.

9. Close the report without saving the changes.

Preview Tab

If you completed the exercises in Chapter 3, then you have seen the Preview tab several times. When the Preview tab is selected, the Preview window is displayed. The Preview tab contains a WYSIWYG (what you see is what you get) view of the report. This is a view of the report as it will actually look when printed; see Figure 4-2.

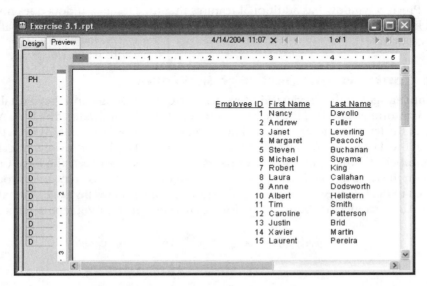

Figure 4-2   Previewing your report

NOTE Your report may look slightly different depending on the printer you have selected. The Preview tab displays the report as it would look on the currently selected printer.

The Preview tab does not exist initially for a report that is created as a blank report or for a report that has been opened but not refreshed. The Preview tab can be displayed as the result of several different actions. As noted earlier, if you use the report wizards to create a report, the result is opened in the Preview window. Other ways to invoke the Preview window are

- Choose the menu options File | Print Preview.
- Press F5.
- Click the Print Preview button.
- Click the Refresh button. (The Refresh button will also reload the report data from the database if you click it when the Preview window already exists.)
- Choose the menu options File | Print | Preview Sample.

NOTE The Preview Sample option allows you to preview the report using any number of database records you desire. This is useful if your report will contain a large number of records, but you only need to see a limited number while designing the report.

Once the Preview tab exists, you may switch between the Preview window and Design window by clicking the appropriate tab.

The Preview window has additional features that the Design window does not possess. It has a page control, more information in its status bar, and it can optionally display a group tree.

Page Controls and Data Age Indicator

In the upper right of the Preview window, across from the Design and Preview tabs, is a group of information called the Page Controls and Data Age indicator. The Data Age indicator at the left side shows the date that the report data was last retrieved from the database. If the data was retrieved today, the indicator will also show the time. The current page number and the total number of pages are displayed between the Page Control buttons in the form n of m. The total number of pages will not be correct unless you have navigated to the last page. Otherwise, it will show the highest number page that has been viewed. Also included are buttons for closing tabs and for stopping report generation.

8/11/2003 16:07 ✕ |◀ ◀   2 of 8   ▶ ▶| ▪

The Page Control buttons are used to navigate through the report. They and the other buttons work as follows:

[X] The Close View button is used to close open tabs. It will not close the Design tab.

[◄|] The Show First Page button displays the first page of the report.

[◄] The Show Previous Page button displays the page immediately preceding the currently displayed page.

[▶] The Show Next Page button displays the page immediately following the current page.

[▶|] The Show Last Page button displays the last page of the report.

[■] The Stop button cancels report page formatting. It is active only when data retrieval or page formatting is occurring. Pressing it will not cancel data retrieval for most data types.

Status Bar

The status bar is displayed at the bottom of the Crystal Reports window, but it shows information about the report currently displayed in the active report window. The status bar is split into four sections. If an object is selected on the report, its name will be displayed at the far left of the status bar. Its size and position will be displayed in the same section but right-aligned. The next section to the right displays the number of records in the report. The next section, which appears blank when a report is finished processing, displays the record count as the records are retrieved from the database. The last section displays the percentage of records retrieved.

Field: Employee.Position	4.3 , 0.6 : 2.5 x 0.2	Records: 15	100%

Display of the status bar can be turned on or off using the menu item View | Status Bar or by right-clicking the status bar (or any toolbar) and clearing its check box on the shortcut menu.

Group Tree

In the Preview window, you can display the Group Tree, shown in Figure 4-3. The Group Tree displays the group values in the report in a hierarchical tree structure. You can expand and contract the nodes of the tree to see lower-level group values or only a higher-level view. The Group Tree option is an aid to report navigation. You can browse the tree and then click a group value to navigate to the report page containing that value.

PART II

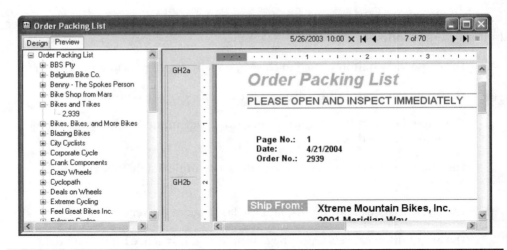

Figure 4-3   Viewing a group tree in the Preview window

    To control display of the Group Tree, use the menu options View | Group Tree or click the Group Tree icon.

Group Tree Shortcut Menu

Right-clicking within the tree displays a shortcut menu. The two commands in this menu are not available through the main menu:

- **Drill Down** opens a drill-down window for the group selected.
- **Hide** closes the Group Tree.

Differences Between Preview and Design

Most capabilities in the Design window also exist in the Preview window. You will see the same menus, shortcut menus, and toolbars in both windows. You have full formatting capabilities in both windows. Actions that you take in one window are immediately reflected in the other window. However, there are a few differences between the windows:

- Preview has only one vertical ruler, whereas the Design window has a vertical ruler for each section. The Preview window can properly show the exact vertical location of an object on the page and so needs only one vertical ruler.
- The display of section names can differ between the windows: In the Design window, you can choose to display either short or long section names. In the Preview window, you can choose to display short section names or to hide the section names; you cannot display long section names.
- Only the Preview window has the Data Age indicator and active Page Controls.

- The Preview window displays more information in the status bar and allows the display of the Group Tree.

- The Preview window displays the page margins as dark gray areas in the rulers. The Design window excludes the margins entirely.

Other differences between the two windows are due to their different natures. In the Preview window, selecting a field selects every value of that field in the report. If you modify the field in some way, the Preview window must redraw the entire report to reflect the change. In the Design window, you are selecting only the field placeholder. Report modifications can be done quicker in the Design window because they are applied only to the placeholder.

Exercise 4.2: Exploring the Preview Tab

1. Open the report that you created in Exercise 3.7.

2. Click the Preview tab to display the Preview window.

3. Click on the Show Next Page button to display the next page of the report. Try the other Page Control buttons.

4. Open the Group Tree if it is not already open. Click Germany in the tree and notice how you are taken to the page where the Germany group begins.

5. Notice the current value of the Data Age indicator, and then click the Refresh button on the Standard toolbar and see how it changes.

6. Click a Customer Name in the Detail section. Notice the field name, size, and position displayed in the Status bar.

7. Close the file without saving the changes.

Crystal Reports Menus

Crystal Reports contains menus similar to most Windows applications. It has a main menu bar and additional shortcut, pop-up, or action menus that are accessible by right-clicking.

 EXAM TIP You should be generally aware of the location of various Crystal Reports commands, but do not try to memorize the menu setups.

The main menu has visual hints that give you more information about some of the commands. If a small right-pointing arrow appears at the right-hand edge of a menu item, it means that there is a submenu for that item. If an ellipsis appears after the item, clicking it will open a dialog box.

Pressing the ALT key will display underlined letters in the names of the main menu items. Pressing one of those letters will then cause that menu item to execute. The underlined letters are called *accelerator keys*. Accelerator keys also appear on submenus.

To use the accelerator keys to pick submenu items, press ALT followed by the main menu accelerator letter and then the submenu accelerator letter. For example, to display the Save As dialog box press ALT-F-A.

Some menu items also have shortcut keys. The key combination for the shortcut is displayed to the right of the menu item, such as CTRL-D for displaying the Design window. You may see button icons or check boxes to the left of menu items. If there is a button icon, then the same icon will appear as a toolbar button on one of the default toolbars. A check box is used to set or clear a property.

File Menu

The File menu has a great number of options, but most will be familiar to you. The File menu is divided into several sections. The top section contains all the commands related to opening, closing, creating, and saving report files. The second section contains a command for saving a subreport. The third section contains several commands related to printing or exporting reports. The fourth section contains a command to e-mail a report. The fifth section contains commands for setting application options and report options, as well as detailed file options. The sixth section contains a list of recently opened files. The last section contains the command for closing Crystal Reports.

NOTE   Menu items that have an icon next to them are also available as buttons on a taskbar.

New

Choosing File | New brings up the Crystal Report Gallery. From the report gallery, you can create a new report using a report wizard or as a blank report. This option creates a new report file.

Open

File | Open opens the familiar Windows Open dialog box. From there you can browse the file system to find any report file and open it in Crystal Reports. By default, the Open dialog box is set to display only Crystal Reports files, but you can change it to display all types of files if desired. A special check box for Crystal Reports called Update Repository Objects, when checked, causes any objects in the selected report file that are connected with the repository to be updated when the file is opened.

Close

Choosing File | Close closes the active report file. If the file is new or has been modified since the last save, you will be prompted to save the changes before closing.

Save

File | Save saves the active report file. If the file has never been saved before, you will be prompted to supply a folder location and name for the file before saving. The Save menu item will be grayed out if no modifications to the file have been made since the last time it was saved.

Save As

Selecting File | Save As allows you to save the active report file with a different name or in a different location. If you change the report filename, the original file is not replaced, but a new file is created. You will then have both the original file with the original name and the new file with the new name on your system.

Save Data with Report

The Save Data with Report check box is unique to Crystal Reports. When a report is previewed, the data it requires is retrieved from the database. If you save a report file with the Save Data with Report option checked, then the data that was last retrieved will be saved with the report file. When you or another user opens the report, it will already be populated with that data.

There are several things to consider when deciding whether to save data with the report. Saving the data can be useful if you are in the process of designing the report and want to avoid retrieving data every time you open the report. You might also save data with the report if you want to give the report to someone who does not have sufficient database privileges to retrieve the data themselves. In this case, when they open the report, the data is already there and no database connection is required. When using Crystal Enterprise and scheduling reports to run at specified times, the data is always set to save with the report so that it is available for users afterwards.

There can be several downsides to saving data with reports:

- The data that is saved takes up space in the report file. Crystal compresses the data, but the size may still be appreciable.

- The data that is saved is old—it is as of the last save. This may or may not be an issue, depending on the report.

- Database security is bypassed. Any user opening the report will see the saved data whether or not they would have had access to the data in the database. However, if the report is published in Crystal Enterprise, Crystal Enterprise security can be attached to it to prevent unauthorized viewing.

Save Subreport As

The Save Subreport As command saves the selected subreport as a main report file. Subreports have not been discussed yet, but when you insert one report into another it is called a *subreport*. The Save Subreport As command allows you to extract a subreport and turn it back into a main report.

Print Preview

Choosing File | Print Preview displays the report in the Preview window.

Print

The Print menu has two submenus, Preview Sample and Printer.

Preview Sample   The Preview Sample option brings up a dialog box where you can choose to preview the report using less than the full record count.

III 4-20

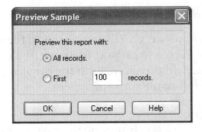

Choosing All Records is equivalent to the Print Preview menu command and opens the Preview window showing all the report's records. Choosing First and entering a number, n, opens the Preview window showing only the first n records retrieved from the database. Limiting the number of records returned is useful if the processing time is long and you only need a sample of records for designing the report.

NOTE   Previewing using a sample of records will create the report using the first n records returned from the database. This will not necessarily be the first n records that would be displayed if the report was run with All Records, so the preview that you see will not be identical to the first pages displayed when running with All Records.

Printer   Choosing the Printer command displays the Print dialog box.

III 4-21

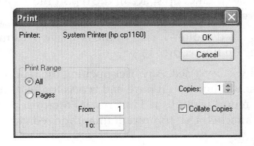

The Print dialog box displays the currently selected printer, but you cannot change it here. In this dialog box, you can choose to print all the report pages or enter a range. In addition, you can choose the number of copies desired and whether the printing should collate those copies or not. Clicking OK sends the report to the printer.

Printer Setup

The File | Printer Setup command brings up the typical Windows Print Setup dialog box, as shown in Figure 4-4. In the Print Setup dialog box, you choose the current printer, paper size, paper source, and orientation. The Properties button can be clicked to set printer-specific options, and when the Reset to Default button is clicked it returns the settings to their default values. The printer selected is applied only to the active report file; any other open report files retain their original printer selections.

Changing the printer options has an immediate impact on the display of the report. If you change the paper size, the page size displayed in the Design and Preview windows changes. If you change the orientation, the orientation changes in the Design and Preview windows. A more subtle change occurs if you change the printer selected. Crystal Reports obtains font metrics such as average character height and width from the selected printer driver and uses this to create the onscreen view of the report.

Page Setup

Choosing File | Page Setup displays the Page Setup dialog box. On the Page Setup box you can set the page margins. The page margins are initially set to the default values for the currently selected printer. Every printer has limits to how close it can print to the edge of a piece of paper; these are used as the printer's default margins. If you change any of the margin settings, the Use Default Margins check box will clear. If you recheck it, the margins will be returned to their default values. The Adjust Automatically check box can be used if there is a possibility of the paper size changing. If checked, the Adjust Automatically option will expand or contract the margins to maintain the same size print area.

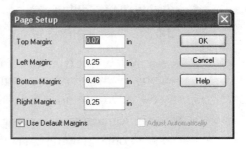

Figure 4-4

Selecting Print Setup options

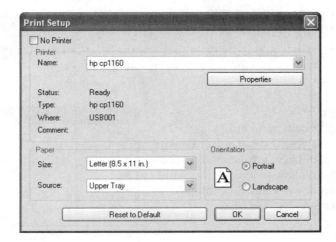

Print Formatting Problems

In many real world situations, reports are created by a developer, on the developer's system, and then run in production by a user on a different system or on a server. Crystal Reports uses information from the printer driver that the report was created for when formatting a report even if the environment the report is running in is different. This can cause very subtle or very obvious problems in the report printouts.

Differences in any of the following components between the development environment and the production environment can potentially be the source of discrepancies:

- Printer
- Printer driver
- Printer driver version
- Operating system
- Use of TrueType or PostScript fonts
- Video driver resolution

To reduce the possibility of problems, follow these recommendations:

- Use common TrueType fonts such as Times New Roman and Arial, which are more likely to be treated consistently by different printer drivers.
- Use the video resolution that is most commonly used by your end users.
- Set specific margins; do not use the printer driver's default margins.
- Size field objects a little larger than necessary to accommodate different font widths on different printers, or check the Can Grow option for the fields. Selecting Can Grow will cause the field to expand vertically and text to be wrapped. This solution may display awkwardly, but it ensures that the entire field value will be displayed.
- Isolate memo fields in their own subsections and set them to Can Grow.

Export

The Export command brings up the Export dialog box. You can export a report to several different formats and destinations by making selections from the two drop-down boxes. Exporting is covered in more detail in Chapter 11.

Send To

The Send To menu has two submenus. One allows you to send a report to an e-mail address. The other sends it to an Exchange folder.

Mail Recipient   The File | Send To | Mail Recipient command opens the Send Mail dialog box as shown in Figure 4-5. To send mail, your default e-mail client must be set to a MAPI-compliant client. Fill in the e-mail address or search for it using the Address button. You can also verify that the address is valid using the Check Names button. Fill in any Cc: addresses, a subject, and create any message you desire. Your report will be sent as an attachment to the e-mail, as an .rpt file, so the recipient must be able to run Crystal Reports to use it.

Exchange Folder   The Exchange Folder command opens the Choose Profile dialog box; from there you can send the report file to an Exchange folder. You must choose a profile to use and pick a folder.

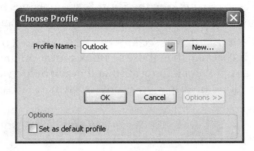

Options

Choosing File | Options opens the Options dialog box. There you can modify settings that apply to the Crystal Reports environment and that act as default values for report settings. Settings for an individual report are set with the Report Options command. The Options dialog box has several tabs.

Figure 4-5
Selecting Send
Mail options

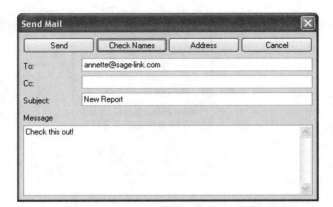

Layout Tab   Figure 4-6 shows the Layout tab of the Options dialog box. Options set in this window affect the display of all reports; it contains several groups of settings. The Design View panel contains settings that affect the display of the Design window:

- **Rulers**   Checking the Rulers box causes the rulers to display. Clearing Rulers removes the rulers and makes it impossible to select guidelines.

- **Guidelines**   Clearing the Guidelines box suppresses the constant display of guidelines. The guidelines still exist but are visible only when they are selected and moved.

- **Grid**   Checking the Grid box displays a grid in the form of evenly spaced dots on the Design window background. The grid is controlled by options in the Grid panel.

- **ToolTips**   If the ToolTips box is checked, short descriptions of button actions display when the mouse is hovered over them.

- **Short Section Names**   Checking the Short Section Names box changes the display of section names in the Design window from full names to abbreviations.

- **Show Hidden Sections**   Report sections can be suppressed or hidden. If Show Hidden Sections is checked, then those sections appear on the Design tab with diagonal lines through them to indicate that they are hidden sections. If it is not checked, those sections are displayed as only a very narrow band across the report.

Figure 4-6

Setting Layout options

The Grid Options panel controls the features of the grid:

- **Snap to Grid** If Snap to Grid is checked, then objects placed in the Design window automatically *snap,* or move, to the nearest grid intersection.

- **Free-Form Placement** If Free-Form Placement is checked, objects may be placed anywhere in the Design window and will not snap to the grid.

- **Grid Size** The Grid Size box allows you to set the interval size for the grid.

The Preview panel contains settings that apply only to the Preview window:

- **Rulers** Checking the Rulers box causes the rulers to display. Clearing Rulers removes the rulers and makes it impossible to select guidelines.

- **Guidelines** Clearing the Guidelines box suppresses the constant display of guidelines. The guidelines still exist but are visible only when they are selected and moved.

- **Grid** Checking the Grid box displays a grid in the form of evenly spaced dots on the Preview window background. The grid is controlled by options in the Grid panel.

- **ToolTips** If the ToolTips box is checked, short descriptions of buttons display when the mouse is hovered over them.

- **Section Names** Checking the Section Names box causes section names to be displayed in the Preview window. Clearing it suppresses the display of section names.

- **Page Breaks in Wide Pages** If Page Breaks in Wide Pages is checked, then indicator lines for page breaks are displayed in the Preview window for reports that are wider than one page. These are typically cross-tabs or OLAP grids.

Choices in the Field Options panel control how field objects are displayed:

- **Show Field Names** The Show Field Names check box controls what is displayed in the field object's frame in the Design window. If it is checked, then the field name is displayed. If it is not checked, an appropriate string of characters is displayed, such as Xs for string fields and 5s for number fields.

- **Insert Detail Field Headings** When Insert Detail Field Headings is checked, a text object containing a column title for a field is created when the field is added to the report. The default heading is the field name. If it is not checked, no column title is created.

- **Insert Group Name with Group** The Insert Group Name with Group option causes Crystal Reports to insert group name objects into the group header when a group is created.

Database Tab   The Database tab of the Options dialog box is covered in Chapter 18.

Editors Tab   Crystal Reports has editors such as the Formula Editor and the SQL Expression Editor. The Editors tab of the Options dialog box controls the display of text in the editors. These options are covered in Chapter 8.

Data Source Defaults Tab   The Data Source Defaults tab allows you to set the default directory where Crystal Reports will look for data files for several database types. These are mostly desktop-type databases such as Access and Paradox.

III 4-25

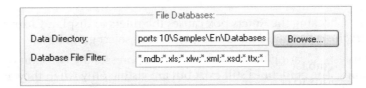

Reporting Tab   The Reporting tab of the Options dialog box contains default settings for the retrieval and storage of data, as shown in Figure 4-7. Settings on the Reporting tab can be overridden for an individual report by modifying that report's Report Options settings (see "Report Options," later in this chapter). If modifications are made to the Reporting tab, they affect all new reports, but do not change any existing reports.

Figure 4-7
Setting Reporting
options

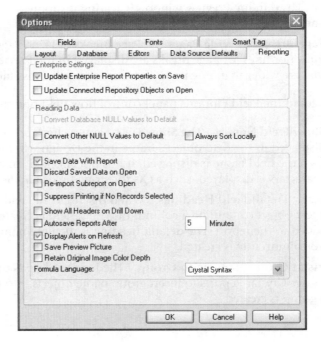

The Enterprise Settings panel contains options that control report behavior in the Crystal Enterprise environment:

- **Update Enterprise Report Properties on Save**   This option affects reports that have been published to Crystal Enterprise. If any report properties that Crystal Enterprise interfaces with, such as parameters, have changed, then checking this option guarantees that those properties are updated in Crystal Enterprise.

- **Update Connected Repository Objects on Open**   If this box is checked, then Crystal Reports will check for and apply any changes made to repository objects that the report uses.

The Reading Data panel controls how Crystal treats null values and handles sorting:

- **Convert Database NULL Values to Default**   Checking this option causes Crystal Reports to convert null string fields to blank and null numeric fields to zero after reading them from the database and before using them in the report.

- **Convert Other NULL Values to Default**   Checking this option causes Crystal Reports to convert other null values to blank or zero. Other values include fields such as formula fields that are not read directly from a database.

- **Always Sort Locally**   If checked, the Always Sort Locally box causes Crystal Reports to sort the report records on the local system whether or not they were sorted by the database via the query that returned them.

The rest of the settings on the Reporting tab affect miscellaneous features:

- **Save Data With Report**   The Save Data with Report option controls the default value for the related File menu option. Saving data with a report is described in the "File Menu" section, earlier in this chapter.

- **Discard Saved Data on Open**   If Discard Saved Data on Open is checked, then any data that was saved with a report is discarded and will be unavailable when the report is opened.

- **Re-import Subreport on Open**   For a report that contains subreports that were imported, this option causes the subreport to be reimported when it is opened.

- **Suppress Printing If No Records Selected**   A report's design or its parameter choices may cause no records to be returned. In this case, no detail sections exist, but the Report Header, Page Header, Report Footer, and Page Footer will still print. If you prefer that the entire report be blank, check the Suppress Printing If No Records Selected box.

- **Show All Headers on Drill Down**   If some sections are suppressed, the user can *drill down* on them to display their contents in a separate tab. Groups can also be drilled down on. By default, the Drill Down tab does not display header sections for the sections above the chosen section. Checking this box causes all higher-level section headers to display in the Drill Down tab.

- **Autosave Reports After __ Minutes** You can set this option and pick a time interval to cause Crystal Reports to automatically save your reports at the chosen time interval.

- **Display Alerts on Refresh** Configured report alerts always display when the report is first opened. Checking Display Alerts on Refresh causes them to be redisplayed if the report is refreshed.

- **Save Preview Picture** If checked, this option saves a thumbnail image of the first page of the report with the report file. This image can be displayed in Windows Explorer or the Open dialog box.

- **Retain Original Image Color Depth** Crystal Reports automatically reduces the color level for images to 8 bits per pixel. To retain the original color depth, check this setting.

- **Formula Language** Crystal Reports allows two different formula syntaxes: its own native syntax and Basic syntax. Use this drop-down box to choose which formula syntax you want to use.

Fields Tab The Fields tab controls the default formatting for the various data types. These format options are covered in Chapter 9.

Fonts Tab The Fonts tab controls the default formatting for the various object types. These format options are also covered in Chapter 9.

Smart Tag Tab Smart tags are a new feature in Office XP. To use Crystal Reports smart tags in Office applications, a web server must be properly set up and configured.

Report Options

The Report Options command differs from the Options command in that its settings apply only to the currently active report. The Report Options dialog box has three sections, as shown in Figure 4-8.

The General Settings panel contains miscellaneous settings for the active report. The behavior of the following settings is identical to the same settings in the Options dialog box (see "Options," earlier in this chapter):

- Convert Database NULL Values to Default
- Convert Other NULL Values to Default
- Show All Headers on Drill Down
- Always Sort Locally
- Save Data With Report
- Suppress Printing If No Records
- Display Alerts on Refresh
- Retain Original Image Color Depth

Figure 4-8
Selecting Report
Options settings

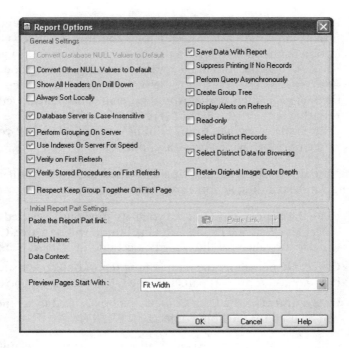

The following settings are all identical to their counterparts on the Database tab of the Options dialog box. They are described in Chapter 5.

- Database Server Is Case-Insensitive
- Perform Grouping on Server
- Use Indexes or Server for Speed
- Verify on First Refresh
- Verify Stored Procedures on First Refresh
- Perform Query Asynchronously
- Read-only
- Select Distinct Records
- Select Distinct Data for Browsing

The other choices in the General Settings panel are as follows:

- **Create Group Tree** Checking Create Group Tree causes Crystal Reports to generate the group information needed to display a group tree during record processing. It does not cause the Group Tree to display.

- **Respect Keep Group Together on First Page**   Crystal Reports has a group formatting option called Keep Group Together. The Keep Group Together option is intended to force a page break before printing a group if that group will not fit on the current page. The downside to this option in previous versions of Crystal Reports was that if the very first group in the report would not fit on the first page, then Crystal would generate a page break before the first group, resulting in the first page of the report being blank. In Crystal Reports 10, by default, the group will begin printing on the first page. If you wish to return to the prior behavior, check this option.

The Initial Report Part Settings panel is used to set the home object for report part viewing. Understanding Report Parts is not an exam objective.

- **Paste the Report Part Link**   If you have previously selected and copied a report object, the Paste the Report Part Link button will be active. Clicking it allows you to paste the values for the copied object into the Object Name and Data Context.

- **Object Name**   Enter the name of the report object that should be used as the home object for report parts into the Object Name text box.

- **Data Context**   The Data Context text box is used to set the specific record that will be used for the home object.

The Preview Pages Start With option allows you to set the default page size for the Preview window. The options are

- **Full Size**   This causes the report to be displayed at 100% magnification.

- **Fit Width**   This causes the report to be displayed at a magnification such that the entire width of the page is viewable.

- **Fit Page**   This causes the report to be displayed at a magnification such that the entire page is viewable.

EXAM TIP   Understand the difference between the File | Options command and the File | Report Options command.

Summary Info

Choosing File | Summary Info displays the standard Windows Document Properties dialog box.

Summary Tab   The Summary tab of the Document Properties dialog box is shown in Figure 4-9. Use this tab to enter information about the file that can later be used for identification. Some of the Summary tab fields appear in the Field Explorer under the Special Fields folder and can be placed on the report. All Document Properties options that you set are visible in Windows Explorer when you choose to view the properties of a selected file. These properties appear on the Summary tab of the Properties dialog box for closed files. They are properties of Windows files and are not specific to Crystal Reports.

Figure 4-9
Entering summary
information about
a report

- **Author** Enter the name of the author of the report. This field is available for use on the report as the special field File Author.

- **Keywords** Enter any words you like. Creating and using standard keywords can help you categorize your report files.

- **Comments** Enter any comments you want to attach to the file. The comments are available for use on the report as the special field Report Comments.

- **Title** This is the report title and is available for use on the report as the special field Report Title.

- **Subject** Enter any words you like. As with keywords, creating and using standard subject descriptions can help you categorize your report files.

- **Template** As of this writing, this field does not function as a real document property. The entry in the Title field automatically appears as the template name.

- **Save Preview Picture** Checking this box saves a thumbnail view of the first page of the report that can be displayed by Windows Explorer, the Crystal Reports Open dialog box, or the Template dialog box. The Preview picture is also called a *snapshot*.

 EXAM TIP Be able to add summary information and a snapshot to a report file.

Once you've entered summary information, it can be displayed in Crystal Reports' Open dialog box by clicking the Properties button, as shown in Figure 4-10. The summary information will also be available in Windows Explorer. Right-click a file and choose Properties, and then select the Summary tab. The summary information will be displayed as shown in Figure 4-11.

Figure 4-10
Viewing report
properties

Properties button

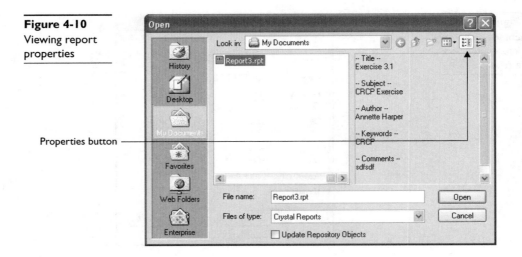

Statistics Tab The Statistics tab of the Document Properties dialog box displays the author, revision number, and several time stamps that may be of interest to the developer, as shown in Figure 4-12. You cannot modify anything on the Statistics tab.

Figure 4-11
Viewing summary
information

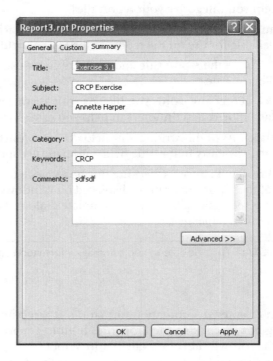

Figure 4-12
Viewing report
statistics

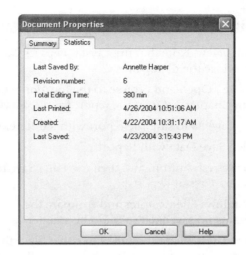

- **Last Saved By**   Last Saved By displays the entry in the author name box from the Summary tab as of the last time the file was saved.

- **Revision number**   The revision number starts at zero at file creation and increments by one each time the report is saved. If no changes were made between saves, it still increments.

- **Total Editing Time**   The Total Editing Time is the accumulation of all the time that the file has been open, whether or not it was actively being edited during that time.

- **Last Printed**   Last Printed displays the last date and time that the report was printed. It does not track previews or exports.

- **Created**   The Created item displays the date and time that the report file was created.

- **Last Saved**   Last Saved shows the date and time that the report file was last saved.

Recently Opened Reports Section
The next to last section of the File menu displays the nine most recently opened reports. You can click a filename to reopen the report.

Exit
The File | Exit command closes Crystal Reports. If any open report files have been modified, you will be prompted to save the changes.

Exercise 4.3: Exploring the File Menu

1. Select File | New. Note that the Crystal Reports Gallery is displayed. Click Cancel to close the dialog box.

2. Choose File | Open and browse to the location where you saved the reports created in Chapter 3. Open the report from Exercise 3.5.

3. Use File | Save As to save the report with a different name.

4. Clear File | Save Data with Report.

5. Click the Refresh button, and then use File | Save to save the new report again. Do not close Crystal Reports.

6. Open Windows File Explorer and compare the file sizes of the two files. The file that contains no saved data should be smaller.

7. Go back to Crystal Reports, and with either file active, Select File | Print | Preview Sample and choose a sample size of 5. Note the record count displayed in the status bar and the different report display.

8. Select File | Print Setup, and change the orientation to Landscape. Note the change in the page on the Preview tab. (This is easier to see if you set Zoom to Full Page.)

9. Select File | Page Setup, and set the top margin to 1 inch. Notice the change in the report.

10. Select File | Options. Then click the Layout tab, and in the Preview panel, check the Grid box. Click OK. Notice the grid pattern now showing on the Preview tab. Remove the grid from the display.

11. Go to File | Summary Info and enter your name as the author on the Summary tab of the Document Properties dialog box.

12. Close all open reports without saving any changes.

Edit Menu

Many entries in the Edit menu will be familiar to Microsoft Office users. The Edit menu is divided into seven sections and contains items for undoing and redoing; cutting, pasting, and deleting; modifying subreport links; working with OLE objects; and searching the report.

Undo

The complete wording of the Undo item changes to reflect the last action that can be undone. For example, it might say "Undo Typing" or "Undo Format Object." Clicking it causes the action to be rolled back. Some actions cannot be undone, in which case the menu item will be grayed out. Undo can be repeated to reverse multiple recent actions.

TIP The Undo toolbar button allows you to undo multiple actions. Click the down arrow to display a list of recent changes and to select how far back you want to undo.

Redo

The Redo button changes dynamically to indicate which actions that have been undone can be redone. Pressing it causes the last undone action to be redone.

Cut

The Cut command removes an object from Crystal Reports and places it on the Windows clipboard.

Copy

The Copy command copies objects to the Windows clipboard.

Paste

Paste is used to paste an item from the Windows clipboard into the report file.

Paste Special

The Paste Special command gives you control over how an object is pasted into the report. It is used primarily with OLE objects.

Delete

Choose Delete to delete an object from the report. The object is not copied to the clipboard as it is with Cut.

Select All

Use Select All to select all the objects in the report. You can then apply other options to them all at once, such as Copy or Delete, format settings, and so on.

Find

Choosing Find displays the Find dialog box, from which you can search for text in the report. The example shows a search for "Peacock." You can specify a case-sensitive search using the Match Case check box or search for only entire words that match using the Match Whole Word Only check box. You can also search the report going forward or backward using the Direction radio buttons. Clicking Find Next displays the page showing the first match and highlights the matching item.

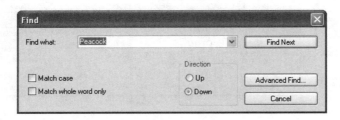

Clicking the Advanced Find button displays the Search Expert dialog box, as shown in Figure 4-13. The Search Expert allows you to search for values in specific fields rather than in the whole report. It also allows you to create multiple search criteria. Figure 4-13 shows a search for the record where the employee's last name is Peacock and first name is Margaret. The Search Expert dialog box works similarly to the Select Expert screen in the report wizards, except that it finds records in the previewed report rather than selecting them to be in the report.

Go to Page

Selecting the Go to Page menu item displays the Go To dialog box, as shown here. Using this dialog box you can jump to any page by selecting the Page radio button, entering a page number, and clicking OK. You can also go directly to the first page or last page by selecting the appropriate radio button.

Edit Report Object

The name of this item changes depending on the type of object that is currently selected in the report. If a text, formula, SQL Expression, Parameter, or Running Total Field object is selected on the report, then choosing Edit | Edit [object type] will allow you to edit the object. For text objects, you will do in-place editing; otherwise an editor will be displayed. The editor will be the Formula Editor, the SQL Expression Editor, the Edit Parameter Field dialog box, or the Edit Running Total dialog box depending on the object type.

 TIP For all object types it is easier to right-click the object and select the corresponding edit option from the pop-up menu.

Figure 4-13
Exploring advanced search options

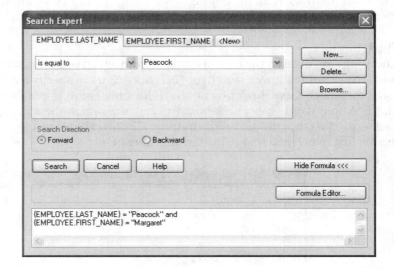

Subreport Links

If a subreport is selected in the report, then the Subreport Links command will display the Subreport Links dialog box where you can modify the link between the main report and the subreport. The dialog box can also be displayed by right-clicking the subreport object.

Object

The Object menu item is only active when an OLE object is selected in the report. The name of the command will change based on the type of object that is selected. Using this command you can edit the OLE object in place, open it in its parent application, change its properties, and so on.

Links

The Edit | Links command is used to modify the link properties for an OLE object.

Exercise 4.4: Exploring the Edit Menu

1. Open the report from Exercise 3.5.

2. Select the chart, and chose Edit | Delete. The chart will be deleted.

3. Select Edit | Undo. The chart will reappear.

4. Select the Print Date field in the Report Header, and click Edit | Copy.

5. Choose Edit | Paste, and click anywhere in the report. The Print Date field will be inserted where you click.

6. Select Edit | Find and enter **Peacock** into the Find What box. Click Find Next. "Peacock" will be highlighted in the record containing it.

7. Select the First Name field in the first record on the report. Then choose Edit | Find, and click the Advanced Find tab. The First Name field should be listed on a tab in the Search Expert. In the first drop-down box, choose Starts With. In the second drop-down box type **A**, and then click Search. The first record meeting the criteria will be highlighted. Press F3. The next matching record will be highlighted.

8. Close the report without saving the changes.

View Menu

The View menu contains options that affect the display of application features in the development environment.

Design/Preview/Other Views

The Design and Preview check boxes act as radio buttons; that is, only one can be checked at a time. The checked box is the currently displayed view. If you select a different item, it becomes the active view and the other view is cleared. If your report includes subreports that have been opened separately for editing or previewing, they will have tabs to the right of the preview tab and the Other Views menu item will be displayed. The Other Views menu will have a submenu listing all other open views. The other open views become part of the same radio group as the Design and Preview windows, so only one view can be checked at a time.

 TIP   Ordinarily you will simply click the tab of the view that you want to display. However, this menu item is useful if you have a large number of open views and need to select one of them.

Close Current View

The Close Current View command closes the active tab.

 NOTE   Views are usually closed using the Close View button on the Page Controls.

Field Explorer, Report Explorer, and Repository Explorer

The Field Explorer, Report Explorer, and Repository Explorer buttons cause the corresponding explorer dialog box to be shown. The Field and Report Explorers are covered in Chapter 5. The Repository Explorer is covered in Chapter 14.

Toolbars

Choosing the Toolbars command displays the Toolbars dialog box. There you can select which toolbars to display, whether they should display regular-size buttons or large buttons, and whether ToolTips should be displayed. The four toolbars—Standard, Formatting, Insert Tools, and Expert Tools—are discussed later in this chapter, in the "Toolbars" section.

Status Bar

The Status Bar command is used to display or hide the status bar at the bottom of the Crystal Report application.

Group Tree

Select the Group Tree menu item to toggle display of the Group Tree in the Preview window.

Zoom

Choosing the Zoom option displays the Zoom dialog box. Using the Zoom dialog box, you can set the magnification from 25% to 400%, or so it will display the entire width of the report (using the Fit One Dimension option), or so it will display the entire report.

Rulers, Guidelines, Grid, and ToolTips

Each of the Rulers, Guidelines, Grid, and ToolTips menu options has two submenus: Design and Preview. The Design and Preview options are check boxes that control the display of the parent menu item. These are equivalent to the like-named File | Options | Layout items and apply to the display of all open report files.

Exercise 4.5: Exploring the View Menu

1. Open the report from Exercise 3.7. Select the Preview tab.

2. Choose View | Close Current View and notice that the Preview tab is closed and is no longer an option on the View menu.

3. Click the Refresh button to reopen the Preview window.

4. Select View | Toolbars and check Large Buttons. Click OK, and notice the changed size of the toolbar buttons. Set the buttons back to small.

5. Clear the View | Status Bar check box, and notice that the status bar at the bottom of the window is removed. Recheck View | Status Bar.

6. Select View | Group Tree. If the Group Tree was displayed, it will be removed. If it was not displayed, it will become visible.

7. Choose View | Zoom and set the magnification factor to **80%**. Notice the change in the display.

8. Close all open reports without saving changes.

Insert Menu

The Insert menu contains options for inserting complex objects or nondatabase objects into a report.

Text Object

The Text Object command creates a text object and puts it on the report where you click the mouse. You can visually track the location with the floating frame attached to the mouse pointer. You can type any text that you like into the Text Object. Text Objects are discussed in detail in Chapter 5.

Summary

Selecting the Summary item displays the Insert Summary dialog box, which allows you to create a summary field and place it in a report section. Summary fields and the Insert Summary dialog box are covered in Chapter 7.

Field Heading

After selecting a database field, you can choose Insert | Field Heading to have the heading for the field inserted into the page header. If you have not disabled the Insert Detail Field Headings option on the Layout tab of the File | Options dialog box, then field headings will be inserted by default when you insert a database field and you will not need to use this option.

Group

Selecting the Group item displays the Insert Group dialog box, which allows you to create a group for the report. Groups and the Insert Group dialog box are covered in Chapter 7.

OLAP Grid

Choosing OLAP Grid displays the OLAP Expert, where you design your OLAP grid object. You can insert multiple OLAP Grids into a single report. OLAP reporting is covered in Chapter 23.

Cross-Tab

Choosing Cross-Tab displays the Cross-Tab Expert, where you design your cross-tab object. You can insert multiple cross-tabs into a single report. Cross-tabs are described in Chapter 12.

Subreport

Selecting Subreport displays the Insert Subreport dialog box. A subreport is a report that is embedded in another report. The subreport may be linked to the main report, in which case the records that it displays are dependent on the main report's records, or it can be completely independent. Subreports are described in Chapter 16.

Line

To draw a horizontal or vertical line on your report, select Insert | Line. The mouse pointer will become a pencil that you can use to draw your line by holding down the right mouse button and moving the mouse. Let go of the mouse button to end the line. Lines can be drawn across section boundaries to make them stretch with the size of the section.

Box

To draw a box on your report, select Insert | Box. The mouse pointer will become a pencil that you can use to draw your box by holding down the right mouse button and moving the mouse. Let go of the mouse button to finish the box. Boxes can be drawn across section boundaries to make them stretch with the size of the section.

Picture

The Picture command can be used to insert graphics files into a report. Selecting Picture will display the Open dialog box where you can browse for image files. Supported file types are metafile, bitmap, JPEG, TIFF, and PNG. The picture will become a static OLE object and cannot be edited in Crystal Reports.

Chart

Choosing Chart displays the Chart Expert. You can use the Chart Expert to design one or more charts that will be added to your report. Charts are covered in Chapter 10.

Map

Choosing Map displays the Map Expert. You can use the Map Expert to design one or more map-based charts that will be added to your report.

OLE Object

To insert an OLE Object into your report, choose Insert | OLE Object. You can insert or link to any type of OLE Object that is available on your system.

Template Field Object

To insert a Template Field Object into your report, choose Insert | Template Field Object. Template Field Objects are similar to database field objects but are not connected to a specific database field. They are used as placeholders for real fields in report files that are used only as templates. Template Field Objects are discussed in Chapter 9.

Format Menu

Commands on the Format menu are used to change the way report objects are displayed. Most of the Format options are covered in detail in Chapter 9, as noted below, but a brief description is given here as a high-level overview.

Format

The Format command changes to indicate the type of report object that is currently selected. Choosing Format displays the Format Editor. Formatting options for the various object types is covered in Chapter 9.

Format Painter

The Format Painter is used to copy format options from one object to another. Use of the Format Painter is described in Chapter 9.

Hyperlink

The Hyperlink command brings up the Hyperlink tab of the Format Editor, which is used to create a hyperlink connected to a field. Hyperlinks are discussed in Chapter 9.

Use Expert

The Use Expert command changes to reflect the type of object that is selected in the report. For example, if a chart is selected, it will say "Chart Expert." Clicking this command displays the appropriate expert to use for editing the object.

TIP It is easier to choose the expert from the pop-up menu available by right-clicking the object.

Highlighting Expert
Selecting this option displays the Highlighting Expert. The Highlighting Expert is used to apply conditional formatting to fields; it is discussed in Chapter 9.

Line Height
The Line Height command is used to adjust the line height of sections where Free-Form Placement is turned off. This option is commonly used to fine-tune the print layout when printing onto forms.

Text Formatting
Selecting a text field and then using various methods to format it ordinarily causes that formatting to be applied to the entire field. However, if you double-click a text field, the cursor is inserted into the field and you can select portions of the field for formatting. After selecting a portion of the field, choose Format | Text Formatting to display the Text Format dialog box. Any changes that you make will apply only to the selected portion of the field.

TIP It is simpler to select the desired text, right-click. and then choose Text Formatting from the pop-up menu.

Move, Align, Size, and Size and Position
Moving, aligning, and sizing objects are described in Chapter 9.

Pivot OLAP Grid
The Pivot OLAP Grid command is used to interchange the rows and columns of an OLAP grid. It is discussed in Chapter 23.

Pivot Cross-Tab
The Pivot Cross-Tab command is used to interchange the rows and columns of a cross-tab grid.

Database Menu
All Database menu options are covered in Chapter 19.

Report Menu

The Report menu contains commands that display experts, set report statistics, create formulas and selection formulas, and manage other report level items. Many of the experts resemble their counterparts in the report wizards.

Select Expert

The Select Expert command displays the Select Expert dialog box. The Select Expert is used to filter the records retrieved for the report. It is discussed in Chapter 6.

Selection Formulas

There are two types of selection formulas: record selection formulas, which are used to select which records will be included in the report; and group selection formulas, which are used to select which groups will be included in the report.

Record   Choosing Report | Selection Formulas | Record brings up the Formula Workshop with the Record Selection Formula Editor displayed. Record selection is covered in Chapter 6.

Group   Choosing Report | Selection Formulas | Group brings up the Formula Workshop with the Group Selection Formula Editor displayed. Group selection is covered in Chapter 7.

Formula Workshop

Select Report | Formula Workshop to open the Formula Workshop. The Formula Workshop will open, allowing you to edit any type of report formula. The Formula Workshop is described in Chapter 8.

Alerts

The Alerts submenus and the use of alerts are covered in Chapter 13.

Report Bursting Indexes

Just as database tables can be indexed to improve access time, the data that Crystal Reports saves with a report can be indexed to improve record selection time. If Save Data with Report is enabled, then you can use the Report Bursting Indexes command to create indexes on the saved data. Unlike database tables, the data saved with Crystal Reports is already sorted appropriately for the report and it has already been retrieved from the database, so the goal of indexing the saved data is not faster retrieval or faster sorting. The main goal that you should consider when indexing saved data is record filtering.

Since the goal is to increase record selection time, the fields that you should consider for indexing are the fields that are used in the record selection formula. Indexing table primary keys or foreign keys will not contribute to the desired result. If the user cannot modify the record selection formula either directly or through the use of parameters, then creating indexes for the saved data will not be helpful.

Choosing Report Bursting Indexes brings up the Saved Data Indexes dialog box, as shown in Figure 4-14. The Available Fields list contains all the fields that can be indexed. Moving a field to the Indexed for Bursting list will cause Crystal Reports to create an index for that field the next time the report is refreshed. Clicking the Auto button will add any fields that are in the record selection formula to the Indexed for Bursting list.

After closing the Saved Data Indexes dialog box, you must refresh the report for the index to be created. If you have a parameter-based record selection formula, then you should set the parameter values such that the largest record set is returned and saved. When your users run the report and modify the parameter values, the result should be a subset of the saved data and not require new data to be retrieved from the database. If new data must be retrieved from the database, then the saved indexes are of no value.

Section Expert

Choosing Report | Section Expert brings up the Section Expert, which allows you to format a report section. Formatting sections is discussed in Chapter 9.

Group Expert and Record Sort Expert

The Group Expert and Record Sort Expert commands display the like-named experts. These experts are used for group creation and modification and record sorting. They are described in Chapter 7.

Figure 4-14

Creating and saving an index

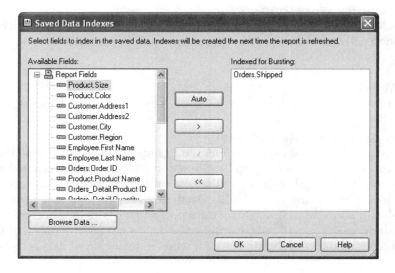

Group Sort Expert

The Group Sort Expert command allows you to order the groups in a report by a group summary field and to suppress the display of groups not in the top or bottom *n* of the summary values. This type of reporting is covered in Chapter 7.

XML Expert

The XML Expert allows you to modify the format of exported XML files.

Template Expert

The Template Expert command displays the Template Expert. You can choose a template to apply to your report. Using templates is explained further in Chapter 9.

OLAP Design Wizard

The OLAP Design Wizard option is only available if an OLAP grid is selected in the report. It displays the OLAP Expert, where you can modify the configuration of the grid. OLAP reporting is examined in Chapter 23.

Hierarchical Grouping Options

The Hierarchical Grouping Options command displays the Hierarchical Group Options dialog box. Sometimes there is a hierarchical relationship between two tables or even within a single table. For example, the Supervisor_ID field in the Employee table is either null or populated with an Employee_ID value from a different Employee record. A link could be created between the Supervisor_ID field and the Employee_ID field in order to determine the name of the supervisor for an employee. However, the supervisor may also have a supervisor, so this is a hierarchical relationship. Hierarchical reporting is covered in Chapter 12.

Show Current Parameter Values

The Show Current Parameter Values command brings up the Current Parameter Values dialog box, as shown in Figure 4-15. This dialog box displays all the report's parameters and their current settings. If you cannot remember the parameters that you last ran the report with, you can examine this dialog box. It is also helpful when the report was saved with data and you need to know what the parameter values at the last save were.

Refresh Report Data

This command will reexecute the report query and retrieve fresh data from the database. If the report has parameters, the Refresh Report Data dialog box will appear, and you can choose to use the same parameter values as last time or pick new parameter values. You might choose to refresh the report data if you believe changes have occurred on the database that are not reflected in the current report data.

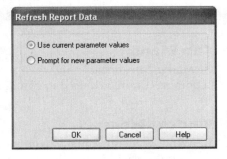

Figure 4-15
Viewing current
report parameters

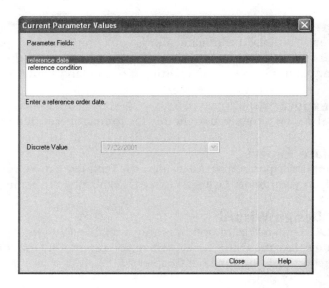

Set Print Date and Time

If you have used the special field Print Date or
Print Time on your report, but you do not want
them to display the actual date and time of the
printing, you can set them to specific values using
the Set Print Date and Time dialog box.

Performance Information

The Performance Information dialog box displays many different types of information about
the processing of the report. These statistics are
described in Chapter 15.

Chart Menu

The Chart menu appears only when a chart is selected in the report. It contains commands used to configure a chart. It is covered in Chapter 10.

Map Menu

The Map menu appears only when a map is selected in the report.
It contains commands used to configure a map.

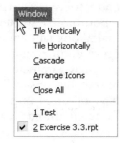

Window Menu

The Window menu contains commands used to manipulate the
open windows within the Crystal Reports environment.

Tile Vertically

The Tile Vertically command places all open windows side by side on the screen. Any files that are open but minimized are placed at the bottom of the screen.

Tile Horizontally

The Tile Horizontally command places all open windows one above the other on the screen. Any files that are open but minimized are placed at the bottom of the screen.

Cascade

The Cascade command places all open windows so that the title bar of each is visible. The bottom window is placed at the upper left of the screen, with subsequent windows placed lower and to the right. Any files that are open but minimized are placed at the bottom of the screen.

Arrange Icons

The Arrange Icons command places all minimized windows at the bottom of the screen in a row.

Close All

The Close All command closes all open windows. If the file has been modified since the last save, you will be prompted to save the changes.

Active Report

Below the Close All command is a section of the Window menu that lists all open reports. The active report has a check mark next to it. To change the active report to a different report, click it. It will come to the front of the display and become the checked report in this section of the Window menu.

Exercise 4.6: Exploring the Window Menu

1. Open the reports from Exercises 3.5, 3.7, and 3.10.

2. Choose Window | Tile Vertically and notice the arrangement of the windows.

3. Minimize the Exercise 3.10 report and select Window | Tile Horizontally. Notice that the 3.10 report stays minimized at the bottom of the screen and the other two windows are tiled.

4. Maximize the Exercise 3.10 report, and choose Window | Cascade. Notice the new window arrangement.

5. Minimize all three windows and move them to random locations on the screen. Then select Window | Arrange Icons. The icons are placed in order at the bottom of the window.

6. Select Window | Close All. Do not save any changes.

Help Menu

The Help menu contains commands related to getting help for the product, configuration of the product, and registration.

Crystal Reports Help

The Crystal Reports Help command opens the Crystal Reports Help file. You can browse the Help file contents, search for a specific word in the index or the whole file, create Favorites, print Help topics, and so on, just as in any Windows Help file.

Context Help

Choosing Help | Context Help causes the mouse pointer to change to the Context Help pointer. Clicking an item in the environment will then display help about that item.

Report Samples

The Report Samples command displays the Open dialog box with the location of the Sample reports shown. You can then open a sample report.

Welcome Dialog

Selecting the Welcome Dialog command displays the welcome dialog box. You can then choose to create a report using a wizard or a blank report or open an existing report. You can also toggle the display of the welcome dialog box at startup using the Show Welcome Dialog at Startup check box.

Register or Change Address

The Register or Change Address command will open the Crystal Reports Registration Wizard which is used to register your product or change your address.

License Manager

The License Manager command displays the Crystal Reports License dialog box of the License Manager. There you can check your license information or add new keycodes.

Crystal Decisions on the Web

The Crystal Decisions on the Web menu item has a submenu with links to several Business Objects web sites, as shown in Table 4-1. Use these links to access web resources for Crystal Reports.

Menu Item	URL
Crystal Decisions Home Page	http://www.businessobjects.com
Technical Support	http://support.businessobjects.com
Licensing Information	http://www.businessobjects.com/products/reporting/ crystalreports/licensing/details.asp
Developer Samples	http://www.businessobjects.com/products/dev_zone
Documentation	http://support.businessobjects.com/library/docfiles/cps10/ docs_en.asp
Web Reporting	http://www.businessobjects.com/products/reporting/ crystalenterprise/default.asp
Consulting and Training	http://www.businessobjects.com/services
Crystal Decisions Solutions	http://www.businessobjects.com/products/reporting/ crystalreports/default.asp

Table 4-1   Online Resources for Crystal Reports

About Crystal Reports

Selecting Help | About Crystal Reports displays the About Crystal Reports dialog box, as shown in Figure 4-16. This dialog box contains contact information and links for Crystal Decisions and Business Objects. The Product Version, Registration Number, and Keycode entries may be of particular interest to you.

If you click the More Info button, the Loaded Modules dialog box displays, as shown in Figure 4-17. This dialog box lists all the program modules (primarily DLLs) that have been loaded for use by Crystal Reports. This list may be useful in troubleshooting some types of reporting problems.

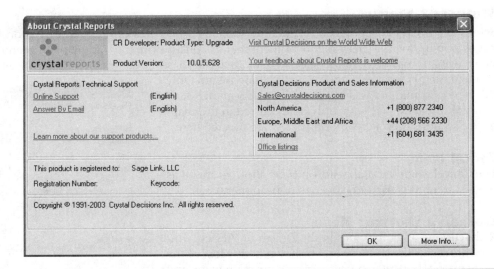

Figure 4-16   Viewing Crystal Reports contact and version information

Figure 4-17
Viewing installed
modules

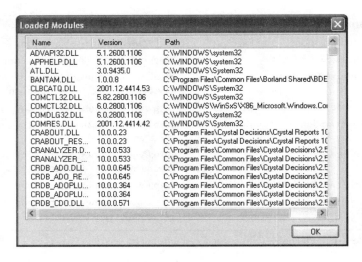

Exercise 4.7: Exploring the Help Menu

1. Choose Help | Crystal Reports Help and click the Index tab. Type **page setup** into the keyword box, and double-click the Page Setup Command entry to open the help for that topic.

2. Select Help | Report Samples. The Open dialog box should display with the location of the Crystal Reports sample files shown. Close the dialog box.

3. Select Help | About Crystal Reports, and note your product version.

Shortcut Menus

Selecting any Crystal Reports object and right-clicking brings up a context-sensitive shortcut or pop-up menu. The contents of these menus consist primarily of any main menu items that are applicable to the selected item. In addition, some commands exist only on shortcut menus and never appear on the main menu. Only this type of command will be covered in this section. Many of the shortcut menu commands are discussed in the chapters or sections they apply to; only a few are covered here.

Cancel Menu

The Cancel Menu item appears on every shortcut menu as the last item. It is used to close the pop-up menu.

Workarea Shortcut Menu

Right-clicking an empty spot in the Design or Preview window brings up the shortcut menu shown here. Most of the items on the shortcut menu also exist on the main menu and were described in previous sections of this chapter. The items that are unique to this menu are described in this section.

Snap to Grid   This shortcut menu command is equivalent to the Snap to Grid check box on the Layout tab of the File | Options dialog box. It causes new objects to align with the grid when they are added to the report.

Show Hidden Sections in Design   This shortcut menu command is equivalent to the Show Hidden Sections check box on the Layout tab of the File | Options dialog box. It causes hidden sections to display on the Design tab with a pattern of vertical lines through them to indicate that they are hidden. If this option is turned off, hidden sections are indicated only by a very small space between section boundaries.

Remove All Vertical Guidelines   The Remove All Vertical Guidelines command causes all vertical guidelines to be hidden. This is *not* equivalent to clearing the Guidelines check box in the Layout tab of the File | Options dialog box, which hides *all* guidelines.

Remove All Horizontal Guidelines   The Remove All Horizontal Guidelines command causes all horizontal guidelines to be hidden. This is *not* equivalent to clearing the Guidelines check box in the Layout tab of the File | Options dialog box, which hides *all* guidelines.

Toolbars

Crystal Reports has four toolbars that contain shortcuts to menu commands. In a few cases, the toolbar option is more powerful than the equivalent menu command, and those are noted in this section. The toolbars can be moved, rearranged, docked to the top, right, or left, or left free-floating by clicking in the far-right or -left area of the bar and holding down the left mouse button while moving the bar to a new location.

Toolbar Shortcut Menu

Right-clicking in the toolbar area under the main menu displays the Toolbar Shortcut menu. On the Toolbar Shortcut menu, you can check the toolbars that you want displayed. Clicking the Toolbars menu item displays the Toolbars dialog box, where you can choose to have large or small buttons and whether to display ToolTips or not. This is equivalent to the View | Toolbars menu command.

   In the following sections, each button on the four toolbars will be listed, along with its menu equivalent and any special notes.

> **NOTE**   Unlike with Microsoft Office applications, you cannot customize the Crystal Reports toolbars by adding or deleting commands, and you cannot create your own toolbars.

Standard Toolbar

The Standard toolbar contains shortcuts to some of the commands on the File, Edit, View, Format, Report, and Help menus.

III 4-44

File | New or CTRL-N
Displays the Crystal Reports Gallery dialog box.

File | Open or CTRL-O
Displays the Open dialog box. Note that clicking the drop-down arrow will display a list of the last nine opened files. You may select one of them to open instead of browsing with the Open dialog box.

File | Save or CTRL-S
Saves the active file.

File | Print | Printer or CTRL-P
Displays the Print dialog box.

File | Print | Preview, click the Preview tab, or View | Preview
Displays the Preview window.

File | Export
Displays the Export dialog box.

Report | Refresh Report Data or F5
Reprocesses the report, gathering fresh data from the database, and displays the Preview window.

Edit | Cut or CTRL-X
Deletes the selected object and places it on the clipboard.

Edit | Copy or CTRL-C
Copies the selected object to the clipboard.

Edit | Paste or CTRL-V
Pastes an object from the clipboard into the report.

Format | Format Painter
Copies the formatting from the selected item and applies it to the next item clicked.

Edit | Undo or CTRL-Z
Undoes the last reversible action. Note that selecting the drop-down arrow displays a list of all reversible actions. You can choose how far back to undo using the list. This capability is not available via any menu item.

Edit | Redo or CTRL-Y
Redoes the last redoable action. Note that selecting the drop-down arrow displays a list of all redoable actions. You can choose how far back to redo using the list. This capability is not available via any menu item.

View | Group Tree
This button toggles the display of the Group Tree. When the Group Tree is displayed, it shows a white background; when the Group Tree is not displayed, it shows a gray background.

View | Field Explorer
Displays the Field Explorer. This button is not a toggle; clicking it again does not close the Field Explorer.

View | Report Explorer
Displays the Report Explorer. This button is not a toggle; clicking it again does not close the Report Explorer.

View | Repository Explorer
Displays the Repository Explorer. This button is not a toggle; clicking it again does not close the Repository Explorer.

Edit | Find or CTRL-F
Displays the Find dialog box.

View | Zoom
The Zoom Control has a drop-down list that allows you to select a limited number of magnifications. The View | Zoom menu item displays the Zoom dialog box where you can choose any magnification you want.

Help | Context Help or SHIFT-F1
Turns the mouse pointer into the Help pointer and displays help for the next item clicked.

Formatting Toolbar

The Formatting toolbar contains shortcuts to many of the Format menu commands.

Format | Format Field | Font tab | font drop-down list
Contains a list of available fonts that can be applied to the selected field.

Format | Format Field | Font tab | size drop-down list
Contains a list of available font sizes that can be applied to the selected field for the font face selected.

TIP   Font sizes not available in the drop-down list can be typed into the font size box.

No direct menu equivalent
Increases the font size by one point each time it is clicked.

No direct menu equivalent
Decreases the font size by one point each time it is clicked.

Format | Format Field | Font tab | Style drop-down list
Applies bold formatting to the selected field.

Format | Format Field | Font tab | Style drop-down list
Applies italic formatting to the selected field.

Format | Format Field | Font tab | Underline check box
Underlines text in the selected field.

Format | Format Field | Common tab | Horizontal Alignment drop-down list
Aligns text in the selected field to the left.

Format | Format Field | Common tab | Horizontal Alignment drop-down list
Aligns text in the selected field to the center.

Format | Format Field | Common tab | Horizontal Alignment drop-down list
Aligns text in the selected field to the right.

Format | Format Field | Common tab | Horizontal Alignment drop-down list
Aligns text in the selected field so that it is *justified* (aligned on both right and left).

NOTE   The four alignment buttons act like radio buttons: only one can be active at a time, and the active button has a white background.

Format | Format Field | Font tab | Color drop-down list
Applies the currently selected color to the selected field. Click the down arrow to change the selected color.

Format | Format Field | Border tab | Left, Right, Top, and Bottom Line Style boxes
Clicking this button applies the currently selected border style to the selected object. To change the border style, click the down arrow and select a different icon.

Format | Format Field | Common tab | Suppress check box
Suppresses the selected object. This button is a toggle: if it is selected the background is white; otherwise it is gray.

Format | Format Field | Common tab | Read-only check box
This button is a toggle. Activating it restricts any formatting changes for the selected object.

Format | Format Field | Common tab | Lock Position and Size check box
Locks the selected report object so that it cannot be moved or resized.

Format | Format Field | Number tab | Display Currency Symbol check box
Toggles the currency symbol for the selected numeric field on or off.

Format | Format Field | Number tab | Customize button | Thousands
Separator check box
Toggles a separator character for thousands for the selected numeric field.

Format | Format Field | Number tab | Customize button | Currency Symbol
tab | Enable Currency Symbol check box, set Currency Symbol to %, and select
Position at the right
Toggles a percent sign for the selected numeric field.

Format | Format Field | Number tab | Customize button | Number tab | Decimals
and Rounding drop-down lists
Adds one decimal place to the display of the selected numeric field and sets the
rounding to the same number of decimal places.

Format | Format Field | Number tab | Customize button | Number tab | Decimals
and Rounding drop-down lists
Subtracts one decimal place from the display of the selected numeric field and
sets the rounding to the same number of decimal places.

Expert Tools

The Expert Tools toolbar contains shortcuts to open various report experts. The experts
are described in other sections and/or chapters, as noted in the "Crystal Reports Menus"
section.

Database | Database Expert
Opens the Database Expert.

Report | Group Expert
Opens the Group Expert.

Report | Group Sort Expert
Opens the Group Sort Expert.

Report | Record Sort Expert
Opens the Record Sort Expert.

Report | Select Expert
Opens the Select Expert.

Report | Section Expert
Opens the Section Expert.

Report | Formula Workshop
Opens the Formula Workshop.

Report | OLAP Design Wizard
Opens the OLAP Expert for the selected OLAP grid.

Report | Template Expert
Opens the Template Expert.

Format | Format Field
Opens the Format Editor for the selected field.

Format | Format Field | Hyperlink tab
Opens the Format Editor with the hyperlink tab active for the selected field.

Format | Highlighting Expert
Opens the Highlighting Expert.

Insert Tools

The Insert Tools toolbar contains shortcuts for inserting many different types of objects onto the report.

III 4-100

ab Insert | Text Object
Inserts a text object into the report where you click.

Insert | Group
Displays the Insert Group dialog box allowing you to create a new group in the report. The Group By field defaults to the field currently selected in the report.

Σ Insert | Summary
Displays the Insert Summary dialog box so that you can create a new summary field. The field to summarize defaults to the field currently selected in the report.

Insert | Cross-Tab
Displays the Cross-Tab Expert, allowing you to create a new cross-tab.

Insert | OLAP Grid
Displays the OLAP Expert so that you can create a new OLAP grid.

Insert | Subreport
Displays the Insert Subreport dialog box, allowing you to create or add a new subreport to the main report.

Insert | Line
The mouse cursor becomes a pencil allowing you to draw a line on the report.

Insert | Box
The mouse cursor becomes a pencil allowing you to draw a box on the report.

Insert | Picture
Displays the Open dialog box so that you can browse for an image file to add to the report.

Insert | Chart
Displays the Chart Expert allowing you to add a new chart to the report.

Insert | Map
Displays the Map Expert allowing you to add a new map to the report.

Chapter Review

This chapter described most of the elements of the Crystal Reports design environment. The Design tab displays a mock-up of the report and lets you see the overall report structure easily. The Preview tab displays a WYSIWYG view of the report using real data. You can do most report development work in either tab. Crystal Reports has menus and toolbars similar to other Windows applications. Many menu options perform identically to their Microsoft Office counterparts, such as File | New, File | Save, and Help | About. Some menu items are unique to Crystal Reports, including View | Field Explorer, Insert | Group, and Report | Alerts. You can customize the development environment using the File | Options dialog box. You cannot customize the toolbars. You can save identification information with report files using the File | Summary Info command. After reading this chapter you should have a general impression of where to look for various report options.

Quick Tips

- The Preview tab displays the report using actual data. The Design tab displays with placeholders for data fields.
- Selecting File | Print | Preview, clicking the Preview tab, choosing View | Preview, or clicking the Print Preview button all cause the Preview window to display. If no saved data exists, these actions will also cause data retrieval.

Clicking the Refresh button, selecting Report | Refresh Report Data, or clicking F5 causes the Preview window to display as well, but it always causes new data to be retrieved from the database.

- Clicking the Refresh button causes Crystal Reports to fetch new data from the database. Clicking the Print Preview button will not fetch new data if saved data exists.

- The order of sections in a report is Report Header, Page Header, Detail, Report Footer, and Page Footer. Group Header and Footer sections are layered around the Detail section if they exist.

- The total page count on the Preview tab is not correct unless the last page has been viewed.

- To save a snapshot of the report, go to File | Summary Info and check the Save Preview Picture check box.

- To save summary information with the report file, go to File | Summary Info and fill in the fields on the Summary tab of the Document Properties dialog box.

Questions

Question may have more than one correct answer. Choose all answers that apply.

1. Which tab allows you to work in a WYSIWIG environment?

   a. Design

   b. Preview

2. What is the first section in a report?

   a. Page Header

   b. Page Footer

   c. Details

   d. Report Header

   e. Report Footer

3. The total number of pages displayed in the Page Control is always correct if data retrieval is complete.

   a. True

   b. False

4. Which tab allows you to work with a schematic view of the report, not with live data?

   a. Design

   b. Preview

5. The Group Tree is available in both the Design window and the Preview window.

    a. True

    b. False

6. The Preview tab always displays current data.

    a. True

    b. False

7. What is always the last section in a report, assuming no core sections are suppressed?

    a. Page Header

    b. Page Footer

    c. Details

    d. Report Header

    e. Report Footer

8. The Data Age indicator is in the status bar.

    a. True

    b. False

9. Choose the option or capability that does not differ between the Design and Preview tabs.

    a. Display of page margins

    b. Vertical rulers

    c. Page Controls

    d. Status bar contents

    e. Field formatting options

10. Which of the following actions always causes database access?

    a. Selecting File | Print | Preview

    b. Clicking the Preview tab

    c. Choosing View | Preview

    d. Clicking the Print Preview button

    e. Clicking the Refresh button

Answers

1. **b.** Preview

2. **d.** The Report Header section is always the first section in a report (although it may be suppressed). The Page Header is second.

3. **b.** False. The total number of pages displayed in the Page Control will not be correct until you have viewed the last page. Crystal Reports counts the pages as it formats them and will not format a page until necessary.

4. **a.** Design

5. **b.** False. The Group Tree is available only in the Preview window.

6. **b.** False. The Preview tab retrieves data from the database the first time the report is run. For later report modifications, it uses saved data unless the data is specifically refreshed using the Report | Refresh Report Data menu option, the Refresh button, or F5. If the report changes require new data, a refresh will happen automatically. The Preview tab may display out-of-date information until a refresh occurs.

7. **b.** The Page Footer section is always the last section in a report (although it may be suppressed). The Report Footer is the next-to-last section.

8. **b.** False. The Data Age indicator is displayed at the top of the Preview window next to the Page Controls.

9. **e.** Field formatting options are identical on both the Preview and Design tabs.

10. **e.** Clicking the Refresh button will always cause new data to be retrieved. The other actions will only cause data to be retrieved if no saved data already exists.

Creating a Report

Exam RDCR200 expects you to be able to
- Plan the layout and content of a report
- Develop a prototype of a report
- Connect to a data source
- Add tables
- Insert objects on a report
- Position and size objects
- Add graphical elements
- Combine text objects with database fields
- Insert fields with prebuilt functions

In Chapter 3, you created reports using the report creation wizards. In this chapter, you will learn about report planning and practice the initial steps needed when creating a report manually.

Planning a Report

Creating a report entails many different steps. Usually there is an initial request, then a requirements-gathering process that includes determining both the data required and the desired format, followed by multiple cycles of development and user refinement until final approval is obtained. At least in theory, the more effort you invest in the planning phase, the shorter the development time and the fewer development cycles needed, reducing overall development time.

Requirements Gathering

Requirements gathering can be very casual or very formal, depending on the environment, but having a checklist of appropriate questions to ask the user is always beneficial and ensures that all important aspects are covered early in the process. Even if you are both the developer and the user, a question list or form will help you plan your report and can act as documentation. If you are in a formal report-development environment, the filled-in questionnaire can be officially signed by the report requester to signify that their requirements have been properly understood and recorded.

Customize the following list of suggested topics for such a questionnaire to fit your specific needs.

- **Title and identification**   Every report needs a title and other identifying information. If you work with only a small number of reports or your reports are all significantly different, then a title may be sufficient to distinguish one report from another. However, if you work with a large number of reports or many similar reports, a report number or other unique identifier is recommended. Users tend to refer to reports in a shorthand manner, such as "the employee report," so you need an easy way to guarantee that everyone is discussing the same report.

- **Description**   A short description of the report that includes most of the main features is helpful as a goal for the requirements-gathering process and as identifying information for later.

- **Audience**   Understanding the audience or end users of a report is essential in developing the report appropriately. It is also beneficial to have a single user or client who is responsible for signing off on the requirements. A single report is often used by many different people, but you do not want to be in a position where you are required to interpret and integrate the desires of several different users if they want very different things.

- **Delivery method(s)**   How the report will be delivered to the user can affect its optimal organization. A report meant to be exported to Excel would be formatted differently than one intended to be displayed on a web site.

- **Page Setup**   Decisions about paper size, orientation, and margins may be made upfront or may be dictated by the report content. For example, if the number and size of fields to display exceed the available row width for letter-size paper in portrait mode, then landscape mode may be required. However, if the report will be displayed on the Web, landscape is not a good option since horizontal scrolling would be required to view the width of the report.

- **Data sources**   The data source or sources correspond to the databases and objects within the database that you must connect to in order to obtain the data for the report. The end user may not know or understand the database structures, in which case you must translate the requirements into concrete data sources. In many cases, however, they will know exactly what they want and have a good understanding of the sources. In any case, you will need to know the database, tables, and linking information required to fulfill the report requirements.

- **Data fields, types, order, and formatting**   The data fields to display—along with their type, required formatting, and order across the page—are the foundation of the report and usually make up the Details section of the report. You will want to note cases where the column title should differ from the default of the corresponding field name.

- **Detail record computations and formatting**   In this section you will want to define any necessary computed fields and special formatting.

- **Record selection and parameters**   Determining the correct record selection can be very difficult for complex reports and will require validation by both the developer and the end user. When discussing record selection it is also appropriate to determine the necessary parameters because parameters are used most often to limit the records returned and therefore become part of the record selection formula. For example, if the user wants to run the report and have it filtered such that only the records for a certain country are displayed and they want to be able to run it for different countries, then you will need to create a parameter for country and embed it in the record selection formula.

- **Grouping and sorting**   Fields to group by and the order of the groups on the report must be determined. Each group has a sort order to determine the sorting of the group values on the report and may have special sorting needs that need to be addressed. For fields that are not used in a group, a sort order can be defined to determine the order of the records within the lowest-level group.

- **Group selection**   Group selection differs from record selection in two ways. It does not filter the records returned by the database; it filters the groups displayed on the report. Group selection can also be used to sort groups based on a summary value for the group rather than on detail field values or on the value of the group-by field itself. For example, if a report that shows only the top five sales amounts by salesperson are desired, then you would sort the report by a summary field for the total amount by salesperson and then select only the top five groups.

- **Summary computations and formatting**   In addition to row-level formulas, which compute a value for each row in the report, a report can contain summary calculations at any group level or for the entire report. For example, a report may have a sum of amounts displayed in the report footer and all group footers.

- **Charts**   A user may desire that some information be displayed visually in a chart. You can add multiple charts to a report, and the chart can show either the same information as that displayed in a columnar format on the report or completely different information.

- **Cross-tabs**   Cross-tabs can be added to a report to display data in tabular format. A report can contain multiple cross-tabs, if desired, although each must be placed in a group section or the Report Header or Report Footer.

- **OLAP grids**   An OLAP grid can be used to add OLAP data to a report. Multiple OLAP grids can be displayed in a single report. OLAP data can be displayed alone or in addition to regular data in the report.

- **Maps**   Some data may be appropriate for display in geographical maps.

- **Alerts**   Crystal can be programmed to display alerts when defined conditions are met in the report. Alerts assist the end user to identify important conditions without searching through the entire report.

- **Flags**   Fields can be flagged by displaying them with special formatting to highlight important values.

After deciding which of these categories are important to your organization, you can create a questionnaire or form to fill out when discussing report requirements with your clients. In most situations, you will need to fill out the form by interpreting the user's needs. You cannot normally expect users to understand the report-design process well enough to fill out the forms by themselves.

Prototyping

Simultaneously with the requirements gathering or as a separate process, it is useful to create a sketch on paper to indicate the approximate placement of fields. This sketch should be done on the same size paper with the same orientation as will be used for the report, and it should show the placement of fields, groups, header information, and so on. Prototyping in this fashion often reveals potential problems, which can then be addressed before development work begins. The prototype can also be used as a sign-off document in the overall reporting process.

For example, suppose that a user requests a report that shows each employee, their birthday, and age, by month and by supervisor, for the current year. Figure 5-1 shows a sample Microsoft InfoPath requirements-gathering form filled out for this report request.

 NOTE   The InfoPath requirements-gathering form is included on the accompanying CD.

Starting with a Blank Report

Once you have your requirements, you can start report development. This chapter introduces report development that starts with a blank report. Using the report wizards to start a report was discussed previously.

 NOTE   Any design that can be created via a report wizard can be duplicated by starting from a blank report. However, if you are creating labels, the Mail Label wizard will let you pick from industry standard label types, whereas if you start from a blank report, you will have to set up the sections for the appropriate label size manually.

As you step through the process of creating a report from a blank report in this chapter, you will read detailed explanations of the Database Expert, Field Explorer, field placement, Report Explorer, and Repository Explorer interspersed throughout the actual development process. Each topic will be discussed as it arises in the process, so several exercises will be required to complete the development of one report.

 TIP   Instead of using a report wizard or starting with a blank report, you can also create new reports by modifying existing reports. To use this method, you must open an existing report and then use File | Save As to save it with a new name. You can then modify it as needed.

Report Requirements   1

Employee Birthdays

Lists employee birthdays and ages, by supervisor for the current year.

Requestor Jill   Request Date 5/12/2004

Documenter Annette   Template None

Keywords   • Employees   Audience   • Supervisors
            • Personal

Subject Employee Personal Information

Comments This report should be considered confidential.

Report Delivery Methods

Printer HP Laserjet III

Page Setup

Right Margin	Left Margin	Top Margin	Bottom Margin
1"	1"	1"	1"

Paper Size ◉ Letter   Orientation ◉ Portrait
            ○ Legal   ○ Landscape

Page Header ☑ Logo ☐ Print Date ☐ Page Number ☐ Total Pages
Page Footer ☐ Logo ☑ Print Date ☑ Page Number ☐ Total Pages

Data Sources

Database	Schema	Source Type	Source Name
Xtreme		Table	Employee

Groups

Group Number	Group On	Sort	Keep Together	Repeat Header
1	Birth Month	Ascending	☐	☑
2	Supervisor ID	Ascending	☐	☑

Fields

Field 1	Type Text	Notes
	Name Employee Name	Concatenate the employees first name and last name.
	Title Employee Name	

Field 2	Type Database	Notes
	Name Birth Date	Format as mm/dd/yyyy.
	Title Birth Date	

Figure 5-1   Report requirements document

Exercise 5.1: Starting from a Blank Report

1. Select File | New or click the New button. The Crystal Reports Gallery will be displayed.

Figure 5-2
Starting from a
blank report in
the Gallery

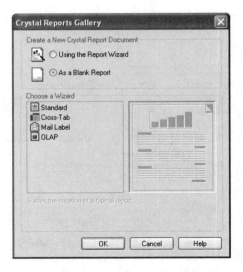

2. Select the As a Blank Report radio button. The Choose a Wizard panel will be grayed out, as shown in Figure 5-2.

3. Click OK. The Database Expert displays.

 NOTE If you click Cancel now, the new report will be created, but you will not have created any new database connections.

Database Expert

The Database Expert is similar to the Data dialog box in the report wizards; it is where you connect to databases and choose tables to use in the report. This section provides a brief overview of the Database Expert. See Chapter 18 for detailed coverage of all Database Expert capabilities and options.

 TIP You can display the Database Expert at any time by choosing Database | Database Expert.

The Database Expert has two tabs: the Data tab and the Links tab. The Links tab is used to create links between tables. The Data tab contains two lists, as shown in Figure 5-3. The list on the left displays Available Data Sources; the list on the right contains the tables selected for use in this report. The top-level folders in the Available Data Sources list are used for grouping; they must be opened to display available data sources. The data

Figure 5-3
Selecting data
sources in the
Database Expert

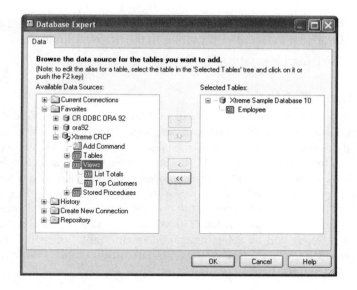

source folders, in turn, must be opened to display the tables that can be selected. Tables
are moved from one list to the other using the arrow buttons or by dragging.

Connecting to the Sample Data

The XTREME sample data is contained in an Access database that you will connect to using
ODBC. New data source connections are created using the Create New Connection folder.
Exercise 5.2 walks you through the steps required to connect to the sample data. You will
also create a Favorites entry for the sample data, to make future connections easier.

Exercise 5.2: Connecting to XTREME

1. Complete Exercise 5.1, and then open the Create New Connection folder.

2. Open the ODBC folder.

3. Select Make New Connection, if necessary.

4. In the ODBC dialog box, choose Xtreme Sample Database 10, and click Finish.

5. Under the ODBC folder, you should now see a folder called Xtreme Sample
   Database 10. Right-click it, and choose Add to Favorites.

6. Scroll until you can see the Favorites folder and open it. If your new entry is not
   displayed, press F5, or close and reopen the folder.

7. Right-click the Favorites entry for Xtreme Sample Database 10, and choose
   Rename Favorite. The entry will be selected and you can modify it. Change
   it to **Xtreme CRCP,** and click somewhere else on the screen.

8. Open the Xtreme CRCP folder. Open the Tables folder and add the Customer, Order, and Order Details tables to the Selected Tables list.

9. Click the Links tab.

Linking Tables

When you use more than one table in a report, you must tell Crystal Reports how to link the tables. Tables are usually linked in Crystal Reports in the same way that they are linked in the underlying database. A field from one table is linked to a field in another table that contains identical field values. For example, the sample data contains an Employee table that has an Employee ID field. It also has an Employee Addresses table that has an Employee ID field. Employee can be linked to Employee Addresses using the Employee ID field. Links are represented by lines drawn between the linked fields, as shown in Figure 5-4.

You can create links for the XTREME sample data by clicking the Link button. Links can also be created by selecting a field in one table, pressing and holding down the mouse button, and then selecting a field in another table. (Table linking is discussed in detail in Chapter 18.)

Exercise 5.3: Creating Links Between Tables

This exercise continues from the end of Exercise 5.2. If necessary, go back and complete that exercise first.

1. You should be on the Links tab with Customer, Orders, and Orders_Detail displayed. Click the Clear Links button, and notice that the links are removed. (If you are asked whether you are sure you want to remove the links, click Yes.)

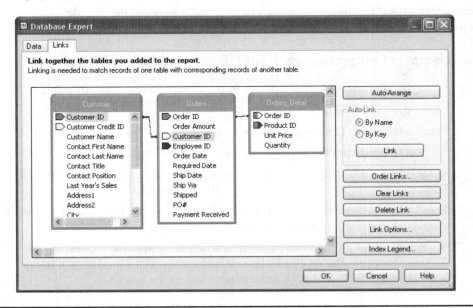

Figure 5-4   Linking tables in the Database Expert

2. Select By Name in the Auto-Link panel, and then click the Link button. Notice that the links reappear.

3. Clear the links again, and then manually create a link from Customer.Customer ID to Orders.Customer ID.

4. Remove all the links again, and then re-create them using the Auto-Link By Name option.

5. Click OK to close the Database Expert. The Design tab will display with a blank report.

6. Save the report as **Exercise 5.3** in your CRCP Exercises folder.

Field Explorer

After completing Exercise 5.3, you will be left in the Design pane with a blank report. To populate the report, you will use the Field Explorer. The Field Explorer is the source for most of the objects you can place on a report. Fields available to place on the report are grouped into category folders in the Field Explorer.

Exploring the Field Explorer

Before starting to place objects on the report, you should understand the features of the Field Explorer window.

Displaying the Field Explorer

If the Field Explorer is not open, open it by choosing View | Field Explorer or clicking the Field Explorer button on the Standard toolbar.

Docking the Field Explorer

The Field Explorer window can be free-floating, or it can be docked to the left, right, or bottom of the Crystal Reports window. To dock the Field Explorer, hold down the left mouse button on its title bar, drag it toward the left, right, or bottom until it is in the position you desire, and then release the mouse button.

The Field Explorer can also be docked with the Report Explorer or Repository Explorer such that tabs are created for each explorer. To create a tabbed explorer, hold down the left mouse button on the title bar and move the mouse into the top area of one of the other explorer windows. It will dock and create tabs as shown here. The tabbed entity can then itself be docked to an edge of the Crystal Reports window. Double-clicking a docked explorer will make it free-floating. Double-clicking a free-floating explorer will redock it in its last docked position.

Toolbar and Shortcut Menu

The Field Explorer window has its own toolbar and shortcut menu. Most commands are available on both the toolbar and shortcut menu, as described in the following list. The commands related to fields always act on the selected field or fields. To select multiple fields, use the SHIFT and CTRL buttons as you would in Windows Explorer.

 Insert to Report   Inserts the selected field into the report. When you click this button or the ENTER key a frame appears on the report. Move the frame to the desired location, and click to place the field at that location. Insert to Report is available for all field types. Once a field has been inserted to the report, a green check mark appears next to it in the Field Explorer tree. You can also insert a field in a report by dragging it.

 Browse Data   Clicking the Browse button displays the contents of the field in a dialog box. The Browse button or Browse Data shortcut command is available only for database fields.

 New   The New button is available for Formula fields, SQL Expression fields, Parameter fields, and Running Total fields. Clicking it allows you to create a new field of that type.

 Edit   The Edit button is available for Formula fields, SQL Expression fields, Parameter fields, and Running Total fields. Clicking it allows you to modify a field of that type.

 Rename   The Rename button (shortcut: F2) is available for Formula fields, SQL Expression fields, Parameter fields, and Running Total fields. Clicking it allows you to change the name of the field.

 Delete   The Delete button (shortcut: DELETE) is available for Formula fields, SQL Expression fields, Parameter fields, and Running Total fields. Clicking it deletes the selected field.

Move Parameter Up   This option applies only to Parameter fields. Selecting it causes the parameter to be moved up in the list of parameters. Parameter values are requested from the user in the order that they are listed.

Move Parameter Down   This option applies only to Parameter fields. Selecting it causes the parameter to be moved down in the list of parameters. Parameter values are requested from the user in the order that they are listed.

Database Expert   Available only for Database fields, this option displays the Database Expert.

Set Datasource Location   This option is only available for Database fields. It displays the Set Datasource Location dialog box, which is used to change the underlying database location for the data source.

Log On or Off Server   This option is available only for Database fields. Selecting it displays the Data Explorer dialog box. The Data Explorer displays the same tree of folders as the Database Explorer. Using it, you can log on or off of data sources, add them to or delete them from the Favorites folder, and set their database options.

Show Field Type   Show Field Type is available only for Database fields. Choosing it toggles display of the field type after the field name in the Field Explorer.

Refresh   Selecting Refresh refreshes the field list in the Field Explorer.

Field Explorer Folders
Each folder in the Field Explorer represents a different type of object that can be added to a report.

Database Fields
The Database Fields folder contains all the data sources that were added to the report using the Database Expert. Expanding a data source displays all the fields in that data source. You can add these fields to the report by dragging them or by using the Insert to Report shortcut command or the Insert to Report toolbar button. You can browse the data in a field using the Browse button or the Browse Data shortcut command. If you would like to see the data type of the fields, you can check the Show Field Types option in the shortcut menu.

Formula Fields
Formula fields are fields that you create using Crystal's Formula Workshop. The Formula Fields folder will initially be empty. After you create a Formula field, it will appear under the Formula Fields folder and can be edited or deleted from there. Once a Formula field exists, it can be added to the report and formatted the same as Database fields. Formula fields are computed locally by Crystal Reports.

SQL Expressions
As an alternative to Formula fields, for SQL databases you can create SQL Expression fields. SQL Expression fields use the SQL dialect of the underlying database and are added to the query that Crystal Reports constructs and sends to the database. They are evaluated on the server, and the result is returned to Crystal Reports with the normal Database fields.

Parameter Fields
Parameter fields are created to gather information from the user. These may have many purposes, but they are often used to limit the records returned from the database and displayed in the report. You can place Parameter fields on the report where they will display the value entered by the report user. This may be done to document the parameters chosen for a report run. Parameter fields are most often used in selection formulas.

Running Totals
Summary fields are used to compute a summary value across a report group or the entire report. A summary field can only be placed in a group section or the Report Header or Report Footer. Running Total Fields are different. They can be placed in the Detail section and display an accumulated value up to the current record. Running Totals can be

reset at chosen points and can accumulate their values dependent on formulas creating conditional Running Totals.

Group Name Fields

Whenever a group is created in a report, a corresponding Group Name field is created. By default the Group Name is equivalent to the field value being grouped on, but it can be customized to suit your needs. The Group Name Fields folder contains all existing Group Names.

When a group is created, the Group Name is added to the Group Header section by default. If you do not want the Group Name added to the Group Header section, you can clear Insert Group Name with Group on the File | Options Layout tab. The Group Name will still exist in the Field Explorer under the Group Name Fields folder.

Special Fields

The Special Fields folder contains fields associated with the report that are not related to the data or content of the report. These fields can be placed on the report and formatted just as any of the other field types.

- **Current CE User ID**   Contains the Crystal Enterprise user ID if you are logged in to Crystal Enterprise.

- **Current CE User Name**   Contains the Crystal Enterprise user name if you are logged into Crystal Enterprise.

- **Data Date**   The date corresponding to the most recent retrieval of data from the database—the most recent refresh.

- **Data Time**   The time corresponding to the most recent retrieval of data from the database.

- **File Author**   The Author field from the Document Properties for the report file.

- **File Creation Date**   The date that the report file was created.

- **File Path and Name**   The filename including the path of the report file.

- **Group Number**   Groups in a report are numbered according to their order in the report. The outermost group is group number 1 and so on. This field displays the number of the group in which it is placed. If a report contains no groups, this field will always display 1.

- **Group Selection Formula**   Contains the Group Selection formula for the report if one exists.

- **Horizontal Page Number**   Cross-tabs and OLAP grids can be too large to fit across a single page. In that case, they expand across multiple pages horizontally.

(They may also expand vertically.) Horizontal Page Number provides a page number that increases by 1 for each horizontal page that is required.

- **Modification Date**   The date of the last modification to the report.

- **Page N of M**   Inserts the current page number (*N*) and the total number of pages in the report (*M*) in the form "Page *N* of *M*."

- **Page Number**   The current page number.

- **Print Date**   The date the report was printed.

- **Print Time**   The time when the report was printed.

- **Record Number**   A sequential number for the records in the report. This number is created by Crystal Reports according to the sort order of the report. It is not a database-related field. If the sort order is changed, the record numbers will also change.

- **Record Selection Formula**   The Record Selection formula, if one exists.

- **Report Comments**   The comments from the Document Properties for the report file.

- **Report Title**   The title from the Document Properties for the report. Using this field in the page header instead of a text object containing the report title will keep the displayed title in the report the same as the title in the file's properties.

- **Total Page Count**   The total number of pages in the report.

 EXAM TIP   Know which Special fields exist and what they are used for.

Exercise 5.4: Using the Field Explorer

1. Open the Exercise 5.3 report.

2. If the Field Explorer is not open, open it using the Field Explorer button or View | Field Explorer.

3. Open the Database Fields folder, and notice that the Customers, Orders, and Orders_Detail tables are listed.

4. Open the Orders folder and notice that all of the Orders fields are listed. Right-click on Orders or one of the Orders fields and select Show Field Types. Notice that the field types are now displayed next to the field names for all tables.

5. Open the Customers folder, right-click on the Contact Title field, and select Browse Data. Examine the dialog that is displayed and then click the Close button.

6. Open the Special Fields folder, and select the Current CE User Name field. Click the Insert to Report button, and place the field in the Report Header section.

7. Dock the Field Explorer to the right side of the environment.

8. If the Report Explorer or Repository Explorer is open, dock the Field Explorer together with one of them to create a tabbed explorer.

9. Save the report as **Exercise 5.4** in your CRCP Exercises folder.

Placing Fields on the Report

Placing a field onto the report is the most basic of the report design steps. When a field is placed on the report in the Design tab, a frame is displayed with the field name inside it. If the field is placed on the Preview tab, the actual value of the field is displayed for every record in the report.

Methods

There are several methods that you can use to place fields onto the report. These methods can all be used with either the Design tab or the Preview tab visible. These methods work for every type of field contained in the Field Explorer.

Single Fields

To place one field onto the report, select it in the Field Explorer and then right-click and choose Insert to Report from the shortcut menu, or click the Insert to Report toolbar button, or drag it onto the report. You can also simply double-click the field. Each method creates an empty frame attached to the mouse pointer. Click or release the mouse to place the field at the desired location.

Multiple Fields

To insert multiple fields onto the report, you must first select them. To select fields in sequential order, select the first field, and then hold down the SHIFT button and select the last field. All the fields from the first to the last will be highlighted. To select other, non-contiguous fields, hold down the CTRL key while clicking each of them. They will all be highlighted. After you have selected the multiple fields, you can drag them onto the report, or use the Insert to Report shortcut command or button. The fields will be placed one after the other, starting where you click the mouse.

Field Headers

By default, when you insert field objects into the Details section of the report, a Field Header text object is also inserted into the Page Header section. If you don't want a Field Header inserted, select File | Options and clear the Insert Detail Field Headings check box on the Layout tab.

Distinguishing the Field Object Type

You can create four types of fields: Formulas, SQL Expressions, Parameters, and Running Totals. When you create a field, you must give it a name. The names must be unique within the field type, but not across field types. For example, this illustration shows one field of each type, where each is named "test." When a field is placed on the report, a symbol is prefixed to its field name to help you distinguish what kind of field it is. Formula fields start with the at (@) symbol. SQL Expression fields start with a percent (%) sign. Parameters are prefixed with a question mark (?). And Running Totals use a pound (#) sign. Crystal Reports adds the symbols to the field name; you do not need to include them when creating the name.

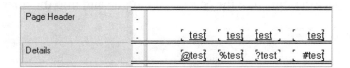

NOTE Each field in the illustration has the same field heading because Crystal Reports uses the field's name for the heading by default.

Fine-Tuning Field Placement and Size

Once a field is placed on the report, you have many different options for moving it around and fine-tuning its placement.

Selecting Multiple Objects

Many of the following placement and sizing functions can operate on multiple field objects. There are several ways to select multiple objects:

- **SHIFT-click or CTRL-click** Select one field, and then hold down the SHIFT or CTRL key and click other fields. Each field will be added to the selection as you click it.

- **Select All Section Objects**   If you right-click in the gray section name area and then choose Select All Section Objects, all field objects in the section will be selected.

- **Lasso or marquee**   You can select multiple objects by drawing a lasso around them with the mouse. With the mouse button situated at one of the corners of the box you want to draw, hold down the left mouse button and then move the mouse diagonally to the opposite corner. You will see a frame being drawn. When you release the mouse button, all the objects enclosed by the frame will be selected and the frame will disappear.

- **Main object**   When you are working with multiple selected objects, the last item selected is considered to be the *main object*. It is important to know which object is the main object when moving, sizing, or aligning multiple objects as explained in the following sections. To change the main object, hold down the SHIFT or CTRL key and click the new main object twice. *Do not double-click.* Click once to unselect the field, and then click again to reselect it as the last item in the selection group.

Moving

If you select a field, the mouse pointer will change to the *move pointer,* a four-way cursor. If you then hold down the left mouse button, you can move the object by moving the mouse. As you move the field, you are given visual clues to help with placement. You will see a frame the same size as the field, as well as vertical and horizontal lines called *tracking guidelines* extending past the edges of the frame and into the ruler area.

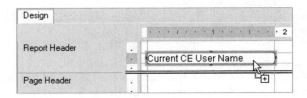

TIP   In Design mode, items can be moved one grid coordinate at a time by selecting them and then using the keyboard arrow keys.

To move multiple objects, select them using any of the methods described in the preceding section, and then hold the mouse pointer over any object until the move cursor appears. Then move the objects to the new location. The objects will stay in the same relative position to each other and move as a block. If you attempt to move multiple objects into a location where they will not all fit, the main object and any others that fit will be moved. If the main object will not fit, then no objects will be moved.

Rulers

Use the horizontal and vertical rulers along with the tracking guidelines when moving an object to place it exactly where you want it on the page.

Guidelines

When you place a field into the Details section of a report, a vertical guideline is auto-matically created and attached to it if Insert Detail Field Headings is checked on the File | Options Layout tab. The field heading is attached to the same guideline. If the field is numeric, the guideline is attached to the right side of the field frame. If the field is a string field, the guideline is attached to the left side of the frame. Guidelines are indicated by an arrow in the ruler area and a dashed line through the report area.

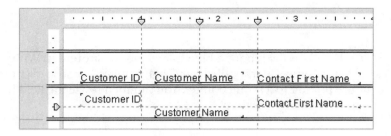

Fields can snap to vertical guidelines at the right side, left side, or middle of the field. To attach a guideline to either side, move the object until its frame overlaps the guideline. To attach a guideline to the center of the field, note that the field frame has a darker square area indicating the middle of the field. Move the field so that this handle is over the guideline. The options for attaching horizontal guidelines are to the top or bottom of the frame or baseline of the text. In this illustration, the Customer ID field is attached vertically on the right and horizontally on the bottom of the frame, the Customer Name field is attached at the middle vertically and at the top horizontally, and the Contact First Name field is attached at the left vertically and to the text baseline horizontally.

If an object is attached to a guideline, it moves with the line when the line is moved. You can tell that an object is attached to a guideline if its frame corners turn red. Attaching multiple items to the same guideline ensures that they are aligned and that they will stay aligned if the guideline is moved. To move a guideline, move the mouse pointer over the arrow until it turns black, then hold down the left mouse button and move the line to a new position. To create a new guideline, click anywhere in either the horizontal or vertical ruler area. To remove a guideline, select it and then move the mouse pointer away from the ruler area. Removing a guideline does not remove any objects attached to it. To detach an object from a guideline, select it and move it away from the guideline.

NOTE   Even if guidelines are not configured to display, they still operate the same way, and the arrows will still appear in the ruler areas for them.

If an object is attached to guidelines on both the right and left side and one guideline is moved, the object will stretch or shrink depending on the direction of the move. This is also the case when guidelines are attached to both the top and bottom of an object.

NOTE   When a summary is created for a field, it is attached to the same guideline that the field is attached to.

Grid

The grid is not visible by default. To display it, select View | Grid | Design or go to File | Options and check Grid in the Design panel of the Layout tab. When the Grid is displayed, you will see a pattern of dots in the background. If Snap To Grid is checked, then any object that you place on the report will move to align itself with the nearest grid intersection. Snap To Grid is enabled by default and affects the placement of guidelines as well as field objects. You can modify the size of the grid by changing the Grid Size option on the Layout tab of the File | Options dialog box.

TIP   You can turn on Snap To Grid whether or not you display the grid. Objects will snap to the grid even if you cannot see the grid pattern.

Sizing

When a field is selected on the report, a blue frame appears around it. Within the blue frame are small darker blue squares called *handles*. Placing the mouse over the handles changes the mouse pointer to a sizing pointer. You can then resize the field by dragging an edge of the frame to a new position.

Customer ID

NOTE   The corner handles display only if a field object is attached to guidelines vertically and horizontally.

To resize multiple objects, first select them all, and then drag the handles on the last object selected (the main object). All the objects will resize by the same amount. To resize multiple objects so that they are the same height, width, or both, select them, then right-click to display the Multiple Selection shortcut menu, and then choose the appropriate option. The objects will be resized relative to the main object. This menu is also available as View | Size.

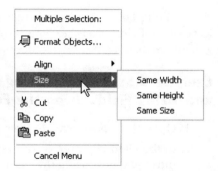

Aligning

To align multiple objects, select them, and then right-click and choose Align from the shortcut menu or choose View | Align. The alignment options are Tops, Middles, Bottoms, Baseline, Lefts, Centers, Rights, and To Grid. All objects will align to the main object.

An alignment command that would cause an object to change sections will fail. For example, if you want to align a field object in the Details section with its corresponding heading in the Page Header, you can align them with Lefts, Centers, Rights, or To Grid, but you cannot align them with Tops, Middles, or Bottoms, because that would cause the objects to be moved into the same section.

Object Size and Position Dialog Box

For the finest control of the size and position of an object, select it, and then choose Size and Position from the shortcut menu or Format | Size and Position. The Object Size and Position dialog box will be displayed. You can modify the object's position there by changing the X and Y values: X is the object's distance from the top margin, and Y is the object's distance from the left margin. To modify the object's size, change the Height or Width.

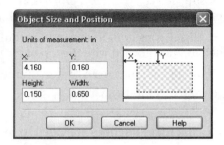

Removing Fields from the Report

You can use several methods to remove objects from a report. You can right-click the object and then choose Delete from the Shortcut menu. You can select the object and then choose Edit | Delete or press the DELETE key. These methods also work with multiple objects. When field objects are removed, their corresponding heading is removed, but their guidelines are not removed because other objects may be attached to the same guidelines.

Exercise 5.5: Placing, Moving, Aligning, and Sizing Fields Using the Field Explorer

1. Open the report saved in Exercise 5.4.

2. In the Field Explorer, open the Customer table and insert the Customer ID field into the report using the Insert to Report toolbar button. Place it as the first object in the Details section, close to the left margin. Notice that a column header and a guideline were created.

3. Drag the Customer Credit ID field onto the report. Again notice that a column header and guideline were created.

4. Remove the Customer Credit ID field by selecting it and then pressing the DELETE key. Notice that its heading was removed but the guideline was not.

5. Remove the guideline that was created for the Customer Credit ID field by selecting its arrowhead and moving it away from the ruler area.

6. In the Field Explorer, select the Customer Name, Contact First Name, Contact Last Name, and Country fields using the CTRL-click method. Then drag them onto the report, placing them immediately after the Customer ID field.

7. Notice that none of the fields placed on the report have been prefixed with a special character: none of them are formulas, SQL expressions, running totals, or parameters.

8. Increase the size of the Details section by dragging the bottom border down.

9. Select the Customer Name field and drag it down in the Details section until it is lower than all the other fields.

10. Select all the fields in the Details section by right-clicking in the gray area of the section and choosing Select All Section Objects. Notice that the Customer Name field is the main object; you can tell because its handles are displayed.

11. Right-click and Select Align | Tops from the shortcut menu. All the other fields will be moved so that their tops are aligned with the top of the Customer Name field.

12. Undo the alignment by clicking the Undo button on the Standard toolbar.

13. Click in the vertical ruler area for the Details section to create a horizontal guideline.

14. Move all the fields so that their baselines are glued to the horizontal guideline.

15. Move the guideline up and down, and notice that all the fields move with it. Then move the guideline as far to the top of the Details section as possible.

16. Reduce the size of the Details section by dragging the bottom border as close to the bottom of the fields as possible.

17. Save the report as **Exercise 5.5** in your CRCP Exercises folder.

Report Explorer

The Report Explorer is an alternative view of the report in a tree structure. Here is the Report Explorer view of the report created in Exercise 5.5.

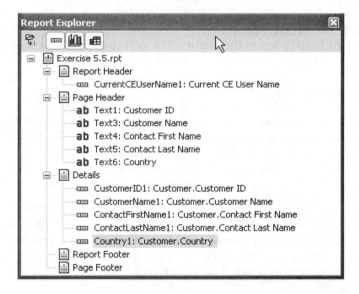

Structure of the Report Explorer

The top node of the tree is the report. The objects at the first level down in the Report Explorer tree are the sections of the report. Under each section, the objects in that section are listed. The Report Explorer tree works just like the Design window or Preview window. If you select an object in the Report Explorer, it is selected in the Design and Preview windows, and you have all the same options for sizing it, formatting it, and so on as you would in the Report window. If you right-click an object in the Report Explorer, you will see the same shortcut menu as you would if you had selected the item in the report window. You can select and manipulate multiple objects using the tree, just as in the report. You cannot insert new objects into the Report Explorer tree (although you can delete them).

Displaying the Report Explorer

To display the Report Explorer, either choose View | Report Explorer or click the Report Explorer icon on the Standard toolbar.

Docking the Report Explorer

The Report Explorer can be free-floating; docked to the right, left, or bottom; or docked with the Field Explorer or Repository Explorer to create a tabbed dialog box.

Shortcut Menus and Toolbar

The Report Explorer has its own toolbar and shortcut menus.

Field Object Shortcut Menu

Right-clicking any field object in the Report Explorer brings up the same shortcut menu you would see if you right-clicked on the object in the report window.

Sections Shortcut Menu

If you right-click on a section node in the Report Explorer tree, you will see a shortcut menu with several options that apply to sections. Some of the options are only available if a section has been split into subsections. The shortcut menu that is displayed in the Report Explorer is the same menu that would be displayed if you right-clicked on the gray section name area in the report window.

Hide/Show (Drill-Down OK)   Selecting Hide causes the section to be hidden when printed or previewed. Hidden sections can be displayed in a separate tab in the Preview window by using drill-down. The mouse cursor will turn into a magnifying glass to indicate that drill-down on a section is possible. Clicking with the magnifying glass will open a separate tab displaying the hidden section.

In the Design window a hidden section will display with a pattern of diagonal lines through it, unless Show Hidden Sections is not checked on the Layout tab of the File | Options dialog box. In that case, the section will be indicated only by a small space between the section divider lines. You can only hide entire sections. If you attempt to hide a subsection, the entire parent section will be hidden.

The node icon for a hidden section changes from the regular section icon to the icon shown here. If a section is hidden, the shortcut menu option changes from Hide to Show. Select Show to reveal the section.

Suppress (No Drill-Down)   Suppress is similar to the Hide/Show option, but does not allow drill-down. Suppress can also be applied to individual subsections. If a section is suppressed, the node icon in the Report Explorer changes to the icon shown here.

Section Expert   Selecting the Section Expert option opens the Section Expert dialog box, which is used to format sections. It is discussed in Chapter 9.

Show Section Names/Hide Section Names   The Show Section Names/Hide Section Names option is available when the Preview window is displayed. Hide Section Names completely removes the section name from the gray area to the left of the report. Show Section Names shows the short section name in the gray area. These options have no effect on the display of section names in the Report Explorer.

Show Short Section Names/Show Long Section Names   The Show Short Section Names/Show Long Section Names option is available when the Design window is displayed. Show Short Section Names shows the short section name in the gray area to the left of the report. Show Long Section Names displays the full name of the section. These options have no effect on the display of section names in the Report Explorer.

Insert Line   The Insert Line option creates a guideline in the selected section.

Delete Last Line   Selecting Delete Last Line removes the bottom guideline in the section and moves up the bottom border of the section to the bottom of the lowest object in the section.

Arrange Lines   The Arrange Lines command moves the guidelines in the section so that they are evenly spaced. This command will add evenly spaced guidelines to the section if none exist.

Fit Section   Choosing Fit Section causes the bottom boundary of the section to move up to the bottom of the lowest object in the section.

Insert Section Below   The Insert Section Below command creates a new section and inserts it immediately below the selected section. The new section will be the same kind of section as the selected section. If a section was not previously subdivided, this action will cause the selected section to become subsection a and the new section to become subsection b. If the section was already subdivided, it simply adds another subsection.

Merge Section Below   Selecting Merge Section Below merges the selected section and the section immediately following it, if they are of the same type. All section objects are retained, the section divider boundary is removed, and all existing subsections are renamed to reflect their new position in the section.

Delete Section   If you choose Delete Section, the selected section will be removed. You can only delete subsections. If no subsections exist in a section, you cannot remove that section.

Select All Section Objects   To select all the objects in a section, select the section, and then choose Select All Section Objects. You can then perform any action that works on a multiple selection.

Moving Sections

Subsections can be moved in the Report Explorer by dragging. Subsections can only be moved within their parent section; they cannot be moved such that they would have to become a different type of section. Subsections can also be moved by dragging in the Preview and Design windows.

Toolbar

The Report Explorer toolbar has four buttons that change the display of the Report Explorer tree:

 Expand opens the selected folder and displays the items under it. This is the same as clicking the plus icon.

 Show/Hide Data Fields toggles the display of field objects (not just database field objects).

 Show/Hide Graphical Objects toggles the display of graphical objects. Charts, maps, boxes, lines, BLOB fields, and OLE objects are graphical objects.

 Show/Hide Grids and Subreports toggles the display of cross-tabs, OLAP grids, and subreports.

Exercise 5.6: Using the Report Explorer

1. Open the Exercise 5.5 report.

2. Open the Report Explorer if it is not already open. Dock it to the left of the report window.

3. Open each section and notice that all the objects on the report are listed in the Report Explorer tree.

4. Click CurrentCEUserName1 under the Report Header section node to select that field, and then press the DELETE key to remove it.

5. Right-click the Report Header node, and select Suppress (No Drill-Down) to suppress the Report Header section. Notice how the node icon changes.

6. Select the Details section. Right-click, and choose Insert Section Below from the shortcut menu. Notice that a new Details section was created and is named Details b. The existing Details section became Details a.

7. Right-click the Details a section and choose Merge Section Below. Notice that the two Details sections were merged back into a single Details section.

8. Right-click the Details section and choose Fit Section. Notice that the extra space at the bottom in the Details section is removed.

9. Save the report as **Exercise 5.6** in your Exercises folder.

Using Object Types Not Available in the Field Explorer

There are several types of objects that can be added to a report that are not available in the Field Explorer.

Text Objects

Text objects are fields that contain text and possibly other fields. The text in the object can be formatted as a single block, or portions of it can be selected and formatted independently of the rest. Text objects are commonly used for report titles, although the special field Report Title can be used instead. Text fields can also be used when you need to concatenate multiple fields instead of creating a formula. They might be used to create a full name from a first name and last name field; to create a City, State, Zip code format for mailing labels; or to create the body of a letter where database fields are embedded to personalize each letter.

Inserting Text Objects

Text objects are created and inserted into a report by choosing Insert | Text Object or clicking the Insert Text Object button on the Insert Tools toolbar. After choosing the menu command or clicking the button, move the mouse pointer onto the report where you want the text object placed, and click. The text object will be created and left in edit mode for you to input the text you want. When the object is in edit mode, the horizontal ruler becomes a ruler just for the text object. Click outside the text object to leave edit mode.

Editing Text Objects

Text objects can be moved, sized, aligned, formatted, and so on, just like other field types. In addition, individual portions of the text can be formatted independently. To edit the text in a text object, double-click the field to put it into edit mode. You can also right-click the text object and choose Edit Text. To get out of edit mode, click outside the text object or press ESC.

Embedding Other Fields into Text Objects

Other field types, including Database fields, Formulas, SQL Expressions, Parameters, Running Totals, Group Name fields, and Special fields can all be embedded within a text object field. To embed a field into a text object you must first create the text object. Once the text object exists, you can drag other fields onto it. When you drag a field over a text object, a bar cursor appears inside the text object to indicate the position where the field can be dropped. You can mix embedded fields with regular text. Here is a text object that combines the City, Region, and Postal Code fields to create an address line. Notice the space and comma have been added as regular text.

{City}, {Region} {Postal Code}

All trailing spaces are removed from any string field that is embedded in a text object. You cannot embed one text object inside of another text object. You can use tabs, returns, soft returns, and so on in text objects for formatting.

Picture Objects

Picture objects are often called "bitmaps," especially in conjunction with the Repository Explorer, but they can hold images in several graphic file formats, not just bitmaps.

Inserting a Graphic

You insert a picture into a report by selecting Insert | Picture or clicking the Insert Picture button on the Insert Tools toolbar. An Open dialog box will appear so that you can select an image file. The supported file types are metafile, bitmap file, TIFF, JPEG, and PNG. Once you select a file and click Open, a frame will appear so that you can place the object on the report, in much the same way that other field types are placed. Placing a graphic into a section that is not large enough to contain it will cause the section to expand to accommodate it.

> **CAUTION** Avoid placing pictures in the Details section—it will cause the image to be displayed in every detail row of the report.

Manipulating Graphics

Picture objects can be moved or deleted just like other objects. Formatting of graphic images is covered in Chapter 9.

Lines

Lines can be drawn on reports to emphasize parts of the report. Lines can be horizontal or vertical. They can be drawn across section boundaries in the Design window, in which case they will stretch across those sections when the Preview window is displayed.

Inserting a Line

To insert a line, click the Insert Line button on the Insert Tools toolbar, or select Insert | Line.

The mouse cursor becomes a pencil shape. Hold down the left mouse button and move the cursor to draw the line. Release the mouse button to complete the line.

Manipulating Lines

A line can be moved by selecting it and then moving it when the move mouse cursor appears. Lines can also be deleted or resized by selecting them and then dragging the sizing handles on either end. Formatting lines is covered in Chapter 9.

Boxes

Like lines, boxes can be drawn on a report to highlight information or to create forms. Boxes can be drawn across section boundaries in the Design window, in which case they will stretch across those sections when the Preview window is displayed.

Inserting a Box

To insert a box, select Insert | Box, or click the Insert Box button on the Insert Tools menu. The cursor will become a pencil. Move the cursor until it is where you want one corner of the box to start. Hold down the left mouse button and move the cursor diagonally to the opposite corner. The box will expand as you move the mouse. Release the mouse button when the box is the size you need.

Manipulating Boxes

Boxes can be moved by selecting them and moving when the mouse pointer becomes the move indicator. Boxes can be resized by selecting them and dragging any of the handles to a new location. Box formatting is described in Chapter 9. Note that a box can also be formatted to round off its corners—anywhere from slightly rounded to an oval or circle.

Exercise 5.7: Working with Text Objects, Pictures, Lines, and Boxes

1. Open the Exercise 5.6 report.

2. Click the Insert Text Object button, and place the text object in the Page Header section above the field headings and to the far left. Type **Exercise 5.6** into the text object.

3. Insert a second text object into the Page Footer section to the far right. Type the word **Page** then a space, and then drag the special field Page Number into the text object. The text object should look like this:

Page {Page Number}

4. Select Insert | Picture and use the Open dialog box to browse to a graphic of your choice. Open it and place it in the Report Header section. If your graphic is more than an inch or two tall, resize it by using the sizing handles until it is less than 2 inches high. If the Report Header section is suppressed or hidden, right-click in the gray area of the section, and choose Don't Suppress or Show to ensure that the Report Header will be visible.

5. Click the Insert Line button, and draw a line about 3 inches long under the report title you added in step 2.

6. Draw a box around the Customer Name header and Customer Name field that extends into the Report Footer section. It should look like this.

Customer Name
Customer Name

7. Preview the report by clicking the Refresh button.

8. The upper right area of the first page should look similar to Figure 5-5.

9. Save the report as **Exercise 5.7** in your Exercises folder.

Chapter Review

This chapter described report planning and requirements gathering. It introduced creating reports by starting with a blank report. The Database Expert and connecting to data sources were explained and used to connect to an ODBC data source. Linking data sources to bring together related data for the report was covered. The Field Explorer was used to add several different field types to a report. Various methods for manipulating report fields were used to move, resize, and align them. The Report Explorer was also described and used to manipulate sections in the report. The use of text objects, lines, boxes, and pictures was explained. You should now be able to create most reports by starting with a blank report.

Figure 5-5
Previewing your
report

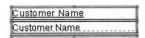

Sage Link, LLC

Exercise 5.6

Customer ID	Customer Name	Contact First Name
1	City Cyclists	Chris
2	Pathfinders	Christine
3	Bike-A-Holics Anonymous	Gary
4	Psycho-Cycle	Alexander
5	Sporting Wheels Inc.	Patrick
6	Rockshocks for Jocks	Heather
7	Poser Cycles	Alex
8	Spokes 'N Wheels Ltd.	Kristina
9	Trail Blazer's Place	Alexandra
10	Rowdy Rims Company	Anthony
11	Clean Air Transportation Co.	Bill

PART II

Quick Tips

- The reporting process should start with a planning phase that includes requirements gathering and prototyping. The planning should result in the early discovery of possible problems, documentation of the requirements, and a better end result.

- The Database Expert is used to manage connections to databases and data sources in the repository. From it you can create connections to any available database. Once connected to a database, you can select tables, views, and so on to use in your report. If you chose more than one data source, you must use the Links tab to create appropriate links between them.

- The Field Explorer is used to add Database fields, Formula fields, SQL Expressions, Parameter fields, Running Total fields, Group Name fields, and special fields to the report. It is also used to create and modify Formula fields, SQL Expressions, Parameter fields, and Running Total fields.

- The Special Fields folder in the Fields Explorer contains fields that can be added to the report but that are not associated with the report data. Some of the fields are related to the file properties, such as the file creation date or user-defined keywords; three are related to page numbers; others are related to the date and time of printing or record retrieval.

- Fields can be placed on a report using the Field Explorer by dragging or by using the Insert to Report toolbar button or shortcut menu option. Multiple objects can be placed on the report using the same options.

- Multiple report objects can be selected in several ways, including CTRL-clicking, SHIFT-clicking, using the Select All Section Objects shortcut command, and using a lasso.

- Fields can be moved, resized, or aligned with other fields. Rulers, guidelines, and the grid are helpful in fine-tuning field placement.

- The Report Explorer represents the report in a tree view. The top of the tree is the report. The first-level nodes are the sections of the report, and the leaf nodes are the objects in the sections of the report. Many of the actions that can be performed on report objects or sections in the Design or Preview window can also be performed in the Report Explorer.

- Report sections can be split, suppressed, unsuppressed, hidden, shown, and deleted. In addition, subsections can be merged and moved.

- Text objects can be added to the report and act as containers for text and other fields. They are often used to create formatted text by mixing typing and embedded fields, for example, to create an address line.

- Images can be added to reports by using the Insert Picture command and opening an image file.
- Lines and boxes can be drawn on a report to highlight certain areas or create forms.

Questions

Questions may have more than one correct answer. Choose all answers that apply.

1. The Database Expert is used to
   a. Connect to Data Sources
   b. Create ODBC DSNs
   c. Add tables to a report
   d. Link the tables used in a report
   e. Add fields to a report

2. To create a Page N of M entry on the report you can use the special field Page N of M or the special fields Page Number and Total Page Count.
   a. True
   b. False

3. To merge sections together, you select multiple sections using the CTRL-click method and select Merge from the section shortcut menu.
   a. True
   b. False

4. Objects can be inserted into the report using the Report Explorer.
   a. True
   b. False

5. Planning a report should
   a. Produce a better report
   b. Speed the development process
   c. Provide documentation
   d. Uncover possible problems
   e. Act as a sign-off point

6. The Field Explorer is not used to add this field type to a report.
   a. Special
   b. Parameter
   c. Summary
   d. Database
   e. SQL Expression

7. When working with multiple objects, the first object selected is considered to be the main object.

   a. True

   b. False

8. Hiding and suppressing a section differ in the following ways:

   a. Hidden sections can be drilled down on; suppressed sections cannot.

   b. Suppressed sections can be drilled down on; hidden sections cannot.

   c. Individual subsections can be suppressed but not hidden.

   d. Individual subsections can be hidden but not suppressed.

9. To place an object anywhere that you like on the report, you must turn off Snap To Grid.

   a. True

   b. False

10. Which of the following is not a way to select multiple report objects?

    a. ALT-click

    b. SHIFT-click

    c. Lasso them

    d. CTRL-click

    e. Select All Section Objects

11. The Group Number special field is null if no groups exist in the report.

    a. True

    b. False

12. A Page Header and Details section can be merged together to create a complex section type.

    a. True

    b. False

13. Which of the following field types cannot be embedded in a text object?

    a. Database

    b. Text object

    c. Formula

    d. Parameter

    e. Special

14. A line or box object cannot cross section boundaries.

    a. True

    b. False

Answers

1. **a, c, d.** The Database Expert is used to connect to data sources, add tables to reports, and link tables. It is not used to create ODBC DSNs or to add fields to a report.

2. **a.** True. Either method will work.

3. **b.** False. To merge sections, you must move them so that they are adjacent to each other and select the Merge Section Below command from the section shortcut menu of the top section.

4. **b.** False. Objects cannot be inserted using the Report Explorer, although they can be deleted.

5. **All.** Planning a report should result in a better report, speed the development process, provide documentation, uncover possible problems, and act as a sign-off point.

6. **c.** The Field Explorer is not used to add Summary fields to a report.

7. **b.** False. The last object selected is considered to be the main object.

8. **a, c.** Hidden sections can be drilled down on, suppressed sections cannot, and individual subsections can be suppressed but not hidden.

9. **a.** True. If Snap To Grid is on, the object will automatically move to a grid intersection; an object cannot be placed off of a grid intersection.

10. **a.** ALT-clicking is not a valid method for selecting multiple objects.

11. **b.** False. The Group Number will display 1 if no groups exist in the report.

12. **b.** False. Only sections of the same type can be merged.

13. **b.** A text object cannot be embedded in another text object.

14. **b.** Lines and boxes can be drawn across section boundaries.

Record Selection and Report Parameters

Exam RDCR200 expects you to be able to

- Define the components of the Select Expert
- Determine the record selection criteria
- Define saved and refreshed data
- Apply record selection
- Apply additional record selection criteria
- Modify record selection
- Apply time-based record selection
- Define and create parameters
- Use edit masks and descriptions
- Build a report with multiple parameters
- Create a date range parameter

A common reporting requirement is to show only certain records in the report. For example, a user may want to see the orders for the current month only, or for the United States only. In Crystal Reports, a *record selection formula* is used to select only those records meeting the defined conditions. In many cases, the record selection formula is converted by Crystal Reports into a SQL WHERE clause that is appended to the report query so that only the needed records are generated by and retrieved from the database engine. In cases where Crystal Reports cannot convert the entire selection criteria into a WHERE clause, some record filtering will be done locally, slowing processing.

NOTE The terms *record selection* and *record filtering* are often used interchangeably. *Record filtering* implies removing unwanted records, whereas *record selection* implies selecting only the desired records. *Record selection* better describes the process used by Crystal Reports.

A *group selection formula* selects only those groups meeting certain conditions for display in the report. Group selection formulas are always based on summary fields instead of detail-level fields. For example, the user might want to see only those customers whose total order amount exceeds $10,000. Since the computation of the total order amount happens at the customer group level, this selection criterion is a group selection criterion. Group selection is always done locally by Crystal Reports and never passed to the database server (unless you use SQL Commands or stored procedures).

There are two methods for creating the selection formulas: using the Select Expert or manually creating the formula.

Select Expert

The Select Expert is an easy-to-use tool that generates simple record or group selection formulas. You do not need to know anything about the Crystal Reports formula language, or SQL, to use it.

Exploring the Select Expert

Before you start creating selection criteria, you need to understand the Select Expert's environment.

NOTE The Record Selection page of the report wizards is similar to the Select Expert, but it lacks some functionality.

Displaying the Select Expert

As with other Crystal Reports experts, you can use a variety of methods to display the Select Expert:

- Click the Expert button on the Expert Tools toolbar.
- Report | Select Expert.
- Right-click a field object, and choose Select Expert,

For the first two options, you may or may not have a field object selected. If you have a field selected, then the Select Expert will appear immediately, ready to create selection criteria for the selected field. If you do not have a field selected, and no previous record selection has been created, the Choose Field dialog box will appear.

Choose Field Dialog Box

If a field is not selected when you open the Select Expert and no selection criterion currently exists, you will see the Choose Field dialog box, shown next. You can select a field and click OK to be taken to the Select Expert with that field chosen, you can cancel the operation, or you can browse the field data. The Fields tree will display all the data sources that have been added to the report, similar to the Database Expert's display. In addition, it will display the fields that are currently being used in the report at the top of the tree under the Report Fields folder. The Report Fields folder will contain all the fields necessary for report generation, not just those actually visible on the report. If a field is used in a formula but not displayed on the report, it will still be listed. Once you use a field in a selection formula, it will become a Report field if it was not one already.

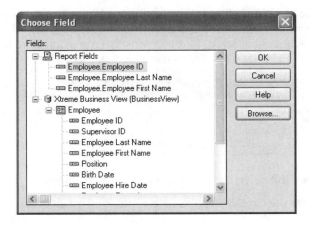

EXAM TIP   You can use any field in the report selection formula; it need not be a field that is displayed on the report or otherwise already used by the report.

Tabs

Once a selection field has been chosen, the Select Expert will appear with the selected field's name displayed on a tab within the Select Expert dialog box.

There will be a tab for each field that has any selection criteria. The drop-down box in the tab will initially be set to "is any value." This is the default, and it really means a record should be selected no matter what the value of the field is. Because this option is equivalent to having no record selection criteria for this field, if you leave the default unchanged, the tab will be removed when the dialog box is closed.

If you are adding a new field to an existing record selection, other tabs may appear. Each will be named after the field to which the selection criterion applies. The last tab is always named <New> and can be selected to create a new criterion based on a new field.

Buttons

The Select Expert dialog box has several buttons.

OK Pressing the OK button applies any changes and closes the Select Expert. If the record selection criteria have changed, the Change In Record Selection Formula dialog box will be displayed, and you must decide whether to use saved data or to refresh the data. (See the "Working with Saved Data" section.)

Cancel Cancel closes the Select Expert and discards any changes.

Help Help displays the Crystal Reports help topic for the Select Expert.

New... Clicking the New button displays the Choose Field dialog box. After you pick a field, you are returned to the Select Expert, where a new tab has been created for the new field.

Delete Clicking the Delete button removes the currently selected tab and the selection criterion associated with it.

Browse... The Browse button displays the familiar Browse dialog box for the field associated with the current tab. If you have chosen an option other than "is any value," such as "is equal to," you can pick a value in the Browse dialog box and paste it into the second drop-down box.

Show Formula >>> The Show Formula/Hide Formula button toggles the display of the actual selection formula at the bottom of the Select Expert. Figure 6-1 shows the Select Expert with the formula area showing. You can manually edit the formula in the Select Expert.

Formula Editor... Pressing the Formula Editor button displays the Formula Workshop, where you can edit the selection formula using all of the features of the Formula Workshop.

The Select Expert can be used to create both record selection formulas and group selection formulas. If you select a detail-level field, the Select Expert will add that criterion to the record selection formula. If you select a summary field, the Select Expert will add that criterion to the group selection formula. Even though both types of tabs appear together in the Select Expert, some may be contributing to the record selection formula and some to the group selection formula. If you click the Show Formula button and the formula area is displayed at the bottom of the dialog box, as shown in Figure 6-1, you can use the radio buttons to toggle between viewing or editing the record selection formula and viewing or editing the group selection formula.

Figure 6-1
Viewing the
formula area in
the Select Expert

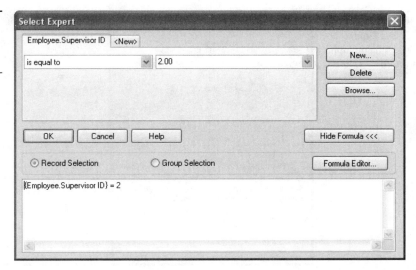

Creating Selection Criteria

Before using the Select Expert to create the record selection formula, you must determine what the selection criteria should be. Your report planning and requirements gathering process should have uncovered and documented the user's need. In most cases, the
selection criteria are relatively straightforward, such as "Display all orders for Alabama."
This statement would translate into a selection formula that selects only those records in
which Region equals "Alabama." Selection criteria can occasionally be quite complex
and difficult to implement. In those cases, you may not be able to use the Select Expert
and might need to use the Formula Workshop instead.

Selection Based on One Field

To select records based on a single field, select the field in the report and click the Select
Expert button, right-click and choose Select Expert, or choose Report | Select Expert. If
the field you need to base your selection on is not in the report, click the Select Expert
button or choose Report | Select Expert and select the field from the Choose Field dialog
box. The Select Expert will open with the name of the selected field displayed on the first
tab. The next step is to select the type of condition you want to apply to the field from the
drop-down box.

CAUTION   If you have selected a summary field, a shortened version of the
summary formula that does not include the group the formula summarizes is
displayed in the tab, as shown in Figure 6-2. This can be very confusing, as you
might see the same title in multiple tabs, but they really apply to summaries at
different group levels. Check the formula itself to verify which is which.

Figure 6-2
Select Expert
showing multiple
summary criteria

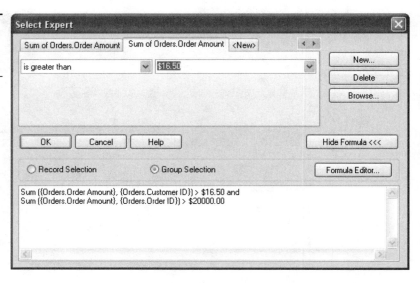

There are many types of comparison conditions that you can apply to create the selection criterion, and each requires additional information. The illustration at left shows the choices for a string field.

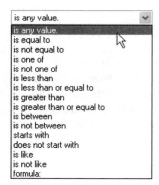

is any value This option is the default condition; it means that Crystal Reports should select a record no matter what value the tabbed field has. This is equivalent to having no selection criterion for the field, so if you leave the condition as "is any value" the tab will be removed automatically when the Select Expert is closed.

is equal to Selecting this option causes a second drop-down box to appear, as shown next. You can pick a value from the drop-down box that has been populated with the browse data for the field, or you can type in a value yourself. Only those records where the field value equals the entered value will be retrieved and displayed on the report. In the illustration, only the records where the value of Orders.Employee ID is 4 will be selected for the report.

is not equal to   This condition is the opposite of "is equal to." Using the previous example, every record where Orders.Employee ID is not 4 will be selected for the report.

is one of   This condition allows you to select records where the field value is one of a list of values. This illustration shows the entries you would need if you wanted to select the records where Orders.Employee ID was 1, 3, or 9.

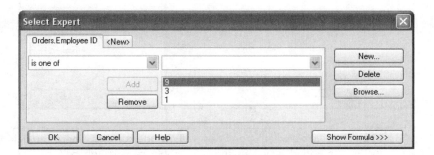

is not one of   As you might expect, this condition is the opposite of "is one of"; it selects all records where the field is not equal to any of the listed values.

is less than   This condition is most commonly used with numeric fields, but it can be used with strings as well. The illustration shows the creation of a selection formula where Orders.Order Amount must be less than $100.

is less than or equal to   Use this condition to select all records where the field is less than or equal to a specific value.

is greater than   This condition is similar to the "is less than" condition, but it selects all records where the field value is greater than the entered value.

is greater than or equal to   This condition selects all records where the field value is greater than or equal to the entered value.

is between   This condition allows you to select records where a field value is between two other values. This illustration shows a selection criterion that will select all records where Orders.Order Amount is between $10 and $20.

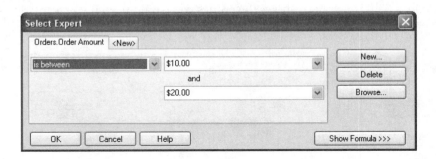

NOTE   The "is between" condition will include records where the field is equal to the boundary values. In the example, records where Orders.Order Amount equals $10 or $20 will be selected.

is not between   This condition is the opposite of the "is between" condition and will select records where the field value is outside of the selected range.

starts with   This condition is available only for string fields. You can use it to select records where the field value starts with one or more specific string values. The illustration shows a selection where Orders.Ship Via must start with "Fe" or "P."

does not start with   This condition is the opposite of "starts with"; it will select records where the field value does not start with any of the listed string values.

is like   This condition is available only for string fields. It allows you to use wildcard characters to create a selection criterion. The next illustration shows a selection where the Orders.Ship Via field must have a *T* somewhere in the string or be three characters long with the second and third characters being *T* and *S,* respectively.

is not like This condition is the opposite of "is like"; it will select all records where the field value differs from the selection string values.

is in the period This condition is available only for date fields. Crystal Reports contains many functions that return date ranges, such as MonthToDate and YearToDate. These functions can be used for record selection using the "is in the period" condition. This illustration shows a selection criterion that will select only records where Orders.Order Date is the current year. See the "Selection Based on a Date Field" section for more on date-based selection formulas.

is not in the period As you might guess, this condition is the opposite of "is in the period." It will select records where the field value is not in the specified period.

is True This condition is available only for Boolean fields. You can use it to select records where a Boolean field is True. This illustration shows a selection where the Orders.Payment Received field must be True.

is False   This condition is also available only for Boolean fields. Use it to select records where a Boolean field value is False.

formula   This will be displayed if the selection condition is too complicated to represent using the earlier options.

Selection Based on Multiple Fields

To create a selection formula based on multiple fields, you can add the new fields by clicking the New tab or the New button or by selecting a different field on the report and re-opening the Select Expert. The selection conditions on every tab must be true for a record to be selected for the report. If you look at the selection formula by clicking the Show Formula button, you will see that the criteria are connected by ANDs; see Figure 6-3. Using the Select Expert, selection conditions are always additive. To create OR conditions you must create or modify the selection formula manually.

Selection Based on a Date Field

Creating selection criteria based on a date or a date-and-time field is similar to creating selection criteria for other field types. You can use most of the same selection conditions, and you also have the "in the period" options.

Date Issues   Most problems with date selection criteria arise because of improper consideration of the time portion of date-and-time fields. For example, if you want to include records in your report where Orders.Order Date is after May 15, 2001, then simply entering 5/15/2001 in the Select Expert (as shown next) may or may not work, depending on how the time portion of the date field is populated.

Figure 6-3
Select Expert showing multiple selection conditions

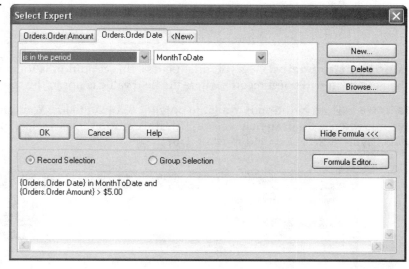

If you reopened the Select Expert, you would see that a default time of 12:00:00AM had been added to the 5/15/2001 date, as shown here.

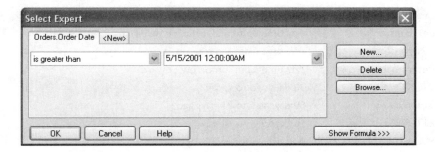

Note that the 12:00:00AM time is midnight, but it is considered the start of the day, not the end. In the XTREME sample database, all date fields are populated with the default time of 12:00:00AM, so the selection criterion would behave as expected and return only records where the date was greater than 5/15/2001. However, if Orders.Order Date were populated with real times, such as 5/15/2001 9:45:00AM, then any records where the date was May 15, 2001 and the time was after midnight would be returned. The example record, with an order date of 5/15/2001 9:45:00AM, would be selected and not filtered out, since 5/15/2001 9:45:00AM is greater than 5/15/2001 12:00:00AM.

The best practice is to specifically set the time portion for your selection conditions. If you want all order dates after May 15, 2001, then you should use the "is greater than" condition and enter 5/15/2001 11:59:59AM, or use the "is greater than or equal to" condition and enter 5/16/2001 12:00:00AM. If you want all order dates before May 15, 2001, then use the "is less than" condition and enter 5/15/2001 12:00:00.

Period Functions   The period functions that Crystal Reports supplies are available in the Formula Workshop and in the Select Expert for the "in the period" conditions. They return a date range. In the Select Expert, if you choose a period function the selected field is checked to determine whether it is in the range. You can always reproduce the selection criterion using the normal "between" conditions with computed start and end points, but the period functions make many common date ranges easily available without necessitating messy date computations. Table 6-1 shows the date ranges for each function.

Function	Date Range
WeekToDateFromSun	Last Sunday to today
MonthToDate	The first day of the current month to today
YearToDate	The first day of the current year to today
Last7Days	Seven days ago to today
Last4WeeksToSun	Four weeks prior to last Sunday to last Sunday
LastFullWeek	Sunday of last week to Saturday of last week
LastFullMonth	First day of last month to the last day of last month
AllDatesToToday	Any time up to and including today
AllDatesToYesterday	Any time up to and including yesterday
AllDatesFromToday	Any time from today onward
AllDatesFromTomorrow	Any time from tomorrow onward
Aged0To30Days	30 days ago to today
Aged31To60Days	60 days ago to 31 days ago
Aged61To90Days	90 days ago to 61 days ago
Over90Days	Any time prior to 90 days ago
Next30Days	Today to 30 days in the future
Next31To60Days	31 days in the future to 60 days in the future
Next61To90Days	61 days in the future to 90 days in the future
Next91To365Days	91 days in the future to 365 days in the future
Calendar1stQtr	January 1 of the current year to March 31 of the current year
Calendar2ndQtr	April 1 of the current year to June 30 of the current year
Calendar3rdQtr	July 1 of the current year to September 30 of the current year
Calendar4thQtr	October 1 of the current year to December 31 of the current year
Calendar1stHalf	January 1 of the current year to June 30 of the current year
Calendar2ndHalf	July 1 of the current year to December 31 of the current year
LastYearMTD	First day of current month last year to the same month and day last year
LastYearYTD	January 1 of last year to today's month and day last year

Table 6-1   Period Functions and Corresponding Date Ranges

Group Selection

Creating group selection criteria is identical to creating record selection criteria, except that you must choose a group summary field instead of a detail-level field. If you have added groups and summaries to your report, then the summary fields will be available on the report or in the Choose Field dialog box. Summary fields are displayed in the Choose Field dialog box preceded by the Σ symbol. After choosing a summary field, you can set its selection condition the same as you would for other detail level fields.

 EXAM TIP Understand the difference between record selection and group selection.

Modifying Record Selection

The selection formula generated by the Select Expert can easily be modified by reopening the Select Expert and deleting, changing, or adding new tabbed selections. The selection formulas can also be modified manually in the formula window or using the Formula Workshop. If you need to use selection formulas that are too complex to construct using the Select Expert, you must create them manually or use the Formula Workshop. The Formula Workshop is covered in Chapter 8.

Case Sensitivity

When using record selection criteria based on string comparisons, you must determine whether the comparison condition should be case sensitive or case insensitive. For example, if the last name field contains the values "Smith" and "SMITH," do you want to select both of them when you create the selection formula? You could use an "is one of" condition and enter all possible variations of the name, but it's simpler if you just declare that you want a case-insensitive comparison. To use Crystal Reports' Database Server Is Case-Insensitive option for an individual report, set it in File | Report Options. To use this option for all new reports, set it on the Database tab of the File | Options dialog box. Note, however, that this setting may not behave as expected, depending on the actual case sensitivity of the server—as opposed to the Crystal Reports setting. The following table shows the possible results of a query for last name on "Smith."

Database Server's Case Setting	Crystal Reports' Case Setting	Database Returns	Report Displays
Sensitive	Insensitive	Smith	Smith
Insensitive	Insensitive	Smith and SMITH	Smith and SMITH
Insensitive	Sensitive	Smith and SMITH	Smith
Sensitive	Sensitive	Smith	Smith

The Database Server Is Case-Insensitive option controls whether Crystal Reports does any further filtering of records after they are returned from the database server. If the database server is set to be case sensitive, then a query for last name on "Smith" will return only those records where the last name is Smith. But if the server is set to be case insensitive, then the same query will return both Smith and SMITH. Conversely, if the server is set to be case sensitive, then it will return only Smith, and the setting of the Database Server Is Case-Insensitive option will have no effect on the records displayed in the report. And so on.

In short, if your database happens to be set for case insensitivity, then setting the Database Server Is Case-Insensitive option can be used to control your desired output. However, most databases are configured to be case sensitive. So how can you create a case-insensitive selection criterion against a case-sensitive database? Simple: you convert the database field to all uppercase and then enter your comparison value in all uppercase. For example, you could create a formula field or a SQL Expression that converts the last name field to uppercase, and then use the formula or SQL Expression in the Select Expert compared to SMITH. SQL Expressions are better choices because the selection will be done on the server rather than locally if you use a formula field.

Working with Saved Data

You know that you can save data with a report by checking the Save Data with Report option on the File menu or by setting the default behavior on the Reporting tab of the File | Options dialog box. These options cause the current result set to be saved to disk with the report definition. However, Crystal Reports also keeps a copy of the report data in memory while the report file is open (after it's been refreshed at least once), no matter what the setting for Save Data with Report is. It is important to understand when the data saved in memory is refreshed.

If you make a modification to a report or change parameter values, the saved data may or may not be refreshed. Some modifications will automatically refresh the data; others will prompt you to see if you want to refresh the data.

- **Refresh** Specifically executing the Refresh command either through toolbar buttons or through menu items will always refresh the data.

- **Change parameters** If you refresh a report that uses parameters, the data will be refreshed.

- **Add fields** If your report modification requires a new field to be retrieved from the database, then the data will be refreshed. A new field may be required if it is used in a formula, for selection, and so on, even if it is not displayed on the report. If you remove fields, the report data will not be refreshed.

- **Drilling down** Drilling down on hidden data will not cause a full refresh. If the report is set up with the Details section hidden and grouping is happening on the server, drilling down on the Details section will cause Crystal Reports to retrieve the extra data required to display the drilled-down-on Details section, but not other Details sections. If grouping is not happening on the server, the detail data will already have been retrieved and no refresh will happen.

- **Changing record selection formula** If you change the record selection formula, the Change in Record Selection Formula dialog box will appear. You can choose whether to use saved data or refresh the data.

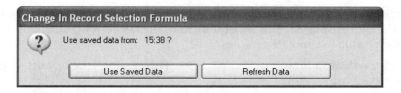

If you choose to use saved data, the records displayed on the report will be the ones available as saved data that also pass the new modified record selection formula. If the record selection formula has been changed such that a subset of the previous result is required, then the correct set of records will be displayed. However, if the modified selection formula requires records that do not exist as saved data, the report display will be incorrect. This situation is sometimes acceptable—or even desirable—during the development process, when a fresh retrieval of data might be time-consuming and not necessary for further report refinement.

Exercise 6.1: Using the Select Expert

1. Create a report using the Orders table that displays the Order ID, Order Amount, Employee ID, Order Date, and Shipped fields with no grouping. Start with a blank report or use the Standard report expert.

2. Preview the report, and note that 2192 records are used in the report.

3. Select the Order Amount field, and open the Select Expert.

4. Choose "is greater than" in the drop-down box.

5. Enter **100** in the second drop-down box, and click OK.

6. Because the new record selection requires a subset of the saved data, click the Use Saved Data button.

7. Note that only records where Order Amount is over $100.00 are now displayed and the record count has changed to 1621.

8. Select the Shipped field, and choose the "is True" condition.

9. Click OK. Then click the Use Saved Data button.

10. Note that only orders that have shipped and have order amounts over $100.00 are now displayed and the record count has dropped to 1571.

11. Reopen the Select Expert, and delete the Shipped tab. Click OK.

12. Click the Use Saved Data button. (Since you have not refreshed the data since the first full data retrieval, all the Orders records are still in memory.)

13. Re-create the record selection on the Shipped field, but click the Refresh Data button this time. The record count will drop to 1571 again.

14. Remove the record selection on the Shipped field, and click Use Saved Data.

15. Notice that the record count is still 1571 and no records with a Shipped value of False are displayed. This is because, as of the last refresh, only Shipped records with a value of True were saved.

16. Click the Refresh button, and choose OK. The missing True records display, and the record count returns to 1621.

17. Save the report as **Exercise 6.1**, but keep it open.

Exercise 6.2: Creating a Group Selection

To create a group selection, you must first create a group. Group creation is covered in more depth in Chapter 7. For now, just follow these instructions.

1. Start with the report from Exercise 6.1. Note that there are 1621 records. Scroll to the last page of the report. There will be approximately 80 pages.

2. Select the Order ID field, and click the Insert Group button.

3. In the Insert Group dialog box, click OK. The group will be created.

4. Select the Order Amount field, and click the Insert Summary button.

5. In the Insert Summary dialog box, choose Group 1 in the Location box and click OK. A summary field will be inserted into the group footer.

6. Select the summary field and click the Select Expert button.

7. The Select Expert will be displayed with a tab called Sum of Orders.Order Amount.

8. Choose the "is less than" condition and type **150** into the second drop-down box.

9. Note that the record count is still 1621, but when you scroll to the end of the report there are only about 10 pages. Group selection does not reduce the number of records retrieved from the database; it just suppresses groups that do not meet the group selection criteria.

10. Save the report as **Exercise 6.2**.

Parameters

Parameters are the mechanism by which you can request information from the user running the report. This information can be used to customize the report in various ways. Parameters are commonly used in selection formulas to allow the user to determine which records are displayed at run time.

Creating Parameters

Parameter fields are created using the Field Explorer. In the Field Explorer, select the Parameter Fields node and either right-click and select New or click the New button on the Field Explorer toolbar. The Create Parameter Field dialog box will be displayed, as shown in Figure 6-4.

Figure 6-4
Creating
parameters

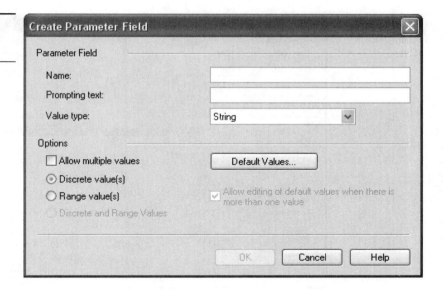

To create a simple single-value parameter, you only need to create a parameter name and choose a data type, although you should also create appropriate prompting text:

- **Name**   You must enter a name for the parameter. When the parameter field is listed in the Fields Explorer or used in a formula a question mark will be prefixed to it to identify it as a parameter field.

- **Prompting Text**   In the Prompting Text box you can enter a short sentence or question to clarify what the user should enter. This prompt will be displayed to the user whenever new parameter values are requested. If you leave Prompting Text blank, the user will only see the parameter field name.

- **Value Type**   In the Value Type drop-down box, you select a data type for the parameter. The available types are Boolean, Currency, Date, DateTime, Number, String, and Time. The value type that you select determines some of the other parameter options.

Parameter Defaults

Instead of requiring your users to type in a parameter value, you can create lists for them to choose from. These are called parameter defaults.

Creating Parameter Defaults

To create parameter defaults, click the Default Values button on the Create Parameter Field dialog box. The Set Default Values dialog box will appear, as shown in Figure 6-5.

The values that will automatically be displayed for the user are those that you put into the Default Values list box. You have three methods for populating the Default Values list. The first is to type values in the text box under Select or Enter Value and then use the arrow button to move them into the Default Values list box.

Figure 6-5
Setting default
values

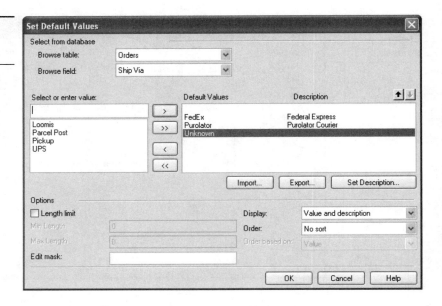

A second option is to select values from a database field. To do this, select the table in the Browse Table drop-down box. Only tables that have been added to the report will be listed. After choosing a table, you must select a field in the Browse Field drop-down box. Only fields that have data types compatible with the parameter's defined data type will be listed. After picking a table, the field values will appear in the Select or Enter Value box, and you can move them to the Default Values list.

 CAUTION When using database values to populate the default list, be aware that additions, deletions, and modifications to the underlying database values will not be reflected in the parameter's default list. You must manually update the default list if the database values change.

A third option is to import the parameter defaults from a text file. To import parameter values, click the Import pick list button, and then browse to the text file. This option is commonly used to import a pick list used in another report. This allows you to save time when the same parameters are used in more than one report.

You can create the Default Values list using just one or any combination of these three methods.

 EXAM TIP Know the various ways of populating the default values for parameters.

Using Descriptions

Descriptions can be added to the default values to supply more information to the user. If you add a description to a value, it will be displayed along with the actual value in the parameter prompting form. To add a description to a default value, select the value and then click the Set Description button. The Define Description dialog box will be displayed, as shown next. Type in the description you want, and click OK to save. If descriptions exist in an import file, they will be imported with the values. If desired, you can display only the description in the prompting form by choosing Description in the Display drop-down box. The default is to display both the value and the description, but if the value is a code and means nothing to the user, you may want to display only the description. The parameter value will be set to the value that corresponds to the description chosen.

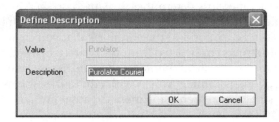

Sorting Parameter Defaults

The list of default values can be sorted manually using the arrow buttons above and to the right of the Default Values list (see Figure 6-5). The default values can also be sorted using the Order and Order Based On drop-down boxes. First choose a sort order in the Order box, and then choose to sort based on either the default values or default descriptions using the Order Based On box. Different data types display different options in the Order box. All data types contain the alphabetically ascending and descending options, which sort values as if they were strings, even if they are not. Under normal circumstances, you should choose the order that corresponds to your parameter's data type.

Restricting User's Choice to the Default List

If you create a list of default values, a check box in the Create Parameter Field dialog box called "Allow editing of default values when there is more than one value" is enabled and automatically checked. When this option is checked, the user can enter a new value or edit an existing default value, as well as choose from the default list. If you want to restrict the user such that they can only pick from the default list, clear this check box.

Refining Parameter Input

For parameter values that are entered manually and not chosen from a list of defaults, you can help ensure that the user enters an appropriate value by using some additional options. These options vary by data type.

String

For string parameters, you can limit the length of the string entered or you can use an edit mask to restrict the user's input, as shown here.

Length Limits   Under Options in the Set Default Values dialog box for string parameters, you will see a Length Limit check box. Checking this box enables the Min Length and Max Length text boxes. Enter a desired minimum and maximum length. Parameter values that are shorter than Min Length or longer than Max Length will not be accepted. Any values listed in the Default Values list must also meet the Min Length and Max Length requirements.

Edit Masks   For string parameters, you can create an *edit mask* to restrict what the user can input. An edit mask inherently determines the length, so the Min and Max Length options are not available when you use edit masks. As with the Length limits, any values in the Default Values list must conform to the edit mask that you create or they will be discarded. Edit masks are strings constructed from the characters listed in Table 6-2.

The edit mask characters act as placeholders that will accept only the defined type of character. When supplying parameter values with edit masks, the user must type something in every space, so be wary when using them to gather numeric data. For example, if the edit mask is #,##0.00 to enter 15.59, the user must type "space space 1 5 5 9."

 EXAM TIP   Know the commonly used mask characters for string parametrs.

Number and Currency

For number or currency parameters, you can set a minimum and maximum allowable value, as shown here.

To restrict number parameters to a specific range of values, check the Range Limited Field box and enter the appropriate numbers in Min Value

and Max Value. Any number a user enters that is outside this range will not be accepted.

Date-Time, Date, Time

Date-Time, Date, and Time parameters can be restricted to a range, much like number parameters, as shown here.

Edit Mask Character	Type of Entry Allowed	Entry Required?
A	Any alphanumeric character.	Yes
a	Any alphanumeric character.	No
0	Any numeric character (0 through 9).	Yes
9	Any numeric character (0 through 9) or a space.	No
#	Any numeric character (0 through 9), the plus or minus sign, or a space.	No
L	Any letter (A through Z, a through z).	Yes
?	Any letter (A through Z, a through z).	No
&	Any alphanumeric character or a space.	Yes
C	Any alphanumeric character or a space.	No
. , : ; - /	These characters are considered to be separator characters and will be retained unchanged in the parameter value. For example, if the edit mask is 000-0000, the user will see ___-____ and can enter 1234567, which will result in 123-4567 as the value of the string parameter.	
<	Inserting the less-than sign into an edit mask will cause all characters after the symbol to be converted to lowercase. The less-than sign will not be visible to the user.	
>	Inserting the greater-than sign into an edit mask will cause all characters after the symbol to be converted to uppercase. The greater-than sign will not be visible to the user.	
\	The backslash must be combined with another character; it causes that character to be displayed in the parameter value the same way that the separator characters are. For example, if you know that the parameter value should have an X in the third position, you could create an edit mask like AA\XAA.	
Password	Entering "Password" as the edit mask causes the parameter value to be displayed as a string of asterisks as it is entered.	

Table 6-2   Edit Mask Characters

PART II

To restrict date-time parameters to a specific range of values, check the Range Limited Field box and select the desired starting and ending date-times. Any value that falls outside of this range will not be accepted.

The Date and Time options are similar to the Date-Time option, but display the Date or the Time only.

Responding to Basic Parameter Prompts

After parameters are created and used in the report, a parameter prompt will appear whenever the report is refreshed. When the report is refreshed, you will be asked whether you want to rerun it with the same parameter values or enter new ones. If you choose to enter new ones, the Enter Parameter Values dialog box will appear. Figure 6-6 shows this dialog box for a report that has five parameter fields.

The Parameter Fields list displays all defined parameters that require values for the report to run. Parameters that are created but not used in the report are not included in the prompt. If you select a different parameter in the Parameter Fields list, the prompting text below the list box changes to display the prompt for the selected field, and the bottom half of the dialog box changes to reflect the options available for the selected field.

Figure 6-6 shows the prompt for the parameter named ShipVia with its default list displayed. Note that the drop-down box is called Discrete Value, signifying that only one value may be selected. Figure 6-7 shows the prompt for OrderDate. Opening the drop-down box for a date displays a calendar from which the user can pick a date. They can also type the date into the text box manually.

Figure 6-6
Basic parameter prompt for a string with default values

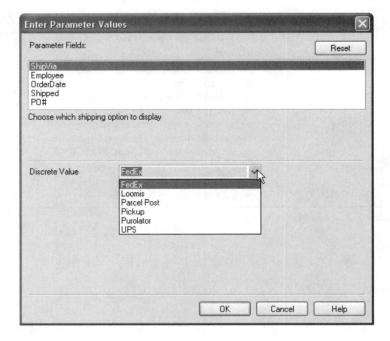

Figure 6-7
Prompt for a date

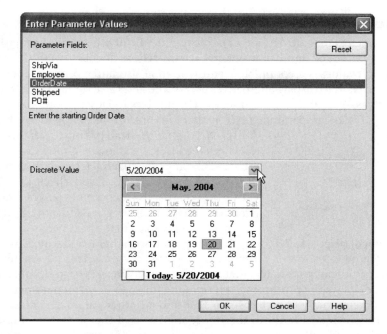

Figure 6-8 shows the prompt for PO#, which has an edit mask. You can tell that there is an edit mask because the field has one underline character for each required character. The figure also shows the error message that is displayed when the user tries to type a letter where a number is required.

Figure 6-8
Prompt for a
number that uses
an edit mask

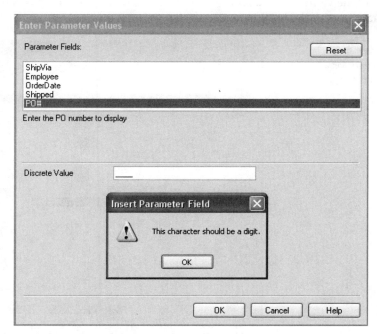

Boolean Parameters

Parameters that are defined as Boolean differ from other parameter types in several ways. They cannot be multivalue or range parameters, as discussed in the next section. The list of default values is prepopulated with True and False, and it cannot be added to or modified. If you want to display alternatives to the True and False values, you can create descriptions such as "Yes" and "No" and set the Display box to Description. In addition, you can use sets of Boolean parameters to create radio button–like choices for the user.

The Options for Boolean parameters are shown here. If you do not check the Place in Parameter Group check box, the parameter is treated like any other parameter, and the user can simply choose the True or False option. If you check the Place in Parameter Group box, this parameter becomes part of a group with any other parameters that have been given the same group number. When a parameter group exists, all the parameters in it are treated as a unit and will be prompted for by the group number rather than individually for each field.

Figure 6-9 shows a prompt for a parameter group. This parameter group consists of three Boolean parameters that have all been given the group number 1. The drop-down box displays the prompting text or name for each Boolean parameter in the group. The parameter that you pick is set to True and all other parameters are set to False.

If your report requires that more than one of the Boolean parameters be True, but they should still be treated as a group, you can clear the Group Is Exclusive check box in the Parameter Creation dialog box. Clearing the box turns off the option for every Boolean parameter in the group. The parameter prompt for a nonexclusive group is shown in Figure 6-10. Every parameter you choose is moved to the Boolean Parameters with True Value list box, and each of those individual parameters is set to True. All other parameters in the group are set to False.

Figure 6-9

Prompts for a parameter group

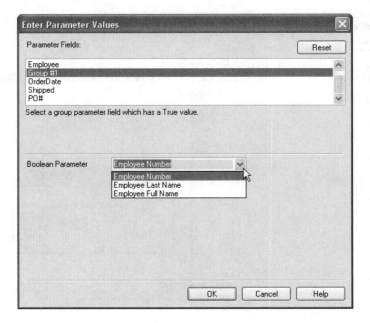

Figure 6-10
Nonexclusive
Boolean
parameter
prompt

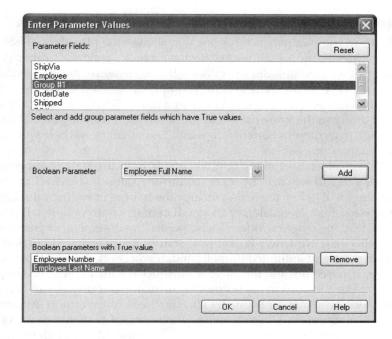

Creating Multivalue and Range Parameters

In addition to simple parameters that hold one value, you can create *multivalue* and *range* parameters. Discrete multivalue parameters are created as arrays of the data type chosen for the parameter and can hold more than one value. *Arrays* are ordered lists of elements (they are discussed in detail in Chapter 17). Range parameters are created as a Crystal Reports range of the defined type. A range is defined by two values, a starting value and an ending value. Multivalue range parameters are created as an array of ranges of the defined parameter type. Multivalue parameters that can contain both discrete values and range values are also created as arrays of ranges. Any discrete values that are chosen are entered into the range with the same starting and ending value.

Creating multivalue or range parameters is controlled with the Options choices on the Create Parameter Field and Edit Parameter Field dialog boxes for non-Boolean parameters, as shown in this illustration. With the Allow Multiple Values check box cleared, you can select either Discrete Value(s), which is the default, or Range Value(s). If you want to allow the user to select more than one discrete value or  range value, you can select the Allow Multiple Values check box. With Allow Multiple Values checked, you can select either Discrete Value(s), Range Value(s), or Discrete and Range Values.

Responding to Complex Parameter Prompts

The most complex parameter is one that allows multiple values of both the discrete and range types. Figure 6-11 shows the prompt for such a parameter. Parameters that allow only ranges or only multiple discrete values will have a subset of the options shown in the figure.

The Discrete Value section of the prompt dialog box is where you can enter or pick individual values. After you select or enter a value, click the Add button to the right to add your choice to the Value list box at the bottom of the dialog box. The section of the dialog box that contains Start of Range and End of Range is where you can create ranges to add to the Value list.

Range values have many options. Beside both the Start of Range and End of Range boxes, you will see check boxes called Include Value. If you check the Include Value box, the range will be constructed to include the starting or ending value entered, in effect creating a less-than-or-equal-to or greater-than-or-equal-to condition. If you clear the Include Value box, the range excludes the end points, like a less-than or greater-than condition. If you check the No Lower Bound box, Start of Range is grayed out and the range is constructed with an unlimited lower bound. If you check the No Upper Bound box, End of Range is grayed out and the range is constructed with an unlimited upper bound.

The Value list box at the bottom of the dialog box displays all currently selected values. You can remove a listing by clicking the Remove button. All values are shown as ranges. If you select a discrete value, it is entered as a range with the same Start and End values. If you select a Start or End value with Include Value checked, the range is constructed with square brackets on that side. If Include Value is cleared, parentheses are used. If No Upper Bound is checked, the range will be blank under End. If No Lower Bound is checked, the range will be blank under the Start.

Figure 6-11

Complex parameter prompt

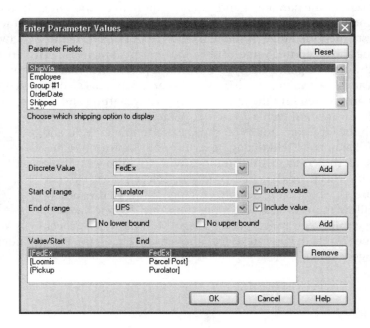

NOTE Creating parameters has no impact on the report until the parameters are used in formulas, selection formulas, or displayed on the report in some manner.

PART II

Modifying Parameters

Once you create a parameter, you can modify it in several ways.

Renaming

You can rename a parameter by selecting it and clicking the Rename button on the Field Explorer toolbar, right-clicking and choosing Rename, or pressing F2. The name will be highlighted and you can change it. Click off the name to complete the change.

Editing

To edit a parameter, select it and click the Edit button on the Field Explorer toolbar, or right-click it and choose Edit. The Edit Parameter Field dialog box will be displayed, which contains all the same options as the Create Parameter Field dialog box. If you modify a parameter, you may be prompted for new parameter values for that parameter when you close the dialog box.

Deleting

To delete a parameter not being used in the report, select it and click the Delete button on the Field Explorer toolbar, right-click it and select Delete, or press the DELETE key. If the parameter is in use in the report, you will be notified and asked if you want all references to it removed.

Changing Prompt Order

Parameters show up in the prompting dialog box in the same order that they appear in the Fields Explorer. To modify the order, select a parameter by right-clicking, and choose Move Parameter Up or Move Parameter Down until the order is correct.

Displaying Parameter Values

You may want to display parameter values on the report. The techniques used for displaying the parameter values differ depending on the type of parameter.

 NOTE The display of array and range parameter values requires the use of formula fields. Creating formula fields is discussed in Chapter 8.

Discrete

You can add discrete parameters of any data type to the report the same as you would any database field: select the parameter field in the Field Explorer and drag it onto the report, or use the Insert to Report button or shortcut menu command. You also can insert a parameter field into a text object if desired. Once the parameter is placed on the report, you have the same formatting options for it as you do for a database field of the same data type.

Range

If you place a range parameter on the report, the display will be empty. To display a range, create a formula to extract the start and end of the range, and place the formula field on the report. Use the Minimum function to obtain the start of the range and the Maximum function to obtain the end of the range. The following is a sample formula, but you may need to format the result of the Minimum and Maximum functions for parameters that are not strings.

```
Minimum({?RangeParam}) & ' to ' & Maximum({?RangeParam})
```

Discrete Multivalue

A discrete multivalue parameter is stored in an array, so you can use array functions in a formula to obtain each value. Several approaches can be used, but the simplest, used for string multivalue parameters, is the Crystal Reports Join function. The Join function extracts each array value and concatenates it into a string using a delimiter of your choice.

```
Join({?StringParam}, ", ")
```

For other data types, you will need to iterate through the array using flow control statements in the formula. This advanced use of arrays is covered in Chapter 17.

Range Multivalue

To display range multivalue parameters, you must create a formula that iterates through the array and takes the Minimum and Maximum of each array element. See Chapter 8 for an example procedure.

 EXAM TIP   Understand how to display the values of each type of parametrs.

Show Current Parameter Values

Crystal Reports provides a method to show the current values of parameter fields to the developer. Select Report | Show Current Parameter Values to display the Current Parameter Values dialog box, as shown in Figure 6-12. You can view the current parameter settings in this dialog box, but you cannot modify them or display them on the report.

Figure 6-12
Viewing current
parameter
settings

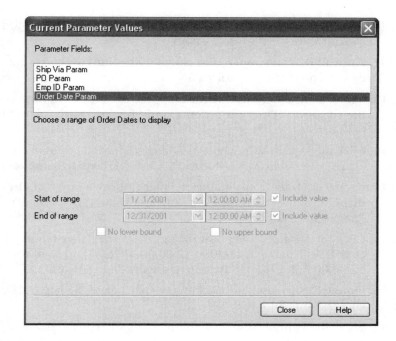

Exercise 6.3: Creating Parameters

1. Create a report based on the Orders table.

2. Include the Order ID, Order Amount, Order Date, Ship Via, Shipped, and PO#
   fields.

3. In the Field Explorer, right-click the Parameter Fields node, and select New.

4. In the Create Parameter Field dialog box, enter **Ship Via Param** as the Name,
   Enter the shipping method to display in the report. as the Prompting text,
   and leave the Value type as String.

5. Click the Default Values button.

6. Select Orders in the Browse Table box and Ship Via in the Browse field box.

7. Use the double arrow button to move all the Ship Via values into the Default
   Values list box.

8. Click OK to close the Set Default Values dialog box, and OK again to close the
   Create Parameter Field dialog box. You will now see the new parameter in the
   Field Explorer.

9. Create a second parameter named PO Param. Make the prompting text **Choose
   PO#s to display**. Leave the type as String, and check the Allow Multiple Values
   box.

10. Click the Default Values button, and browse the PO# field. Add all PO#s to the Default Values list. Click OK twice.

11. Since all PO#s are four digits, enter **0000** as the edit mask; this will require the user to enter four numeric characters.

12. Create a third parameter named EmpID. For the prompting text, type in **Enter the employee ID whose orders should be displayed.** Change the Value type to Number.

13. Click the Default Values button, and check the Range Limited Field box. Set Min Value to **1** and the Max Value to **15**. Click OK twice to complete the process.

14. Create an Order Date parameter. Enter **Choose a range of Order Dates to display.** for the prompting text. Then set Value Type to DateTime and select the Range Values radio button.

15. Click the Default Values button, and check the Range Limited Field box. Set Start Date-Time to 2/18/2000 12:00:00 AM and End Date-time to 4/9/2002 12:00:00 AM. Click OK twice to close the dialog boxes.

16. On the Design tab, right-click in the gray area of the Report Header section, and choose Don't Suppress.

17. Select the EmpID parameter and press F2. Change the name to **Emp ID Param** to be consistent with the other parameter names (even though using "Param" in the name is a little redundant since all parameters will be prefixed with a question mark anyway).

18. Drag each of the parameters into the Report Header section.

19. Click the Refresh button. When the Refresh Report Data dialog box appears, select Prompt for New Parameter Values, and click OK.

20. The Enter Parameter Values dialog box appears with the four parameters listed.

21. For Ship Via Param choose Parcel Post.

22. For the PO Param, enter **1119**, **1282**, and **5569** by typing the values in the Discrete box and then clicking the Add button. Type in **256** and click Add. You should get an error message because of the four-digit edit mask on the PO Param. Make the entry **2569** and click Add.

23. For Emp ID Param, enter **25**, and then select the Order Date Param. You should get an error message. Change the value to **10**.

24. For Order Date Param, set the range to 1/1/2001 12:00:00 AM to 12/31/2001 12:00:00 AM. Click OK.

25. You will be returned to the report, and some of the parameter choices will be displayed. The Ship Via Param will display Parcel Post. The PO Param will display the first value of the multiple values, which is 1119. The Emp ID Param will display 10. The Order Date Param will be blank because it is a range parameter and cannot be displayed directly.

26. Select Report | Show Current Parameter Values and scan the parameter listing. Then click Close.

27. Save the report as **Exercise 6.3**.

Using Parameters in Record Selection

Parameters are used often in record selection to allow the user to control which records are displayed on a report. The parameters that were created in the previous section had no effect on the records displayed in the report, since they were not used in a record selection formula. This section describes how to use parameters with the Select Expert, but you can also use parameter fields when constructing selection formulas using the Formula Workshop.

Using a Discrete Parameter

To use a single-value discrete parameter in the Select Expert, select the field that you want to filter on and open the Select Expert. Choose any available comparison condition other than "is any value," and then open the second drop-down box. You will notice that any parameters that are type compatible with the database field appear in the list in addition to the normal database field values, as demonstrated in this illustration for the Ship Via field.

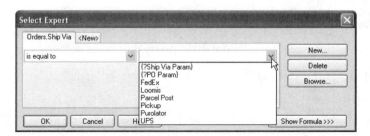

You can select the parameter field just as you would a database field value, and the selection formula will be constructed using the parameter in place of a specific value. When the report is refreshed, the value supplied for the parameter by the user will be substituted into the selection formula before the query is sent to the database server.

For single-value discrete parameters, you can use any of the comparison conditions; they will behave exactly as they would if you had chosen a specific field value.

Using Range-Value Parameters

Range-value parameters can only be used with the "is equal to" or "is not equal to" conditions. When a range-value parameter is used with an "is equal to" condition, it will be interpreted as "is in the range." Likewise, when used with an "is not equal to" condition, it will be interpreted as "is not in the range." The Crystal Reports selection formula will use the equal sign or not-equal sign, but the database query that is constructed will convert the comparison into a range-type comparison appropriate for the specific database. The following examples show a comparison for a Microsoft Access database.

The selection formula is

```
{Orders.Order Date} = {?Order Date Param}
```

But the WHERE clause of the database query is

```
WHERE 'Orders'.'Order Date'>={ts '2001-01-01 00:00:00'}
   AND 'Orders'.'Order Date'<{ts '2001-12-31 00:00:01'}
```

Notice that the database query is constructed with the actual parameter values chosen by the user, not the parameter field placeholder.

Using Multivalue Discrete Parameters

In order for multivalue discrete parameters to be available for use in the Select Expert, you must choose the "is equal to" or "is not equal to" condition. The "is equal to" condition can be thought of as "is one of," and "is not equal to" can be thought of as "is not one of." When you choose "is equal to" the database query will be constructed with a WHERE clause containing a series of comparisons connected with ORs, as shown here.

```
WHERE ('Orders'.'PO#'=1119
    OR  'Orders'.'PO#'=1282
    OR  'Orders'.'PO#'=2569
    OR  'Orders'.'PO#'=5569)
```

If you choose "is not equal to," the database query will be as shown here.

```
WHERE NOT ('Orders'.'PO#'=1119
    OR  'Orders'.'PO#'=1282
    OR  'Orders'.'PO#'=2569
    OR  'Orders'.'PO#'=5569)
```

Using Multivalue Range Parameters

To use multivalue range parameters in the Select Expert, you must choose either the "is equal to" or "is not equal to" condition. The "is equal to" condition can be thought of as "is in one of the ranges," and "is not equal to" can be thought of as "is not in one of the ranges." The database query is constructed as shown here for "is equal to." A NOT would be prefixed for the "is not equal to" condition.

```
WHERE (('Orders'.'Order Date'>={ts '2001-04-09 00:00:00'}
        AND 'Orders'.'Order Date'<{ts '2001-05-09 00:00:01'})
    OR  ('Orders'.'Order Date'>={ts '2002-04-09 00:00:00'}
        AND 'Orders'.'Order Date'<{ts '2002-04-09 00:00:01'}))
```

Exercise 6.4: Using Parameters in Selection Formulas

1. Open the Exercise 6.3 report.

2. Select the PO# field and open the Select Expert. Choose the "is not equal to" condition, and pick the {?PO Param} field from the second drop-down box.

3. Click the New button, and choose the Ship Via field. Choose the "is equal to" condition, and pick the {?Ship Via Param} field from the second drop-down box.

4. Click the New button, and choose the Order Date field. Choose "is equal to" condition, and pick the {?Order Date Param} field from the second drop-down box.

5. Click the Show Formula button. You should see the following as the formula.

```
{Orders.PO#} <> {?PO Param} and
{Orders.Ship Via} = {?Ship Via Param} and
{Orders.Order Date} = {?Order Date Param}
```

6. Click OK to close the dialog box. Click Refresh Data. The report will run and you will see 154 records displayed.

7. Select Database | Show SQL Query to see how the selection formula was converted in the database query. The query should look like this.

```
SELECT  'Orders'.'Order ID', 'Orders'.'Order Amount',
        'Orders'.'Order Date', 'Orders'.'Ship Via',
        'Orders'.'Shipped', 'Orders'.'PO#'
FROM    'Orders' 'Orders'
WHERE   NOT ('Orders'.'PO#'=1119 OR 'Orders'.'PO#'=1282 OR
            'Orders'.'PO#'=2569 OR 'Orders'.'PO#'=5569)
        AND ('Orders'.'Order Date'>={ts '2001-01-01 00:00:00'} AND
            'Orders'.'Order Date'<{ts '2001-12-31 00:00:01'})
        AND 'Orders'.'Ship Via'='Parcel Post'
```

8. Save the report as **Exercise 6.4**.

Chapter Review

This chapter covered two very important aspects of report development, the Select Expert and parameters. The Select Expert is used to create simple record and group selection formulas that are used to filter the records displayed in the report. Parameters are used to gather information from the user of the report at run time. Combining parameters with selection formulas allows you to create dynamic reports whose records change depending on the user's selection.

Quick Tips

- The Select Expert is an easy-to-use tool that generates record selection formulas and group selection formulas.

- Crystal Reports saves the current result set in memory. Some modifications to a report force a refresh of the saved data; others allow you to choose whether to use saved data or retrieve new data.

- After modifying the selection formulas using the Select Expert, you will be prompted whether to use saved data or to refresh data. The report display can be incorrect if you choose to use saved data but not all of the required data is available in memory.

- You can create selection criteria for multiple fields. If you do, *each* criterion must be true for a record to pass the selection process. The selection formula that is generated will use ANDs to connect the selection criteria for each field.

- The record selection formula is usually passed to the database and modifies the number of records retrieved. The group selection formula does not modify the number of records retrieved; it only modifies the number of records displayed. Changes in the record number indicator can be monitored as a check on the changed record selection formula.

- Care must be taken when using dates in selection formulas. Many date fields include a time portion even if it is not used, and this can cause unexpected results. Always set the appropriate time value when using dates in selection formulas.

- Parameters are used to obtain input from the user. Parameters can be created with several data types and they can be discrete values or range values. Both discrete-value parameters and range-value parameters can be single entries or arrays of values. Parameters can be given default values so that the user can choose the value they want from a list.

- Parameter fields have no effect on the report until they are used in formulas or selection formulas or are displayed on the report.

- The values that the user can input for parameters can be restricted in several ways. The user can be forced to pick from the default values list. All parameter types except the Boolean type can be limited to values between an upper bound and lower bound. String parameters can have an edit mask that restricts the input to specific types of characters.

- To display single-value discrete parameters, you can place the field directly on the report or into a text object. To display other parameter types, you must create a formula that extracts the parameter values. The functions Minimum and Maximum are used to obtain the end points of range parameters. Multivalue parameters are stored in arrays, and you must use array logic to extract them.

- Parameter fields are often used in selection formulas to create dynamic user-defined record selections.

- Discrete parameter fields can be used exactly the same as regular database values in the Select Expert, but range parameters and multivalue parameters can only be used with the "is equal to" or "is not equal to" condition.

Questions

Questions may have more than one correct answer. Choose all answers that apply.

1. Which two tools can be used to create record selection formulas?

   a. Database Expert

   b. Formula Workshop

   c. Select Expert

   d. Selection Formula tool

   e. Record Sort Expert

2. Modifying the record selection formula using the Select Expert forces a data refresh.

   a. True

   b. False

3. When using the Select Expert and multiple selection fields, you can choose whether the criteria should be ANDed together or ORed together by clicking a radio button.

   a. True

   b. False

4. Which of the following records will be selected if the selection formula is DateField>3/25/2003?

   a. 3/31/2003 12:00:00AM

   b. 3/25/2003 12:00:00AM

   c. 3/24/2003 23:59:59PM

   d. 3/25/2003 8:15:00AM

   e. 3/26/2003 3:30:00PM

5. Which of the following fields is a parameter?

   a. {Param}

   b. {%Param}

   c. {?Param}

   d. {@Param}

   e. {#Param}

6. Which of the following values cannot be entered with this edit mask? ###,#00.00 (Think of the following choices as strings of characters being typed with any required spaces added to the front; no decimal point is included, but it will be in the final number because it is in the edit mask.)

   a. −10050

   b. 526

    c. 123456789

    d. 2590099

    e. +526

7. To extract the starting and ending values of a range parameter, you use the Maximum and Minimum functions.

    a. True

    b. False

8. Parameters can be given default values in order to

    a. Keep the user from having to type values

    b. Mask the user's entry to restrict what can be entered in each place

    c. Keep the user from entering incorrect values

    d. Give the user a longer definition of coded values

    e. Limit the length of the user's entry

9. Parameter fields can be used in place of hard-coded values in selection formulas to create user-definable record selections.

    a. True

    b. False

10. Select the comparison conditions in the Select Expert that can be used with a multivalue discrete parameter.

    a. is equal to

    b. is not equal to

    c. is one of

    d. is not one of

    e. is less than

Answers

1. **b, c.** The Select Expert generates simple selection formulas. The Formula Workshop can be used to create complex selection formulas.

2. **b.** False. After making changes in the Select Expert, you will be prompted whether to use saved data or to refresh data.

3. **b.** False. The Select Expert always ANDs multiple criteria together, although you can modify this manually in the formula window.

4. **a, d, e.** Answer b will not be selected because it is equal to but not greater than the comparison value; c will not be selected because it is less than the comparison value.

5. **c.** Parameter fields are prefixed with a question mark when displayed on a report or used in a formula.

6. **b, c, e.** Answer b is too short: the zeros require an entry, so at least four digits must be entered. Answer c is too long: the mask allows a maximum of 8 digits. Answer e is also too short: the zero mask character does not allow the plus or minus sign (but the # does).

7. **a.** True, you use the Minimum and Maximum functions to extract the starting and ending values of a range.

8. **a, c, d.** Answer b is a feature of edit masks; e is the Length Limit feature, not a feature of default lists.

9. **a.** True. This is the primary use for parameter fields.

10. **a, b.** Only "is equal to" or "is not equal to" can be used with multivalue parameters. Crystal Reports will translate this into multiple WHERE clauses connected by ORs in the report query.

Grouping, Sorting, and Summarizing

Exam RDCR200 expects you to be able to

- Sort records
- Group records
- Summarize data

Sorting records so that they display in a particular order on a report is often an aid to finding information within the report. Grouping records is an extension of sorting in that all records with the same value for a particular field are displayed together in a block on the report. Summarizing data involves computing some value across all the records in a group or the entire report, such as the total amount of sales by region.

You have created report groups with the report wizards in Chapter 3. This chapter will teach you how to create groups without using the wizards.

Groups

Every report except the very simplest of list reports or specially formatted reports like mailing labels or form letters will have one or more groups. Very often, the entire purpose of a report is to group data in a particular way and compute summaries for the groups. A group in Crystal Reports is indicated by a Group Header section and a connected Group Footer section. The group name is usually displayed in the Group Header section and summaries for the group are usually displayed in the Group Footer section. Groups can be created with two methods, the Insert Group command or using the Group Expert.

Insert Group

The Insert Group command can be executed by clicking this button on the Insert Tools toolbar, selecting Insert | Group from the menu, or clicking the Insert Group button on the Insert Summary dialog box. If a field is selected when the Insert Group command is executed, it will automatically be set as the field to group by, although you can change it once the Insert Group dialog box is displayed. When you first create a group, the Insert Group dialog box has two tabs, Common and Options.

Common

The Common tab contains two or three options you need to configure. For all field types, you must set the field to group by and the group sorting options. Date fields and Boolean fields have a third option that can be set.

Group by Field   This illustration shows the Insert Group dialog box for a number field. The first drop-down box lists all fields that can be grouped. The list includes fields currently on the report as well as those available in any data source being used by the report. Memo fields cannot be used to group by and so will not show up in the list. Choose the field that you want to group by.

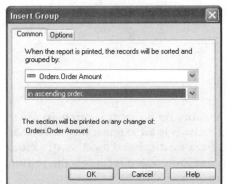

NOTE   You can group by the same field more than once, although it is not usually desirable. One exception is grouping on a date field; you might group by the same field twice, once with an option for months and once with an option for days. See the "Date-Time Options" section, coming up shortly.

Group Sort Order   The second drop-down box on the Insert Group dialog box is where you choose the sort order that you want for the group. This sort order determines how the group is sorted in the report—not how the records within a group are sorted. The sort order options are ascending, descending, "specified," and original.

- In Ascending Order sorts the group-by field from smallest to largest value.
- In Descending Order sorts the group-by field from largest to smallest value.
- In Specified Order sorts the group-by field in a user-defined order. See the "Custom Grouping" section for more information.
- In Original Order does not sort the group; instead, it leaves the records in the order in which they were retrieved from the database.

CAUTION   Using In Original Order can produce unexpected results, since records are not usually ordered when stored in a relational database.

Date-Time Options   When you choose a date-time field to group by, a third drop-down box is added to the Insert Group dialog box as shown next.

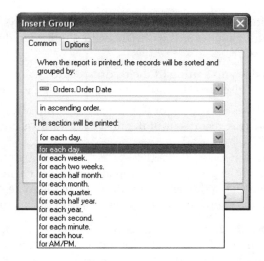

When you choose to group by a date field, it is grouped into whole days by default using the For Each Day option. To group by another interval you can change the date grouping to any of the other choices shown in the preceding illustration.

Boolean Options   If you group by a Boolean field, the third drop-down box on the Insert Group dialog box is used to set the grouping options for the field, as shown here.

The Boolean options require further explanation. Groups created on every other field type cause the records to be sorted such that records with identical values in the sort field are together. Only the default Boolean option (On Any Change) does this type of record sort. The Boolean options behave as follows:

- On Any Change is the default and sorts the group as expected with all True values together and all False values together.

- On Change to Yes does no sorting of the records but creates a new group every time that a True value is encountered after a False value.

- On Change to No does no sorting of the records but creates a new group every time that a False value is encountered after a True value.

- On Every Yes does no sorting of the records. A group always ends with a True value and includes any records with False values that precede it back to the last previous True value.

- On Every No does no sorting of the records. A group always ends with a False value and includes any records with True values that precede it back to the last previous False value.

- On Next Is Yes does no sorting of the records. A group always starts with a True and includes all False records until the next True value is encountered.

- On Next Is No does no sorting of the records. A group always starts with a False and includes all True records until the next False value is encountered.

Custom Grouping

Using the In Specified Order group sort option allows you to create a custom sort order when the simple ascending or descending options are inadequate. It is also used to create custom groups that are supersets or ranged groupings of existing field values.

User-Defined Sort Order   To create a user-defined sort order, select In Specified Order on the Common tab of the Insert Group dialog box. A new tab called Specified Order will be created. The Named Group drop-down box will contain every value for the group-by field, as shown here.

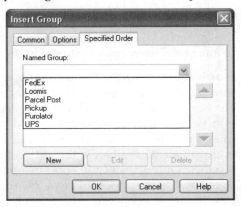

As you select values from the Named Group box, they are added to the list box at the bottom. The order of values in the list box determines the order of the groups on the report. After adding values, you can change the order using the arrow buttons to the right of the list box.

After you have added one value to the list box, a fourth tab called Others appears, as shown next.

The options on the Others tab determine how any values not specifically added to the list box on the Specified Order tab are sorted. There are three possible treatments for the other values:

- Discard All Others discards any group value whose sort order is not listed on the Specified Order tab.

- Put All Others Together, with the Name groups all values that are not listed on the Specified Order tab together and gives the group the name shown in the text box. The default name is Others, but you can change it.

- Leave in Their Own Groups displays all groups that were specified on the Specified Order tab first and then displays the remaining groups in ascending order.

User-Defined Groups In addition to creating a custom sort order with the In Specified Order option, you can also create custom groupings. Custom grouping is limited because the groups must be based on a single report field. You can create groups that are supersets of the report field values. For example, you could create sales regions such as West, East, Midwest, and South from a state field by creating the four named

groups and picking the states that belong in each. You could create rankings such as Big Order, Normal Order, and Small Order by creating ranges based on the order amount. Alternatively, you can create groups with complex conditions such as that the Ship Via field must start with F or be greater than T to be in the first group.

Creating custom groups requires two steps: creating the group names and then specifying the content of the named group. After creating a group and choosing In Specified Order, you must type a name into the Named Group box, as shown on the right.

Then press the New button, and the Define Named Group dialog box will appear. Enter the condition as you would in the Select Expert, as shown here for the Tiny group.

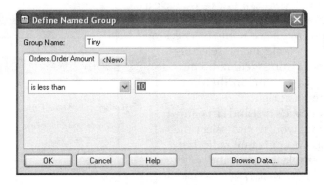

If you select the <New> tab, a new tab will be created where you can enter another condition. Unlike the Select Expert, the conditions on multiple tabs of the Define

Named Group dialog box all refer to the same field and are connected with ORs, as shown in this illustration, and you cannot modify the formula or use parameters.

After you create your custom groups, the report will be reprocessed, and you will see your named groups.

Options

The Options tab of the Insert Group dialog box contains three check boxes, as shown here. These options control the group name and paging for the group.

Customize Group Name Field The Customize Group Name Field option allows you to use the value of another field or the result of a formula for the group name instead of the value of the group-by field. For example, if you have a group on Employee ID, you can make the group name be the employee's last name by checking Customize Group Name Field, selecting the Choose From Existing Field radio button, and picking Last Name in the drop-down box, as shown at right.

To use the employee's first and last name as the group name, you would select the Use a Formula as Group Name radio button, click the formula button, and enter `{Employee .First Name}&' '&{Employee.Last Name}`. The formula button will change as shown here to indicate that a formula has been entered, and your report will group by the Employee ID but display the employee's first and last name

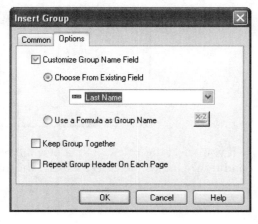

as the group name. The formula that you enter must return a string and cannot use any fields that must be evaluated at run time, such as a running total field.

Keep Group Together   The Keep Group Together option is intended to keep all parts of a group together on a single page if possible. The sections that the option affects start with the group header for the selected group, end with the group footer for the selected group, and include all sections in between: the details sections and any lower-level group sections. If the group is too large to fit completely on the current page, it will move to the next page. If the group is still too large to fit on the page, then it will break across pages as necessary.

In earlier versions of Crystal Reports, if the very first group in a report was too large to fit on the first page, it was moved to the next page, leaving a blank first page. By default, Crystal Reports 10 will start the first group on the first page even if it will not all fit. However, a new File | Report option called Respect Keep Group Together on First Page can be checked to mimic the behavior of previous versions.

Repeat Group Header on Each Page   If groups break across pages, you may have detail data at the top of a page with no indication of what group it belongs to. To repeat the group header at the top of each page that contains part of the group, check Repeat Group Header on Each Page.

Group Expert

The Group Expert can be used to modify existing groups or create new groups. Click the Group Expert button or select Report | Group Expert to open the Group Expert. The Group Expert has two list boxes, Available Fields and Group By, as shown in Figure 7-1.

The Group By list displays the existing groups in a hierarchy to indicate the group levels for the various fields. To create a new group, select a field in the Available Fields list and move it to the Group By list. If you use the arrow buttons to move the field, it will be added at the bottom of the Group By list and become the innermost group. If you drag

Figure 7-1
Viewing existing groups in the Group Expert

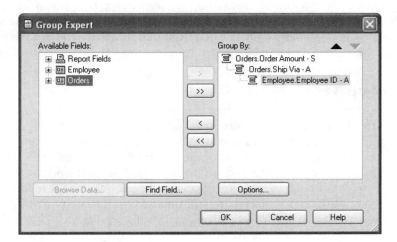

the field, you can drop it at any position in the hierarchy. If you click the Options button with a Group By field selected, the Change Group Options dialog box will be displayed. This dialog box is identical to the Insert Group dialog box.

Modifying Groups

Groups can be modified in a variety of ways using several different methods.

Deleting Groups   To delete a group, move it from the Group By list back to the Available Fields list in the Group Expert, or right-click in the gray area of the Group Header or Group Footer section and select Delete Group.

Changing a Group   To display the Group Options dialog box, where you can modify a group's settings, open the Group Expert, select a group, and click the Options button, or right-click in the gray area of the group's section and select Change Group. You can change any of the group options, including the field that it is grouped by.

Changing the Order of Groups   There are two ways to change the order of groups in your report. In the Group Expert dialog box, you can use the up and down arrows or drag groups to change the group order in the Group By list. The second way is to rearrange the group sections by dragging. Selecting the Group Header or Group Footer section selects both with a small area connecting them. You can then drag the group to a new location. Here, Group #2 is selected and is being moved outside of Group #1, as indicated by the thick line.

Group Name

By default, the group name for the group is inserted into the Group Header when a group is created. The group name is the value of the group by field unless it has been modified using settings in the Group Options dialog box. If you do not want the group name inserted by default, then you must clear the Insert Group Name with Group check box on the Layout tab of the File | Options dialog box. Insert Group Name with Group is a global option and will be applied to all groups you create in the future.

Group Tree

The Group Tree is available when viewing the Preview tab. The Group Tree button toggles the display of the Group Tree on and off. You can also display the Group Tree by selecting View | Group Tree. The Group Tree is a hierarchical tree view of the groups in the report. It is displayed to the left of the report window, as shown in Figure 7-2.

Clicking a box next to a node value opens and closes the node so that you can see the inner nodes or hide them. Clicking on a node value causes the report display to jump to that area of the report. In Figure 7-2, the user has clicked on "Margaret Peacock." The Group Tree is a valuable navigation aid for long reports.

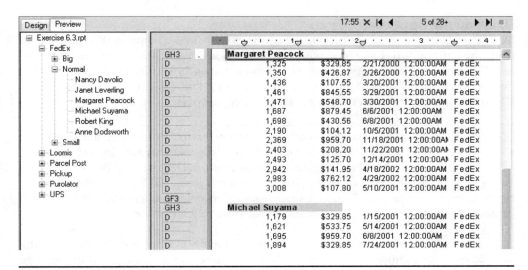

Figure 7-2 Navigating using the Group Tree

Drill-Down

When the Details section and any lower-level groups are hidden (not suppressed) for a group, the user has the option to drill down when viewing the report. When the mouse pointer is positioned over a hidden group, it will change to a magnifying glass.

Double-clicking on a group header when the cursor is a magnifying glass causes another tab to open displaying the contents of the group. The name of the new tab will be the group name that you clicked, and only the contents of that group will be displayed in the new tab. If there are multiple levels of hidden groups, you can drill down again to display the lower-level group values in their own new tabs. To close an open tab, click the Close View button next to the page controls at the top of the window.

Printing Drill-Down Views

Drill-down views are printed independently of the main report view. The user must choose to print each drill-down view separately; there is no command that will print the main report and all drill-down views.

NOTE Creating a drill-down report is not the same as creating a report that can dynamically expand and contract according to the user's choice. If the requirement is a report that can be displayed with various levels of detail visible for the *entire report*, then a method of conditionally suppressing sections dependent on a parameter must be used. Drill-down will not accomplish this.

DrillDownGroupLevel

DrillDownGroupLevel is a print state function available in the Formula Workshop. It returns the current drill-down level where the highest level, which is the Preview window itself, is zero. The DrillDownGroupLevel always matches the number of the group being drilled down on. If you are drilling down on Group #1, DrillDownGroupLevel will be 1. If you are drilling down on Group #2, DrillDownGroupLevel will be 2.

 NOTE The GroupNumber special field or Formula Workshop function is not the same as DrillDownGroupLevel. The GroupNumber function returns the count of the different group values up to the current point in the report. For example, if you had only a Group #1 and this group had four different values at run time, the first instance of Group #1 would have a GroupNumber equal to 1, the second instance of Group #1 would have a GroupNumber equal to 2, and so on.

DrillDownGroupLevel is often used to conditionally format the View tab for the drill-downs. For example, since column headers are commonly displayed in the Page Header section, and the Page Header section is not displayed in drill-down views, you can create another section in the group header that repeats the column headings but only displays them when the group is drilled down on.

Grouping on a Formula Field or SQL Expression Field

You can create groups based on formula fields or SQL Expression fields. If you're basing the group on a formula field, the formula cannot contain any expressions that must be evaluated at print time. The methods for creating and manipulating groups based on formula fields or SQL Expressions are identical to the methods for database fields. Creating groups based on formulas or SQL Expressions gives you even more flexibility than creating custom groups, since you can use very complex formulas that reference multiple fields, perform computations, contain parameters, and so on.

Exercise 7.1: Creating and Modifying Simple Groups

1. Create a new report as a blank report using the Customer, Employee, and Orders tables.

2. Place the Order Amount field in the Details section of the report.

3. Click the Insert Group button, and choose the Customer.Country field to group by. Click OK. A group will be created.

4. Click the Group Expert button, and move the Order Date and the Customer Name fields into the Group By list.

5. Drag Customer Name up so that it is the middle group.

6. Select Order Date, and click the Options button.

7. Select the For Each Quarter option.

8. Click the Options tab, and check the Repeat Group Header on Each Page option. Then click OK.

9. Click OK to close the Group Expert.

10. Preview the report. Use the Group Tree to navigate to the USA node. Open it, and then open the Alley Cat Cycles node. Notice the group names for the quarters. The quarter name is the first month and the year of the quarter, so you will see 1/2001, 4/2001, 7/2001, and 10/2001 instead of quarters numbered 1 through 4.

11. Save the report as **Exercise 7.1**.

Exercise 7.2: Creating a Specified Group Order

1. Open the Exercise 7.1 report if it is not already open.

2. Right-click in the gray area of Group Header #1, and choose Change Group.

3. Select In Specified Order; the Specified Order tab will appear.

4. In the Named Group drop-down box, choose Canada, England, and USA. Reorder the list so that it is USA, Canada, England.

5. Click the Others tab, and choose Discard All Others. Click OK to close the Change Group Options dialog box.

6. Preview the report. You should see only three groups in the Group Tree; records for countries other than USA, Canada, and England should be excluded from the report.

7. Save the report as **Exercise 7.2**.

Exercise 7.3: Setting Group Names

1. Open Exercise 7.2 if it is not already open.

2. Right-click in the gray area of Group Header #3, and choose Change Group.

3. Click the Options tab, select Use a Formula as Group Name, and then click the Formula button.

4. Enter this exact formula into the Formula Workshop:

```
ToText(DatePart ('q', {Orders.Order Date}), '0') & 'Q' &
ToText(DatePart ('yyyy', {Orders.Order Date}), '0000')
```

5. Close the Formula Workshop.

6. Click OK to close the Change Group Options dialog box.

7. Browse again to USA and Alley Cat Cycles. Notice that the Order Date group now shows 1Q2000, 1Q2001, 2Q2001, and so on. The quarters are in the proper date order even though the group names would sort differently.

8. Save the report as **Exercise 7.3**.

Exercise 7.4: Creating Custom Groups

1. Open the Exercise 7.3 report if it is not already open.

2. Click the Group Expert button to open the Group Expert.

3. Create a new group based on the Ship Via field using the drag-and-drop method. Place the new group immediately after the group on Country and before the existing group on Customer Name.

4. Select the new group, and click the Options button.

5. Choose the In Specified Order sort option.

6. On the Specified Order tab, type **Commercial Shipper** into the Named Group box, and click the New button.

7. In the Define Named Group dialog box, choose Is One Of, and then add FedEx, Loomis, Purolater, and UPS to the list. Click OK to close the dialog box.

8. Click the Others tab, and select Leave in Their Own Groups.

9. Click OK twice to complete the change.

10. Preview the report, and notice that the Ship Via group has three possible values: Commercial Shipper, Parcel Post, and Pick Up.

11. Save the report as **Exercise 7.4**.

Exercise 7.5: Grouping on Formula Fields

1. Open Exercise 7.4 if it is not already open.

2. Right-click Formula Fields in the Field Explorer, and choose New. Formula creation has not been covered yet, so follow these instructions explicitly.

3. In the Formula Name dialog box, type **Customer Initial,** and click the Use Editor button.

4. Type the following formula into the window, and then close the Formula Workshop:

```
UpperCase ({Customer.Customer Name}[1])
```

5. Click the Insert Group button, and choose Customer Initial from the drop-down box on the Common tab.

6. Click OK to close the Insert Group dialog box.

7. The new group will be Group #5. Select the Group Header #5 section and move it so that it becomes the third group.

8. Preview the report, and notice that the customer names are now grouped together by their starting letter. This is most easily seen in the Group Tree.

9. Save the report as **Exercise 7.5**.

NOTE Grouping by the customer's initial could have been set up with the In Specified Order group sort option, but you would have to create a named group for each letter of the alphabet to accomplish it.

Sorting Records

Sorting records enables the user to quickly find the information they need. Browsing an unordered report can be frustrating and time-consuming. Sorting is accomplished through two mechanisms in Crystal Reports. Any groups in the report have sort orders associated with them. The group sort order will sort based on the group-by field and the chosen sort order. If no groups exist or if sorting within groups is desired, you can do a record sort. Records are sorted using the Record Sort Expert.

You can sort by database fields, formula fields, and SQL Expression fields. Memo fields cannot be used for sorting. A sort direction must be chosen for each field in the sort. Ascending is the default. For ascending sorts, string fields are sorted as if they were padded with blanks on the right so that they are equal in length, and then blanks are considered the lowest value, followed by symbols, numbers, uppercase letters, and then lowercase letters. Numeric fields are sorted by value from lowest to highest. Dates, times, and date-times are sorted from earliest to latest. Booleans sort with False before True. Null is considered lower than any value. For descending sorts, these orders are reversed.

Record Sort Expert

 The Record Sort Expert can be opened by clicking the Record Sort Expert button on the Expert Tools toolbar or by selecting Report | Record Sort Expert. The Record Sort Expert contains an Available Fields list and a Sort Fields list, as shown in Figure 7-3. You can move fields from the Available Fields list to the Sort Fields list using the arrow buttons or by dragging. For each field in the Sort Fields list, you must set the Sort Direction radio button to Ascending or Descending.

Figure 7-3
Setting up a sort in the Record Sort Expert

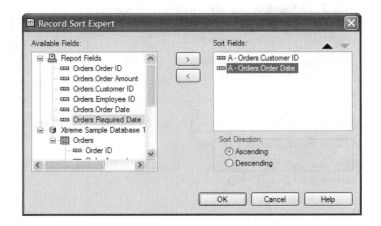

PART II

Sorting Without Groups

To create a sort for a report that is not grouped, simply open the Record Sort Expert and create the sort as described in the preceding paragraph. You can rearrange the sort fields using the arrow buttons or by dragging.

Sorting with Groups

Sorting a report that contains groups is very similar to a record sort. The only difference is that each group-by field will be listed in order in the Sort Fields list before any record sort fields, as shown here. The groups are listed showing the group icon, the group number, and the group-by field name. The group sort order is appended as a single letter to the listing. Record-level sorts are listed last, have a different icon, and have the record sort order shown by a prefixed A or D.

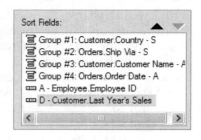

Exercise 7.6: Sorting a Report with No Groups

1. Open the Exercise 3.1 report.

2. Open the Record Sort Expert by clicking the Record Sort Expert button.

3. Move Last Name and First Name into the Sort Fields list.

4. Click OK to close the dialog box.

5. Preview the report, and notice that it is sorted by the employee's last name. (Since no two employees have the same last name, you cannot see that the second-level sort on first name is happening, but you can trust Crystal Reports on this.)

6. Save the report as **Exercise 7.6**.

Exercise 7.7: Sorting a Report with Groups

1. Open the Exercise 7.4 report.

2. Add Employee ID and Ship Date to the report.

3. Open the Record Sort Expert by selecting Report | Record Sort Expert.

4. Add Employee ID in ascending order to the Sort Fields list.

5. Add Ship Date in descending order to the Sort Fields list.

6. Click OK to close the dialog box.

7. Preview the report, and notice that the records are sorted within the quarters by Employee ID and Ship Date.

8. Save the report as **Exercise 7.7**.

Summarizing

Most reports have some type of summary information. The summary might be the count of employees, the total order amount by customer, the average sales per quarter, and so on. Summaries involve an aggregation of the data from multiple records. The summary can be computed for all the records in a report or for report groups.

Summary Operations

Crystal Reports includes many different summary types or operations. Some summary operations are available only for numeric (or currency) fields, while others are available for all field types. Some summary types can be displayed as percentages of a higher-level group summary. For example, you could show the total order amount for each country as the percentage of each country's order amount divided by the grand total order amount.

Table 7-1 lists the summary operations, the field types for which the operation is available, and whether or not it can be used as a percentage.

Operation	Field Types Operator Is Available For				Can Be Used as a Percentage?
Sum	Number				Yes
Average	Number				Yes
Sample variance	Number				No
Sample standard deviation	Number				No
Maximum	Number	Date	String	Boolean	Yes
Minimum	Number	Date	String	Boolean	Yes
Count	Number	Date	String	Boolean	Yes
Distinct count	Number	Date	String	Boolean	Yes
Correlation with	Number				No
Covariance with	Number				No
Median	Number				No
Mode	Number	Date	String	Boolean	No
Nth largest	Number	Date	String	Boolean	No
Nth smallest	Number	Date	String	Boolean	No
Nth most frequent	Number	Date	String	Boolean	No
Pth Percentile	Number				No
Population variance	Number				No
Population standard deviation	Number				No
Weighted average with	Number				No

Table 7-1 Summary Operations

Insert Summary

Summary fields are created using the Insert Summary dialog box, which can be displayed using three different methods. To display the Insert Summary dialog box, you can click the Insert Summary button on the Insert Tools toolbar, select Insert | Summary from the main menu, or right-click a detail-level field on the report and choose Insert | Summary. If a field is selected when the Insert Summary dialog box is opened, it will be listed as the field to summarize. You can change the field to summarize if desired. The Insert Summary dialog box is shown in Figure 7-4.

A field will be selected in the Choose the Field to Summarize drop-down box. You can either accept it or choose another field. Memo fields will not be listed in the drop-down box and cannot be used to create summaries. A summary operation will be selected in the Calculate This Summary drop-down box. You can change it if you like. The default summary operation differs depending on the data type of the field to summarize. For numeric fields, the default is Sum. For string, date, and Boolean fields, the default is Maximum.

The Summary location drop-down box always contains a choice for a Grand Total that will be placed in the Report Footer section if it is chosen. In addition to the Grand Total, a choice for each group that exists in the report will be listed. If you choose a group as the location, the summary will be computed for that group and placed in the Footer section for that group. After making or confirming these three choices, you can click OK to create the summary field.

The Insert Summary dialog box contains some optional choices. If you wish to create summaries for groups that do not exist in the report, you can click the Insert Group button to display the Insert Group dialog box, where you can create new groups. After the Insert Group dialog box is closed, the new group will be available in the Insert Summary dialog box.

If your report contains more than one group, you have selected a valid summary operation (as shown in Table 7-1), and you have chosen a location other than the Grand Total, then the Show as a Percentage of check box will be available. If you choose to show your summary as a percentage, you must select the level that will be used as the

Figure 7-4

Choosing a field to summarize

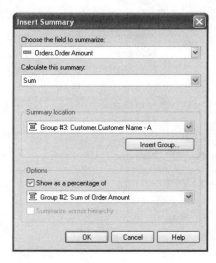

divisor for the percentage. You can choose any group level that is higher than the Summary location. The percentage will be computed as the summary at the Summary location level divided by the summary at the Show as a Percentage of location.

Working with Summary Fields

After you create a summary field using the Insert Summary dialog box, it becomes a report field. It is displayed on the report in a frame like other fields. Its name is a combination of the summary operation and the name of the field being summarized, such as Sum of Order Amount or Count of Customer ID. The summary field is placed in the group footer for the group to which it applies and is snapped to the same guideline that the field being summarized is connected to, as shown here.

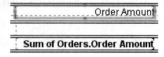

You can place summary fields inside text objects just as you can other field types.

Summary fields are not displayed in the Field Explorer, but they are available in the Formula Workshop and are displayed in the Report Explorer. You can format summary fields just as you can any other field. You can move a summary field within the Group Footer section or move it to the Group Header section. You cannot move a summary field into the Details section. If you move a summary field into the header or footer section for a different group, it will become a summary for the new group level.

To modify a summary field, select it. Then right-click and choose Edit Summary, or choose Edit | Edit Summary from the main menu. The Edit Summary dialog box will appear, as shown here.

The Edit Summary dialog box is identical to the Insert Summary dialog box except that you cannot change the summary location. If you need to change the summary location, you can just move the summary field into a different group header or footer.

Summarizing Formula Fields

Most formula fields can be summarized in the exact same fashion as database fields. Any formula that uses only detail-level fields or parameters can be summarized. Formula fields that contain running totals or other run time–computed fields cannot be summarized.

Exercise 7.8: Creating Summaries

1. Open the Exercise 7.7 report.

2. Select the Order Amount field in the Details section, and click the Insert Summary button.

3. Change the summary location to Group #1, and click OK. You will see a new field added in the Group Footer #1 section aligned with the Order Amount field.

4. Insert subtotals for the Order Amount field for Group #2, Group #3, and Group #4.

5. Insert a grand total for the Order Amount field.

6. Create a summary on the Ship_Date field. Use Minimum as the summary operation, and locate it in Group #4.

7. Preview the report.

8. Save the report as **Exercise 7.8**.

Exercise 7.9: Modifying Summaries

1. Open the Exercise 7.8 report.

2. Unsuppress the Report Header section.

3. Move the grand total for the Order Amount from the Report Footer into the Report Header. Place a text field next to the grand total. The text field should say "Grand Total."

4. Move the Order Amount summaries from each group footer to the corresponding group header.

5. Preview the report, widening the fields, if necessary, to see the entire summary value.

6. Right-click the Order Amount summary in Group Header #1, and choose Edit Summary.

7. In the Edit Summary dialog box, check the Show as a Percentage of box, and click OK.

8. Preview the report, and notice that the Group #1 summary is now a percentage.

9. Move the summary on the Ship Date from the Group Footer #4 into Group Header #1.

10. Preview the report, and notice that the Ship Date summary has changed and is now computed across the Country group instead of the Order Date group.

11. Save the report as **Exercise 7.9**.

Exercise 7.10: Summarizing Formula Fields

1. Open the Exercise 7.7 report.

2. Right-click the Formula Fields folder in the Field Explorer and select New.

3. In the Formula Name dialog box, type **Discount**, and click Use Editor.

4. Construct or type the following formula into the Formula Workshop, and then close the Formula Workshop.

```
{Orders.Order Amount}*0.15
```

5. Place the Discount field on the report after the Order Amount.

6. Right-click the Discount field, and select Insert | Summary.

7. Choose Average as the summary type, and locate it in the Country group.

8. Click OK to close the Insert Summary dialog box.

9. Preview the report and scroll to see the average discount by country.

10. Save the report as **Exercise 7.10**.

Group Sorting and Selection

Groups can be sorted or selected for based on the values of group summary fields.

Group Sort Expert

Groups are ordinarily sorted by the values in the group-by field, in either ascending or descending order, as configured on the Insert Group dialog box. However, you can also sort groups according to the value of a summary field for the group. For example, instead of sorting the Country group alphabetically by the country name, you could sort it by the total order amount by country in descending numerical order. This would display the country with the highest total order amount first on the report, followed by the country with the second highest total order amount, and so on.

Reports can also be configured to display only those groups that fall at the top or bottom of the report numerically. If you choose the Top N, Bottom N, Top Percentage, or Bottom Percentage options, then the group is sorted based on a summary field, and all groups that do not meet the condition are suppressed.

To sort a group based on a summary value, you use the Group Sort Expert, shown in Figure 7-5. The Group Sort Expert can be invoked by clicking the Group Sort Expert button or choosing Report | Group Sort Expert from the main menu. The Group Sort Expert dialog box contains a tab for each group that exists in the report. You use the options on each tab to configure the sorting for that group. There are six sort options: No Sort, All, Top N, Bottom N, Top Percentage, and Bottom Percentage.

Figure 7-5

Sorting by group

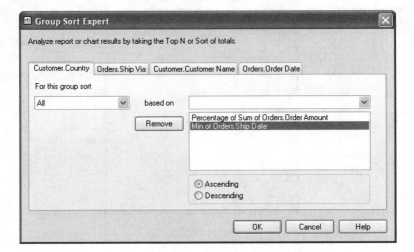

No Sort   No Sort is the default value. If you leave a group at No Sort, it will be sorted according to the options that were set when the group was created.

All   If you choose All, no groups will be suppressed and you will only configure group sorting. Figure 7-5 shows the Group Sort Expert dialog box with the All option selected. From the Based On drop-down box, you can choose any existing summaries for the group to use for group sorting. If you choose multiple summaries, the group will be sorted first on the first summary, then on the next summary, and so on. For each summary you must choose whether to sort in ascending or descending order.

Top N   If you choose Top N, the Group Sort Expert will look like Figure 7-6. Unlike the All option, you can choose only one summary to base the Top N sort on. You must set the value for N in the Where N Is box. If you want to see the top 5 groups, then enter 5, if you want to see the top 10, enter 10. Clearing the Include Others box will cause all groups that are not in the designated range to be suppressed, and they will not appear on the report. If the Include Others box is checked, all other groups will be grouped together under the name you enter, similar to using Named Groups. Check the Include Ties box to allow tying groups in the designated range to be displayed. If you include ties in a top 5 report and two groups are tied for fifth place, they will both be displayed.

CAUTION   If you do not include ties, then one of the tied groups will be displayed and the other will be suppressed. You have no control over which group is displayed.

Bottom N   The Bottom N option is the same as the Top N option, except that it displays the lowest summary values instead of the highest ones, according to the number you enter.

Figure 7-6

Setting up a Top N sort

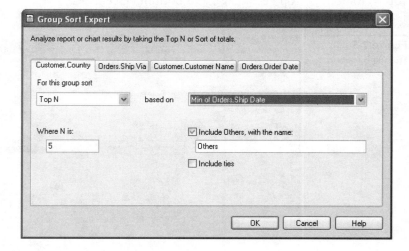

Top Percentage   The Top Percentage option is similar to the Top N option, except that you enter a percentage instead of a count, and all groups that fall within the chosen percentage are displayed. For example, if you choose the top 10 percent based on order amount, then the group would be sorted based on the order amount summary, 10 percent of the total orders would be computed, and groups would be displayed until the running total of their order amounts met the 10 percent limit.

Bottom Percentage   The Bottom Percentage is identical to the Top Percentage except that it displays the bottom-most groups until the percentage is met.

Group Selection Formulas

The Group Sort Expert can be used to filter out groups that are not in the Top N, Bottom N, Top Percentage, or Bottom Percentage of the report. Group selection formulas can be used to filter out groups based on any conditions that you can create in the Select Expert or manually in a group selection formula.

To create group selection based on a summary field, you use the same techniques that

Group Selection can be based on the Group Name or on group summaries. The Group Name is the value of the group by field unless custom group names have been created. The Group Name field for each group is available in the Field Explorer under the Group Name Fields folder. The Group Name is available in formulas using the GroupName function. Basing a group selection on a Group Name is necessary only when you have created named groups and want to select based on your custom names. Otherwise, the Group Name is identical to the detail field value and you can use record selection instead. For example, suppose that you have a group on the Country field with no custom groups created. A group selection formula using the Group Name might be `GroupName ({Customer.Country})=-'USA'`. But, since group selection is never pushed to the server, a better option would be to use a record selection formula like `{Customer.Country}='USA'`.

To create group selection based on a summary field, you use the same techniques that you would for record selection, but you choose a summary field instead of a detail-level field. For example, to create a group selection formula that filters out all countries with less than $1,000 in total order amount, you would create a total order amount summary for the Country group, and then select the summary and click the Select Expert button. Then in the Select Expert, choose Is Greater Than, and enter **1000**. All groups that do not have at least $1,000 in total order amount will be suppressed. For complex conditions that cannot be created in the Select Expert, you can create or modify the Group Selection formula in the Formula Workshop.

CAUTION   Group Selection formulas suppress groups that do not meet the defined conditions; they do not filter records out of the report. Due to this behavior, summaries for the entire report will contain the totals for the suppressed groups.

Exercise 7.11: Using the Group Sort Expert

1. Open the Exercise 7.8 report.

2. Open the Group Sort Expert.

3. On the Customer.Country tab, select Bottom N, set N to **2**, and include others with the name **Others**.

4. Click OK to close the Group Sort Expert, and then preview the report.

5. You should see England, then Canada, and then Others as the top-level groups in the preview.

6. Save the report as **Exercise 7.11**.

Exercise 7.12: Using a Group Selection Formula

1. Open the report from Exercise 7.8.

2. Select the Min of Orders.Ship Date summary field.

3. Open the Select Expert, choose Is Greater Than or Equal To, and enter **1/1/2002 12:00:00AM**.

4. Click OK to close the Select Expert, and preview the report.

5. Note that the record count does not change, but only groups with a Ship Date of or after January 1, 2002 are displayed.

6. Save the report as **Exercise 7.12**.

Chapter Review

Grouping, sorting, and summarizing skills are essential for the report developer. This chapter described Crystal Reports features and capabilities that you can use to group reports, sort groups and records, and create summary values.

Quick Tips

- Groups can be created using the Insert Group button or menu command or using the Group Expert. To create a group, you must choose the field to group by, and you can optionally choose a sort order or create a custom sort order.

- You can create groups based on formula fields as long as the formula is not evaluated at print time.

- When grouping on a date-time field, the default is to group in intervals of one day. You can change the option to other periods such as weeks, months, or hours.

- Keep Group Together is a group option that is used to instruct Crystal Reports to start a group on a new page if it will not fit on the current page.

- The In Specified Order group sort option allows you to specify the sort order for the field. It also allows you to create your own custom groups by defining conditions that will generate supersets of the group-by field's values.

- The Group Tree is a hierarchical tree display listing the groups in a report. It can be turned on or off, and users can expand and collapse the nodes as desired. The Group Tree serves as a navigation aid, since double-clicking a value in the tree takes you directly to that section of the report.

- Group Names can be customized by choosing the value of another field or using a formula that returns a string.

- Groups can be reordered using the Group Expert or by dragging the group sections.

- Hidden group details can be drilled down on when the mouse pointer turns into a magnifying glass. Drilling down causes a new tab to be created for the drill-down view.

- The report's record sort order is defined using the Record Sort Expert. For reports with groups, the group sort order is applied first and then the record sort order is applied. Each sort-by field can have either an ascending or descending sort order.

- Summary fields are created using the Insert Summary dialog box, which can be displayed using the Insert Summary button or the Insert | Summary menu command or by right-clicking on a field and choosing Insert | Summary.

- A single summary field can apply to only one group or to the whole report. If you need summaries at every level in a report, you must create multiple summary fields, one for each group and one for the grand total.

- Several summary operations are available, including Sum, Count, Average, and so on. However, some operations are not available for date, Boolean, or string fields.

- The default summary operation for a numeric field is Sum; for other field types, it is Maximum.

- Memo fields cannot be summarized.

- Moving a summary field into a different group changes the summary so that it applies to the new group. Summary fields cannot be moved into the Details section.

- Summary fields can be modified by right-clicking and choosing Edit Summary.

- Summary fields can be configured to display as percentages of a higher-level summary.

- The Group Sort Expert can be used to sort groups based on summary values. It can also be used to create reports showing only those groups at the top or bottom numerically.

- Group Selection formulas are based on the Group Name or on summary values for groups. They suppress any groups that do not meet the defined conditions.

Questions

Questions may have more than one correct answer. Choose all answers that apply.

1. The group sort option that allows you to customize the group sort order is called
   a. In Manual Order
   b. In Specified Order
   c. In Custom Order
   d. In Dynamic Order
   e. In Original Order

2. Groups can be created by
   a. Choosing Report | Group Expert
   b. Clicking the Insert Group button on the Insert Summary dialog box
   c. Clicking the Insert Group button
   d. Choosing Insert | Group
   e. Clicking the Group Expert button

3. Which options are true when Repeat Group Header on Each Page is checked?
   a. The group values will be displayed in a tree that the user can use to navigate the report.
   b. A page that contains Details sections will always start with a group header (after the page header).
   c. Crystal Reports will attempt to keep all sections of a group together on the report.
   d. The report will be longer.
   e. The user can tell what group details belong to without paging backward in the report.

4. The Group Tree allows users to expand and collapse the display of groups on the report.
   a. True
   b. False

5. Which combination of conditions might cause the first page of a report to display no records?
   a. Keep Group Together is checked.
   b. Keep Group Together is cleared.
   c. Respect Keep Group Together on First Page is checked.
   d. Respect Keep Group Together on First Page is cleared.
   e. Repeat Group Header on Each Page is checked.
   f. Repeat Group Header on Each Page is cleared.

6. The group sort options are

   a. In Original Order

   b. In Ascending Order

   c. In Descending Order

   d. In Specified Order

   e. In Custom Order

7. The Group Tree can be used in the Preview window to navigate to the area of a report where a group begins.

   a. True

   b. False

8. You have which of the following options when you group by a date-time field?

   a. For Each Week

   b. For Each Two Weeks

   c. For Each Half Month

   d. For Each Month

   e. For Each Two Months

9. When creating custom groups, the Define Named Group dialog box works exactly like the Select Expert.

   a. True

   b. False

10. The group name for a group can be

    a. A string constant

    b. The numeric result of a formula

    c. The value of the group-by field

    d. The value of another field

    e. The string result of a formula

11. Groups can be reordered by which of the following methods?

    a. Using the Group Expert

    b. With the Insert Group command

    c. By dragging

    d. Using the Group Sort Expert

    e. Using the Sort Order Expert

12. A drill-down report is one that contains suppressed Detail sections.

    a. True

    b. False

13. Which of the following formulas could not be used as a group-by field?

    a. `{Last Name}&' '&{First Name}`

    b. `Sum ({Orders.Order Amount},{Orders.Customer ID})`

    c. `{Orders.Order Amount}*1.1`

    d. `NextIsNull ({Orders.Courier Website})`

    e. `RecordNumber`

14. Which is applied first, the record sort order or the group sort order?

    a. Record sort order

    b. Group sort order

15. When you choose Ascending or Descending in the Record Sort Expert, it is applied to every sort field.

    a. True

    b. False

16. The default summary operation for a Date field is

    a. Sum

    b. Count

    c. Maximum

    d. Minimum

    e. Average

17. A report with no groups can have summaries.

    a. True

    b. False

18. A report with no groups can have summaries shown as percentages.

    a. True

    b. False

19. In the Edit Summary dialog box, you can modify which parts of a summary?

    a. The field being summarized

    b. The summary operation

    c. The summary location

    d. The Show as a Percentage Of field

    e. The group the summary applies to

20. The Group Sort Expert is used to sort records within groups.

    a. True

    b. False

21. You can create new groups within the Group Sort Expert if desired.

    a. True

    b. False

22. Which of the following Group Sort Expert options allow you to sort based on more than one summary field?

    a. No Sort

    b. All

    c. Top N

    d. Bottom N

    e. Top Percentage

    f. Bottom Percentage

23. Group Selection formulas may or may not be passed to the server, depending on their definition.

    a. True

    b. False

Answers

1. **b.** The group sort option that allows you to specify the group sort order is called In Specified Order.

2. **All.** Groups can be created using any of these methods.

3. **b, d, e.** Answer a refers to the Group Tree; c refers to the Keep Group Together option.

4. **b.** False, users can expand and collapse groups within the Group Tree, but this has no effect on the report itself.

5. **a, c.** If Keep Group Together and Respect Keep Group Together on First Page are checked, Crystal Reports will mimic the behavior of earlier version and start the first group on the second page if it will not fit on the first page.

6. **a, b, c, d.** In Custom Order is not an actual option, although you can use In Specified Order to create a custom sort order.

7. **a.** True, the Group Tree cannot be used in the Design window.

8. **a, b, c, d.** Answer e is not an available choice.

9. **b.** False, the Define Named Group dialog box is similar to the Select Expert, but each tab is related to the same field, the conditions are connected with ORs, and you cannot modify the resulting formula.

10. **a, c, d, e.** Answer b is not a valid choice, because a formula for a group name must return a string. Answer a is valid because a string constant could be the result of a formula.

11. **a, c.** Groups can be reordered using the Group Expert or by dragging.

12. **b.** False, a drill-down report must have hidden sections.

13. **b, d, e.** Answer b contains a summary function. Answers d and e contain functions that are evaluated at print time. Note that IsNull may be usable even though it is defined as a print-time function.

14. **b.** The record sort order is applied within the lowest-level group.

15. **b.** False, each sort field has its sort order applied independently of the other sort fields.

16. **c.** The default summary operation for a Date field is Maximum.

17. **a.** True, a report with no groups can still have grand total summaries.

18. **b.** False, to show summaries as percentages, at least one group must exist because the percentage must be computed over a second, higher level summary. For a report with only one group, the percentage must be over the grand total.

19. **a, b, d.** In the Edit Summary dialog box, you cannot change the Summary location, which is the same thing as the group the summary applies to. To change the group the summary applies to, you can move the summary field into the group header or group footer for a different group.

20. **b.** False. The Group Sort Expert is used to sort groups based on summary values.

21. **b.** False. At least one group and one summary field for the group must exist before the Group Sort Expert can be used. You cannot create new groups or summaries within the Group Sort Expert.

22. **b.** Only the All option allows you to sort a group based on more than one summary field.

23. **b.** False. Group Selection formulas are never passed to the server.

Creating Formula Fields

Exam RDCR200 expects you to be able to

- Define a formula
- Create a formula
- Apply Boolean formulas
- Apply If-Then-Else formulas
- Apply date calculations
- Apply number calculations
- Apply string manipulation
- Use functions and operators
- Define control structures available in Crystal Syntax
- Use variables
- Use arrays

Formula fields are report fields that you create using the Formula Workshop. There will be times when no existing field in your database meets your reporting need exactly. You may need to combine fields or compute new values using existing fields. When you need to create a new value, you can use a formula or a SQL Expression. Choosing which field type to create depends on the needed computation and your experience. SQL Expressions will be evaluated on the server as part of the report query, with the result passed back to Crystal Reports. Formulas are always evaluated locally by Crystal Reports, but that is usually less efficient.

To create any but the simplest SQL Expression you need to know the SQL dialect of your database. Creating a formula requires knowledge of the Crystal Reports Formula Workshop. SQL Expressions for most databases will be limited to fewer possible options than a Crystal Reports formula. In addition, if you need to create a computation that refers to records other than the current record, you will probably need a Crystal Reports formula, although some databases have introduced analytical functions that can be used for this purpose.

Formula fields can be used in a report in many of the same ways that a database field can be used. They can be placed on the report and formatted as desired. If a formula does not use any other formulas or fields that must be evaluated at run time, you will be able to group and summarize on it. Formulas can be simple one-line calculations or complex miniprograms. Chapter 17 covers some advanced formula topics that are not covered in this chapter.

Formula Workshop

All Crystal Reports formula types can be created using the Formula Workshop. This chapter will concentrate on regular formula fields, but the Formula Workshop can also be used to create record or group selection formulas, SQL Expression fields, formatting formulas, and custom functions.

Opening the Formula Workshop

The Formula Workshop can be opened in several different ways, as this table shows.

From	Steps	Formula Workshop Result
Main menu	Select Report | Formula Workshop.	No formula field is active. You can select a formula or create a new formula of any type.
Toolbar	Click the Formula Workshop button.	No formula field is active. You can select a formula or create a new formula of any type.
Field Explorer	Select a Formula field or SQL Expression, and then click the Edit button or choose Edit from the right-click menu.	The selected formula will be active.
Field Explorer	Select a Formula field, SQL Expression, the Formula Fields node, or the SQL Expression node. Then click the New button or choose New from the right-click menu.	You will be asked to create a name for the formula and the new formula will be active.
Preview or Design window	Select a Formula field or SQL Expression, and then choose Edit from the right-click menu.	The selected formula will be active.
Select Expert	Click the Show Formula button and then the Formula Editor button.	The record selection formula will be active.
Format Editor	Click any Formula button displayed on any tab.	The format formula for the selected attribute will be active.

Exploring the Formula Workshop

Figure 8-1 shows the Formula Workshop open with the Discount formula from the Exercise 7.10 report active. The Formula Workshop has several toolbars, four special areas, and the main formula creation window. The formula is created in the lower right-hand window. You can type in this area or select items from the other areas to make entries into the formula.

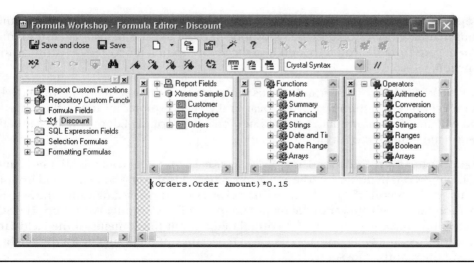

Figure 8-1 Constructing formulas in the Formula Workshop

Workshop Tree

The *Workshop Tree* is a tree view of all formulas in the report or available via the repository. It is docked at the left side of the
Formula Workshop by default, but you can
move it as you like. Existing formulas are
shown under a category folder, as shown on
the right.

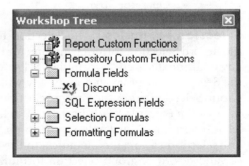

The Workshop Tree behaves much like
the Field Explorer. In addition to creating
new formulas using the Field Explorer, you
can create new formulas in the Formula Workshop by selecting a node of the Workshop
Tree and clicking the New button or selecting New from the right-click menu. You can
delete or rename existing formulas by selecting the formula and clicking the appropriate
toolbar button or selecting the appropriate option from the right-click menu.

This chapter concentrates on the Formula Fields folder, but other types of formulas
can also be manipulated with the Formula Workshop.

Report Custom Functions *Report custom functions* are user-created functions
that are stored in the current report. They may have been created in the report or copied
into the report from the repository. Once a custom function is available to a report, it
can be used in the same way as the functions supplied with Crystal Reports. Report custom functions appear in the Workshop Tree under the Report Custom Function folder
and in the Function Tree under the Custom Functions folder. Select a function in the
Workshop Tree to edit it; select it in the Function Tree to use it in your formula.

Repository Custom Functions   *Repository custom functions* are custom functions that have been stored in the repository. In order to use a repository custom function in your formula, you must add it to the report, so that it becomes a report custom function.

Formula Fields   The Formula Fields folder contains all user-defined formula fields in the report. These formulas also appear in the Field Explorer for use in the report. If you edit an existing formula or create a new one, the Formula Editor will appear in the right-hand pane of the Formula Workshop.

SQL Expression Fields   The SQL Expression Fields folder contains all user-defined SQL Expressions in the report. The SQL Expression fields also appear in the Field Explorer for use in the report. If you edit an existing expression or create a new one, the SQL Expression Editor will appear in the right-hand pane of the Formula Workshop. The SQL Expression Editor is similar to the Formula Editor, but the contents of the Field Tree, Function Tree, and Operator Tree change to reflect the options available for the database type of the report's data source.

 NOTE   The SQL Expression Editor may not accurately reflect the functions and operators available for a particular database type. In most cases, you can enter any valid options even if they are not displayed in the Function Tree or Operator Tree.

Selection Formulas   The Selection Formulas node contains two entries, one for the Record Selection formula and one for the Group Selection formula. You cannot add any additional selection formulas. Selection formulas may be created and edited with the Select Expert or created manually within the Formula Workshop. If you select the Group Selection node, the Group Selection Formula Editor will appear in the right-hand pane of the Formula Workshop. If you select the Record Selection node, the Record Selection Formula Editor will appear in the right-hand pane of the Formula Workshop. The selection editors look identical to the Formula Editor, but will enforce the creation of valid record or group selection formulas. For example, the result of a selection formula must be a Boolean.

Formatting Formulas   The Formatting Formulas folder of the Workshop Tree lists each section of the report. Under each section folder, all objects that appear in that section are listed. After selecting a report object, you can create new formatting formulas for that object. A single report object can have formatting formulas for each attribute of the object that can be formatted, such as its font or color. The formatting formulas for an object will appear as children under the object after they have been created. Formatting formulas are created and edited with the Format Formula Editor.

Formula Workshop Toolbars
The Formula Workshop has no menu, so all actions must be completed using the toolbars or other window options. There are individual toolbars in the Formula Work-

shop. By default, they are all docked at the top of the window, but they may be undocked and moved about as desired.

Save Toolbar   The Save toolbar contains two buttons, Save and Close, and Save. Clicking the Save button saves the formula. Clicking the Save and Close button saves the formula and closes the Formula Workshop.

General Toolbar   The General toolbar contains buttons that let you create new formulas, change the display of the Formula Workshop, or open the help file.

The New button lets you create a new formula. You select the type of formula that you want to create from the drop-down list.

The Hide/Show Workshop Tree button toggles the display of the Workshop Tree. The Workshop Tree is displayed to the left by default and lists all the formulas that exist in the report.

The Toggle Properties Display button switches between displaying the properties and the definition of a custom function when a custom function is selected.

The Use Expert/Editor button toggles the display between the Formula Expert and the Formula Editor for regular formula fields. The Formula Expert is discussed in Chapter 17.

Pressing the Help button opens the online help for the Formula Workshop.

Workshop Tree Toolbar   The Workshop Tree toolbar contains buttons that act on the Workshop Tree or items within it.

Use the Rename button to rename formulas, SQL Expressions, or report custom functions.

Click the Delete button to delete the selected formula, SQL Expression, or report custom function.

The Expand Node button expands the selected node or nodes of the Workshop Tree.

Click the Show Formula Formatting Nodes Only button to toggle between displaying all report objects under the Formatting Formulas node or only those objects that have an associated formatting formula.

The Add to Repository button is active if a report custom function is selected. Clicking it allows you to add the selected function to the repository.

The Add to Report button is active if a repository custom function is selected. Clicking it allows you to add the selected repository function to the report.

Expression Editor Toolbar   The Expression Editor toolbar contains buttons that act on the formula.

Click the Check button to have Crystal Reports check the formula for syntax errors.

The Undo button will undo the last change made to the formula.

The Redo button redoes the last action that was undone with the Undo button.

The Browse Data button is active when a database field is selected. Clicking it will display data values for the selected field.

Clicking the Find or Replace button displays the Find dialog box. You can use the Find dialog box to search for expressions in the Fields, Functions, and Operators windows or in the formula itself. If you elect to search the formula text, you can also replace the found items with new text.

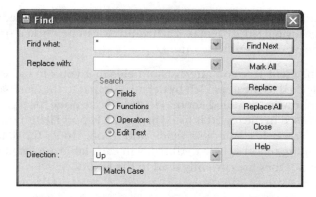

Clicking the Toggle Bookmark button inserts a bookmark at the current line of the formula. If the current line already has a bookmark, clicking this button will remove it. Setting bookmarks helps you find parts of the formula quickly.

The Next Bookmark button will move the cursor to the next bookmark in the formula.

The Previous bookmark button will move the cursor to the previous bookmark in the formula.

Click the Clear All Bookmarks button to remove all bookmarks in the formula.

The Sort Trees button causes the nodes of the Fields, Functions, and Operator Trees to sort in alphabetical order. It is a toggle; clicking it twice will return the sort order to its original state.

The Field Tree button toggles the display of the Field Tree window on and off.

The Function Tree button toggles the display of the Function Tree window on and off.

The Operator Tree button toggles the display of the Operator Tree window on and off.

Use the Syntax drop-down box to choose the syntax for the formula. The options are Crystal Syntax or Basic Syntax.

The Comment/Uncomment button inserts or removes the comment characters (//) from the start of the current formula line. If more than one line is highlighted, it acts on all highlighted lines.

Formula Workshop Trees

Three windows are available with some of the formula editors: the Field Tree, Function Tree, and Operator Tree. As the names imply, each of these windows contains a tree view of options. Clicking a node inserts code into the formula for you, speeding formula development and ensuring proper syntax. Each window can be docked or floating or can be hidden from view using toolbar buttons.

Field Tree The Field Tree contains lists of fields that you can use in your formula. This window is docked to the upper left by default. Similar to the Database Explorer, the Field Tree contains one node called Report Fields and one node for each connected data source. Each field used in the report is listed under the Report Fields node, including database fields, formula fields, summary fields, and so on. Under the data source nodes, each table used in the report is listed. All fields in each table are listed under the table name whether or not they are currently used in the report.

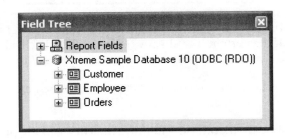

Function Tree The Function Tree contains lists of functions that you can use in the formula. This window is docked in the upper middle by default. The functions are grouped into categories to make them easier to find. *Functions* contain commonly needed computations and return a value. When a function exists that does an operation you require, you can use the function instead of writing the logic yourself.

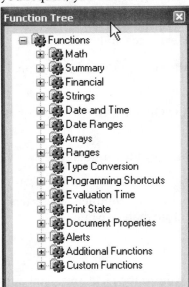

The formula text window can "auto-complete" functions and operators for you. If you type the first few letters of a function and then press CTRL-SPACEBAR, a pop-up list of functions that start with the same letters will appear in the Formula Workshop. You can select one from the list to complete the function name.

Operator Tree The Operator Tree contains a list of operators that you can use in your formula. It is docked to the upper right by default. The operators are grouped by type to make them easier to locate. Operators are similar to functions but use symbols instead of words to represent their actions. Common examples are the arithmetic operators +, –, *, and / (plus, minus, multiply, and divide), but the Formula Workshop contains many other types as well. See the "Operators" section for more information.

Options—Editors

Display of the formula text in the Formula Workshop can be customized using the Editors tab of the File | Options dialog box, as shown in Figure 8-2. You can select a font using the Font drop-down box. (Only fixed-width fonts are available for use in the editors.) You can set the font size in the Font Size drop-down box. The tab size can be set using the Tab edit box. In addition to these overall settings, you can set the foreground and background colors separately for comments, keywords, text, and selected text using the options in the Color panel.

Figure 8-2
Controlling the appearance of formula text

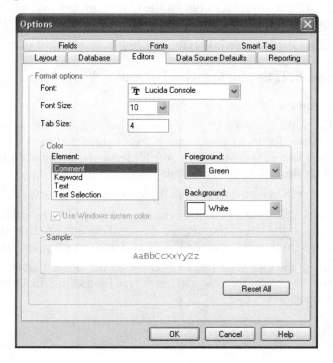

Exercise 8.1: Opening the Formula Workshop

1. Open the Exercise 7.10 report.

2. In the Fields Explorer, select the Discount formula under the Formula Fields folder. Right-click and choose Edit. The Formula Workshop will open with the Discount formula open in the Formula Editor. Close the Formula Editor.

3. Click the Formula Workshop button on the toolbar. The Formula Workshop will open with a blank right-hand pane. Open the Formula Fields node and select the Discount formula. The right-hand pane will now display the Discount formula. Close the Formula Editor.

4. Right-click the SQL Expression Fields node in the Field Explorer and select New. Type **Test** for the name, and click OK. The Formula Workshop will open with the SQL Expression Editor displayed in the right-hand pane. Close the Formula Editor.

5. Click the Select Expert button on the toolbar. In the Choose Fields dialog box, select Customer.Country, and click OK. On the Customer.Country tab of the Select Expert, set the condition to "is equal to" and the country to USA. Click the Show Formula button, and then click the Formula Editor button. The Formula Workshop will appear with the Record Selection formula node selected. Close the Formula Workshop and Cancel the Select Expert.

6. Select the Order Amount field in the Details section of the report. Right-click and choose Format Field. Select the Font tab. Click the Formula button next to the Style box. The Formula Workshop will open with the Format Formula Editor active. The Font Style format formula for the Order Amount in the Details folder will be created and selected. Close the Formula Workshop. Cancel the Format Editor.

7. Close the Exercise 7.10 report without saving the changes.

Exercise 8.2: Exploring the Formula Workshop

1. Open the Exercise 7.10 report.

2. Open the Formula Workshop using the Formula Workshop button on the toolbar. Explore the Workshop Tree. Notice that there are formulas under only two of the Workshop Tree folders—the Formula Fields folder and the Repository Custom Functions folder.

3. Select the Discount formula under the Formula Fields folder.

4. Dock the Field Tree at the bottom of the window by clicking on the double lines at the left of the tree window and dragging to the bottom of the Formula Workshop. Now drag the Field Tree back to the upper left.

5. Close the Operator Tree by clicking on the small black × in the upper left of the tree window. Open the Operator Tree by clicking the Operator Tree button in the toolbar.

6. Explore the trees by opening each node and examining the options available.

7. Close the Formula Workshop.

8. Close the Exercise 7.10 report without saving the changes.

Exercise 8.3: Customizing the Formula Editors

1. Open the Exercise 7.10 report.

2. Choose File | Options and select the Editors tab.

3. Change the font, font size, and tab if desired.

4. Select Keyword in the Element list, and change the foreground color to purple.

5. Click OK to close the Options dialog box.

6. Open the Formula Workshop, and select the Discount formula.

7. Add a second line to the formula by pressing ENTER at the end of the current line. In the Function Tree, open the Math node, and double-click the Abs function.

8. The Abs function will be added to the function, and the letters will be purple because it is a keyword.

9. Close the Formula Workshop without saving the changes.

10. Reset the Keyword color back to blue if desired.

11. Close the Exercise 7.10 report without saving changes.

Formula Fundamentals

A Crystal Reports formula does some computation and returns a value. It consists of one or more statements, and it may contain comments.

Syntax

Crystal Reports formulas are created using a language, much as you would create a program using other programming languages. Two syntaxes are available. You can use the Crystal syntax or the Basic syntax. Most requirements can be met equally well with either syntax, and neither is faster or slower than the other. If you are familiar with Visual Basic, you may prefer the Basic syntax since it is modeled on Visual Basic. Otherwise, you may find the Crystal syntax more user-friendly. The Crystal syntax is used throughout this book.

EXAM TIP   Know that there are two formula syntaxes.

To set a default formula syntax for all reports, choose File | Options, click the Reporting tab, and choose an option from the Formula Language drop-down box. To override the default syntax for an individual formula, set the syntax in the drop-down box on the Expression Editor toolbar of the Formula Workshop while that formula is the active formula. Any given formula can use only one syntax, but formulas using Basic syntax and formulas using Crystal syntax can be used together in the same report.

The syntax that you choose dictates the grammar for the formula. It determines how the components of a formula can be combined. The components of a formula can be fields, literals, variables, operators, functions, control structures, comments, and other syntax elements.

Return Value

A formula must return a value of a simple data type. The allowed types are Number, Currency, String, Boolean, Date, Time, and DateTime. The return value cannot be a complex type such as a range or array. The result of the last executed statement in the formula is the return value. If the result of the last statement in a formula is not a simple type, you will receive an error message.

Boolean Formulas and Expressions

A *Boolean formula* is a formula that returns a Boolean value (True or False). Boolean results are required for some formula types. Record Selection and Group Selection formulas must be Boolean formulas. The condition that is evaluated in Control Structures such as an If statement must be a Boolean expression; it must result in a True or False value. The implementation of formula logic usually requires the use of Boolean expressions.

Here are some examples of Boolean expressions.

```
True

{Ship Date} > {Order Date}

{Employee.Salary}*1.08 <= 50000

({Ship Date} > {Order Date}) and ({Employee.Salary}*1.08 <= 50000)
```

Statements

A Crystal Reports formula can consist of one or more *statements* that are evaluated sequentially. A statement consists of a combination of functions, operators, field references, variables, and so on that results in a value. A formula statement is like a sentence. Statements conclude with a semicolon, but the last statement in a formula does not require a semicolon. Statement components other than string literals are not case sensitive. Statements may break across lines or be indented for readability. Crystal Reports will consider a statement to include any text up to the semicolon, no matter how many lines are required.

NOTE The Crystal Reports help files use the term *expressions* instead of *statements*.

Comments

Comments can be added to a formula by using double forward slashes (//). Comments can be used to add explanatory text, instructions, warnings, or any other documentation the developer thinks is important. Any text after the double slash on a line will be considered a comment and ignored by Crystal Reports. If the double slash starts the line, the entire line is a comment. If it is in the middle of a line, all text after the double slash is a comment. Comments do not flow to the next line; each comment line must have a separate comment character.

Fields

Most field types can be used in formulas. Any database field in any connected data source can be used in a formula, whether or not it is currently used in the report. Existing formula fields can be used in a new formula unless the new formula must be evaluated before the existing formula. SQL Expression fields can be used in formulas in the same manner as database fields. Parameter fields can also be used in formulas, but you must treat the parameter type correctly. Multivalue parameters are arrays. Running total fields can be used in record-level formulas. Special fields can be used in formulas, but they are called Print State or Document Properties functions in the Formula Workshop. If you insert a Summary field into a formula, it is replaced with an equivalent summary function.

Fields inserted into formulas are shown surrounded by braces—{ and }—and prefixed with the appropriate type indicator character, as shown in Table 8-1.

Literals

Literals are actual values such as the number 3 or the string "Tomorrow" and can be used in formulas. Numeric literals are entered into the formula by simply typing the numbers, including a decimal point and negative sign if needed. Using a currency sign will cause the number to be treated as a currency field. String literals must be enclosed with single or double quotation marks. To include a single or double quote inside a string literal, type it twice. For example `'Joe''s'` would be treated as the string "Joe's." To include a single quote in a string literal, you can use double quotes for the string definition, as in `"This`

Table 8-1	Field Type	Example
Prefix Characters for Inserted Fields	Database	{*Tablename.Field Name*}
	Formula	{*@Formula Name*}
	Parameter	{*?Parameter Name*}
	SQL Expression	{*%Expression Name*}
	Running Total	{*#Running Total Name*}
	Summary Fields	*EquivalentFunctionName()*
	Special Fields	*EquivalentFunctionName*

string's an example.1" To include a double quote in a string literal, you can use single quotes for the string definition, as in 'He said, "What?"' Boolean literals are True and False or Yes and No; they do not need to be surrounded by quote marks.

Date-time literals must be preceded and followed by pound signs (#). Many different date-time formats are recognized by Crystal Reports. For example, #October 31, 1961# will be properly recognized, as will #10/31/61#. However, due to possible misinterpretation, it is recommended that you use Crystal Reports functions to create datetimes rather than relying on date-time literals.

 CAUTION   Literals created using the # symbols are date-times, not dates.

Complex types can also be used as literals. Range literals can be created using the range operators, such as To and UpFrom. For example, 4 To 10 is a range literal. Array literals are created by surrounding a comma-delimited list with square brackets. For example, [30, 40, 50] is an array literal. You can even create arrays of ranges: [10 To_ 20, 20 To_ 30, 30 To_ 40] is an array of ranges.

Operators

Operators perform an action on one or more arguments and result in a new value. Operators are similar to functions, but they usually use shorthand symbols rather than text names. For example, the addition operation is represented by the plus sign.

Some operator categories are discussed in their own sections, later in this chapter. These include variable declarations, scope, and control structures. The rest are described here.

Arithmetic Operators

The arithmetic operators act on numbers and behave as expected. The arithmetic operators are shown in Table 8-2, along with comments for the less frequently used operators. The letters x and y are used as placeholders for the operator's arguments.

Table 8-2 Arithmetic Operators	Operator	Results in
	$x+y$	Addition: the sum of x plus y
	$x-y$	Subtraction: the result of y subtracted from x
	$x*y$	Multiplication: the result of x multiplied by y
	x/y	Division: x divided by y
	$x\backslash y$	Integer division: the integer part of x divided by y (x and y are rounded to integers before the division)
	$x\%y$	Percentage: $(x/y) \times 100$
	x mod y	Modulus: the remainder of x divided by y (x and y are rounded to integers before the division)
	$-x$	Negation: $(-1) \times x$ (the negative of x)
	$x^\wedge y$	Exponentiation: x^y (x raised to the power of y)

Arithmetic operators are evaluated in the following order of precedence:

1. Exponentiation
2. Negation
3. Multiplication, division, percentage
4. Integer division
5. Modulus
6. Addition, subtraction

After any higher precedence operations are evaluated, the operations at the same level are evaluated from left to right. To override the default order of precedence, use parentheses. Operations inside parentheses are evaluated first. If parentheses are nested, they are evaluated from the inside out.

String Operators

Several common string operators are used to combine strings, extract characters from strings, and check for the existence of one string inside another.

The appending of one string to another is called *concatenation*, and it can be accomplished using the string operators + or &. The ampersand always does string concatenation, even if it is passed two numbers. It will convert all arguments to string and then concatenate. The plus sign will only work for string concatenation if all the arguments are already strings.

Crystal Reports treats strings as arrays of characters, so you can use the array subscript operator to extract characters from a string. For example, if the value of your string called *x* is "Yesterday" then x[2] is "e" and x[7 to 9] is "day." To test for the existence of a substring within a string, you can use the In string operator. To test the existence of "day" in our string *x* above, you would write 'day' In x, and the result would be True. The In operator is a Boolean operator, since it returns True or False.

Pattern Operators

The two pattern operators work only on strings and return only True or False, so they are Boolean operators. The pattern operators are commonly used in selection formulas, but they can be used wherever a Boolean can be used. The StartsWith operator checks to see if string *x* starts with string *y*. It is written as x StartsWith y. If *y* is "Y" and *x* is "Yesterday" then x StartsWith y returns True.

The Like operator is usually used with wildcard characters in the comparison value. A question mark (?) is used as a wildcard character for any single character, and the asterisk (*) is used as a wildcard for any number of characters. For example if *x* is "Yesterday" then x Like 'Y*d?y' is True.

Conversion Operators

There is one conversion operator, $, which converts a number value to a currency value. This operator does not affect formatting of the formula result; it just converts a value from the number data type to the currency data type. Currency types are stored and rounded differently than number types.

Comparison Operators

The comparison operators compare one value to another and return True if the values meet the condition and False if they do not. If either value is null, the result of the comparison will be null. The comparison operators are equal (=), not equal (<>), less than (<), less than or equal to (<=), greater than (>), and greater than or equal to (>=). Comparison operators have lower precedence than all arithmetic operators, and all comparison operators are considered to have the same precedence.

Comparison operators can be used to return Boolean values, but they are more commonly used in conditional statements such as If statements to evaluate a condition and cause branching of the statement logic.

Boolean Operators

The Boolean operators take Boolean values as arguments and return a Boolean value. Boolean operators have different precedences, but are all considered to be lower in precedence than the comparison operators, which are lower than the arithmetic operators. The Boolean operators in order of precedence are shown in Table 8-3.

Range Operators

All but one of the range operators are used to create ranges. The other is used to check whether a value is in a range. The range creation operators are described in Table 8-4.

The In range operator is a Boolean operator that returns True if the test value falls in the range and False otherwise. For example, 6 In 1 To 10 is True. The In operator can be used with all types of ranges and not just with numbers.

Table 8-3	Operator	Results in
Boolean Operators	Not x	If x is True, Not x is False. If x is False, Not x is True.
	x And y	If x and y are both True, then x And y is True. If either x or y is False, then x And y is False.
	Or	If x and y are both False, then x Or y is False. If either x or y is True, then x Or y is True.
	Xor	If x and y are both True or both False, then x Xor y is False. Otherwise, x Xor y is True.
	Eqv	If x and y are both True or both False, then x Eqv y is True. Otherwise, x Eqv y is False.
	Imp	If x and y are both True or both False, then x Imp y is True. If y is True, then x Imp y is True.

Table 8-4	Operator	Results in
Range Creation Operators	x To y	Creates a range going from x to y and including both x and y. x and y must be of the same type, but can be Number, Boolean, Currency, Date, Time, DateTime, or String.
	x _To y	Creates a range going from x to y that does not include x.
	x To_ y	Creates a range going from x to y that does not include y.
	x _To_ y	Creates a range going from x to y that does not include either x or y.
	upTo x	Creates a range that includes all values up to and including x.
	upTo_ x	Creates a range that includes all values up to but not including x.
	upFrom x	Creates a range that includes all values up from and including x.
	upFrom_ x	Creates a range that includes all values up from but not including x.

Array Operators

Array operators are used to create or resize arrays, to extract elements of the array, and to check for the existence of an element in an array. To create an array, you surround a comma-delimited list of elements with square brackets. All elements of an array must be of the same data type. For example, `[1,2,3,4,5]` and `['Red','Blue','Green']` are arrays. To extract an element from an array, you can use a *subscript*. The subscript is placed in square brackets following the array name. For example, if this preceding color array is saved in a variable called Colors, then `Colors[2]` is `'Blue'`. You can also use subscripting to return portions of an array. `Colors[1 To 2]` is equal to the array `['Red','Blue']`. The In array operator is a Boolean operator that returns True if the test value is in the array and False otherwise. `'Yellow '` In `Colors` returns False.

Functions

The Function Tree in the Formula Workshop contains all the functions that you can use in your formula. To use a function, double-click it in the tree to add it to your formula, drag it into your formula, or type its name into your formula. Some functions require arguments; others do not. If the function you are using has arguments, you must enter them in the proper order in parentheses following the function name. If you double-click or drag to add the function, the parentheses will be created for you.

You will see some functions listed more than once in the Function Tree, with different numbers of arguments. In this case, some of the arguments are optional. Choose the version of the function that best fits your situation.

Functions can be nested. Any function argument can be another function as long as it returns the appropriate type.

There are a large number of functions covering many needs. Before creating your own complex logic, check the functions list to see if what you need is already available.

Math Functions

The Math folder contains all the mathematical functions. Look here for trigonometric, logarithmic, exponential, and other math-related functions. Commonly used math functions are Round and Truncate. The constant value for pi is also available in this folder.

Summary Functions

The Summary functions compute an aggregate across a group of records or an array. The same summary operations that are available when you create Summary Fields are available in the Summary function folder. If you use a Summary Field in a formula, it will be converted to its summary function equivalent when it is displayed in the formula.

Most Summary functions have several variants. For example the Sum function has four variants, Sum(*fld*), Sum(*fld, condfld*), Sum(*fld, condfld, cond*), and Sum(*x*), where the terms inside the parentheses are the arguments of the function and will be replaced with values, fields, or variables, when the function is used. Sum(*fld*) is used to obtain the total of a report field (*fld*) across the entire report. Sum(*fld, condfld*) is used to compute the total of a report field grouped by another field. The *condfld* must be a report field that already has a group created for it. The Sum(*fld, condfld, cond*) variant is used when grouping by Date, Time, DateTime or Boolean fields to specify a nondefault grouping interval. For example, if you use a Date field as *condfld*, it will group into daylong intervals by default. If you want to group by weeks, you can use the *cond* argument to specify weekly. The options available for the *cond* argument are listed under the Summary folder, under Boolean Conditions, Date Conditions, and Time Conditions. The Sum(*x*) variant is used to obtain the total of values in a numeric array where *x* is the array.

Financial Functions

The Financial folder contains a wealth of functions that can be used to compute finance-related values. There are functions related to interest calculation, depreciation, bond valuation, and so on.

String Functions

Many of the available string functions are commonly used. You will find functions for obtaining the length of a string, for stripping out parts of a string, for changing the case of a string, for converting a string to a number, and for checking to see if a string is in another string. Several string functions act on string arrays. You can join the elements of the array to create a string or create an array by parsing a string.

Several string functions are listed in Table 8-5 along with descriptions and examples.

Function	Description	Example
Length(*string*)	Returns the length of a string	`Length('Yesterday') =` **9**
UpperCase(*string*)	Returns the string in all uppercase	`UpperCase('Yesterday')` **= "YESTERDAY"**
LowerCase(*string*)	Returns the string in all lowercase	`LowerCase('Yesterday')` **= "yesterday"**
Left(*string, n*)	Returns the left *n* characters from a string	`Left('Yesterday', 3) =` **"Yes"**
Right(*string, n*)	Returns the right *n* characters from a string	`Right('Yesterday', 3) =` **"day"**
Mid(*string, x, n*)	Returns *n* characters from the string starting at *x*	`Mid('Yesterday', 4, 3) =` **"ter"**
Trim(*string*)	Removes leading and trailing spaces from the string.	`Trim('  Yesterday  ')` **= "Yesterday"**
Replace(*string, oldchars, newchars*)	Replaces *oldchars* in string with *newchars*. Replace has additional optional parameters.	`Replace('Yesterday', 'Yester', 'To') =` **"Today"**
Instr(*string, findchars*)	Finds the first occurrence of *findchars* in *string* and returns its position in the string. Instr has additional optional parameters.	`InStr('Yesterday', 'day') =` **7**
ToText(*x, y*)	Converts a number to a string with *y* decimal points. ToText has additional optional parameters and can be used with other data types.	`ToText(234.56, 0) =` **"235"**

Table 8-5   Common String Functions

Date and Time

The Date and Time functions are essential when working with dates. There are functions that return the current date and time, convert dates and times to strings or strings to dates and times, extract the parts of a date or time, check if a number or string is a valid date, add or subtract intervals from dates or times, and so on.

Date computations are sometimes quite complex. The date functions supplied with Crystal Reports can help simplify date logic when they are used appropriately. Some commonly used Date functions and operators are listed in Table 8-6, along with explanations and an example.

Function	Description	Example
CurrentDate	Returns the current date.	
Year	Extracts the year portion of the date.	`Year(#6/30/2004#) =` **2004**
Month	Extracts the month portion of the date.	`Month(#6/30/2004#) =` **6**

Table 8-6   Common Date Functions

Function	Description	Example
Day	Extracts the day portion of the date.	`Day(#6/30/2004#)` = **30**
DateDiff	Returns the number of intervals between two dates. You choose the type of interval you want returned.	`DateDiff('yyyy', #7/15/1999#, #6/30/2004#)` = **5** In this case the number of years is returned. Note that the year difference is based solely on the year components of the two dates, so the answer is 5 even though there are less than 5 years between the two dates.
DateAdd	Returns a date-time after adding the number of intervals of the type specified.	`DateAdd('m', 8, #6/30/2004#)` = **2/28/2005** Eight months were added to 6/30/2004. Since February has only 28 days, the day of the result was set to 28. This function can also subtract intervals.
Date	Converts other data types to date.	`Date('6/30/2004')` = **the date 6/30/2004** `Date(40000)` = **7/6/2009** (this form uses the number of days since 12/30/1899) `Date(#6/30/2004#)` = **the date 6/30/2004** (rather than the date-time) `Date(2004, 6, 30)` = **the date 6/30/2004**
IsDate	Checks to see if a string or number can be converted to a date.	`IsDate('6/30/2004')` = **True** `IsDate(40000)` = **True**
DateSerial	Creates date values given year, month, and day values. Each argument is converted to a number of days, then they are added together to return a new date.	`DateSerial(2004, 6, 30)` = **6/30/2004** `DateSerial(2004, 6+8, 30)` = **3/2/2005** `DateSerial(2004, 6, 90)` = **8/29/2004**

Table 8-6   Common Date Functions *(continued)*

To obtain the difference in days between two dates, you can use the minus sign or subtraction operator.

```
CurrentDate - {Birthdate}
```

You can add or subtract a number of days from a date to obtain another date.

```
{Ship Date} + 2

{Ship Date} - 4
```

However, using the addition and subtraction operators may return unexpected results if your dates are really date-time types and include some time portion.

Date Range Functions

The Date Ranges folder contains functions that return various date ranges based on the current date. For example, the YearToDate function returns a range that starts with January 1 of the current year and goes up to today. These functions are often used with the In operator to determine if a date falls within a given range.

Array Functions
The Arrays folder contains only one unique function, UBound. The other functions listed here also appear under other folders. The array creation functions are also listed under the Array folder in the Operator Tree, and the array summary functions are listed under the Summary folder. The UBound function returns the subscript of the last element in the array.

Range Functions
The range functions are used to determine the type of range. They all return Boolean values. There are functions that determine if a range has an upper or lower bound and whether the range includes the upper or lower bound.

Type Conversion Functions
The type conversion functions are used to convert values from one data type to another.

Programming Shortcut Functions
The Programming Shortcuts folder contains three functions that can sometimes be used to replace multiple expressions in a conditional statement.

 NOTE In some cases, using the programming shortcuts functions allows Crystal Reports to convert the formula into SQL in the report query.

Evaluation Time Functions
The evaluation time functions are used to force a formula to evaluate at a particular point in the report processing.

Print State Functions
Most of the print state functions return values that concern the report itself and not the database data. For example, the PageNumber function returns the current page number. Several of the print state functions allow you to access data in the next or previous rows within your formula.

IsNull differs from the other print state functions because it can be evaluated when the database records are retrieved. (The others cannot be evaluated until the report formatting is processed.) IsNull returns True if a value is null and False otherwise. Null values in formulas can be the cause of unexpected errors. For example, $x + y$ returns null if y is null. To avoid problems, use the IsNull function to check for null values and provide alternative processing.

Document Properties Functions

The Document Properties folder contains functions that return other report values. For example, all the special fields from the Field Explorer are available for use in your formulas as functions under Document Properties.

Alerts Functions

The Alerts folder contains functions related to report alerts. The use of alerts is covered in Chapter 13.

Additional Functions

Functions available to the report from UFLs (user function libraries) are listed in the Additional Functions folder. Crystal Reports ships with several of these, and you can create your own libraries.

Variables

You can create variables to hold intermediate values during the calculation of your formula. *Variables* are containers that hold a specific type of value. The value of a variable can change during the processing of a formula. Variables must be *declared* before they are used, and they can optionally be defined with a specific *scope:* local, global, or shared.

Variable Types

Variables can be simple, single-value entities; ranges; or arrays.

Simple Variables   Simple variables of any of the usual Crystal Reports data types can be created. The variable data type for each Crystal Reports data type is listed in Table 8-7.

Range Variables   A range variable can hold a continuous sequence of values of any of the simple data types. Ranges are created using range operators.

Array Variables   An array variable can hold an ordered collection of simple data types or ranges of simple data types. Each element of the array must be the same data type. The elements of the array are numbered starting with 1 up to the upper bound of

Table 8-7	Crystal Reports Data Type	Variable Data Type
Variable Types	Boolean	BooleanVar
	Number	numberVar
	Currency	currencyVar
	Date	dateVar
	Time	timeVar
	Datetime	datetimeVar
	String	stringVar

the array. These numbers are called the *index*. Array elements are referenced using the array name followed by the index in square brackets: `ArrayName[Index]`. You can assign a list of values to the entire array by setting the array equal to an array literal. You can assign a value to a single element of an array by using an array subscript.

 NOTE Crystal Reports array variables can have a maximum of 1000 elements.

Range Array Variables   A range array variable can hold a collection of ranges of any of the simple data types.

Variable Scopes

Variables can be declared with a scope of local, global, or shared. The scope determines where the variable is available. The scope can be typed in or selected from the Operator Tree under the Scope folder.

Local   A local variable is available only in the formula in which it is declared, and it is reset each time the formula is executed. If two formulas declare local variables with the same name, they are two different variables.

Global   This is the default scope and will be assumed if no scope is declared. A global variable is available to any formula in the main report but not to subreports. If two formulas declare a global variable with the same name and data type, there is really only one variable that shares its value between the formulas.

Shared   Shared variables maintain their value across all formulas in the main report and any subreports. The shared variable must be declared and initialized in the main report before it can be used in a subreport.

Declaring Variables

Declaring a variable sets aside a storage area to hold the variable's value. It also determines its name and data type, which allows the variable to hold only values of that data type. The possible variable declarations are listed in the Operator Tree under the Variable Declarations folder, or they can be entered manually. You can assign an initial value to a variable in the declaration.

```
Scope Datatype [Range] [Array] Name [:= InitialValue] ;
```

To declare a number variable, you would type the following:

```
numberVar  VariableName;
```

VariableName has a scope of global because you did not declare a scope. To declare a number variable with local scope, use

```
Local numberVar  VariableName;
```

And to declare a Local number variable and initialize it to zero, you would use

```
Local numberVar   VariableName := 0;
```

You can then refer to the variable as needed in your formula. You can also use the assignment operator to assign values to the variable.

Variable names must be shorter than 255 characters and cannot contain spaces. Variables in the same formula must have different names. Global variables with the same name but different data types cannot be declared. Variable names cannot be the same as any Crystal Reports keyword.

Assignment

The Crystal Reports assignment operator is := (a colon and an equal sign). *Assignment* means setting the value of a variable equal to the right-hand argument. The := sign is used for assignment to differentiate it from the equal comparison operator. For example, if your statement uses the equal sign, as shown here,

```
NumberVar TestVal; //Variable declaration.
TestVal = 1000;
```

then the result will be a Boolean value of True or False, indicating whether TestVal is equal to 1000. But if your statement uses the assignment operator,

```
NumberVar TestVal; //Variable declaration.
TestVal := 1000;
```

the value of TestVal will be set to 1000.

Control Structures

Processing of a Crystal Reports formula progresses sequentially from one statement to the next. You can create branches or loops in the flow using *control structures.* (Loop control structures are discussed in Chapter 17.)

If Statements

The If statement allows you to execute different statements as the result of a Boolean expression. The syntax for the If statement is shown here:

```
If Expression Then TrueStatements [Else FalseStatements];
```

Expression must evaluate to the Boolean True or False. *TrueStatements* is one or more statements that should execute if *Expression* is True. *FalseStatements* is one or more statements that should execute if *Expression* is False. The Else part of the statement is optional. If you do not include that part and the *Expression* is False, the result of the If statement will be the default value for the result data type of the Then part.

 EXAM TIP   Understand what value an If statement will return if the condition is false but no Else part exists.

If *TrueStatements* or *FalseStatements* contains multiple statements, they must be enclosed in parentheses. If you do not use parentheses to group the series of statements, then Crystal Reports will assume that the If statement ends with the first encountered semicolon, very likely causing a syntax error to be generated.

Every Crystal Reports formula statement must result in a value, so the If statement must result in a value. The purpose of an If statement is to conditionally execute other statements—not usually to return some result itself—so this causes some confusion and may result in hard-to-understand error messages. The result of an If statement is considered to be the result of last statement executed in either the *TrueStatements* or *FalseStatements* sequences. Because of this restriction, the last statement in *TrueStatements* and last statement in *FalseStatements* must return the same data type. For example, the following statement would cause "A string is required here" error for the Else part of the statement. Because the Then part of the statement results in a string, the Else part must also result in a string.

```
NumberVar Discount:=0;
StringVar Message:='';

If ({Orders.Ship Date}-{Orders.Order Date} > 5) Then
   (Discount := .05;
    Message := 'Late shipment discount';)
Else
   (Message := 'On time';
    Discount := .03;);

{Orders.Order Amount}*Discount;
```

Reordering the assignment statements in the Else part will correct the error. However, since the result of the If statement is not used, you could also correct it by adding an arbitrary last statement to both parts.

```
NumberVar Discount:=0;
StringVar Message:='';

If ({Orders.Ship Date}-{Orders.Order Date} > 5) Then
   (Discount := .05;
    Message := 'Late shipment discount';
    True;)
Else
   (Message := 'On time';
    Discount := .03;
    False;);

{Orders.Order Amount}*Discount;
```

You can use True and False to indicate which part of the If statement was executed, as shown here, or any other statement you desire as long as it results in the same data type.

Nested If Statements

If statements can be *nested*; that is, the branches of an If statement can be other If statements. For example, the following is a nested If statement where the same condition is compared to different values:

```
NumberVar Discount:=0;
StringVar Message:='';
```

```
If ({Orders.Ship Date}-{Orders.Order Date} > 10) Then
   (Discount := .15;
    Message := 'Very Late shipment discount';)
Else If ({Orders.Ship Date}-{Orders.Order Date} > 5) Then
   (Discount := .05;
    Message := 'Late shipment discount';)
Else
   (Discount := .03;
    Message := 'On time';);

{Orders.Order Amount}*Discount;
```

Here is a nested If statement where different conditions are tested:

```
NumberVar Discount:=0;
StringVar Message:='';

If {Customer.Country} = 'USA' Then
   If ({Orders.Ship Date}-{Orders.Order Date} > 5) Then
       Discount := .05
   Else
       Discount := .03
Else
   If ({Orders.Ship Date}-{Orders.Order Date} > 10) Then
       Discount := .05
   Else
       Discount := .03

{Orders.Order Amount}*Discount;
```

Select Statements

The Select statement can be used as a shortcut for the first type of nested If statement shown in the preceding section, as shown here:

```
Select Expression
  Case CaseList1: StatementList1
  Case CaseList2: StatementList2
  Case CaseList3: StatementList3
  . . .
 [Default: DefaultList];
```

Expression is some statement to be evaluated. The *CaseLists* are one or more possible values in a comma-delimited list. The data type of *Expression* must match the data types in the *CaseLists*. The *CaseLists* can use range values if needed. The *StatementLists* are one or more statements that should be executed if *Expression* equals a value in the corresponding *CaseList*. If multiple statements need to be executed, they must be enclosed in parentheses, as in the If statement. No semicolon is required between cases. The Default case is optional. It executes if *Expression* does not equal any of the cases.

The nested If in the previous section could be converted to the following Select statement:

```
NumberVar Discount:=0;
StringVar Message:='';

Select ({Orders.Ship Date}-{Orders.Order Date})
  Case UpFrom_ 10 :  (Discount := .15;
```

```
                        Message := 'Very Late shipment discount';)
Case UpFrom_  5 :   (Discount := .05;
                        Message := 'Late shipment discount';)
Default          :   (Discount := .03;
                        Message := 'On time';);

{Orders.Order Amount}*Discount;
```

This example uses range operators in the case definitions, but single values such as 5, or simple lists such as 10, 11, 12, can also be used.

Exercise 8.4: Creating Literals

1. Open the report from Exercise 3.1.

2. Create a formula called Test by selecting the Formula Fields node in the Field Explorer and clicking the New button. Enter **Test** as the formula name, and click Use Editor.

3. In the formula window, type a string literal containing your name.

4. Close the Formula Workshop, and place the Test formula onto the report.

5. Preview the report to verify that your literal is displaying as expected. (Hint: Enclose the string in single or double quotes.)

6. Edit the Test formula to remove your name. Create a date-time literal containing your birth date. Close the Formula Workshop and verify that the Test formula now displays your birth date.

7. Edit the Test formula to remove your birth date. Create a number array containing your guess for the lottery (put six two-digit numbers in the array), and use a subscript to extract the third element. It should look similar to this: [44, 45, 20, 29, 31, 8][3]. Close the Formula Workshop and verify that the Test formula displays the third element of your array.

8. Save the report as **Exercise 8.4**.

NOTE This exercise is intended to be practice for creating literals. You would not normally create a formula that was just a literal.

Exercise 8.5: Using Operators

1. Open the Exercise 8.4 report.

2. Edit the Test formula by replacing any existing text with **5+10**. Close the Formula Workshop, and verify that the Test formula displays 15.

3. Edit the Test formula by replacing any existing text with {**Employee.First Name**} + ' ' + {**Employee.Last Name**}. You can double-click fields in the Field Tree to enter the field names. Close the Formula Workshop, and verify that the Test formula displays the full names of the employees.

4. Edit the Test formula by replacing any existing text with {**Employee.Employee ID**} + ' ' + {**Employee.Last Name**}. Check the formula by clicking the Check button on the toolbar. You will receive an error message. Change the plus signs to ampersands, and recheck the formula. Close the Formula Workshop, and verify that the Test formula displays the new result.

5. Edit the Test formula by replacing any existing text with {**Employee.First Name**} = {**Employee.Last Name**}. This creates a Boolean formula using the equal comparison operator. Close the Formula Workshop, and verify that the Test formula displays False for each employee, since no employee's first name equals his or her last name.

6. Close the report without saving, or continue on to the next exercise.

Exercise 8.6: Creating Simple Formulas

1. Open the Exercise 8.4 report, if necessary.

2. Edit the Test formula by removing any existing text.

3. The supervisor is determining raises for this year and wants everyone to get at least as much as inflation. Inflation is 3% this year. You need to create a formula that shows the minimum new salary for each employee, so enter {**Employee.Salary**} * 1.03 as the new formula text.

4. Right-click the Test formula in the Workshop Tree, and choose Rename. Rename the formula **MinSalary**.

5. Close the Formula Workshop.

6. The cap on salary increases for the year is 8%. Create a new formula called **MaxSalary** using {**Employee.Salary**} * 1.08. Close the Formula Workshop, and place MaxSalary on the report.

7. Move fields on the report to improve legibility, and save the report as **Exercise 8.6**. Close the report.

Exercise 8.7: Creating Complex Formulas

You have been requested to create a report that displays the name, birth date, and hire date of each employee. The report needs to calculate and display the age at hire and current age of each employee. Follow these steps:

1. Create a new report using the Standard wizard. Use the Employee table and place the First Name, Last Name, Birth Date, and Hire Date on the report.

2. Create a formula called **BirthYear** equal to **Year(**{**Employee.Birth Date**}**);** (you will use this formula in other formulas, but it will not be displayed on the report).

3. Create a new formula called **AgeAtHire** to compute each employee's age on their hire date.

```
Local numberVar HireYear;
Local dateVar BirthdayInHireYear;
```

```
HireYear:=Year({Employee.Hire Date});
BirthdayInHireYear:=
  Date(HireYear,Month({Employee.Birth Date}),
       Day({Employee.Birth Date}));
//If the employee had not had their birthday at hire
//Then subtract a year.
If BirthdayInHireYear < {Employee.Hire Date} Then
  HireYear-{@BirthYear}
Else
  HireYear-{@BirthYear}-1;
```

Note the use of date functions, comments, and the BirthYear formula in this formula.

4. Create a new formula called **CurrentAge**, as shown here:

```
Local numberVar CurrentYear;
Local dateVar BirthdayInCurrentYear;

CurrentYear:=Year(CurrentDate);
BirthdayInCurrentYear:=
  Date(CurrentYear,Month({Employee.Birth Date}),
       Day({Employee.Birth Date}));
//If the employee has not had their birthday this year
//Then subtract a year.
If BirthdayInCurrentYear < CurrentDate Then
  CurrentYear-{@BirthYear}
Else
  CurrentYear-{@BirthYear}-1;
```

5. Place AgeAtHire and CurrentAge on the report. Do not be concerned with formatting.

6. Your result should show the ages, as shown in Figure 8-3.

7. Save the report as **Exercise 8.7**.

Last Name	First Name	Birth Date	Hire Date	AgeAtHire	CurrentAge
Davolio	Nancy	12/8/72	3/29/91	18	31
Fuller	Andrew	2/19/69	7/12/91	22	35
Leverling	Janet	8/30/71	2/27/91	19	32
Peacock	Margaret	9/19/73	3/30/92	18	30
Buchanan	Steven	3/4/75	9/13/92	17	29
Suyama	Michael	7/2/63	9/13/92	29	40
King	Robert	5/29/72	11/29/92	20	32
Callahan	Laura	1/9/74	1/30/93	19	30
Dodsworth	Anne	1/27/76	10/12/93	17	28
Hellstern	Albert	3/13/68	3/1/93	24	36
Smith	Tim	6/6/73	1/15/93	19	31
Patterson	Caroline	9/11/79	5/15/93	13	24
Brid	Justin	10/8/77	1/1/94	16	26
Martin	Xavier	11/30/75	1/15/94	18	28
Pereira	Laurent	12/9/70	2/1/94	23	33

Figure 8-3   Exercise 8.7 result

Exercise 8.8: Sharing Variables Between Formulas

In Exercise 8.7, we created a BirthYear formula and used it in two other formulas, but we did not use it on the report. Since it was not used on the report, it could have been created as a global variable and shared between the two formulas. This exercise demonstrates sharing variables between formulas.

1. Open the Exercise 8.7 report.

2. Rename the BirthYear formula to **ComputeGlobalVars,** and edit it by modifying the formula to the following:

```
//Compute global variables for use in other formulas.

Global numberVar BirthYear;
Global numberVar BirthMonth;
Global numberVar BirthDay;

BirthYear := Year({Employee.Birth Date});
BirthMonth := Month({Employee.Birth Date});
BirthDay := Day({Employee.Birth Date});
```

3. In the Formula Workshop, select the AgeAtHire formula. Click Yes when asked if you want to save the changes to the ComputeGlobalVars formula.

4. Add declarations for the three global variables and substitute the new BirthYear variable for the old BirthYear formula. Use the BirthMonth and BirthDay variables in the formula rather than recomputing the values. In addition, since the new global variables need to be calculated before the age is calculated, insert the EvaluateAfter statement, as shown. The new formula should look like this:

```
EvaluateAfter ({@ComputeGlobalVars});

Global numberVar BirthYear;
Global numberVar BirthMonth;
Global numberVar BirthDay;
Local numberVar HireYear;
Local dateVar BirthdayInHireYear;

HireYear := Year({Employee.Hire Date});
BirthdayInHireYear := Date(HireYear,BirthMonth,BirthDay);
//If the employee had not had their birthday at hire
//Then subtract a year.
If BirthdayInHireYear < {Employee.Hire Date} Then
  HireYear-BirthYear
Else
  HireYear-BirthYear-1;
```

5. Make similar changes in the CurrentAge formula:

```
EvaluateAfter ({@ComputeGlobalVars});

Global numberVar BirthYear;
Global numberVar BirthMonth;
Global numberVar BirthDay;
Local numberVar CurrentYear;
Local dateVar BirthdayInCurrentYear;
```

```
CurrentYear := Year(CurrentDate);
BirthdayInCurrentYear := Date(CurrentYear,BirthMonth,BirthDay);
//If the employee has not had their birthday this year
//Then subtract a year.
If BirthdayInCurrentYear < CurrentDate Then
  CurrentYear-BirthYear
Else
  CurrentYear-BirthYear-1;
```

6. Close the Formula Workshop, and verify that the results have not changed.

7. Save the report as **Exercise 8.8**.

Chapter Review

This chapter introduced Crystal Report's Formula Workshop and formula-building concepts. Formulas can be used to create new fields for use in the report, to filter record selection, and to conditionally format fields. The Formula Workshop is also used to create SQL Expression fields and custom functions.

Quick Tips

- There are two formula syntaxes, Crystal and Basic.

- The Formula Workshop can be used to create and modify report custom functions, formula fields, SQL Expression fields, selection formulas, and formatting formulas. Each formula type has its own editor. Repository custom functions can be created by adding report custom functions to the repository.

- There are many ways to open the Formula Workshop: choosing Report | Formula Workshop, clicking the Formula Workshop toolbar button, selecting Edit or New in the Field Explorer for formula fields or SQL Expression fields, and using the Select Expert or Format Editor.

- Three tree views with formula options are available in the Formula Workshop. The Field Tree contains fields that may be used in the formula. The Function Tree includes Crystal Reports–supplied functions and report custom functions usable in the formula. The Operator Tree includes operators and other syntax elements that may be used in the formula.

- Crystal Reports formulas are composed of one or more statements. Each statement except the last must end with a semicolon. The statements are executed sequentially unless a branching or looping control structure is encountered.

- The result of a formula is the result of the last statement executed in the formula.

- Comments can be included in formulas using a double forward slash (//). Everything from the slashes to the end of the line is considered comment text.

- Crystal Reports formula variables have three possible scopes: local, global, and shared. Local variables are visible only to the formula that declares them. Variables of the same name declared in other formulas are different variables. Global variables are available to any formulas in the main report. If a global variable of the same name and data type is declared in more than one formula, it is the same variable. Global is the default scope. Shared variables are available to all formulas in the report, including any subreports.

- Variables must be declared before they are used. Variables may be declared with a scope. If no scope is given, global is assumed. Variables may be initialized at the same time they are declared. Declarations of array variables must include the keyword array.

- Assignment is done in formula statements using the assignment operator, := (the equal sign by itself is used as a comparison operator).

- Operators are evaluated in statements in the order of their precedence.

- Strings can be concatenated using the plus sign (+) or the ampersand (&). If you use the plus sign, you must ensure that all the arguments are strings. If you use the ampersand, Crystal Reports will convert every argument to string automatically.

- A specific element of an array, or a specific character of a string, can be accessed using subscript notation in Crystal Reports formulas. For example, `Colors[2]` will result in the element stored in the second position of the Colors array.

- A Boolean formula is one that results in a Boolean value. Record and Group Selection formulas are Boolean formulas.

- The Boolean operators AND, OR, and NOT are used to combine two Boolean expressions and the result is a Boolean.

- Variables can be used in formulas. The syntax of variable declaration is

  ```
  Scope Datatype [Range] [Array] Name [:= InitialValue] ;
  ```

- Variables can be any of the simple Crystal Reports data types, ranges, arrays, or range arrays.

- If and Select statements are used to execute different sets of statements depending on the evaluation of a condition. They are conditional statements.

Questions

Questions may have more than one correct answer. Choose all answers that apply.

1. Which of the following are syntaxes available in the Crystal Reports Formula Workshop?

   a. C

   b. Crystal

   c. Basic

   d. Visual Basic

   e. Java

2. The Formula Workshop cannot be used to create record selection formulas. Though viewable and editable in the Formula Workshop, they must be created with the Select Expert.

   a. True

   b. False

3. Which of the following show the proper use of comments?

   a. `//Declare and initialize variables`

   b. `/*Declare and initialize variables*/`

   c. `i:=i+1; //Increase counter variable`

   d. `i:=i+1; Increase counter variable`

   e. `i:=i+1; /*Increase counter variable*/`

4. Formula fields, Record Selection formulas, and SQL Expression fields are all edited using the Formula Editor.

   a. True

   b. False

5. Which of the following would not be found in the Function Tree?

   a. Round

   b. Maximum

   c. +

   d. UpperCase

   e. CurrentDate

6. Which scope will be assumed if no scope is declared for a variable?

   a. Local

   b. Global

   c. Shared

7. Which statement will result in an error?

   a. `'Grand Total ' & Sum ({Orders.Order Amount});`

   b. `'Grand Total ' + Sum ({Orders.Order Amount});`

   c. `'Grand Total ' + ToText(Sum ({Orders.Order Amount}), 2);`

8. Which of the following is not a valid variable declaration?

   a. `booleanVar Found;`

   b. `Local numberVar Counter := 0;`

    c. `dateTimeVar range InSession := #1/1/2004# to #6/30/2004#;`

    d. `dateVar range InSession := #1/1/2004# to #6/30/2004#;`

    e. `stringVar range array ValidProducts := ['SA111' to 'SA999','PA111' to 'PA999'];`

9. In an array called Colors, equal to `['Red', 'Blue', 'Green', 'Yellow']`, `Colors[2]`, will equal which of the following?

    a. "Red"

    b. "Blue"

    c. "Green"

    d. "Yellow"

    e. Error

10. Which of the following are valid array declarations?

    a. `stringVar array ValidProducts := ['SA111' to 'SA999','PA111' to 'PA999'];`

    b. `stringVar ValidProducts := ['SA111' to 'SA999','PA111' to 'PA999'];`

    c. `stringVar ValidProducts := ['SA111','SA999','PA111','PA999'];`

    d. `stringVar array ValidProducts := ['SA111','SA999','PA111','PA999'];`

    e. `stringVar array ValidProducts := ['SA111','SA999','PA111','PA999'][2];`

11. Which of the following items require a Boolean formula or expression?

    a. Record Selection formulas

    b. The condition in an If statement

    c. Group Selection formulas

    d. The condition in a Do While statement

    e. The counter variable in a For loop

12. Given that A=5, B=4, C=10, and D=0, which of the following is True?

    a. B>A

    b. (B>A) AND (C>D)

    c. (B>A) OR (C>D)

    d. (B>A) OR NOT (C>D)

    e. NOT (C>D)

13. Which of the following components can be used in formulas?

    a. Database fields

    b. Formula fields

    c. Functions

    d. Operators

    e. Literals

14. What is the result of this formula

    ```
    Discount = {Order.Amount}*.10;
    ```

    if `Discount` was 15 before this statement executes and `{Order.Amount}` is $200.00?

    a. 20

    b. True

    c. False

    d. 35

    e. An error

15. Subtracting one date from another date results in (select the best answer)

    a. A date

    b. A number

    c. An error

    d. A number of days

    e. A number of intervals

16. `If {Country} = 'USA' Then {Amount}*.10 Else {Amount}*.15` is what kind of statement?

    a. Boolean

    b. Conditional

    c. Comment

    d. Looping

    e. Arithmetic

17. Which of the following statements would extract "day" from "Yesterday"?

    a. `Right('Yesterday', 3)`

    b. `Mid('Yesterday', 7, 3)`

    c. `Left('Yesterday', 3)`

    d. `'Yesterday'[7 to 10]`

    e. `InStr('Yesterday', 'day')`

18. Length('CRCP')-5 returns what value?

    a. Error

    b. 4

    c. 1

    d. −1

19. Which function would you use to obtain the difference in weeks between two dates?

    a. − (Subtraction operator)

    b. DateAdd

    c. DateSerial

    d. Week

    e. DateDiff

20. What is wrong with this formula?

```
Select {Orders.PO#}[1 to 2]
  Case UpTo_ 30 : 'Autoprocess'
  Case UpTo_ 60 : 'Process manually'
       Default : 'Bad PO#'
```

    a. You cannot use a range as a subscript.

    b. There is no ending semicolon.

    c. Null PO# is not trapped and will cause errors.

    d. {Orders.PO#}[1 to 2] is a string, but the case conditions are numbers.

    e. The range operator UpTo_ cannot be used in a case list.

21. What is the result of this formula

```
{Order.Amount}-{@Discount}*{Quantity}+20/100
```

if {Order.Amount} is 200, {Quantity} is 3, and {@Discount} is 5?

    a. 6.05

    b. 185.20

    c. 624.00

    d. 184.80

22. This is a valid statement.

```
Replace(Replace ({Customer.Customer Name}, 'Mrs.', 'Ms.')
                , 'Jr.', 'Junior')
```

    a. True

    b. False

23. Your report contains a group on Country, and you have created a summary field for the total order amount by country. You create a formula and insert the group summary field into your report. How will the summary field be shown in the formula text?

   a. `{Sum of Orders.Order Amount}`

   b. `Sum ({Orders.Order Amount}, {Customer.Country})`

   c. `{Customer.Country - Sum of Orders.Order Amount}`

Answers

1. **b, c.** Crystal and Basic are the syntaxes available in the Crystal Formula Workshop.

2. **b.** False. Selection formulas can be created in the Formula Workshop as well as with the Select Expert.

3. **a, c.** // is the comment character.

4. **b.** False. Formula fields use the Formula Editor, SQL Expression fields use the SQL Expression Editor, and Record Selection formulas use the Record Selection Formula Editor.

5. **c.** The plus sign is an operator, not a function, and would be found in the Operator Tree.

6. **b.** Global scope is the default; it means that the variable is available to all formulas in the main report but not to the subreports.

7. **b.** When using the plus sign for string concatenation, you must ensure that all the arguments are strings.

8. **d.** When using the pound sign (#) to create literals, the result is always considered a date-time, not a date.

9. **b.** Crystal Reports arrays are 1-based, so `Colors[2]` is "Blue."

10. **d, e.** Answer a is a range array, but it is missing the keyword range. Answers b and c are missing the keyword array. Answer d is correct, as is Answer e, although it results in an array of only one item.

11. **a, b, c, d.** The counter variable in a For loop must be numeric.

12. **c.** Answer a is 4>5, which is False. Answer b is (4>5) AND (10>0), or False AND True, which is False. Answer c is (4>5) OR (10>0), or False OR True, which is True. Answer d is (4>5) OR NOT (10>0), or False OR NOT (True), or False OR False, which is False. Answer e is NOT (C>D), OR NOT (10>0), OR NOT (True), which is False.

13. **All.** All the listed components can be used in formulas.

14. **c.** Discount is being compared to `{Order.Amount}*.10`, not set to `{Order.Amount}*.10`.

15. **d.** Subtracting one date from another results in a number of days.

16. **b.** The statement is a conditional statement. It contains a Boolean expression but does not result in a Boolean value.

17. **a, b, d.** Any of these three would extract "day" from "Yesterday."

18. **d.** `Length('CRCP')-5` is `-1`.

19. **e.** DateDiff is used to obtain the difference between two dates for many different interval types.

20. **d.** The result data type of the Select expression must match the data type of items in the Case lists.

21. **b.** The expression should be evaluated as `{Order.Amount}-({@Discount}*{Quantity})+(20/100)`, since multiplication and division have higher precedence than addition and subtraction, so $200 - (5 \times 3) + (20/100) = 200 - 15 + 0.2 = 185.20$.

22. **a.** True. The functions are properly nested.

23. **b.** The summary field will be converted to use the summary function.

Formatting

Exam RDCR200 expects you to be able to

- Format objects
- Add hyperlinks to a report
- Format sections
- Create a summary report
- Use sections
- Use group-related functions to format sections
- Use Section Underlay
- Use multiple-column reporting
- Apply a Crystal Reports template
- Build a template without a data source
- Remove templates
- Format data conditionally
- Format individual elements of a text object
- Apply specialized formatting

Crystal Reports lets you make a report look exactly the way you want by formatting many different elements. You can customize the display of the fields that you place on the report. You can create and format report sections or apply formatting conditionally based on a formula. You can add lines, boxes, and graphic elements to your report. Finally, by creating a template you can save a report format and apply it to another report.

Formatting Field Objects

You can format the display of any field that you can place on a report, including database fields, formula fields, SQL Expression fields, group name fields, summary fields, special fields, running total fields, and parameter fields. There are several methods that you can use to format fields, and many attributes of fields that can be modified.

NOTE The term *object* is often used instead of *field* when discussing formatting. These terms are interchangeable for most report items, but *object* better conveys the fact that Crystal Report fields include many attributes not usually associated with the font used to display them and whether they have borders. These formatting attributes are part of the Crystal Report object just as the actual value of the field is.

Methods

To format an object, you can use the Format toolbar, the Format Editor, or the Format Painter. Select an object or multiple objects, and then invoke the method you want to use.

Formatting Toolbar

The Formatting toolbar contains buttons for many commonly used formatting commands, as shown here.

Select one or more objects and then click the button, or choose an option from a drop-down box to apply the format.

 Use the Font Face drop-down box to select a new font for the selection.

 Use the Font Size drop-down box to pick from a list of commonly used font sizes.

 Click the Increase Font Size button to increase the font size of the selection one point. Each subsequent click increases the font size by another point.

 Click the Decrease Font Size button to decrease the font size of the selection one point. Each subsequent click decreases the font size by another point.

 The Bold button toggles the bold attribute on and off. Click once to set the font to bold; click again to turn bold off.

 The Italics button toggles the italic attribute on and off.

 The Underline button toggles the underline attribute on and off.

 Click the Align Left button to align the contents of the selected object to the left margin.

 Click the Align Center button to center the contents of the selected object between its right and left margins.

Click the Align Right button to align the contents of the selected object to the right margin.

Click the Justify button to align the contents of the selected object with both its right and left margins.

Click the Font Color button to apply the color displayed to the selection. To change the selected color, click the down arrow on the button and pick a new color.

Click the Outside Borders button to apply the displayed outside borders to the selected object. To change the borders, click the down arrow, and choose another border option from the choices shown.

Click the Suppress button to toggle suppression of an object on and off.

Click the Lock Format button to lock or unlock the selected object's formatting, depending on its current state (this button is a toggle). If the formatting is locked, it must be unlocked before any formatting changes are allowed. Locking the format helps to avoid accidental changes.

Click the Lock Size/Position button to lock or unlock the selected object's size and position (this button is also a toggle). If an object's size and position are locked, it cannot be moved or resized.

Click the Currency button to toggle the display of a currency sign on and off. This button is available only for numeric fields.

Click the Thousands button to toggle the display of a thousands separator on and off (for numeric fields).

Click the Percent button to toggle the display of a percent sign on and off (for numeric fields).

Click the Increase Decimals button once to add one decimal place to the display of a number. Click again to add another decimal place, and so on.

Click the Decrease Decimals button once to remove one decimal place from the display of a number. Click again to remove another decimal place, and so on.

Format Editor

The Format Editor is a tabbed dialog box that allows you to set the format options available for the selected object. To invoke the Format Editor, select one or more objects, and then choose Format | Format Field from the main menu or Format Field from the right-click menu, or click the Format button on the Expert Tools toolbar. Alternatively, you can select the object in the Report Explorer, right-click, and choose Format Field.

The various options you can apply are described in the "Format Editor Options" section.

Format Painter

The Format Painter is used to copy formatting from one object and apply it to one or more other objects. If you have several objects that require the same formatting, use the Format Painter to quickly copy the format from the first object and apply it to the other objects:

1. Format one object as required.

2. Select the formatted object.

3. Invoke the Format Painter by clicking the Format Painter button on the Standard toolbar, choosing Format | Format Painter from the main menu, or right-clicking and choosing Format Painter.

4. The mouse cursor will become a paintbrush when it is placed over an object that can accept the format.

5. Click the unformatted object to apply the new formatting.

To apply the formatting to multiple objects, hold down the ALT key when clicking the target object(s).

The Format Painter will copy all format options between objects of the same type. If you copy the formatting from one object to an object of a different type, only the common options will be copied. Here are some examples of the restrictions:

- The Format Painter does not copy hyperlink properties. (See "Hyperlink Tab," later in the chapter.)

- You can copy formats from repository objects to report objects, but not from report objects to repository objects.

- The Format Painter cannot copy formats created with the Highlighting Expert. (The Highlighting Expert is covered in the "Conditional Formatting" section.)

- Formatting cannot be copied from text objects or template objects to database fields.

 EXAM TIP Understand the process required to use the Format Painter.

Format Editor Options

After invoking the Format Editor using one of the methods described in the previous section, you can use the options on the various tabs to modify the display of selected objects. Some of the tabs are displayed for every data type, and some are type-specific. Many formatting options have the Formula button next to them. Options with the Formula button can be formatted conditionally using a formula.

Each of the tabs includes a Sample area at the bottom that shows an example of how the formatting will look when it's applied to the selected object.

EXAM TIP Be familiar with the location of the various formatting options in the Format Editor.

PART II

Common Tab

This tab, shown in Figure 9-1, is available for all data types. It is used to set some of the formatting options that are identical across all object types and data types.

Object Name   Crystal Reports assigns a default name to each object that you place on the report. The name for a database field will be the field name with embedded blanks removed and a number appended, 1 for the first time the field is placed on the report, 2 for the second time the field is placed on the report, and so on. The object name is displayed in the Report Explorer and is used when adding items to the repository or creating report parts. You can change the Object Name if desired.

CSS Class Name   CSS stands for cascading style sheets. If you want to format a field to use a particular CSS class when it is displayed online, enter the class name in this field. This field can be set conditionally using a format formula.

Read-only   Checking the Read-only check box is equivalent to clicking the Lock Format button on the toolbar. If you set the field to read-only, you cannot modify its formatting. If a field is read-only and you need to make changes to it, clear the Read-only check box. Use this setting to protect fields from accidental changes.

Lock Position and Size   Checking the Lock Position and Size check box is equivalent to clicking the Lock Size/Position button on the toolbar. If you lock an object's position and size, it cannot be moved or resized until you unlock it.

Figure 9-1
Setting common
format options

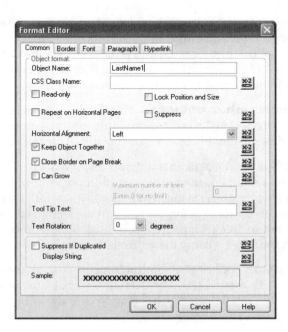

Repeat on Horizontal Pages   This option is applicable to reports containing cross-tabs or OLAP grids. If the grid is too large to fit across a page, the report will expand horizontally to as many pages as needed. If you want an object to appear on every horizontal page, check this box. Common objects that you might want to repeat are the contents of the Page Header or Footer section.

Suppress   To make an object invisible in the Preview window, exports, and printouts, check the Suppress box. This option is often used with a formula to suppress a field conditionally, depending on the result of a formula. The object will still be visible in the Design window.

Horizontal Alignment   The Horizontal Alignment drop-down box is equivalent to the Align Left, Align Center, Align Right, and Justify buttons on the toolbar. Select the alignment you want. If you choose the Default value, the field will be aligned to the left for text fields and to the right for number fields.

Keep Object Together   This option is used when an object is breaking across a page and you do not want it to. If Keep Object Together is selected and an object will not fit on the current page, it will be moved to the next page. If the object is bigger than one page, it will break across a page anyway. This option is commonly set for graphics objects or memo fields.

Close Border on Page Break   If you place a border around an object and the object breaks across a page, the part at the bottom of the first page will have no bottom border and the part at the top of the next page will have no top border. If you want both pieces of the object to have a complete border, check Close Border on Page Break.

Can Grow   When you place an object on a report, you set the size of the field by expanding or reducing the size of the frame. The contents of the field will be displayed inside the frame. If the contents cannot be completely displayed in the frame, they will be truncated. To allow the field to expand vertically, check the Can Grow option. Can Grow is often used with large text fields to allow each record to expand as needed. Can Grow allows the field height to differ from record to record.

Maximum Number of Lines   This is used in conjunction with the Can Grow option. If you check Can Grow, you can limit the amount of expansion to the specified number of lines using this option. The default, 0 (zero), means there is no limit.

Tool-Tip Text   A *tool tip* is text that is displayed when you place the cursor over an object on the screen. It is used to supply additional information to the user. The default tool tip for a report object is the field name. If you want to display some other text as the tool tip, use this option. Tool tips display on the Design tab and Preview tab and will appear in the report viewers if the report is displayed that way. The tool tip text can be created with a formula by using the Formula button.

Text Rotation   Choose an option from the Text Rotation drop-down box to format your object with rotated text. The default, 0 (zero), and means no rotation. The other options are 90 or 270 degrees. Choosing 90 degrees will cause the text to run vertically from the bottom to the top of the field frame as if it had been turned 90 degrees to the right. Choosing 270 degrees has the opposite effect: the text will run from the top to the bottom as if it had been turned 90 degrees to the left.

Suppress If Duplicated   If sequential records contain the same value in a field, you can check the Suppress If Duplicated box to suppress the second and subsequent displays of the value.

Suppress Embedded Field Blank Lines   Suppress Embedded Field Blank Lines appears only when you are formatting text object fields. Check it to suppress any blank lines caused by blank fields embedded in the text object.

Display String   The Display String option allows you to customize the display of a field. To use the Display String option, you must create a formula that results in the string you want displayed. For example, if you want to insert a hyphen after the first letter of the employee's last name, you could use the following formula:

```
CurrentFieldValue[1]
   &'-'&CurrentFieldValue[2 to Length(CurrentFieldValue)]
```

The CurrentFieldValue function is a formatting function that returns the value of the field that is being formatted.

Border Tab
This tab, shown in Figure 9-2, is available for all data types. Use this tab to create a line around an object or add a drop shadow.

Figure 9-2
Creating object
borders

Line Style   The Line Style panel contains a drop-down box for each side of an object: top, bottom, left, and right. For each side, you can choose to have no line, a single line, a double line, a dashed line, or a dotted line.

Tight Horizontal   The border lines are usually drawn at the field's frame edges. If you want the border to change depending on the width of the field, check the Tight Horizontal box.

Drop Shadow   To create a drop shadow for a field, check the Drop Shadow box. You can create a drop shadow even if the object has no border lines.

Color   The Color panel has two options, one for the border and drop shadow color and one for the background color. The background color is not activated by default; to activate it, check the Background box. Choose a color from the drop-down boxes to apply it to the border or background.

Font Tab

This tab, shown in Figure 9-3, appears for all field types except graphics or OLE objects. Use the options on the Font tab to select a font, font style, font size, font color, apply underlining or strikeout, and change the character spacing.

Font   Select a typeface from the Font drop-down box to apply it to the selected object(s).

Figure 9-3
Selecting font
attributes

PART II

Style   The Style drop-down box allows you to select from the styles available for the selected font. Commonly available are Regular, Bold, Italic, and Bold Italic, although the list may differ for different fonts.

Size   Select a font size from the drop-down list or enter your own size number. You can enter fractional font sizes, but Crystal Reports will round to the nearest half point.

Color   Use the Color drop-down box to select a color for the display text of the field. If you want a color that is not shown, click More and the Color dialog box will be displayed. You can create and save custom colors in the Color dialog box.

Strikeout   Checking the Strikeout box causes the display text of the object to be shown with a line through it.

Underline   Checking the Underline box causes all characters in the display text of the object to be underlined.

Character Spacing Exactly   The Character Spacing Exactly option sets the character spacing to the number of points that you enter. The default, 0 (zero), leaves the character spacing at its normal value for the chosen font. Most fonts use variable character spacing, taking up more space for wide characters like *w*, and less space for thin characters like *i*. Setting this option results in each character taking up the same amount of space, giving you a *monospace* font. This may be useful for creating a report that prints on forms. Setting it to less than the font's point size will result in overlapping characters. Setting it to more than the font's point size will result in extra space between characters.

Hyperlink Tab

This tab, shown in Figure 9-4, appears for all object types. It allows you create hyperlinks attached to the object. When the mouse is passed over an object with a hyperlink, the cursor turns into a pointing hand, and the user can click it to go use the hyperlink. Hyperlinks can be static or can change dynamically based on a formula or field value.

Hyperlink Type   Several different types of hyperlinks can be created, depending on the type of the selected object:

- **No Hyperlink**   This is the default value.
- **A Website on the Internet**   Linking to a web site will cause a browser window to open at the URL given in the Hyperlink Information section. The URL can be a relative address.
- **Current Website Field Value**   If the selected object is a text field containing a web site address, you can use this option to create a link to that address.
- **An E-Mail Address**   Use this option to create a mail-to link to an e-mail address.
- **A File**   The File option links to a file on any accessible computer. The file will be opened or executed as if the link information were entered at the Windows | Start | Run command.

Figure 9-4
Creating
hyperlinks

- **Current E-Mail Field Value**   If the selected object is a text field containing a valid e-mail address, you can use this option to create a mail-to link to the address contained in the field object.

- **Report Part Drilldown**   The Report Part Drilldown option is used to emulate Crystal Reports' drill-down functionality using the Report Part Viewer. The hyperlink must be created for a group-level field and the target must be in a lower-level group.

- **Another Report Object**   You can create a link to another report object in the current report or another report if it is managed by Crystal Enterprise.

Hyperlink Information   The information required for the hyperlink changes depends on the Hyperlink Type:

- **No Hyperlink**   No information is required.

- **A Website on the Internet**   A URL is required. You can enter it or create it using the Formula button.

- **Current Website Field Value**   No information is required.

- **An E-Mail Address**   An e-mail address is required. You can enter one or create one using the Formula button.

- **A File**   A filename and path are required. You can enter it, use the Browse button to locate it, or create it with the Formula button. You can also use relative addressing to indicate the path to the file.

- **Current E-Mail Field Value**   No information is required.

- **Report Part Drilldown**   Information about what report object to display is required.

- **Another Report Object**   Information about what report object to display is required.

Helpful Hint   This section displays tips about creating the type of hyperlink chosen in the Hyperlink Type section.

Number Tab

The Number tab of the Format Editor is displayed for number or currency fields only. It is used to set format options that are unique to numbers, as shown in Figure 9-5.

Style   The Style list box of the Number tab contains predefined styles that you can apply to the selected object. The System Default Number Format option applies the number setting from the Regional Options of the Windows Regional and Language Options in the Control Panel. The other options format the number as displayed in the list. The

Figure 9-5

Setting number formats

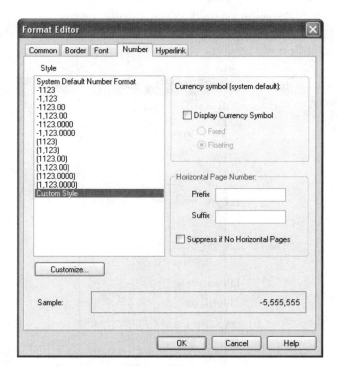

list of predefined styles is different for number fields and currency fields. The choices for currency fields all include the currency symbol. The Custom Style list item is highlighted if the object has been given a customized format.

Currency Symbol   Check the Display Currency Symbol check box to have a currency symbol displayed with the selected field. Choose Fixed to have the currency symbol appear in the same location no matter what the width of the field is. Choose Floating to have the currency symbol position vary with the size of the field.

Horizontal Page Number   The Horizontal Page Number panel is displayed only if the object being formatted is the special field Horizontal Page Number. You can place characters in the Prefix or Suffix text boxes to have them prefixed or appended to the horizontal page number. Check the Suppress If No Horizontal Pages check box to suppress the display of the horizontal page number if the report does not spread across more than one page horizontally.

Customize   Click the Customize button if none of the available styles meets your needs. The Custom Style dialog box will be displayed. It contains two tabs, described in the following sections.

Custom Currency Symbol Tab   The Currency Symbol tab contains options for customizing the display of the currency symbol, as shown in Figure 9-6:

- **Enable Currency Symbol**   Check the Enable Currency Symbol box to display a currency symbol with the selected field.

- **Fixed**   Choose Fixed to display the currency symbol in the same position regardless of the width of the field.

Figure 9-6
Customizing
currency symbol
display

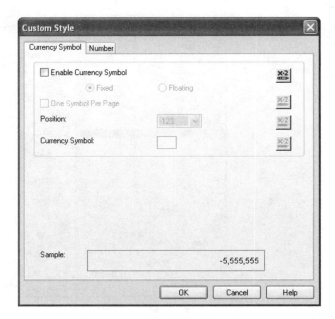

- **Floating**   Choose Floating to display the currency symbol with no space between it and the number. The location of the symbol will change depending on the width of the field.

- **One Symbol per Page**   Check the One Symbol per Page box to cause the currency symbol to be displayed only with the first occurrence of the selected field on each page.

- **Position**   Choose the position where you want the currency symbol displayed. It can be displayed before or after the number, but the specific options depend on the choice selected for displaying negative numbers.

- **Currency Symbol**   Type in the symbol that you want to use for currency.

 NOTE   The Currency Symbol options are often used to display percent signs.

Custom Number Tab   The Number tab of the Custom Style dialog box is used to control configurable elements for numbers other than the currency symbol. The Number tab is shown in Figure 9-7.

- **Use Accounting Format**   Check the Use Accounting Format box if you want to use the predefined accounting format. The accounting format will use the negative indicator defined in the Windows Regional Options, display a fixed currency symbol, and show zero values as dashes.

Figure 9-7
Formatting
numbers

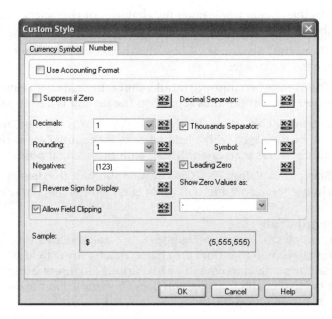

PART II

- **Suppress If Zero**   Check the Suppress If Zero box if you want nothing to print if the field value is zero.

- **Decimals**   Choose an option from the drop-down box to set the number of decimal places that you want displayed for the field. You can chose from 1 to 10 decimal places.

- **Rounding**   Choose an option from the drop-down box to set the place to which the field will be rounded. You can round to any place from 0.0000000001 to 1,000,000.

NOTE   You will usually want Decimals and the Rounding to be set to the same number of decimal places.

- **Negatives**   Select an option from the drop-down box to configure the display of negative numbers. You can use a minus sign at the front or back of the number, enclose negatives in parentheses, or even display no indicator so that negative numbers are indistinguishable from positive numbers.

- **Reverse Sign for Display**   Check the Reverse Sign for Display box if you want negatives to appear as positives and positives to appear as negatives.

- **Allow Field Clipping**   When Allow Field Clipping is checked, numeric fields that are too wide to fit in their frames are truncated. When Allow Field Clipping is turned off (the default), numbers that are too large are displayed as a string of pound signs to indicate that the full value cannot be shown.

- **Decimal Separator**   Enter the character or characters that you want to use as the decimal separator. The default is a decimal point.

- **Thousands Separator**   Check the Thousands Separator box to enable a thousands separator character.

- **Thousands Separator Symbol**   Enter the character or characters that you want to use as the thousands separator. The default is a comma.

- **Leading Zero**   When the Leading Zero box is checked, numbers less than one will be displayed with a leading zero. If Leading Zero is cleared, the display for numbers less than one will start with the decimal point.

- **Show Zero Values As**   Choose an option for the display of zeros. You can choose the zero value, a dash, or enter a different character.

Paragraph Tab

The Paragraph tab, shown in Figure 9-8, is displayed for string fields and memo fields. The Font tab is used to format the characters of a string field. The Paragraph tab is used to format the paragraphs contained in a string field. Every string field is assumed to have at least one paragraph. A paragraph break is assumed at the end of the field and at any return character within the field.

Figure 9-8
Formatting
paragraphs

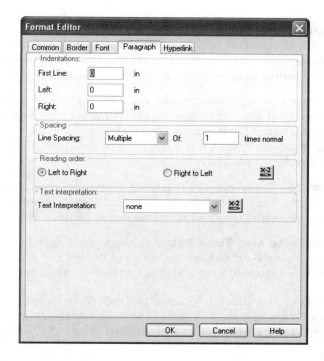

Indentations   Use the options in the Indentations panel to set an indentation for the first line of a paragraph and for the right and left margins. The indentations are entered in inches and are relative to the frame of the object. For example, if you set the Left indentation to .25, all the lines in the field will be indented a quarter-inch from the left side of the field.

Spacing   The Spacing options are used to set the amount of space between lines in a paragraph. Use the Line Spacing drop-down box to choose whether the spacing should be in multiples of the normal spacing for the current font or in exact points. If you choose Multiple, then enter the multiplier in the Times Normal box. For example, if you set the multiplier to 2, the paragraph will be double-spaced. If you choose Exact, then enter the number of points that you want each line to take up in the Pts box. If you enter a point size that is less than the font size, the characters will be truncated at the top. A minimum blank space between lines will be maintained.

Reading Order   You can set the Reading Order to Right to Left or Left to Right. Left to Right would be used for languages that are normally read from left to right.

Text Interpretation   The Text Interpretation options can be used to tell Crystal Reports that a string field contains formatting information. The formats that Crystal Reports can recognize and display correctly are plain text, rich text format (RTF), and HTML. There are limits to the HTML tags that Crystal Reports can understand. The default is None for plain text. Select one of the other two if your field contains that type of formatting information.

Date and Time Tab

When you open the Format Editor for Date and Time fields, the Date and Time tab will be visible, as shown in Figure 9-9. It works much like the Number tab—you can choose a predefined format or create your own with the Customize button.

Style From the Style box, you can select a predefined style. Only styles applicable to the selected field type are displayed. The Windows-level System Default Long Format and System Default Short Format can be chosen if you want to use the default format configured on your system. If you create a new style using the Customize button, it will be added to the list as Custom Style.

Customize If none of the predefined styles is appropriate, you can define your own style using the Customize button. Click the Customize button to display the Custom Style dialog box for Dates and Times, shown in Figure 9-10.

Custom Date and Time Tab The Date and Time tab is used to set options applicable to both the Date and Time portions of the field.

The following options are available on the Date and Time tab.

- **Order** The Order drop-down box contains the options for the display order of the Date and Time portions of the field. You can choose Date Then Time, Time Then Date, Only Date, or Only Time.

Figure 9-9
Formatting dates and times

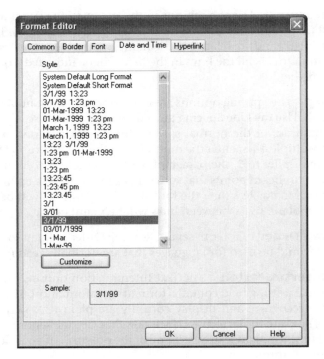

Figure 9-10
Creating custom
date and time
formats

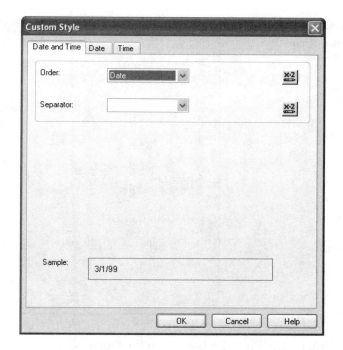

- **Separator** In the Separator drop-down box, you can select a character to use to separate the Date and Time portions of the field, or you can enter your own character(s).

Custom Date Tab The Date tab, shown in Figure 9-11, is used to format the date portion of the field:

- **Date Type** The date type will usually be Custom since you are customizing a format. You could select the Windows Default Short or Windows Default Long options to set the properties to match those formats, but those options are already available as predefined styles.

- **Calendar Type** If your operating system supports multiple calendar types, they will be listed in the Calendar Type drop-down box. Choose the type you want to use.

- **Format** Use the drop-down boxes in the Format panel to set the format for the month, day, year, and era parts of the date. For month, you can choose two fixed digits, variable digits (one or two depending on the month number), the month name, the three-character month abbreviation, or None. For Day, you can choose two fixed digits, variable digits (one or two depending on the day number), or None. For Year, you can choose two digits, four digits, or None. Your choices for Era are Short, Long, and None. Some calendar types use eras, the common Gregorian calendar does not.

Figure 9-11
Creating custom
date formats

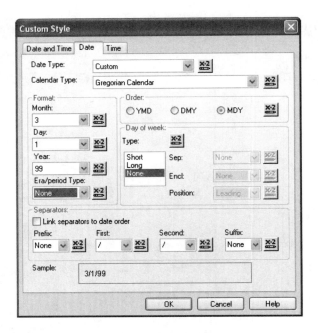

- **Order**   Use the radio buttons in the Order panel to select the order in which you want the date elements listed. You can choose MDY for month, day, year; DMY for day, month, year; or YMD for year, month, day.

- **Day of Week**   The options in the Day of Week panel are used to add and configure a day-of-the-week string to the date format. The Type can be Short, Long, or None; None is the default. Short displays a three-character abbreviation for the day. Long displays the entire day name. In the Sep box, pick from one of the available separator options, or enter your own. The separator character(s) entered will be used to separate the day of the week from the rest of the date. The Encl drop-down box has options for enclosing the day of the week in parentheses or brackets. Choose Leading or Trailing from the Position drop-down box to place the day of the week before or after the date, respectively.

- **Separators**   Use the options in the Separators panel to configure the characters used to separate the month, day, and year date elements and add a prefix or suffix to the date. For each separator, you can choose an existing option from the drop-down box or type in your own. If you check the Link Separators to Date Order box, the separators you enter will be considered part of the date when it is sorted.

Custom Time Tab   The Time tab of the Custom Style dialog box, shown in Figure 9-12, is used to format the time portion of the selected field.

- **Use System Default Format**   Check the Use System Default Format box to set the Time options to match the default time format defined in Windows.

Figure 9-12
Creating custom
time formats

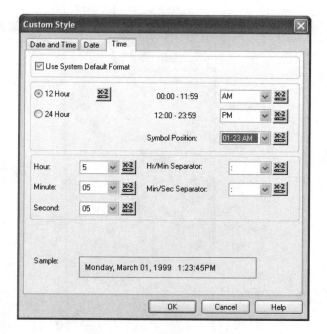

- **12 Hour**   Choose 12 Hour to display the time in 12-hour format with AM and PM options.

- **24 Hour**   Choose 24 Hour to display the time in 24-hour format with no AM and PM options.

- **00:00 – 11:59**   For the 12 Hour option, set the characters that you want displayed for the AM hours. You can choose an available option or enter your own. The default is AM.

- **12:00 – 23:59**   For the 12 Hour option, set the characters that you want displayed for the PM hours. You can choose an available option or enter your own. The default is PM.

- **Symbol Position**   For the 12 Hour option, choose whether you want the AM/PM characters displayed before or after the time.

- **Hour**   Select an hour formatting option from the drop-down box: two fixed digits, variable digits, or None.

- **Minute**   Select a minute formatting option from the drop-down box: two fixed digits, variable digits, or None.

- **Second**   Select a second formatting option from the drop-down box: two fixed digits, variable digits, or None.

- **Hr/Min Separator**   Select a separator for hours and minutes, or enter your own.

- **Min/Sec Separator**   Select a separator for minutes and seconds, or enter your own.

Figure 9-13
Formatting
Boolean values

Boolean Tab

When you format Boolean fields, the Boolean tab shown in Figure 9-13 will be available. On the Boolean tab, you configure how you want the Boolean values displayed.

Boolean Text   The Boolean Text drop-down box is used to select the display format of the True and False values of a Boolean field. The choices are True or False, T or F, Yes or No, Y or N, and 0 or 1. These options only affect the display of the field; they have no impact on the way the field is stored.

Picture Tab

If you choose to format a graphic field, the Picture tab of the Format Editor will be displayed, as shown in Figure 9-14. Use the Picture tab to crop, scale, or resize the graphic.

Crop From   The Crop From panel contains options for the Left, Right, Top, and Bottom. Enter a positive number in the boxes to have the graphic cropped that amount (in inches) on that side. If you enter a negative number, white space will be added to the graphic.

Scaling   Use the Height and Width options in the Scaling panel to shrink or expand the graphic in either or both dimensions. Entering numbers over 100 expands the graphic; numbers under 100 shrink the graphic. The scaling percentages are always applied to the original size of the graphic. When you change the scale, the measurements in the Size panel will change to display the new size.

Figure 9-14
Formatting
graphics

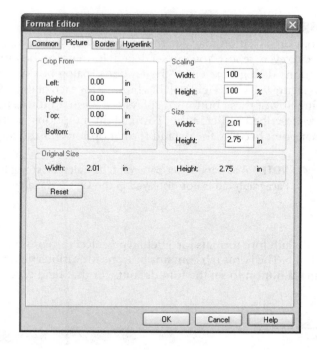

Size   Use the Height and Width options in the Size panel to resize the graphic. Enter the new Height or Width, and the graphic will stretch or shrink to the new values. When you change the Size options, the Scaling options will change accordingly.

Original Size   The Original Size panel displays the original size of the graphic.

Reset   Click the Reset button to return the graphic to its original size.

Working with Multiple Objects

You can format more than one object at a time. Select multiple objects using the SHIFT or CTRL key, or lasso them and then invoke the Format Editor. Any Format Editor tabs that apply to all the selected objects will be visible, and you can make changes that will affect all the objects.

Alternatively, you can use the Format Painter to copy the format from one object to several other objects by holding down the ALT key when clicking the target objects. Click the source object and then the Format Painter button. The cursor becomes the paint-brush to signify that the formatting from the source can be applied to other objects. When you click a second (target) object, the formatting is applied to it, and the cursor returns to normal. However, if you hold down the ALT key when you click a target for the Format Painter, the source format information is retained, the mouse cursor stays as the Format Painter brush, and you can then click another target.

Setting Defaults for Format Attributes

You or your organization may determine some standard formatting options that should be applied to every report. You can set default formats for the various field types using the File | Options dialog box. Open the Options dialog box and select the Fields tab. As shown in Figure 9-15, the Fields tab has buttons for each of the Crystal Reports data types.

Clicking any of these buttons displays the Format Editor, where you can set format options as described earlier in the "Format Editor Options" section. The options you select at that point become the default format options for the selected field type.

 NOTE You cannot set paragraph defaults for string fields because the Paragraph tab is not displayed in the Options dialog box.

To set default font formats for a field type, select the Fonts tab rather than a button on the Fields tab. The Fonts tab contains buttons for various field types, as shown in Figure 9-16. Click a button to set the font defaults for that field type.

Figure 9-15
Setting default
field formats

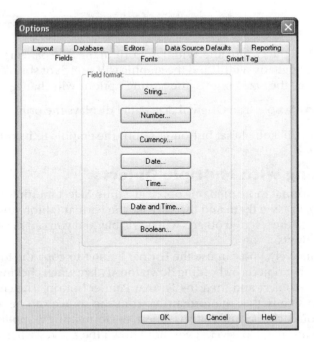

Figure 9-16
Setting default
fonts by field type

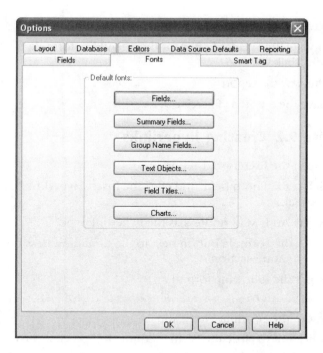

Exercise 9.1: Applying Common, Border, and Font Formatting Options

1. Open the Exercise 8.8 report.

2. Right-click the gray area of the Details section and choose Insert Section Below.

3. Add the Photo field to Details b, and attach it to the guideline for the last name field.

4. Add the Notes field to Details b, and attach it on the left to the guideline for the hire date field. Expand the field frame, and attach it to the guideline for the current age formula.

5. Right-click the Notes field, and select Format Field. Select the Common tab. Check the Can Grow option. Click OK.

6. Preview the report, noticing that the Notes field expands vertically to display the entire contents of the field. In addition, its height varies from record to record.

7. Right-click in the Photo field, and choose Format Graphic. Select the Border tab. Set the Right, Left, Top, and Bottom drop-down boxes to Double, and check the Drop Shadow box. Click OK.

8. Preview the report.

9. Invoke the Format Editor for the AgeAtHire formula field. Set the Style to Bold, and click OK.

10. Preview the report.

11. Save the report as **Exercise 9.1**.

Exercise 9.2: Creating Hyperlinks

1. Open the Exercise 9.1 report.

2. Select the Photo field, and click the Insert Hyperlink button on the Expert Tools toolbar.

3. Select An E-Mail Address as the hyperlink type.

4. Click the Formula button next to the E-mail Address box in the Hyperlink Information section.

5. Enter the following formula:

```
'mailto:'&{Employee.First Name}&'.'&{Employee.Last Name}&'@xtreme.com'
```

6. Close the Formula Workshop.

7. Click OK to close the Format Editor, and preview the report.

8. Move the mouse over a photo and click.

9. Your e-mail program should start with an e-mail addressed to the person whose photo you clicked. (This may not work if your e-mail is incompatible or not properly configured.)

10. Save the report as **Exercise 9.2**.

Exercise 9.3: Applying Type-Specific Formatting Options

1. Open the Exercise 9.2 report.

2. Open the Format Editor for the Notes field. Set First Line to .5, Left to .25, and Right to .25. Click OK to close the dialog box. You should see the Notes field with the new indentations on the Preview tab.

3. Place the Salary field on the report next to CurrentAge. Right-click, and choose Format Field. On the Number tab, select the $(1,123) style. Click OK. You should see the Salary field on the Preview tab, formatted with no decimal places.

4. Open the Format Editor for Salary again, and click the Customize button. In the Custom Style dialog box's Number tab, change the rounding to 10,000. Click OK twice. You should see that the salaries have all been rounded to multiples of $10,000.

5. Create a formula called Percent of Total Salary. Use the Editor and enter this formula:

```
100*{Employee.Salary}/Sum ({Employee.Salary})
```

6. Place Percent of Total Salary on the report. Click the Percent button on the Formatting toolbar. A percent sign will be added to the number.

7. Open the Format Editor for Percent of Total Salary. Note that it is using the Custom Style. Click the Customize button. Select the Currency Symbol tab. Notice that the percent sign is being used as the currency symbol. Click OK twice.

8. Format the birth date field. Select the March 01, 1999 style, and then click Customize. Select the Date tab in the Custom Style dialog box. Choose 1 for the Day format. Click OK twice. Move or resize fields, if necessary, to view the entire birth date field.

9. Create a formula field called 21 At Hire. Use the following formula:

```
{@AgeAtHire} >= 21
```

10. Place 21 At Hire on the report in the Details b section attached to the salary field's guideline. Open the Format Editor for 21 At Hire, and change the Boolean text to Yes or No. Click OK. Preview the report, and notice that 21 At Hire is either Yes or No.

11. Open the Format Editor for the Photo field. Select the Picture tab. Crop the picture by entering 1 in the Bottom edit box. Click OK, and notice that the picture has been cropped.

12. Right-click in the gray area of the Details b section, and select Fit Section.

13. Save the report as **Exercise 9.3**.

Exercise 9.4: Formatting Multiple Objects

1. Select the first name, last name, birth date, hire date, AgeAtHire, CurrentAge, and Salary fields.

2. Click the Format button on the toolbar to open the Format Editor. (Or right-click and choose Format Objects.)

3. Select the Font tab, and change the font. Click OK. You will see that the font has changed for all the selected fields. Since you did not change the font style, the boldface on AgeAtHire did not change.

4. Select the AgeAtHire field. Click the Format Painter button. Then hold down the ALT key and click the CurrentAge field. It will now be boldface.

5. The cursor is still the paintbrush. Click the 21 At Hire field. It is now bold and the cursor has returned to normal.

6. Save the report as **Exercise 9.4**.

PART II

Formatting Other Objects

In addition to the object types discussed in the "Formatting Field Objects" section, text objects, lines, and boxes can also be formatted.

Text Objects

Text objects that you place on the report can be formatted identically to any string field using the Format Editor. This method formats the entire contents of the text object at once. However, text objects have additional formatting options. When a text object is in edit mode, you can select a portion of the text or a field embedded in the text and format it separately from the rest of the field. (Embedding fields in text objects is covered in Chapter 5.)

Formatting Embedded Fields

To format an embedded field, you must put the text object in edit mode by double-clicking it; selecting it, right-clicking, and choosing Edit Text; or selecting it and choosing Edit | Edit Text. Then you must select only the embedded field. Selecting the embedded field is easier in the Design tab. The embedded field will be enclosed in brackets. Select everything from the opening bracket to the closing bracket, and then invoke the Format Editor. If you have correctly selected the embedded field, right-clicking will display a choice of Edit {*fieldname*}, as will the Format menu, and either choice will display the Format Editor. You can also click the Format button.

After the Format Editor is displayed for the embedded field, you can format it the same as you would if it were not embedded in a text object. The formatting will apply only to the instance of the field embedded in the text object and not to any other instance of the field elsewhere on the report.

Text Format Dialog Box

To format only a portion of the text in a text object (which can include an embedded field), select Format | Text Formatting or right-click and select Text Formatting. The Text Format dialog box will be displayed, as shown in Figure 9-17. This dialog box has three tabs for formatting the font or paragraph and for adding tabs to a text object.

Font Tab   The Font tab of the Text Format dialog box is similar to the Font tab of the Format Editor. You can set the font face, font style, size, and color. You can add strikeout or underline effects, and you can set the font spacing to an exact number of points.

Paragraph Tab   The Paragraph tab of the Text Format dialog box is similar to the Paragraph tab of the Format Editor shown in Figure 9-8. You can set the indentation, line spacing, and reading order the same as you can in the Format Editor. The Text Format dialog box adds the ability to set the paragraph's horizontal alignment; you can choose Right, Left, Centered, or Justified.

Tabs Tab   Use the Tabs tab, shown in Figure 9-18, to set tabs in a text object:

- **Tab Stop Position**   Enter the position where you want a tab in the Tab Stop Position box. Click Set to create the tab.

Figure 9-17
Formatting all or part of a text object

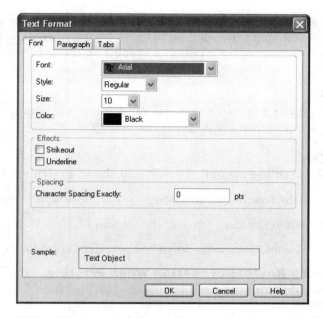

- **Alignment**   Choose the alignment for the selected tab stop: Left, Right, Center, or Decimal.
- **Set**   The Set button creates a tab once the position has been entered.
- **Delete**   Click Delete to remove the selected tab.
- **Delete All**   Click Delete All to remove all tabs.

Figure 9-18
Setting tabs in a text object

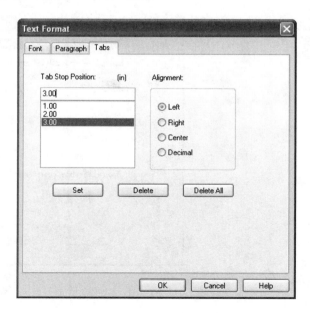

You can also create tabs in text objects when the object is in edit mode. Click on the ruler, and a tab stop will appear on the ruler. You can then move the tab by dragging it to a new position or remove a tab by dragging it off the ruler.

Lines

After adding lines to your report, you can format them with the Format Editor. First select the line, and then invoke the Format Editor.

Line Tab

The Line tab will be the only tab visible, as shown in Figure 9-19.

Style   In the Style drop-down box, you can choose None, Single, Dashed, or Dotted.

Width   For Single lines, you can choose a width from Hairline to 3.5 points.

Color   Use the Color drop-down box to select a color for the line.

Extend to Bottom of Section When Printing   The Extend to Bottom of Section When Printing option is primarily used for horizontal lines in sections that may expand due to fields formatted with the Can Grow option. If Extend is checked, the line will be moved to the bottom of the section no matter how much the section grows. When it is applied to a vertical line, the line is extended to the bottom of the section.

Suppress   Check the Suppress box to hide the line. It will still exist but be invisible.

Figure 9-19
Formatting line
objects

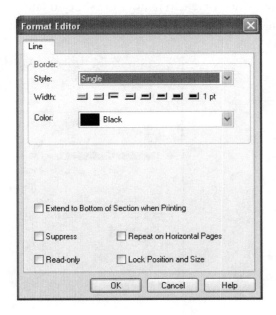

Read-Only   If Read-Only is checked, no other formatting options are available. Clear Read-Only to allow formatting for the line. Use this option to protect against accidental changes.

Repeat on Horizontal Pages   Check Repeat on Horizontal Pages if you want your line to appear on overflow pages created by cross-tabs or OLAP grids.

Lock Position and Size   Use the Lock Position and Size check box to protect against accidental movement or resizing of the line.

Boxes

Boxes can be formatted using the Format Editor. When you are editing a box, two tabs are available, as shown in Figure 9-20.

Box Tab

The Box tab has many of the same formatting options as the Line tab. The other options are Drop Shadow, Fill Color, and Close Border on Breaks.

Drop Shadow   Check Drop Shadow to draw a shadow below and to the right of your box in the selected color.

Fill   Use the Fill check box to add a fill (background) color to your box. Check Fill and then choose a color from the drop-down box that appears.

Figure 9-20
Formatting boxes

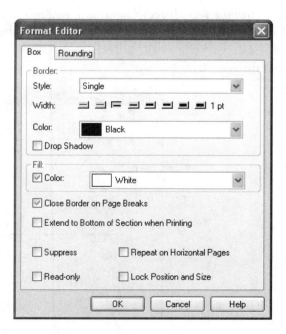

Close Border on Breaks   The Close Border on Breaks option draws a closing border for boxes that extend across a page break. The part of the box on the first page will be given a bottom border and the part of the box on the next page will be given a top border.

Rounding Tab

The Rounding tab, shown in Figure 9-21, is used to round the corners of boxes. Use the Rounding drop-down box or the slider bar to set a percentage for the rounding: 0 leaves the box rectangular; 100 creates an oval; values in between give rounded corners.

Exercise 9.5: Formatting Other Objects

1. Open Exercise 9.4.

2. Place a text object on the report in the Details b section, to the right of the Notes field.

3. Type **Was over 21 when hired?** followed by a space, as the text, and then drag the 21 At Hire field that is already on the report into the text field. The result should look like this in the Design tab.

   ```
   Was over 21 when hired? {@21 At Hire}
   ```

4. Double-click the text object to put it into edit mode. Select the string "over 21," right-click, and choose Text Formatting.

5. Set the font style to italic, and click OK.

6. Double-click the text object to put it into edit mode. Select {@21 At Hire}, right-click, and choose Format {@21 At Hire}. Set the Boolean Text to Y or N, and click OK.

7. Preview the report.

Figure 9-21

Creating rounded boxes and ovals

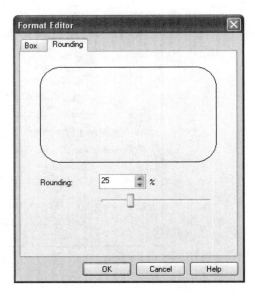

8. Draw a box around the text field.

9. Select the box and invoke the Format Editor.

10. Make the box color green and set its rounding to 100. Click OK.

11. Preview the report.

12. Save the report as **Exercise 9.5**.

Section Expert

Entire sections of a report can be formatted as well as report objects. Section formatting can be used to determine which sections appear on a report, fine-tune page breaks, use colors and graphic underlays to enhance the report presentation, and to create mailing label type reports. (Creating, moving, merging, and deleting sections is discussed in Chapter 5.)

Invoke the Section Expert by clicking the Section Expert button on the Expert Tools toolbar, selecting Report | Section Expert, or right-clicking the gray area of a section and choosing Section Expert. The Section Expert will appear with two tabs, as shown in Figure 9-22.

Sections Area

The Sections area of the Section Expert displays a tree list of all report sections. For any of the five core sections (Report Header, Page Header, Details, Page Footer, and Report Footer) that have subsections, the subsections will be displayed as lower-level nodes. Formatting can be applied to all subsections by formatting the parent node. Sections can be inserted, deleted, merged, and moved using the buttons in the Sections area. The formatting options on the tabs area are applied to the section selected in the Sections area.

Figure 9-22
Formatting
report sections

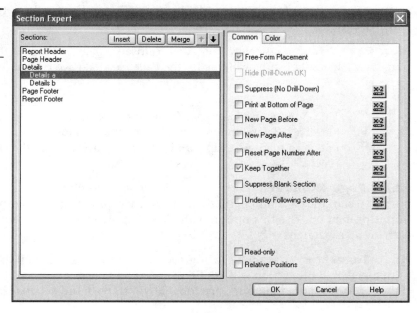

Common Tab

The Common tab contains the following options, although what you see on screen will vary depending on the selected section's type.

Free-Form Placement   Free-Form Placement is checked by default. It ensures that report text objects print where you placed them on the report, even if the printer driver causes text elements such as the width or height of the font to change. If you clear Free-Form Placement, Crystal decides where text elements should be placed vertically on the page based on the line-spacing attributes of the font. If a section contains subsections, only the subsections have the Free-Form Placement option available.

Hide (Drill-Down OK)   Check Hide to suppress a section in the preview but allow it to be displayed in a drill-down tab. Hide is not available for subsections.

Suppress (No Drill-Down)   Checking Suppress will suppress a section and not allow drill-down. Suppress is available for parent sections and subsections, and it is often used with a formula to conditionally suppress sections.

EXAM TIP   Suppressing or hiding all Details sections results in a summary report.

Print at Bottom of Page   Print at Bottom of Page causes the selected section to print at the bottom of the page and be followed by a page break. This option is not available for Page Header or Page Footer sections. Use Print at Bottom of Page to show group totals at the bottom of the page and continue with the next group on the next page.

New Page Before   Use New Page Before to insert a page break before the selected section. New Page Before is not available for the Report Header, Page Header, or Page Footer sections.

New Page After   Use New Page After to insert a page break after the selected section. New Page After is not available for the Page Header, Page Footer, or Report Footer sections.

TIP   You can use formatting formulas containing NOT OnFirstRecord for the New Page Before option or NOT OnLastRecord for the New Page After option to suppress extra page breaks at the beginning or the end of the report.

Reset Page Number After   Check Reset Page Number After to cause Crystal Reports to restart the page numbering at 1 on the page following the page the selected section is printed on. Use this option with New Page After for group footers to paginate each group separately.

Keep Together   Use the Keep Together option to ensure that all lines of a section print together. If the section will not fit on the current page, it is moved to the next page. If the section is more than one page long, it will start on the next page and take up as many pages as necessary. If you check Keep Together for a parent section, all subsections will be kept together.

 CAUTION Keep Together applies to sections only. If you want an entire group from the group header to the group footer to stay together, use the corresponding group option.

Suppress Blank Section   If every object in a section is blank and Suppress Blank Section is checked, then the section will not print. This option is commonly used when a memo field is placed in its own subsection. If the memo field is the only field in the section and its value is null, the section will be suppressed.

Underlay Following Sections   The Underlay Following Sections option is commonly used to place a graphic or chart behind data in other sections. Place the object(s) in a section of its own, and then check Underlay Following Sections. Subsequent sections will print on top of the underlay section.

Format with Multiple Columns   Check Format with Multiple Columns to create mailing label reports. This option is only available for the parent-level Details section. Checking it causes the Layout tab to be displayed so that you can format the columns.

Reserve Minimum Page Footer   Reserve Minimum Page Footer is only visible for the Page Footer parent section and only applies if there are multiple page footers and some of them are conditionally suppressed. By default, Crystal Reports will make the page footer as tall as the combined height of all the page footer sections that are not unconditionally suppressed. If you check this option, Crystal Reports will reserve only enough space to contain the tallest page footer based on the suppression formulas.

Read-Only   Setting a section to read-only locks the format and position of every object in the section. Setting a parent section to read-only locks the format and position of every object in every subsection. Use this option to help prevent accidental changes to the objects.

Relative Positions   If you place an object to the right of a cross-tab or OLAP grid and the grid grows horizontally, the object may be overwritten by the grid. Check Relative Positions to allow Crystal Reports to move objects to the right of grids when the grid expands.

Color Tab
The Color tab, shown in Figure 9-23, is used to change the background color of a section. Check the Background Color box, and then choose a color for the section. The color will extend from the left margin to the right margin.

Layout Tab
The Layout tab, shown in Figure 9-24, only appears if the Format with Multiple Columns option is checked for the parent Details section. Multiple column reports are commonly called mailing label reports. Use the options on the Layout tab to configure the columns.

Figure 9-23

Applying a background color to a section

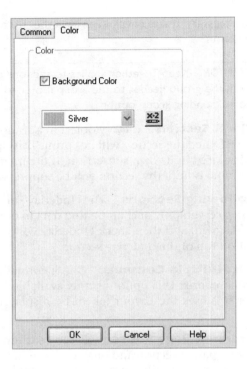

Figure 9-24

Formatting mailing labels

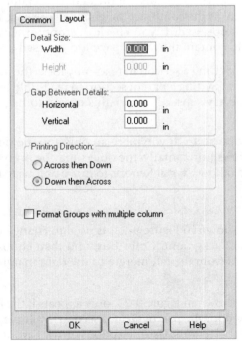

Detail Size   The options in the Detail Size panel are used to set the height and width of one detail section. Think of this as the size of the label.

Gap Between Details   Use the Horizontal and Vertical options in the Gap Between Details section to set the size of the space between detail sections—the gap between labels.

Printing Direction   The Printing Direction options are Across Then Down and Down Then Across.

Format Groups with Multiple Column   If your report has groups, the Group sections will occupy a full row by default. If you want the Group sections to be the same size as the Details sections, check Format Groups with Multiple Columns.

Exercise 9.6: Creating a Summary Report

1. Create a new report using the Standard report wizard.
2. Use the Customer and Order tables.
3. Include the customer name, order ID, and order amount on the report.
4. Group by the customer name.
5. Create a summary for the total order amount by customer.
6. Preview the report.
7. Use the Section Expert to hide the Details section.
8. Preview the report. It is now a summary report.

NOTE   If you check the SQL query, you will see that it contains a group-by clause and is not returning the detail rows that the original report returned.

9. Since we hid the Details section, you can drill down for more information. Drill down on Alley Cat Cycles.
10. Save the report as **Exercise 9.6**.

Exercise 9.7: Creating a Report with an Underlay

1. Open the report from Exercise 9.6.
2. Right-click the page header, and choose Insert Section Below.
3. Move the new section so that it becomes Page Header a.
4. Insert a graphic into Page Header a. Resize it if it is more than about 3 inches high.
5. Right-click on the gray area of Page Header a, and choose Section Expert.

PART II

6. Check Underlay Following Sections.

7. Click OK, and preview the report. Move fields if they are obscured by the graphic. Your report should look something like this.

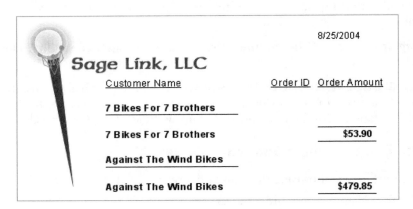

8. Save the report as **Exercise 9.7**.

Exercise 9.8: Creating a Multicolumn Report

1. Create a new report as a blank report.

2. Use the Employee and Employee Addresses tables.

3. Suppress the Report Header and Report Footer sections.

4. Drag the bottom border of the Details section until it is approximately 5/8 of an inch tall.

5. Create a guideline at the left margin and at 2 ½ inches.

6. Place a text object into Details a, attach it to both guidelines, and stretch it to the height of the section.

7. Embed the employee's first and last name fields, with a space in between, into the text object. Type **ENTER** in the text object to embed a carriage return.

8. Place Address1 into Details, and embed a carriage return.

9. Place Address2 into Details, and embed a carriage return.

10. Embed the city, region, and postal code into the text object. Add a comma and space between the city and region. Add two spaces before the postal code.

11. Open the Section Expert and select the Details section.

12. Check the Format with Multiple Columns box.

13. Select the Layout tab, and set the width to **2.5** and the horizontal and vertical gaps to **.25**. Set the Printing Direction to Across Then Down.

14. Click OK, and preview the report.

15. You will see the label report. There are undesirable blank lines appearing when the Address2 field is blank.

16. Select the text object, right-click, and choose Format Text. Check the Suppress Embedded Field Blank Lines box. Preview the report.

17. Save the report as **Exercise 9.8**.

Templates

You can apply the field formatting and layout from one report to another report. When you do this, the source report is called a *template*. The format and placement of the template's fields, group fields, text objects, and simple summaries is copied to the target report's matching objects, including conditional formatting formulas. Group charts, graphics, lines, boxes, and special fields that exist in the template are added to the target report. Group charts can replace existing group charts. (Charting is described in Chapter 10.)

If a template has more sections or more fields than the target file, the extra items are not used. If there are more fields in the target's Details section than in the template's Details section, a new Details section will be created and the extra fields will be moved into it. They are not lost.

Applying a template makes many formatting changes simultaneously. You can undo the changes immediately after applying the template. You can also apply multiple templates or the same template more than once. However, once the report has been saved or any other action has occurred, you cannot remove the template.

There are three categories of templates you need to understand. Predefined templates are Crystal Reports–supplied reports intended for use as templates. Regular reports created to fulfill user needs can also be used as templates. You can also create special-purpose reports that are only used as templates and not for displaying data.

Using Predefined Templates

Crystal Reports ships with several predefined templates. These templates can be applied via the report creation wizards or the Template Expert.

Report Wizards

The last page of the report wizards is the Template screen, shown in Figure 9-25. You can pick from the available template files or browse to find another report file. A preview of the report formatting is displayed in the Preview pane.

Template Expert

For an existing report, you can apply a template using the Template Expert. Click the Template Expert button on the Expert Tools toolbar, or choose Report | Template Expert from the menu to display the Template Expert. The Template Expert is shown in Figure 9-26.

Figure 9-25

Applying a template from a report wizard

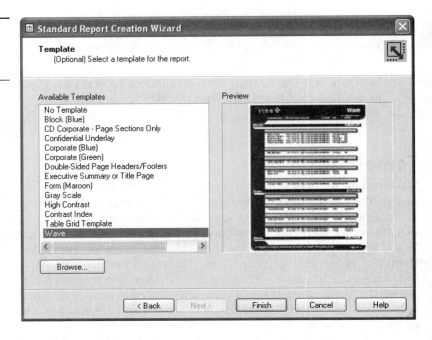

Figure 9-26

Applying a template from the Template Expert

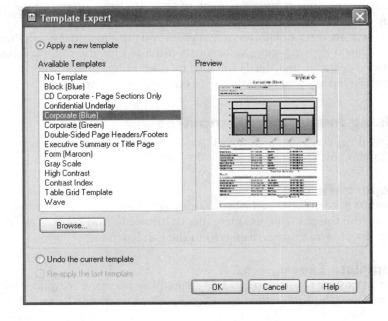

Available Templates   The Available Templates list displays all report files that are stored at \Program Files\Crystal Decisions\Crystal Reports 10\Templates. Crystal Reports installs with several templates stored in this directory. The name shown in the list is taken from the Title field in the document properties for the report file. Choose a template to apply it to your report.

Preview   The Preview window displays the thumbnail image saved with the selected template file.

Apply a New Template   Apply a New Template is the default action when the Template Expert opens. The other options are Undo the Current Template and Re-apply the Last Template. Use Apply a New Template to apply the selected template to your report.

Browse   Click Browse to search for a template file in another directory.

Undo the Current Template   Select Undo the Current Template to undo the application of the most recent template.

Re-apply the Last Template   You can select Re-apply the Last Template if changes to the report have been made and the same template needs to be applied to format them.

Using Reports as Templates
If you have a report whose formatting you wish to apply to another report, you can use it as a template.

Browse
To use any report file as a template, search for it using the Browse button in the report creation wizards or the Template Expert.

Add to Template List
You can add your own reports to the Available Templates list in the report wizards or the Template Expert by saving them to the template directory, \Program Files\Crystal Decisions\Crystal Reports 10\Templates. The report file's Title document property will be displayed in the list if it has a Title, otherwise it will be listed as Unnamed Template 1.

Include Preview
To include a preview picture when saving report files as templates, be sure to check Save Preview Picture on the Summary tab of the Document Properties dialog box. Open the Document Properties dialog box by choosing File | Summary Info.

Creating Templates
You can create report files whose only purpose is to serve as templates. Start with a regular report file and modify it for use as a template, or create a file from scratch that has no data sources and uses Template Field Objects instead of real database fields.

Template Field Objects

Template field objects are used as placeholders for real field objects in a template file. They are a special type of formula field. Selecting Insert | Template Field Object creates the ob-

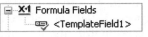

ject and places it on the report. A new formula field will then appear in the Field Explorer, as shown in this illustration. The angle brackets on either side of the name indicate that this field is a template object. You can create groups on template field objects to create groups in your generic template file.

When you display the Format Editor for a template field object, all tabs for every data type are displayed, as shown here. You can create and format the object as any data type you like. When the template is applied, the formatting for the matching data type will be used. If you preview a report with template field objects, the object will appear blank by default.

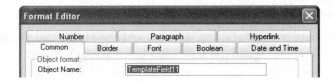

Template field objects will be applied to database fields, parameter fields, SQL Expression fields, and formula fields in the target file, but not to any special fields.

Sample Data　You may want to create sample data for template field objects to better judge how they will appear on a report. Locate the template field in the Field Explorer under the Formula node, and edit it. You will see something like the following formula:

```
//Crystal Report Template Field
WhileReadingRecords;Space(10)
```

The Space(10) part of the formula is supplying the sample data, but since it is just spaces, it is not very useful. You can replace the Space(10) with a literal or database field of any type to see how the formatting would look when the template is applied. To use a database field, you must connect to a data source.

Exercise 9.9: Using Predefined Templates

1. Open the Exercise 9.6 report.

2. Click the Template Expert button to open the Template Expert.

3. Select the Confidential Underlay template and click OK.

4. Preview the report.

5. Save the report as **Exercise 9.9**.

Exercise 9.10: Using a Report as a Template

1. Open the Exercise 9.6 report.

2. Click the Template Expert button to open the Template Expert.

3. Click the Browse button and select the Exercise 9.7 report. Click Open, and then click OK.

4. Preview the report. The underlay that you created in Exercise 9.7 should be applied to the report.

5. Save the report as **Exercise 9.10**.

Exercise 9.11: Creating a Template

1. Create a new report as a blank report, and do not connect to any data sources.

2. Suppress the Report Header section.

3. Insert the Xtreme logo from the repository into the page header.

4. Insert the Powered by Crystal graphic from the repository into the page footer.

5. Insert three template field objects into the Details section.

6. Group by the first template field object.

7. Increase the font size of Group#1 Name to 14 points.

8. Insert the Page N of M special field into the page footer, and format it in italics.

9. Select all the template Field Objects and their associated field headings. Open the Format Editor and choose a different font.

10. Close the Format Editor.

11. Preview the report. (You must preview the report in order to create a preview picture.)

12. Select File | Summary Info, and enter **Xtreme** as the Title. Check Save Preview Picture, and click OK.

13. Save the report as **Exercise 9.11 Template**.

14. Save the file again into the Template directory as **Xtreme Template**.

15. Open the Exercise 9.6 report.

16. Open the Template Expert, and select Xtreme Template from the list.

17. Click OK, and the template will be applied.

18. Preview the report.

19. Save the report as **Exercise 9.11**.

Conditional Formatting

As you read the previous sections, you probably noticed the Formula button next to many of the options on the Format Editor and the Section Expert. Wherever the Formula button appears, you can set the formatting for the attribute conditionally, based on a formula. Conditional formatting is used for many purposes. You can highlight values that reach a certain goal by changing the font color. You can display flags or messages when certain conditions are met. This type of formatting is commonly called *stop lighting.* You can also use conditional formatting to improve the readability of a report by alternating row colors or printing a "continued" message for groups that span pages. You might also use conditional formatting to make a particularly complex report request possible.

Highlighting Expert

Use the Highlighting Expert to create conditional formatting for several field attributes at the same time.

CAUTION   The Highlighting Expert is a third-party add-in and does not create Crystal Reports formatting formulas. The conditional formatting applied by the Highlighting Expert cannot be modified in the Formula Workshop and is applied after all other report processing.

 Open the Highlighting Expert by clicking the Highlighting button on the Expert Tools toolbar, choosing Format | Highlighting Expert from the menu, or selecting Highlighting Expert from the right-click menu for a field. The Highlighting Expert contains two panels, the Item List and the Item Editor, as shown in Figure 9-27.

Figure 9-27
Creating conditional formatting with the Highlighting Expert

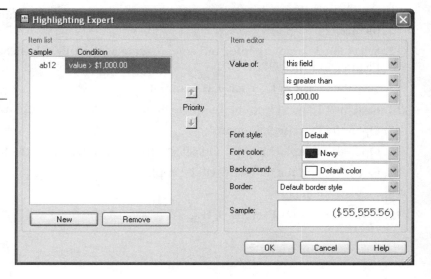

Item List

The Item List panel displays the conditions you create and an example of what applying them will look like.

Sample   The Sample column of the Item List panel displays sample text formatted with the options that will be applied if the condition is True.

Condition   The Condition column displays the comparison condition that you create using options in the Item Editor.

Priority   If you create more than one condition, use the Priority buttons to arrange the conditions in the correct priority. Conditions higher in the list have higher priority.

New   Click the New button to add a condition to the Highlighting Expert.

Remove   Click Remove to delete a condition.

Item Editor

The options in the Item Editor panel are used to create the conditions you want to use to format your field.

Value Of   In the Value Of drop-down box, select the field that you want to use in the comparison condition. You can choose This Field to base the condition on the value of the field you are formatting. You can choose any report field from the drop-down box to base the formatting of this field on the value of another report field. Or you can choose Other Fields to open the Choose Field dialog box and pick a field from any connected data source.

Comparison Condition   After choosing a field, you must select a comparison condition in the second drop-down box. The available options are shown here.

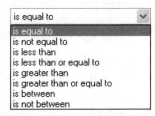

Compare To   In the third drop-down box, you pick the value to compare to. The drop-down box will be populated with the current contents of the Value Of field. You can pick one of those values or type in your own to complete the condition statement.

Font Style   In the Font Style box, choose the font that you want the field value to use if the condition is True.

Font Color   Choose the font color that you want the field value to have if the condition is True using the Font Color drop-down box.

Background   To change the background color if the condition is True, pick a color in the Background drop-down box.

Border   You can highlight the field using a border by
selecting a border style from the Border drop-down box.
The available options are shown here.

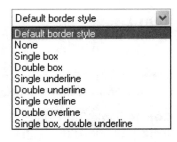

Format Formulas

To create more complex conditional formatting than is
possible with the Highlighting Expert, you must create
format formulas.

Creating Format Formulas

You can create a format formula using the Format Editor, the Section Expert, or the Formula Workshop. If you click the Formula button next to a property on the Format Editor
or Section Expert, the Formula Workshop will open with a format formula for the property displayed in the Workshop Tree. For example, if you click the Formula button next
to the Style property on the Font tab of the Format Editor, the Formula Workshop will
open, as shown in Figure 9-28. You would then create a formula to control the formatting of the font style for the field.

EXAM TIP   If you create a format formula for a property, it will be applied
regardless of the state of the associated check box. If the Format button is
red, indicating that a formula exists, the formula will be applied whether or not
the box is checked.

Formatting Functions

Notice that the Functions tree in Figure 9-28 has two new nodes: Formatting Functions and
Font Style Constants. Each node lists functions that you can use in your formatting formula.

CurrentFieldValue   This function returns the current value of the field being formatted. CurrentFieldValue is used often in formatting formulas to change the format de-

Figure 9-28
Creating a format
formula in the
Formula
Workshop

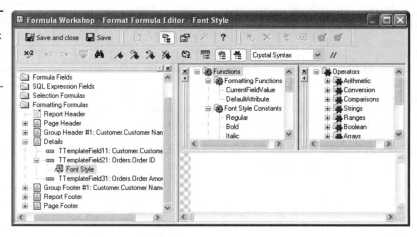

pending on the value of the field. For example, our font style formula could be the following:

```
If CurrentFieldValue > 1000 then crBold else DefaultAttribute
```

DefaultAttribute   DefaultAttribute returns the default value of the attribute being formatted. For example, the default attribute for Font Style is Regular. DefaultAttribute is often used in the Else part of formatting formulas to ensure that the attribute is set to the default value if the condition is False. Using DefaultAttribute means that you do not have to know what the default attribute is for a particular field.

> **NOTE**   DefaultAttribute returns the value the attribute would have if the format formula did not exist. The default value changes depending on the options chosen in the Format Editor or Section Expert. For example, if Font Style is set to Bold in the Format Editor, then Bold is the default attribute for Font Style for the selected field. If Can Grow is not checked, then the default attribute for Can Grow is False.

GridRowColumnValue   GridRowColumnValue is similar to CurrentFieldValue, but it applies to the values in a cross-tab or OLAP grid.

Property Type Constants   Each format element that is not Boolean has a set of valid options. The appropriate set will appear in the Formula Workshop for the field you are formatting so that you can use them in your formula. For example, when you are creating a format formula for the Font Style property, the Font Style constants will be available.

Boolean Properties
If you create a format formula for a property that is set with a check box in the Format Editor or Section Expert, then your formula must return the Boolean value True or False. This is also called an *On or Off property*.

Multivalue Properties
If you create a format formula for a property that has several possible values displayed in a drop-down box, the result of your formula must be one of the type constants for that property. This is also called an *Attribute property*.

Fill-in Properties
If you create a format formula for a property whose value is typed into an edit box, then the return value of your formula must be of the appropriate data type for the property.

Exercise 9.12: Using the Highlighting Expert

1. Open the Exercise 9.11 report.

2. Insert a summary field that is the total order amount by customer.

3. Open the Highlighting Expert for the summary field.

4. Click the New button to create a new condition.

5. Set the condition so that it is Value < 100, and set the Font color to Red.

6. Create another condition that it applies to values under 1000, and set the Font color to Green.

7. Create another condition that it applies to all values equal to or above 1000, and set the Font color to Purple.

8. Preview the report.

9. Save the report as **Exercise 9.12**.

Exercise 9.13: Alternating Row Colors

1. Open the Exercise 9.12 report.

2. Open the Section Expert for the Details section, and select the Color tab.

3. Click the Background Color Formula button to open the Formula Workshop.

4. Enter the following formula.

```
If RecordNumber mod 2 = 0 then crSilver else DefaultAttribute
```

 NOTE RecordNumber mod 2 will return 1 for odd numbered rows and 0 for even numbered rows, since it is the remainder after dividing by 2.

5. Close the Formula Workshop and preview the report.

6. Save the report as **Exercise 9.13**.

Exercise 9.14: Suppressing a Details Section Conditionally

1. Open the Exercise 9.3 report.

2. Create a Boolean parameter called Show Details.

3. Open the Section Expert for the Details b section.

4. Click the Formula button next to the Suppress property.

5. Enter the following formula:

```
If {?Show Picture} then False else True
```

6. Close the Formula Workshop and the Section Expert.

7. Select False for Show Picture, and click OK. The report will be displayed with the Details b section suppressed.

8. Refresh the report, and choose True for Show Picture. The report will be displayed with the Details b section showing.

9. Save the report as **Exercise 9.14**.

Exercise 9.15: Adding a "Continued" Line

1. Open the Exercise 9.13 report.

2. Right-click in the gray area of the Group Header, and select Change Group.

3. On the Options tab of the Change Group Options dialog box, check Repeat Group Header On Each Page. Then click OK.

4. Preview the report. You should see the group header repeated at the top of the next page if a group breaks across pages. However, it is not easy to tell if the group starts on a page or if it has been continued from the previous page.

5. Insert a text object in the Group Header section toward the right side of the page. Type **Continued** into the text object.

6. Open the Format Editor for the text object, and click the Formula button next to the Suppress property.

7. Enter the following formula into the Formula Workshop:

```
Not InRepeatedGroupHeader
```

8. Close the Formula Workshop and the Format Editor.

9. Preview the report. You should see the word "Continued" when the group breaks across a page.

10. Save the report as **Exercise 9.15**.

 EXAM TIP Know how to use the InRepeatedGroupHeader function.

Chapter Review

Understanding how to modify a report's formatting is essential to meeting user needs. This chapter covered formatting field objects, formatting graphical objects, formatting sections, using templates, and creating conditional formatting.

Quick Tips

- Formatting can be applied to report objects using the Format Editor, the Formatting toolbar, or the Format Painter.

- The Format Editor contains four tabs that are available for all field types except graphic objects: Common, Font, Border, and Hyperlink. The String, Memo, and Text Object fields add the Paragraph tab. Number and Currency fields add the Number tab. Boolean fields add the Boolean tab. Date, Time, and DateTime fields add the Date, Time, and Date and Time tabs, respectively. OLE objects have Common, Border, Hyperlink, and Picture tabs. Lines have the Line tab, and Boxes have the Box and Rounding tabs.

- Custom Styles can be created for number, date, and time fields.

- The Can Grow option on the Common tab is used to allow a field to expand vertically to accommodate the current field value. It is often used with memo fields.

- The Format Painter copies all applicable formatting options from a source object to one or more target objects. Select the source, click the Format Painter, and then click the target. To copy to multiple targets, you must hold down the ALT key when clicking the target objects.

- You can create hyperlinks to web sites, e-mail addresses, files, report parts, or other report objects. If you link to a file, it will be opened with its associated program executable.

- Hyperlink targets can be static or they can change based on the result of a formula or the value of a report field. Hyperlinks to files or web sites can use relative addressing.

- Multiple objects can be formatted by selecting them and then invoking the Format Editor. All options that apply to all the selected objects will be visible and can be set simultaneously.

- You can set default formats for all field types by using the Fields tab of the File | Options dialog box.

- Field objects embedded in text objects can be formatted separately from the rest of the text. To format the embedded field, put the text object in edit mode, select the embedded field, and invoke the Format Editor.

- Sections of text fields can be formatted individually by selecting them when the field is in edit mode and invoking the Text Format dialog box. You can format font- or paragraph-related items and set tabs.

- Lines and boxes can be formatted using the Line, Box, and Rounding tabs of the Format Editor. The Rounding tab allows you to round off the corners of boxes.

- The Section Expert is used to format sections and contains at most three tabs: Common, Color, and Layout.

- The Common tab of the Section Expert is used to hide or suppress sections, insert page breaks, set the Keep Together option, create underlays, and create multicolumn reports (mailing labels).

- The Color tab of the Section Expert is used to set the background color for a section.

- The Layout tab of the Section Expert is used to configure the columns of multicolumn reports.

- A summary report is one where all the detail sections are suppressed and only summary information is displayed.

- When you apply the formatting from one report to another, the source file is called a template. Any Crystal Reports .rpt file can be used as a template.

- Crystal Reports ships with several report files installed in the Template directory. These files appear in the Template Expert and can be applied to other reports as templates.

- You can create reports to use as templates using template object fields. Template object fields are placeholders for the real fields in the target file. You can set formatting options for them as if they were of any data type. All the data type–specific tabs appear for template object fields in the Format Editor.

- To create sample data for a template object field, you edit the associated formula and enter a literal value or database field.

- The Highlight Expert is a tool that you can use to set the font style, font color, background color, or border for a field conditionally. You can create format conditions based on the value of the selected field or another field. If you create multiple conditions, you can set their priorities.

- Conditionally format field or section properties by creating format formulas for them. Use the Formula buttons next to properties in the Format Editor or Section Expert to create the format formula in the Formula Workshop.

- There are three types of properties that can be conditionally formatted, and each requires a different type of formula result. Check box properties require a Boolean result. Drop-down choice properties require a property type constant as the result. Typed-in properties require a result data type appropriate for the property type.

- Special functions are available in the Formula Workshop when you are editing a format formula. CurrentFieldValue returns the current value of the field being formatted. DefaultAttribute returns the property's default attribute. In addition, property type constants for the selected property will be available.

Questions

Questions may have more than one correct answer. Choose all answers that apply.

1. The Format Painter is used to change the font, background, and border colors for an object.

   a. True

   b. False

2. A numeric amount field on your report is being truncated. For example, the value 19,345 is displaying as 9,345. Which of these options will prevent the user from assuming that the correct value is 9,345?

   a. Expand the size of the field to display the maximum value required.

   b. Check Allow Field Clipping on the Number tab of the Format Editor.

   c. Clear Allow Field Clipping on the Number tab of the Format Editor.

   d. Reformat the field to remove the comma thousands separator.

   e. Reduce the font size until the maximum value can be displayed.

   f. Check the Can Grow option on the Common tab of the Format Editor.

3. The Can Grow option is available for which field types?

    a. String

    b. Memo

    c. Number

    d. Currency

    e. Date and Time

    f. Boolean

4. Which options can be used to display percent signs with number fields?

    a. Display Percent Sign check box on the Number tab

    b. Display Currency Symbol check box on the Number tab

    c. The Currency Symbol tab of the Custom Style dialog box

    d. The Percent Sign tab of the Custom Style dialog box

    e. The Percent button on the Formatting toolbar

5. Using number-formatting options, which of the following could never result for the number –125?

    a. –125

    b. 125–

    c. (125)

    d. (125)

    e. 125

6. Hyperlink targets can be which of the following?

    a. Static web site address

    b. Formula

    c. Relative website address

    d. File with a static path

    e. File with a relative path

    f. Field value

7. You can create hyperlinks to which of the following?

    a. http://www.sage-link.com

    b. mailto:annette@sage-link.com

    c. AgeAtHire1 from the average age at hire by supervisor

    d. MaxofFirstName1 in the current report

    e. ..\..\Business Objects\crcp_program.pdf

    f. c:\CRCP\Page Count.xls

8. You can format a field embedded in a text object by selecting the object, right-clicking, and choosing the Format {*fieldname*} option.

   a. True

   b. False

9. You can center align the middle paragraph in a text object containing three paragraphs and leave the other two left-justified.

   a. True

   b. False

10. Checking the Extend to Bottom of Section line-formatting option will

    a. Cause a horizontal line to stretch to the bottom of the section when previewed or printed (becoming wider)

    b. Cause a horizontal line to move to the bottom of the section when previewed or printed

    c. Have no impact on a horizontal line

    d. Cause a vertical line to stretch to the bottom of the section when previewed or printed

    e. Have no impact on a vertical line

11. Boxes can be

    a. Rectangular

    b. Rounded

    c. Oval

    d. Left open across page breaks

    e. Closed across page breaks

12. To create a page break after a group is printed, you should check

    a. Keep Together for the Group Header and Group Footer sections

    b. Keep Group Together option for the group

    c. Page Break Before for the Group Header section

    d. Page Break After for the Group Footer section

13. If you have multiple Details sections and you want them to always print together, you should check the Keep Together option for each section.

    a. True

    b. False

14. Checking the Read-Only option for a section will

    a. Lock the formatting of all objects in the section

    b. Lock the position of all objects in the section

    c. Lock the position of the section relative to other sections

    d. Make all objects in the section be grayed out in the preview

15. You can set the color for all objects in a section using the Color tab of the Section Expert.

    a. True

    b. False

16. To create a watermark on a report, you would use the following option.

    a. Section Overlay

    b. Watermark

    c. Imprint

    d. Transparent Graphic

    e. Section Underlay

17. To create a mailing label report, you need to check the Format with Multiple Columns option on the Layout tab of the Section Expert.

    a. True

    b. False

18. You have two narrow Details sections and want to print more than one record across the page to save space. Your report also contains a group, but you want the group sections to print normally, taking up the entire row of the report. Which options do you need to check?

    a. Format with Multiple Columns for Details a

    b. Format with Multiple Columns for Details b

    c. Format with Multiple Columns for Details

    d. Format Groups with Multiple Column

19. A summary report is the result of

    a. Inserting groups and summary fields into a report

    b. Hiding all detail sections

    c. Suppressing all detail sections

    d. A group-by query

20. A template file is created by choosing File | Save As Template.

    a. True

    b. False

21. How do you save a preview picture with a template file?

    a. Choose File | Save As Template, and check Save Preview Picture in the Save As dialog box.

b. Check Save Preview Picture in the report's Summary Info, and then choose File | Save As Template.

c. Check Save Preview Picture in the report's Summary Info, and then choose File | Save As.

22. If a template file Details section has more subsections and more (nongraphical) fields than the target file

 a. The extra sections will be added to the target.

 b. The extra sections will be ignored.

 c. The extra fields will be added to the target.

 d. The extra fields will be discarded.

 e. The template application will fail.

23. You can use any report file as a template by

 a. Clicking the Browse button of the Template Expert

 b. Clicking the Browse button of the Template screen of the report wizards

 c. Saving the file to the template directory and then picking it from the Available Templates list of the Template Expert

 d. Saving the file to the template directory and then picking it from the Available Templates list of the Template screen of the report wizards

 e. Choosing File | Apply Template and clicking the Browse button

24. When you apply a template file that contains Template Field Objects to a target file, which field types will not be reformatted to match the template?

 a. Database fields

 b. Formula fields

 c. SQL Expression fields

 d. Parameter fields

 e. Special fields

25. How would you create sample data for a template field object?

 a. Enter a string into the Sample box of the Format Editor.

 b. Right-click the template field object and select Sample Data.

 c. Right-click the template field object on the report, select Edit Template Field Object, and enter sample data in the Formula Editor.

 d. Right-click the template field object in the Field Explorer, select Edit, and enter sample data in the Formula Editor.

 e. Right-click the template field object in the Report Explorer, select Edit, and enter sample data in the Formula Editor.

26. Fields can be formatted conditionally using which of the following methods?

    a. Highlighting Expert

    b. Format Expert

    c. Formula Expert

    d. Format formulas created in the Formula Workshop

    e. Highlighting formulas created in the Formula Workshop

27. If a section has a conditional format formula attached to its New Page Before property, and the New Page Before property is checked, then

    a. A page break will always be inserted before the section.

    b. A page break will be inserted if the format formula returns True.

    c. The DefaultAttribute function will return True.

    d. The DefaultAttribute function will return False.

28. If this is your format formula, what type of property is being formatted?

```
Select CurrentFieldValue
Case upTo   100: crBlack
Case upTo 1000: crGreen
Case upTo 10000: crRed
    Default: DefaultAttribute;
```

    a. On or Off

    b. Attribute

29. Which properties can be conditionally formatted using a format formula but not with the Highlighting Expert?

    a. Font face

    b. Font style

    c. Font color

    d. Background color

    e. Border

30. To allow drill-down on a section based on a parameter value, you could create a Format Formula on the Hide property.

    a. True

    b. False

Answers

1. **b.** False, the Format Painter is used to copy formatting from one object to another.

2. **a, c, e, f.** Answer a, expanding the field, is the best solution. Answer b is incorrect because Allow Field Clipping must already be checked, since the field

is being truncated. Answer c, clearing Allow Field Clipping, will display pound signs if the number does not fit; this will prevent the user from assuming the truncated value is correct. Answer d, removing the comma, may or may not free enough space to display the whole number. Answer e, reducing the font, can be used and will meet the requirement, but is probably not desirable for aesthetic reasons. Answer f, checking the Can Grow option, will let the field expand vertically to accommodate the entire number and so meet the requirement, but it will result in the number wrapping to two lines.

3. **All.** The Can Grow option is on the Common tab of the Format Editor and is available for all the listed field types.

4. **c, e.** To display a percent sign with a number, you can use the Percent button on the Formatting toolbar or the Currency Symbol tab of the Custom Style dialog box. (Answer b might be correct in the rare circumstance that your currency symbol is a percent sign by default.)

5. **d.** The negative formatting options include the negative sign before or after the number, enclosure in parentheses, and no sign. Using parentheses with extra spaces is not an option.

6. **All.** A hyperlink can be any of the listed options.

7. **All.** Each choice is a valid hyperlink target.

8. **b.** False. You must first put the text object into edit mode and select only the embedded field.

9. **a.** True. You can select the middle paragraph and format it separately.

10. **b, d.** A horizontal line will be moved to the bottom of the section, and a vertical line will extend to the bottom of the section.

11. **All.** Each option is true for a box.

12. **d.** None of the other choices will guarantee a page break after every Group Footer section.

13. **b.** False. Checking the Keep Together option for a section only ensures that everything in the selected section will print together. In this case, you should check the Keep Together option for the Details parent section.

14. **a, b.** The Read-Only section option locks the formatting and position of all objects in the section.

15. **b.** False, you can set the background color for a section but not the color of objects in the section.

16. **e.** Use the section Underlay option to create a watermark.

17. **b.** False. You need to check the Format Multiple Columns option on the Common tab of the Section Expert.

18. **c.** The Format with Multiple Columns option is set at the parent Details section only. You do not need to check Format Groups with Multiple Columns because you want the group sections to print normally.

19. **b, c.** A summary report can be created by hiding or suppressing all detail sections.

20. **b.** False. A template file is a regular .rpt file.

21. **c.** Check Save Preview Picture in the Document Properties dialog box, and then save the file normally.

22. **b, d.** Extra sections and fields will be ignored.

23. **a, b, c, d.** Only Answer e is not a valid method.

24. **e.** Template field objects are not applied to special fields.

25. **d.** Editing of template field objects is only available from the Field Explorer.

26. **a, d.** Conditional formatting can be created using the Highlighting Expert or by creating format formulas.

27. **b, c.** Since the property is checked, DefaultAttribute will return True. Since a format formula exists, it will determine whether a page break is inserted.

28. **b.** The return value is a property type constant, so the property must be a multivalue or Attribute property, not an On/Off or Boolean property.

29. **a.** The font face cannot be modified using the Highlighting Expert.

30. **b.** The Hide property cannot be formatted conditionally.

Charting

Exam RDCR200 expects you to be able to
- Create a chart using the Chart Expert
- Modify a chart
- Customize a chart
- Determine trends in data

Charts of important report data help the user understand trends, exceptions, relationships, and so on, quickly. Crystal Reports has powerful charting tools that make creating visual representations of information quick and easy. The Chart Expert is used to create regular charts, and the Map Expert is used to create geographical charts.

EXAM TIP   Mapping is not an exam objective.

Creating a Chart

To create a chart, you open the Chart Expert and choose the options you want. After a chart is created, you can modify the Chart Expert options, reposition the chart, format the chart with the Format Editor, or customize the chart with the Chart menu options.

Opening the Chart Expert

Open the Chart Expert by selecting Insert | Chart from the menu or clicking the Insert Chart button on the Insert Tools menu. If a chart already exists, you can open the Chart Expert by selecting it and then choosing Chart Expert from the right-click menu or Format | Chart Expert from the main menu.

Using the Chart Expert

The Chart Expert is a tabbed wizard. You configure a chart by setting the various options on the Chart Expert tabs. The Chart Expert options are discussed in detail in the "Chart Expert" section of this chapter.

Chart Location

The location of the chart in the report determines what data is charted in much the same way that the location of a summary field determines what data is summarized. If you place a chart in the Report Header or Report Footer sections, it will contain data for the entire report. If you place it in a group header or footer, it will contain data for the group.

After creating the chart, you may need to move or resize it. Resize a chart by selecting it and dragging one of its resizing handles. You can also move the entire chart by dragging within the same section, to another group section, or to the Report Header or Report Footer section.

Drill-Down

If your chart contains groups, you will be able to drill down on it just as you could drill down on a group with hidden detail sections. If there is only one group, you can double-click on the chart to drill into the group's details. If there are multiple groups, double-click on the legend to drill into the group you want. If the Details section is suppressed, drill-down will display only the summary value.

Modifying a Chart

To modify a chart, select it, and then choose Chart Expert from the right-click menu or select Format | Chart Expert from the main menu.

Formatting a Chart

If you invoke the Format Editor with a chart selected, you can modify options on the Common, Border, and Hyperlink tabs. No other tabs are available.

Customizing a Chart

Individual components of a chart can be customized using the Chart menu options. The Chart command appears on the main menu when a chart is selected, and the same options are visible on the right-click menu. The Chart menu options are described in the "Chart Menu" section of this chapter.

Chart Expert

After opening the Chart Expert, you will see several tabs. The Type, Data, and Text tabs are always visible. The Axes and Options tabs are available if you are setting chart options manually. The OK button will become active once the Data tab has been selected.

Type Tab

The Type tab, shown in Figure 10-1, is where you select the chart type, set its orientation, and choose whether to let Crystal Reports set some options for you or whether you want to set all the options yourself.

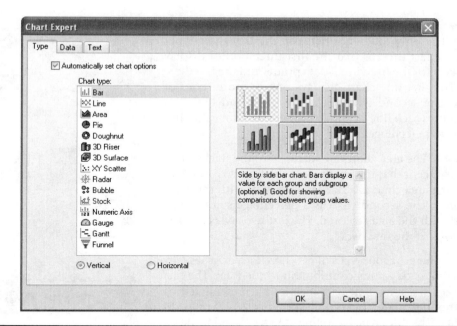

Figure 10-1   Choosing a chart type and orientation

Automatically Set Chart Options

Automatically Set Chart Options is checked by default. Clearing it causes the Axes and Options tabs to appear; there you can configure the chart's axes and set other display options.

Chart Type

The Chart Type list box contains the types of charts that Crystal Reports can create. Different chart types are appropriate for different types of data. When you select a chart type, a set of buttons appears to the right. These buttons display the available styles for the chart type selected. The list box below the buttons describes the chart style and gives recommendations for when it should be used. The more commonly used chart types are listed first.

Bar   Six types of bar chart are available. The first is a simple bar chart showing one set of summary values. The second is a stacked bar chart that shows the components of a total value in different colors. The components might be summary subtotals or detail values. The third type of bar chart shows the components of a total value as a percentages of the total. The remaining three types are identical to the first three types but displayed with 3-D bars.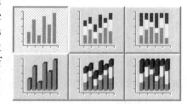

Line   The available types of line charts are shown here. The only difference between the first three types and the last three is that the first three do not display markers for the individual data points and the last three do. The first line chart displays one or more series of data. The second type stacks the lines, and the third computes each line's contribution to the total value and displays percentages.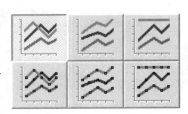

Area   The area charts are identical to the stacked line charts except that the area below the line is colored in. The first area chart is a stacked line chart with the areas colored. The second chart is a percentage stacked line chart with the areas colored. The last two styles are 3-D versions of the first two.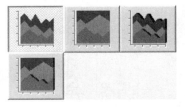

Pie   There are four types of pie chart. Pie charts visually represent each value's contribution to the total. The first type is just a simple pie with pie pieces representing each contributing value. The second type is just a 3-D version of the first. The third type is multiple pies representing the totals for different groups, with each group's components shown as pie pieces. The fourth type refines the second type by sizing each group's pie in proportion to the group's contribution to the overall total.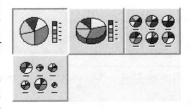

Doughnut   These chart styles are identical to the pie chart styles except that the shape used is a torus rather than a circle, and the simple 2-D style is not separately available.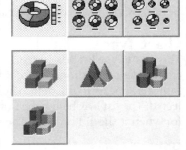

3D Riser   These charts are three-dimensional bar charts where the bars are displayed one behind the other as well as next to each other. The bars can be rectangular, pyramidal, octagonal, or rectangular with cut corners.

3D Surface   You can use three variations of a 3-D surface chart. These charts produce a surface by using three sets of data. The first style option displays only the surface. The second displays the area under the surface as a solid color. The third option adds lines to the surface.

XY Scatter   This chart category contains only one style option, as shown here. An XY scatter chart simply plots points. You can use it to show relationships or trends in the data visually.

Radar These charts take the values that are usually plotted on the X axis, and plot them in a circle. The Y values are then plotted from the center of the circle out, and the points are connected. There are two radar styles, regular and stacked.

Bubble There is only one type of bubble chart, as shown here. The bubble chart is similar to a scatter chart, but the size of the points is determined by a third set of data values.

Stock There are two styles of stock charts: The high-low chart displays a bar for each stock, where the bar stretches from the low price for the day to the high price for the day. The high-low-open-close chart adds an indicator for the opening and closing prices. You can use these chart types for other kinds of data where you want to display similar information.

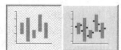

Numeric Axis Most of the preceding chart types used fixed intervals for the X axis. The numeric axis types plot the X coordinates according to their values. There are six numeric axis types. The first three are a bar chart, line chart, and area chart that use numbers on the X axis. The last three are similar but use dates on the X axis.

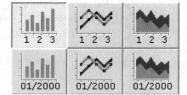

Gauge The gauge chart looks like an automobile fuel gauge; use it to display one value per gauge. You can display multiple gauges and color wedges of the gauge differently to indicate warning levels. You might use a gauge to display today's sales.

Gantt There is only one style of Gantt chart. A Gantt chart is commonly used in project management processes. It displays a horizontal bar stretching from a start date to an end date for a set of tasks.

Funnel A funnel chart is a single stacked bar in the shape of a funnel. There is only one style of funnel chart. The height of each bar represents its percentage contribution to the total value. The width of the bar is of no significance.

Vertical/Horizontal

The Vertical and Horizontal radio buttons are available for bar, line, and area charts. The default is Vertical. If you chose Horizontal, the chart will be turned so that the bars are horizontal instead of vertical.

Data Tab

Use the Data tab to choose the data for the chart, the placement of the chart, and the chart layout. The layout chosen determines the data options.

Placement

The Placement panel of the Data tab is used to set the location of the chart in the report, as shown in Figure 10-2 for the Group option. The chart can be moved after creation by dragging or by modifying the placement options.

Location The Location drop-down box contains an option for once per report and an option for each group in the report, if the Advanced button is selected. Fewer choices are listed for the Group, Cross-Tab, and OLAP options.

Header/Footer Use the Header and Footer radio buttons to have the chart placed in the header or footer section related to the location selected. If Once per Report is chosen, the Header option will place the chart in the report header and the Footer option will place the chart in the report footer. If a report group is chosen, the chart will be placed in the Group Header or Footer sections.

NOTE When using the Group Layout option, a chart can only be placed in the header or footer section for a group that is higher in the group hierarchy than the group used in the On Change Of field.

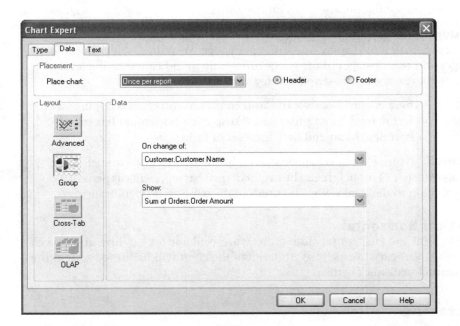

Figure 10-2 Setting the placement of a chart on a group

Layout

Charts can be created on detail data, group data, cross-tabs, and OLAP grids. Use the Layout area to pick the type of data that you want to use in the chart. In some cases, you can change the chart layout after the chart has been created. There are four buttons in the Layout panel, as shown here.

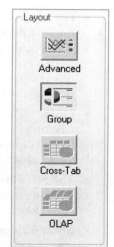

Group   Use the Group layout when your report contains groups and you want to chart on group summary values that already exist.

Advanced   Use the Advanced option to chart on detail-level data or summary-level data. You can use database fields, formulas, or running total fields. In addition, you can create summaries in the Chart Expert for use only in the chart.

Cross-Tab   The Cross-Tab option is available when a cross-tab exists in your report. Use it to create a chart based on the cross-tab cells.

OLAP   The OLAP option is available if an OLAP grid is used in your report. It is similar to the Cross-Tab option, but works for OLAP grids.

Data

The Data area of the Data tab is used to configure the data sources for the chart. The options available in the Data panel change depending on the layout type selected.

Group   The Group option requires the least configuration; you only need to pick a group field and a summary field (see Figure 10-2).

- **On Change Of**   The On Change Of drop-down box lists all the groups that exist in the report. Pick the group that you want the chart to use as the X values.

- **Show**   The Show drop-down box lists all the summary fields that exist in the report for the group you selected. Pick the summary that you want the chart to use as the Y values.

Advanced   Use the Advanced option when you need more flexibility than is provided by the Group option. Figure 10-3 shows the Data tab with the Advanced option selected. The Data area of the Data tab for the Advanced option has many items that you can customize to create exactly the chart you need.

- **Available Fields**   This is a tree view of the existing report fields and the fields from all connected data sources. You populate the On Change Of list and the Show values list from this list by using the arrow buttons or by dragging.

- **Browse**   This button is available when any database field is selected. Click it to see a sample of the contents of the field.

- **On Change Of**   This drop-down box contains three options. On Change Of is the default; when it is selected, you must add one or more fields from the Available Fields box to the list box below On Change Of. Choosing On Change Of creates a chart based on summary values. The second option is For Each Record; it is used to create a chart based on detail values. The last option is For All Records; it creates a chart based on grand total values.

- **Order**   This button becomes available when an On Change Of field is selected. Clicking it opens the Chart Sort Order dialog box, which is very similar to the Group Options dialog box. Using the Chart Sort Order dialog box, you can select a sort order: ascending, descending, specified, or original.

- **Top N**   This button is also available when an On Change Of field is selected. Clicking it displays the Group Sort Order dialog box, where you can create Top N or Bottom N groupings for your chart.

- **Show Values**   The values in this list box are used as the data points or Y coordinates. Move fields into this box from the Available Fields list box.

- **Don't Summarize**   This button is available for formula fields. If you want formula fields summarized, clear the box and then set the summary operation with the Set Summary Operation button.

- **Set Summary Operation**   Click this button to change the type of summary that is computed for the selected Show Values field. Clicking the button opens the Edit Summary dialog box, where you can change the summary type and choose whether to make it a percentage summary of a higher-level group.

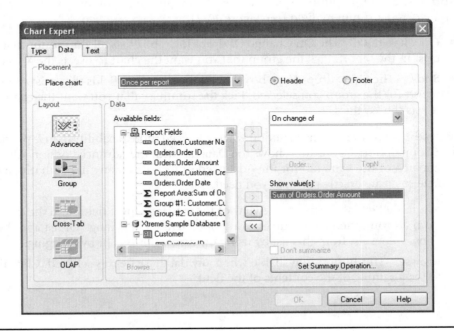

Figure 10-3   Customizing a chart design

Cross-Tab   When you select the Cross-Tab button, the Data panel changes, as shown in Figure 10-4. To create a chart based on a cross-tab you need to set three items:

- **On Change Of**   This drop-down box contains the list of all row and column fields used in the cross-tab. Select one to use as the primary X value for the report.
- **Subdivided By**   This drop-down box contains the list of row and column fields from the cross-tab, except for the value used in the On Change Of box. You can select None or one of the fields to use as the secondary X value for the report.
- **Show**   This drop-down box lists the summary values used in the cross-tab cells. Pick one to use in your chart.

OLAP   Figure 10-5 shows the Data tab of the Chart Expert when the OLAP layout is selected. For a chart based on an OLAP grid, there are four items to set:

- **Chart Off Entire Grid**   Check this option if you want the chart to mimic the settings for the grid. Clear it to customize the settings.
- **On Change Of**   Pick the dimension that you want across the X axis in the On Change Of drop-down box.
- **Subdivided By**   After you pick a dimension in the On Change Of box, the other dimensions, as well as the None option, will be listed in the Subdivided By drop-down box. Choose one to add a secondary field to the X axis.
- **Other Dimensions**   Click this button to display the Format Other Dimensions dialog box. In this dialog box, you can select one of the unused dimensions and set the value it should have for the chart display.

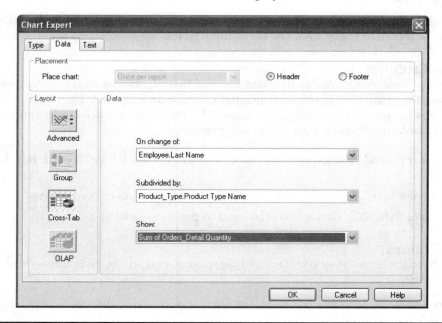

Figure 10-4   Creating a chart based on a cross-tab

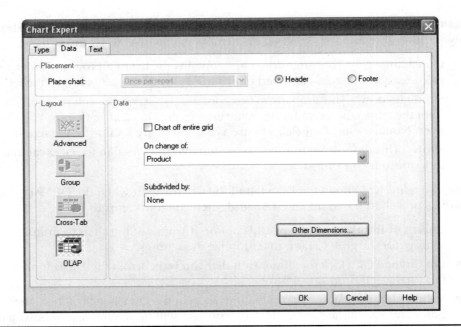

Figure 10-5   Creating a chart based on an OLAP grid

Axes Tab

If you clear the Automatically Set Chart Options check box on the Type tab, the Axes tab will appear, as shown in Figure 10-6. Use the options on this tab to configure the chart's axes.

Show Gridlines

The Show Gridlines panel of the Axes tab has two or three options, depending on whether the chart type is two-dimensional or three-dimensional. Each option has a check box for Major and Minor. Check Major if you want a major tick mark to appear on the axis, or Minor if you want a minor tick mark.

- **Group Axis**   The group axis corresponds to the On Change Of field; it is the X axis.
- **Series Axis**   The series axis only appears for three-dimensional charts.
- **Data Axis**   The data axis corresponds to the Show field; it is the Y axis.

Data Values

Options in the Data Values panel control the spacing, end points, and number format of the data axis.

Auto Scale   Check this box to have Crystal Reports determine the best spacing for the labels on the X axis.

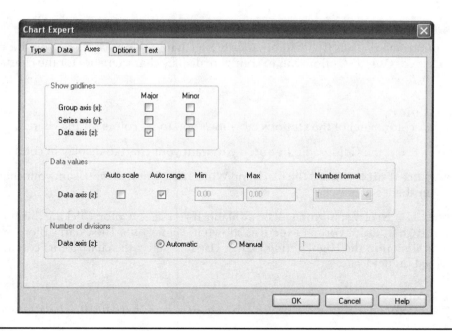

Figure 10-6   Configuring chart axes

Auto Range   Check Auto Range to have Crystal Reports compute the starting and ending values for the data axis from the chart values.

Min   Clear Auto Range and enter a number into the Min edit box to set the starting point for the data axis manually.

Max   Clear Auto range and enter a number into the Max edit box to set the ending point for the data axis manually.

Number Format   If Auto Range is cleared, the Number Format drop-down box will be available. Select the option that gives you the number display you want. You can select from the options shown here.

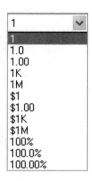

Number of Divisions

In the Number of Divisions panel of the Axes tab, you choose whether to let Crystal Reports decide the number of intervals or to manually set the number of intervals for the data axis. Select the Automatic radio button to have Crystal Reports set the number of divisions. Select the Manual radio button and enter a number to set the divisions manually.

Options Tab

The Options tab appears if the Automatically Set Chart Options check box on the Type tab is cleared. Use the Options tab to configure display characteristics for the chart. See Figure 10-7.

Chart Color

The Chart color panel of the Options tab allows you to set colors for the chart.

Color   Select the Color radio button if you want your chart to display in color.

Black and White   Select the Black and White radio button if you want your chart to display in shades of gray.

Format   The Format button will be available if you select Color. Clicking this button opens the Chart Color Format Expert, as shown in Figure 10-8. The Chart Color Format Expert is similar to the Highlighting Expert. Use it to select the chart colors conditionally, based on field values.

Data Points

The Data Points panel of the Options tab is used to configure the display of the data point markers.

Show Label   If you check Show Label, the name of the field being charted will be displayed next to each point on the chart.

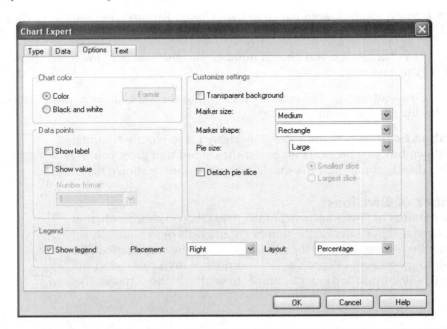

Figure 10-7   Manually configuring chart display options

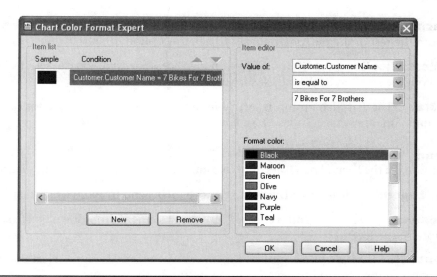

Figure 10-8   Chart Color Format Expert

Show Value   If you check Show Value, the value of the data point will be displayed next to the point marker.

Number Format   If you check Show Value, the Number Format drop-down box will become available, and you can pick a format for the display value.

Customize Settings
The options in the Customize settings panel change depending on the chart type.

Transparent Background   Check Transparent Background to make the background of the chart clear, allowing objects behind the chart to be seen.

Marker Size   Choose an option from the Marker Size drop-down box to set the size of the data point markers: Small, Medium Small, Medium, Medium Large, or Large.

Marker Shape   Select an option from the Marker Shape drop-down box to choose a shape for the data point markers: Rectangle, Circle, Diamond, or Triangle.

Viewing Angle   The Viewing Angle option appears for three-dimensional chart types. The choices are shown in this illustration. Changing the viewing angle changes the perspective from which the chart is viewed.

Pie Size   The Pie Size option is available for pie and doughnut charts. Select a size for your pie: Minimum, Small, Average, Large, or Maximum.

Detach Pie Slice　For pie and doughnut charts, you can have a slice shown pulled out from the rest of the pie for emphasis. Check this option to detach a pie slice.

Smallest Slice/Largest Slice　If Detach Pie Slice is checked, you can select whether to pull out the smallest or the largest slice using these radio buttons.

Bar Size　The Bar Size option is available for bar charts. Select a size for the bars: Minimum, Small, Average, Large, or Maximum.

Legend

The options in the Legend panel are used to configure the display of the chart's legend.

Show Legend　Clear Show Legend to remove the legend from the chart display.

Placement　If Show Legend is checked, use the Placement drop-down box to select a location for the legend.

Layout　The Layout option appears for some chart types. Use it to select the values that appear in the Legend box: Percentage, Amount, Both, or None.

Text Tab

Use the Text tab options, shown in Figure 10-9, to configure how the chart's text items are displayed.

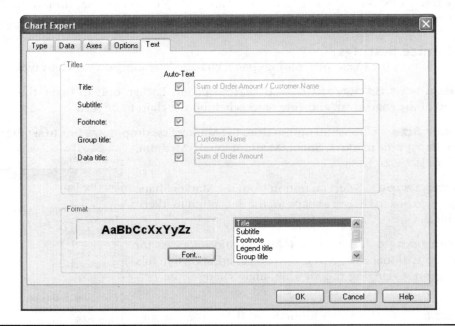

Figure 10-9　Configuring chart text

Titles

The Titles panel lists all titles that exist for the current chart type. You can change the default titles assigned by Crystal Reports if you like.

Auto-Text   Each title has an Auto-Text check box. If you want Crystal Reports to assign a title automatically, check the box. If you want to assign a title manually, clear it.

Title   The entry in this box is the text that will appear at the top of the chart.

Subtitle   The text in this box will appear immediately below the title, usually in a smaller font.

Footnote   This text will appear at the bottom of the chart, as a note.

Group Title   The Group Title text is the title of the X axis.

Data Title   The Data Title text is the title of the Y axis.

Series Title   The Series Title option will appear for three-dimensional charts. This text is the title of the third axis.

Format

The Format panel of the Text tab is used to format the text of the chart's titles.

Title List Box   The Title list box contains an entry for every title that exists in the report. Select the title you want to format.

Font   After selecting the title that you want to format, click the Font button. The Font dialog box will appear, and you can set the font face, style, and size and add strikeout or underline effects.

Sample Area   The sample area of the Format panel displays a sample of the selected font format.

Exercise 10.1: Creating a Group Chart

1. Open the Exercise 9.15 report.

2. Create selection criteria such that only records where the region is CA and the order date is after 4/1/2002 are included. The selection formula should look like this:

   ```
   {Orders.Order Date} >= DateTime (2002, 04, 01, 00, 00, 00) and
   {Customer.Region} = "CA"
   ```

3. Click the Insert Chart button to open the Chart Expert.

4. Select Bar as the Chart type, and then press the button for the side-by-side, three-dimensional bar chart.

5. Select the Data tab, and notice that Crystal Reports has entered the customer name in the On Change Of field and the sum of the order amount in the Show field.

6. Click OK to create the chart. Note that the display of the chart on the Design tab is just a generic rendering. You will not see the actual chart until you click the Refresh button.

7. Click the Refresh button.

8. Select the chart object and drag the right side until the chart is as wide as the page.

9. Right-click the chart, and choose Chart Expert.

10. Select the Text tab, and clear the Auto-Text box for the title. Type **Orders by Customer** for the title.

11. On the Type tab, clear the Automatically Set Chart Options check box.

12. On the Options tab, check the Show Value box and select the $1K option in the Number Format drop-down box.

13. Click OK. Preview the report.

14. Save the report as **Exercise 10.1**.

Exercise 10.2: Creating an Advanced Chart

1. Open the Exercise 9.14 report.

2. Click the Insert Chart button to create a chart.

3. Select Pie as the chart type, and click the 3-D pie chart button.

4. Select the Data tab. Notice that the Advanced option is selected because no groups exist in the report.

5. Move the Hire Date field into the On Change Of list box. Then select it in the list box, and click the Order button. Set the section to be printed for each year, and click OK.

6. Move the Employee ID field into the Show Value(s) list box. Select it, and click the Set Summary Operation button.

7. Change the summary operation to Count, and click OK.

8. Click OK to close the Chart Expert. Preview the report.

9. Save the report as **Exercise 10.2**.

Exercise 10.3: Creating a Cross-Tab Chart

1. Open the Exercise 3.8 report.

2. Select the cross-tab, and then choose Insert | Chart from the menu to open the Chart Expert.

3. On the Type tab, select the 3-D riser chart, and press the octagon button.

4. On the Data tab, select the Cross-Tab option in the Layout panel.

5. The On Change Of box should be set to the Employee.Last Name field, and the Show field should be the Sum of Orders_Detail.Quantity. Set the Subdivided By field to Product_Type.Product Type Name.

6. Click OK to close the Chart Expert. Preview the report.

7. Save the report as **Exercise 10.3**.

Chart Menu

You can use commands available on the Chart menu to enhance chart viewing in preview mode, to customize the chart in ways that are not available via the Chart Expert, to save the chart as a template chart, and to add trend lines to a chart. The Chart menu is available on the main menu when a report is selected. Its options are also added to the right-click menu for charts.

Movement Options

The four movement commands, shown here, act as radio buttons: only one can be selected at a time. Not all movement commands are available for all report types.

Select Mode   Choose the Select Mode option to have mouse clicks select chart objects. In select mode the mouse pointer is a magnifying glass.

Zoom In   Choose the Zoom In option to use the mouse to zoom in on a smaller portion of the data. Draw a box with the mouse pointer, and the graph will be redisplayed showing only the selected area. The mouse pointer in Zoom In mode is a magnifying glass with a plus sign.

Zoom Out   Choose the Zoom Out option to use the mouse to zoom out. Click the chart with the Zoom Out pointer, and the chart will be redisplayed showing more data. The Zoom Out option is only available if the chart has previously been zoomed in on. The mouse pointer in Zoom Out mode is a magnifying glass with a minus sign.

Pan   The Pan option is only available if the chart has been zoomed in on. The Pan option allows you to scroll the chart: hold down the mouse button and drag to the right or left. The mouse pointer is a double-ended arrow in Pan mode.

Save Options

Use the Save options shown here to apply customizations to all chart instances, discard custom changes, or to save a chart as a template.

> Apply Changes to All Charts
> Discard Custom Changes
> Save as Template...

Apply Changes to All Charts   When you customize a chart using Chart | Chart Options in the Preview window, the changes apply only to the specific chart instance that you selected. (There will be more than one chart instance if the chart is in a group header or footer section.) You can execute Apply Changes to All Charts to replicate the change you made to all chart instances.

NOTE If you make a change using the Chart Options in the *Design* window, the change will automatically apply to all chart instances.

Discard Custom Changes If you customize an instance of a chart and wish to undo those customizations, select Discard Custom Changes. Discard Custom Changes will not be available if you have previously executed Apply Changes to All Charts.

Save As Template You can save a chart as a user-defined template by selecting Save As Template. The chart template will be saved to a special directory and can be applied to other reports by using the Chart Options | Template command.

Edit Axis Label

The series labels on the X axis may be difficult to read. To modify the name of a single label, in the Preview window, select the label on the X axis, right-click and choose Edit

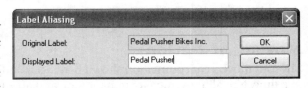

Axis Label. The Label Aliasing dialog box will appear, as shown here. Change the name and click OK. You can then choose to apply the change to all chart instances if you like.

Trend Lines

Trend lines are additional lines drawn on a chart to show trends in the data. To show a trend line on a bar chart, select a bar, and then choose Trendlines from the Chart menu or the right-click menu. The Trendlines dialog box shown in Figure 10-10 will open.

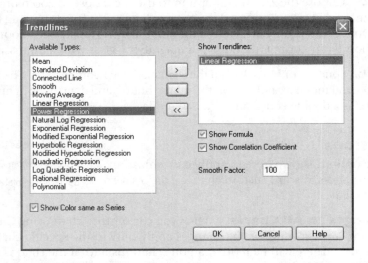

Figure 10-10 Including trend lines in a chart

NOTE To show trend lines on a line chart, you must first remove the line and show only the data point markers. This is a bug and should be fixed in a service pack.

Available Types

The Available Types list box shows the types of trend lines that Crystal Reports can create. To have a specific trend line displayed on your chart, move it to the Show Trendlines list box. Some of the common types are described here.

Mean The Mean option draws a horizontal line at the mean value of the data points.

Standard Deviation To show a horizontal line at the standard deviation of the data points, select the Standard Deviation option.

Connected Line The Connected Line option is a line connecting one data point to the next. This is the same as showing the line in a line chart.

Smooth The Smooth option draws a smooth line connecting all the data points. You control the amount of smoothing.

Moving Average The Moving Average option computes a moving average and connects the moving average points. The number of values you want averaged is entered in the Order edit box.

Linear Regression To create a straight line that best fits the data points, select Linear Regression. A line of the form $y = mx + b$ will be created and m and b will be computed. This is the same as a first-degree polynomial.

Power Regression The Power Regression option will create a line of the form $y = mx^b$ and m and b will be computed.

Natural Log Regression The Natural Log Regression option will create a line of the form $y = m \ln(x) + b$ and m and b will be computed.

Exponential Regression The Exponential Regression option will create a line of the form $y = mb^x$, and m and b will be computed.

Quadratic Regression The Quadratic Regression option will create a line of the form $y = ax^2 + bx + c$, and a, b, and c will be computed. This is the same as a second-degree polynomial.

Log Quadratic Regression The Log Quadratic Regression option will create a line with the form $\ln(y) = ax^2 + bx + c$, and a, b, and c will be computed.

Polynomial The Polynomial option will create a line with the form $y = a + bx + cx^2 + dx^3\ldots$, where there will be as many x terms as the order entered in the Order edit box.

Show Trendlines
Move any trend line types that you want displayed in the report to the Show Trendlines list box.

Show Formula
To display the formula of the selected trend line on the chart, check the Show Formula check box.

Show Correlation Coefficient
To display the Correlation Coefficient on the chart, check the Show Correlation Coefficient check box.

Smooth Factor
Enter a value for Smooth Factor for the trend line types that allow it. The higher the number, the smoother the resulting line will be.

Show Color Same as Series
Check the Show Color Same as Series box to draw the line in the same color as the selected data point.

Order
The Order box is used for different purposes, depending on the trend line type. For a moving average, it is the number of values in each average. For a polynomial, it is the order, or degree, of the polynomial.

Financial/Scientific
For a Moving Average trend line, Financial places the average at the last point contained in the average. Scientific places the average at the midpoint of the averaged values.

Chart Options
The options on the Chart Options submenu allow you to customize a chart in ways that are not available in the Chart Expert. You can also apply predefined or user-defined templates to charts.

 TIP If you press the Help button in any of the Chart Options dialog boxes, the Chart Help file will open. This file is separate from the common Crystal Reports help file and has its own contents list.

Template
Choosing the Template option opens the Choose a Chart Type dialog box shown in Figure 10-11. It has two tabs, one for picking a chart type from the gallery, and one for picking a custom chart template.

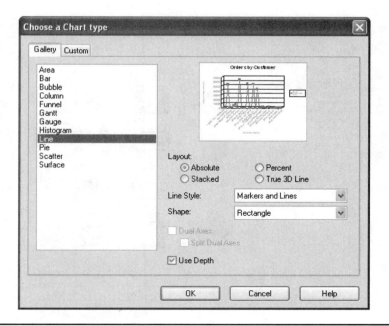

Figure 10-11   Choosing a chart type

Gallery   The Gallery tab contains all the possible chart types. When a chart type is selected, the options that apply to that chart type are displayed and you can modify them. The Gallery options are more flexible than the chart type options available in the Chart Expert.

Custom   The Custom tab is shown in Figure 10-12. You can apply these report templates to your charts. They are organized by category. Any chart templates that you create with the Save As Template command are shown in the User Defined category.

General

If you select General from the Chart Options submenu, the Chart Options dialog box will be displayed, as shown in Figure 10-13. The Chart Options dialog has several tabs where you can fine-tune the chart settings. The tabs are General, Layout, Data Labels, Numbers, Dual Y Options, Look, Display Status, and Titles. The specific properties displayed on the tabs change depending on the chart type.

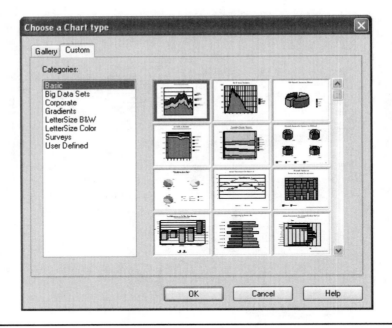

Figure 10-12   Choosing a custom chart type

Series

The Series command is available if a data series is selected. Selecting it opens the Series Options dialog box. The Series Options dialog has tabs for General, Data Labels, Numbers, and Trendline, as shown here. Properties on the tabs change depending on the chart type.

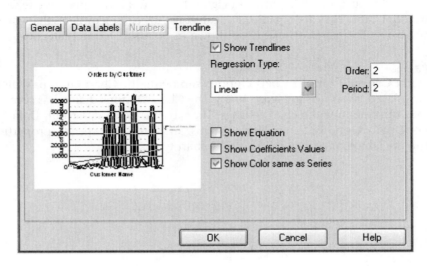

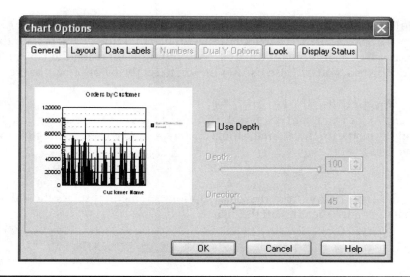

Figure 10-13 Selecting chart options

Grid

Select Grid from the Chart Options submenu to display the Numeric Axis Grids & Scales dialog box. This dialog box has tabs for General, Scales, Labels, Numbers, and Grid, as shown here. Use the properties on these tabs to format the axes and gridlines.

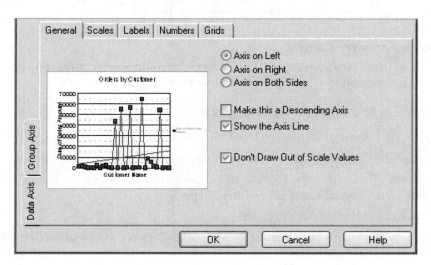

Selected Item

Choosing the Selected Item command displays the Formatting dialog box for the chart item that is selected. You can set the font, line, and fill color using the tabs of the For-matting dialog box. You can also use this option to set the color of bars or pie slices.

Viewing Angle

The Viewing Angle command displays the Choose a Viewing Angle dialog box. This op-tion is only available for three-dimensional chart types and is used to fine-tune the angle of perspective.

Titles

Selecting the Titles option from the Chart Options submenu displays the Titles dialog box. Use it to change the titles on the chart.

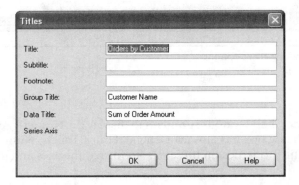

Auto-Arrange Chart

If you move or resize a chart object in the Preview window, select Auto-Arrange Chart from the Chart menu to return it to its original size and position.

Exercise 10.4: Customizing a Chart

1. Open the report from Exercise 10.1.

2. Select the chart, right-click, and select Chart Options and then Template.

3. Select Column from the Gallery, and choose True 3D Riser from the Layout area. Pick Floating Cube as the Riser Shape.

4. Click OK and preview the report.

5. On the chart, select the highest floating cube, then right-click and select Chart Options | Selected Item.

6. On the Fill tab, select a pattern, and make the background color white.

7. Click OK twice to return to the chart.

8. Save the report as **Exercise 10.4**.

Chapter Review

This chapter covered charting in Crystal Reports. Charting is done primarily with the Chart Expert and fine-tuned with the Chart menu options.

Quick Tips

- Charts are created with the Chart Expert. The tabs available on the Chart Expert are Type, Data, Axes, Options, and Text.
- Charts can be further customized using the Chart menu options.
- The Chart type is chosen on the Type tab. The data to include in the chart is selected on the Data tab. The Axes tab is used to set options for the chart's axes. The Options tab is used to set chart color, format the legend, and set other properties. Chart titles are set on the Text tab.
- The location of a chart determines the data it contains. If it is placed in the Report Header or Footer, it includes all data in the report. If it is placed in a group section, it contains data for the group.
- The Data tab of the Chart Expert contains four layouts: Advanced, Group, Cross-Tab, and OLAP. The Group option can be used for reports that contain groups and summary fields. The Cross-Tab option is used to create a chart from a cross-tab. The OLAP option is used to create a chart from an OLAP grid.
- Charts created using the Group layout can be drilled down on.
- The Advanced layout option can be used in a report that does not contain any groups. Summary values for the chart are created on the Data tab.
- Chart templates can be created and applied with options from the Chart Options submenu.

Questions

Questions may have more than one correct answer. Choose all answers that apply.

1. You can use the Advanced layout to create charts with summary data, but you will not be able to drill down on the summaries.
   a. True
   b. False

2. In the Chart Expert, you can select the following layouts:
   a. Group
   b. Detail
   c. Advanced
   d. Cross-Tab
   e. OLAP

3. Charts cannot be placed in which of these sections?

   a. Report Header

   b. Report Footer

   c. Details

   d. Group Header

   e. Group Footer

4. Moving a chart from the Report Header to a Group Header changes the data displayed in the chart.

   a. True

   b. False

5. On a line chart, you can display

   a. Both the line and point markers

   b. Only the line

   c. Only the markers

   d. Neither the line or the markers

6. Checking the Show Label option of the Chart Expert displays the data point value next to the marker.

   a. True

   b. False

7. Which of the following tabs are available on the Chart Expert?

   a. Type

   b. Data

   c. Axes

   d. Options

   e. Text

8. If your report contains groups, but no cross-tabs or OLAP grids, you can use which of the following layout option(s)?

   a. Advanced

   b. Group

   c. Cross-Tab

   d. OLAP

9. Various chart properties can be formatted using the

   a. Chart Editor

   b. Format Editor

   c. Chart Expert

   d. Chart menu

   e. Chart Properties Editor

10. You can change the color of individual pie slices using the

   a. Options tab of the Chart Expert

   b. Selected Item command of the Chart Options menu

   c. Slice Colors button on the Template Gallery

Answers

1. **a.** True. You can create a chart using the Advanced layout that looks similar to a chart using the Group layout, but you will not be able to drill down into the details.

2. **a, c, d, e.** Detail is not an available chart layout. Detail charts are created with the Advanced layout.

3. **c.** Charts cannot be placed in the Details section.

4. **a.** The location of a chart determines the data it contains.

5. **a, b, c.** You can show Lines Only, Markers Only, or Markers and Lines.

6. **b.** The Show value option causes the data value to be displayed on the chart.

7. **All.** Type, Data, and Text are always visible. Axes and Options are available if Automatically Set Chart Options is not selected on the Type tab.

8. **a, b.** If your report contains groups, you can use the Group or Advanced layout.

9. **b, c, d.** Different Chart properties can be set with the Format Editor, Chart Expert, and Chart menu options.

10. **b.** Individual pie slices can be colored using the Selected Item command from the Chart Options menu.

CHAPTER 11

Report Distribution

Exam RDCR200 expects you to be able to

- Export a report
- Save a report to Crystal Enterprise

Reports can be distributed in several ways. They can be printed and then distributed as hard copies. They can be exported to various file formats and then distributed via e-mail, web sites, or file servers. Or they can be saved to Crystal Enterprise and then distributed via the Crystal Enterprise web client or any of the other Crystal Enterprise distribution options. Printing reports was covered in Chapter 4; exporting reports and saving reports to Crystal Enterprise are covered in this chapter.

Exporting Reports

To export a report, you select File | Export, or click the Export button on the Standard Toolbar. The Export dialog box will open, as shown here. You must choose a destination and a format for the export file.

Destination

The destination determines where the exported file will be saved.

Disk File

Choosing Disk File exports the report to a file on disk. You will be prompted for a file location and other necessary options for the format chosen. The location can be any directory that you have access to; it need not be local.

Application

The Application option saves the report to your Temp directory, in the format you select, and then opens it with the application associated with that format's file extension. The usual file extensions and associated applications are listed in Table 11-1, but your system could have different associations configured. Once the file is opened in the application, you may want to save it to a different directory with a different name.

Exchange Folder

If Microsoft Exchange is properly installed and configured on your system, you will be able to export to an Exchange Folder. After setting any required options for the format you have chosen, the Exchange dialog box called Choose Profile will appear. You must select a profile or create a new one, and then select a folder. The report will be exported to the selected Exchange folder.

Lotus Domino

To export to a Lotus Domino database, you must have the Lotus client installed and properly configured. In addition, you must create a special form in the database that you want to export to. The form must be named Report Form, and it must have a field called Comments. You must create a view that contains the default # column and a reference to the form's Comments field.

After choosing a format and selecting Lotus Domino as the destination type from the Export dialog box, you will be prompted for any settings required by the selected format.

Format	File Extension	Commonly Associated Application
Acrobat Format (PDF)	.pdf	Adobe Acrobat or Adobe Acrobat Reader
Crystal Reports (RPT)	.rpt	Crystal Reports
HTML 3.2	.htm or .html	Web browser or HTML editor
HTML 4.0	.htm or .html	Web browser or HTML editor
MS Excel 97-2000	.xls	Microsoft Excel
MS Excel 97-2000 (Data Only)	.xls	Excel
MS Word	.doc	Microsoft Word
ODBC	None	File is saved into the selected database; no application is opened.
Record Style (Columns No Spaces)	.rec	None
Record Style (Columns with Spaces)	.rec	None
Report Definition	txt	Notepad
Rich Text Format	.rtf	Word
Separated Values (CSV)	.csv	Excel
Tab-Separated Text	.ttx	None
Text	.txt	Notepad
XML	.xml	Web browser

Table 11-1   Export File Extensions and Associated Applications

The Lotus Domino dialog box will then display, and you can select the database you want to export to. You will be prompted to enter something for the Comments field. Click OK to close the dialog box and complete the export. The report will be available in the Domino database as a hyperlink.

Lotus Domino Mail

If the Lotus Domino Mail client is properly installed and configured on your system, you will be able to export a report as an attachment to a Lotus mail message. After filling in the prompts required by the format you have chosen, you will be prompted for your Lotus password. The Send Mail dialog box then appears, and you can fill in the recipient and any other options you require.

MAPI (Microsoft Mail)

If you have a MAPI-compliant mail client such as Microsoft Mail, Outlook, or Outlook Express installed and properly configured, you will be able to export a report as an attachment to an e-mail message. The MAPI client should be set up as your default mail client. You can verify the default mail client in the Tools option of Internet Explorer. After filling in the prompts required by the format you have chosen, the Send Mail dialog box will appear, and you can fill in the recipient and any other options you require.

Format

Crystal Reports supplies many export file formats. The formats that you see in your export dialog box depend on the options you chose during installation. Some export formats require additional information and will display dialog boxes to obtain the necessary settings.

There are two distinct types of formats: the first attempts to create a duplicate of the display seen in Crystal Reports and is meant primarily for report viewing; the second extracts the report data and is meant primarily for importing into other applications. Some applications can place objects anywhere in their documents, similar to Crystal Reports. These types will best duplicate the look of the original report and include the PDF format. Other formats must move objects to the nearest line; an example is text. Microsoft Excel exports move objects to the nearest cell. Formats meant to export the report data only will preserve the least report formatting; these include Excel (Data only), ODBC, Record Style, CSV, Tab-separated text, and XML. All export types except RPT may lose *some* formatting.

Acrobat Format (PDF)

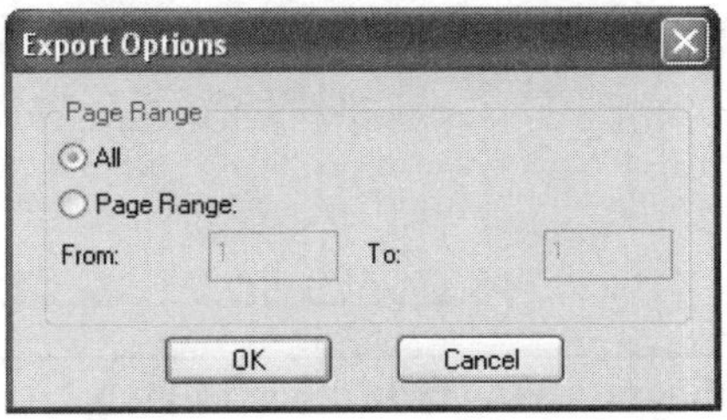

If you choose to export to PDF, the Export Options dialog box will be displayed as shown here. The PDF format most closely reproduces the look of the original report.

You can choose to export all pages of the report or select a range of pages. After closing the Export Options dialog box, a file dialog box will appear.

Choose the location, set the name for the export file, and click Save to start the export. A progress box will be displayed while the export is happening and then you will be returned to Crystal Reports.

CAUTION Interactive elements such as hyperlinks and drill-down will not work when exported to PDF.

If you need to fine-tune your PDF exports, optimize them for web viewing, create tagged PDFs, or add security to them, you can purchase the full Adobe Acrobat product and use the Print to PDF option.

Crystal Reports (RPT)

The RPT export creates a new Crystal Reports file, in the location and with the name you specify. The result is the same as using the File | Save As command, except that the open report file does not change to the new name. The open report retains its name and another file is created with the new name.

HTML 3.2

When you choose the HTML 3.2 export format, the Select Export File dialog box shown in Figure 11-1 will appear. Use the properties in the dialog box to configure the output options for the HTML file. If your report contains graphics, multiple files will be created for the HTML export, even if you clear the Separate HTML Pages check box. In that case, there will be one HTML file plus any required graphic files.

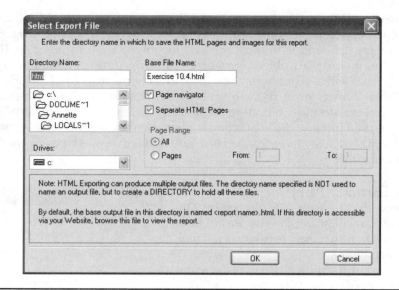

Figure 11-1   Exporting to HTML 3.2

Directory Name   The files created by the HTML export will be saved into a directory of your choice. Enter the name of the directory in the Directory Name box. You can enter a new name to create a new directory. The name you enter will be created under the directory displayed in the directory list box.

Directory List Box   Use the Directory list box to browse to the location where you want the export files created.

Drives   Use the Drives drop-down box to select the drive where you want the export files created.

Base File Name   Base File Name defaults to the report filename with an .html extension. You can change it if you like.

Page Navigator   If you check the Page Navigator box, page navigation links will be added to the HTML page(s), as shown here.

[<<First Page]   *[<Previous Page]*   *[Next Page>]*   *[Last Page>>]*

The page navigation links will be added whether or not you select Separate HTML Pages. If only one HTML page is created, the links will appear where the page breaks would normally occur.

Separate HTML Pages   If you check the Separate HTML Pages box, each page of the report will be exported to its own HTML page. A page number will be appended to the filename to indicate the page number. If you clear the Separate HTML Pages box, only one HTML page will be created. The pages of the report will be placed in sequence in the single HTML page.

Page Range   In the Page Range panel, you can select the All option to export all pages of the report or the Pages option to select a range of pages. If you choose Pages, you must then enter page numbers in the From and To boxes.

Notes Panel   The Notes panel of the dialog box displays helpful information about the HTML settings.

 CAUTION   Justified text will appear as left-justified only in the HTML file.

HTML 4.0
The options for HTML 4.0 are identical to the options for HTML 3.2; see the preceding section.

MS Excel 97-2000

If you elect to export to Microsoft Excel 97–2000, the Excel Format Options dialog box shown in Figure 11-2 will be displayed. The effects of the various properties on the exported file are discussed next.

EXAM TIP Exam questions tend to concentrate on the Excel export formats.

Column Width The options in the Column Width panel configure the method that Crystal Reports will use to determine the Excel column widths:

- **Column width based on objects in the:** This option sizes the Excel columns based on objects in the part of the report you select. You can choose Whole Report, Report Header, Page Header, Details, Page Footer, Report Footer, or the group header or footer sections in your report.

- **Constant column width (in points):** This option sets all the columns to the width that you enter.

Export Page Headers and Footers The options in the Export Page Headers and Footers drop-down box are used to determine where the page header and footer information will appear in the Excel file:

- **None** Choose None if you want no header or footer information to appear in the export file.

- **Once Per Report** If you select Once Per Report, the header fields will appear once at the top of the file and the footer fields will appear once at the bottom.

- **On Each Page** If you choose On Each Page, the header and footer fields will appear in the Excel file where the top and bottom of each page in the report would be.

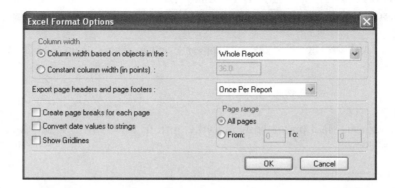

Figure 11-2 Exporting to Microsoft Excel

Create Page Breaks for Each Page   Check the Create Page Breaks for Each Page option if you want Crystal Reports to insert page breaks in the Excel file. This will cause page breaks to appear where they are in the report. If you clear this check box, page breaks will be determined by settings in Excel.

Convert Date Values to Strings   Check Convert Date Values to Strings if you want Crystal Reports to convert the report's dates into strings in the export file. This option preserves the date formatting from the report; otherwise, the dates will be formatted according to the Excel date settings.

Show Gridlines   Clear the Show Gridlines check box to remove the display of gridlines from the Excel file. Removing the gridlines will cause the Excel file to look more like the report.

Page Range   In the Page Range panel, you can select the All option to export all pages of the report or the Pages option to select a range of pages. If you choose Pages, you must then enter page numbers in the From and To boxes.

MS Excel 97-2000 (Data Only)

The Excel Format Options dialog box is different for the Data Only format, as shown in Figure 11-3.

Excel Format   The Excel Format panel contains three options. Two of the options act as shortcuts to choosing a particular set of options:

- **Typical**   Choose Typical to select the most commonly used options. Typical uses a column width based on the Details section, uses worksheet functions for summaries, maintains column alignment, exports the page header and page footer, and simplifies page headers.

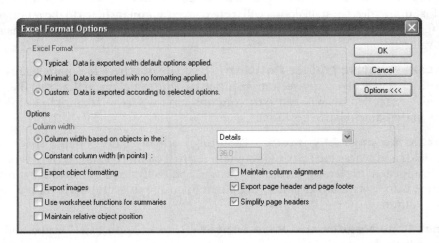

Figure 11-3   Exporting data only to Excel

- **Minimal**   Choose Minimal to export with no formatting. Minimal uses a column width based on the Details section and uses worksheet functions for summaries.

- **Custom**   Choose Custom to set the export options manually. If you have previously chosen Typical or Minimal, the settings for those options will be the starting point. If you choose Typical or Minimal and then change an individual option, the format will become Custom.

Options Button   The Options button acts as a toggle to display or hide the individual options area of the Excel Format Options dialog box.

Column Width   The options in the Column Width panel configure the method that Crystal Reports will use to determine the Excel column widths:

- **Column width based on objects in the:**   This option sizes the Excel column widths based on objects in the part of the report you select. You can choose Whole Report, Report Header, Page Header, Details, Page Footer, Report Footer, or the group header or footer sections that exist in your report. The Details option is commonly chosen when exporting data only to Excel.

- **Constant column width (in points):**   This option sets all the columns to the width that you enter.

Export Object Formatting   Check Export Object Formatting to have Crystal Reports export as much formatting as possible to the Excel file.

Export Images   Check Export images to have Crystal Reports export any images in the report to the Excel file. The images may be database fields or inserted pictures.

Use Worksheet Functions for Summaries   If you check Use Worksheet Functions for Summaries, Crystal Reports will try to convert summary fields in the report to use Excel functions. If no matching function exists, the summary will be exported as a numeric value.

Maintain Relative Object Position   If you do not check Maintain Relative Object Position, every object in a section will appear in the same row in the Excel file. If it is checked, Crystal Reports will add extra columns and rows in an attempt to keep report objects in the same relative positions.

Maintain Column Alignment   Exporting normally ignores blank space to the left of fields and places the first field found in the first column. This can cause summary fields to appear in the left-most columns instead of directly under the field they are summarizing. Check Maintain Column Alignment to ensure that summaries appear in the correct column.

Export Page Header and Page Footer   Check Export Page Header and Page Footer to have the page header and footer fields appear once at the top and bottom of the Excel file.

Simplify Page Headers   If Simplify Page Headers is checked, only the last row of objects in the page header is exported to the Excel file. This is commonly the field headers. If Simplify Page Headers is not checked, all objects in the page header are exported to the same row in the Excel file, possibly causing the field headers to be offset from their related fields.

MS Word
To export a report to Microsoft Word, you only need to choose All or specify the desired page range in the Export Options dialog box, and pick a filename and location in the file dialog box.

ODBC
When you choose ODBC as the export format, the export destination is grayed out. Clicking OK displays the ODBC Formats dialog box shown in Figure 11-4.

It lists all the system's defined ODBC DSNs (data source names). Choose a DSN to export to, and then enter the name that you want used for the report data in the Enter ODBC Table Name dialog box, as shown here.

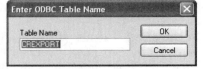

The report will be exported to the table you entered, in the selected DSN.

Record Style (Columns No Spaces)
Choosing Record Style (Columns No Spaces) displays the Number and Date Format dialog box shown here. This format exports each field in a fixed width with no spaces between columns.

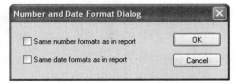

Same Number Formats as in Report   Check the Same Number Formats as in Report option to export the numbers in the report with their numeric formatting maintained.

Same Date Formats as in Report   Check the Same Date Formats as in Report option to export the dates in the report with their date formats maintained.

Figure 11-4
Selecting an
ODBC DSN

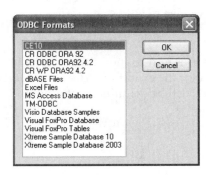

Record Style (Columns with Spaces)

Choosing Record Style (Columns with Spaces) displays the same Number and Date Format dialog box just shown. The Columns with Spaces format exports each field in a fixed width and adds a space before and after each column.

Report Definition

When you choose to export to the Report Definition format, you only need to supply a name and location for the export file. A report definition file is exported with a .txt file extension and contains a textual definition of the report, including its subreports.

Rich Text Format

To export a report to rich text format, you only need to choose All or specify a page range in the Export Options dialog box, and pick a filename and location in the file dialog box. Rich text format files can be opened in Microsoft Word and other applications that recognize it.

Separated Values (CSV)

Selecting the Separated Values format displays the Character-Separated Values dialog box shown here. Use it to choose the characters to use as separators and delimiters in the export file.

Separator   You can choose to separate fields with a character or with a tab. If you want to use a character, you must enter that character in the Character edit box.

Delimiter   In the Delimiter box, you can enter a character to use to enclose the fields in the report. The delimiter character appears before the field content and after the field content. All fields are delimited, not just string fields. The typical delimiter is the double quote.

Number and Date Format   After you close the Character-Separated Values dialog box, the same Number and Date Format dialog box is displayed as for the Record Style formats. Set the number and date options, and then choose a filename and location.

The resulting export file will contain a row for each record in the report. Each row will start with the fields from the report header, followed by the detail field names, followed by the detail field values.

Tab-Separated Text

When you choose to export to the Tab-Separated format, you only need to supply the name and location for the export file. The output file will have fields separated by tabs, and the string fields will be delimited with double quotation marks.

Text

If you choose the Text format, the Lines Per Page dialog box will appear, as shown on the left. Select the number of lines that you want on each page in the export file. The Export to Text dialog box will then appear, as shown on the right.

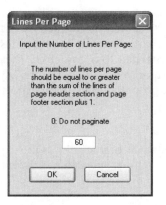

In the Export to Text dialog box, you must choose the characters per inch for the export file. Enter a value or accept the default. The exported file is a text file with fixed-width columns. Field data may be truncated.

XML

To export to XML, you must create a directory to hold the output files using the Export to Directory dialog box shown in Figure 11-5. The resulting XML file can be read by any XML-aware application and contains all the report data.

Figure 11-5
Exporting to an
XML file

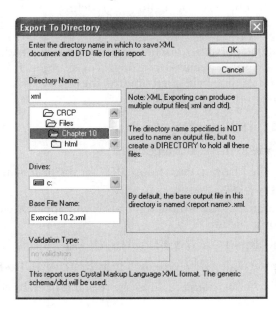

PART II

Formatting Tips for Exported Reports

When you are designing a report that will be exported, especially to another application, you can take steps to help guarantee that the exported file contains what you expect, where you expect it to be.

Free-Form Placement

The section formatting option called Free-Form Placement is checked by default. It allows you to place objects on a report in any location. If you clear it, guidelines appear in the section and nongraphical objects must be attached to a guideline. Clearing Free-Form Placement for all the sections of your report, or in the File | Options Layout tab as the default setting, will ensure that your fields are properly lined up for export types that require a line orientation.

Reduce Empty Space in Sections

If a section contains empty space, this may translate as blank lines in the export. Place fields toward the top of sections, and eliminate any empty space below them by resizing the section.

Do Not Overlap Objects

Overlapping objects may cause unexpected results in the export file. Eliminate any overlapping.

Guidelines

Snap all objects that you want on the same line to horizontal guidelines. In addition, verify that all objects are the same height by snapping the tops to a second horizontal guideline, or use the Format | Size commands to set the size of multiple objects.

You can use vertical guidelines to ensure that every object in a column is the same width: snap the objects to right and left guidelines.

Alignment

To help Crystal Reports decide where columns start and end, verify that every object in a column has the same alignment settings. For example, if a detail field is right-aligned and a related summary field is left-aligned, the fields may appear in different columns in the export file.

Exercise 11.1: Exporting to PDF

1. Open the Exercise 10.2 report.

2. Select File | Export, and choose PDF for the format and Disk File for the location. Click OK.

3. The parameter-prompting dialog box will appear. Select True to show the employee picture.

4. On the Export Options dialog box, choose All, and click OK.

5. In the file dialog box, save the file as **Exercise 11.1.pdf**, and click Save.

6. The file will be exported. Find the file, and open it with Adobe Acrobat.

Exercise 11.2: Exporting to Excel

1. Open the Exercise 10.2 report.

2. Select File | Export, and choose MS Excel 97-2000 for the format and Disk File for the location. Click OK.

3. Leave all the Excel format options at their defaults, and click OK.

4. Save the file as **Exercise 11.2a.xls**.

5. Open the saved file in Excel. Notice that it looks very similar to the report preview.

6. Return to Crystal Reports, and click the Export button.

7. Choose MS Excel 97-2000 (Data Only) for the format and Disk File for the location. Click OK.

8. Select Typical Excel Format, and then check Export Images.

9. Click OK, and then save the file as Exercise **11.2b.xls**.

10. Open the saved file in Excel. Notice that it does not look like the report preview, but that the data is properly aligned in rows and columns. The images overlap, but they exist in their same relative positions.

Working with Crystal Enterprise Folders

To distribute a report using Crystal Enterprise, you must save the report to a Crystal Enterprise folder.

 NOTE Chapter 14 covers the integration of Crystal Reports into the Crystal Enterprise environment. Other methods of publishing reports to Crystal Enterprise are covered there.

Saving a Report to Crystal Enterprise

In order to save a report to a Crystal Enterprise folder, you must be logged on to a Crystal Management Server. You will be asked to log on when you open Crystal Reports if Crystal Reports detects a Crystal Enterprise server, but if you did not log on then, you can log on later from the Save As dialog box.

To save a report to a Crystal Enterprise folder, select File | Save As. In the Save As dialog box, click the Enterprise button displayed in the lower left-hand corner. If you are not logged on to a Crystal Management Server, the Log On to Crystal Enterprise dialog box will appear, as shown here, so that you can log on.

Figure 11-6

Selecting a Crystal Enterprise folder to save a report in

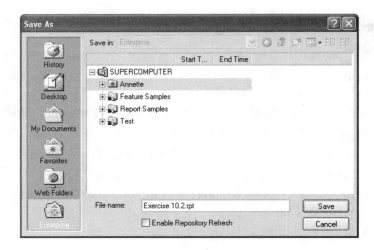

After you successfully log on, the Save As dialog box will display Enterprise Folders, as shown in Figure 11-6.

Select a folder in which to save your report or, if you have sufficient privileges in Crystal Enterprise, you may create a new folder. The Save As dialog box contains a check box called Enable Repository Refresh. Check it if you want the repository objects in your report updated when the report is opened or when it is run in Crystal Enterprise.

 NOTE The Enterprise button will not be visible in the file dialog boxes if Crystal Enterprise was not detected.

Opening a Crystal Enterprise Report

You can open a report that was saved to a Crystal Enterprise folder in much the same way that you would any report. In the Open dialog box, select the Enterprise button in the lower left-hand corner, and then browse the folders to find the report you want, as shown in Figure 11-7. The Enterprise option in the Open dialog box has a special right-click menu, shown here.

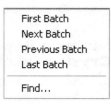

Enterprise folders often store a large number of reports. The right-click menu options that include the word "Batch" can be used to display files in batches of 100, instead of the entire list. The Find command can be used to search for specific files by filename or by entering the starting characters of the filename.

Viewing a Report in Crystal Enterprise

To view a report in Crystal Enterprise, follow these steps:

1. Select Start | Programs | Crystal Enterprise 10 | Crystal Enterprise User Launchpad.

2. Click the Launch Crystal Enterprise web desktop link.

3. Log on to Crystal Enterprise.

4. Browse the folders to find the report you want, and then click it. A pop-up menu with three options will appear. Choose the View option.

5. The report will be displayed in a separate browser window. If the report has parameters, you will be prompted for them. Many of the navigation options that you have in Crystal Reports will also be available in the web viewer.

Optimizing Reports for Crystal Enterprise

Reports viewed in Crystal Enterprise are displayed in a web browser using a web server. It is important to consider that your report will be viewed on the Web when designing it. Your goal should always be to display the least amount of information in the fastest time, while still meeting the users' needs.

Several strategies will help you accomplish this optimization.

Use Summary Reports with Drill-Down

Using summary reports that allow drill-down can speed report viewing for users. A summary is displayed first, and then users can drill into only the groups they need details for. This strategy is helpful because it limits the amount of information that needs to be displayed. Instead of displaying the entire report and letting users navigate to the parts of interest, only the parts of interest are displayed. The drawback to this strategy is that printing of drill-down tabs is limited to the displayed tab. Each drill-down window has to be printed separately.

Figure 11-7

Opening a Crystal Enterprise report

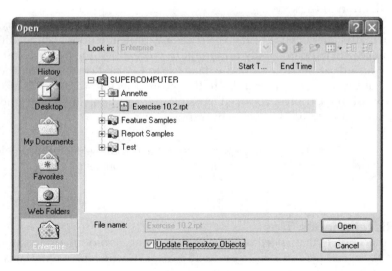

Save Reports with Data

Reports can be configured to save data using the File | Report Options, Save Data with Report check box. If these reports are scheduled to run in Crystal Enterprise with a particular set of parameters, the result data will be saved with the report. If users then need to view the report, it is immediately available—no database interaction is required, speeding processing time.

However, there are situations where this strategy is not appropriate, for example, if data changes often or report parameter choices for each user tend to be different. In these cases, saving data with the report is not very useful because the report needs to be refreshed anyway.

Update Your Reports to Crystal Reports 10

Crystal Reports 10 contains many processing enhancements. Simply saving your older format reports as version 10 reports will improve their performance. If you open an older version report in Crystal Reports 10 and then save it, it will be updated.

NOTE To keep a report from being updated to version 10, use the Save As command.

Push All Possible Processing to the Database Server

For all reports, but particularly for reports that do not save data, it is important to push all possible processing to the database server. There are many methods, covering many different topics, that affect where processing occurs. For example, Crystal Reports formulas are always evaluated locally. Try to substitute SQL Expressions if possible, to force the evaluation to the server.

Record selection criteria may or may not be added to the report query. Check the report query, and if it does not contain all criteria, explore methods to change it. The record selection criteria are particularly important to processing time because you want to return as few records as possible from the database to Crystal Reports. A common problem is the use of Crystal Reports formulas in the record selection formula. Replace these with SQL Expressions as noted above, if possible. In addition, investigate the use of database stored–procedures to implement complex report logic.

NOTE *Crystal Reports 9 on Oracle* (McGraw-Hill Osborne Media, 2003) covers report optimization in an Oracle environment.

Miscellaneous Tips

Other choices may speed your report processing. Avoid subreports, the use of the Page N of M special field in long reports, and maps. Cache report templates, if the same template is used for multiple reports.

Exercise 11.3: Saving a Report to Crystal Enterprise

1. Open the Exercise 10.2 report.

2. Select File | Save As.

3. Click the Enterprise button in the Save As dialog box, and log on to Crystal Enterprise using the user ID created earlier, if necessary.

4. You should see a folder with an asterisk on it. This is your personal folder. Select it.

5. Check the Enable Repository Refresh box, and then click Save. The report will be saved to Crystal Enterprise.

Exercise 11.4: Viewing a Report in Crystal Enterprise

1. Select Start | Programs | Crystal Enterprise 10 | Crystal Enterprise User Launchpad.

2. Click the Launch Crystal Enterprise web desktop link.

3. Log on to Crystal Enterprise.

4. Select the folder with the asterisk, and then click it. A pop-up menu with three options will appear. Choose the View option.

5. You will be prompted for the parameter value. When you have entered it, the report will be displayed in a separate browser window.

Chapter Review

This chapter covered report distribution via the Export command and via Crystal Enterprise folders.

Quick Tips

- To export a Crystal Report, choose File | Export or use the Export button.

- Crystal will export to several formats, including PDF, Microsoft Word or Excel, text, CSV, HTML, rich text, and XML.

- To create a report definition file, use the Report Definition export format.

- To create another copy of the report file with a new name, use the Crystal Reports (.rpt) export format.

- There are two main export types. One produces a file that looks very similar to the report preview and is intended primarily for report viewing. The second produces a file that can be easily imported into another application; this is intended primarily for data transfer.

- You can export report data into a database using the ODBC export format.

- In addition to exporting to a file, you can export to an application, a Lotus Domino location or Exchange folder, or to e-mail using MAPI or Lotus Domino Mail.

- If a report is being designed for data export, it should follow certain design tips such as using guidelines, not using Free-Form Placement, and not overlapping objects.

- There are two Excel export formats, one that closely reproduces the look of the report, and one that is intended for data transfer.

- Exporting to an application causes the export file to be saved to your Temp directory and then opened in the application associated with the file extension.

- Reports are saved to Crystal Enterprise folders using the Save As dialog. Selecting the Enterprise option in the bottom left-hand corner will display Enterprise folders, and you can save reports to them.

- Reports that have been saved to Enterprise folders can be opened for modification in Crystal Reports using the Open dialog box. Select the Enterprise button to display Enterprise folders and select a report.

- Check the Enable Repository Refresh box in the Save As or Open dialog boxes to have the report's repository objects refreshed when it is opened or run.

- It is important to optimize reports for the web if they will be distributed via Crystal Enterprise.

Questions

Questions may have more than one correct answer. Choose all answers that apply.

1. Knowing that comma-delimited files or fixed-format files can be imported to Oracle, to move report data into an Oracle database, you could

    a. Export to CSV and then import into Oracle.

    b. Export to Report Definition format and then import into Oracle.

    c. Export to an Oracle ODBC DSN.

    d. Export to PDF and then import to Oracle.

    e. Export to Record Style and then import into Oracle.

2. If you choose to export images with the MS Excel 97-2000 (Data Only) export format, which option will you be using?

    a. Typical

    b. Minimal

    c. Custom

3. Which export format most closely resembles the original report?

    a. XML

    b. DOC

c. PDF

d. Rich Text

e. HTML 4.0

4. When exporting to an application, you must choose

a. The file location

b. The filename

c. The file location but not the filename

d. The filename but not the file location

e. Neither the filename nor the file location

5. You initially save a report from Crystal Reports to a Crystal Enterprise folder by

a. Using the Save dialog box

b. Using the Save As dialog box

c. Using the File | Publish to Crystal Enterprise command

d. Using the Publish button on the toolbar

e. Using the Open dialog box

6. To display Enterprise folders in the Save As dialog box, you

a. Browse to an Enterprise folder.

b. Select Enable Repository Refresh.

c. Set the Enterprise option on the File | Options dialog box.

d. Select the Web Folders button.

e. Select the Enterprise button.

7. If the Enterprise button is not visible in the Save As dialog box, it means that

a. You are not logged on to Crystal Enterprise.

b. Crystal Enterprise was not detected by Crystal Reports.

8. Reports can be optimized for web viewing using which of the following strategies:

a. Using subreports instead of linking tables

b. Avoiding maps

c. Using the Page N of M special field to help users understand how many pages are in the report

d. Saving reports as version 10

e. Avoiding reports with drill-down capabilities

9. When designing reports for web viewing, it is important to push as much processing as possible to the database server.

   a. Usually true

   b. Never true

Answers

1. **a, c, e.** CSV will produce a comma-delimited file, and Record Style will produce a fixed-format file; either could be imported to Oracle. You could export directly to an Oracle table using the ODBC format. Report Definition files do not contain data. A PDF is formatted for viewing, not for data exchange.

2. **c.** Neither Typical nor Minimal includes images. If you include images, you will be using a custom format.

3. **c.** The PDF format most closely resembles the preview of the original report.

4. **e.** When you export to an application, the export file is saved to the system's defined Temp directory with an automatically generated name.

5. **b.** Reports are saved to Crystal Enterprise using the Save As dialog box.

6. **e.** To see Enterprise folders, you must select the Enterprise button in the Save As dialog box.

7. **b.** If Crystal Enterprise was detected, the button will be displayed. If you click the button and are not logged on, you will be prompted to log on.

8. **b, d.** Answers a, c, and e will not optimize web report viewing.

9. **a.** This is usually true, though there might be unusual circumstances that override the general strategy.

Nonstandard Report Types

Exam RDCR200 expects you to be able to
- Build a basic cross-tab
- Format a cross-tab
- Create a form letter

You can create reports in Crystal Reports that do not have the usual columnar format. You can create cross-tabs for a spreadsheet-like report. You can create reports that look like customized letters. In addition, you can create reports that are grouped hierarchically.

EXAM TIP   Although understanding hierarchical reports is not an exam objective, it is discussed in this chapter because it solves a particular reporting need.

Cross-Tabs

You were introduced to cross-tabs in previous chapters. This chapter will delve more deeply into cross-tab creation, customization, and formatting.

Cross-tabs have three elements, each of which can contain more than one field. The values in the fields chosen for the row elements are displayed as the row headers. They are displayed in the leftmost columns of the cross-tab. The values in the fields chosen for the column elements are displayed across the top of the cross-tab. A cross-tab displays one or more summaries by the row field(s) and across the column field(s) in its cells.

Using the Cross-Tab Expert

Creating a cross-tab is very simple. You created one in Chapter 3 using the Report Creation wizard. Using the wizard gave you a report where the cross-tab was the entire content. You can also add a cross-tab, or multiple cross-tabs, to an existing report using the Cross-Tab Expert. Display the Cross-Tab Expert by selecting Insert | Cross-Tab or by clicking the Insert Cross-Tab button on the toolbar.

Cross-Tab Tab

The Cross-Tab Expert will open to the Cross-Tab tab, as shown in Figure 12-1. Use the options on this screen to create the cross-tab. The Cross-Tab tab is divided into two sections.

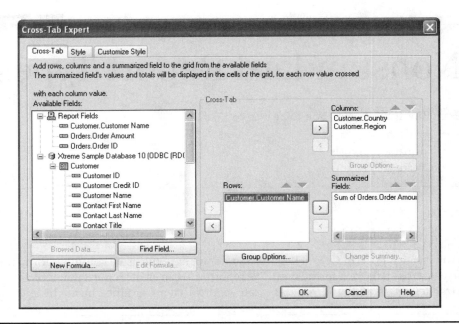

Figure 12-1   Creating a cross-tab using the Cross-tab Expert

The section to the left is used to find or create fields to use in the cross-tab. The Cross-Tab panel to the right defines the cross-tab. Move fields using the arrow buttons or by dragging.

Available Fields   The Available Fields list box contains all the fields currently in the report or available via a connected data source. Move fields from this list into boxes in the Cross-Tab panel to add them to the cross-tab.

Browse Data   To see a sample of the data in any field, select it in the Available Fields list, and then click the Browse Data button. A dialog box will appear listing a sample of the values in the field.

Find Field   Use the Find Field button to find a field in the Available Fields list. Click the button and then enter the field name, or part of the field name, and click OK. The first matching field will be highlighted.

New Formula   If you want to create a new formula field to use in your cross-tab, click the New Formula button. You will be prompted to enter a formula name and then the Formula Workshop will appear. After creating the formula, you will be returned to the Cross-Tab Expert.

Edit Formula   You can edit a formula field by selecting it in the Available Fields, Rows, Columns, or Summarized Fields list and clicking the Edit Formula button.

Rows   Add fields to the Rows box to create the rows of the cross-tab. You can adjust the order of the fields using the arrows at the upper right-hand corner of the list. The row fields act like group-by fields and the order in the box determines the group hierarchy. The first field will become the outermost group, the second field will become the next group, and so on, until the last field becomes the innermost group.

Columns   Add fields to the Columns box to create the columns of the cross-tab. You can adjust the order of the fields using the arrows at the upper right-hand corner of the list. The column fields act like group-by fields, and the order in the box determines the group hierarchy.

Summarized Fields   The Summarized Fields list contains the fields that will appear in the cells of the cross-tab. If you select more than one field, the summaries will be displayed one on top of the other by default.

Group Options   The Group Options button is available if you select any field in the Rows or Columns lists. Selecting a field and clicking the Group Options button will open the Cross-Tab Group Options dialog box. Use the dialog box to change the sort order of the group fields or to customize group names.

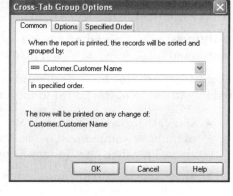

Change Summary   When you move a field into the Summarized Fields list, a default summary operation is selected. If you want to change the summary operation, select the field and then click the Change Summary button. The Edit Summary dialog box will be displayed.

You can modify the summary properties using the options in the Edit Summary dialog box:

- **Choose the Field to Summarize**   You can pick the field to summarize using the Choose the Field to Summarize drop-down box.

- **Calculate This Summary**   If you want to change the summary operation, select a new one from the Calculate This Summary drop-down box.

- **Options Panel**   Check the Show as a Percentage Of box to have the summary computed as a percentage. Select the field to use as the denominator in the drop-down box. Choose Row or Column to indicate whether the denominator should be taken from the row total or the column total.

After filling in the Cross-Tab tab options, click OK to create the cross-tab or select the Style or Customize Style tabs to format the cross-tab.

Style Tab

Select the Style tab to apply a predefined style to your cross-tab. The Style tab is shown in Figure 12-2. Select different styles to preview their formatting options. When you find a style that you like, you can modify it with the Customize Style tab or accept it by clicking OK, which will close the Cross-Tab Expert.

Customize Style Tab

The Customize Style tab, shown in Figure 12-3, is used to format the cross-tab grid. Some options apply to the selected row or column field; others apply to the entire grid.

Rows   The Rows list box displays each row field and an entry for the row grand total. Select a row field to format it using the Group Options panel.

Columns   The Columns list box displays each column field and an entry for the column grand total. Select a column field to format it using the Group Options panel.

Summarized Fields   The Summarized Fields panel will be unavailable unless more than one field was added to the Summarized Fields list on the Cross-Tab tab.

- **Vertical/Horizontal**   Choose Vertical or Horizontal to determine the placement of multiple summarized fields. The default is Vertical, which places them one above the other. The Horizontal option will place them side by side.

- **Show Labels**   Check Show Labels to include the field name of each summarized field in the row header or column header area.

Group Options   The properties in the Group Options panel apply to the selected field in the Rows or Columns list boxes.

- **Suppress Subtotal**   Suppress Subtotal is not available for the grand total fields or the innermost group-by field. If you suppress a subtotal, the row or column that would have contained the subtotal is omitted from the report.

- **Suppress Label**   Suppress Label is available if Suppress Subtotal is checked. Check Suppress Label to remove the group-by field's label from the row header or column header area.

- **Alias for Formulas**   The Alias for Formulas box contains the name of the selected field. You can create an alias for the original field name by changing the name in the Alias for Formulas box. The alias can be used in the Highlighting Expert to simplify the creation of conditional formatting formulas.

- **Background Color**   Use the Background Color drop-down box to select a color for the background of the selected row or column field.

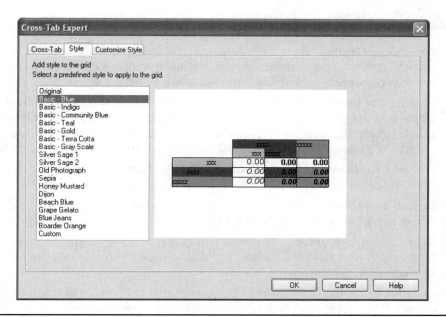

Figure 12-2   Applying a predefined style to a cross-tab

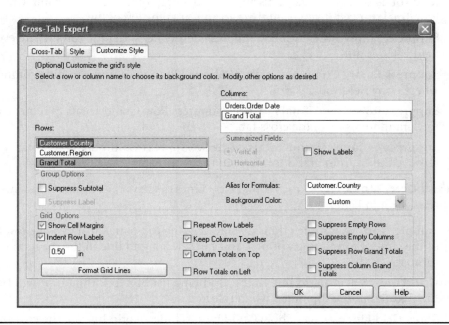

Figure 12-3   Customizing a cross-tab's formatting

Grid Options   Properties in the Grid Options panel apply to the entire grid.

- **Show Cell Margins**   Show Cell Margins is checked by default; it causes blank space to surround the contents of cells. If you clear Show Cell Margins, space between cells, both vertical and horizontal, will be removed.

- **Indent Row Labels**   Each field in the Rows list is indented from the field above it in the row headers, by a customizable amount. Clear Indent Row Labels to stop indentation. It is checked by default and the indent is set to ½ inch. You can set the amount of indentation to a different value if you like.

- **Format Grid Lines**   Click the Format Grid Lines button to modify the display of the lines in the cross-tab. See the next section for details.

- **Repeat Row Labels**   Cross-tabs may spill across multiple pages horizontally. Check Report Row Labels to have the row headers repeated on each page.

- **Keep Columns Together**   For cross-tabs that spill across multiple pages horizontally, check Keep Columns Together to prevent horizontal page breaks in the middle of columns.

- **Column Totals on Top**   Column totals appear at the bottom of columns by default. Check Column Totals on Top if you want them to appear at the top of the column.

- **Row Totals on Left**   Row totals appear at the right of the row by default. Check Row Totals on Left if you want them to appear at the left of the row.

- **Suppress Empty Rows**   Check Suppress Empty Rows to hide rows where every field value is null.

- **Suppress Empty Columns**   Check Suppress Empty Columns to hide columns where every field value is null.

- **Suppress Row Grand Totals**   Check Suppress Row Grand Totals to remove the row grand totals from the cross-tab.

- **Suppress Column Grand Totals**   Check Suppress Column Grand Totals to remove the column grand totals from the cross-tab.

Format Grid Lines   Clicking Format Grid Lines displays the Format Grid Lines dialog box, shown in Figure 12-4.

- **Sample Grid**   A sample grid is displayed in the top panel. It shows the results of the current formatting options. You can select a grid line in the diagram to format it.

- **Grid Line**   Select a grid line in the Grid Line list box to format it. It will be highlighted in the top panel when selected.

- **Show Grid Lines**   Clear Show Grid Lines to hide all grid lines in the cross-tab.

- **Color**   Select a color for the selected grid line using the Color drop-down box.

- **Style**   Select a style for the selected grid line using the Style drop-down box. The options are Single, Dashed, and Dotted.

- **Width**   Select a width for the selected grid line using the Width drop-down box. The options go from Hairline to 3.5 points in increments of a half point.
- **Draw**   Clear the Draw check box to hide the selected grid line.
- **Draw Grand Total Line Only**   Check the Draw Grand Total Line Only check box to hide the grid lines for lower-level groups but show one for the grand total.

Cross-Tab Location

When you close the Cross-tab Expert after creating a new cross-tab, you will see a cursor with a frame attached to it. Click the area of the report where you want the cross-tab placed and it will be created. Cross-tabs can be placed in the Report Header or Report Footer section or in any group header or footer section. If you drop a cross-tab in an in-valid location, it will be moved to the nearest valid location. The location determines the data used in the cross-tab. If the cross-tab is placed in the report header or footer, it will use all data in the report. If it is placed in a group header or footer, it will use data only for that group.

Editing a Cross-Tab

Many different elements of a cross-tab can be edited. Different elements are edited using different tools or methods.

Invoking the Format Editor

To format the Common, Border, or Hyperlink properties for the whole cross-tab, select the cross-tab and then invoke the Format Editor. (Use of the Format Editor is described in Chapter 9.)

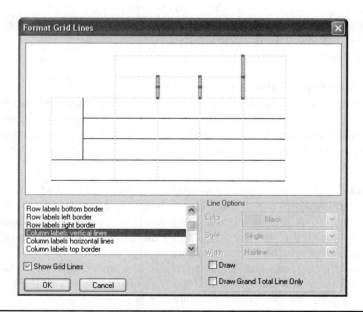

Figure 12-4   Formatting grid lines

Invoking the Cross-Tab Expert

To modify properties that were set with the Cross-tab Expert, select the cross-tab and then invoke the Cross-Tab Expert. (See "Using the Cross-Tab Expert," earlier in this chapter.)

Using the Right-Click Menu

If you right-click a cross-tab, the menu that appears includes the commands shown here. The commands are also available on the Insert and Format menus.

> ⚡ Group Sort Expert...
> 📊 Insert Chart...
> 🌐 Insert Map...
> Pivot Cross-Tab

Group Sort Expert   Select the Group Sort Expert to apply a group sort to the rows of the cross-tab. The group sort applies only to the rows and cannot apply to the columns of the cross-tab. The Group Sort Expert allows you to create Top-N type reports; it is covered in Chapter 7.

Insert Chart   Choose the Insert Chart command to create a chart based on the cross-tab contents. The Chart Expert will appear with the cross-tab layout selected.

Insert Map   Choose the Insert Map command to create a map based on the cross-tab contents. The Map Expert will appear with the cross-tab layout selected.

Pivot Cross-Tab   Select Pivot Cross-Tab to interchange the row fields and column fields of the cross-tab—to change columns to rows, and vice versa.

Moving Row and Column Fields

To move individual row and column fields, select a field from the row or column header and drag it to another position in either the row or the column header area. An orange line will appear when the mouse is in a position where the field can be dropped, as shown here.

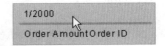

Editing Individual Elements

You can edit individual elements of a cross-tab by selecting them and then opening the Format Editor. This type of editing is easier to do using the Design tab. Figure 12-5 shows a sample cross-tab displayed in the Design window. Each element in the cross-tab is contained in a frame so that you can select it easily. There are two types of elements in each cross-tab, text objects and data fields.

Text Objects   The parts of the cross-tab that are text fields include the labels for the total columns and rows. In Figure 12-5, everywhere "Total" appears is a text field. In addition to the total labels, if there are multiple summaries in the cross-tab cells, the labels for the summary fields are also text fields. In Figure 12-5, the Order Amount and Order ID fields in the column header section are summary fields.

You can edit the cross-tab text fields just as you can any other report text object. You can double-click them and change the text. You can format them with the Format Editor. And you can resize them using the frame handles.

	Column #1 Name			Total
	Column #2 Name	Total		
	Column #3 Nar	Total		
	Order AOrder	Order AmOrder I	Order Ar Order ID	Order AmOrder ID
Total	Amount der ID	r Amount Order ID	Amount Order ID	Amount Order ID
Row #1 Name	Amount der ID	r Amount Order ID	Amount Order ID	r Amounts.Order ID
Row #2 Name	Amount der ID	r Amount Order ID	Amount Order ID	r Amounts.Order ID

Figure 12-5   Editing individual cross-tab elements

Data Fields   The other fields in a cross-tab contain data and each has a particular data type. You can format them the same as you would if they were placed elsewhere in the report. The summarized fields are all summary formulas, as are the total fields. The row and column fields are like group-by fields. For example, you would see "Group #1 Name" in a regular report. In the cross-tab, you will see "Row # 1 Name" or "Column # 1 Name." Select one and invoke the Format Editor. The proper tabs for that data type will appear.

TIP   To change the text of the row or column header labels, select them and then create a Display String formula to create the desired output.

Highlighting Expert   The Highlighting Expert can be used on the data fields of a cross-tab just as it is used with regular report fields.

Formatting Formulas   The elements of a cross-tab can be conditionally formatted using the formula buttons in the Format Editor—in the same way that other report fields are formatted. However, a special function is available in the Formula Workshop when you are creating format formulas for cross-tabs. The CurrentFieldValue and DefaultAttribute functions are available just as for regular fields, and they behave in the expected manner. In addition, the GridRowColumnValue function and the accompanying Row or Column Names constants are available. The CurrentFieldValue function lets you create logic that is dependent on the current value of the selected field. The GridRowColumnValue lets you create logic that is dependent on the value of a row or column field related to the current cell.

For example, if you wanted to color a field green where the value was over $1000, you would create the following font-color format formula for your field:

```
If CurrentFieldValue > 1000 then crGreen else DefaultAttribute
```

If you had a cross-tab where one of the row fields was Country and you wanted to color the field green if the row pertained to the United States, you would use the following formula:

```
If GridRowColumnValue("Customer.Country") = 'USA'
  then crGreen else DefaultAttribute
```

Of course, this formula would accomplish the same thing:

```
If {Customer.Country} = 'USA' then crGreen else DefaultAttribute
```

One advantage to using the GridRowColumnValue method is that you use the field aliases created in the Cross-Tab expert instead of the actual field names. (In the preceding example, no field alias was created, so it was the same as the field name.) The aliases are available in the Formula Workshop when you are creating a format formula for a cross-tab object; look in the Function Tree, under a folder called Row or Column Names.

Cross-Tab Printing Tips

Cross-tabs have unique printing concerns, especially those that spill across pages horizontally. Several features are available to help you make such cross-tabs easy to understand and visually appealing:

- **Relative Positions** Any object placed to the right of a cross-tab may be overlapped by the cross-tab if it grows horizontally. To make the object move with the cross-tab, invoke the Section Expert for the section that includes the cross-tab and the object. On the Common tab, check Relative Positions. The object will now stay in the same position relative to the cross-tab, no matter how much the cross-tab grows.

- **Repeat Row Labels** Column labels are repeated on overflow pages by default. Row labels are not. To have row labels print on each horizontal page, check Repeat Row Labels on the Customize Style tab of the Cross-Tab Expert.

- **Keep Columns Together** To prevent columns from splitting across a page, check Keep Columns Together on the Customize Style tab of the Cross-Tab Expert.

- **Horizontal Page Number** The Page Number special field contains the usual vertical page number. The Horizontal Page Number special field contains a number that indicates the count of pages horizontally. This field can be used to identify a page's location horizontally in the report. If you are designing a report containing a cross-tab or OLAP grid that will spill across pages horizontally, you could insert a text object in the footer that contained something like this:

```
Page {Page Number} - {Horizontal Page Number}
```

Note that this technique will not work if the cross-tab is placed in a section that will not print with page footers, such as the Report Header.

- **Repeat on Horizontal Pages** If you have report objects that you want repeated if the cross-tab spills across pages, you can check the Repeat on Horizontal Pages option on the Common tab of the Format Editor. This option is commonly used for objects in the page header or page footer that you want to display on every page.

Exercise 12.1: Creating a Cross-Tab

1. Open the report from Exercise 9.9.
2. Click the Insert Cross-Tab button to open the Cross-Tab Expert.
3. Place the Customer Country and Region in the Rows list.
4. Place the Order Date in the Columns list, then select it, and click the Group Options button.
5. Set the column to be printed for each year and click OK.
6. Put the Order Amount and Order ID in the Summarized Fields list.
7. Select the Order ID, and click the Change Summary button. Change the summary operation to Count, and click OK.
8. Click the Style tab.
9. Select Silver Sage 1.
10. Click the Customize Style tab.
11. In the Summarized Fields panel, select Horizontal, and check Show Labels.
12. Clear Indent Row Labels.
13. Click OK, and place the cross-tab in the Report Header section.
14. Select the cross-tab, right-click, and choose Group Sort Expert.
15. Show the top three countries based on the order amount, leave the rest in others, and include ties.
16. Show the top five regions based on the order amount, leave the rest in Others, and include ties. Click OK to close the Group Sort Expert.
17. Select Row # 1 Name, right-click, and choose Format Field. On the Common tab, set the text rotation to 90 degrees, and click OK.
18. Narrow the width of the Row # Name field as much as possible.
19. Preview the report.
20. Select the Region field, and reduce its width as much as possible.

21. Change the Order Amount label to **Amount**. Change the Order ID label to **Orders**.

22. Remove the currency sign and decimal places from all the amount fields. (You can format multiple objects at the same time.)

23. Reduce the width of the numeric fields until the grid does not spill onto multiple pages.

24. Save the report as **Exercise 12.1**.

Exercise 12.2: Creating a Conditional Formatting Formula for a Cross-Tab

1. Open the Exercise 12.1 report.

2. On the Design tab, select the Order Amount field next to Row #2 Name.

3. Open the Format Editor, and go to the Font tab.

4. Click the Formula button next to the Color property.

5. Type the following formula.

```
If CurrentFieldValue > 1000000 then crGreen else DefaultAttribute
```

6. Close the Formula Workshop and the Format Editor.

7. Preview the report, looking for items that are green.

8. Save the report as **Exercise 12.2**.

Form Letters

Form letters can be created with Crystal Reports for many purposes. The result should look like a professional letter, but it will be customized for each recipient. Large text objects are commonly used to produce the body as well as the address block and salutation of the letter. Fields can be embedded in the text objects to produce the appropriate result, and section formatting can be used to display the appropriate text. Exercise 12.3 creates a form letter using techniques discussed in previous chapters.

Exercise 12.3: Creating a Form Letter

This form letter report should create a letter for each supplier with whom Xtreme has units on order. For each order, if the order has been received and paid for, a request will be sent for acknowledgment of payment. If the order has been received but not paid for, a letter will be sent with the payment. If the order has not been received, a letter requesting an expected arrival date will be sent.

1. Select File | Options to open the Options dialog box. On the Layout tab, clear the Free-Form Placement option, and click OK. (This step is not required, but it will cause lines to be drawn on the report for easy placement of objects and visualization of the spacing in the form letter.)

2. Create a new report as a blank report.

3. Use the Products, Purchases, and Suppliers table. Accept the automatic linking.

4. Create a selection criterion to exclude records where the Units on Order field equals zero.

5. Set all margins to 1 inch using the File | Page Setup dialog box.

6. Suppress the Report Header, Report Footer, and Page Footer sections.

7. Use the Section Expert to insert a page break after the Report Header section.

8. Place vertical guidelines at the right and left margins and at 3 and 3¼ inches.

9. Place the Xtreme logo (from the Images folder in the repository) in the Page Header so that its right side snaps to the guideline at 3 inches. The graphic is taller than the section's original height, so the section is expanded to accommodate it. However, there are no lines in the expanded section. Right-click in the gray area of the section, and click Insert Line until the entire section has lines.

10. Place a text object in the Page Header section. Position and size it such that its left side is glued to the guideline at 3¼ inches, its bottom is glued to the last line in the section, and it is approximately 2 inches wide and four lines tall.

11. Enter the following text into the text object:

    2020 Mountain View Drive
    Denver, CO 12345
    (123) 456-7890

12. This is the return address; it stays constant for every letter.

13. Create a new Page Header section using the Insert Section Below command. Insert lines until there are three lines in the new section. Place the special field Print Date on the middle line in the new section. Format the date so that it displays using the format March 1, 1999.

14. Create a group on the Supplier Name.

15. Remove the Group Name field. Insert lines until the group header section has seven lines.

16. Insert a text object into the group header section, and size it so that it is glued to the left margin, the guideline is at 3 inches, and it is six lines tall. Populate it as shown here:

    {Supplier Name}
    {Address1}
    {Address2}
    {City}, {Region} {Postal Code}

    Greetings:

17. Format the text field, and check Suppress Embedded Blank Field Lines to suppress the line when the Address2 field is blank. Note that the hard-coded blank line before the greeting will not be suppressed.

18. Open the Section Expert for the Group Footer section. Check New Page After to insert a page break after each supplier.

19. Insert lines into the Group Footer section until there are seven lines. Insert a text object. Size it so that it snaps to the left margin, the guideline is at 3 inches, and it is seven lines tall. Insert the following text:

Sincerely,
four blank lines for signature

your name
Purchasing Supervisor

20. Preview the report. It looks good now—except for the complete lack of content!

21. There are three different conditions that an order might have, each of which requires a different message. Create two additional Details sections, one for each condition.

22. Create a formula to determine which condition is true for each order. Call the formula **MessageType**, and use the following:

```
If {Purchases.Received} then \\ Nested If-Then statement
  (If {Purchases.Paid} then
     'AckReceipt'
   Else
     'Pay')
Else
  'RequestDate'
```

23. Insert lines into the Details a section until it is four lines tall. Insert a text object and snap it to the right and left margins. Size it to the height of the section, and enter the following text, embedding the fields where shown.

Thank you for your timely processing of purchase order number {PO#}. We received the order on {Expected Receiving Date} and promptly submitted payment. A response from you indicating your receipt of the payment would be appreciated.

24. Format the PO# field to exclude commas. Format the date field to the 1-Mar-1999 format.

25. Open the Section Expert for the Details a section. Create a formula for the Suppress property, as shown here, to suppress the section if MessageType is not equal to AckReceipt:

```
{@MessageType} <> 'AckReceipt'
```

26. Insert lines into the Details b section until it is three lines tall. Insert a text object and snap it to the right and left margins, and size it to the height of the section. Then enter the following text, embedding the fields where shown.

Purchase order number {PO#}, for {Units on Order} units of {Product Name} was received on {Expected Receiving Date}. Attached to this letter you will find our check for the amount due.

27. Format the PO# field to exclude commas. Format the date field to the 1-Mar-1999 format.

28. Open the Section Expert for the Details b section. Create a formula for the Suppress property, as shown here, to suppress the section if MessageType is not equal to Pay:

`{@MessageType}<>'Pay'`

29. Insert lines into the Details c section until it is three lines tall. Insert a text object, snap it to the right and left margins, and size it to the height of the section. Then enter the following text, embedding the fields where shown:

Purchase order number {PO#}, for {Units on Order} units of {Product Name}, has not been received. Please respond with an expected ship date. If the order has been shipped, please disregard this request.

30. Format the PO# field to exclude commas.

31. Open the Section Expert for the Details c section. Create a formula for the Suppress property, as shown here, to suppress the section if MessageType is not equal to RequestDate:

`{@MessageType}<>'RequestDate'`

32. Preview the report.

33. Save the report as **Exercise 12.3.**

Hierarchical Reports

Data sometimes has a hierarchical relationship. When Crystal Reports uses the term *hierarchical* it is not referring to master-detail relationships between tables but to an internal reference within a table. For example, the Employees table contains an Employee ID field as the primary key, but it also has a Supervisor field that is populated with the employee ID of the supervisor. Therefore, a hierarchical relationship exists between the Supervisor field and the Employee ID field.

Hierarchical Grouping Options

To create a hierarchy in Crystal Reports, you must first create a group on the child field. This seems counterintuitive, but it is necessary. Once you have created the group on the child field, the Hierarchical Grouping Options command on the Report menu becomes active. Selecting it opens the Hierarchical Group Options dialog box. Use the properties in this dialog box to configure hierarchical grouping.

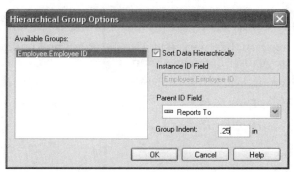

Available Groups   The Available Groups list box contains all the groups in the report. Select the group that you want to configure hierarchically.

Sort Data Hierarchically   Check the Sort Data Hierarchically box to implement hierarchical sorting for the selected group.

Instance ID Field   Instance ID Field displays the selected group-by field for reference.

Parent ID Field   The Parent ID Field drop-down box lists all fields of the same data type as that shown in Instance ID Field. Select the one that contains the parent key. If Parent ID Field is null, the instance is listed first in the hierarchy.

Group Indent   Enter the amount in inches you want to indent each child group. Note that the entire row is indented, causing fields to be misaligned from the field headers. Click OK and your report will be hierarchically grouped.

Summary Fields for Hierarchical Groups

If your report is grouped hierarchically, the Insert Summary dialog box will display, with the Summarize Across Hierarchy option available, as shown in Figure 12-6. Check that option to create sums that include the values for the lower levels of the hierarchy.

Exercise 12.4: Creating a Hierarchical Report

1. Open the Exercise 9.14 report.

2. Remove Age At Hire and Current Age from the report, and move the Salary and Percent of Total fields to the left.

3. Format the Salary field as $(1,123).

4. Create a group on the Employee ID field.

5. Select Report | Hierarchical Grouping Options to open the Hierarchical Group Options dialog box.

6. Select the Employee ID field from the Available Groups list, and check the Sort Data Hierarchically check box.

7. Select Report To from the Parent ID Field drop-down box, and set the indentation to .25.

8. Click OK, and preview the report without showing the picture.

9. Insert a summary on the Salary field. Use the group on Employee ID, and check the Summarize Across Hierarchy option.

10. Suppress the group header, for readability.

11. Save the report as **Exercise 12.4**.

Figure 12-6
Creating
summary fields
for hierarchical
groups

Chapter Review

This chapter covered the nonstandard report types of cross-tabs, form letters, and hierarchically grouped reports.

Quick Tips

- Cross-tabs are created with the Cross-Tab Expert.

- Cross-tabs display summary values grouped by the row fields and summarized across the column fields in a grid. The cells of a cross-tab are the summarized values by the row fields and the column fields.

- Cross-tabs can be placed in the Report Header or Report Footer section or in a group header or footer. The location of the cross-tab determines what data is included.

- You can create new formulas to use in cross-tabs from the Cross-Tab Expert.

- You can format the row and column groups using the Group Options dialog box.

- A cross-tab can be formatted with the Format Editor either as a whole object or by selecting any cross-tab element.

- You can turn the columns of a cross-tab into rows, and vice versa, using the Pivot Cross-Tab menu command or by dragging the row or column fields.

- Elements of a cross-tab can be conditionally formatted using the Highlighting Expert or by creating format formulas. The special function GridRowColumnValue is available when creating format formulas.

PART II

- Form letters can be created using text objects with embedded fields. They can be customized for different purposes using multiple text objects and conditional suppression.

- Hierarchically grouped reports are created using the Hierarchical Group Options dialog box. You must supply the field containing the parent and specify an indentation measurement.

- If hierarchies exist in your report, you can create summaries that calculate across the levels of the hierarchy.

Questions

Questions may have more than one correct answer. Choose all answers that apply.

1. The Cross-Tab Expert can be displayed in which of the following ways?

   a. Select Insert | Cross-Tab from the menu.

   b. Click the Insert Cross-Tab button.

   c. Right-click in a blank area of a valid section in the design window, and select Insert Cross-Tab.

   d. Right-click on an existing cross-tab and select Cross-Tab Expert.

   e. Select Report | Insert Cross-Tab

2. Fields are moved from the Available Fields list into which of the following list boxes to create a cross-tab?

   a. Totals

   b. Rows

   c. Columns

   d. Cells

   e. Summarized Fields

3. You can edit which of the following field types directly from the Cross-Tab Expert?

   a. SQL Expression fields

   b. Running Total fields

   c. Formula fields

   d. Database fields

   e. Parameter fields

4. Cross-tabs are not location-dependent. If you move a cross-tab from the Report Header to a group header, the contents will not change.

   a. True

   b. False

5. Cross-tabs can be created in which of the following sections?

    a. Report Header

    b. Page Header

    c. Group Header

    d. Details

    e. Group Footer

    f. Page Footer

    g. Report Footer

6. If you try to drag a cross-tab into a Details section you will get an error and must move the cursor to a valid section.

    a. True

    b. False

7. Individual cross-tab formatting properties can be set on which of the following tabs of the Cross-Tab Expert?

    a. Cross-tab

    b. Format

    c. Customize Style

    d. Style

    e. Template

8. When creating format formulas for the elements of a cross-tab, which of the following special functions or constants are available?

    a. CurrentFieldValue

    b. DefaultAttribute

    c. GridRowColumnValue

    d. Row or Column Names

    e. Attribute constants

9. Column totals in a cross-tab can be placed at the top of the grid or at the bottom of the grid.

    a. True

    b. False

10. Which of the following are commonly used in the construction of a form letter?

    a. Suppress Embedded Blank Lines option

    b. Text objects with embedded fields

    c. Indented paragraph formatting

    d. Text objects with constant text

    e. Conditional section suppression

11. You can open the Hierarchical Group Options dialog box in which of the following ways?

   a. Right-click a group and choose Hierarchical Grouping Options from the menu.

   b. Select Report | Hierarchical Grouping Options.

   c. Click the Summarize Across Hierarchy button in the Group Options dialog box.

   d. Select Insert | Hierarchical Group.

12. Since hierarchical groups are not real Crystal Reports groups, you cannot create summary fields that show the group totals.

   a. True

   b. False

Answers

1. **a, b, d.** These are the only valid methods.

2. **b, c, e.** Move fields into the Rows, Columns, and Summarized Fields lists to create cross-tabs.

3. **c.** You can edit formula fields by clicking the Edit Formula button when a formula field is created. (You can also edit any other type of formula after the Formula Workshop is open.)

4. **b.** False. Cross-tabs are location-dependent. The contents will change if you move a cross-tab.

5. **a, c, d, e, g.** Cross-tabs cannot be used in a Page Header, Page Footer, or Details section.

6. **b.** False. If you try to drop a cross-tab into an unacceptable section, it will automatically move to an acceptable one.

7. **c.** The Customize Style tab is the only tab of the Cross-Tab Expert where you can set individual formatting properties.

8. **All.** All the items listed are available when creating a format formula for a cross-tab element.

9. **a.** The default is at the bottom but it can be changed using the Column Totals On Top check box on the Customize Style tab of the Cross-tab Expert.

10. **All.** All the options listed are commonly used to construct form letters.

11. **b.** The only way to open the Hierarchical Group Options dialog box is by selecting Hierarchical Grouping Options from the Report menu.

12. **b.** Use the Summarize Across Hierarchy option in the Insert Summary dialog box to sum across the levels of the hierarchy.

CHAPTER 13

Special Reporting Features

Exam RDCR200 expects you to be able to
- Use the Running Total Expert
- Build a report with alerts

In this chapter, you will learn how to create cumulative summary fields using the Running Total Expert and an alternative method involving formulas. In addition, you will learn how to add pop-up messages, called alerts, to reports. There is also a brief introduction to smart tags and using OLE objects, although these topics are not on the exam.

Running Totals

Running totals display the cumulative summary of some value up to the current record. There are two ways to create running totals in Crystal Reports: you can create either a Running Total field or a set of Formula fields with specific properties.

Before using either method to create running totals, it is important to understand how they work.

Cumulative Tally

A *running total* is a cumulative tally. Crystal Reports takes the value for the current record and adds it to the total from all previous records. The order of the records is important since the running total will differ if the sort order of the records changes. The running total for the last record will equal the value of a regular summary of the field. A simple running total is shown here.

Order ID	Amount	Running Total
1002	10	10
1003	125	135
1004	2380	2515
1005	36	2551

The summary operation need not be a sum; it could be any operation that is valid for the data type of the field being summarized. Since a running total accumulates record by record for the records contained in the report, it can be used to get the proper total for reports that have records suppressed due a group selection formula. (Remember that the report grand total is computed before the record suppression caused by group selection formulas.)

Reset

The tally can be restarted when some condition is met. For example, the following shows a running total that resets when the country changes. You can cause running totals to reset when report group values change or reset them independent of the report's groups.

Country	Order ID	Amount	Running Total
USA	1002	10	10
USA	1003	125	135
Canada	1004	2380	2380
Canada	1005	36	2416

Conditional Tally

The tally can include a record's value only when some condition is met. For example, here is a running total for orders from the United States only.

Country	Order ID	Amount	Running Total
USA	1002	10	10
Canada	1003	125	10
USA	1004	2380	2390
Canada	1005	36	2390

Creating Running Total Fields

You use the Create Running Total Field dialog box to create a Running Total field. This dialog box is opened from the Field Explorer by selecting the Running Total Fields folder and clicking the New button or by selecting New from the right-click menu. The dialog box is shown in Figure 13-1.

 EXAM TIP The exam objectives call this the Running Total Expert, but the Crystal Reports help files do not classify it as an Expert, merely as a dialog box.

Available Tables and Fields

The Available Tables and Fields list shows all fields that can be used in the running total. It shows both existing report fields and all fields from connected data sources. Use the arrow buttons to move fields into the Field to Summarize box, or use the On Change of Field boxes in the Evaluate and Reset sections.

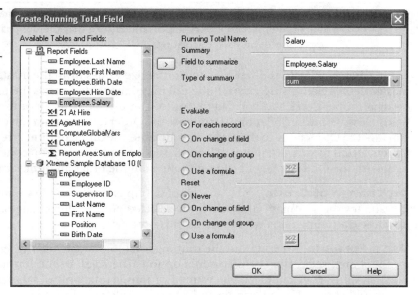

Figure 13-1
Creating running
totals

Running Total Name

Enter a name for your Running Total field in the Running Total Name box. This name
will appear in the Field Explorer. When you place a Running Total field on the report, a
pound sign will be prefixed to it.

Summary Section

In the summary section of the dialog box, you choose the field to summarize and the
summary operation to use.

Field to Summarize   Move a field from the Available Tables and Fields list into
the Field to Summarize box using the arrow button or by dragging. The running total
will be based on this field.

Type of Summary   Select a summary operation from the Type of Summary drop-
down box. The available options change based on the data type of the field the running
total is based on.

Evaluate

The Evaluate section contains four radio buttons, as shown in Figure 13-1. Choose one
to determine when the tally will be executed.

For Each Record   Choosing For Each Record causes the running total operation to
happen for every record in the report.

On Change of Field   Choosing On Change of Field causes the running total operation to happen only when the value of the selected field changes. Place the field that
you want to use in the box next to the On Change of Field radio button.

CAUTION On Change of Field executes when a field value changes, so the order of the records is very important. Ensure that the designated sort order is appropriate for your calculation.

On Change of Field is often used to summarize values from the master table when a master-detail relationship exists. If the linking of the tables causes the master record to occur multiple times and you only want to sum one occurrence of the master record field, use this option. For example, suppose the Order table contains an order amount. If you link the Order table to the Orders Detail table, the order amount is repeated for each Orders Detail record, even though it applies to the entire order. You could use a running total with the On Change of Field option to sum the order amount properly.

On Change of Group On Change of Group is similar to On Change of Field, but it evaluates the summary only when the selected group value changes. Select a group from the drop-down box when you use this option.

Use a Formula If you want the running total to evaluate only when a certain condition is met, select the Use a Formula option. The result of the formula should be a Boolean value. For example, if you wanted a running total only of salaries over $50,000, you would choose Use a Formula and enter the following formula:

```
{Employee.Salary} > 50000
```

Reset
In the Reset area, you must choose when you want your running total set back to zero.

Never Never is the default. It causes the running total never to reset.

On Change of Field Choose On Change of Field to have the running total reset when the value of the selected field changes. Add the field you want to use to the adjacent box.

On Change of Group Choose On Change of Group to have the running total reset when the value of the selected group changes. Select the group you want to use from the drop-down box.

Use a Formula Choose Use a Formula and create a Boolean formula to have the running total reset when a specific condition is met.

Placement of Running Total Fields
Once you create a Running Total field, you can place it in your report. The location of the Running Total field affects the value displayed. If you place the field in the Details section, it behaves as previously discussed. If you place it in some other section of the report, it computes using the records available to it when that section is printed:

- In the Report Header section, it will evaluate using only the first record of the report.
- In a Page Header, it will use all records up to the first record to be printed on the current page.

- In a Group Header, it will use all records up to the first record of the current group.
- In a Group Footer, it will use all records up to the last record in the group.
- In a Page Footer, it will use all records up to the first record on the next page.
- In the Report Footer, it will use all records in the report.

Creating Manual Running Totals

Manual running totals are running totals created with Formula fields. Use a manual running total if your logic is too complex to represent in a Running Total field, if you want to include values from suppressed records, or if you want a running total based on a Formula field that is itself evaluated at print time.

 EXAM TIP   Manual running totals are not an exam objective.

Manual running totals require three formulas and use global variables: One formula is created to do the summary operation. One is created to reset the summary. And one is created to display the result.

Summary Formula

The summary formula should look like the following. Use the proper variable type for your field, usually number or currency.

```
WhilePrintingRecords;
numberVar Tally;
Tally := Tally + {Field to summarize};
```

If you want the summary evaluated conditionally, add the condition to the formula. For example, use a statement similar to this:

```
If condition then
   Tally := Tally + {Field to summarize}
Else
   Tally;
```

The condition can be a comparison of some value in the current record to a value in the previous record, if you want to implement an On Change of Field or On Change of Group evaluation. If you want to use a different summary operation, adjust the formula accordingly.

Place the summary formula in the Details section if you want it evaluated for every record. Be wary of placing it in other sections. For example, if you placed the formula in a Group Footer section, it would show a running total of the last record in each group. If you want the accumulation to happen for every record, but not be displayed for every record, you should place it in the Details section and then suppress it.

Reset Formula

The reset formula simply sets the global variable to zero. Use something similar to the following:

```
WhilePrintingRecords;
numberVar Tally := 0;
```

Place the Reset formula where you want the reset to occur. If you are never resetting, you do not need a reset formula. If you want to reset conditionally, you can add a condition like this:

```
WhilePrintingRecords;
numberVar Tally;
If condition then Tally := 0;
```

Display Formula

The display formula simply returns the current value of the global variable. The display formula should look like this:

```
WhilePrintingRecords;
numberVar Tally;
```

Place the display formula where you want the running total displayed, but not reevaluated, such as in a Group Footer to show a group total or the Report Footer to show a grand total. You may not need a display formula if you are only displaying the running total in the Details section.

Exercise 13.1: Creating a Simple Running Total

1. Open the Exercise 8.8 report.

2. Place the Salary field on the report as the rightmost field.

3. Right-click the Running Total Fields folder in the Field Explorer, and choose New.

4. Enter **Salary** into the Running Total Name box.

5. Select Salary as the field to summarize, and leave the summary operation set at sum.

6. Click OK to close the dialog box, and place the field to the right of the existing fields in the Details section.

7. Preview the report.

8. Create a new folder for the exercises in this chapter, and save the report as **Exercise 13.1** within that folder.

Exercise 13.2: Creating a Conditional Running Total

1. Open the report from Exercise 13.1.

2. Right-click the #Salary field, and select Edit Running Total to open the Running Total dialog box.

3. In the Evaluate section, choose Use a Formula, and enter the following formula:

   `{@CurrentAge} < 40`

4. Close the Formula Workshop and the Running Total dialog box.

5. Preview the report. Notice that Michael Suyama's salary is not added to the total.

6. Save the report as **Exercise 13.2**.

Exercise 13.3: Resetting the Running Total

1. Open the Exercise 13.2 report.

2. Add the Reports To field to the report, and sort the report by it. (Change field widths if needed to accommodate all the fields.)

3. Edit the Running Total field and reset the Evaluate option to For Each Record.

4. In the Reset section, select On Change of Field, and add the Report To field to the adjacent box.

5. Preview the report, and notice when the running total resets.

6. Save the report as **Exercise 13.3**.

Alerts

Alerts are messages that Crystal Reports displays when some user-defined condition is met. You can use alerts to draw attention to a condition or to give instructions when a condition is met. Alerts are created from the Create Alerts dialog box and viewed in the Report Alerts dialog box. Both dialog boxes can be opened from the Alerts submenu of the Report menu.

Creating Alerts

To open the Create Alerts dialog box, select Report | Alerts | Create or Modify Alerts. The dialog box will open, shown in Figure 13-2, listing any existing Alerts. From this dialog box you can create new alerts, edit existing alerts, or delete alerts.

New

Clicking the New button opens the Create Alert dialog box, shown here. This is where you name and configure the alert.

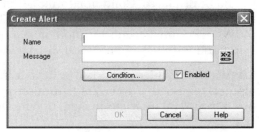

Name   Enter the name you want for the alert in the Name box.

Message   Enter the message that you want displayed when the alert is triggered in the Message box. Note that the message is displayed only once, even if multiple records are triggered. You can create a message consisting of a formula by clicking the

Figure 13-2
Working with
alerts

Formula button. If you use a formula, the text that you enter into the Message box is returned from the DefaultAttribute function for the formula. The message can be up to 254 characters and can be left blank if desired, in which case only the name of the alert will be displayed, with no detailed description.

Message Formula   Click the Formula button to open the Formula Workshop and create a formula for the alert message. The Workshop Tree will have a folder called Alerting Formulas that lists the alerts that use formulas, as shown here.

Alerts can have two types of formulas, one for the message and one for the condition. You can create an alert message formula that uses report fields to customize the message display, but be aware that the message displayed will be the one computed for the first record that triggers the alert.

Condition   Clicking the Condition button in the Create Alert dialog box opens the Formula Workshop; there you can create a Boolean formula describing when the alert should be displayed. Condition formulas cannot use any field that is computed at print time (during Pass 2). This excludes Running Total fields and Formula fields that contain the WhilePrintingRecords function or are otherwise required to compute at print time. Condition formulas can use local variables but not global or shared variables.

Enabled   Enabled is checked by default and causes the alert to be evaluated when the report is refreshed. If you want to turn off an alert temporarily, clear the Enabled check box. If you want to delete an alert, use the Delete button.

Edit
Selecting an alert and clicking Edit opens the Edit Alert dialog box. Except for the name, the Edit Alert dialog box is identical to the Create Alert dialog box just described.

Delete

Select an alert and click the Delete button to delete the alert.

Creating Report Alerts

The Report Alerts dialog box, shown here, displays the alerts that are currently triggered for the report.

The Report Alerts dialog box is displayed automatically when a report is refreshed, if any alerts are triggered. You can also display it by selecting Report | Alerts | Triggered Alerts.

Report alerts will not be displayed unless the Display Alerts on Refresh check box of the Report Options dialog box for the report is checked. Report Options is opened from the File menu. The default setting for the Display Alerts on Refresh property is set on the Reporting tab of the Options dialog box.

Alert List

The Alert list box displays triggered alerts and their messages. The alert is displayed only once, no matter how many records met the alert condition.

View Records

Select an alert and then click the View Records button to open a new report tab that displays all records that triggered the alert. If you select more than one alert, records that satisfy all the alert conditions are displayed.

Adding Alerts to Formulas

Some special Formula Workshop functions and alert constants exist to make alert information available in formulas. These elements appear after an alert has been created, as shown here.

Alert Functions

The three alert functions give you programmatic access to the status of the alert and the alert message:

- **IsAlertEnabled(*alertName*)**   IsAlertEnabled returns True or False, indicating the enabled state of the listed alert. This value will be constant for the entire report.

- **IsAlertTriggered(*alertName*)**   IsAlertTriggered returns True or False, indicating whether the alert condition is True or False for the current record. This value will vary from record to record. If you have an alert based on a summary, the value will be constant for every record in the group the summary is related to.

- **AlertMessage(*alertName*)**   AlertMessage returns the text message configured for the alert. This value will be constant for the report.

Alert Names

The Alert Names folder of the Function Tree lists the names of any existing alerts for use as the parameter for the alert functions.

Exercise 13.4: Creating an Alert

1. Open the report from Exercise 13.3.
2. Select Report | Alerts | Create or Modify Alerts.
3. Click the New button.
4. Enter **Too Young At Hire** for the alert name and **Employee was under 18 when hired.** as the message.
5. Click the Condition button, and enter the following formula:

```
DateAdd ('yyyy', 18, {Employee.Birth Date}) >= {Employee.Hire Date}
```

 NOTE   You cannot use the AgeAtHire formula because it is a print time formula.

6. Close the Formula Workshop and the alert creation dialog boxes.
7. Preview the report. In the Report Alerts dialog box, click the View Records button to see the records that triggered the alert.
8. Save the report as **Exercise 13.4**.

Exercise 13.5: Creating an Alert on a Summary Field

1. Open the report from Exercise 13.4.
2. Create a group on the Reports To field.
3. Create a summary on the Salary field for the Reports To group.
4. Create a new alert called **Group Salary Too High**. Set the message to **The Salary total for a group is over $125,000.**
5. Set the condition to the following formula:

```
Sum ({Employee.Salary}, {Employee.Reports To}) > 125000
```

6. Close all dialog boxes, and preview the report. View the records for the new alert. Note that every record for each of the groups that met the condition is displayed.

7. Save the report as **Exercise 13.5**.

Exercise 13.6: Using Alert Functions in a Formula

1. Open the report from Exercise 13.5.

2. Create a formula called **SalaryAlertTriggered** using the following formula:

```
If IsAlertTriggered ("Group Salary Too High") then '*' else ' ';
```

3. Place the Formula field next to the Salary summary field in the Group Footer section, and size it to just one character wide. Remove the associated field header.

4. Place a text object in the Page Footer, and enter this text: *** Group's salary total is over $125,000.**

5. Preview the report. This method creates alerts that show up in the printed output as well as when the report is previewed online.

6. Save the report as **Exercise 13.6**.

Smart Tags

Crystal Reports report objects can be embedded in Microsoft Office applications as *smart tags*. A smart tag is simply a link to the original report. The user can refresh the object, view the original report, or remove the tag. You can embed single values, such as a report total or text object, or charts.

To create a smart tag, select the text field, report field, or chart that you want to use in the report file. Then right-click and choose Copy Smart Tag, open the Office application, and paste the smart tag in the desired location. Figure 13-3 shows a Crystal Reports smart tag in an Excel spreadsheet with the pop-up menu open. The smart tag pop-up menu has options that allow you to refresh the value or view the source report.

Some special configuration is required to make smart tags work. Properties on the Smart Tag tab of the Options dialog box must be properly configured, and users must have the Crystal Reports Smart Tags code. See Crystal Reports documentation for more details.

OLE Objects

Object Linking and Embedding (OLE) is a Microsoft standard; it can be used to incorporate application files or parts of files from one application in another. Crystal Reports can act as an *OLE container*; that is, OLE objects can be embedded in Crystal Reports documents. To embed an object, select it in the source application, and copy it to the clipboard. Then open the report that will act as the container, and select Paste or Paste Special.

Figure 13-3

Opening a Crystal Reports smart tag in an Excel spreadsheet

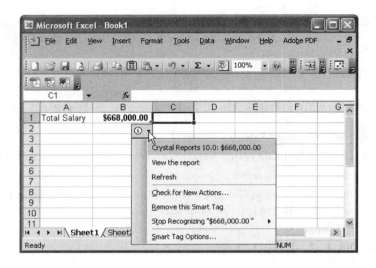

Click at the location in the report where you want the object embedded. If the source application can act as an OLE server, the object will be embedded into the report as an OLE object. If you want to control how the object is pasted, select Paste Special. The Paste Special dialog box, shown here, will be displayed.

Check the Display as Icon box if you want the object displayed as

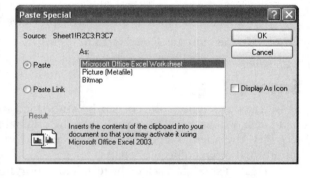

a small icon in the report. Choose the Paste Link option if you want the object to update when the underlying document is updated. Linked objects cannot be edited in place. If you double-click an OLE object, the source application opens in place, in the report, and you can edit the object.

Chapter Review

This chapter covered several reporting features, primarily Running Totals and Alerts that need to be understood for the exam. It also briefly introduced smart tags and OLE objects.

Quick Tips

- Running Total fields are created with the Create Running Total Field dialog box (sometimes called the Running Total Expert).
- The Create Running Total Field dialog box is opened using the New command in the Field Explorer while the Running Total Fields folder or one of its entries

is selected. The Edit Running Total Field dialog box is identical and opens when you edit a Running Total field.

- To create a Running Total field, you must select the field to summarize, the summary operation to use, when to evaluate the summary, and when to reset the summary.
- Conditional Running Total fields can be created by choosing the Use a Formula option in either the Evaluate or the Reset section of the dialog box, and then creating a Boolean formula.
- Running Total fields can be placed anywhere on the report, but they will display only the summary evaluated as of the current record.
- Alerts are messages that you can cause to appear when certain conditions are met.
- Alerts are created using the Create Alerts dialog box, which is opened by selecting Report | Alerts | Create or Modify Alerts.
- When you create an alert, you give it a name, enter the message to display, and define the condition that will trigger it.
- The alert message can be created via a formula.
- You can enable or disable alerts.
- Alerts are displayed in the Report Alerts dialog box when a report is refreshed or can be viewed by selecting Report | Alerts | Triggered Alerts.
- You can click the View Records button in the Report Alerts dialog box to open a report tab displaying the records that met the alert condition.
- Three alert-related functions exist so that you can use alert information in formulas. They are IsAlertEnabled, IsAlertTriggered, and AlertMessage.

Questions

Questions may have more than one correct answer. Choose all answers that apply.

1. Running totals can be created using which of the following?
   a. Insert | Running Total menu option
   b. Running Total Expert
   c. Create Running Total Field dialog box
   d. Formula Workshop
   e. Insert Running Total button

2. What are the three sections of the Create Running Total Field dialog box?
   a. Evaluate
   b. Restart
   c. Reset
   d. Conditions
   e. Summary

3. The options for resetting the Running Total field are

   a. For Each Record

   b. On Change of Field

   c. On Change of Group

   d. Use a Formula

   e. Never

4. Say that you have a Running Total field defined as the sum of a currency field, evaluated for each record, and reset when Group 1 changes. What result would you get if you placed the field in the Group 1 Header section?

   a. Zero

   b. The total for Group 1

   c. The total of all records up to the first record in Group 1

   d. The amount from the first record in Group 1

   e. The total for the previous Group 1

5. Running totals can be used to create totals that exclude records suppressed by a group selection formula.

   a. True

   b. False

6. Manual running totals are created by using which three types of formulas?

   a. Initialization

   b. Aggregation

   c. Reset

   d. Display

   e. Summary

7. Alerts can be disabled but not deleted.

   a. True

   b. False

8. Every record that triggered an alert is displayed

   a. With highlighting in the report.

   b. In the Report Alerts dialog box.

   c. Via the View Records button in a report tab.

   d. With a footnote in the report.

   e. By creating a formula.

9. Report alerts are displayed by default in the Report Footer when the report is printed.

   a. True

   b. False

10. To create an alert, you must provide the following items.

   a. Name

   b. Message

   c. Message formula

   d. Condition

Answers

1. **b, c, d.** Answers a and e do not exist. You create the Running Total field using the Create Running Total Field dialog box, which is sometimes called the Running Total Expert. You can create manual running totals using formulas created with the Formula Workshop.

2. **a, c, e.** The field to summarize and the summary operation are set in the Summary section. When to evaluate and when to reset are set in the Evaluate and Reset sections.

3. **b, c, d, e.** For Each Record is an Evaluate option, but not a Reset option.

4. **d.** The Running Total field would display the amount from the first record in Group 1.

5. **a.** True. Use running totals to calculate summaries of only the records displayed in a report that uses a group selection formula.

6. **c, d, e.** To create a manual running total, you create summary, reset, and display formulas.

7. **b.** False. Alerts can be deleted or disabled.

8. **c.** To see every record that triggered an alert, you must click the View Records button in the Report Alerts dialog box, and the records will be displayed in a report tab.

9. **b.** Report Alerts are not displayed in the print version of a report unless the developer uses formulas to display them.

10. **a, d.** Only a name and condition formula are required.

Crystal Reports in the Crystal Enterprise Environment

Exam RDCR200 expects you to be able to
- Manage the Crystal Repository
- Add folders to the repository
- Add objects to the repository
- Update the connection to repository objects in a report
- Delete objects in the repository
- Connect to your own repository
- Create a report from a SQL Command
- Create a report from a Business View
- Define how Crystal Reports fits into the Crystal solution
- Use the Crystal Publishing wizard
- View parameterized reports in Crystal Enterprise

When you use Crystal Reports in a Crystal Enterprise environment, several new capabilities are revealed. You can store report objects in a central location for sharing and reuse among reports and report developers. You can base your reports on Business Views that were created to help simplify or automate report development. And you can publish your reports to Crystal Enterprise so that they will be available to all users in the enterprise.

Repository Explorer

The Crystal Repository is a database contained within Crystal Enterprise where you can store some types of objects for reuse in multiple reports. The Repository Explorer allows you to browse objects that have been saved in the repository and use them in your report. Repository objects that are added to reports maintain their link to the repository and can be automatically updated if the repository object is updated. For example, assume that your company has a logo that is displayed on every report. The logo graphic can be stored in the repository and then used in each report. If the logo ever changes, you only need to make sure that the reports are configured to update their repository objects when they are run, and then all the reports will get the new logo automatically. You use the Repository Explorer to add, use, and organize most repository objects.

 NOTE Administration of the repository database is handled via the Business View Manager.

Exploring the Repository Explorer

The Repository Explorer is similar to the Field Explorer or Report Explorer. It has its own toolbar and shortcut menus and can be docked in the same ways.

Displaying the Repository Explorer

If the Repository Explorer is not open, you can open it by clicking the Repository Explorer button on the Standard toolbar, or by choosing View | Repository Explorer. If you are not already logged on to Crystal Enterprise, you will be asked to log on. If you did the exercises in Chapter 1, then your Repository Explorer should look similar to this illustration.

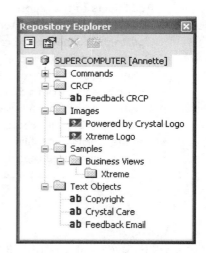

Toolbar

The Repository Explorer toolbar has only four buttons:

 Clicking the Change View Settings button displays the View Setting dialog box, shown in Figure 14-1, which allows you to customize the display of the Repository Explorer tree. You can choose to display or not display bitmap objects, SQL Commands, and text objects, and you can modify the sort order.

 The Advanced Filtering button toggles the display of filtering options at the bottom of the Repository Explorer dialog box, as shown in Figure 14-2. You can filter to items containing specified text in their name or that have a particular author.

 The Delete the Item/Folder button is available when you have selected a folder or item; it deletes that folder or item. Deleting a folder deletes all the items stored in it. Deleting objects from the repository does not delete the corresponding objects from the report files. Reports that use deleted repository items will display an error when next run, and the report fields can then be disconnected from the repository. You must have the appropriate Crystal Enterprise privileges to delete items and folders.

 Use the Insert a New Folder button to create a new folder. You must have the appropriate Crystal Enterprise privileges to create a new folder.

Figure 14-1
Customizing the
Repository
Explorer tree

Docking
The Repository Explorer can be free-floating, docked to the right, left, or bottom, or docked with the Report Explorer and Field Explorer to create a tagged dialog.

Shortcut Menu
As shown here, the shortcut menu displayed for folders (left) differs slightly from that displayed for items (right).

Figure 14-2
Repository
Explorer showing
filtering options

Note that some of the shortcut commands require appropriate privileges for the repository folders or items.

- **Rename**   Allows you to rename a folder or item
- **New Folder**   Creates a new folder under the selected folder
- **Refresh**   Rereads repository information from the repository database
- **Expand All**   Opens all folders under the selected folder
- **Advanced Filtering**   Displays the filtering options at the bottom of the Repository Explorer
- **Change View Settings**   Displays the View Settings dialog box, where you can customize the display of items in the Repository Explorer
- **Delete**   Deletes the selected folder or item
- **Properties**   Displays the Properties dialog box for the item. The Properties dialog box contains the item's name, type, description, and last modification date.

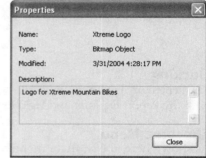

Tooltips

A repository item's description appears as a tooltip in the Repository Explorer.

Using Folders

Repository objects are organized by placing them in folders. The structure of the folder system is completely up to you. The sample objects are arranged into object type folders, but you can create any folder hierarchy that you need. Once a Crystal Enterprise administrator has granted you edit privileges to a folder via the Business Views Manager, you can add items or more folders to that folder.

New folders can be added by using the toolbar button or shortcut menu option. When you add a new folder it is given the name New Folder, but you can immediately change the name to anything you desire. Folders can be deleted using the DELETE key, the toolbar button, or the shortcut menu option. Folders can be moved to a new location by dragging.

Repository Object Types

The repository holds only a few object types, and their creation and use depends on the type. After your folder hierarchy is created, you will need to add objects to the repository, and then you will be able to use those objects in your reports. You may also periodically need to modify the objects in the repository and update existing reports that use those objects.

Repository Naming Conventions

You must name each item that you add to the repository. The name you create cannot contain the following characters: # " { } ; /

Text Field and Bitmap Objects

Text field and bitmap repository objects are the simplest repository objects. They are regular report text objects or picture objects that have been added to the repository.

Adding to the Repository To add a text field object or picture field object to the repository, select the field in a report and drag it to a repository folder. Alternatively, you can select the field and then choose Add to Repository from the shortcut menu.

If you drag the field to a repository folder, the Object Information dialog box is displayed, as shown in Figure 14-3. You must create a name for the repository item. The author field will default to your Crystal Enterprise user ID, and you can enter a description to help identify the item. Click OK to complete the process.

If you right-click a text field or picture field and choose Add to Repository, the Add Item dialog box will appear, as shown in Figure 14-4. In addition to completing the fields in the Object Information dialog box, you must choose a folder for the object to be added to.

 EXAM TIP The four types of objects that can be added to the repository from Crystal Reports are text objects, bitmaps, custom functions, and SQL Commands.

Adding to a Report To use a text object or picture object from the repository in your report, simply select the object in the Repository Explorer and drag it onto the report.

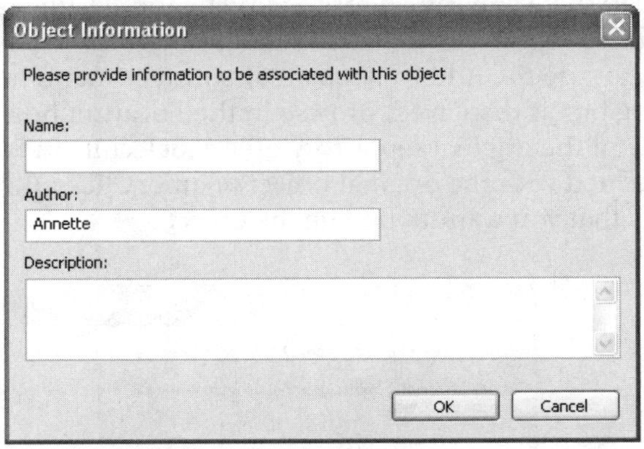

Figure 14-3

Adding an object to a repository folder

Object Information

Please provide information to be associated with this object

Name:

Author:

Annette

Description:

OK   Cancel

Figure 14-4

Adding an item
to the repository

Updating Once a report field has been added to the repository, it becomes read-only in the report. Modifying a repository object requires multiple steps:

1. You must disconnect the report object from the repository by selecting the report object and choosing Disconnect from Repository from the shortcut menu.

2. Modify the report object as needed.

3. Now put the object back in the repository by dragging it onto the existing repository entry for that item. The Add or Update Object dialog box will appear; there you can choose to update the existing repository object with the modified report object or add it as another new repository object. Alternatively, you can use the Add to Repository shortcut menu item. When the Add Item dialog box is displayed, browse in the Location box until you can select the name of the original repository object. Select it, and the Name text box will be populated with the original object's name. Click OK, and you will be asked to verify that you want to update the object.

NOTE You cannot undo any actions that affect the repository, such as adding objects, updating objects, or deleting objects.

Custom Functions

Custom functions are not displayed in the Repository Explorer and cannot be added directly to a report. They are used and maintained via the Formula Workshop and are discussed in Chapter 8.

SQL Commands

SQL Commands stored in the repository cannot be dragged onto a report like text objects or picture objects. SQL Commands are database queries that can be used as data sources for a report, similar to tables or views. They are managed in the Database Expert.

Adding to the Repository   To add a SQL Command to the repository, use the following steps. A SQL Command must have previously been created and exist in the Selected Tables list for the report.

1. Open the Database Explorer.
2. Right-click on the SQL Command in the Selected Tables list, and select Add to Repository.
3. The Add Item dialog box will appear, where you must create a name for the repository item and choose a folder location for it. The description defaults to the text of the database query.
4. Click OK to complete the process.

Adding to a Report   Using a repository SQL Command in a report is similar to using any other type of data source:

1. Open the Database Expert.
2. Open the Repository folder.
3. If you have not already used any repository SQL Commands in the report, the Crystal Enterprise Explorer will open immediately. If you have used other repository SQL Commands, click the Make New Connection node to display the Crystal Enterprise Explorer.
4. Browse the Crystal Enterprise Explorer until you find the SQL Command that you want to use. Only Command and Business View items are available, even though all folders will be displayed.
5. Select the SQL Command you want, and click Open.
6. Add the SQL Command to the Selected Tables list, as you would any normal table.

Updating   To modify a SQL Command stored in the repository, follow these steps:

1. Open the Database Expert.

2. In the Selected Tables list, right-click the SQL Command and choose Disconnect from Repository.

3. Right-click the SQL Command, and choose Edit Command. Make the desired changes to the query.

4. Right-click the SQL Command again, and choose Add to Repository. In the Add Item dialog box, browse the repository tree in the Location box to select the original repository object. The Name box will populate automatically with the name of the selected original object.

5. Click OK. You will be asked if you are sure you want to update the object. Click Yes.

Business Views

Business Views are created, modified, and maintained with the Crystal Enterprise tool Business View Manager.

Adding to a Report   Using a Business View in a report is similar to using any other type of data source:

1. Open the Database Expert.

2. Open the Repository folder.

3. If you have not already used any repository SQL Commands or Business Views in the report, the Crystal Enterprise Explorer will open immediately. If you have used other repository SQL Commands or Business Views, click the Make New Connection node to display the Crystal Enterprise Explorer.

4. Browse the Crystal Enterprise Explorer until you find the Business View that you want to use. Open the Business View to display its contained data sources.

5. Select the data source that you want to use.

6. Add it to the Selected Tables list, as you would any normal table.

Note that you cannot mix Business View data sources with other types of data sources in the same report.

 EXAM TIP   All you need to know for the RDCR200 exam is how to use an existing Business View as a data source for a report.

Updating Reports That Use Repository Items

To make sure that reports containing repository items are updated with the current version of the items, check the Update Connected Repository Objects on Open check box on the Report tab of the File | Options dialog box. If you do not set this global option, you can update an individual report's repository items by checking the Update Repository Objects check box on the File | Open dialog box.

The update happens when the report is opened in the Crystal Reports designer environment, not when a report is run. Crystal Enterprise can also be set to update the reports appropriately.

Exercise 14.1: Setting Up a Repository Folder

To set up a repository folder that you can use for practice, follow these steps. (You do not need to know how to do this for the exam.)

1. Open the Business View Manager and log on using the Administrator account that you created in Chapter 1.

2. Cancel the welcome dialog box if it appears.

3. In the Business View Manager's Repository Explorer, select the root node, right-click, and choose New Folder.

4. A new folder will be created. Change the name of the new folder to **CRCP**.

5. Right-click the CRCP folder, and select Edit Rights. The Edit Rights dialog box will be displayed.

6. Click the Add Users button, as shown here.

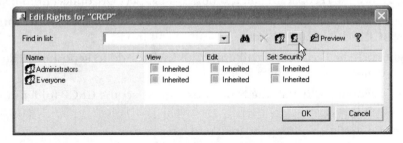

7. In the Add Users dialog box, select the account you created in Chapter 1, and click Add. Then click Close to return to the Edit Rights dialog box. Your account will now show up.

8. Click the check boxes for your account in the View, Edit, and Set Security columns until a check mark appears and the text changes to "Granted," as shown here.

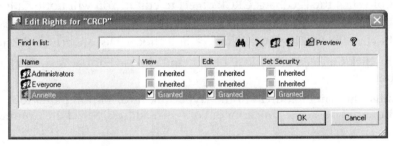

9. Click OK to close the Edit Rights dialog box.

10. Close the Business View Manager.

Exercise 14.2: Using the Repository

1. Close and then reopen Crystal Reports.

2. Choose the Exercise 5.6 report from the welcome dialog box to open it.

3. Log on to Crystal Enterprise using your user ID (not Administrator).

4. You should now see the CRCP folder in the Repository Explorer.

5. Right-click in the gray area of the Page Header section, and choose Insert Section Below. A new Page Header subsection will be created.

6. Drag the Page Header b section until it is above the Page Header a section, and drop it there. This will reverse the position of the two sections.

7. Open the Images folder of the Repository Explorer. Grab the Xtreme Logo item, drag it into the now-empty Page Header a section, and drop it close to the left margin.

8. Open the Text objects folder, and drag the Feedback Email item into the Page Footer section.

9. Right-click the Feedback Email text object, and select Disconnect from Repository.

10. Double-click the Feedback Email object to edit it. Change the word "Samples" to **CRCP**. Click off the object to get out of edit mode.

11. Right-click the Feedback Email object, and select Add to Repository. The Add Item dialog box will appear.

12. Type **Feedback CRCP** in the Name box, and select the CRCP folder in the Location tree.

13. Click OK to finish adding the item to the repository.

14. Look in the CRCP folder of the repository. You should see the new item there.

15. Save the report as **Exercise 14.2**, and close it.

16. Open Exercise 5.6.

17. Drag the Feedback CRCP text object into the Page Footer.

18. Double-click the Feedback CRCP object to edit it. You will not be allowed to edit it.

19. Right-click the Feedback CRCP object, and choose Disconnect from Repository.

20. Right-click the Feedback CRCP object, and choose Format Text. Click the Hyperlink tab.

21. Change the e-mail address in the Hyperlink Information panel to **mailto:annette@sage-link.com** or your own address. Select the Common tab,

and change the tool tip text to **annette@sage-link.com** or your own address. Click OK to close the Format Editor.

22. Drag the Feedback CRCP text object back into the repository on top of its original entry.

23. In the Add or Update Object dialog box, click the Update button. Click OK in the Modify Item dialog box.

24. Close the Exercise 5.6 report, saving your changes.

25. Select File | Open. In the Open dialog check the Update Repository Objects check box and select the Exercise 14.2 report. Click the Open button.

26. Hover the mouse cursor over the Feedback CRCP text object. The tool tip should now say "annette@sage-link.com," indicating that the object has been updated to match the repository.

27. Save the report, and close it.

Exercise 14.3: Creating a Report Based on a SQL Command

1. Click the New button to create a new report.

2. Choose the Standard report wizard, and click OK.

3. On the Data screen of the wizard, open the Repository folder or click Make New Connection to display the Crystal Enterprise Explorer. (You may need to log on to Crystal Enterprise.)

4. Open the Commands folder, and select the EmployeeInfo command. Click Open.

5. A folder named EmployeeInfo should now appear under the Repository folder in the Available Data Sources list. Move the query that is under the EmployeeInfo folder to the Selected Tables list. Click Next.

6. On the Fields screen, move Employee ID, Last Name, and First Name to the Selected Fields list, and click Finish.

7. Save the report as **Exercise 14.3**.

Exercise 14.4: Creating a Report Based on a Business View

1. Click the New button to create a new report.

2. Choose the Standard report wizard, and click OK.

3. On the Data screen of the wizard, open the Repository folder or click Make New Connection to display the Crystal Enterprise Explorer. (You may need to log on to Crystal Enterprise.)

4. Open the Samples folder, then Business Views, then the Xtreme folder, and select the Xtreme Business View. Click Open.

5. A folder named Xtreme Business View should now appear under the Repository folder in the Available Data Sources list. Select Employee, and move it to the Selected Tables list. Click Next.

6. On the Fields screen, move Employee ID, Employee Last Name, and Employee First Name to the Selected Fields list, and click Finish.

7. Save the report as **Exercise 14.4**.

Using the Publishing Wizard

The Crystal Publishing wizard is an easy-to-use wizard that steps you through the process of saving files to a Crystal Management Server database. In a previous chapter, you saved reports to Crystal Enterprise folders directly from the file dialog box in a report. Both are valid methods. The Publishing wizard allows you to save file types other than Crystal Reports' (.rpt) and has other capabilities. You can also use the Crystal Management Console to copy objects into the database.

Select Start | Crystal Enterprise 10 | Crystal Publishing Wizard. The wizard will open at the welcome screen. Click Next.

Log On to Crystal Enterprise

The Log On to Crystal Enterprise screen will appear. Log on to the Crystal Enterprise system where you want to publish items with a user name, password, and authentication method that has appropriate privileges. Click Next.

Select A File

The Select A File screen will appear, as shown in Figure 14-5. It is used to select the files that you want to publish to Crystal Enterprise.

Figure 14-5
Selecting a file in the Publishing wizard

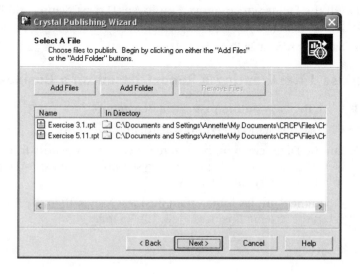

NOTE Crystal Enterprise can handle the following file types in addition to report files: Adobe Acrobat, Microsoft Excel, Microsoft Word, Microsoft PowerPoint, text, rich text format, and executables.

File List

In the center of the dialog box is a list box showing the selected files' names and directory locations. You add and remove items from this list using the buttons.

Add Files

Clicking the Add Files button displays an Open dialog box where you can browse to and select files for publishing to Crystal Enterprise. In the Open dialog box, you can filter the displayed files to the type for which you are searching. The available file types are shown in this illustration.

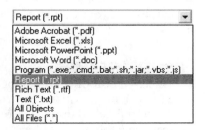

Add Folder

If you want to add every file in a folder, click the Add Folder button. The Browse for Folder dialog box, shown in Figure 14-6, will be displayed. To include files in subfolders of this folder, check the Include Subfolders box. You can select a specific file type using the drop-down box at the bottom of the dialog box, or if you want to add all file types, select All Objects.

Remove Files

To remove files from the list, select them, and click the Remove Files button. You can remove files one at a time or select multiple files for removal. When you are finished selecting files, click the Next button.

Figure 14-6
Adding a folder

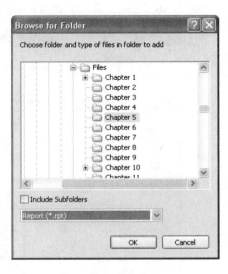

PART II

Specify Object Type

If you attempt to publish a file with an extension that Crystal Enterprise does not recognize, the Specify Object Type screen will be displayed. Select each file in the list, and choose a file type for it from the drop-down box. Click Next to continue.

Folder Hierarchy

If you selected folders and subfolders, the Folder Hierarchy screen will be displayed. Select Yes if you want the folder hierarchy maintained or No if you want all files placed in the same folder. If you want to create an object package, select No. Click Next to move to the next screen.

Specify Location

The Specify Location screen appears, as shown in Figure 14-7. Folders for which you have full privileges will appear. You can select an existing folder or create a new one to hold your published files. The icons to the upper right of the directory window are used to create new folders and object packages and to delete folders.

 Click the New Folder button to create a new folder in the tree. The folder icon for new folders is green. You can also choose New Folder from the right-click menu.

 Click the New Object Package button to create a new object package in the tree. The package icon for new packages is green. You can also choose New Object Package from the right-click menu.

 The Delete button will be available if a new folder or package is selected; you cannot delete existing folders or packages. Click Delete to remove the selected folder or package. Delete is available on the right-click menu for new folders and packages.

Click Next to continue to the next screen of the wizard.

Figure 14-7
Selecting a location for published files

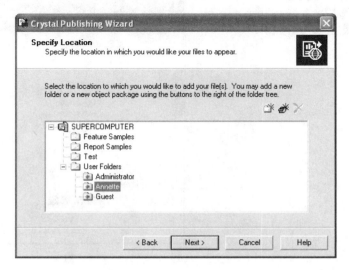

Location Preview

Use the Location Preview screen, shown in Figure 14-8, to rearrange files and folders. You can also create new folders and packages here. You can move files and folders by dragging or using the arrow buttons. The New Folder, New Object Package, and Delete buttons function the same way they do on the Specify Location screen, described in the preceding section.

 The Show File Names/Show Titles button toggles the display between the complete filename and the file title.

 Click the Move Down button to move a file or folder into the next folder in the tree.

 Click the Move Up button to move a file or folder into the preceding folder in the tree.

All button functions are also available as commands on the right-click menu. In addition, the Rename option is available on the right-click menu. You can rename folders and packages and retitle files using the Rename option. Click Next to continue.

Schedule Interval

The Schedule Interval screen has a list of the published objects and three radio button options, as shown in Figure 14-9. Select one or more objects to create the schedule for them. The default is Let Users Update the Objects, which requires no additional configuration.

Run Once Only

If you select Run Once Only, the Run Once Only panel will appear. In this panel, you can choose to have the objects run once when the wizard is finished or once at a scheduled time. If you choose At the Specified Data and Time, you must enter a date and time in the boxes provided.

Figure 14-8
Working with folders and packages

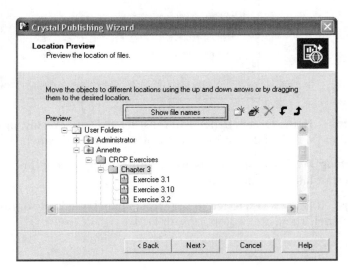

Figure 14-9
Scheduling when
objects run

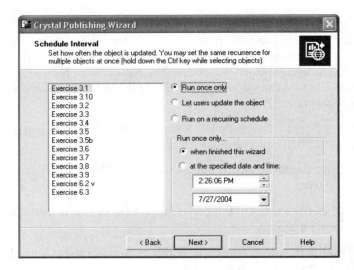

Let Users Update the Object

Let Users Update the Object is the default option and requires no further information.
Users will be able to schedule the object themselves.

Run on a Recurring Schedule

If you select Run on a Recurring Schedule, the Set Recurrence button will appear. Clicking Set Recurrence opens the Pick a Recurrence Schedule dialog box, shown here.

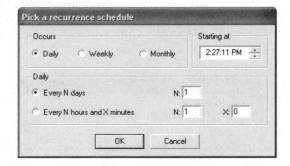

Occurs   In the Occurs panel, you must select Daily, Weekly, or Monthly. The option
picked in this panel determines the display of the third panel.

Starting At   The Starting At box defaults to the current time. If you want the schedule to start later, change the time.

Daily   If Daily was selected in the Occurs panel, the Daily options will appear in the
third panel. There are two options for Daily:

- **Every N Days**   Choose the Every N Days option to have the object run, for example, every third day. Enter a value for N.

- **Every N Hours and X Minutes**   Choose this option to run the object, for example, every 2 hours and 30 minutes every day. Enter a value for N and X.

Run Weekly   If Weekly was selected in the Occurs panel, the Run Weekly options will appear in the third panel. A check box appears for each day of the week; check the days on which you want the object to run. You can select one day or several, and the object will run every week on the selected days.

Run Monthly   If Monthly was selected in the Occurs panel, the Run Monthly options will appear in the third panel. There are two options for Run Monthly:

- **Nth Calendar Day**   Choose this option to run the object once a month on the selected date. Select the day from the drop-down box.

- **Nth Weekday**   Choose this option to run the object once a month on the selected weekday. You configure the day by selecting First, Second, Third, Fourth, or Last from the first drop-down box and then selecting a day of the week from the second drop-down box. For example, you might schedule the report to run on the second Monday of each month. In addition to a choice for each day of the week, there is a choice called Weekday that can be used to pick the first or last weekday of the month, or any weekday in between. For instance, you might schedule a report to run on the last weekday of the month.

After scheduling each object, click Next to continue to the next screen of the wizard.

Repository Refresh

If any of your published objects are reports, the Repository Refresh screen will appear. Select an object or multiple objects, and check the Use Object Repository When Refreshing Report box to enable the repository to refresh the report when it is run from Crystal Enterprise. To enable repository refresh for all the reports you are publishing, click the Enable All button. To disable repository refresh for all reports, click the Disable All button. Then click Next to continue.

Program Type

Each executable file that you selected for publishing will appear in the list on the Program Type screen. Select the radio button for the appropriate program type:

- **Binary/Batch**   Select Binary/Batch if the file is a command line executable such as .com, .exe, .bat, or .sh file.

- **Java**   Select Java if the file is a Java program. Java programs usually use .jar as the file extension.

- **Script**   Select Script if the file is a JScript or VBScript file.

Click Next to continue to the next screen of the wizard.

Program Credentials

All program files will be listed in the Program Credentials screen. Select each program that requires credentials, and enter a user name and password for it. Click Next.

Change Default Values

The Change Default Values screen contains two options: Publish Without Modifying Properties, and Review or Modify Properties. If you want to modify the logon credentials, parameters, or title and description of the files you are publishing, select Review or Modify Properties. Click Next to continue.

Review Object Properties

In the Review Object Properties screen, shown in Figure 14-10, you can change the title and description of the published objects. Select the object, and enter the title and description you want in the Title and Description boxes. If a preview picture is available, you can check the Generate Thumbnail Image box to display a preview in Crystal Enterprise. Click Next.

Database Logon Information

The Database Logon Information screen is shown in Figure 14-11. Each report file is listed in the box on the left half of the screen. Each data source used in each report file is listed under the report file. You must set logon information for each data source that requires it:

- **Database**   For file-based databases, you can change the database the report uses in the Database box.
- **Logon User Name**   Enter the user name that you want Crystal Enterprise to use when logging on to the selected data source.

Figure 14-10
Changing object properties

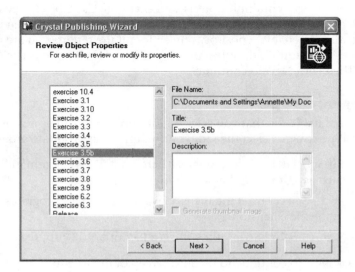

Figure 14-11

Setting logon
information

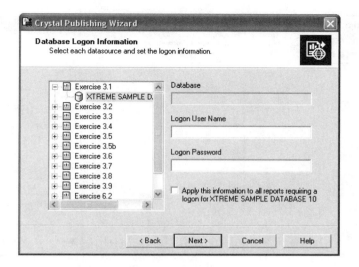

- **Logon Password**   Enter the Password that you want Crystal Enterprise to use when logging on to the selected data source.
- **Apply the Information to All Reports Requiring a Logon for** *data source*   If you have multiple reports that use the same data source, you can check this option to have the logon credentials copied to all the reports.

Click Next to continue.

Set Report Parameters

Each report that you are scheduling and that has parameters will be displayed on the Set Report Parameters screen, as shown in Figure 14-12.

- **Report List**   The list box to the left of the screen displays each report whose parameters must be set.
- **Parameter List**   The list box to the upper right displays the parameters contained in the selected report. The second column displays the current value picked for the parameter.
- **Edit Prompt**   For each parameter, you must select the value(s) for the parameter using the Edit Prompt button. The Set Parameter Values dialog box will be displayed; it is similar to setting parameter values in Crystal Reports. Choose the values you want for each parameter. You may select multiple values if the parameter allows it.
- **Set Prompts to NULL**   Click the Set Prompts to NULL button to set each nullable parameter to NULL.

Click Next when you are finished setting parameters.

Figure 14-12
Setting report
parameters

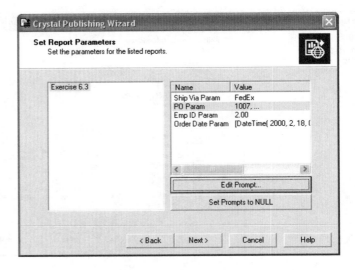

Schedule Format

For each published report, you can select the format that you want the output created in. These are the same formats available as export formats in Crystal Reports. After you select a format, other options appropriate to the type may appear. Set them as you would for a Crystal Reports export file. Then click Next.

Extra Files for Program

The Extra Files for Program screen appears if you are publishing any program files. If your program requires any files in addition to the executable, use the Add button to add them to the list. Click Next to continue.

Command Line for Program

The Command line for Program screen appears, listing all the program files that you are publishing. Select a program, and enter any required command line arguments in the Command Line box. Click Next.

Final

The final screen of the wizard lists all the files that you are publishing along with an icon symbolizing whether it is scheduled or not. Click Next to publish the objects. The Finish screen will appear, listing each published object. To display the details about an object, select it. Messages concerning the object will appear in the Details box at the bottom of the screen. Click Finish to close the wizard.

Exercise 14.5: Using the Crystal Publishing Wizard

1. Open all the Chapter 13 reports, and turn off Save Data with Report if it is on. Resave the reports. Do the same for the Exercise 6.3 report.

2. Select Start | Programs | Crystal Reports 10 | Crystal Publishing Wizard.

3. Click Next.

4. Log on to Crystal Enterprise, and click Next.

5. Click Add Files, and browse to find the Exercise 6.3 report. Click Open to add it.

6. Click Add Folder, and select the folder where you stored the reports for Chapter 13. Click OK.

7. Click Next.

8. Select Yes to duplicate the folder hierarchy, and click Next.

9. On the Specify Location screen, select your personal folder, and click the New Folder button.

10. Call the new folder **CRCP Exercises**, and click Next.

11. Explore the Location Preview screen, and then click Next.

12. Select the Exercise 13.1 and 13.2 reports, and then select Run Once Only.

13. Select the Exercise 6.3 report, and then select Run on a Recurring Schedule.

14. Click the Set Recurrence button. Select Monthly and choose the 20th of the month.

15. Click OK, and then Next.

16. Click Enable All, and then click Next.

17. Select Review or Modify Properties, and click Next.

18. Change the titles and descriptions of the reports, if desired, and click Next.

19. None of these reports require logon information, so click Next.

20. The Exercise 6.3 report will be displayed in the Set Report Parameters screen. Select each parameter, click the Edit Prompt button, and choose a parameter value. Click Next.

21. On the Schedule Format screen, select the Exercise 13.1 report, and choose Adobe Acrobat. Click Next.

22. Click Next. Browse the details for the published objects, and then click Finish.

Viewing Reports in Crystal Enterprise

To view reports in Crystal Enterprise, open the user launchpad. Then from the browser page, click the Crystal Enterprise link and log on. Then Browse the folders until the report you want to view is displayed. The report will be displayed in a new browser window when you select View from the pop-up menu. If the report you select to view has parameters, you will be prompted for them before the report is displayed.

Exercise 14.6: Viewing Reports in Crystal Enterprise

1. Select Start | Programs | Crystal Enterprise 10 | Crystal Enterprise User Launchpad.

2. Click the Crystal Enterprise link and log on.

3. Click the Favorites folder.

4. You should see the CRCP Exercises folder. Open it, and the open the Chapter 13 folder.

5. Select the Exercise 13.1 report. Click View in the pop-up menu.

6. The report will open in a separate browser window.

7. Close all browser windows.

Chapter Review

This chapter discussed Crystal Reports' integration with Crystal Enterprise. The use of the Crystal Repository for object reuse and the Crystal Publishing wizard for publishing reports to Crystal Enterprise were also covered.

Quick Tips

- Text objects, bitmap objects, SQL Commands, custom functions, and Business Views can be stored in the repository for use in multiple reports.

- Repository objects used in a report can be automatically updated to reflect changes in the stored objects when a report is opened.

- Text objects and bitmap objects can be added to the repository by dragging or using the Add to Repository shortcut menu command.

- Custom functions are added to the repository from the Formula Workshop.

- SQL Commands are added to the repository from the Database Expert.

- Objects in a report must be disconnected from the repository before they can be edited.

- You can use Business Views as data sources for a report.

- Repository folders can be created and deleted in the Repository Explorer using a toolbar button or shortcut menu option.

- You need to check Update Repository Objects in the Open dialog box to cause repository objects in the report to update if the global option is not set.

- To always update repository objects, check the Update Connected Repository Objects on Open check box on the Report tab of the File | Options dialog box. This is the global option.

- You can publish reports to Crystal Enterprise by using the Save As option in Crystal Reports or the Crystal Publishing wizard.

- The Crystal Publishing wizard walks you through the steps needed to publish files to Crystal Enterprise and is available in the Crystal Enterprise 10 program group.

- Reports can be viewed using the Crystal Enterprise web interface by logging in, browsing to the report, and selecting a view option.

Questions

Questions may have more than one correct answer. Choose all answers that apply.

1. Which items can be stored in the repository?

   a. SQL Commands

   b. Formulas

   c. Text objects

   d. Bitmaps

   e. Parameters

   f. Custom functions

   g. Business Views

2. If you change your mind after deleting a repository folder, you cannot click the Undo button to restore it.

   a. True

   b. False

3. Deleting an object from the repository will

   a. Delete the object from every report that uses it the next time the report is opened.

   b. Cause an error message to display the next time a report that uses it is opened.

   c. Have no impact on the reports that use it; the object will be automatically disconnected on the next open.

4. Select the methods that can be used to publish reports to Crystal Enterprise.

   a. Choose Save from Crystal Enterprise.

   b. Choose Save As from Crystal Enterprise.

   c. Use the Crystal Publishing Wizard.

   d. Use the Windows File Explorer to copy report files to the Crystal Enterprise folders.

   e. Use the Crystal Management Console.

5. For reports that contain nullable parameters, you can set a parameter to NULL in the Crystal Enterprise wizard by

   a. Typing the word NULL as the parameter value.

   b. Clicking the Set Prompts to NULL button.

   c. Leaving the parameter value empty.

6. Select the object types that can be added to the repository by dragging.

   a. SQL Commands

   b. Formulas

   c. Text objects

   d. Bitmaps

   e. Parameters

   f. Custom functions

7. To create a report from a SQL Command stored in the repository or a Business View, you select the data source from the Crystal Enterprise Explorer, which appears after you select the Repository folder in the Database Expert.

   a. True

   b. False

Answers

1. **a, c, d, f, g.** Formula fields and parameter fields cannot be stored in the repository; all the other types can.

2. **a.** True. Undo does not work for repository actions.

3. **b.** An error message will be displayed when you open a report that uses repository objects that have been deleted. You will then be able to disconnect the objects from the repository to fix the report.

4. **b, c, e.** You can use the Save As command from Crystal Reports, the Crystal Publishing wizard, or the Crystal Management Console.

5. **b.** Use the Set Prompts to NULL button to set the parameter value to NULL.

6. **c, d.** Only text objects and bitmap objects can be added to the repository by dragging.

7. **a.** True.

PART III

Exam RDCR300, Advanced Reporting

Report Processing

Exam RDCR300 expects you to be able to

- Describe multipass reporting
- Use evaluation time functions

In order to optimize report generation it is essential to understand how Crystal Reports processes reports. Crystal Reports uses a *multipass report-processing* model, with specific actions occurring at each step. When you create formulas, you can use *evaluation time functions* to force your custom processing to occur at the appropriate step.

Multipass Report Processing

A *pass* is an operation that involves "touching" each report record. Crystal Reports processing makes at most three passes. In addition to the processing done during a pass, other processing is done before or between passes. There are two prepass operations. The fewer passes that a report must go through, the faster it will process.

Prepass 1

Any operation that does not require access to the data and is constant for the entire report is handled in the Prepass 1 stage. There are several categories of Prepass 1 operations.

Parameter Retrieval Before any other report processing, for reports that contain parameters, the parameter values are gathered from the report user. The rest of the report processing happens with the selected parameter values plugged in wherever they are used in the report.

Constant Formulas Constant formulas are formulas whose value does not vary from record to record in a given report. Any formula that references a database field is not a constant formula. Print state functions and alert functions cannot be evaluated in the Prepass 1 stage. A constant formula may reference a parameter field. Here are two constant formulas:

```
60*24; //Minutes in a day

If {?Param} = 'C' then 'Country' else 'Region';
```

Query Generation   Since report queries commonly use parameters in the selection criteria, they must be generated after parameter values are retrieved but before the query is sent to the database. This happens in Prepass 1. For example, if you have a selection criterion that the country must equal the value of the {?Country} parameter, and if the user chooses USA for the parameter, the Where clause of the query will look like this:

```
WHERE Country = 'USA'
```

 NOTE   Crystal Reports documentation mentions only constant formula evaluation for Prepass 1. However, for your own optimization work be aware that parameter retrieval and query generation must happen before Pass 1 as well.

Pass I

Pass 1 occurs during the fetching of records from the database. The query has been sent to the server and Crystal Reports is reading the result set. Several processes happen as each record is read.

Detail Level Formula Evaluation   Formulas that use only values available at this stage, such as individual field values, are evaluated as each record is read. Formulas that refer to summarized fields cannot be evaluated yet.

Local Record Selection   Any record selection that could not be incorporated into the report query is applied during this stage. Commonly, these selection criteria refer to formula fields. They can then be evaluated, since formulas have been computed. Records that do not meet the selection criteria are read but not saved.

Record Sorting, Grouping, and Summarizing   As records are read, they are grouped as defined by the report, sorted within the groups, and summaries are computed. Think of Crystal Reports as reading a record, storing it in the proper group bin in the proper order, adding its values to the summary fields, and then reading the next record.

Detail-Level Cross-Tab, Chart, and Map Creation   Cross-tabs, charts, and maps that do not require running totals or the results of formulas that will be evaluated in Pass 2 are generated during Pass 1.

Saving Data   Crystal Reports saves the report data, both detail records and computed summaries, while it is reading records. This data is saved in memory or to temporary files, whether or not you have chosen to save data with the report. Any further report processing will use this saved data until the report is refreshed. If you choose to save data with the report, the data will also be saved in the report file.

Running Total Fields   Running Total fields (as opposed to manual running totals) are also computed during Pass 1, if sorting is done on the server.

 EXAM TIP   For the exam, always assume that running totals are evaluated during Pass 2.

Prepass 2

After Pass 1 is complete, all the record-level data and regular summary fields are available. In Prepass 2, group sorting and hierarchical grouping can occur. Since the group summary fields now exist, they can be used in any group sorting required for the report. Groups not matching the group sort conditions are suppressed to obtain Top N/Bottom N–type reports. Special sorting required for hierarchical grouping can also be done during Prepass 2.

NOTE   The grand total or other outer-level summaries are not recomputed, even if some groups are suppressed due to the group sort properties. This results in some totals displaying incorrectly.

Pass 2

Pass 2 consists of all further operations required to create the values needed to display or print a page. Pass 2 is optional and will not occur if all the necessary values were computed in Pass 1.

NOTE   Crystal Reports uses "print on demand" and will not format a page until it is required. If a report is printed or exported, all pages will be formatted. If a report is viewed, not all pages will necessarily be formatted. Any page that the viewer specifically requests will be fully formatted. All previous pages must be partially formatted to determine the proper contents of the requested page.

Group Selection Formula Evaluation   Group selection formulas depend on summary fields computed in Pass 1. Since those summaries now exist, group filtering based on the group selection formula can now be done. Groups that do not meet the criteria are excluded from the report.

Running Total Field Evaluation   Since running total fields depend on the sort order of records, they cannot be evaluated in Pass 1 (unless sorting is done on the server). Records are read and processed in Pass 1, in the order in which they are returned by the database query, not necessarily in the order defined in the report. Therefore, running total fields are evaluated during Pass 2.

Print Time Formula Evaluation   Any formula that could not be evaluated during Pass 1 is evaluated during Pass 2. Commonly, these formulas reference summary fields or other print time formulas. Manual running totals are print time formulas because they use the WhilePrintingRecords evaluation time function.

Cross-Tabs, Charts, and Maps That Could Not Be Created Earlier

Cross-tabs, charts, and maps that could not be created during Pass 1 are created during Pass 2. They may require running totals or print time formulas and so cannot be created until Pass 2. Charts based on cross-tabs must be created in Pass 2 because the cross-tab itself was created in Pass 1.

OLAP Grids   OLAP grids are always processed in Pass 2.

Subreports   Subreports are created in Pass 2. Each instance of each subreport is processed in the same manner as the main report and goes through the same phases. Therefore, if a subreport is located in a report section that appears more than once in the report, it will be processed more than once, each time with the new link parameter values applied. An exception is on-demand subreports. The report processing for an on-demand subreport happens only if and when the associated link is clicked. Subreports are discussed in detail in the Chapter 16.

Pass 3

A third pass is required if the report uses the TotalPageCount or PageNofM special field. The third pass computes the total page count and makes it available for use on any page of the report.

Evaluation Time Functions

An evaluation time function can be used in a formula to cause the formula to process sometime after its default processing time. The evaluation time functions appear in the Formula Workshop, in the Function Tree, under the Evaluation Time folder, as shown here.

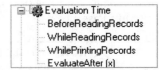

Default Formula Evaluation Time

When you create formulas Crystal Reports determines the earliest possible time that they can be evaluated and processes them at that time. As discussed in the section "Multipass Report Processing," constant formulas are evaluated during Prepass 1, formulas that require only record level data are processed during Pass 1, and all other formulas are evaluated during Pass 2.

A formula can never be evaluated earlier than its default time, but you can use the evaluation time functions to cause a formula to be evaluated later than its default time. If you attempt to force an earlier evaluation, you will receive an error in the Formula Workshop.

BeforeReadingRecords   The BeforeReadingRecords evaluation time function causes the formula to be processed during Prepass 1. If you use BeforeReadingRecords, it should be the first statement in the formula. It has no arguments.

NOTE   Any formula that can be evaluated in Prepass 1 should default to Prepass 1, so this evaluation time function is not necessary. You can use it for clarification or consistency, to document the processing time.

WhileReadingRecords   The WhileReadingRecords evaluation time function causes the formula to be processed during Pass 1. If you use WhileReadingRecords, it needs to be the first statement in the formula, and it has no arguments. Since constant formulas are the only type of formula that can be evaluated in Prepass 1, they are the only type of formula that would be affected by this function. You could use it with Pass 1 formulas as documentation, but you would get an error if you used it in a formula whose default processing time is Pass 2.

WhilePrintingRecords   WhilePrintingRecords is the most commonly used evaluation time function. You can use it to force formulas that would normally be evaluated in Prepass 1 or Pass 1 to be evaluated in Pass 2. If you use this function, it should be the first statement in the formula, and it has no arguments.

 EXAM TIP   Any formulas that do not reference database fields will not automatically calculate for each record in the report. This is a common occurrence when a global variable is used as a counter. In this situation, use WhilePrintingRecords to force the formula to evaluate for every record in the report.

EvaluateAfter(x)   The EvaluateAfter function does not correspond to a report-processing stage. It is used to force one formula to evaluate after another formula. This might be necessary for two formulas that are processed in the same pass, but you need one to evaluate first to compute the proper result. If you use EvaluateAfter, it should be the first statement in your formula. It requires one parameter, which must be the name of the formula that should be evaluated before this formula.

Exercise 15.1: Using WhileReadingRecords

1. Create a new report using the Standard report wizard. Use the Orders and Customers table.

2. Use the Country, Customer Name, Order ID, Order Date, and Order Amount fields.

3. Group by country and customer name.

4. Change Summaries on Order ID to use the Count operation instead of the Sum operation.

5. Click Finish after completing the Summaries page.

6. Create a formula field called **Count** using the following:
   ```
   Global numberVar Count;
   Count := Count + 1;
   ```

7. Place the Count formula in the Details section of the report, and preview the report. Note that the value displayed for Count is always 1. Since the Count formula does not reference any database or summary fields, Crystal Reports assumes that it is a constant formula and evaluates it only once for the report.

8. Modify the Count formula to look like this:
   ```
   WhileReadingRecords;
   Global numberVar Count;
   Count := Count + 1;
   ```

9. Preview the report. Notice that the Count formula is counting each record.

10. Save the report as **Exercise 15.1**.

Exercise 15.2: Using WhilePrintingRecords

1. Open the report from Exercise 15.1.

2. We want to reset the Count variable when the customer name changes, so create a formula called **Reset** with the following code:

   ```
   Global numberVar Count := 0;
   ```

3. Place the Reset formula in the Customer Name Group Header section, and preview the report.

4. The Reset formula is always displaying as zero, and the Count formula is not being reset. This is occurring because the Reset formula is a constant formula, so it is being evaluated only once, during Prepass 1.

5. Change the Reset formula to the following:

   ```
   WhilePrintingRecords;
   Global numberVar Count := 0;
   ```

6. Preview the report. It is still not resetting the Count variable correctly because we used WhilePrintingRecords in the Reset formula. The Count formula accumulates its values during Pass 1, or while reading records, but the reset happens after that, during Pass 2, while printing records.

7. Change the Count formula to the following:

   ```
   WhilePrintingRecords;
   Global numberVar OrderCount;
   OrderCount := OrderCount + 1;
   ```

8. Preview the report. Now the Reset formula is working as expected. Both the accumulation and the reset are happening during the same report-processing pass.

 NOTE Setting both formulas to WhileReadingRecords does not work.

9. Save the report as **Exercise 15.2**.

Exercise 15.3: Running Totals and Top N/Bottom N reports

1. Open the Exercise 15.2 report, and delete the Count and Reset formulas.

2. Create a new formula called **RunningTotal** using the following:

   ```
   WhilePrintingRecords;
   Global currencyVar RunningTotal;
   RunningTotal := RunningTotal + {Orders.Order Amount};
   ```

3. Note that while reading records is the default evaluation time for this formula because it references a database field.

4. Place the RunningTotal formula in the Details section.

5. Create a new formula called **Reset** using the following:

```
WhilePrintingRecords;
Global currencyVar RunningTotal := 0;
```

6. Place Reset in the Country Group Header section, and suppress it using the Format Editor.

7. Create a new formula called **DisplayRunningTotal** using the following:

```
WhilePrintingRecords;
Global currencyVar RunningTotal;
```

8. Place DisplayRunningTotal in the Country Group Footer section.

9. Suppress the Details section.

10. Make sure that the Order count summaries line up under the Order ID field and the Order Amount summaries line up under the Order Amount field.

11. Preview the report, noting that the last value of the RunningTotal formula in each Country group matches the summary field on the amount.

12. Open the Group Sort Expert. For the Country group, choose the top 5 based on the Amount field, and exclude others. For the Customer Name group, choose the top 10 percent based on the Amount field, and exclude others.

13. Preview the report.

14. Note that the summary field on Order Amount still displays the total by country, as if no group sorting were being done, but the RunningTotal field displays the total of only the customers displayed on the report.

15. Use the Format Painter to copy the formatting from the Order Amount summary field to the DisplayRunningTotal field. Remove the summary field on Country for the Order Amount, and move the DisplayRunningTotal field into its place.

16. Save the report as **Exercise 15.3**.

 NOTE   Refer to Chapter 8, Exercise 8.8, for an example of using the EvaluateAfter function.

Performance Information

Crystal Reports makes some performance information available to you. This information is displayed in the Performance Information dialog box and may help you diagnose performance problems. It is also helpful in determining the number of passes required for report processing.

 EXAM TIP   Performance information is not an exam objective.

Open the Performance Information dialog box by selecting Report | Performance Information. It has two main panes, as shown in Figure 15-1. The tree in the left side of the dialog box lists the report and the information categories that are available under the report. Some categories are not available until the report is previewed. Subreports, if any, are listed under the main report; each has its own information categories.

 NOTE The Performance Information dialog box is not well documented. The explanations presented here are as accurate and complete as possible at this writing.

Report Definition

The Report Definition node is shown in Figure 15-1. It contains information about the report as it is currently defined. This information is not dependent on previewing the report. The Comments column may point out opportunities to enhance report performance, as shown in the figure, for the Number of Database Fields entry.

Number of Database Fields   Number of Database Fields shows the count of database fields, exclusive of BLOBs (binary large objects), that are retrieved from all data sources. This may be higher than the number of fields displayed on the report. The fewer fields retrieved, the better, although it may be difficult to reduce them. Converting formulas into SQL Expressions may be helpful. You should also eliminate any unnecessary fields.

Number of Memo/Blob Fields   Number of Memo/Blob Fields contains the count of memo and BLOB fields in the report. These types of fields can be very large and should be used only when needed.

Number of Running Total Fields   Running Total fields that require processing during Pass 2 should only be used when no other method will give the desired result.

Figure 15-1
Viewing
performance
information

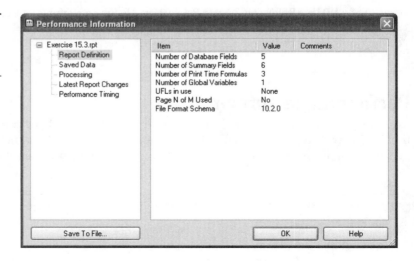

Number of Running Total Fields Using Distinct Count   The Distinct Count operation requires not only accumulating some value but also comparison with all previous values to determine distinctness. This is more processing intensive than other summary operations and should be avoided if possible.

Number of Summary Fields   Number of Summary Fields displays the count of summary fields in the report. Each summary field must be computed and its data stored, so reducing this number is somewhat helpful, but usually not significantly. Summary fields are preferred over Running Total fields.

Number of Print Time Formulas   Print Time formulas must be evaluated during Pass 2. Eliminating the need for Pass 2 can result in a significant performance gain. Evaluate print time formulas, looking for other alternatives.

Number of Global Variables   Variables with global scope are not as efficient as local variables. Since global is the default scope, you may have global variables that could be converted to local variables.

UFLs in Use   User-defined function libraries are DLLs containing user-defined functions. These appear in the Function Tree of the Formula Workshop and can be used in formulas. However, their use requires calling into the DLL and is less efficient than using native Crystal Reports functions.

Number of Subreport Objects   Subreports can be particularly damaging to report processing speed. In some cases, subreports can be replaced by doing table joins and appropriate grouping. Always place subreports where they will be processed as few times as necessary and consider using on-demand subreports.

Page N of M Used   If the report requires the total page count, Pass 3 must be executed. Eliminate the use of TotalPageCount and PageNofM if possible.

File Format Schema   The File Format Schema displays the version of the Crystal Reports file format used in the report. Version 10 files will have better performance than earlier file formats.

Saved Data

The Saved Data node displays information about the data currently saved for the report, as shown in Figure 15-2. This is not the data saved with a report file, but the data currently in memory or temporary files for the open report preview.

Number of Data Sources   If a report uses more than one data source, significantly more processing must be done locally. This increases processing time and consumes more system resources.

Unicode Saved Data   If the fonts used in the report are unicode fonts, Unicode Saved Data will be Yes. Unicode fonts require more storage space per character than nonunicode fonts.

Figure 15-2
Viewing Saved
Data
performance
information

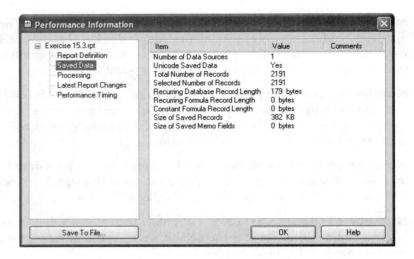

Total Number of Records   Total Number of Records shows the total number of records retrieved from the database at the last refresh. This is the saved data.

Selected Number of Records   Selected Number of Records shows the record count for the current report configuration. This number will differ from that shown for Total Number of Records if a change is made that affects the number of records contained in the report but no refresh was selected. This happens when Use Saved Data is selected in the Change In Record Selection Formula dialog box.

Recurring Database Record Length   Recurring Database Record Length entry displays the length, in bytes, of the detail records. This excludes any memo or BLOB fields that are saved.

Recurring Formula Record Length   Recurring Formula Record Length shows the bytes required to store all formulas computed in Pass 1.

Constant Formula Record Length   Constant Formula Record Length shows the bytes required to store all formulas computed in Prepass 1.

Size of Saved Records   The total size of the saved data, exclusive of memo and BLOB fields, is displayed in the Size of Saved Records entry.

Size of Saved Memo Fields   The total size of all saved memo and BLOB fields is displayed in the Size of Saved Memo Fields entry.

Processing
The Processing node is shown in Figure 15-3. This node is particularly interesting if you are exploring ways to optimize your report.

Figure 15-3
Viewing
Processing
performance
information

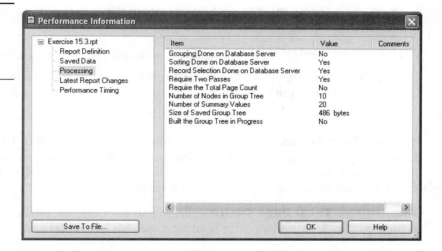

Grouping Done on Database Server   If you create a summary report (one in which the Details section is suppressed), then your goal should be to have grouping done on the server. If it is, then the detail records are not returned to Crystal Reports and only the lowest level summary information is returned. This results in less data for Crystal Reports to manipulate and save as well as less data traveling the network.

For grouping to be done on the server, the report query must contain a Group By clause, the Details section must be hidden or suppressed, and the Perform Grouping on the Server report option must be checked. In addition, only databases accessed using SQL can perform grouping on the server.

When users view a report where grouping is done on the server, they can still drill down to see the details. A separate query is sent to the database server at drill-down to return only the detail records needed. In this way, the least amount of data is retrieved.

NOTE   If your report is not a summary report or you are not using a SQL database, Grouping Done on Database Server will always be No.

Sorting Done on Database Server   If record sorting is done on the database server, less work must be done locally and Running Total fields can be computed in Pass 1. For sorting to be done on the server, the report option Use Indexes or Server for Speed must be checked.

Record Selection Done on Database Server   Forcing record selection to the server is one of the most important optimization techniques. When record selection is done on the server, only the desired report records are returned to Crystal Reports, resulting in less resource usage and processing time. You might see "Partial" here, indicating that parts of the record selection are being passed to the server and parts are being done locally. Here are a few guidelines:

- Avoid the use of Crystal Reports functions in the record selection formula.
- Avoid referencing Crystal Reports formula fields in the record selection formula; use SQL Expression fields instead.
- Check the report option Use Indexes or Server for Speed.

Require Two Passes   A report that requires only one pass will be faster than a report that requires two passes. Look for print-time formulas that can be changed to read-time formulas. Avoid using group selection formulas by using a SQL Command. Use summary fields instead of Pass 2 Running Total fields, if possible.

Require the Total Page Count   Reports that contain the total page count must go through Pass 3. Avoid using the TotalPageCount or PageNofM special fields.

Number of Nodes in Group Tree   The Group Tree is held in memory, so the fewer nodes, the better. However, a group tree makes navigation easier, so you must determine the trade-offs.

Number of Summary Values   Summary values require computation and storage, so the fewer, the better. However, the cost of summary values is usually not high enough to warrant much attention.

Size of Saved Group Tree   The Group Tree is held in memory, so the smaller, the better.

Build the Group Tree in Progress   Building the Group Tree while processing the report is desirable. If it cannot be built in that process then it must be built later, in an additional process.

Latest Report Changes

The Latest Report Changes node, shown in Figure 15-4, displays the most recent changes to the report—those that required the report to be reprocessed. The changes may or may not have required new data to be retrieved.

Performance Timing

The Performance Timing node, shown in Figure 15-5, shows several performance statistics. For each statistic, the lower the number, the better.

Open Document   The Open Document figure is the time it took to open the report file in the Crystal Reports environment. This statistic is not very important, but does give an indication of the complexity of the report file.

Run the Database Query   This is the measure, from Crystal Reports' point of view, of how long the database query took to execute. It is the execution time and does

Figure 15-4
Viewing Latest
Report Changes
performance
information

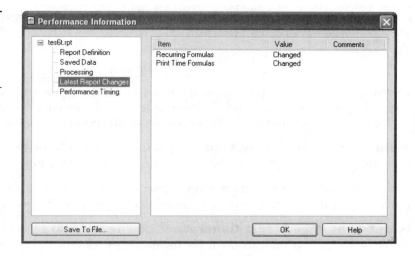

not include the time taken to fetch the result set. This may not match the time given by the database itself. For queries against SQL databases, you should see this number decrease if the report is refreshed without modifying the database query. That is, the first time the query is run it will take longer because of the setup required. The second and subsequent times should be faster.

Read Database Records   Read Database Records indicates the time taken to fetch the results of the report query from the database. The relationship between the time taken to run the query and the time taken to fetch the records depends on the report. A report that requires complex processing on the server but results in few records may have an execution time that is longer than the record fetch time. A simple query that returns many records will have a short execution time and a long fetch time.

Figure 15-5
Viewing
Performance
Timing
information

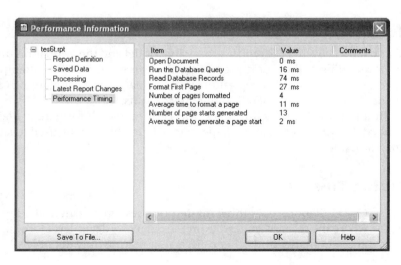

NOTE The query and fetch times will be affected by the server's and network's current workload.

Format First Page   Formatting the first page of the report will take longer than formatting any subsequent pages. A report is initially displayed showing the first page, so this time is relevant to the user's perception of the report-processing time.

Number of Pages Formatted   The Number of Pages Formatted entry shows the total number of pages that have been viewed since the last refresh.

Average Time to Format a Page   Average Time to Format a Page is the computed average display time of the total number of pages viewed since the last refresh.

Number of Page Starts Generated   If a user skips to a page in the report by using the Group Tree or other methods, the pages between the last viewed page and the new page do not need to be fully formatted. They must be partially formatted, however, and this is referred to as a *page start*. Number of Page Starts Generated will show the number of pages that were skipped over.

Average Time to Generate a Page Start   Average Time to Generate a Page Start is the computed average time required for the number of page starts generated.

Save to File
You can click the Save to File button to create a text file containing the current values of the entries in the Performance Information dialog box. You might do this to compare to values after making some optimization changes, but be aware that some of the values are influenced by things the report design does not control.

Chapter Review
This chapter covered the report-processing model and the evaluation time functions. An understanding of the report-processing model is essential when attempting to optimize report performance. Appropriate use of evaluation time functions can affect performance as well as the generation of correct results.

In addition to the exam topics, the Performance Information dialog box was described. Performance data available in this dialog box can be used to support your optimization efforts.

Quick Tips
- Crystal Reports uses three main processes when generating reports: Pass 1 is where the records are read from the database, detail-level formulas are computed, and summaries and other objects that require only detail-level data are created.

The optional Pass 2 is where all computations that require summaries or other Pass 1 results are done, including running total fields. Pass 3 is optional; it is where the total page count is computed.

- In addition to the three main stages, two other stages are recognized by Crystal Reports: Prepass 1 and Prepass 2. In Prepass 1, constant formulas are computed. Prepass 2 is used for group sorting and hierarchical grouping.

- User-defined formulas can contain evaluation time functions to force evaluation in a particular pass, but they cannot force a formula to evaluate before its default evaluation time.

- BeforeReadingRecords is related to Prepass 1.

- WhileReadingRecords is related to Pass 1.

- WhilePrintingRecords is related to Pass 2.

- EvaluateAfter is used to force a formula to evaluate after some other formula; it is not related to a particular pass.

Questions

Questions may have more than one correct answer. Choose all answers that apply.

1. Which stages of report processing will every report go through?

   a. Prepass 1

   b. Pass 1

   c. Prepass 2

   d. Pass 2

   e. Pass 3

2. A report that requires two passes is better than a report with the same output that requires one pass.

   a. True

   b. False

3. If your report contains running total fields, what is the minimum number of passes required for report processing?

   a. 1

   b. 2

   c. 3

4. If your report uses the PageNofM special field in the Report Footer section, what is the minimum number of passes required for report processing?

   a. 1

   b. 2

   c. 3

5. What operations happen in Pass 1?

   a. Detail-level formula evaluation

   b. Record selection that was not incorporated in the database query

   c. Running total field evaluation

   d. Creation of cross-tabs, charts, and maps that require only detail-level data

   e. Saving data

6. What operations happen in Prepass 2?

   a. Group Sorting (Top N/Bottom N)

   b. Group selection formula evaluation

   c. Running total field evaluation

   d. Hierarchical grouping

   e. Saving data

7. What operations happen in Pass 2?

   a. Sorting, grouping, and summarizing

   b. Group selection formula evaluation

   c. Print time formula evaluation

   d. Creation of OLAP grids

   e. Generation of subreports

8. Evaluation time functions can be used to force a formula evaluation during any pass of the report processing.

   a. True

   b. False

9. Which evaluation time function is used when creating manual running total fields?

   a. BeforeReadingRecords

   b. WhileReadingRecords

   c. WhilePrintingRecords

   d. EvaluateAfter

10. Which pairs are not correct?

   a. Prepass 1 and BeforeReadingRecords

   b. Pass 1 and WhileReadingRecords

   c. Prepass 2 and WhilePrintingRecords

   d. Pass 2 and WhilePrintingRecords

   e. Pass 3 and EvaluateAfter

Answers

1. **b.** Every report must go through Pass 1. If you consider that query generation is part of Prepass 1, then every report goes through Prepass 1 as well.

2. **b.** False. Fewer passes means faster processing.

3. **b.** Running total fields are evaluated during Pass 2.

4. **c.** The total page count is computed during Pass 3.

5. **a, b, d, e.** Running totals are evaluated in Pass 2.

6. **a, d.** Group sorting and hierarchical grouping happen in Prepass 2.

7. **b, c, d, e.** Sorting, grouping, and summarizing happen in Pass 1.

8. **b.** False. You can only force a formula to evaluate at a later stage than it would by default; you cannot force it to evaluate at an earlier stage.

9. **c.** Manual running totals must use WhilePrintingRecords.

10. **c, e.** Prepass 2 has no equivalent evaluation time function, and EvaluateAfter is not related to a pass.

Subreports

Exam RDCR300 expects you to be able to

- Define subreports
- Create an unlinked subreport
- Create a linked subreport
- Create an on-demand subreport
- Use shared variables in a subreport
- Use subreports to link "unlinkable" data

This chapter covers creating subreports, using linked or unlinked subreports, creating on-demand subreports, using shared variables with subreports, and using subreports to link data that is otherwise not linkable.

Definition and Use of Subreports

A subreport is a report that has been embedded inside another report. The subreport may have been created from the start to be a subreport, or it may have been an independent report. A subreport can be linked to data fields in the main report, or not. Subreports are identical in structure to main reports except that a subreport cannot contain a subreport. When subreports are generated, their Page Header and Page Footer sections are suppressed; only the main report's Page Header and Page Footers are displayed.

Unlinked Subreports

An unlinked subreport is one that is placed inside another report but is not directly connected to the data in the main report. This type of subreport might be used when you want to combine multiple reports into a single report. For example, a dashboard report might contain unlinked subreports, each showing a different measure of interest. The main report can simply be a container used to group together multiple subreports. Unlinked subreports should always be placed in the Report Header or Report Footer section so that they are generated only once.

Linked Subreports

Linked subreports are connected to data in the main report via parameters. For example, if you have a report that shows orders by country and another report that shows top salespeople, you could insert the top salespeople report into the country group header section of the orders report and link them on the country field. The result will be that the top salespeople for each country are shown in the group header sections of the orders report.

Using Crystal Reports–Generated Parameters

In the preceding example, if the subreport had no country parameter defined, but you linked the subreport to the main report on the country field, Crystal Reports would create a country parameter in the subreport and add a criterion to the selection formula to limit the rows to records that match the country parameter. When the country group header needed to be generated, Crystal Reports would execute the subreport, passing it the current value of the country field. In this fashion, the now parameterized subreport is executed once for each country in the main report.

 NOTE It is important to understand that the subreport is executed multiple times, once for each instance of the section in which it is placed. It is not run once, then somehow burst apart, and merged into the main report. This behavior, in addition to the extra resources required, is the source of subreport inefficiency. Placing subreports in the Details section should be particularly avoided, since they would be executed once for *each record* in the main report.

Using Existing Report Parameters

If you use an existing report that already contains parameters as a subreport, you can use the existing parameters to link the subreport to the main report, rather than letting Crystal Reports generate the subreport parameters for you. Continuing our example, if you already have a top salespeople report that has a country parameter and selection criteria based on the parameter, you can insert the report as a subreport and link the country field in the main report to the country parameter in the subreport. In this case, it is very important to use the existing parameters, otherwise Crystal Reports will generate its own parameters, causing duplication, and it will prompt for parameter values for the subreport each time it is executed. In addition to using parameters for linking, you can also pass other information from the main report to the subreport using parameters.

 NOTE In general, subreports should not be placed in Page Header or Page Footer sections. The Page Header and Page Footer sections cannot span pages, so if a subreport might be longer than a page, it should be placed elsewhere.

Using "Unlinkable" Fields

Occasionally, you may not be able to link tables the way you need to using the Database Expert. The link fields might have different data types, for example. You can use subreports to link fields that are normally not linkable, but you should avoid the use of subreports for this purpose in favor of other solutions, where possible. It may be possible to convert fields to linkable data types via a view or by using SQL Expressions.

On-Demand Subreports

An on-demand subreport can be either linked or unlinked and is represented in the report as a hyperlink. The subreport is not generated until the user clicks the hyperlink. When the hyperlink is activated, the subreport opens in a separate preview tab. On-demand subreports should not be used if the primary report distribution method is printing or exporting, since user interaction is required.

Insert Subreport Dialog Box

Subreports are created using the Insert Subreport dialog box. You can open the Insert Subreport dialog box by selecting Insert | Subreport from the menu or by clicking the Insert Subreport button, shown here, on the Insert Tools menu. The Insert Subreport dialog box has two tabs, the Subreport tab and the Link tab.

Subreport Tab

The Subreport tab, shown in Figure 16-1, is used to select or create the subreport.

Choose an Existing Report

Select the Choose an Existing Report button to insert an existing report into the current report as a subreport. Selecting this option makes the File Name edit box and Browse button available.

File Name

If you select Choose an Existing Report, the report's filename must be entered into the File Name box. You can type the filename or browse to locate it.

Figure 16-1
Selecting or creating a subreport

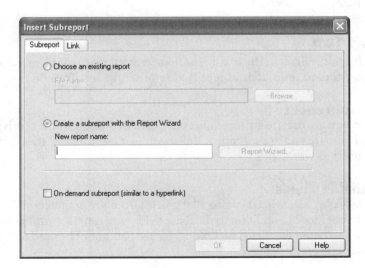

Browse

Clicking the Browse button opens a file dialog box that you can use to locate and select an existing report file to use as a subreport.

Create a Subreport with the Report Wizard

If you want to create a new report to use as a subreport, select the Create a Subreport with the Report Wizard button. The New Report Name edit box and Report Wizard button will become available.

New Report Name

Enter a name for the new report in the New Report Name edit box. The name that you enter will not be used as the filename for the new report, since the new report will not be saved separately from the main report. The report name is simply used to identify the subreport within the main report.

Report Wizard

Once you have entered a new report name, you can click the Report Wizard button to open the Standard report wizard. Create a report as described in Chapter 3. You will then be returned to the Insert Subreport dialog box.

 NOTE Only a standard report type can be developed using this report wizard. If the desired report format is a cross-tab, mailing label, or OLAP grid, it would have to first be developed independently of the main report and then embedded in the main report.

On-Demand Subreport

Check the On-Demand Subreport box if you want your report to be an on-demand subreport. If you check this box, then a hyperlink will be created at the position where you place the subreport.

Link Tab

A subreport's links to the main report are created on the Link tab, shown in Figure 16-2. If you want an unlinked subreport, do not set up any links on the Link tab.

For Subreport

When you are first inserting a subreport, the For Subreport list box is not available. Later, when you are editing subreport links, you can use this box to select the subreport that you want to work with.

Available Fields

The Available Fields list contains all the fields from the main report that you can use to link to the subreport. In addition to database fields, you can use formula fields, SQL Expression fields, and parameter fields for linking. Fields that cannot be used due to incompatible data

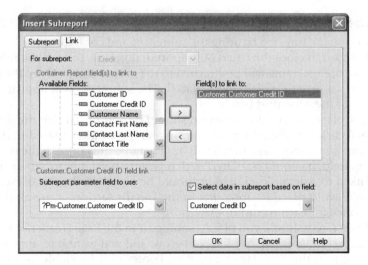

Figure 16-2
Setting a
subreport's links

types are not listed. Choose a field and move it into the Field(s) to Link To box to create a
link using that field.

Field(s) to Link To

The Fields to Link To list contains all the fields from the main report that you have selected
to use in linking to the subreport. When a field is selected in the Field(s) to Link To list, the
specific link definition for it is displayed in the bottom panel of the dialog box.

Subreport Parameter Field to Use

In the Subreport Parameter Field to Use drop-down box, you must choose the
subreport parameter to use when linking to the main report field selected in the Fields
to Link To list. If the subreport that you selected or created has parameter fields defined,
they will be listed in this box. In addition, Crystal Reports will generate a parameter called
?Pm-*field name* where *field name* is the name of the selected field in the Fields to Link
To list. If you choose not to use that parameter, it will not be created in the subreport.

Select Data in Subreport Based on Field

Selecting a subreport parameter field ensures that the subreport will get the value of the
field from the main report. The Select Data in Subreport Based on Field check box and
drop-down list are used to create the selection formula entry that will limit the
subreport data based on the value of the linking parameter:

1. Check the box to have a selection criterion added to the subreport.

2. Then in the drop-down box, select the subreport field that should be linked to
   the value of the subreport parameter. The selection formula will created such
   that the selected subreport field must equal the selected subreport parameter
   for the record to be included in the report.

Subreport Placement

Once you are finished creating the subreport and configuring its links, you can click the OK button to close the Insert Subreport dialog box. You will be returned to the report, and an orange frame will be attached to the mouse cursor. Drop the frame in the section where you want the subreport placed. The subreport will appear as a frame with the name of the subreport inside.

The placement of the subreport should be appropriate for the links created. As mentioned earlier, if the subreport is unlinked, it should be placed in the Report Header or Report Footer section so that it will be generated only once. If the subreport is linked to a group field, it should be placed in that group's header or footer section. If the subreport is linked to a detail-level field, it should be placed in the Details section. However, you should avoid placing subreports in the Details section, if possible, since they will execute once for each record in the report.

Only rarely should you place a subreport in the Page Header or Page Footer section. If the subreport is small, not likely to grow, and you want it to appear on each page, then placing it in the Page Header or Page Footer may be viable. But remember that if the subreport is linked, it will be executed once for each page of the report, even if its contents do not change.

Exercise 16.1: Creating an Unlinked Subreport

In this exercise, you will create a report that combines three charts with different information into one report. A report like this might used as a dashboard report.

1. Create a new report as a blank report. Do not connect to any data sources.

2. Add new sections to the Report Header until there are four sections.

3. Suppress all sections other than the Report Header sections.

4. Insert a text object into Report Header a. Type **Performance Over the Last Seven Days** into the text object.

5. Set the font size to 16, and expand the text box across the width of the report. Click the Center button to center the text.

6. Since the XTREME data is old, you need to set the print date to an old date. Select Report | Set Print Date and Time. Choose Other, and set the date to 4/28/2002, which is the last date in the XTREME data. Click OK to close the dialog box.

7. Click the Insert Subreport button, and choose to create a new subreport. Call the subreport **Orders**, and click the Report Wizard button.

8. Add the Orders table, and click Next.

9. Add the Order Date and Order Amount fields, and click Next.

10. Group on Order Date, and click Next.

11. Click Next on the Summaries screen.

12. Click Next on the Group Sorting screen.

13. Select Bar on the Chart screen, and set the Chart Title to **Orders**.

14. Create a record selection criterion on the Order Date. Set it so that order dates greater than CurrentDate−7 are included.

15. Click Finish. Click OK.

16. Place the subreport in the Report Header b section.

17. Click the Orders tab, and suppress all the report sections except the one containing the chart.

18. Insert a new subreport, and call it **Top Customers**. Click the Report Wizard button.

19. Add the Customers and Orders tables, and click Next.

20. Click Next on the Link screen.

21. Choose to display Customer Name and Order Amount, and then click Next.

22. Group by Customer Name, and click Next.

23. Click Next on the Summaries screen.

24. Select Top 5 groups on the Group Sorting screen, and click Next.

25. Select Bar Chart, and set the chart title to **Top Customers**. Click Next.

26. Filter on Order Date, and set it to greater than CurrentDate−7. Click Finish.

27. Click OK, and place the subreport in the Report Header c section.

28. Select the Top Customers tab, and suppress all report sections except the one containing the chart.

29. Insert a new subreport, and call it **Top Products**. Click the Report Wizard button.

30. Add the Orders, Orders Detail, Product, and Product Type tables and click Next.

31. Click Next on the Link screen.

32. Choose to display Product Type Name and Order Amount, and then click Next.

33. Group by Product Type Name, and click Next.

34. Click Next on the Summaries screen.

35. Select Top 5 groups on the Group Sorting screen, and click Next.

36. Select Bar Chart and set the chart title to Top Product Types. Click Next.

37. Filter on Order Date, and set it to greater than CurrentDate−7. Click Finish.

38. Click OK, and place the subreport in the Report Header d section.

39. Select the Top Product Types tab, and suppress all report sections except the one containing the chart.

40. Preview the report.

41. Save the report as **Exercise 16.1**.

Exercise 16.2: Creating a Linked Subreport

1. Open the Exercise 13.1 report.

2. Create a new Details section below the current Details section.

3. Insert a subreport called Address, and click the Report Wizard button.

4. Add the Employee Addresses table.

5. Do not select any fields. Click Finish.

6. Select the Link tab, and choose the Employee ID field as the field to link to.

7. Accept the default settings in the bottom panel of the dialog box. They will link the Employee ID field in the main report to a parameter in the subreport and use that parameter for record selection in the subreport.

8. Click OK, and place the report in the Details b section.

9. Select the Address tab. Remove the Print Date field, and suppress all sections except the Details section.

10. Place a text object in the Details section, and add the Address1, Address2, City, Region, and Postal Code fields to it with line breaks, commas, and spaces added as necessary.

11. Format the text object, and check Suppress Embedded Field Blank Lines to suppress lines when the Address2 field is null. Resize the text object so that all fields are visible.

12. Preview the report. You will see each employee's address in a box below his or her detail row.

13. Save the report as **Exercise 16.2**.

Exercise 16.3: Creating an On-Demand Subreport

1. Open the Exercise 16.2 report.

2. Select the Address subreport. Right-click, and choose Format Subreport.

3. On the Subreport tab, check the On-Demand Subreport box.

4. Click OK.

5. Preview the report.

6. Click one of the hyperlinks.

7. Save the report as **Exercise 16.3**.

Exercise 16.4: Linking "Unlinkable" Data

In real life you will undoubtedly have more unlinkable data than you want, but for this exercise, we must create some.

1. Open the XTREME database in Microsoft Access.

2. Select the Supplier table, right-click, and select Copy.

3. Select Edit | Paste, and use Supplier2 as the name of the new table. Be sure that structure and data are copied. Click OK.

4. Open the Supplier2 table in Design view, and change the Supplier ID field to text.

5. Close Access.

6. Create a new report using the Standard report wizard. If the Supplier2 table is not visible, right-click and select Refresh.

7. Add the Supplier2 and Product tables to the report.

8. On the Link tab, link the tables on the Supplier ID field.

9. The link will fail because the fields are not of the same data type.

10. Cancel report creation.

11. Create a new report using the Standard wizard.

12. Choose the Product table, and use the Product ID, Product Name, Price, and Supplier ID fields.

13. Group by Supplier ID.

14. Click Finish to create the report.

15. Create a formula called Supplier2ID using the following formula:

    ```
    ToText({Product.Supplier ID},0)
    ```

16. Insert a subreport called **SupplierInfo**. Use the Supplier table, and display the supplier name and phone.

17. Finish the report.

18. Select the Link tab, and choose the Supplier2ID field as the field to link to.

19. Use the generated parameter, but set Select Data in Subreport Based on Field to Supplier2.Supplier ID.

20. Click OK, and place the report in the Group Header #1 section next to the group name.

21. Select the SupplierInfo tab, and suppress all sections except the Details section.

22. Preview the report. You should see the supplier name and phone number.

23. Save the report as **Exercise 16.4**.

Subreport Maintenance

After a subreport is inserted, you may need to change it, modify its links, format its appearance in the main report, or delete it.

Editing a Subreport

A subreport has its own Design and Preview tabs. The subreport's Design tab appears automatically after the subreport is inserted into the main report. If the subreport's Design tab is closed and you want to reopen it, double-click on the subreport in the Design window of the main report. You can also select the subreport in either the Design or Preview tab of the main report and then choose Edit Subreport from the right-click menu or the Edit menu.

Once the subreport is displayed in the Design tab, you can modify it as desired. The Design tab of the subreport does not have Page Header and Page Footer sections, but is otherwise identical to the Design window of the main report. Any parameters that were generated by Crystal Reports for linking the subreport to the main report are listed in the Field Explorer and can be used, modified, and even renamed, if desired.

Refreshing a Subreport

When the main report is refreshed, all subreports are also refreshed, with one exception: on-demand subreports are only refreshed when their hyperlink is clicked. If the current window is a subreport Design or Preview tab, then clicking the Refresh button will refresh only the subreport. If the subreport contains parameters, either user-defined or generated by Crystal Reports, you will be prompted for them. You can enter any valid values, and one instance of the subreport will be generated. In addition, you can double-click an instance of a subreport in the Preview window of the main report. The subreport will open in its own tab. In this fashion, you can open multiple instances of the same subreport.

Modifying Subreport Links

If you want to change a subreport's links after the subreport has been inserted, select the subreport, and then either right-click and choose Change Subreport Links or else select Subreport Links from the Edit menu. The Subreport Links dialog box will open. This dialog box is identical to the Link tab of the Insert Subreport dialog box, except that the For Subreport drop-down box is now available. If your report contains more than one subreport, you can use this list to select the subreport whose links you want to modify.

Formatting a Subreport

The Format Editor for a subreport is invoked by clicking the Format button or by selecting Format Subreport from the Format menu or the right-click menu. A Subreport tab is available in addition to the Common, Border, and Font tabs, as shown in Figure 16-3.

The options on the Subreport tab are used to configure properties that are specific to subreports.

 NOTE The subreport's border is set to single lines on all sides by default, but you can change that using the Border tab.

Figure 16-3
Formatting a
subreport

Subreport Name   The subreport name is how the subreport is identified in the Report Explorer. You can change the name using this option. The name is not displayed in the report preview unless the subreport is an on-demand subreport and the default caption is used.

On-demand Subreport   If you want to change an existing subreport to an on-demand subreport, check the On-demand Subreport box. The subreport border will be removed, and the subreport name will be displayed as a hyperlink in the subreport frame in both the Design and Preview tabs. You can customize the text of the hyperlink in the Preview window, using the On-demand Subreport Caption formula button.

On-demand Subreport Caption   The On-demand Subreport Caption formula button is used to create a custom hyperlink for the subreport. Click the formula button and then create a string formula to use as the hyperlink text when previewing the main report. You can use report fields in the formula to create hyperlinks that change for each instance. For example, if the subreport displays an employee's address, you might create a formula like this:

```
'Click here for '
&{Employee.First Name}&' '&{Employee.Last Name}&'''s address'
```

Subreport Preview Tab Caption   The Preview tab for a subreport uses the Subreport Name plus the word *Preview* as its caption. To customize the caption on the Preview tab, use the Subreport Preview Tab Caption formula button to create a caption. Any type of subreport can be opened in a Preview tab, but since this is the only way to view on-demand subreports, setting a caption for them is more important than setting the caption for a subreport whose content is already displayed in the main report's Preview tab.

Re-import When Opening   If you created a subreport from an existing report, you can check the Re-import When Opening box to have the subreport reimported each time the main report is opened. Any changes in the file will be reflected in the subreport. The location of the file must stay constant for Crystal Reports to be able to find and reimport it. This option applies only to the selected subreport; it does not affect any other subreports that might exist in the main report.

Suppress Blank Subreport   Check Suppress Blank Subreport if you want the sub-report suppressed when it returns no records. If no records are returned, the subreport will be blank—all headers, footers, group fields, and so on will be suppressed. Suppress Blank Subreport is often used in conjunction with Suppress Blank Section to hide the entire section when the subreport is empty.

Deleting a Subreport

A subreport can be deleted by selecting it and then clicking the DELETE key or choosing Delete from the right-click menu. Deleting a subreport can be undone.

Extracting a Subreport

There may be times when you want to take a subreport and turn it into a main report. You can do this using the Save Subreport As command that is available from the File menu or right-click menu when a subreport is selected. Selecting Save Subreport As opens the Save As dialog box, where you can choose a name and location for the new report. The subreport will be saved into the new file, but not removed from the current report.

Reimporting a Subreport

For subreports that were created from an existing file, you may need to reimport the report file to obtain any changes that have been made to the source report.

Default Setting

If you want all subreports reimported whenever a report is opened, you can set the default behavior using the Options dialog box. Open the Options dialog box by selecting File | Options. On the Reporting tab, check the Re-import Subreport on Open box.

Automate Reimporting for a Specific Subreport

If you have one subreport that you want to set up so that it is always reimported when its main report is opened, you can use the Format Editor to configure this behavior. Select the report, and then open the Format Editor. Go to the Subreport tab, and check the Re-import When Opening box.

Manual Reimport

To reimport a subreport manually, select the subreport and then choose Re-import Subreport from the right-click menu.

Exercise 16.5: Formatting a Subreport

1. Open the Exercise 16.2 report.

2. Select the Address subreport, right-click, and choose Format Subreport.

3. Select the Borders tab, and remove all the lines.

4. Select the Font tab, and set the font to Italic.

5. Preview the report.

6. Note that the font setting applied only to the subreport name, not to the contents of the subreport.

7. Save the report as **Exercise 16.5**.

Exercise 16.6: Formatting an On-Demand Subreport

1. Open the Exercise 16.3 report.

2. Select the Address subreport. Right-click, and choose Format Subreport.

3. Click the formula button next to On-demand Subreport Caption.

4. Enter the following formula:

```
'View '&{Employee.First Name}&' '&{Employee.Last Name}&'''s Address'
```

5. Close the Formula Workshop.

6. Click the formula button next to Subreport Preview Tab Caption, and enter the following formula:

```
'Address for '&{Employee.First Name}&' '&{Employee.Last Name}
```

7. Close the Formula Workshop.

8. Click OK.

9. Preview the report.

10. Click several of the hyperlinks, and note the names of the tabs that open.

11. Save the report as **Exercise 16.6**.

Shared Variables

Some information can be passed between a main report and a subreport using parameters. Parameters are primarily used to pass values needed for record selection, but they can be used to pass other types of information as well. The use of shared variables for passing information to and from a subreport is straightforward and easy to implement.

The contents of variables declared with the shared scope are available to the main report and any of its subreports. Declaring a shared variable in the main report and a subreport with the same name will access the same memory location. The main thing to remember is the processing order. The value of the shared variable is changed whenever Crystal Reports generates the section of the report where a formula containing the shared variable resides. Therefore, if you want to pass a value to a subreport, you must place a formula in a section *before* the subreport, to set the value of the shared variable. If you want to return a value from the subreport to the main report, set the value in a formula in the subreport and access it in a formula in the main report that resides in a section that comes *after* the subreport section.

For example, suppose you want to display the phone numbers of the employees and the customers in the same report and you cannot create a union in a SQL Command. You also want the total count of phone numbers in the report. You would create a main report displaying the customer phone numbers and place the count of customer phone numbers in a shared variable. Then create a subreport that displays the employee phone numbers and a total count of phone numbers obtained by adding the value of the shared variable to the count of employee phone numbers.

Exercise 16.7: Using Shared Variables with Subreports

1. Open the Exercise 16.1 report.

2. Remove suppression from the Report Footer section.

3. Create a formula called DisplayMessage using the following formula:

   ```
   Shared stringVar Message;
   ```

4. Place DisplayMessage in the Report Footer section. Format it so that it can grow and stretch it across the width of the report.

5. Edit the Orders subreport, and create a formula called **OrdersMessage** using the following formula:

   ```
   Shared stringVar Message;
   If sum({Orders.Order Amount}) > 10000 then
    Message:=Message & 'Great week for Orders! '
   else
    Message:=Message;
   ```

6. Place the formula field in the section with the chart. Use the Suppress option on the Common tab of the Format Editor to suppress its display.

7. Edit the Top Customer subreport. Create a formula called **CustomerMessage** using the following formula:

   ```
   Shared stringVar Message;
   Message:=Message & {Customer.Customer Name} & ' was a top customer. '
   ```

8. Place the formula in the Group Header #1 section.

9. Preview the report, and notice the message in the footer.

10. Save the report as **Exercise 16.7**.

Chapter Review

Subreports can be the solution to otherwise unsolvable reporting problems. This chapter covered how to create subreports and when to use them.

Quick Tips

- Subreports are reports that are embedded in another report.
- Subreports can be unlinked, meaning that their data is not directly connected to the data in the main report.
- Subreports can be linked. A linked subreport has parameters that take on values in the main report. It usually uses those parameters in a selection formula, so the data in the subreport is customized for the current related values in the main report.
- Subreports are created using the Insert Subreport dialog box. You can choose to use an existing report, or you can create a new report using the Standard report wizard.
- Subreport links are defined on the Link tab of the Insert Subreport dialog box for new subreports or in the Subreport Links dialog box for existing subreports.
- An on-demand subreport is displayed as a hyperlink. The subreport is not run until a user clicks the hyperlink. Any subreport can be configured to be an on-demand subreport using options in the Insert Subreport dialog box or on the Format Editor Subreport tab.
- Subreports should not be placed in the Details section unless absolutely necessary, because they will run once for every record in the report.
- The values of variables declared with the shared scope are available to the main report and any subreports.
- Subreports can be used to link data that is normally unlinkable. For example, if you want to link a field in a table to a formula field, you cannot use the Database Expert, but you can link them using a subreport.
- Subreports can be formatted using the Format Editor. The Common, Border, and Font tabs plus a Subreport tab are available.

Questions

Questions may have more than one correct answer. Choose all answers that apply.

1. A subreport whose information is not directly connected to the main report is
   a. An unlinked subreport
   b. A linked subreport

2. Subreports can be nested; that is, a subreport can contain another subreport.

   a. True

   b. False

3. A subreport that gets its parameter values from fields in the main report is a

   a. Unlinked subreport

   b. Linked subreport

4. On-demand subreports are or can be

   a. Linked

   b. Unlinked

   c. Executed when the user clicks the hyperlink

   d. Opened in-place in the report

   e. Opened in their own Preview tab

5. Assume that subreports exist in the following sections and that there are 100 records in the report, 10 group instances, and five pages. Order the sections starting with the section that would cause a subreport to be evaluated the least number of times and ending with the section that would cause the subreport to be evaluated the most number of times.

   a. Report Header

   b. Page Header

   c. Group header

   d. Details section

6. The report query for an on-demand subreport is sent to the database only when the user clicks the hyperlink.

   a. True

   b. False

7. Which methods can be used to share data between a report and a subreport?

   a. Selection formulas

   b. Parameters

   c. Global variables

   d. Shared variables

   e. Stored procedures

8. To open a subreport in a Design window you can

   a. Select the subreport in the Design window of the main report, right-click, and choose Edit Subreport.

   b. Select the subreport in the Preview window of the main report, right-click, and choose Edit Subreport.

   c. Select the subreport in the Design window of the main report and then select Edit | Subreport.

   d. Select the subreport in the Design window of the main report and then double-click.

   e. Select the subreport in the Preview window of the main report and then double-click.

9. A shared variable must be declared in the main report before it is used in a subreport.

   a. True

   b. False

Answers

1. **a.** If the subreport is not connected to the main report data, it is unlinked.

2. **b.** False. Subreports cannot be nested.

3. **b.** Linked subreports get (at least some of) their parameter values from fields in the main report.

4. **a, b, c, e.** On-demand subreports can be linked or unlinked, are not executed until the user clicks the hyperlink, and open in their own Preview tab.

5. **a, b, c, d.** A subreport in the Report Header will be evaluated once. A subreport in a group header will be evaluated 10 times. A subreport in the Page Header will be evaluated 5 times. And a subreport in the Details section will be evaluated 100 times.

6. **a.** True. An on-demand subreport is not executed until the user clicks the hyperlink.

7. **b, d.** Data can be exchanged between a report and its subreports using parameters or shared variables.

8. **a, b, c, d.** Double-clicking the subreport in the Preview window of the main report will open the subreport in its Preview window, not in its Design window.

9. **b.** A shared variable can be declared in a subreport first.

CHAPTER 17

Complex Formulas and Custom Functions

Exam RDCR300 expects you to be able to

- Use a dynamic array
- Create complex formulas
- Use loop control structures
- Use array functions and loops
- Use nested functions
- Create, use, and modify custom functions
- Explain the effects of NULLs in formulas

In Chapter 8, you learned the basics of formula creation. In this chapter, you will learn several advanced formula concepts, including the use of custom functions.

Complex Formula Elements

Most formula elements were covered in Chapter 8. The complex topics of nesting functions, using print state functions, loop control structures, and dynamic arrays are described in more detail in this chapter.

NULLs in Formula Fields

A NULL in a formula field statement will cause the entire statement to evaluate to NULL. For example, if you have {Orders.Order Amount}*{@Discount} and the Order Amount field is NULL, the result of the statement will be NULL. If you have {Orders .Order Amount}+{@Tax} in a statement and the Order Amount field is NULL, the result will be NULL.

An exception exists for the summary functions: NULL values used in summary functions are ignored. Therefore, if you are summing or averaging a field and some of the records contain NULL for the field, those values will be excluded from the summary operation. The effect for the summing operation is the same as if the field was treated as zero, but differs for many of the other summary operations. For example, if the report contains 10 records and one of the records contains NULL in a field, then a count of that field would return 9.

You can cause Crystal Reports to treat NULL values as zeros or blanks for a specific report using settings in the Report Options dialog box or for all new reports using the Report tab of the Options dialog box. The Convert Database NULL Values to Default option will convert all NULL numeric database fields to zero and NULL string fields to blank. The Convert Other NULL Values to Default option will convert all other NULL report fields to zero or blank.

 EXAM TIP   Some SQL databases treat an empty string as equivalent to a NULL. For the exam, consider that an empty string is *not* the same as a NULL string.

Nesting Functions

Any Crystal Reports function, whether built-in or user-defined, that returns a value can be used as the argument to another function that requires the same type of value. This is called *nesting functions*. For example, to find an employee's birthday this year, you need to create a date using the month and day of their birth date and the current year, as shown here:

```
Date(Year(CurrentDate),
    Month({Employee.Birth Date}),
    Day({Employee.Birth Date}))
```

The Year, Month, and Day functions are nested inside the Date function. CurrentDate itself is a function nested inside the Year function, which is nested inside the Date function. It is not necessary to do the inner computations, save the results in variables, and use the variables in the outer function. Nesting functions is efficient and usually easy to understand.

Print State Functions

A collection of print state functions is available in the Function Tree of the Formula Workshop. Print state functions return values that are only known for the report during Pass 2 or while printing records. Using any of the print state functions in a formula field makes the formula a print time (Pass 2) formula.

IsNull (fld)   The IsNull function returns the Boolean values True or False. If the value of the field argument is NULL, then it will return True, otherwise it will return False. (Note that NULL is not the same thing as zero for a number field, and may not be the same as an empty string for string fields.) If the IsNull function is used in a record selection formula for a SQL database, it will be passed to the database and evaluated there. In that case, it is the one print state function that is *not* a print state function! When used in a regular formula field, it is evaluated at print time as expected.

PreviousIsNull (fld)   PreviousIsNull returns the Boolean value True or False, depending on the value of the field argument in the preceding record. The preceding record is the detail record immediately before the current record in the report. The preceding record in the report might be different from the preceding record in the database result set if sorting was not done on the server. PreviousIsNull always returns NULL for the first detail record in the report because a previous record does not exist.

NextIsNull (fld)   NextIsNull is similar to PreviousIsNull, but it looks at the value of the field argument in the next record. NextIsNull always returns NULL for the last record in the report because no next record exists.

Previous (fld)   Use the Previous function if you need the value of a field in the preceding record. For example, if you want to compare the country in this record to the country in the preceding record, you could use the Previous function, like so:

```
If Previous({Country}) = {Country} then ...
```

Next (fld)   Next is similar to Previous, but returns the field value in the next record.

PageNumber   Use the PageNumber function if you need to use the current page number in a formula. This function returns the same value as the Page Number special field.

TotalPageCount   The TotalPageCount function returns the total number of pages in the report. If you use this function in a formula, the report processing will require Pass 3. This function returns the same value as the Total Page Count special field.

PageNofM   It is unlikely that you would use the PageNofM function in a formula because it returns a string like "Page *n* of *m*," where *n* is the current page number and *m* is the total page count. This function is equivalent to the Page N of M special field. If you use PageNofM in a formula, a third pass will be required to process the report.

RecordNumber   The RecordNumber function returns the record number of the current record. The records are numbered starting at one in the sort order of the report. The RecordNumber function is equivalent to the Record Number special field.

GroupNumber   The GroupNumber function returns the number of the group instance as counted for the lowest-level group in the report. It is the same as the Group Number special field.

RecordSelection   The RecordSelection function returns the report's record selection formula as a string. It is equivalent to the Record Selection Formula special field.

GroupSelection   The GroupSelection function returns the report's group selection formula as a string. It is equivalent to the Group Selection Formula special field.

InRepeatedGroupHeader   InRepeatedGroupHeader is a Boolean function that returns True if it is placed in a group header section that has repeated. It returns False for the first instance of a particular group header. It will never be True unless the group option Repeat Group Header on Each Page is checked. You can use this function to create a formula that notifies the user when a group has been continued from the previous page.

EXAM TIP Understand the use of InRepeatedGroupHeader.

OnFirstRecord The OnFirstRecord Boolean function returns True if the current record is the first record in the report and False otherwise.

OnLastRecord The OnLastRecord Boolean function returns True if the current record is the last record in the report and False otherwise.

DrillDownGroupLevel The DrillDownGroupLevel function returns a number indicating the depth of the current drill-down. If no drill-down has been executed, it will return 0. If the highest-level group has been drilled into, it will return 1. The next lower group will return 2 when drilled into, and so on. This function is often used to format headers for drill-down tabs.

Loop Control Structures

Using loop control structures in a formula allows you to repeat the same block of statements multiple times. There are three loop control structures available in Crystal Reports formulas: For, While Do, and Do While.

For

Use the For statement when you need to execute the same statement multiple times. The syntax for the statement is

```
For Counter := StartValue to EndValue [Step StepValue] Do StatementList;
```

Counter is a numeric variable that you must declare prior to using the For statement. The name of the variable is not important. *StartValue* is the first value that you want *Counter* to take on. It can be a constant, expression, or other variable. *EndValue* is the last value that you want *Counter* to take on. The Step clause is optional. *Counter* will increase by one unless you set the Step value. *StepValue* can be negative to step down from *StartValue* to *EndValue*. *StatementList* is one or more statements that should be executed for each value of *Counter*. Use parentheses for multiple statements.

The For statement is often used to process strings character-by-character or to process the elements of an array, as shown here:

```
stringVar array Colors := ['Blue', 'Green', 'Light Blue', 'Navy Blue'];
numberVar Counter := 0;
numberVar MatchCount :=0;

For Counter := 1 to UBound(Colors) Do
  (If 'Blue' in Colors[Counter] then
    MatchCount:=MatchCount+1
  else
    MatchCount:=MatchCount+0;);

MatchCount;
```

Exit For   The Exit For statement can be used inside the Do part of a For statement to stop execution of the For statement and continue processing at the next statement following the For statement, as shown here:

```
stringVar array Colors := ['Blue', 'Green', 'Light Blue', 'Navy Blue'];
numberVar Counter := 0;
booleanVar Found := False;

For Counter := 1 to UBound(Colors) Do
  If 'Blue' in Colors[Counter] then
    (Found := True;
     Exit For;);

Found;
```

While Do/Do While

The For statement executes a specific number of times based on the *Counter* variable. While loops execute until *Condition* evaluates to False. The syntax of the While Do statement is

```
While Condition Do StatementList;
```

Condition is some expression that evaluates to the Boolean value True or False. If *Condition* is True, the statements in *StatementList* are executed. If *Condition* is False, the statement ends and processing continues with the next statement following the While Do statement. If *Condition* is False when the statement is first executed, *StatementList* will never execute. The *StatementList* operations must somehow modify *Condition* or the statement will loop repeatedly until it reaches the maximum allowed loop count.

```
stringVar array Colors := ['Blue', 'Green', 'Light Blue', 'Navy Blue'];
numberVar Counter := 1;
booleanVar Found := False;

While (Found = False and Counter<=UBound(Colors)) Do
  (If 'Blue' in Colors[Counter] then Found := True;
   Counter := Counter + 1;);

Found;
```

The Do While loop is very similar, but *Condition* is evaluated after *StatementList* is executed, as shown here, so *StatementList* is executed at least once.

```
stringVar array Colors := ['Blue', 'Green', 'Light Blue', 'Navy Blue'];
numberVar Counter := 1;
booleanVar Found := False;

Do
  (If 'Blue' in Colors[Counter] then Found := True;
   Counter := Counter + 1;)
While (Found = False and Counter<=UBound(Colors));

Found;
```

Use a Do While loop if *StatementList* should be executed at least once before *Condition* is evaluated. In the examples given, both statements will give the same result, but that is not always the case.

Option Loop   The maximum number of times that Crystal Reports will evaluate a loop is 100,000. This is a safety mechanism to trap loop processing that will never get to an exit condition. You can set the loop maximum to a different value if you need more than 100,000 iterations or want to limit the processing to fewer than 100,000. To set the loop maximum, you use the Option Loop statement, as shown here:

```
Option Loop MaxIterations;
```

MaxIterations is the number that you want to set as the maximum loop counter. To use the Option Loop statement, enter it as the first statement in any formula.

Exit While   The Exit While statement can be used to break out of a While loop, as shown here:

```
stringVar array Colors := ['Blue', 'Green', 'Light Blue', 'Navy Blue'];
numberVar Counter := 1;
booleanVar Found := False;

While Found = False Do
  (If 'Blue' in Colors[Counter] then Found := True;
   Counter := Counter + 1;
   If Counter > UBound(Colors) then Exit While);

Found;
```

Arrays

Array variables, operators, and functions were mentioned in Chapter 8, and array parameters were discussed in Chapter 6. This section covers array topics in depth.

 NOTE   Arrays can have a maximum of 1000 elements, and the first element is referenced using 1 as the index. (Crystal Reports arrays are one-based rather than zero-based.)

Array Operators

Array operators are used to manipulate arrays and are available in the Operator Tree of the Formula Workshop.

Make Array   Arrays can be created by surrounding a comma-delimited list of items with square brackets. Each element in the list must be of the same data type. The elements can be expressions. For example, the following snippets all create arrays:

```
[123, 456, 789]

[Date(1960,1,31), Date(1961,7,29), Date(1984,1,8)]
```

```
['Top', 'Bottom']
```

```
[{Employee ID}, {Supervisor ID}+2, 1, 745/5}
```

Subscript   A particular element of an array can be accessed using subscripts. The syntax is

```
ArrayName[index]
```

where *index* is the number of the element that you want to return. Arrays are indexed starting with one and not zero. For example, the following formula would return "Blue":

```
stringVar array Colors := ['Red', 'Blue', 'Yellow'];
Colors[2]
```

In   The In function tests to see if a value is contained within an array. It will return the Boolean value True if the element exists and False otherwise. The following example will return True:

```
stringVar array Colors := ['Red', 'Blue', 'Yellow'];
'Blue' in Colors
```

Redim   Static arrays are arrays that are created with a certain number of elements, and the number of elements is never changed. Dynamic arrays are arrays whose number of elements is changed programmatically after the array has been declared.

 NOTE   Some Crystal Reports documentation calls an array dynamic if its *contents* change during the execution of the report, but this is not the typical definition.

The Redim function is used to change the size of an array. The number of elements can be increased or decreased. The syntax is

```
Redim ArrayName[NewSize];
```

Redim destroys any elements that already exist in the array. Each element is set to the default value for the data type of the array. The following example will return an empty string:

```
stringVar array Colors := ['Red', 'Blue', 'Yellow'];
Redim Colors[5];
Colors[2]
```

Redim Preserve   Use the Redim Preserve function to change the size of an array but maintain the values of any existing elements. The syntax is

```
Redim Preserve ArrayName[NewSize];
```

The following example will return "Blue":

```
stringVar array Colors := ['Red', 'Blue', 'Yellow'];
Redim Preserve Colors[5];
Colors[2]
```

Array Functions

Array functions are used to create arrays, obtain the size of arrays, summarize the elements in an array, and create a string from the elements of an array. MakeArray, UBound, and the summary functions are found under the Array folder in the Function Tree of the Formula Workshop. Join and Split are found under the String folder.

MakeArray MakeArray is a function that returns an array. You can use the function or create an array using brackets. The MakeArray function might be used to differentiate the process of constructing an array from the process of subscripting an array, since both operations can be done with brackets and might cause confusion. Here is an example of array construction using the MakeArray function:

```
stringVar array Colors := MakeArray('Red', 'Blue', 'Yellow');
Colors[2]
```

And here is the same example without using the function:

```
stringVar array Colors := ['Red', 'Blue', 'Yellow'];
Colors[2]
```

UBound The UBound array function returns the size of the array. The size of the array is the index of the last element in the array. The following example returns 3:

```
stringVar array Colors := MakeArray('Red', 'Blue', 'Yellow');
UBound(Colors)
```

NOTE UBound will return 1 for an empty array.

Summary Functions The summary functions Average, Count, DistinctCount, Maximum, Minimum, PopulationStdDev, PopulationVariance, StdDev, Sum, and Variance can be used with arrays. The summary will be computed across the elements of the array. The following example will return "Yellow" because "Yellow" falls last when the elements are sorted alphabetically:

```
stringVar array Colors := MakeArray('Red', 'Blue', 'Yellow');
Maximum(Colors)
```

Join Use Join to create a single string containing all the elements of an array. Join takes an array as its first argument and an optional second argument defines the separator to use for the string. For example, the result of the following formula is "Red, Blue, Yellow":

```
stringVar array Colors := MakeArray('Red', 'Blue', 'Yellow');
Join(Colors, ', ')
```

Split Split is the opposite of Join. It will take a string and parse it, storing the results in an array. Since an array cannot be the result of a formula, the following example uses Join to return the resulting array. The result is "Red, Blue, Yellow."

```
stringVar ColorStr := 'Red/Blue/Yellow';
stringVar array Colors;
Colors := Split(ColorStr, '/');
Join(Colors, ', ');
```

Split has optional parameters. The delimiter argument used in the example is optional. If it is deleted, a single space character is considered the delimiter. The next optional argument can be used to limit the number of elements returned. Just enter the number of elements you want and Split will return no more than that. The last optional argument is used to indicate whether the delimiter should be considered case sensitive or not.

Common Array Uses

Arrays are used in many different ways in Crystal Reports formulas. You often need to loop through arrays, accumulate values in arrays, and extract array parameter values for display.

Looping Through an Array   Since arrays contain sequences of elements, it is common to loop through them for various computations. The UBound or Count function can be used to determine the number of elements in an array for use in a For statement, and the counter variable can be used as the index of the array as shown in this example. The result is "Reds, Blues, Yellows."

```
stringVar array Colors := MakeArray('Red', 'Blue', 'Yellow');
numberVar Counter := 0;
For Counter := 1 to UBound(Colors) do
  Colors[Counter]:=Colors[Counter]&'s';
Join(Colors, ', ');
```

Populating an Array with Report Values   Suppose you need to collect some item from each record, as the report is processed. For example, say you want to list the names of customers who purchased more than $10,000 for the reporting period as a note in the Report Footer section. You would compute the total for the customer using a summary field in the Customer group footer. Then you could use an array to collect only the customer names that meet the criteria.

You would need to initialize the array in one formula, add to it in a formula placed in the group footer, and display it with a third formula in the Report Footer. The initialization formula would look like this:

```
WhilePrintingRecords;
stringVar array CustomerNames;
numberVar Counter := 0;
```

 NOTE   The initialization formula is not required. If you do not create one, the variables will be created when the accumulation formula for the first record is executed.

The accumulation formula would look like this:

```
WhilePrintingRecords;
stringVar array CustomerNames;
numberVar Counter;
```

```
If Sum ({Order.Order Amount}, {Customer.Customer Name}) > 10000 then
  (Counter := Counter + 1;
   Redim Preserve CustomerNames[Counter];
   CustomerNames[Counter] := GroupName ({Customer.Customer Name});)
```

And the display formula would look like this:

```
WhilePrintingRecords;
stringVar array Names;
'The following customers ordered over $10,000: '
  &Join(CustomerNames, ', ');
```

The whole sequence of formulas must be evaluated at print time because the summary value used in the accumulation formula would not be available before that time. (The accumulation formula would be evaluated at print time by default and so does not really need the WhilePrintingRecords evaluation time function; it is included for consistency.)

Extracting Array Parameters   Parameter fields are commonly placed in the report header or footer as documentation of the values used to run the current report. Single-value parameters are straightforward and display their value when inserted in the report. Multivalue parameters will display only their first element when placed directly on a report. You must create a formula that uses the Join function or loops through the array to create a display string that shows all the parameter values. (The top and bottom of range-valued parameters can be displayed using the Minimum and Maximum functions.)

Exercise 17.1: Using Dynamic Arrays and Loop Control Structures

The report from Exercise 3.3 displays employees by position with a count of employees in each position. You need to identify positions that have more than one employee in a note in the report footer.

1. Open the Exercise 3.3 report.

2. Create a formula called **Init** using the following code, and place it in the Report Header section.

   ```
   WhilePrintingRecords;
   stringVar array Names;
   numberVar Counter := 0;
   ```

3. Create a formula called **Accum** using the following code, and place it in the Group Footer #1 section.

   ```
   WhilePrintingRecords;
   stringVar array Names;
   numberVar Counter;
   If Count ({Employee.Employee ID}, {Employee.Position}) > 1 then
     (Counter := Counter + 1;
      Redim Preserve Names[Counter];
      Names[Counter] := GroupName ({Employee.Position});)
   ```

4. Open the Format Editor for the Accum field, and check the Suppress option on the Common tab.

5. Create a third formula called Display using the following code:

```
WhilePrintingRecords;
stringVar array Names;
'There is more than one employee with the following job titles: '
   &Join(Names, ', ');
```

6. Place the Display formula in the Report Footer, and format it to Can Grow.

7. Preview the report. You should see "There is more than one employee with the following job titles: Sales Representative" as the result of the Display formula.

8. You can refine the message display to use *title* instead of *titles* if there is only one element. Modify the formula as shown here:

```
WhilePrintingRecords;
stringVar array Names;
stringVar Title;
If Count(Names) > 1 then
   Title := 'titles'
Else
   Title := 'title';
'There is more than one employee with the following job '
   & Title & ': '&Join(Names, ', ');
```

9. You can further customize the message so that, if there is more than one element in the array, the last element is appended to the string with *and*, as shown here:

```
WhilePrintingRecords;
stringVar array Names;
numberVar i;
stringVar Message :=
   'There is more than one employee with the following job ';
If Count(Names) > 1 then
   Message := Message & 'titles: '
Else
   Message := Message & 'title: ';
For i := 1 to Count(Names) do
   Select i
     Case 1: Message := Message & Names[i]
     Case Count(Names): Message := Message & ', and ' & Names[i]
     Default : Message := Message & ', ' & Names[i];
Message := Message & '.';
Message;
```

The Case statement treats the first and last elements of the array differently when creating the message.

10. Preview the report.

11. Save the report as **Exercise 17.1**.

Custom Functions

You have seen and used many of Crystal Reports' built-in functions. They are listed in the Function Tree of the Formula Workshop. Each function may actually require many computations to accomplish its purpose, but you do not need to know or understand what those computations are. In this way, a function encapsulates a block of reusable code.

Functions of all types have a couple of common characteristics. Each function returns a single result and may require input in the form of arguments. The return value of a function is one data item, although it may be in the form of an array. A function is called using its name and any required arguments in parentheses.

You can create your own functions and then reuse them in the same report or save them to the repository for use in other reports or by other developers. You can use functions created by other developers that were stored in the repository. Functions created by users are called *custom functions*.

 TIP Custom functions are wonderful options for sharing or reusing commonly needed operations; however, you should consider creating database functions in preference to custom functions where possible. They have the same advantages, can be used easily in SQL Expression fields, and will execute more efficiently. In situations where database functions are not usable, as in formatting formulas, custom functions are the best alternative.

Creating Custom Functions

A custom function can be created using two methods, either by using the Custom Function Editor or by extracting it from an existing formula.

Custom Function Syntax

The syntax of custom function is similar to formulas, except that the function arguments must be identified in the first line of code. The Function statement identifies a block of code as a function and defines the function arguments.

```
Function (argument1, argument2 ...)
```

Function here is the word *Function*—not a placeholder for a function name. Also, the parentheses that follow it are required even if no arguments are listed.

 NOTE This section describes Crystal syntax for functions; Basic syntax differs.

The arguments are normal variable declarations with a couple of extra features, as shown here:

```
[Optional] datatype [Range] [Array] argumentName [:= default value]
```

Elements in brackets are optional. The keyword Optional can be added to an argument's definition to make the argument optional. Optional arguments must be given default values, and required arguments cannot be given default values. All arguments following an optional argument must also be optional. The data type can be any of the Crystal Reports types that you can use in variable declarations. The Range keyword can be added to create a range argument. The Array keyword can be added to create an Array argument. Creating a default value is similar to giving a variable an initial value, but the default value will only be used for optional arguments that are omitted when the function is called. If the function is passed a value for an argument, that value will be used even if a default value was defined.

The following rules apply to custom functions:

- Variables can be declared and used inside a function as in a normal formula. However, the default scope of variables declared in functions is local, not global. You cannot declare or use any global or shared variables in a function. They can be passed in as arguments to the function, but not used directly.

- You also cannot use any fields in a function, and the Field Tree will not be displayed in the Formula Workshop when you are using the Custom Function Editor. Your completed function can take fields as arguments, but you must declare the arguments as you would regular variables of the proper type in the Function statement. Using a field would make the function dependent on a particular report.

- You cannot use any function that is report dependent. These include the formatting functions CurrentFieldValue, DefaultAttribute, and GridRowColumnValue; the evaluation time functions; print time functions; and the document properties functions.

- A function cannot call itself.

- Unlike a Crystal Reports formula, a custom function can return an array or range type as its result.

Custom Function Editor

You create custom functions using the Custom Function Editor of the Formula Workshop. (Open the Formula Workshop using Report | Formula Workshop.) To create a new custom function, select Custom Function from the New button's drop-down list or right-click in the Report Custom Function node of the Workshop Tree and choose New. The Custom Function Name dialog box will appear, as shown here.

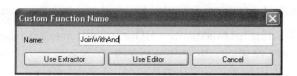

Enter a name for your custom function; you cannot use spaces. Once the name is entered, the Use Extractor and Use Editor buttons will be available. See the next section, "Custom Function Extractor," for a discussion of the Use Extractor button. Click the Use Editor button to create a custom function from scratch.

The Formula Workshop will invoke the Custom Function Editor and create the Function statement for you, as shown here.

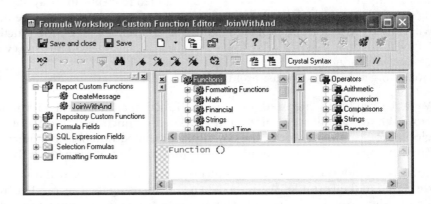

Note that the title of the Formula Workshop now indicates that the Custom Function Editor is active and lists the name of the function. The Formula Workshop looks and behaves much as it does when you are creating formulas. One exception is that the Field Tree is not available.

Create any statements required to implement your function's logic and return the result in the final statement.

Custom Function Extractor

If you have a formula whose logic you would like to encapsulate in a function, you can use the Custom Function Extractor. When applied to a formula, it converts all fields in the formula to arguments and creates a new function. The Extractor cannot create functions that return ranges or arrays because formulas cannot return ranges or arrays. Many formulas cannot be converted; you will receive a message indicating the reasons. One common reason is the use of print time functions in the formula. Another is the use of global variables in the formula.

To use the Extractor, create a new custom function using the Custom Function option of Formula Workshop's New button, or right-click in the Report Custom Function node of the Workshop Tree and choose New. The Custom Function Name dialog box will appear. Enter a name for your custom function, and then click the Use Extractor button. The Extract Custom Function from Formula dialog box will appear, as shown in Figure 17-1.

Formula   The Formula list box displays all formulas that exist in the report. Select the formula that you want to use as the source of your new custom function.

Custom Function Name   The name that you entered for the custom function is displayed in the Custom Function Name edit box. You can change the name if desired. Function names cannot include spaces and cannot start with a number.

Enter More Info   Clicking the Enter More Info button opens the Custom Function Properties dialog box. You can modify several of the custom function's properties,

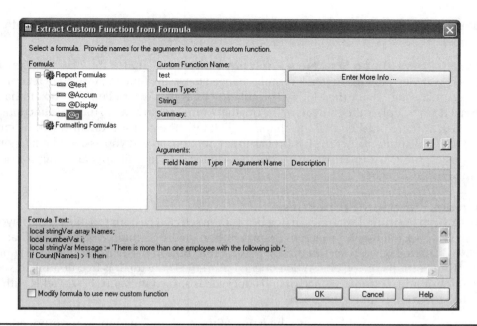

Figure 17-1   Extracting a custom function from a formula

including its category and help text using this dialog box. It is covered in detail in the "Custom Function Properties" section.

Return Type   The Return Type displays the return type of the new function. This will be the data type of the result of the last statement in the original formula. You cannot change it.

Summary   The Summary text box can be used to add descriptive commentary to your function. It is good practice to fully describe the proper use of the function and point out any exception cases or other issues here.

Arguments   The Arguments grid displays all fields of the original formula that are going to be converted to arguments.

- **Field Name**   The Field Name displays the name of a field in the original formula. You cannot modify it.

- **Type**   The Type column displays the data type of the original field.

- **Argument Name**   Argument Name is the name of the new argument that is replacing the original field. You can change the Argument Name from its default (v1, v2, and so on). Argument names should be as descriptive as possible to help guide the user.

- **Description**   You can enter a description of the argument in the Description column.

Formula Text   The Formula Text area is used for display only. It shows the original formula.

Modify Formula to Use New Custom Function   Once the new function is created, you may want the original formula changed to use the function instead of retaining the formula code. Check the Modify Formula to Use New Custom Function box to have Crystal Reports replace the contents of the original formula with a call to the new function.

When you are finished making changes, click OK. The custom function will be created and will appear under the Report Custom Functions tree. If you assigned a category to it using the Custom Functions Properties dialog box, it will appear under a node named for its category.

Custom Function Properties

The Custom Function Properties dialog box for the selected custom function is displayed when you click the Toggle Properties Display button on the Formula Workshop toolbar. It is also displayed when you click the Enter More Info button in the Extract Custom Function from Formula dialog box. When opened from the Extractor, it is free-floating. If you open it from the Formula Workshop, it is docked, as shown in Figure 17-2. Fields with a white background can be modified.

Name   The Name field displays the name of the custom function. You cannot edit it here. If you need to change the name, right-click the custom function in the Workshop Tree and select Rename.

Summary   The Summary area is used to enter important information about the function. You should describe the intended purpose of the function and any other commentary that would be of interest to a user. Remember, an important advantage of using custom functions is that they can be shared among developers. You should create every function with this in mind and provide adequate documentation.

Category   Custom functions available for use in a report are displayed in the Report Custom Functions node of the Workshop Tree. Just like the Function Tree, the Report Custom Functions node can have lower-level folders that are used to categorize the functions. You create the folders using the Category edit box. Existing categories are available in the drop-down list. You can create new ones by entering a new value in the box. If you want to have a multiple-level category, use a slash to separate the folder names. In Figure 17-2, notice that the category is String/Array and the function appears in the Array folder under the String folder.

Repository   If a custom function has been saved to a repository, the name of the repository will be shown in the Repository box.

Author   The Author field is entered by the user. Enter your name so that other developers will know that you are the owner of this custom function.

Return Type   The Return Type field displays the data type of the function result. You cannot change it here. To modify the return type, you must modify the function code so that it returns a different data type.

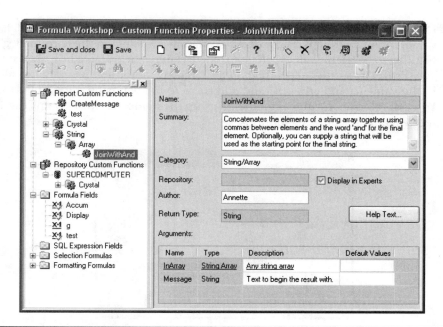

Figure 17-2   Setting custom function properties

Help Text   Clicking the Help Text button opens the Help Text dialog box for the function, as shown here. The help text will be visible to users if they use the Formula Expert to create a formula. Enter any information that would be helpful for the user.

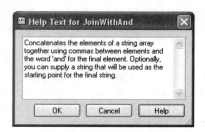

Arguments   The grid in the Arguments area lists the function's arguments.

- **Name**   The Name column displays the names of the arguments. You cannot change the names here.

- **Type**   The Type column displays the data type of the arguments. You cannot change the data type here.

- **Description**   You can enter a description for each argument. The description will be visible to a user when the Formula Expert is used to create a formula.

- **Default Values** You can use the Default Values column to define sets of default values for an argument. These defaults are only available in the Formula Expert. Clicking in a Default Values cell opens the Default Values dialog box, shown here. The display may differ depending on the data type of the argument. Enter values in the Value to Add edit box, and add them to the list using the Add button. You can remove any unwanted items using the Remove button. Items can be reordered using the arrow buttons.

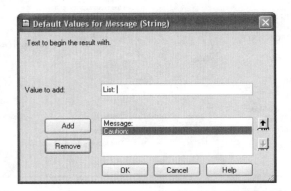

Display in Experts Check the Display in Experts box to make the custom function available in the Formula Expert. Clearing the box will remove the function from use in the Formula Expert, but it will still be available in the Formula Editor.

Sharing Custom Functions Using the Repository

Saving a custom function to the repository makes it available to other report developers. Sharing custom functions allows code reuse and standardization. Custom functions linked to the repository can also be automatically updated when their underlying code changes, easing maintenance work.

Report Versus Repository Custom Functions

Report custom functions are custom functions that reside in a report. Only report custom functions can be used in report formula fields. Repository custom functions are custom functions that are stored in the repository. A repository custom function must first exist as a report custom function before it can be saved to the repository. If a repository custom function is used in a report formula or report custom function, it automatically becomes a report custom function. A link is maintained between report custom functions and their related repository custom functions.

Granting Edit Privileges to the Repository

In order to save custom functions to the repository, you must have edit rights to the Custom Functions folder of the repository. To grant edit rights follow these steps:

1. Select Start | Programs | Crystal Enterprise 10 | Business View Manager to open the Business View Manager.

2. Log in to Crystal Enterprise as the administrator.

3. If the welcome dialog box opens, click Cancel to close it.

4. The Business View Manager will open with the Repository Explorer on the right.

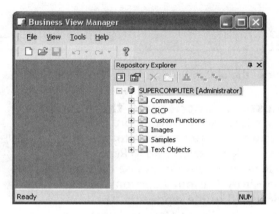

5. Right-click the Custom Functions folder, and select Edit Rights.

6. The Edit Rights dialog box will open, as shown here.

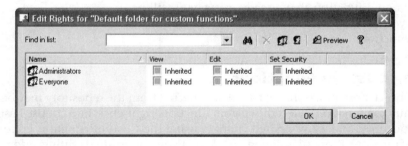

7. You could grant the edit right to everyone by checking the Edit box next to the Everyone group. However, to grant the right only to your user account, click the Add Users button.

8. Click your user name and then the Add button. Click Close.

9. In the Edit Rights dialog box, click the Edit check box next to your account until it says "Granted."

10. Click the Preview button to verify that you now have both view and edit rights, as shown here.

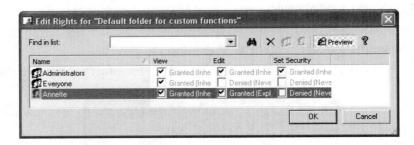

11. Click OK to close the dialog box, and then close the Business View Manager.

Saving Report Custom Functions to the Repository

In the Formula Workshop, select the report custom function that you want to add to the repository in the Workshop Tree. Right-click and select Add to Repository or click the Add to Repository button, or else drag the function to the Repository Custom Functions folder. The function will be added to the repository. The icon next to the function in the Report Custom Functions folder will change to indicate that it is linked to the repository, and the function will appear in the Repository Custom Functions folder, as shown here.

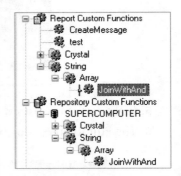

If you add a function that already exists, you will be asked if you are sure you want to update the repository custom function.

Editing Custom Functions

Only report custom functions that are disconnected from the repository may be edited. To disconnect a function, select the custom function, right-click, and choose Disconnect from Repository. Make any desired changes using the Custom Function Editor or the Custom Functions Properties dialog box. When you are finished editing, add the function back to the repository.

Using Custom Functions

Just like built-in functions, custom functions cannot be used directly in a report. They must be used in a formula field or within another custom function.

Using a Custom Function in a Formula Field

Report custom functions appear in the Function Tree of the Formula Workshop, similar to the built-in functions. They appear under the Custom Functions folder in their defined categories, as shown here.

Note that functions created with optional arguments are displayed multiple times, once for each valid combination of optional parameters.

If you want to use a repository custom function in a formula, you must first add it to the report. Select the function in the Workshop Tree, right-click and choose Add to Report, or click the Add to Report button. If the selected custom function relies on any other custom functions, they will be added to the report as well.

Using a Custom Function Within a Custom Function

You can use report custom functions in new custom functions. Just choose them from the Function Tree as described in the preceding section.

Using the Formula Expert

The Formula Expert can be used to create a formula that relies solely on a custom function. Create a new formula field and choose the Use Expert button from the Formula Name dialog box. The Formula Expert will open in the Formula Workshop, as shown in Figure 17-3. The Formula Expert will also appear for existing formulas if you click the Toggle Properties Display button. If you select a custom function, the original formula will be replaced.

Custom Function Supplying Logic   The Custom Function Supplying Logic list box displays all custom functions available to you, both report custom functions and repository custom functions. Select the custom function that you want to use in the formula. If you select a repository custom function, it will automatically become a report custom function.

Return Type   The Return Type displays the return data type of the selected custom function.

Function Arguments   The Function Arguments grid displays the selected custom function's arguments. The Name, Type, and Description fields are read-only. The Value column is used to select or enter the value for the argument. You can enter a value or select one from the drop-down list. All fields of the proper type are listed, as well as any defined default values. If the argument is optional and you do not select a value, the optional default value will be used.

Summary   The Summary area displays the summary text of the selected custom function.

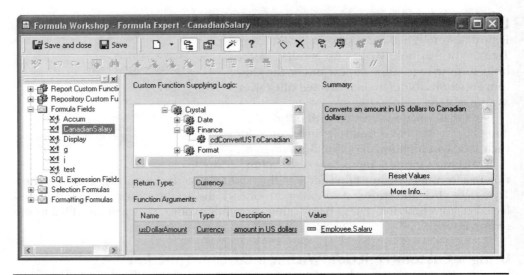

Figure 17-3   Using the Formula Expert

Reset Values   Click the Reset Values button to return all the argument values to their defaults.

More Info   The More Info button displays the Custom Function Properties dialog box.

 After creating a formula with the Formula Expert, you can toggle the Use Expert/Editor button to open the formula in the Formula Editor for further customization.

Updating Repository Custom Functions in Reports

For reports containing links to repository custom functions, the functions will be updated when the report is opened if Update Repository Objects is checked in the Open dialog box or the global option Update Connected Repository Object on Open is checked on the Reporting tab of the Options dialog box.

Exercise 17.2: Creating a Custom Function

1. Open the report from Exercise 17.1.

2. Select Report | Formula Workshop to open the Formula Workshop.

3. Right-click the Report Custom Functions node of the Workshop Tree, and select New.

4. Enter **JoinWithAnd** as the function name. This function will operate like the Join function, except that it will use the word *And* to connect the last element of the array to the list.

5. Click the Use Editor button.

6. Enter the following code:

```
Function (stringVar array ArrayIn)
local numberVar i;
local stringVar Result := '';
For i := 1 to Count(ArrayIn) do
  Select i
    Case 1: Result := Result & ArrayIn[i]
    Case Count(ArrayIn): Result := Result & ', and ' & ArrayIn[i]
    Default : Result := Result & ', ' & ArrayIn[i];
Result
```

7. Click the Save button.

8. Browse the Custom Functions folder of the Function Tree, and notice that the JoinWithAnd function is listed.

9. Close the Formula Workshop.

10. Save the report as **Exercise 17.2**.

Exercise 17.3: Using a Custom Function

1. Open the report from Exercise 17.2.

2. Open the Formula Workshop, and select the Display formula in the Workshop Tree.

3. Modify it to use the new custom function as shown here:

```
WhilePrintingRecords;
stringVar array Names;
numberVar i;
stringVar Message :=
    'There is more than one employee with the following job ';
If Count(Names) > 1 then
  Message := Message & 'titles: '
Else
  Message := Message & 'title: ';
Message := Message & JoinWithAnd2 (Names);
Message := Message & '.';
Message;
```

4. Close the Formula Workshop, and notice that the result of the Display formula is the same.

5. Save the report as **Exercise 17.3**.

Exercise 17.4: Adding a Custom Function to the Repository

1. Open the report from Exercise 17.3.

2. Select the JoinWithAnd custom function under the Report Custom Functions folder of the Workshop Tree.

3. Click the Toggle Properties Display button.

4. Enter descriptive text in the Summary field.

5. Enter **String/Array** in the Category field.

6. Right-click, and select Add to Repository.

7. Notice that the function is added to the Repository Custom Functions folder under the Array folder, under the String folder.

8. Close the Formula Workshop.

9. Save the report as **Exercise 17.4**.

Chapter Review

Complex formula topics were covered in this chapter. The use of arrays, print state functions, loop control structures, and custom functions were described.

Quick Tips

- NULL values in formula statements will cause the statement to evaluate to NULL.

- NULLs in summary formulas are ignored.

- NULLs can be converted to zero or blank using the Convert NULL Database Values to Default or Convert Other Values to Default options.

- Functions can be nested. You can use one function as an argument for another function, if it returns the proper data type.

- Print state functions are functions whose values are only known at print time. They include IsNull, functions that reference fields in the previous or next records, record numbers, group numbers, page numbers, and so on.

- The loop control structures are For, While Do, and Do While. For loops a specific number of times. While loops until a condition is True.

- Loops can be exited using an Exit For or Exit While statement.

- The Option Loop statement can be used to limit the number of iterations of a loop.

- Arrays can be resized with the Redim function.

- You can loop through the elements of an array using the For statement.

- The size of an array is returned by the UBound function and the Count function.

- Many summary functions can be used with arrays, such as Count, Sum, Minimum, and Maximum.

- Custom functions encapsulating business logic can be created in the Formula Workshop using the Custom Function Editor or the Extractor.

- When a custom function is added to the repository, it is called a Repository Custom Function. It retains its link to the report custom function. If a repository custom function is added to a report, it becomes a Report Custom Function and the link is retained. Only report custom functions can be created, edited, or used in formulas.

- To edit a custom function, you must disconnect it from the repository.
- The Custom Function Extractor creates a custom function from an existing formula.
- The code for custom functions cannot use fields, print time functions, or global variables.
- Custom functions can return ranges and arrays in addition to simple data types.
- Custom functions can be used in formula fields or other custom functions.
- The Formula Expert can be used to easily create a formula based on a custom function.

Questions

Questions may have more than one correct answer. Choose all answers that apply.

1. If Convert Other NULL Values to Default is checked, then
   a. NULL numeric formulas will return zero.
   b. NULL string formulas will return blank.
   c. NULL numeric database fields will display as zero.
   d. NULL string database fields will display as blank.

2. What is the result of the following formula if Quantity is NULL, Price is $1.50, and all report options are at their defaults?
   ```
   {Quantity}*{Price}
   ```
   a. Zero
   b. $1.50
   c. NULL
   d. An error
   e. 1

3. There are three records in a report. The values of FieldA are 100, NULL, and 50. You insert a summary on FieldA and choose Average. What will the average be?
   a. 75
   b. 50
   c. NULL
   d. An error
   e. Zero

4. The following is a valid formula.
   ```
   UpperCase(LowerCase('Yesterday'))
   ```
   a. True
   b. False

5. You should limit the use of print state functions when possible, because

   a. They require more resources than normal functions.

   b. They must be evaluated during Pass 2.

   c. Their value changes depending on the printer selected.

   d. They cannot be pushed to the server.

6. Which print state function, when used in the selection formula, can be passed to a SQL database server?

   a. IsNull

   b. NextIsNull

   c. PreviousIsNull

   d. RecordNumber

   e. OnFirstRecord

7. Which functions will return the size of an array?

   a. UpperBound

   b. UBound

   c. Count

   d. Last

   e. SizeOf

8. A For loop always executes a set number of times.

   a. True

   b. False

9. Which statement always executes *StatementList* at least once?

   a. While Do

   b. Do While

10. If you use a While Do loop and forget to use any code that modifies the test condition, what will happen?

    a. The loop will run until the system memory is exhausted.

    b. You will get an error.

    c. The loop will execute 100,000 times and then stop.

11. You have a multivalue parameter. How do you print the parameter values?

    a. Use Minimum and Maximum.

    b. Use Join.

    c. Use Split.

    d. Loop through and concatenate the values together.

    e. Just place the parameter field on the report.

12. Custom functions are created in the repository and then used in reports.

    a. True

    b. False

13. Report custom functions can be used in

    a. Formula fields

    b. Report custom functions

    c. Record selection formulas

    d. Formatting formulas

    e. Group selection formulas

14. Add custom functions to the repository

    a. To encapsulate business logic

    b. To share them with other developers

    c. To implement standards

    d. To make report maintenance easier

    e. To speed report processing

15. The following items are allowed in custom functions

    a. Print time functions

    b. Field references

    c. Local variables

    d. Global variables

    e. References to other custom functions

16. The Extractor can create a custom function from any formula.

    a. True

    b. False

17. The default scope of variables declared in custom functions is local.

    a. True

    b. False

18. Custom function arguments cannot

    a. Be simple data types

    b. Be arrays

    c. Be optional

PART III

    d. Have default values

    e. Be separated by semicolons

Answers

1. **a, b.** The "Other" option does not apply to database fields.

2. **c.** A NULL in a formula statement will cause the result to be NULL unless an option is set telling Crystal Reports to treat NULLs as the default value.

3. **a.** The NULL value will be ignored, so the average will be (100 + 50) / 2, or 75.

4. **a.** True. It does not make much sense, but you can nest functions in this manner.

5. **b.** Print state functions are evaluated during Pass 2. (They cannot be pushed to the server, either, but no Crystal Reports formula field can.)

6. **a.** For many database types, the IsNull function is passed to the server when it is used in a selection formula.

7. **b, c.** UBound and Count will both return the size of an array.

8. **b.** False. A For loop may not complete its iterations if an Exit For is encountered.

9. **b.** Do While will always execute *StatementList* at least once.

10. **c.** The default loop maximum is 100,000; you can change it with the Option Loop statement.

11. **b, d.** A multivalue parameter is stored in an array, so you can use the Join function or manually loop through it to concatenate the values.

12. **b.** Custom functions must be created in a report.

13. **All.** Report custom functions can be used in any of the listed formulas.

14. **b, c, d.** Adding custom functions to the repository will not speed report processing. Even report custom functions encapsulate business logic.

15. **c, e.** Local variables and references to other custom functions are allowed in custom functions.

16. **b.** False. The Extractor cannot create a custom function from a formula that contains any items not allowed in custom functions, such as global variables or print time functions.

17. **a.** True. Unlike regular formulas, the default scope of variables in custom functions is local.

18. **e.** Custom function arguments are separated by commas.

The Database Expert

Exam RDCR300 expects you to be able to

- Describe the Database Expert
- Understand the Database Expert tabs
- Link multiple tables
- Apply joins
- Create a report from a SQL Command
- Create a report from a Business View

As you know from earlier chapters, the Database Expert is where you connect to databases and choose tables to use in the report. You will explore the Database Expert in depth in this chapter.

You open the Database Expert by selecting Database | Database Expert or by clicking the Database Expert button shown here. The Database Expert also appears when you create a new report or select Database Expert from the right-click menu of the Field Explorer with any node of the Database Fields folder selected. The Database Expert has two tabs: the Data tab and the Links tab. The Links tab will be visible only if more than one table is selected in the Data tab.

Data Tab

The Data tab contains two list boxes, as shown in Figure 18-1. The list box on the left displays Available Data Sources; the list box on the right will contain the tables selected for use in this report. Tables are moved from one list box to the other using the arrow keys or by dragging. You can simultaneously connect to as many data sources as you like using the Database Expert. No matter how many data sources you are connected to, the report will access only the data sources necessary for the fields you insert into the report or that are otherwise used in the report.

Folders

The Available Data Sources list box contains a tree view with several folders, as you can see in Figure 18-1. Some folders are used to contain different types of data sources. Other folders categorize data connections so that you can more easily use them in the future.

Figure 18-1
Viewing data
sources and
options

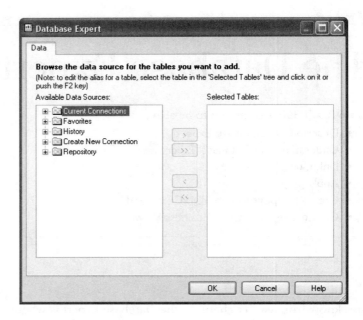

Opening a data source may display tables directly or other folders. You may see folders that organize all the tables, views, and stored procedures together. In databases that use the schema concept, you will see the list of schema names, and under each schema name, you will see tables or the list of Tables, Views, and Stored Procedures folders. You may also see a folder called Qualifiers. This folder is used to hold packages that contain individual stored procedures. In all cases, the lowest level, or *leaf*, entries in the tree are individual entities that you can move into the Selected Tables list and use in your report.

Current Connections

The Current Connections folder lists all the data sources that you are currently connected to. This illustration shows connections to the Xtreme Business View and the Xtreme Sample Database 10. Connections stay current until the Crystal Reports session ends, you specifically log off, or you are disconnected by the database. You can create or modify multiple reports without reconnecting to the database each time.

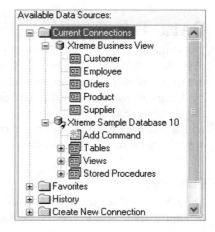

Favorites

The Favorites folder contains any data sources that you have copied there. If you right-click a data source, the shortcut menu contains the option to add it to the Favorites folder. Since favorites are shortcuts to specific data sources, not data source types, you must completely configure the data source before you can add it to the Favorites folder. For some data sources, this means you must connect to the data source. For example, to add an ODBC data source to the Favorites folder, you must click the Make New Connection node and pick an ODBC DSN. The DSN will be added to the ODBC folder, and you can then right-click and add it to the Favorites folder. At this point, you are connected to the ODBC data source. If you wanted to make a native Oracle connection a favorite, you would open the Oracle Server folder and connect to an Oracle instance. The Oracle data source would appear under the Oracle Server folder, and you could add it to the Favorites folder. The History folder contains data sources that are completely configured, so any entry in the History folder can be added to the Favorites folder, whether it is currently connected or not. Business Views cannot be added to the Favorites folder.

 EXAM TIP   For the exam, consider that Database File data sources require a connection before they can be added to the Favorites folder and that ODBC data sources do not.

History

The History folder lists the last five data sources that you have connected to. This list is maintained even if Crystal Reports is closed. You can reconnect quickly to a recently used data source by finding it in the History folder.

Create New Connection

The Create New Connection folder lists all the possible connection types that you can create. These are dependent on the options that you chose during the installation of Crystal Reports—and in some cases on whether the appropriate database drivers, ODBC DSNs, and so on, exist on your system. Each folder under the Create New Connection folder represents a type of data source. Opening one of the folders for the first time will display the connection dialog box for that type of data source. If at least one connection for a data source type already exists, it will be displayed under the data source type's folder, and a node called Make New Connection will also be added, as shown here. To create other new connections for the same data source type, select the Make New Connection node.

 NOTE   You may have heard the term *native* applied to some connection types. *Native* is used to distinguish connection types that do not use ODBC from those that do. For many database types, it is possible to connect using an ODBC driver or natively. Other than the possible exception for Wire Protocol ODBC drivers, a native connection is usually faster and more feature rich.

Repository

The Repository folder displays connections to SQL Commands and Business Views stored in the repository, as shown here. When you first open the folder or when you select Make New Connection, the Crystal Enterprise Explorer dialog box, shown in Figure 18-2, is displayed. You can browse the repository content there. Only SQL Commands and Business Views are available for use as data sources; other repository objects are not displayed. You can select SQL Commands or Business Views to use as data sources, just as you can select a database table.

Add Command

If you are connected to a data source that allows queries to be used as data sources, you will see the Add Command option under the data source's folder and before the Tables folder, as shown here. The Add Command option is used to create a SQL query in the connected database's own SQL syntax. Crystal Reports will send the query to the database without any modification other than the substitution of current values for parameters embedded in the query.

If you understand the query language of the database, you can create commands containing more complex queries than Crystal Reports can generate by itself. You can take advantage of SQL options, such as the UNION set operator, that Crystal Reports cannot

Figure 18-2

Selecting SQL
Commands and
Business Views

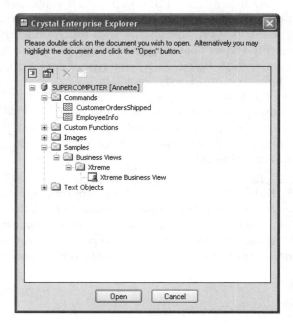

create using regular data sources. You can, in many cases, use existing queries that have been built in other query tools by business analysts.

A few of the Crystal Reports native drivers—specifically DB2, Sybase, and Informix—do not support the Add Command feature. The Add Command is supported for other native drivers, for ODBC, and for some desktop databases such as Access.

After the command is created, you can select it as a data source, the same as you would a table. If it contains parameters, their values will be prompted for immediately because Crystal Reports must execute the query once to obtain the field list to display in the Field Explorer. Chapter 22 covers SQL Commands in detail.

Data Sources Shortcut Menu

Right-clicking any object in the Available Data Sources list box displays this shortcut menu. Items not applicable to the object that is currently selected will be grayed out.

Add to Report   If the selected object is a leaf node, such as a table or view, the Add to Report option will be available; selecting it will cause the object to be copied to the Selected Tables list. The object is copied to the Selected Tables list, not moved. It is not removed from the Available Data Sources list, and the same object can be added to the Selected Tables list multiple times.

 NOTE   You can select tables from multiple data sources for use in a single report, but it is not recommended. Linking between the disparate data sources will be done locally by Crystal Reports in this situation, and performance will suffer. Record selection may also need to be performed locally. Crystal Enterprise Business Views may be appropriate in this situation. Business Views are discussed in Chapter 27.

Add to Favorites   If the selected object is a connected data source, an entry for it can be added to the Favorites folder. It is not removed from its original location; instead, another listing for it is added to the Favorites folder. The entry that is added to the Favorites folder is a specific connection, not the data source type. The values other than logon credentials needed to make the connection are saved with the Favorites entry, saving you considerable time if you use the same connection repeatedly.

Remove from Report   Remove from Report is the opposite of Add to Report; it removes the selected data source from the Selected Tables list.

Properties   Choosing the Properties option for a data source displays the Properties dialog box. The contents of the dialog box differ depending on the type of the data source.

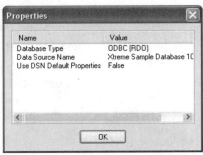

Rename Favorite   If you select a data source in the Favorites folder, the option to rename it is available. Renaming a favorite can be very helpful, since the names that Crystal Reports uses may not be user friendly. In addition, if you want to add two connections to the same database to the Favorites folder, you must rename the existing one; Crystal Reports will not allow two favorites with the same name.

Delete Favorite   Delete Favorite removes the entry for the connection from the Favorites folder but does not remove it from other folders.

Remove from Repository   Remove from Repository removes the object from the repository.

Rename Repository Object   The Rename Repository Object command allows you to rename the object.

Options   Selecting Options displays the Database Options dialog box. This is the same as the Database tab of the File | Options dialog box; it is discussed in the "Options—Database Tab" section.

Refresh   Choosing Refresh causes Crystal Reports to reload the Available Data Sources list. For example, you may need to refresh if you have added favorites and they are not appearing under the Favorites folder or if stored procedures have been added to the data source and they are not appearing in the list.

Options—Database Tab

The Database tab of the Options dialog box, shown in Figure 18-3, can be displayed in two ways. You can use the File | Options method and click the Database tab, or you can choose the Options command from the Database Expert shortcut menu. These options control both the appearance of the data source in the Database Expert and the processing of the report query.

Tables and Fields

Items in the Tables and Fields section configure how tables and fields are displayed in Crystal Reports:

- **Show Name**   Show Name is the default; it causes Crystal Reports to display only the table or field name.

- **Show Description**   The Show Description option displays the description associated with tables and fields for Business Views, OLAP data, and ERP data.

- **Show Both**   The Show Both option displays both the object name and its description.

- **Sort Tables Alphabetically**   Sort Tables Alphabetically is checked by default; it causes Crystal Reports to display tables in alphabetical order. If this setting is cleared, table names are displayed in the order they are retrieved from the database.

Figure 18-3
Choosing display
and processing
options

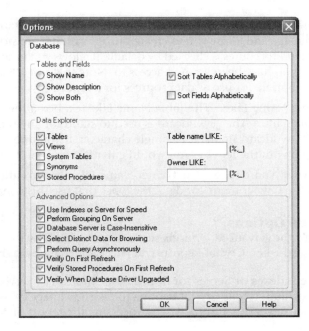

- **Sort Fields Alphabetically**   Sort Fields Alphabetically is not checked by
  default. Checking it causes Crystal Reports to display fields in alphabetical
  order under their table name folder. If this setting is cleared, field names are
  displayed in the order they are retrieved from the database.

Data Explorer

Options in the Data Explorer section determine which database objects are displayed in
the Database Expert:

- **Tables**   Tables is checked by default. It causes Crystal Reports to include regular
  tables in the Database Explorer listings.

- **Views**   Views is also checked by default. It causes Crystal Reports to include
  views in the Database Explorer listings.

- **System Tables**   Checking System Tables causes Crystal Reports to display the
  database's own internal tables, such as the catalog tables. System Tables is not
  checked by default. You must also be granted the right to view system tables
  before they will appear in the list.

- **Synonyms**   Some databases allow objects to have aliases or synonyms. Checking
  Synonyms causes the alias to display in the Database Explorer along with the true
  name of the object. Synonyms is not checked by default.

- **Stored Procedures**   Some database types have an internal programming language and allow you to create procedures that are stored in the database. Stored Procedures is checked by default; it allows you to see any stored procedures that you have been granted access to. Note that not all stored procedures are appropriate for use as data sources for a report.

- **Table Name Like**   The Table Name Like text box allows you to enter a filter for table names. The % wildcard is used to stand for any number of characters, and the _ wildcard stands for a single character. If you only want to see tables that begin with the letter P, you would enter P% into the Table Name Like text box.

- **Owner Name Like**   The Owner Name Like text box allows you to create a filter on the Owner name for database types that use this concept.

Advanced Options

Options in the Advanced Options section determine how the database queries will be executed and when Crystal Reports will check for changes in the database structure:

- **Use Indexes or Server for Speed**   Use Indexes or Server for Speed is checked by default. It tells Crystal Reports to take advantage of database indexes and other server capabilities when processing the report query.

NOTE   SQL databases will use indexes when processing the query, whether or not this option is checked.

- **Perform Grouping on the Server**   Perform Grouping on the Server is not checked by default. If this option is checked and no detail records are displayed in the report, the detail rows will not be retrieved from the database; instead, only the group-level items (group values and summary values) will be retrieved, enhancing report execution times. If any detail sections of the report are visible, this option will have no effect.

- **Database Server is Case-Insensitive**   This option controls whether Crystal Reports does any further filtering of records when there is a selection formula involving string matching. If the database server is configured to be case sensitive, then it will return only those records whose values match exactly to the comparison value, including their case. So a search for "brown" will not return a record whose value is "Brown." If the database server is set to be case sensitive, then this option will have no effect. On the other hand, if the database server is configured to be case insensitive, it would return both "brown" and "Brown." Checking Database Server is Case-Insensitive will cause Crystal Reports to use both "brown" and "Brown" in the report. Clearing this option will cause Crystal Reports to filter the data further and use only "brown" in the report.

- **Select Distinct Data for Browsing**   Field data can be browsed in Crystal Reports to help you better understand the field, to create the proper formatting for it, and so on. When field data is browsed, up to 500 field values are retrieved from the database. If Select Distinct Data for Browsing is checked, the first 500 unique field values are requested from the database. If this option is cleared, the first 500 records (regardless of field value) are requested from the database, and Crystal Reports displays the unique values from among those records. If by chance all of the first 500 records had the same field value, only one unique value would be displayed in the browse dialog box.

- **Perform Query Asynchronously**   This option allows a query to be processed asynchronously. The main advantage of this option (for database types that allow it) is that it enables you to cancel long-running queries without having to wait for the complete retrieval of all the report data.

- **Verify on First Refresh**   Setting this option causes Crystal Reports to verify and update the database structures the first time a report not based on stored procedures is refreshed. If database changes have been made that affect the report, such as the dropping of a field used in the report, then the report will need to be modified to account for the changes.

- **Verify Stored Procedures on First Refresh**   Setting this option causes database verification for reports based on stored procedures the first time the reports are refreshed.

- **Verify When Database Driver Upgraded**   This option causes a database verification if the database driver is changed.

NOTE   The advanced options can be overridden for an individual report using the Report Options dialog box. Choose File | Report Options to display it.

Selected Tables Shortcut Menu

The shortcut menu for items in the Selected Tables list varies depending on the object type. For commands, the Edit Command, View Command, Add to Repository, and Disconnect from Repository options are available. For other objects such as tables and views, only Rename and Properties are available.

Rename   Crystal Reports creates an alias for all tables, views, stored procedures, and so on that are used in a report. By default, the alias is the same as the table name. If the same table is added to the Selected Tables list more than once, an underscore and number is appended to the table name. You can change the table alias to anything you want by choosing the Rename option.

Properties   The Properties option displays the properties for the data source. These are the data source properties and are the same for every table used from the same data source.

Edit Command   Select the Edit Command option to display the Modify Command dialog box, where you can modify the SQL query in the command.

View Command   Choosing View Command displays the View Command dialog box. You can see the text of the SQL query there, but you cannot modify it.

Add to Repository   The Add to Repository option displays the Add Item dialog box, where you can connect the SQL Command to the repository.

Disconnect from Repository   Selecting Disconnect from Repository disconnects the SQL Command from the repository, allowing you to edit it. You must add it back to the repository if you want any changes reflected in the repository version of the command.

Exercise 18.1: Viewing System Tables

1. Create a new report using the Standard wizard. Use the Employee table and put the Employee ID, First Name, and Last Name fields on the report.

2. Open the Database Expert. Note that a report must be open to access the Database Expert, even though connections are maintained if all report files are closed.

3. Right-click the Xtreme CRCP data source, and choose Options.

4. Check System Tables, and click OK.

5. Notice that there is now a System Tables folder under the Xtreme CRCP data source. Open the System Tables folder, and browse the tables listed there. You could now use those tables in a report.

6. Save the report as **Exercise 18.1**.

Exercise 18.2: Using Table Aliases

1. Open the Exercise 18.1 report.

2. Open the Database Expert.

3. Add the Employee table to the Selected Tables list again. You will receive a message saying that the Employee table has already been added and verifying that you want to add it again. Click Yes.

4. You will see Employee and Employee_1 in the Selected Tables list. You are going to use the second instance of the Employee table to get the supervisor's name, so right-click Employee_1, click Rename, and enter **Supervisor**.

5. Click the Links tab.

6. Click the Clear Links button, and choose Yes from the message box.

7. Link Supervisor ID in the Employee table to Employee ID in the Supervisor table.

8. Click OK to close the Database Expert.

9. Click OK to refresh the report.

10. Add the Last Name field from the Supervisor table to the report, and change the field heading to **Supervisor**.

11. Save the report as **Exercise 18.2**.

Links Tab

The Links tab of the Database Expert is used to define the links between tables. The Links tab appears if more than one table is added to the Selected Tables list on the Data tab.

Link Display Area

Each table that has been selected is displayed in the Links tab with a default linking already created. Indexed fields in each table are indicated by colored flags next to them. The link is represented by a line connecting a field in one table to a field in another table, as shown in Figure 18-4.

Creating Links Manually

To create a link, select the link field in the first table, hold down the left mouse button, and move the mouse cursor over the link field in the second table. Then release the mouse button, and the link will be created. Links can only be created between fields of the same data type.

Field Shortcut Menu

Selecting a field in any of the displayed tables and right-clicking will cause a shortcut menu to appear. The two options on the menu are Browse Field and External Indexes.

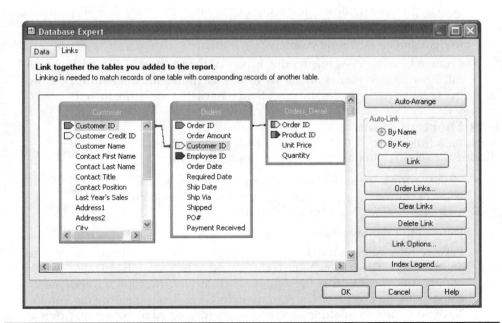

Figure 18-4 Viewing default links in the Database Expert

Selecting Browse Field will display a dialog box containing information about the field. The name of the field is displayed in the title of the dialog box. The data type and length are shown below the title, and a sample of the field contents is displayed in a list box.

Display Area Shortcut Menu

Right-clicking anywhere in the link display area other than on a field or a link opens the corresponding shortcut menu. The options work as follows:

- **Smart Linking by Key** uses foreign key information to link the tables.

- **Smart Linking by Name** links the tables using identically named fields in pairs of tables.

- **Clear Links** removes all existing links.

- **Order Links** displays the Order Links dialog box, where you can change the order in which links are processed. See "Options—Link Tab" for more information.

- **Index Legend** displays the Index Legend dialog box.

- **Locate Table** displays the Locate Table dialog box, which lists all the tables. Selecting a table name in the list highlights that table in the link display area.

- **Rearrange Tables** causes the tables to rearrange so that the links go from left to right and all tables are visible.

- **Change Linking View** toggles the display of field names within tables on and off. Turning field names off allows you to see more tables at a time, as shown in Figure 18-5, but hides the exact field names that are being linked.

Link Shortcut Menu

Selecting a link causes it to display as a wider blue line. Right-clicking the selected link displays the corresponding menu:

- **Link Options** opens the Link Options dialog box, where you can choose the type of link you want to use. See "Join and Link Options," later in this chapter.

- **Delete Link** removes the selected link.

- **Reverse Link** changes the direction of the link. A link goes from one table to another table. The starting table is considered to be the left-hand table, and the ending table is considered the right-hand table. Link direction is important when using Left Outer or Right Outer joins, enforcing joins using only the From or To options, and when using link types other than equal or not equal. (Joins are described in the "Join and Link Options" section, later in this chapter.)

- **Remove All Links** deletes the selected link.

Figure 18-5
Viewing links with
field names not
displayed

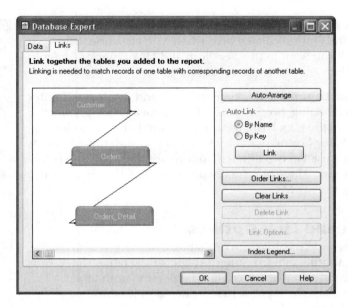

PART III

Options—Link Tab

Many of the actions that were described in the "Link Shortcut Menu" section are also available via buttons on the Link tab.

Auto-Arrange   Clicking the Auto-Arrange button causes Crystal Reports to re-arrange the tables displayed in the link display area such that links go from left to right and all tables are visible.

Auto-Link   The Auto-Link panel has two options: By Name or By Key. Choosing By Name causes Crystal Reports to create links based on identical field names in different tables. Selecting By Key causes Crystal Reports to use foreign key information to link the tables.

Order Links   The Order Links button is available if more than one link exists (more than two tables are linked). Selecting Order Links displays the Order Links dialog box, where you can change the order in which links are processed. Link order is not important if you are using inner joins and equal link types, but it can affect the resulting data

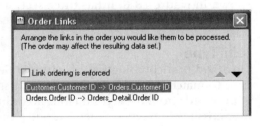

set if you use outer joins or nonequal join types (see "Join and Link Options," later in this chapter).

Clear Links   Clicking the Clear Links button removes all existing links.

Delete Link   Clicking Delete Link removes the selected link. This button is available only when a link is selected.

Link Options Clicking the Link Options button displays the Link Options dialog box, where you can choose the type of link you want to use. See "Join and Link Options," later in this chapter.

Index Legend Clicking Index Legend displays the Index Legend dialog box. Colored flags appear next to indexed fields in the Link Display Area, as shown here. The Index Legend dialog box maps a color to the index. Most notably, fields that are used in two different indexes display with both colors in the flag. These are usually primary key fields that are also foreign key fields.

Join and Link Options

A *join* causes records from one table to be merged with records from another table, creating a single virtual table. The records of the virtual table can contain fields from both tables.

For example, suppose that the two simple tables shown here are joined. The resulting virtual table could contain all the fields from both tables. The joined virtual table could have records that contain Order.Order ID, Order.Product ID, Order.Quantity, Product.Product ID, and Product.Product Name. The columns that will exist in the result set are database fields that are displayed on the report or needed for any computations or groupings.

The rows contained in the result set are dependent on the link options. Clicking the Link Options button on the Links tab displays the Link Options dialog box for the selected link, as shown in Figure 18-6. It has three sections that control the processing of the link.

Order Table

Order ID	Product ID	Quantity
47	12	3
48	3	1
49	5	10
50	10	2
51	3	4

Product Table

Product ID	Quantity
3	Stapler
5	Pencil
9	Pen
12	Ruler

Join Type

One field or a combination of multiple fields is used to match up the records from the first table with records from the second table, according to the join type and link type. There are four possible join types: inner, left outer, right outer, and full outer.

Inner Join The virtual table created from an inner join will contain only records in which the join type condition was satisfied—that is, where a record from the first table matched a record from the second table according to the join type. If an inner join using an equal link type on the Product ID field is done from the Order to the Product table defined earlier, the resulting set will look like the following. Inner join is the default join type for all SQL databases, any ODBC data source, and some desktop databases.

Order.Order ID	Order.Product ID	Order.Quantity	Product.Product ID	Product.Product Name
47	12	3	12	Ruler
48	3	1	3	Stapler
49	5	10	5	Pencil
51	3	4	3	Stapler

Left Outer Join   In a left outer join, in addition to the result set of an inner join, all records from the left-hand table that did not have a match in the right-hand table will be added to the result set. For the records from the left-hand table that had no match in the right-hand table, the value of any field in the resulting virtual table that came from the right-hand table will be NULL. If a left outer join is done from Order to Product, the result will look like the following. A left outer join is the default for some desktop databases.

Order.Order ID	Order.Product ID	Order.Quantity	Product.Product ID	Product.Product Name
47	12	3	12	Ruler
48	3	1	3	Stapler
49	5	10	5	Pencil
50	10	2	NULL	NULL
51	3	4	3	Stapler

Figure 18-6

Selecting link and join options

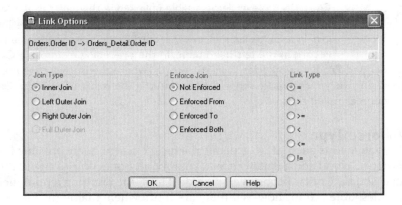

Right Outer Join   A right outer join is similar to a left outer join, except that all records from the right-hand table will be in the result set whether or not they had a match in the left-hand table. If a right outer join is done from Order to Product, the result will look like the following. Right outer joins are commonly used for data quality checking, to find child records that have no parent record.

Order.Order ID	Order.Product ID	Order.Quantity	Product.Product ID	Product.Product Name
47	12	3	12	Ruler
48	3	1	3	Stapler
49	5	10	5	Pencil
51	3	4	3	Stapler
NULL	NULL	NULL	9	Pen

Full Outer Join   A full outer join will contain the inner join result set plus any records from both tables that did not match given the link type, as shown here.

Order.Order ID	Order.Product ID	Order.Quantity	Product.Product ID	Product.Product Name
47	12	3	12	Ruler
48	3	1	3	Stapler
49	5	10	5	Pencil
50	10	2	NULL	NULL
51	3	4	3	Stapler
NULL	NULL	NULL	9	Pen

CAUTION   Never leave a table unlinked in the Link tab. If a table is selected for use in a report but is not linked to any other table, it will cause a *Cartesian join*. In a Cartesian join, every record in the right-hand table is joined to every record in the left-hand table. In the preceding example, a Cartesian join of Order and Product would result in 20 records, where the majority are nonsense. Cartesian joins only very rarely make sense; they are usually the result of an error. Cartesian joins are sometimes called *cross joins*.

Enforce Type

Crystal Reports attempts to generate the most efficient query possible for your report. For instance, if you add a data source to your report but never use any of the fields from that data source, Crystal Reports will exclude it from the resulting report query. This is usually the desirable action; however, there are times when a table may be needed in a query merely to act as a link to other tables. In this case, even though you do not directly use any fields from the table, it must be left in the query to obtain the correct result. The Enforce Type settings are used to modify Crystal Reports' default behavior and keep the tables in the query.

- **Not Enforced** This is the default option. It lets Crystal Reports remove any tables from the query if none of their fields is used in the report.

- **Enforced From** If fields from the right-hand table (the "to" table) are in the report, but no fields from the left-hand table are used, this option guarantees that the left-hand table (the "from" table) will still be included in the report query.

- **Enforced To** If fields from the left-hand table ("from") are in the report, but no fields from the right-hand table are used, this option guarantees that the right-hand table ("to") will still be included in the report query.

- **Enforced Both** If at least one field from either the left-hand table or right-hand table is used in the report, the option will guarantee that both tables are included in the report query.

Link Type

By far the most commonly used link type is the equal (=) link. You will rarely need to use any other type. The equal link type causes the join to happen when the value in the link field from the left-hand table is identical to the value in the link field in the right-hand table.

The other link types (see Figure 18-6) are used in only very special circumstances. The not-equal (!=) link type, for example, creates merged records only when the link fields *do not* match. Think back to a Cartesian join, in which every record in the left-hand table is joined to every record in the right-hand table. An equal join would filter the result of a Cartesian join to only those records where the link fields were identical. A not-equal join would be all the other Cartesian join records.

The other link types are similar. For each type, assume you are starting with a Cartesian join and then removing all the records where the relationship between the link fields does not satisfy the link type. For example, for a greater than (>) link, all records where the value of the link field in the left-hand table is greater than that of the link field in the right-hand table will be retained.

Exercise 18.3: Using a Left Outer Join

1. Open the report from Exercise 18.2.

2. Open the Database Expert.

3. Click the Links tab.

4. Select the link, and click the Link Options button.

5. In the Link Options dialog box, select Left Outer Join.

6. Click OK three times to return to the report.

7. Notice that employee number 2, Andrew Fuller, has appeared on the report even though he has no matching supervisor record.

8. Save the report as **Exercise 18.3**.

Exercise 18.4: Using a Right Outer Join

1. Open the Exercise 18.3 report, and preview it.

2. Note that all 15 employees appear once on the report and each employee's supervisor is listed, even if the entry is NULL.

3. Open the Database Expert.

4. Click the Links tab.

5. Select the link, and click the Link Options button.

6. In the Link Options dialog box, select Right Outer Join.

7. Click OK three times to return to the report.

8. Notice the changes in the report. With a left outer join, you saw each employee once along with his or her supervisor. With the right outer join, you are seeing a record for the combination of each supervisor and all the employees that report to that supervisor. Some employees are not supervisors, so they show up as NULL employee fields.

 NOTE You could have accomplished the same thing by reversing the link direction, except that the employees who were not supervisors would not have appeared in the Supervisor field.

9. Save the report as **Exercise 18.4**.

Chapter Review

The Database Expert, including all its options and features, was described in this chapter. In addition, your options when linking data sources together for the report were covered.

Quick Tips

- The Database Expert is used to connect to data sources. It is also used to select and link the tables, views, stored procedures, SQL Commands, and Business Views to be used in the report.

- The Available Data Sources list contains five folders: Current Connections, Favorites, History, Create New Connection, and Repository. Current Connections contains all currently connected data sources. You can add and delete data sources from the Favorites folder for quick access. History contains the last five data sources that were connected. Create New Connection is used to create a new data source connection. Repository lists SQL Commands and Business Views stored in the repository that can be used in reports.

- When you use tables, views, and stored procedures as data sources, Crystal Reports generates the report query for you. If you use a SQL Command, you must write the query or use one created by another developer. If you use a Business View, logic stored in the repository is used. You cannot edit a Crystal Reports–generated query in version 10 (although you could in versions prior to 9). You can edit SQL Commands.

- Right-clicking a data source in the Database Expert will display a menu that you can use to add data sources to the report or the Favorites folders, delete data sources from the Favorites folder, rename favorites, display data source properties, rename or remove data sources from the repository, refresh the Data Sources list, and display a data source's Options dialog box.

- A data source's Options dialog box settings control how tables and fields appear in the Database Expert, what database objects are displayed, and how the report query is processed.

- Tables, views, and stored procedures appear by default. You must check the appropriate option to see system tables and synonyms.

- The list of database objects can be filtered using the Table Name Like and Owner Name Like options.

- All database objects are given aliases in Crystal Reports. By default, the alias is the same as the table name. A number is added to the alias if you select the same table more than once. You can change the alias using the Rename command on the right-click menu for the Selected Tables list of the Database Expert.

- The right-click menu for the Selected Tables list also allows you to view and edit SQL Commands and to add or disconnect a SQL Command from the repository.

- The Links tab of the Database Expert is used to define how related tables should be joined.

- Links are created with the Auto-Link option or manually, by using the mouse to connect a field in one table to a field in another table. Auto-Link can link by matching field names or using defined database keys.

- Each link must have a join type. The default join type is inner, which retains only records from each table that match on the join field. If there are multiple matching records, there will be multiple occurrences of the matching records in the result set.

- A left outer join will retain all records from the left-hand table and matching records from the right-hand table.

- A right outer join will retain all records from the right-hand table and matching records from the left-hand table. It is commonly used to find orphaned child records.

- A full outer join will retain all records from each table.

- A link must have a link type. The default link type is an equal link. In an equal link, the link fields must be equal. Other link types such as not equal, greater than, less than, and so on are possible, but are rarely used.

- Clicking the Index Legend button will display a legend defining the colored tabs next to the indexed fields in the tables.

Questions

Some questions have more than one correct answer. Choose all answers that apply.

1. The Database Expert can be displayed by

   a. Clicking the Database Expert button

   b. Creating a new report as a blank report

   c. Creating a new report with the Standard wizard

   d. Selecting Database Expert from the right-click menu of the Database Fields folder of the Field Explorer

   e. Selecting Database | Database Expert

2. Which of the following data source types are selected for use in a report via the Database Expert?

   a. Tables

   b. Views

   c. Stored procedures

   d. SQL Commands

   e. Business Views

3. The Current Connections folder lists

   a. Data sources used in the active report file

   b. Data sources used in all open report files

   c. Connected data sources for the active report file

   d. Connected data sources for all open report files

   e. All connected data sources

4. The Current Connections folder will list the most recently used data source.

   a. True

   b. False

5. SQL Command data sources are available only from the Repository folder.

   a. True

   b. False

6. Business View data sources are available only from the Repository folder.

   a. True

   b. False

7. Data sources in the Favorites folder can be renamed.

   a. True

   b. False

8. Which database objects appear by default in the Database Expert?

    a. Tables

    b. Views

    c. System tables

    d. Synonyms

    e. Stored procedures

9. The same table can be used only once in a report.

    a. True

    b. False

10. If you want the result set to contain only the records from each table that match on the link fields, which join type would you use?

    a. Inner join

    b. Left outer join

    c. Right outer join

    d. Full outer join

11. If you want the result set to contain all the records from each table, whether they match on the link fields or not, which join type would you use?

    a. Inner join

    b. Left outer join

    c. Right outer join

    d. Full outer join

12. Which join type is used to ensure that all records from the parent table are retained?

    a. Inner join

    b. Left outer join

    c. Right outer join

    d. Full outer join

13. Which join type is commonly used to find child records that have no matching parent records?

    a. Inner join

    b. Left outer join

    c. Right outer join

    d. Full outer join

14. The default join type when connecting to Oracle differs if you use ODBC or native connections.

   a. True

   b. False

15 The Add Command is not supported for which of the following database types?

   a. Oracle

   b. DB2

   c. SQL Server

   d. Informix

   e. Sybase

Answers

1. **a, b, d, e.** The Data screen of the Standard wizard is displayed when you use the report creation wizards, not the Database Expert.

2. **All.** All data source types are selected with the Database Expert.

3. **e.** The Current Connections folder lists all connected data sources, whether or not any report file that uses it is open.

4. **b.** Current Connections will only list it if it is still connected. The History folder will display the most recently used data source, whether or not it is connected.

5. **b.** False. SQL Commands are available from the Repository folder and most SQL database data sources.

6. **a.** True. Business View data sources are only available in the Repository folder.

7. **a.** True. Data sources in the Favorites folder can be renamed.

8. **a, b, e.** System tables and synonyms do not display by default.

9. **b.** False. A table can be selected more than once. Each occurrence is given a new alias.

10. **a.** An inner join will retain only the records that matched on the join field.

11. **d.** A full outer join will retain all the records from each table, whether they match on the link fields or not.

12. **b.** A left outer join retains all records from the left-hand or parent table.

13. **c.** Right outer joins are used to find orphaned child records.

14. **b.** The default join type for native connections to SQL databases is inner, and the default join type for ODBC is also inner.

15. **b, d, e.** The Add Command option is not supported for DB2, Informix, or Sybase.

Data Sources

Exam RDCR300 expects you to be able to

- Understand ODBC versus native data connections
- Configure ODBC
- Apply database changes

Connecting to a data source is the first step in report creation. The data is the primary building block and essential element of all reports. Crystal Reports can use an astonishing array of data source types and several connection methods. Each type-connection combination has different requirements and configuration needs. You need an understanding of the setup, configuration, and connection properties of the commonly used types to be a professional report developer.

Connection Types

There are two general categories of connection types. *Direct* or *native* connections require only the database client drivers and Crystal Reports–specific DLLs for the database type. Non-native connections add another layer of drivers that must be used, and they adhere to a database connectivity standard. The primary example of non-native connections is ODBC, but the category also includes OLE DB and JDBC. Non-native connections use a Crystal Reports DLL for the connectivity standard rather than a specific DLL for the database type.

A single report can use multiple data sources, but this should be avoided if possible. For example, you might need some forecast data from an Excel spreadsheet combined with actual data from a SQL Server database. Using more than one data source prevents Crystal Reports from pushing some processing to the server. For example, if you join a table in one data source to a table in another data source, Crystal Reports must process the join locally.

Native

Native connections are generally faster than non-native connections, although there may be exceptions. They require the installation of fewer components to function. They allow you to use the SQL dialect that is specific to the database type when creating SQL Commands. And native connections use the Crystal Reports drivers specifically written for the database type. (But note that these drivers are not always up-to-date with current upgrades to the database engine.)

Native connections require three layers to function: the Crystal Reports layer, a data translation layer, and the database layer. The Crystal Reports layer is the Crystal Reports engine and is always installed when you install the product. The data translation layer is a DLL or set of DLLs that Crystal Reports supplies for communication with the various databases it supports natively. These are chosen during installation and differ for each database type. The database layer consists of the files, DLLs, and executables required by the database. For example, for Access, the database layer is the .mdb file; for Oracle, it is the Oracle client and the database server; for Paradox, it is the .db file.

For most native connection types, when you install Crystal Reports you need to install only the Crystal Reports data access component for the data source. SQL databases and some of the other database types require that you install the database client as well.

Database Files
Native connections to database files require that you use indexed fields for linking and use a left outer join as the default join type. The data sources in this category include Access, dBase, Excel, XML, Paradox, Btrieve, and Data Link (.udl files).

SQL Databases
The SQL databases that Crystal Reports can access natively are Oracle, Sybase, Informix, and IBM DB2. SQL Server is accessible only via ODBC or OLE DB in Crystal Reports 10. Native access to all SQL databases requires the installation of the database client software.

Other Databases
Other database types that Crystal Reports can connect to natively include ACT!, Exchange, Outlook, Microsoft CRM, XML, and Lotus Domino.

Nondatabase Sources
In addition to the traditional databases, Crystal Reports can use other file types as data sources. These include field definition files (.ttx), COM objects, the Windows file system, and several Windows system log files.

Connectivity Standards
Each database type has unique methods that must be used to attach to, query, and manipulate the data it contains. Programmers, being the impatient and inventive people that they are, quickly tired of learning so many different interfaces and created a standard interface. Each of the connectivity standards works in the same way. A translation layer that converts calls to the standard interface into calls to a specific database is placed between the application and the database, allowing the developer to learn only the standard and yet be able to manipulate any database.

To understand how this works, imagine the translators at the United Nations. In order to understand everything that is said in a meeting, each translator would have to know every language being spoken. Suppose there is a meeting with representatives of the United States, France, Spain, and China. A translator would need to know English, French, Spanish, and Mandarin in order to communicate the meeting content to the U.S. representative. Now suppose instead that as each representative speaks, his or her words are translated into French by a translator. So the Spanish representative's remarks are translated to French, the Chinese representative's remarks are translated to French, and the American representative's remarks are translated to French. Now each translator only needs to know one language in addition to French.

This is exactly how the connectivity standards work. In place of a translator, a database driver exists that can translate the native API of the database into a common standard. Then developers only need to know the common standard to use any database. The analogy can be extended as well. Errors in translation can happen, with unexpected results. An individual database may have features that do not exist in the standard and so are untranslatable. The translation driver may not be up-to-date. Multiple translation drivers may exist, each of which gives different results. Adding the translation layer can slow down processing time. The trade-offs when using a standard must be weighed against the difficulty of learning the native API.

IDAPI

The first data connectivity standard was the Integrated Database Application Programming Interface (IDAPI) created by Borland. Developers using Borland languages could work with any database using the same commands. Borland supplied IDAPI drivers that could connect to any of the major SQL databases. Crystal Reports can use IDAPI via the Borland Database Engine (BDE) for the desktop databases Paradox and dBase.

ODBC

The Open Database Connectivity (ODBC) standard is the most widely used connectivity standard. It was created by Microsoft. Almost every database has an ODBC driver, which allows it to be accessed and manipulated with the ODBC standard commands. Crystal Reports can access any database that has an ODBC driver, although it works best with the ODBC drivers that are supplied with Crystal Reports. For example, to connect to an Oracle database using ODBC, you could use the Oracle ODBC driver for Oracle, the Microsoft ODBC driver for Oracle, or one of the DataDirect ODBC drivers (normal or wire protocol) for Oracle. Crystal Reports licenses the DataDirect drivers and ensures that they are compatible with Crystal Reports. You will get the best results using the DataDirect drivers.

ODBC connectivity from Crystal Reports requires five layers: the Crystal Reports layer, the ODBC translation layer, the ODBC layer, the DBMS translation layer, and the database layer. The Crystal Reports layer and the database layer are the same as for native connections. The ODBC translation layer is a Crystal Reports DLL called crdb_odbc.dll that allows the product to generate ODBC standard SQL queries. The ODBC layer consists of DLLs that are installed with the Windows operating system or the Microsoft Data Access Components (MDAC). The DBMS translation layer consists of the ODBC drivers for specific databases. Crystal Reports supplies DataDirect ODBC drivers for all the

PART III

major SQL databases; these are installed with Crystal Reports if they are selected. The DataDirect ODBC drivers will be prefixed with "CR" to distinguish them from other ODBC drivers for the same databases.

 NOTE The DataDirect ODBC wire protocol drivers do not require the database client to be installed, and they may perform as fast as or faster than the associated native connection types.

OLE DB

OLE DB is similar to ODBC in that a translation layer is required. In addition, OLE DB can be used to access nonrelational data, such as e-mail systems and hierarchical databases. It was created to support modern multitier applications and makes possible the exposure of the database's complete native functionality. OLE DB is the foundation for ActiveX Data Objects (ADO) and ADO.NET.

 NOTE The actual functionality available is dependent on the OLE DB provider.

OLE DB requires four layers: the Crystal Reports layer, the OLE DB consumer layer, the OLE DB provider layer, and the database layer. The Crystal Reports layer and the database layer are identical to the corresponding ODBC layer. The OLE DB consumer is implemented in the Crystal Reports DLL called p2soledb.dll. Crystal Reports does not supply any OLE DB providers.

ADO

ActiveX Data Objects (ADO) adds a COM interface to OLE DB providers. ADO exposes less of the database's native functionality than OLE DB.

JavaBeans and JDBC

Java DataBase Connectivity (JDBC) is similar to ODBC, but ODBC is for the Windows platform, whereas JDBC is for the Java platform. JavaBeans are components used to manipulate databases, similar to ADO.

Business Views

Business Views are Crystal Enterprise components that encapsulate database complexity and present a simpler view of information to the report developer. Business Views are available through the Repository folder of the Database Expert. Business Views are created using the Business View Manager application.

SQL Designer Queries

The Crystal SQL Designer application is no longer supported by Business Objects. However, Crystal Reports can still use the query files generated by SQL Designer as data sources. SQL Designer was used to create queries against ODBC data sources. You could save the data with the query or not, much as you can with a Crystal Report. The SQL Command feature of current Crystal Reports versions can be used instead of SQL Designer to create database queries against both ODBC and native sources.

Crystal Dictionary Files

Crystal dictionary files are no longer supported by Business Objects, but existing dictionary files can still be used as data sources for Crystal Reports. A Crystal dictionary is a simplified view of a database. Business Views replace Crystal dictionary files in the current version of Crystal Reports.

Configuring ODBC Data Sources

Using an ODBC data source in Crystal Reports is a two-step process. The ODBC Data Source Name (DSN) must be created outside of Crystal Reports, and then a new ODBC connection must be created in Crystal Reports using the defined DSN. The only exception is that using connections strings instead of DSNs eliminates the first step.

ODBC data sources require that certain parameters or attributes be supplied before a connection can be made. These attributes are configured in the ODBC Data Source Administrator and stored as DSNs, but they can be supplied directly in Crystal Reports using a connection string. The ODBC Data Source Administrator, along with the other core ODBC DLLs, is usually installed with the operating system. If it has not been installed, it can be installed with Crystal Reports or via Microsoft's latest MDAC version.

DSNs

To create a DSN, open the ODBC Data Source Administrator. This application is usually found in the Control Panel or the Administrator Tools window, depending on your version of Windows. The ODBC Data Source Administrator will open, as shown in Figure 19-1. You can create three types of DSNs: user, system, and file.

Data Sources
(ODBC)

- User DSNs are available only to the user who created them and only on the system where they were created.

- System DSNs are available to anyone logged into the system where they are defined.

- File DSNs are stored in plain text files and are accessible to anyone with read privileges to their disk location. File DSNs will work for anyone who has the ODBC driver that the DSN uses installed.

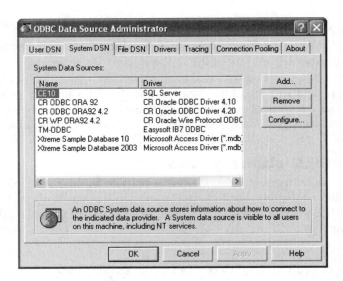

Figure 19-1
Opening the
ODBC Data
Source
Administrator

User and System DSN Tabs

The User DSN and System DSN tabs of the Microsoft ODBC Administrator are identical. The only difference in the resulting DSN is the users who can access it.

- **User/System Data Sources** The main list displayed on the tab is called either User Data Sources or System Data Sources, depending on the tab selected. This list has two columns. The Name column shows the names of existing DSNs. The Driver column shows which ODBC database driver was used to create the DSN.

- **Add** Click the Add button to create a new DSN.

- **Remove** Click the Remove button to delete the selected DSN.

- **Configure** Click the Configure button to modify the properties of the selected DSN.

- **OK** Click OK to apply any changes and close the dialog box.

- **Cancel** Click Cancel to discard any changes and close the dialog box.

- **Apply** Click Apply to apply any changes but leave the dialog box open.

- **Help** Click Help to receive context-sensitive help for the dialog box.

Creating a User or System DSN

From the User DSN or System DSN tab of the ODBC Administrator, click the Add button. The Create New Data Source dialog box will be displayed, as shown in Figure 19-2. A list of all ODBC drivers installed on the system appears. You can scroll to see version and source information for each driver. Note that the drivers prefixed with "CR" are the DataDirect drivers installed with Crystal Reports.

Select the driver that you want to use for the new DSN, and click Finish. A new dialog box specific to the selected driver will appear. This dialog box contains the options that

Figure 19-2
Selecting an
ODBC driver

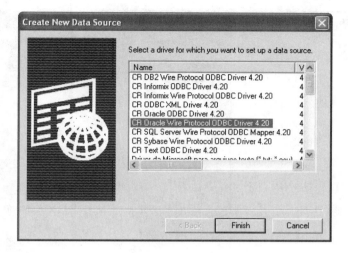

must or can be set for the DSN. The dialog boxes differ depending on the database and the vendor, but most have General, Advanced, and About tabs. Most also have a Test Connection button that can be used to verify that the settings work.

Each DSN requires a name and can have a description, so all the dialog boxes must ask for a data source name and description. The data source name is user definable and will be the name you see in Crystal Reports when creating a new ODBC connection. Databases that require authentication will ask for a user name and password or other authentication method. If you do not enter authentication information in the DSN, it will be requested when the DSN is used. A Help button is available to access the specific requirements of the selected ODBC driver. Depending on the requirements, you may need the assistance of a DBA to create the DSN. When you are finished setting the properties and have successfully tested the connection, click OK to close the dialog box.

Creating a File DSN

Creating a file DSN is similar to creating a User or System DSN but requires a few more initial steps. To create a file DSN, select the File DSN tab of the ODBC Administrator; see Figure 19-3. In addition to the Add, Remove, and Configure buttons of the User and System DSN tabs, you will see a Look In drop-down box and a Set Directory button.

Look In   The Look In drop-down box displays the current default folder for storing file DSNs. The list of DSNs displayed are the file DSNs found in this directory. You can change the directory using the drop-down box and the file folder button. When you create a new file DSN, this will be the default location, but you can place the new DSN in any directory that you can access.

Set Directory   If you have changed the directory settings and want the new location to become the default location for storing file DSNs, click the Set Directory button.

When you click the Add button to create a new file DSN, you will see the same Create New Data Source dialog box that appears for the other DSN types. After selecting a driver, a new dialog box requesting a filename will be displayed. You can use the Browse button in

PART III

Figure 19-3
Creating a file
DSN

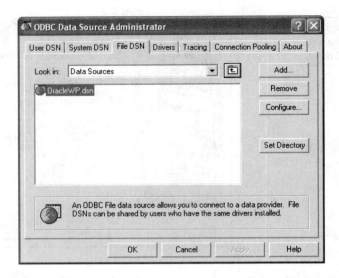

this dialog box to place the file in a different location. Click Next, and a dialog box displaying the filename and driver will appear. Click Finish. The driver-specific dialog box will then display. Enter the properties required by the driver, and click OK to close the dialog box.

ODBC Connections in Crystal Reports

Once the DSN has been created, or if you are going to use connection strings, the next step is to create a new ODBC connection in Crystal Reports. From the Database Expert Data tab or the Data screen of one of the report creation wizards, open the Create New Connection folder. Browse to the ODBC (RDO) folder and open it. The Data Source Selection dialog box shown in Figure 19-4 will open.

Figure 19-4
Creating a new
ODBC
connection

This dialog box contains three radio buttons: Select Data Source, Find File DSN, and Enter Connection String. You must select one of these options.

Select Data Source   If you choose Select Data Source, the Data Source Name list box becomes active and you can select a DSN to use from the list. This list displays all the DSNs that you can use, including user DSNs, system DSNs, and any file DSNs in the default directory for file DSNs.

Find File DSN   If you select Find File DSN, the File DSN edit box and associated browse button become active. You can type in a file DSN (its filename and path) or browse for it using the browse button.

Enter Connection String   If you select Enter Connection String, the Connection String edit box becomes active and you can enter a connection string into it. The entries required in connection strings vary depending on the ODBC driver. The same entries that are created in a file DSN are needed in a connection string, so you can create a working file DSN and then refer to it to create a connection string. Each line of the file DSN contains an attribute and its value. For the connection string, add a semicolon and concatenate these entries together.

For example, a file DSN to connect to the Xtreme sample data looks like this:

```
[ODBC]
DRIVER=Microsoft Access Driver (*.mdb)
UID=admin
UserCommitSync=Yes
Threads=3
SafeTransactions=0
PageTimeout=5
MaxScanRows=8
MaxBufferSize=2048
FIL=MS Access
DriverId=25
DefaultDir=C:\Program Files\Crystal Decisions\Crystal Reports 10\
Samples\En\Databases
DBQ=C:\Program Files\Crystal Decisions\Crystal Reports 10\
Samples\En\Databases\xtreme.mdb
```

Therefore, the connection string would look like this:

```
DRIVER=Microsoft Access Driver (*.mdb);UID=admin;UserCommitSync=Yes;
Threads=3;SafeTransactions=0;PageTimeout=5;MaxScanRows=8;MaxBufferSize=2048;
FIL=MS Access;DriverId=25;DefaultDir=C:\Program Files\Crystal Decisions\
Crystal Reports 10\Samples\En\Databases;DBQ=C:\Program Files\
Crystal Decisions\Crystal Reports 10\Samples\En\Databases\xtreme.mdb
```

Connection string requirements are also defined in the *DataDirect Connect for ODBC Reference* that should be included with the Crystal Reports database drivers. This guide can also be found on the DataDirect web site (http://www.datadirect.com).

Exercise 19.1: Configuring an ODBC Connection to Access

1. Open the Microsoft ODBC Administrator.

2. On the User DSN tab, click Add.

PART III

3. Select the Microsoft Access Driver (*.mdb), and click Finish.

4. The ODBC Microsoft Access Setup dialog box appears, as shown in Figure 19-5.

5. Enter **Xtreme** as the data source name and **Crystal Reports sample data** as the description, as shown in Figure 19-5, and then click the Select button in the Database panel.

6. In the Select Database dialog box, browse to the xtreme.mdb file at C:\Program Files\Crystal Decisions\Crystal Reports 10\Samples\En\Databases\, and click OK.

NOTE   Many other options can be set for the Access DSN; see the help file for descriptions.

7. Click OK again to close the ODBC Microsoft Access Setup dialog box and return to the User DSN tab.

8. You should see your new DSN in the list.

9. Close the ODBC Administrator or leave it open for the next exercise.

Exercise 19.2: Configuring an ODBC Connection to SQL Server

For this exercise, you need access to a SQL Server database. If you installed Crystal Enterprise as described in Chapter 1, you can use that database.

1. Open the ODBC Administrator if it is not already open.

2. Click the System DSN tab.

3. Click the Add button.

4. Select the CR SQL Server Wire Protocol ODBC Mapper 4.20 driver, and click Finish.

Figure 19-5

Creating an Access DSN

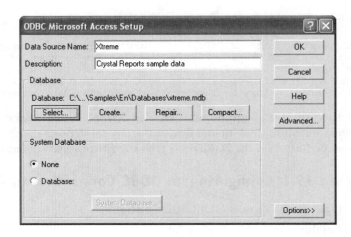

Figure 19-6
Creating a SQL
Server DSN

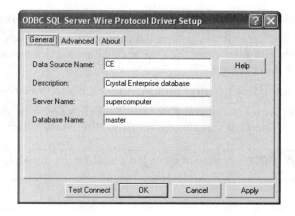

NOTE Other SQL Server ODBC drivers will require different properties from those described here.

5. The dialog box shown in Figure 19-6 will be displayed. Enter the **CE** as the data source name and **Crystal Enterprise database** as the description.

6. Enter the name of the computer where the database is installed in the Server Name box.

7. Enter the Database Name.

8. Click Test Connection to verify that the settings are correct.

9. After successfully connecting, click OK to close the dialog box.

10. Close the ODBC Administrator or leave it open for the next exercise.

Exercise 19.3: Configuring an ODBC Connection to Oracle

For this exercise, you will need an Oracle database to connect to and the Oracle client properly set up and configured on your workstation.

NOTE If you use the CR Oracle Wire Protocol ODBC Driver, you do not need the Oracle client installed, but the required properties are different from those described here.

1. Open the ODBC Administrator if it is not already open.

2. Select the System DSN tab.

3. Click the Add button.

4. Select the CR Oracle ODBC Driver 4.20, and click Finish.

5. The ODBC Oracle Driver Setup dialog box will be displayed.

6. On the General tab, enter a data source name and description. In the Server Name edit box, enter the Oracle database service name. (Consult your DBA for the proper entry.)

7. Click the Test Connect button. A logon box will be displayed.

8. Enter a user name and password, and click OK. You should get a message that the connection was successful. Close the message box.

 NOTE   Advanced settings are available on the Advanced and Performance tabs.

9. Click OK to close the ODBC Oracle Driver Setup dialog box.

10. Click OK to close the ODBC Administrator application.

Exercise 19.4: Using ODBC DSNs in Crystal Reports

1. Create a new report using the Standard wizard.

2. On the Data screen, open the Create New Connection folder.

3. Open the ODBC (RDO) folder, and double-click the Make New Connection entry.

4. In the Data Source Selection dialog box, select Xtreme.dsn, which you created in Exercise 19.1, and click Next.

5. A Connection Information dialog box will appear. You do not need to supply a password because the sample database does not require it. Click Finish.

6. Xtreme.dsn will now appear in the Available Data Sources list, and you can use it in your report.

7. Click Cancel to close the wizard.

Database Menu Items

Commands on the Database menu are used to verify the structure of databases, log on or off databases, browse data in data sources, change the location of data sources, and display the report query. There are also shortcuts for setting two report options on this menu.

Database Expert

Selecting the Database Expert command opens the Database Expert. The Database Expert is covered in Chapter 18.

Set Datasource Location

The Set Datasource Location command opens the Set Datasource Location dialog box, shown in Figure 19-7. If a database has changed location or you wish to use a different database that has the same structure, or almost the same structure, for your report, you can use this dialog box to tell Crystal Reports where the new database is. For example, a common situation requires that you change the source for the report from the test database to the production database. The Set Datasource Location dialog box can be used to reset an entire data source or any table within the data source.

The Set Datasource Location dialog box contains two lists and an Update button. To change a data source's location, select the database or table that you want to change in the Current Data Sources list, select the database or table you want to change to in the Replace With list, and then click the Update button.

- **Current Data Source**   This list displays data sources used in the report. Under each data source there is a Properties node and a node for each table or view used in the report. Each table or view also has a Properties node. Database properties show information about the database connection. Table properties show information about the table. You can select one database or table from the list.

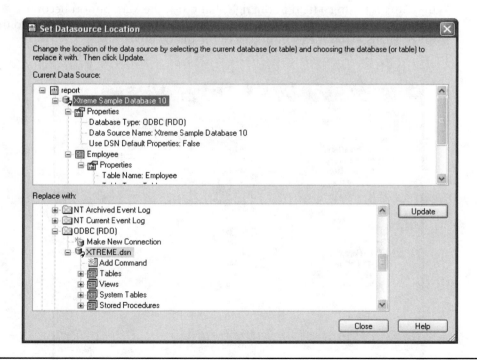

Figure 19-7   Changing a data source location

- **Replace With** This list displays the Database Expert folders. You select a new data source from one of the folders. You may be prompted for connection information. After connecting, you can leave the selection at the database level or choose a table or view.

- **Update** If the type of item selected (database or table) matches in the Current Data Source list and the Replace With list, the Update button will be available. Click the Update button to change the data source location.

Mapping Fields

The current data source and the new source may both contain all the same, identically named fields (and tables, if replacing an entire database) used in the report. If the two sources do not match, however, the Map Fields dialog box, shown in Figure 19-8, will appear after Update is clicked. Field mapping will always be required if you change the location from a desktop database to a SQL database. Mapping employs the following options:

- **Unmapped Fields** The left-hand list in the Unmapped Fields area displays the report fields that Crystal Reports could not match to fields in the new data source. The right-hand list displays the fields in the new data source that have the same data type as the selected report field in the left-hand list.

- **Map** After selecting a field in the right-hand list, the Map button becomes available. Clicking the Map button will move the matched pair of fields into the Mapped Fields list in the bottom part of the dialog box.

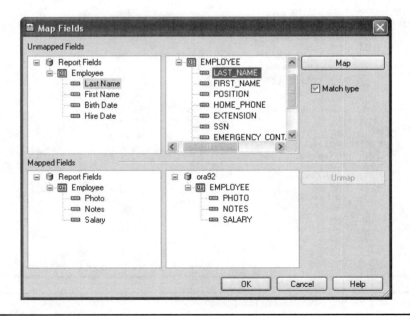

Figure 19-8   Mapping fields

NOTE When fields are mapped, the report field's alias does not change. By default the report field's alias is the field name in the original data source, although it may have since been altered by the developer.

- **Match Type** The Match Type box is checked by default. It causes only fields with matching data types to display in the right-hand mapping list. If you want to map a report field to a field in the new data source that has a different data type, clear the Match Type box.

- **Mapped Fields** The Mapped Fields area of the dialog box displays fields that were mapped by Crystal Reports or by the developer. When you select a field in the right-hand or the left-hand list, the related field is highlighted in the other list.

- **Unmap** To remove a field mapping, select the field in one of the Mapped Fields lists and click the Unmap button. The fields will be unmapped and moved back into the Unmapped Fields lists.

When you are finished mapping, click OK to close the Map Fields dialog box and return to the report.

Log On or Off Server

Selecting the Log On or Off Server command opens the Data Explorer dialog box, shown in Figure 19-9. Options in the Data Explorer allow you to log on or off data sources, maintain your Favorites folder, and set database options. Except for logging off data sources, all the capabilities of the Data Explorer can be accomplished using other methods.

- **Data Sources List** The list box in the Data Explorer displays the same folders as the Database Expert. Select a data source in this list before clicking any of the buttons.

Figure 19-9
Using the Data
Explorer dialog
box

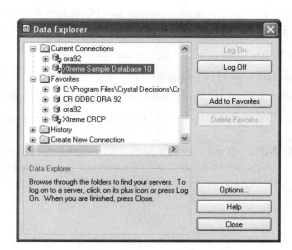

- **Log On**   Click the Log On button to log onto the selected data source. If a user name and password are required, you will be prompted for them.

- **Log Off**   Click the Log Off button to disconnect from the selected data source.

- **Add to Favorites**   This button adds the selected data source to the Favorites folder.

- **Delete Favorite**   If you select a data source in the Favorites folder, the Delete Favorite button is available. Click it to remove the data source from the Favorites folder.

- **Options**   Click the Options button to display the Database Options dialog box for the selected data source. Database options are described in Chapter 18.

Browse Data

Select a database field in the report, then choose Database | Browse Data to display a sample of the data contained in the field. The action of this command is the same as the Browse button of the Field Explorer.

Set OLAP Cube Location

Select the Set OLAP Cube Location command to change the location of an OLAP cube used in the report.

Verify Database

Select the Verify Database command to have Crystal Reports compare the current structure of the report's data sources to the structure used in the report. If the structure of the data sources has not changed, you will receive a message saying that the database is up-to-date. If changes to the underlying databases that require field remapping have occurred, the Map Fields dialog box will appear. You can remap fields as described earlier in the "Mapping Fields" section. Crystal Reports will automatically correct for the following types of changes:

- New fields have been added to the database.
- Field data types have changed.
- Fields not used in the report have been dropped from the database.
- The order of fields in the database tables has changed.

 NOTE   If the report option Verify on First Refresh is checked, a Verify Database command will be executed the first time a report is refreshed during a session.

Show SQL Query

Use the Show SQL Query command to open the Show SQL Query dialog box, shown here.

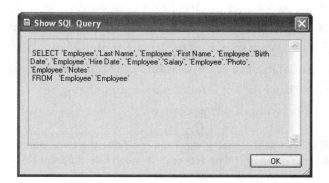

The query that Crystal Reports generated or that you created using a SQL Command will appear in the dialog box exactly as it will be sent to the database server. Current parameter values will be included if they are used in the selection formula, and SQL Expressions will appear as expressions in the query's select list. Use Show SQL Query to examine the query and ensure that it is as you expect.

Perform Grouping On Server

The Database | Perform Grouping On Server option is a check box. Check it if you want Crystal Reports to perform grouping operations on the server. Clear it if you want grouping performed locally. This option is identical to the like-named option on the File | Report Options dialog box. It applies only to the current report. Grouping can be performed on the server only if groups exist and the Details section is hidden.

Select Distinct Records

The Select Distinct Records menu option is a toggle. Check it if you want to exclude duplicate records from the report. Clear it if you want duplicate records returned. Checking this option adds the DISTINCT keyword to the database query. A record in the result set is considered a duplicate only if every field in the record matches the corresponding field in another record. The File | Report Options dialog box contains the same Select Distinct Records option. It is repeated on the Database menu for ease of use.

 TIP Verify that your joins are correct before applying Select Distinct Records. You may see duplicates due to errors in the join configuration.

Exercise 19.5: Changing a Data Source Location

1. Open the report from Exercise 18.4.

2. Select Database | Set Datasource Location.

3. In the Current Data Source list, select the current data source (not a table).

4. In the Replace With list, open Create New Connection, and open ODBC (RDO).

5. Scroll to Xtreme DSN (created in Exercise 19.1), then select it, and click Finish.

6. Select the Xtreme data source in the Replace With list, and click Update.

7. Note that the data source in the Current Data Source list has changed.

8. Click Close to close the Set Datasource Location dialog box.

9. Close the report without saving changes.

 NOTE No field mapping was required since the two sources were actually the same database being accessed through two different DSNs.

Exercise 19.6: Showing a SQL Query

1. Open the report from Exercise 18.4.

2. Select Database | Show SQL Query.

3. The Show SQL Query dialog box will appear; the contents should look like this.

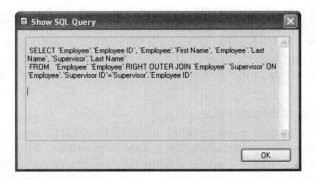

4. Examine the query, and then click OK to close the dialog box.

Chapter Review

This chapter expanded your knowledge of database connections, taught you how to create ODBC data sources for use in Crystal Reports, and covered data source maintenance issues such as handling changes in the database and relocation of the database.

Quick Tips

- Crystal Reports supports both native connections and connections based on a standard API, such as ODBC.

- You can use multiple data sources in a report.

- A native connection requires three layers: the Crystal Reports layer, a data translation layer, and the database layer.

- An ODBC connection requires five layers: the Crystal Reports layer, the ODBC translation layer, the ODBC layer, the DBMS translation layer (ODBC drivers), and the database layer.

- An OLE DB connection requires four layers: the Crystal Reports layer, the OLE DB consumer, OLE DB provider, and the database layer.

- Using native drivers is generally faster than using ODBC drivers, due to the added layers.

- Crystal Reports can connect to any data source that has an ODBC driver installed.

- Crystal Reports includes DataDirect ODBC drivers for the major SQL databases.

- Business Views are available as data sources via the Repository folder of the Database Expert.

- To use ODBC connections in Crystal Reports, you must first create an ODBC DSN for the data source or know the proper connection string.

- DSNs are created with the Microsoft ODBC Administrator found in the Control Panel or Administrator Tools.

- There are three types of DSNs: user, system, and file. User DSNs are available only to the user who created them. System DSNs are available to any user logged into the system where they are defined. File DSNs are stored in text files and can be used by anyone who has access to the file and who has the required ODBC driver installed.

- Each ODBC driver requires specific properties to be set. These vary from driver to driver.

- The Set Datasource Location command of the Database menu allows you to change the location of a report's data sources.

- The Verify Database command checks the database structure information stored in the report against the current state of the database.

- If existing database structure information does not match the new database structure information when using Set Datasource Location or Verify Database, the Map Fields dialog box will be displayed. You can use this dialog box to tie existing field aliases to a field in the new or updated data source.

PART III

- The Log On or Off Server command of the Database menu opens the Data Explorer dialog box. You can use this dialog box to log on or off of data sources, maintain your Favorites folder, or change database options.

- The Show SQL Query dialog box displays the query that Crystal Reports will send to the database server.

Questions

Questions may have more than one correct answer. Choose all answers that apply.

1. You can join a SQL Server table to an Oracle table in a Crystal Report.

   a. True

   b. False

2. Select methods that you could use to connect to an Oracle database.

   a. Native

   b. ODBC using Oracle's ODBC driver

   c. OLE DB using Microsoft's OLE DB Provider for Oracle

   d. ODBC using DataDirect's ODBC driver

   e. ODBC using DataDirect's wire protocol ODBC driver

3. Crystal Reports can connect to an ODBC data source only if a DataDirect ODBC driver is used.

   a. True

   b. False

4. Which connection type will probably be the fastest?

   a. Native

   b. ODBC using Oracle's ODBC driver

   c. OLE DB using Microsoft's OLE DB Provider for Oracle

   d. ODBC using DataDirect's ODBC driver

   e. ODBC using Microsoft's ODBC driver

5. OLE DB is similar to ODBC except that

   a. No database layer is required.

   b. An OLE DB provider is required instead of an ODBC driver.

   c. Crystal Reports does not supply OLE DB providers.

   d. Crystal Reports does not supply ODBC drivers.

   e. OLE DB only works against Microsoft databases.

6. Crystal Reports can connect to a database via ODBC using

    a. A user DSN

    b. A system DSN

    c. A file DSN on the local computer

    d. A file DSN on a remote computer

    e. A connection string

7. A specific DSN is ODBC driver independent.

    a. True

    b. False

8. The Verify Database command will prompt you to remap fields when which of the following changes has occurred?

    a. A new field is added to a table used in the report.

    b. A field that is not used in the report is dropped from the database.

    c. A field used in the report undergoes a name change.

    d. A field that was not previously indexed is indexed.

    e. The order of fields in the table has changed.

9. The Set Datasource Location command is used to move the database used in a report.

    a. True

    b. False

10. The Set Datasource Location command will prompt you to remap fields when which of the following changes has occurred?

    a. A matching field name in the new data source is not found for some report fields.

    b. The new data source contains more fields than the old data source.

    c. The new data source has a different primary key than the old data source.

    d. The location is changed from a desktop database to a SQL database.

    e. The order of fields in the current data source does not match the order of fields in the new data source.

11. The Set Datasource Location dialog box can be displayed by

    a. Clicking the Set Datasource Location button on the toolbar

    b. Selecting File | Report Options and modifying the properties on the Location tab

    c. Right-clicking a data source in the Database Expert and selecting Change Location

    d. Selecting Database | Set Datasource Location

    e. All of the above

PART III

12. In the Map Fields dialog box, you can map only fields that have the same data type. (Select the *best* answer.)

   a. True

   b. If Match Type is cleared

   c. If Match Type is checked

   d. False

13. Set Datasource Location is not needed in which of the following scenarios?

   a. A report uses a native connection to an Access database and the database has been moved to a new directory.

   b. A report uses an ODBC connection to an Access database, the database has been moved to a new directory, and the DSN has been modified to reflect the new location.

   c. You received a report file in an e-mail from a third-party vendor, and your database environment differs from theirs.

   d. A report using a native connection to a SQL database in the test environment needs to be changed to use production data

Answers

1. a. True. You can use multiple data sources in Crystal Reports.

2. All. Any of the listed options could be used to connect to Oracle.

3. b. False. Crystal Reports can use any data source that has an ODBC driver.

4. a. Native connections are generally faster, although wire protocol ODBC drivers may be faster.

5. b, c. For an OLE DB connection, an OLE DB provider is required instead of an ODBC driver. Crystal Reports does not supply any OLE DB providers.

6. All. Any of the options can be used by Crystal Reports.

7. b. False. A DSN is created for a specific ODBC driver.

8. c. The only change listed that requires remapping is the change of a field name.

9. b. False. Set Datasource Location does not move databases. You use it to tell Crystal Reports where the new location is.

10. a, d. You must remap if a field name match is not found or when changing from a desktop database to a SQL database.

11. d. The Set Datasource Location dialog box is opened by choosing Database | Set Datasource Location.

12. c. If Match Type is checked, then you can only map fields with matching data types.

13. b. The change in location is handled in the DSN.

Optimizing the Use of SQL Databases

Exam RDCR300 expects you to be able to

- Optimize record selection
- Use SQL Expressions
- Group on the server
- Test the SQL query and returned data

Each database type that Crystal Reports can use has its own unique characteristics. Understanding and exploiting those characteristics to create accurate, fast, scalable reports is the often unstated, but vital, responsibility of the report developer. All databases that are accessed via SQL, including true SQL databases and those non-SQL databases that you access via ODBC, have many characteristics in common. This chapter describes how to best use Crystal Reports to generate an optimal SQL query and lists other important report optimization strategies.

Overview

When you use a native connection to a SQL database, or an ODBC connection to any database type, Crystal Reports generates a SQL query, sends the query to the database server for execution, and retrieves the result set. Decisions that you make in the Crystal Reports development environment affect the content of the generated query. The only exceptions are when you use SQL Commands or stored procedures. In the case of SQL Commands, you write the query; it is not generated for you. In the case of stored procedures, Crystal Reports generates an execute statement, and not a query.

Goals

There are three goals for any report query. Primarily, it needs to return the correct result. Secondarily, it needs to return the result as quickly as possible. Query speed has three components that can be influenced by the report developer: the number of records returned; the best use of database objects such as indexes, views, and stored procedures;

and the number of computations done on the server versus locally. (The report developer usually does not directly influence other speed-related issues such as network bandwidth or server memory.) The third goal is scalability. The report developer should strive to generate queries that use a minimum of server resources.

Crystal Reports Query Generation

The first step in report query optimization is understanding how Crystal Reports generates the query. As described in Chapter 19, the query that Crystal Reports generates is visible in the Show SQL Query dialog box. Select Database | Show SQL Query to display the query. Subreports generate their own queries and can be viewed in the same manner. The Show SQL Query dialog box is read-only.

NOTE   The Show SQL Query command will not be available if multiple data sources are used in the report or if the data sources are not accessed via SQL (such as in the case of native access to desktop databases).

Basics

The SQL SELECT statement is used to retrieve information from the database. The clauses that Crystal Reports can generate are as follows:

```
SELECT SelectList FROM TableList WHERE Conditions
  GROUP BY GroupList ORDER BY OrderList
```

Crystal Reports generates a query such that every database report field or SQL Expression field is listed in *SelectList,* and all tables used in the report are contained in *TableList.* Parts of the selection formula that can be converted to SQL become *Conditions.* Table-joining commands will be in *TableList* or *Conditions,* depending on the database's syntax. The GROUP BY clause will exist only if the report is doing grouping on the server. Crystal Reports will create an ORDER BY clause if report sorting is specified.

All tables will be given an alias. The alias follows the table name in the FROM clause and is prefixed to the fields from that table in the select list. The alias will equal the table name shown in the Database Expert. The table name defaults to the actual table name, but it can be renamed by the report developer. The table name will also differ if the same table is added to a report more than once—Crystal Reports will append a number to the table name to indicate that it is used more than once.

Syntax Differences

The query that you see in the Show SQL Query dialog box is written in the SQL dialect of the connected database or in standard ODBC SQL if you are using ODBC. Crystal Reports knows the basic syntax requirements of the various SQL databases and uses the proper join terminology and so on. However, Crystal Reports may not be up-to-date with the current versions, so you may see a query that could be written a different way. In addition, Crystal Reports does not take advantage of any SQL extensions available in the database; it uses only core SQL elements.

NOTE Basic SQL syntax is covered in Chapter 22.

Parameter Substitution

If your report uses parameter fields in the selection formula and that part of the selection formula is added to the report query, then any needed parameter fields will be prompted for and the user-selected values will be placed in the query before it is sent to the server.

Treatment of Formulas

Crystal Reports formula fields are never added to the report query. Some or all of the record selection formula may be added as the WHERE clause, but regular formula fields are not added to the select list. If you want a formula's computations to happen on the server, use a SQL Expression instead.

SQL Commands

If a SQL Command is the only data source for a report, then the report query will be the SQL Command after any necessary parameter substitution. If multiple data sources are used and one of them is a SQL Command, then the report query will not be displayed.

CAUTION When you use a SQL Command, every field or expression in the select list will be returned whether or not it is used in the report. This may add unnecessary overhead to the report.

Exercise 20.1: Examining the SQL Query

1. Open the report from Exercise 9.7.

2. Select Database | Show SQL Query to display the report query.

3. The query will look like this:

```
SELECT 'Customer'.'Customer Name',  SUM('Orders'.'Order Amount')
FROM    'Orders' 'Orders' INNER JOIN 'Customer' 'Customer'
        ON 'Orders'.'Customer ID'='Customer'.'Customer ID'
GROUP BY 'Customer'.'Customer Name'
ORDER BY 'Customer'.'Customer Name'
```

Note that it is a summary query. It returns the customer name and the total order amount.

4. Click OK to close the Show SQL Query dialog box.

5. Display the Details section.

6. Look at the SQL query again. Notice that the GROUP BY clause has been removed and Order ID has been added. (Order ID was excluded from the summary query because it had no related summary fields.)

7. Add Ship Date to the report.

8. Look at the SQL query again. Notice that Ship Date has been added to the select list.

9. Create a discrete date parameter called **Ship Dates After**.

10. Create a record selection formula like this:

```
{Orders.Ship Date} > {?Ship Dates After}
```

11. Open the Show SQL Query dialog box. You will be prompted for the Ship Dates After parameter. Enter **8/27/2000**.

12. The report query is now the following:

```
SELECT 'Orders'.'Order ID', 'Orders'.'Order Amount',
       'Customer'.'Customer Name', 'Orders'.'Ship Date'
FROM   'Orders' 'Orders' INNER JOIN 'Customer' 'Customer'
       ON 'Orders'.'Customer ID'='Customer'.'Customer ID'
WHERE  'Orders'.'Ship Date'>={ts '2000-08-27 00:00:00'}
ORDER BY 'Customer'.'Customer Name'
```

13. Notice that a WHERE clause was created and the parameter value was used in it.

14. Close the report without saving changes.

Minimize the Record Count

The fewer records in a report, the faster it will run. This is obvious, of course, but needs to be stated as a report design goal. A report needs to contain the records that meet its stated requirements, but there may be design considerations that can reduce the average number of report records actually viewed by the user. In addition, more records may be retrieved from the database than are used in the report. This needs to be minimized.

By Report Design

There are two extremes in report length. One is the old-style green-bar report model, where every possible bit of information and every possible record is included in the report. Users then browse the report for the information they need. It works, and it is still a valid model in a few circumstances (such as when saving data with a report). The other extreme is a completely customized report showing the bare minimum of information that a single user needs right now. Most reports you design should use the second model.

Use Parameters

The simplest way to customize a report for each user (or use) is to use parameters in the selection formula. By creating parameters and then filtering the report data based on the parameter values, you should be able to construct a report that contains the fewest number of records that satisfy the user's need.

Creating parameters and adding them to the record selection formula was covered in Chapter 6. Creating a record selection formula that contains parameters does not guarantee where the record filtering will happen. It could be done on the server, or it could be done locally by Crystal Reports. Pushing it to the server is most desirable (see the "Push Record Selection to the Server" section, later in this chapter). Nevertheless, there is some benefit to doing the filtering locally: Crystal Reports will filter out the unneeded records in Pass 1, so all processing done in the later passes will benefit.

Use Summary Reports with Drill-Down

Detail data is often included in a report *just in case* the user wants to see the lowest level of data granularity. Suppose the primary goal is the report summaries. In this situation, the majority of detail data is ignored. If the report can be run in an interactive fashion by the user (using Crystal Enterprise or a report viewer), you should design a summary report that allows drill-down, to optimize report processing. Only the summary information and any specifically requested detail information (drilled-down sections) would need to be retrieved from the database and processed by Crystal Reports.

A summary report is a report where the Details section is hidden or suppressed. A performance boost is realized if the report does not have to fetch and process every record that contributes to the summary but instead can use summaries computed on the server. When summaries are processed on the server, the report query will contain a GROUP BY clause and no detail rows will be retrieved.

A SELECT query that contains a GROUP BY clause returns only summary-level data. All items in the select list, except those that are used as the group-by fields, must be summary functions. The summary is computed for the combination of fields listed in the GROUP BY clause. For example, this is a summary query that returns the total order amount by customer name.

```
SELECT 'Customer'.'Customer Name', SUM('Orders'.'Order Amount')
   FROM  'Orders' 'Orders' INNER JOIN 'Customer' 'Customer'
         ON 'Orders'.'Customer ID'='Customer'.'Customer ID'
GROUP BY 'Customer'.'Customer Name'
ORDER BY 'Customer'.'Customer Name'
```

If the Details section is hidden (not suppressed), the user will still be able to drill down to view the detail records for a particular group value. When the user requests a drill-down view, a second query will be sent to the server to retrieve only the needed detail records. In this fashion, the user has access to any required details, but record processing is minimized. If it is the case that a large portion of the groups are likely to be drilled into, then it would be more efficient to return all detail records and do the grouping locally.

Several conditions must be met to ensure that grouping happens on the server. The central requirement is to guarantee that no detail-level fields are required for any report processing.

Perform Grouping on Server The Perform Grouping on Server option must be checked for the report. This option can be set globally on the Database tab of the File | Options dialog box. Alternatively, for the current report it can be set in the Report Options dialog box available from File | Report Options.

TIP You could also select Database | Perform Grouping on Server if the Use Indexes or Server for Speed option is checked in the File | Options or File | Report Options dialog box.

Groups Exist　　You must have at least one group in your report. If you have multiple groups, the lowest-level group that is not completely suppressed will determine the GROUP BY clause sent to the server. All higher-level grouping and summarizing will be done by Crystal Reports locally.

Details Section Hidden　　For grouping to be performed on the server, the Details section of the report must be hidden or suppressed. If the Details section is not hidden, then detail-level data must be retrieved from the database and a GROUP BY clause cannot be added to the report query. If a report has multiple groups, the lowest-level group that is displayed in the report preview will be the group level of the report query.

No Groups on Formula Fields　　Formula fields are computed locally, so if a report contains groups based on formula fields, that grouping cannot be performed on the server. In that case, convert the formula to a SQL Expression and group on that.

No Summaries on Formula Fields　　None of the summary fields in the lowest-level group section that is displayed can be based on formula fields. You can create formulas that are based on the summaries returned from the server, but you cannot have the server return a summary based on a formula field. Use SQL Expression fields instead.

No Top N Type Group Sorting　　If you use the group sort expert and choose Top N, Bottom N, Top Percentage, or Bottom Percentage, grouping will not be performed on the server.

No Running Totals on Detail Fields　　Running total fields are computed locally, so you cannot use a running total that is based on detail-level data. You can use a running total that is based on the summary fields returned from the database.

No Record Selection That Must Be Performed Locally　　If your report contains any record selection criteria that cannot be pushed to the server, it must retrieve the detail records in order to do the local filtering.

No Groups "in Specified Order"　　Grouping "in specified order" is done locally based on the options you configure. It cannot be passed to the server. You may be able to create a SQL Expression that mimics the specified order settings and group on that instead.

Summary Operation Is Sum, Count, Maximum, or Minimum　　Using any of the other Crystal Reports summary operations will result in all detail records being retrieved, and the summary will be computed locally.

TIP Check the Show SQL Query dialog box to verify that the report query contains a GROUP BY clause.

Push Record Selection to the Server

Ensuring that record selection is pushed to the server is the most important step in optimizing the use of SQL databases. The result is fewer records that must travel the network and less work to be done locally by Crystal Reports. The record selection formula, created either manually in the Formula Workshop or generated by the Select Expert, should be your primary focus. Crystal Reports attempts to convert the entire record selection formula to the WHERE clause of the report query. Some types of criteria cannot be converted by Crystal Reports and so are not added to the WHERE clause. In that case, more records are returned than necessary and Crystal Reports does further filtering locally. There are several easy steps you can take to ensure that as much filtering as possible is done on the server.

Use Indexes or Server for Speed

Record selection will not be passed to the server if this option is cleared. Set it globally on the Database tab of the File | Options dialog box or for the active report on the File | Report Options dialog box.

Do Not Use Formula Fields in the Selection Formula

Crystal Reports allows you to use formula fields in the record selection formula. For example, say the report contained a formula called @Taxed that computed the order amount plus tax as {Orders.Order Amount}*1.05. The selection formula for the report could be @Taxed > 2000. In this case, the selection formula could not be converted to the WHERE clause, all records would be returned from the database, and Crystal Reports would process the record selection locally.

Formula fields can often be converted to equivalent SQL Expression fields. SQL Expression fields in selection formulas *are* converted to the WHERE clause. In our example, if @Taxed were changed to a SQL Expression field, %Taxed, and %Taxed was used in the selection formula as %Taxed > 2000, then the WHERE clause would become WHERE ('Orders'.'Order Amount' * 1.05)>2000.

Avoid Most Functions and Operators in the Selection Formula

Many simple formulas that would work unchanged in a SQL query are not passed into the WHERE clause. For example, if you wrote a selection formula like this, ({Orders.Order Amount} + .5) > 500, it would not become part of the WHERE clause, even though virtually all SQL databases would understand it as written. Instead, create a SQL Expression field to do the computation, and then use that in the selection formula.

The Comparison operators (=, <>, <, <=, >, >=); the AND, NOT, and OR Boolean operators; and the Pattern operators, StartsWith and Like, can be used in selection formulas and will be translated into the report query's WHERE clause. Other operators, including the brackets for array subscripting, will not. The Range operator In will work with date ranges and number ranges, but not as a string operator.

Use of most of the Crystal Reports functions in the selection formula will result in that part not being added to the WHERE clause. This is true even if the database server has an identically named function. Use a SQL Expression field instead. Some Crystal Reports functions that simply return constants, such as CurrentDate, can be used in the selection formula without harm. The IsNull function can be used and will be converted to the database's equivalent function. The Programming Shortcut functions can be used successfully with some database types.

 TIP   Always check Show SQL Query to determine if the criteria are being passed to the server.

Use OR Carefully

Crystal Reports passes whatever parts of the selection formula it can to the database server. If there is a three-part selection formula like this,

```
{Orders.Order Amount} > $500.00 and
{Orders.PO#}[2 to 3] = "12" and
{Orders.Order Date} in Date(2000, 02, 18) to Date(2000, 02, 21)
```

then only the first and third condition will be added to the WHERE clause, as shown here:

```
WHERE  'Orders'.'Order Amount'>500 AND
('Orders'.'Order Date'>={ts '2000-02-18 00:00:00'} AND
 'Orders'.'Order Date'<{ts '2000-02-22 00:00:00'})
```

When using ANDs, each part can be treated independently, since a record must pass each condition to be included in the report. Crystal Reports can pass the first and third conditions to the database, retrieve the result set, and then perform the filtering for the second condition itself.

The situation is more complex when using ORs. Consider two conditions connected with an OR. A record will be retained if it meets one condition *or* the other. If Crystal Reports cannot pass one of the conditions to the database, then it must not pass either of the conditions to the database, because a record that should be selected due to the condition that must be performed locally might be filtered out by the condition that was passed to the database.

Substituting an OR for the first AND in the previous example, and adding parentheses to guarantee that the first two conditions are evaluated first, gives you the following record selection formula,

```
({Orders.Order Amount} > $500.00 or
 {Orders.PO#}[2 to 3] = "12") and
{Orders.Order Date} in Date(2000, 02, 18) to Date(2000, 02, 21)
```

which will result in the following WHERE clause:

```
WHERE  ('Orders'.'Order Date'>={ts '2000-02-18 00:00:00'}
    AND 'Orders'.'Order Date'<{ts '2000-02-22 00:00:00'})
```

This WHERE clause includes only the third condition. Neither of the other conditions was passed to the database.

TIP The parentheses are required due to the precedence order of the Boolean operators. Boolean operators are performed in this order: NOT, AND, OR.

Exercise 20.2: Investigating Summary Reports

In this exercise, you start with a summary report and change it in ways that prevent it from doing grouping on the server.

1. Open the report from Exercise 9.6.

2. Preview the report and check the record count (268).

3. Check the SQL query. It includes a GROUP BY clause, as shown here:

```
SELECT 'Customer'.'Customer Name',  SUM('Orders'.'Order Amount')
FROM    'Orders' 'Orders' INNER JOIN 'Customer' 'Customer'
        ON 'Orders'.'Customer ID'='Customer'.'Customer ID'
GROUP BY 'Customer'.'Customer Name'
ORDER BY 'Customer'.'Customer Name'
```

4. Clear the Perform Grouping on Server option of the Database menu.

5. Refresh the report. The record count is now 2191, but the same records are displayed as before.

6. Recheck the SQL query.

7. The GROUP BY clause has been removed.

8. Select File | Report Options, and check the Perform Grouping on Server option. The record count returns to 268.

9. Select the Design tab, and create a formula called **Discount**. Use the following code, and place the formula in the Details section.

```
If {Orders.Order Amount}>1000 then {Orders.Order Amount}*.15
else {Orders.Order Amount}*.05
```

10. Select Discount, right-click, and choose Insert | Summary.

11. Change the Summary Location to the Customer Name group, and click OK.

12. Preview the report, and check the SQL query. There is no GROUP BY clause because of the summary on a formula field.

13. Create a SQL Expression called **Discount** using this code.

```
SWITCH('Orders'.'Order Amount'> 10000,'Orders'.'Order Amount'*.15,
       'Orders'.'Order Amount'<=10000,'Orders'.'Order Amount'*.05)
```

SWITCH is the Microsoft Access equivalent for Crystal Reports' Select Case statement.

14. Place the SQL Expression in the Details section.

15. Right-click the summary on the Discount formula, and choose Edit Summary.

16. In the Choose the Field to Summarize drop-down box, select the Discount SQL Expression field.

17. Preview the report, and look at the SQL query. It should look like this:

```
SELECT 'Customer'.'Customer Name',  SUM('Orders'.'Order Amount'),
        SUM(SWITCH('Orders'.'Order Amount'> 10000,
                    'Orders'.'Order Amount'*.15,
                    'Orders'.'Order Amount'<=10000,
                    'Orders'.'Order Amount'*.05))
    FROM   'Orders' 'Orders' INNER JOIN 'Customer' 'Customer'
        ON 'Orders'.'Customer ID'='Customer'.'Customer ID'
    GROUP BY 'Customer'.'Customer Name'
    ORDER BY 'Customer'.'Customer Name'
```

18. Notice that the contents of the Discount SQL Expression have been added to the select list and the GROUP BY clause has reappeared.

19. Right-click the Discount summary field, and choose Edit Summary.

20. Change the summary operation to Average.

21. Check the SQL query. The GROUP BY clause has been removed.

22. Change the summary operation back to Sum, and save the report as **Exercise 20.2**.

Exercise 20.3: Pushing Record Selection to the Server

1. Open the report from Exercise 20.2.

2. Create the following record selection formula:

```
{@Discount} > $2000.00
```

3. Check the SQL query. No WHERE clause has been added to implement the record selection.

4. Change the record selection formula to the following:

```
{%Discount} > $2000.00
```

5. Check the SQL query. It will now have a GROUP BY clause, as shown here:

```
SELECT 'Customer'.'Customer Name',  SUM('Orders'.'Order Amount'),
    SUM(SWITCH('Orders'.'Order Amount'> 10000,'Orders'.'Order Amount'*.15,
        'Orders'.'Order Amount'<=10000,'Orders'.'Order Amount'*.05))
    FROM   'Orders' 'Orders' INNER JOIN 'Customer' 'Customer'
        ON 'Orders'.'Customer ID'='Customer'.'Customer ID'
    WHERE  (SWITCH('Orders'.'Order Amount'> 10000,'Orders'.'Order Amount'*.15,
                'Orders'.'Order Amount'<=10000,'Orders'.'Order Amount'*.05)
            )>2000
    GROUP BY 'Customer'.'Customer Name'
    ORDER BY 'Customer'.'Customer Name'
```

6. Save the report as **Exercise 20.3**.

TIP You can also check the Report | Performance Information and look at the Processing node. The Grouping Done on Database Server and Record Selection Done on Database Server will tell you where these two processes are happening.

Minimize Processing Time

As discussed in the preceding section, report run time is influenced by the number of records that must be processed. It is also affected by the division of labor between the database server and the local machine (as well as network transfer time, and so on). The database server is usually the most efficient location for data processing, so your goal should be to move as much of the report processing to the server as possible. In addition, the database query should be written such that it returns the result set in the minimum amount of time.

Query Optimization

The query that Crystal Reports generates to gather the data for a report has a significant impact on the speed of report creation. You can take several steps to improve the query, as described in the sections that follow.

Use the Fastest Connection Method

For some databases, you will have three or more possible connection choices: a native connection, one or more ODBC drivers, and one or more OLE DB providers. In most cases, the native connection will be the fastest and most feature rich. However, you should investigate each option to determine the one that meets your needs in the most efficient manner. The wire protocol ODBC drivers may outperform native connections. Several vendors probably offer ODBC drivers for your database; some will be better than others. If you need to use OLE DB, you should determine which provider works best in your environment.

When choosing a database connection method in a Crystal Enterprise environment it is also important to verify that the driver you choose is thread-safe. Using a thread-safe driver allows multiple report queries to be processed at the same time. See the Crystal Reports documentation to verify the thread safety of the drivers it supplies.

Use Indexed Fields

Using indexed fields for linking and record selection, although not required for SQL databases, will improve query performance. The database server's SQL engine will determine what indexes to use to achieve the required results, but you can help by picking fields you know to be indexed when linking or creating the record selection formula.

 TIP SQL queries will use appropriate database indexes for the report query whether or not the Use Indexes or Server for Speed option is checked in the Options or Report Options dialog box.

Avoid Sorting or Grouping on a Formula Field

If the Use Indexes or Server for Speed option is checked, Crystal Reports will add an ORDER BY clause to the report query, resulting in a sorted result set. If Crystal Reports knows that the result set is already sorted, it will not re-sort it, and it can process grouping and summarizing faster. If you sort or group on a formula field, Crystal Reports must sort the result set locally.

Use SQL Expressions

Using SQL Expressions instead of formula fields was recommended in the record selection formula to ensure that record selection happens on the server. A second use of SQL Expression fields is simply to move processing to the server. A formula field will be evaluated locally. If the processing is resource intensive, it might perform better if moved to the server.

The text of Crystal Reports SQL Expression fields is appended to the select list of the report query. The text of the SQL Expression is also added to the WHERE clause with the defined condition if it is used in a record selection formula. SQL Expression fields are created in the Formula Workshop using the SQL Expression Editor and can contain any expression that is valid for the connected database.

TIP You can insert parameter fields into SQL Expressions, but the result will be an error.

New SQL Expressions can be created from the Field Explorer by selecting the SQL Expression folder and using the New button or by right-clicking and selecting New. They can be created in the Formula Workshop in the same manner. Existing SQL Expressions can be edited by selecting them and then clicking the Edit button or by choosing Edit from the right-click menu. SQL Expression fields can be deleted in the same ways as formula fields.

This illustration shows the SQL Expression Editor active in the Formula Workshop.

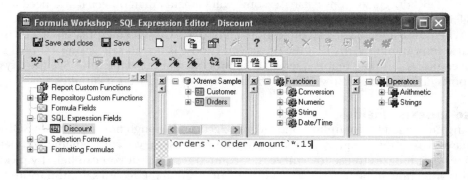

The Field Tree, Function Tree, and Operator Tree are available, just as they are for formula fields, but the contents of the Function Tree and Operator Tree are different. The Function Tree will list functions that are specific to the connected database's SQL syntax. However, the SQL Expression Editor may not list all the database's available functions. If you want to use a database function that is not listed, just type it in. The Operator Tree likewise contains operators that are valid for the connected database's SQL syntax.

CAUTION   The Function Tree and Operator Tree may contain some items that are not valid for your database. If so, you will get an error when the SQL Expression is checked.

Create the SQL Expression as you would a formula field, using components from the trees or typing in a valid expression. Note that what you need to type in is only an expression, not a complete SELECT statement. You can type in anything that would be allowed as an expression in the select list for your database. Some databases allow complete select statements as expressions in the select list of another SELECT statement. In that case, you can type in a complete SELECT statement, but understand what is happening. If you want to write your own complete report query, you need to use a SQL Command, not a SQL Expression.

NOTE   SQL Expressions may not be available if your data source is a stored procedure.

Subreports

Subreports and their impact on the report query were discussed in Chapter 16. Each instance of a subreport generates its own report query. You should strive to minimize the number of queries needed by attempting to eliminate subreports, placing subreports in the highest-level report section possible, and using on-demand subreports.

Use Database-Specific Features

Crystal Reports–generated report queries are generally more limited than the database itself would allow. However, Crystal Reports allows you to take advantage of the specific features of your database in several ways.

SQL Commands

If you are familiar with your database's SQL syntax, you can write your own report query using a SQL Command. In this way, you can create SQL statements that Crystal Reports cannot generate. SQL Commands are discussed in Chapter 22.

Views

You can base a report on a database view. Views are queries that are stored in the database. Using a view that is identical to the report query will not improve performance. However, there can be advantages to using views. Views could be created by database analysts who are more familiar with the database and know best how to retrieve the report data. In that case, Crystal Reports is used primarily for formatting. The existence of a view will make query optimization for the DBA more straightforward as he or she will not need to capture the report query. Permissions to select from a view can differ from the select permissions on the underlying tables, allowing you to fine-tune data access.

Stored Procedures

Stored procedures are programs that are stored and executed in the database. Stored procedures that return data sets can be used as data sources by Crystal Reports. Long, complex processing logic can be moved to the server using stored procedures. In addition, database functions that are defined in stored procedures can be used in SQL Expressions and SQL Commands. Stored procedure requirements differ across database types; see the Crystal Reports documentation for more information.

Preprocessed Data

In some cases, the logic required to create the data for a report is so intense that processing it on demand is not practical. In that case, you might create database processes that generate the data and store it in a new table specifically for use in a report.

Exercise 20.4: Exploring Connection Types

In this exercise, you will compare run times for several different connection types. Since you are using a local Access database, the differences between the connection methods will be small. However, the same method can be used to compare connection methods for your SQL database.

1. Open the report from Exercise 20.3.

2. Refresh the report at least twice; then open Report | Performance Information. (The first time a query is run, there may be overhead due to query parsing and data loading.)

3. Select the Performance Timing node, and record the value listed for the Run Database Query and Read Database Records statistics.

4. Select Database | Set Datasource Location, and open the Create New Connection node.

5. Open the Access/Excel (DAO) node. In the Connection dialog box, in the Database Name box, click the Browse button and locate the Xtreme sample database. Select it and click Open. Then click Finish.

6. Select the new connection, and click the Update button.

7. Close the Set Datasource Location dialog box.

8. Refresh the report a few times, and then check the performance timing. Record the new values.

9. Change the data source again. This time, set up a new connection under the Database Files node of the Create New Connection folder. This will be a native or direct connection to the Access database.

10. Refresh the report a few times, and record the timing statistics.

11. Change the data source again, this time to an OLE DB connection.

12. Refresh the report a few times, and record the timing statistics.

13. The following shows some sample values. As expected, they do not vary much. Close the report without saving changes.

Connection Method	ODBC	DAO	Native	OLE DB
Run the Database Query	23 ms	23 ms	22 ms	24 ms
Read Database Records	8 ms	8 ms	8 ms	8 ms
Total query time	31 ms	31 ms	30 ms	32 ms

CAUTION Do not make a connection method choice based purely on the timing statistics for one report. You also need to investigate the available feature set of each driver, use many different types of reports, evaluate the effect of multiple users, and take into account the restrictions of your particular environment.

Exercise 20.5: Removing a Subreport

In this exercise, you will create a report that uses a subreport, and then you will rewrite the report to eliminate the subreport.

1. Create a new report using the Standard wizard.

2. Use the Customer and Orders tables.

3. Put Customer Name, Order ID, Order Amount, Order Date, and Ship Date on the report.

4. Group by Customer Name and Order ID.

5. On the Summaries screen, remove the summaries for the Order ID field.

6. Click the Finish button.

7. On the Design window, split the Group Footer #2 section so that the summary fields are placed in the lower section (2b).

8. Insert a subreport.

9. Create a new subreport called **OrderDetail**, and click the Report Wizard button.

10. Select the Orders Detail and Product tables, and accept the default linking.

11. Choose the Product Name, Unit Price, and Quantity fields, and click Finish.

12. Select the Link tab, and move the Order ID field into the Field(s) to Link To list.

13. Click OK, and place the subreport in the Group Footer #2a section.

14. Select the OrderDetail tab. Remove the print date field, suppress or delete the Report Footer b section, and move the field headings to the top of the Report Header b section. Resize the Report Header b section.

15. Arrange the Design window until it looks like this.

16. Preview the report. Print the first and last pages for later reference.

17. Check the time. Now, using the page control buttons, scroll to the last page of the report. Watch the status bar as it runs the subreport for each record in the main report. Check the time when the report is finished scrolling. The process will take a noticeable amount of time.

18. Save the report as **Exercise 20.5a**.

19. On the Design tab, remove the subreport.

20. Open the Database Expert.

21. Add the Orders Detail and Product tables to the report. Click OK. Click OK if asked to refresh the report data.

22. Insert a group on the Orders Detail.Product ID field.

23. Create a new detail section, and put Product Name, Unit Price, and Quantity into it.

24. Delete the Group #3 Name field from the report, and preview it.

25. You will see the same information as previously, but if you scroll down to an order that contains more than one product, you will see that the Order Amount, Order Date, and Ship Date are repeating for each product in the order. This is the result of joining the Order table to the Orders Detail table.

26. Scroll to the last page. Notice that the grand total is different from that of the original report. Again, this is because the order amount is getting duplicated for every order that contains more than one product.

27. You could simply move Order Amount, Order Date, and Ship Date into the next higher section, and they would print only once because Crystal Reports

displays the first record in the group when a field is placed in the group header. However, that would just mask the fact that the Orders records are being duplicated. So instead, create summaries for them.

28. For Order Date and Ship Date, create summary fields at the Order ID using the Maximum function. Move the summary fields into the Group Header #3 section to mimic their place in the original report.

29. You could create the same kind of summary for the Order Amount, but it makes more sense to recompute it from the values in the Orders Detail table. Create a formula called LineOrderAmount that is Unit Price times Quantity. Place the formula in the Details b section.

30. Insert a summary in the formula field using the Sum operation and Order ID level. Move the summary field into the Group Header #3 section.

31. Suppress the Details a section.

32. Suppress the Group Footer 2a section.

33. Remove the LineOrderAmount formula field from the Details b section.

34. Insert a Group Header #3b section.

35. Select the Product Name field, right-click, and choose Insert | Field Heading. The heading will appear in the Page Header section. Move it into the Group Header #3b section.

36. Repeat step 35 for Unit Price and Quantity.

37. Select the summary field for Order Amount in the Group Footer #1 section, and change the field summarized to the LineOrderAmount formula. Repeat for the summary in the Report Footer section.

38. Preview the report.

39. Move or format fields to more closely match the original report.

40. Scroll to the last page, and note that the grand total now matches that of the original report. In addition, notice that scrolling to the last page is now much faster.

41. Save the report as **Exercise 20.5**.

Other Optimization Considerations

Several report optimization strategies are not specific to SQL databases.

Use a Group Tree

If your report contains a group tree, your users can jump directly to the node they need to see. Otherwise, they will have to browse page by page through the report until they find the portion they need. Hitting every page is time-consuming, since each page displayed must be fully formatted. Pages that are skipped over and not displayed need only minimal formatting.

Use Current Crystal Reports Versions and Drivers

The current version of Crystal Reports processes reports faster than previous versions. Make sure that you are using the current version and that all your report files are saved in the current version. To upgrade older report files, open them in Crystal Reports 10 and then save them. The file version will change to reflect the new version and the reports will run faster.

Avoid Maps

Map generation is *single-threaded* (only one map can be generated at a time), so maps should be used sparingly in a multiuser environment.

Avoid Using Total Page Count

As discussed in Chapter 15, using the Total Page Count or the PageNofM special fields requires an extra report-processing pass. Avoid this if possible.

Avoid Using Multiple Data Sources

Whenever a report uses multiple data sources, Crystal Reports must send a separate query to each database and then merge the results. If possible, avoid reports with multiple data sources. Some of the major SQL databases allow you to create internal connections to other databases. If you need to do this type of processing, investigate your back-end alternatives; they will probably result in better performance than relying on Crystal Reports to merge the data sources.

Use Saved Data When Appropriate

Using saved data completely eliminates the data retrieval process for the user. Only record selection and report formatting are required.

When to Use Saved Data   You should save a report with data when the underlying data is not updated frequently, when viewing old data is acceptable for some reason, or data is updated on a regular schedule. (You can schedule a report to run at regular intervals and save data. Then any access to the report will see the data as of the last run.) In addition, saved data should only be used if security is not a concern or you are using Crystal Enterprise security, because the data stored with the report is available to all report users.

Parameters and Saved Data   If a report has a selection formula based on parameters, you should run it so that the widest possible result set is returned and saved. When a user requests the report and enters parameter choices, the saved data will be filtered according to their choices. All the saved data will be retained and is available to another user with different parameter values.

Drill-Down and Saved Data   If your report is a summary report that allows drill-down, you should make sure that the drill-down data is saved with the report by disabling grouping on the server. If grouping is done on the server, no detail data will be available to save. If the detail data is not saved, then the drill-down will cause a new query to be sent to the database.

Use Saved Data Indexes   For reports with a large amount of saved data, you can improve report performance by indexing the saved data. Saved data indexes are created in the Saved Data Indexes dialog box that opens when you select Report | Report Bursting Indexes. If your saved data is not indexed, Crystal Reports must read every saved record when the report is run to determine which records should be included in the report. When creating indexes on saved data, you should not index fields that contain unique values. An index on such a field would have as many entries as there are records in the saved data. You should create saved indexes on fields that are used in the record selection formula, as these will speed data retrieval. See the Crystal Reports documentation for more information on Saved Data indexes.

Exercise 20.6: Creating Saved Data Indexes

1. Open the report from Exercise 20.5.

2. Create a discrete string parameter called **Customer**.

3. Create a record selection formula using the following formula:

   ```
   {Customer.Customer Name} like '*'&{?Customer}&'*'
   ```

4. Test the selection formula by refreshing the report and entering **Cat** when prompted for a customer.

5. Refresh the report, and leave the parameter blank. All records will be returned.

6. Select File | Save Data with Report, then select File | Save As, and save the report as **Exercise 20.6**.

7. Use Windows Explorer to check the size of the file.

8. Select Report | Report Bursting Indexes to open the Saved Data Indexes dialog box.

9. Click the Auto button.

10. The Customer.Customer Name field will be placed in the Indexed for Bursting list because it is used in the selection formula.

11. Click OK to close the dialog box.

12. Refresh the report, and leave the parameter blank. All records will be returned.

13. Select File | Save to resave the report. The saved data indexes will be created and saved with the report.

14. Use Windows Explorer to check the size of the file. The file increased due to the space required for the saved data indexes.

15. If the report is rerun with a new parameter value (and without refreshing the data), the index will be used to quickly return the requested records.

16. Close the report.

Chapter Review

This chapter covered topics specific to the use of SQL databases, including optimization of record selection, using SQL Expressions, grouping on the server, and the effect of NULLs.

Quick Tips

- For all data access methods that use SQL, Crystal Reports generates a SQL SELECT statement using the proper syntax for the database, unless the report is based on a SQL Command or stored procedure. If the report is based on a SQL Command, Crystal Reports will use the exact text of the SQL Command as the report query. If the report is based on a stored procedure, Crystal Reports will use a command to execute the stored procedure instead of a SELECT command.

- Report fields are put in the select list of the report query, data sources are listed in the FROM clause, and record selection is represented in the WHERE clause.

- Minimizing the number of records that Crystal Reports must retrieve to satisfy a report query is a major optimization goal. You can do this by using parameters in the selection formula and by choosing to use summary reports (with grouping on the server) when they are appropriate.

- In a summary report, grouping will be performed on the server if the following conditions are met: the Perform Grouping on Server option is checked, groups exist in the report, and the Details section is hidden. Other conditions that will prevent grouping done on the server include groups on formula fields, summaries on formula fields, Top N-type grouping, running totals on database fields, record selection that must be performed locally, groups "in specified order," and summary fields that use operations other than Sum, Count, Minimum, and Maximum.

- Ensuring that record selection happens on the server will result in faster report generation for the user.

- Check the SQL query (using the Show SQL Query command) to verify that the record selection is represented in the WHERE clause of the report query.

- Record selection cannot be passed to the server if the Use Indexes or Server for Speed option is cleared, if formula fields or (most) Crystal Reports functions or operators are used in the record selection formula, or if a condition is connected to another condition using an OR and the other condition cannot be passed to the server.

- Formula fields in the record selection formula can be replaced with SQL Expression fields to allow the record selection to be passed to the server.

- These operators can be used in the record selection formula and still allow it to be passed to the server: =, <>, <, <=, >, >=, AND, NOT, OR, StartsWith, Like, and (for dates and numbers) In.

- The IsNull function can be used in record selection formulas that are passed to the server.

- Using indexed fields for linking and record selection will speed report processing.

- Many formula fields can be converted to SQL Expressions to push the processing to the server.

- Whenever possible, you should use SQL Expressions to push processing to the server. SQL Expressions are similar to formulas but use the SQL syntax of the database and are appended to the select list of the report query. SQL Expressions are created with the SQL Expression Editor of the Formula Workshop.

- Subreports can be detrimental to report processing time, particularly if they are placed in the Details section.

- Reports can be saved with data to decrease the report processing time for users, but the saved data will always be as of the last refresh.

- Report Saved Data can be indexed to further increase performance when using parameters in the record selection formula.

- When using Saved Data with parameterized reports, you should run the report so that the widest possible result set is obtained before saving the report. Subsequent calls to the report will then find the data needed, no matter what parameter values are used.

Questions

Questions may have more than one correct answer. Choose all answers that apply.

1. Which of the following SELECT statement clauses might Crystal Reports include in a generated report query?

   a. FROM

   b. GROUP BY

   c. ORDER BY

   d. HAVING

   e. UNION

2. The best method to allow users to specify the records contained in a report is to use

   a. A group tree

   b. Parameters in section suppression formulas

   c. Parameters in the record selection formula

   d. Parameters in the group selection formula

   e. Constants in the record selection formula

3. Which command opens the Saved Data Indexes dialog box?

   a. Report | Saved Data Indexes

   b. File | Saved Data Indexes

   c. Report | Report Bursting Indexes

   d. Database | Report Bursting Indexes

   e. File | Save As

4. Which of the following conditions will prevent grouping from happening on the server in a summary report?

   a. Groups on formula fields

   b. Top N–type grouping

   c. Record selection that must be performed locally

   d. Groups "in specified order"

   e. Summary fields that use operations other than Sum, Count, Minimum, and Maximum

5. How can you verify that grouping is happening on the server?

   a. Check the Processing node of the Performance Information dialog box.

   b. Examine the Show SQL Query dialog box.

   c. Check the record count in the status bar.

   d. Check the Performance Timing node of the Performance Information dialog box.

   e. Examine the SQL Command dialog box.

6. Record selection cannot be passed to the server if

   a. The Use Indexes or Server for Speed option is checked.

   b. There are formula fields in the record selection formula.

   c. The CurrentDate function is used in the record selection formula.

   d. ORs are not used in the record selection formula.

   e. IsNull is used in the record selection formula.

7. Which of the following could be used in a record selection formula that is passed to the server?

   a. @Discount

   b. %Discount

   c. #Discount

   d. ?Discount

   e. IsNull

8. SQL Expression fields should be used instead of formula fields for which of the following reasons?

 a. They are generally more flexible.

 b. They are easier to write.

 c. They guarantee no conversion problems when changing data sources.

 d. When used in record selection, they are passed to the server.

 e. They force computations to happen on the database server instead of locally.

9. Saving a report with data will be of little benefit if

 a. The main report is a one-page summary report (grouping not done on the server) that allows drill-down.

 b. Report security is required and you are using Crystal Enterprise.

 c. The main report is a one-page summary report (grouping done on the server) that allows drill-down.

 d. The report is parameterized and the last refresh saved only a subset of the possible result set.

 e. The report must display up-to-the-minute data.

Answers

1. **a, b, c.** Crystal Reports will always generate a FROM clause, and it might generate a GROUP BY or ORDER BY clause. It cannot generate HAVING or UNION clauses.

2. **c.** To give users control over the records displayed in a report, create a parameter and then use the parameter in the record selection formula. Parameters in the group selection formula will have no effect on the records in the report because group selection only suppresses records.

3. **c.** The Report | Report Bursting Indexes command opens the Saved Data Indexes dialog box.

4. **All.** Any of the listed conditions will prevent grouping from happening on the server.

5. **a, b.** To verify that grouping is happening on the server, check the SQL query in the Show SQL Query dialog box or check the Grouping Done on Database Server entry of the Processing node of the Performance Information dialog box.

6. **b.** The record selection formula cannot be passed to the server if it contains formula fields.

7. **b, d, e.** SQL Expression fields, parameter fields, and the IsNull function will not prevent the record selection from being passed to the server.

8. **d, e.** SQL Expressions are usually more limited than Crystal Reports functions, they require knowledge of the SQL syntax of the database, and they will fail if the report is converted to use another database type.

9. **c, d, e.** If the drill-down must access the database, then performance gains will be minimal. If the saved data is not adequate for all users' requests, then the database must be queried anyway. If the report requires real-time data, saving data is not beneficial.

CHAPTER 21

Troubleshooting

Exam RDCR300 expects you to be able to
- Find self-service resources for solving problems
- Use utilities to confirm or resolve problems

Crystal Reports ships with help files covering the application's use and features. These should be your first reference when you have problems or questions. However, for in-depth help with specific problems, for up-to-the minute documentation, for insight from other users, and for patches and file updates, you have many resources available to you.

Business Objects Support Web Site

The Business Objects support web site at http://support.businessobjects.com contains many different types of information that you may find helpful. The categories of reference material are shown as a menu to the left of the home page, as shown in Figure 21-1.

 NOTE Business Objects occasionally updates its web site, so the pages you see may not be identical to those shown in this chapter.

Search Engine

The support web site can be searched using basic search parameters or advanced search parameters.

Search String

When using either the basic search or the advanced search, you must enter a string for the engine to use to match articles. Here are some guidelines for forming the search string:

- **Wildcard character**   You can use an asterisk (*) as a wildcard character in your search string. A search on "ERR*" will return any articles containing words that start with "err," such as "Error," "erroneous," and "ErrNo."

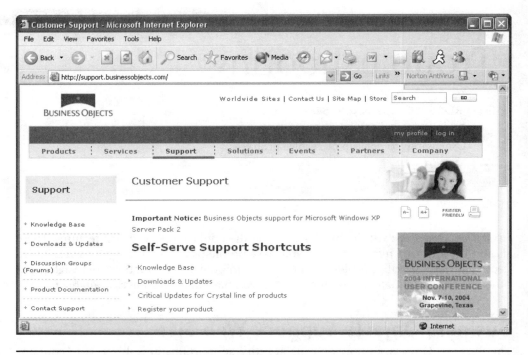

Figure 21-1 Browsing the Business Objects support page

- **Case-insensitivity** The search engine makes no distinction for case. It will find matches to your search string regardless of case. A search on "odbc" will return any articles containing "odbc," "ODBC," "ODbC," and so on.

- **Multiple word search** If you enter more than one word in your search string, by default, the search engine will return only the articles that contain *all* the words.

- **Using OR** If you want to search for one word *or* another, you can use the word OR in your search string.

- **Excluding words** You can create a search that includes excluding words by placing a minus sign in front of them. For example, to search for articles on ODBC but not Microsoft, you would use "ODBC -Microsoft" as your search string.

- **Search for phrases** When entering more than one word, the search engine assumes that you want all files that include both words, anywhere in the article. To search for a specific phrase, you must use quotation marks. For example, to search for advanced charting options, you would enter "advanced charting" (including the quotes).

Basic Search

If you select the Knowledge Base link, the Basic Criteria box will be displayed, as shown here. Enter a search string, and click the Search button. Links to matching articles will be displayed.

Basic criteria:

Search for (required)

☑ All content types
☐ Knowledge base
Advanced search ☐ Files and updates
☐ Technical papers

Search

PART III

The search engine is a combination of three search engines: one on the knowledge base, one on technical papers, and one on files and updates. You can choose to search all three sources or select any combination of them.

- **Knowledge base** The knowledge base consists of documents describing particular problems or questions and gives solutions or workarounds. Knowledge base articles are categorized by product, version, and topic area.

 NOTE When you call technical support level one, this is the resource they will use to research the problem.

- **Technical papers** The technical papers category includes technical briefs, FAQ lists, and product guides. Technical briefs are longer and more detailed than knowledge base articles. They can cover problems in detail or more fully describe a product feature. FAQs contain common questions and their answers for a product. Product guides give an overview of a product and may contain guidelines for using or evaluating the product.
- **Files and updates** The files and updates category contains files that you can download, such as sample reports, sample applications, sample databases, utilities, user function libraries, hot fixes, service packs, and database drivers.

Advanced Search

You can use an advanced search to narrow your search to a particular product, version, or topic area. To initiate such a search, select the Advanced Search link in the Basic

Criteria box or in the left-hand menu. The resulting page consists of several boxes in which you set the search options, as shown in Figure 21-2.

- **Basic Criteria** This box contains the same elements as the previous Basic Criteria box, except that it adds a Reset link. Clicking the Reset link returns all options in the search page to their original values, except for the search string.

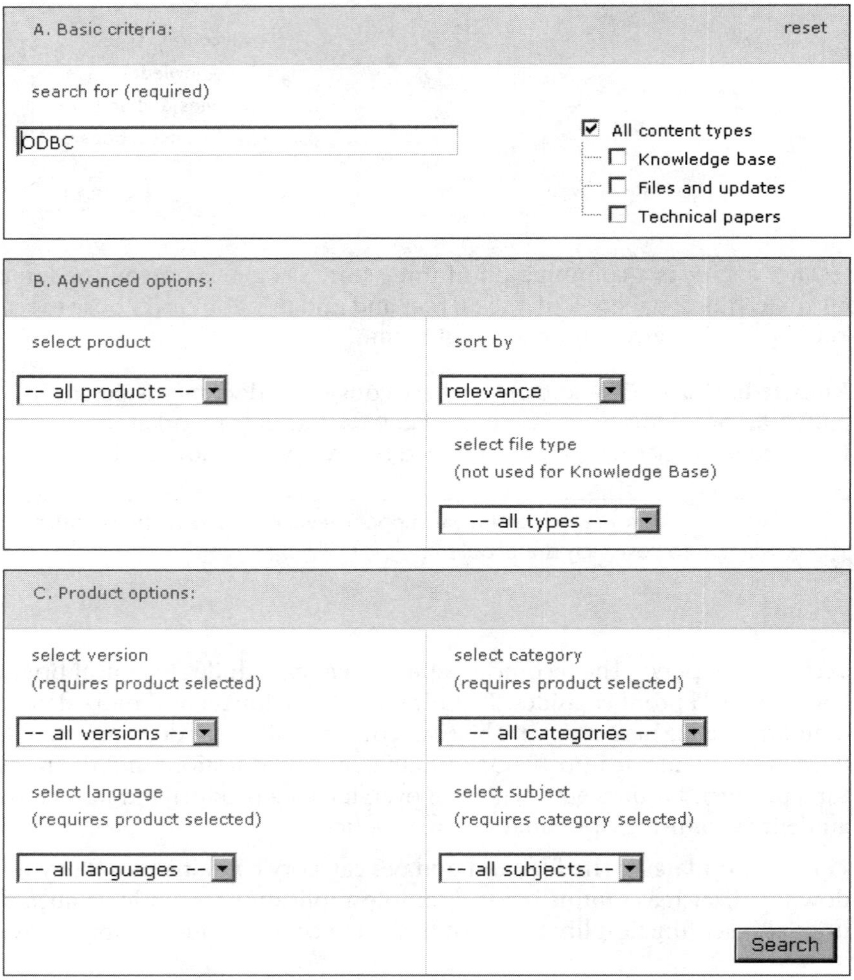

Figure 21-2 Using Advanced Search options

- **Advanced Options**   This box contains drop-down lists where you can choose to search only for documents or files that apply to a particular product. You can choose to have the result list sorted by relevance, date published, or first by relevance and then by date published. In addition, you can search for particular file types by selecting a type from the Select File Type drop-down box. This list is empty if you are searching the knowledge base or any combination of the knowledge base, technical papers, and files and updates. If you select only technical papers or files and updates, it will be populated with appropriate choices.

- **Product Options**   This box allows you the further narrow your search to a particular version of the product selected in the Advanced Options box. You can select a language to receive results that apply only to a particular language version of the product. You can select a broad category if you have previously selected a product. After selecting a product, you can narrow your search by selecting a subject.

The Advanced Search options give you great control over your search results. Click the Search button when you have made your selections.

Search Results

After clicking the Search button, the Results page will be displayed, as shown here. At the top of the page, you will see the search term along with the number of results and the amount of time that the search required.

Searched for **ODBC join**.   Results **1 - 10** of about **61**. Search took **0.04** seconds.
Previous page|Basic search|Advanced search

Title	Product Version	Article ID / File Name	Content Type
Specifying Outer **Join** Syntax for an **ODBC** Driver Without ...	**Seagate Crystal Reports 7**	c2003023	**Knowledge Base**
Creating a report through an ODBC driver generates one of various error messages. Examples of the various error messages are:ODBC ERROR:"Query contains an illegal outer-join request" or"Syntax Error"or "Expected lexical element not found: **[Published Date:2004/01/05]**			

If the results require more than one page, you will see page navigation links at the bottom of the page.

1 2 3 4 5 6 7 Next

Each result is displayed in its own box with its title, the product and version that it applies to, the name of the file, the content type, and a description of the contents. Click the title to display a knowledge base article. Technical papers are usually PDFs. When you select either a technical paper or a file, a second page will appear, and if you click the title again, it will either open in the browser or prompt you to download or open the file, depending on your browser setting.

Downloads and Updates

The Downloads and Updates page contains links to the most commonly needed files.

- **Critical Updates**   Critical updates are applications or SDK patch files necessary to ensure that security is maintained. You should investigate and apply these patches.

- **Service Packs**   Service packs are used to apply many patches and updates using only one file. They are released occasionally and incorporate the monthly hot fixes.

 CAUTION   Service packs are generally safe, but they should be tested before installation on production systems.

- **Monthly Hot Fixes**   Monthly hot fixes are groups of patches and updates that are released on a scheduled monthly basis. They should be tested before implementation. You can sign up to receive an e-mail when monthly hot fixes are released.

- **Merge Modules**   Merge modules are used to deploy applications that incorporate Crystal Reports functionality. Different files are used for different application platforms.

- **Crystal Reports Samples**   This link takes you to the Crystal Reports Samples page, where you can download report samples and application samples for several development environments.

Discussion Groups (Forums)

The Discussion Groups link takes you to the Forums page. The forums are intended for user-to-user interaction; they are not the proper place to post questions if you need a response from Business Objects. There are several forums, divided into topic areas, for each product. In addition to the English forums, there are also French and German language forums. You can browse the existing posts, post your own messages, or reply to other posts. You must register in order to make any posts on the forums.

You can search the forum message threads using the Search the Forums link. After clicking Search the Forums, this form will be displayed.

Search Online Forums

For messages containing this exact phrase:

[   ]   Submit Search

Search these forums (select at least one):
☑ Select all forums

☑ Ask the Community

☑ Seagate Analysis

☑ Seagate Info

☑ Crystal Reports

☑ Graphs & Maps	☑ Formulas
☑ Exporting	☑ Data Connectivity
☑ Web Components	☑ Subreports

You can enter a search term and select the forums that you want searched. A list of messages containing the term will be listed, and you can click them to see the entire message.

Forums Search

Search Results: Sorted by date, descending   Search Again

Subject	Name	Date
Can	donnie.dallas	8/27/2004 4:27:54 PM
Windows Trusted Connection when using Crystal Acti...	valdny	8/27/2004 10:29:47 AM
New Stored Procedure Parameter Not Listed...	EAC	8/27/2004 6:17:56 AM
Problem changing datasource location...	Own	8/27/2004 3:26:16 AM
native SQL v. ODBC drivers	al maragni	8/26/2004 9:07:18 AM
Error 20599 Cannot oper SQL Server...	anonymous	8/26/2004 7:07:03 AM
Mysql Problem	Matt Martin	8/26/2004 5:50:06 AM

Product Documentation

The Product Documentation link displays the Product Documentation on the web page, where you can browse to documentation files related to your product. You can change languages by clicking one of the language buttons aligned vertically on the right side of the page. The documents displayed on this page are the current versions of the documentation files that are shipped with the product.

Contact Support

Selecting the Contact Support link opens the Contact Support page. Three types of support contacts are available from this page:

- **Answers by Email**   To use Answers by Email, you must first register your product. Follow the screen prompts to send a question to customer support. You will receive an answer via e-mail.

PART III

- **Report a Bug** Use the Report a Bug form to report bugs in your product to Business Objects. They will not necessarily respond to your bug report, or fix your bug, but the report will be logged and compiled with all other bug reports.
- **Remote Diagnostics Service** Crystal Reports support representatives can use the Webex tool, available from this link, to get a real-time view of your system in order to facilitate problem solving.

Popular Technical Content

Selecting the Popular Technical Content link will open a page that lists the top 10 knowledge base articles.

Top 10 Knowledge Base Articles

Following are our most viewed articles, updated every month.

1. Runtime File Requirements for the Report Designer Component Version 9

2. Error message: "Cannot find keycodev2.dll or invalid keycode" appears in Visual Studio .NET

3. How do you deploy an application that uses Crystal Reports and Visual Studio .NET?

Top 10 technical briefs

Top 10 files and updates

What's new

You can browse this list to see what problems are occurring most often and click the articles to read about workarounds or solutions. To the right of the list are links to the top 10 technical briefs, the top 10 files and updates, and the What's New page.

What's New

On the What's New page, you select your product to display links to the newest related information, as shown here.

What's New – Crystal Reports

Technical support information for Crystal Reports published in the last full month.

- Product documentation on the web
- Critical Updates
- Crystal Reports 10 Monthly Hot Fixes
- Development
- Installation
- Report Application Server (RAS)
- Report Designer
- Web

Exercise 21.1: Doing a Basic Search

1. Open a web browser and go to http://support.businessobjects.com.

2. Click the Knowledge Base link to open the search page.

3. Enter **templates** as the search string, and click the Search button.

4. Browse the returned items. Go forward a page or two.

5. Find the article that tells you how to apply templates to a report. Print it for reference.

Exercise 21.2: Doing an Advanced Search

1. Open a web browser and go to http://support.businessobjects.com.

2. Click the Knowledge Base link to open the search page.

3. Click the Advanced Search link.

4. Search for **templates** in the technical papers area. Search for articles related only to the English version of Crystal Reports 10.

5. Search again, but use version 9. Note that the version 9 articles apply equally well to version 10, but were excluded from the search on version 10.

 TIP   Be wary of too much filtering. Articles of interest to you may be excluded.

Exercise 21.3: Retrieving Current Application Updates

1. Open a web browser, and go to http://support.businessobjects.com.

2. Click the Downloads and Updates link.

3. Click Critical Updates, and then Crystal Reports 10.

4. Download the update file.

5. Click the Service Packs link, and then click Crystal Reports Service Packs.

6. Download the service pack.

7. Click the Monthly Hot Fixes link, and then click Crystal Reports.

8. Scroll down to the Crystal Reports 10 area.

9. You will see updates for several different Crystal Reports components. Download cr10win_en.zip (report designer), common10win_en.zip (common components), dbex10win_en.zip (database and export drivers).

10. Unzip and install the updates if you wish.

Business Objects Developer Sites

Business Objects provides two specialized sites for report developers.

Developer Zone

The Developer Zone (http://www.businessobjects.com/products/dev_zone) is a web site devoted to Crystal Reports and Crystal Enterprise developers. Those users who are integrating Crystal Reports or Crystal Enterprise into an application or web site will find many useful resources and samples there. The Developer Zone is divided into four main areas, depending on the development environment: a .NET zone, a Java zone, a zone for ASP or COM developers (Visual Basic, Delphi), and a zone for users of the Data Integrator product.

Report Design Zone

The Report Design Zone (http://www.businessobjects.com/products/dev_zone/reporting) is a new web site for report designers. It can be reached via links from several Business Objects web sites. Here you will find resources of specific interest to report designers, including samples, technical documents, and tips and tricks.

Utilities

Several utilities are available to help you troubleshoot specific types of Crystal Reports problems. The utilities discussed here are used to help diagnose installation problems or database connectivity problems.

SQLCon

SQLcon32 is a Delphi application developed by Crystal Reports engineers to test ODBC connectivity. It is not supported and not frequently updated. You can use it to test your ODBC connections. It sends the same types of ODBC commands to the data source as Crystal Reports, enabling you to determine if your problem is specific to Crystal Reports, or is due to the ODBC configuration. If you are using a connection method that requires a database client, you should first verify that the client is fully functional before using SQLCon32 to check the ODBC functionality.

Download and Installation

To download the SQLCon32 utility, search the Business Objects support site for SQLCon32.zip. The zip file contains the application and a readme file. Unzip it. No installation is required; simply click the executable to launch the application.

File Menu

The application's File menu contains three options:

- **Clear Window** erases the content of the application window.
- **Save to File** saves the contents of the window to a text file with a .log extension. You must choose a name and location for the file.
- **Exit** closes the application.

Server Menu

The Server menu is used to test connections to ODBC data sources. It has four options. In order to understand the different connection choices, you must understand the connection process that Crystal Reports uses and that SQLCon32 mimics.

For every connection attempt, Crystal Reports first attempts to connect using only the information stored in the ODBC DSN (without requesting logon credentials from the user). For desktop databases, the initial connection uses the SQLConnect command. For SQL databases, the initial connection uses the SQLDriverConnect command.

If the initial connection fails, Crystal Reports will attempt to connect a second time, this time requesting logon information. The second connection attempt uses the ODBC SQLDriverConnect command and prompts for logon information. You can choose one of the connection options to connect to your ODBC data source to verify that the ODBC driver and DSN are properly configured for connections. If the connection is successful, connection information will be displayed. If the connection is unsuccessful, error messages will display.

Driver Connect (SQLDriverConnect)   This connection option corresponds to the second connection attempt that Crystal Reports makes. If you choose this option, the Select Data Source dialog box will be displayed. System and file DSNs are available for testing. Select one, and click OK. The logon prompt for that data source will be displayed. Enter the user ID and password (or leave them blank if credentials are not required), and click OK. If the connection is successful, some information will be displayed in the window, as shown here for a connection to the sample database.

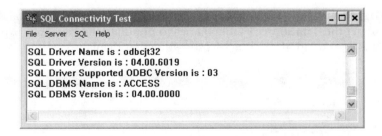

Simple Connect (SQLConnect)   This connection option corresponds to the initial connection attempt to desktop databases that Crystal Reports makes. The dialog box shown here will be displayed; there you can select a DSN and enter a user name and password. Click OK, and the connection will be made. Connection information will display in the window.

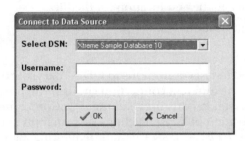

Silent Connect (SQLDriverConnect)   This connection option corresponds to the initial connection attempt to SQL databases that Crystal Reports makes. When you select Silent Connect, this dialog box will display. You can only choose a DSN; you cannot enter a user name and password. If the data source requires a user name and password, they must be saved with the DSN.

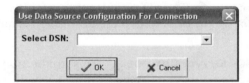

Disconnect   This command disconnects you from the currently connected ODBC data source.

SQL Menu
Each command on the SQL menu sends a query to the connected data source.

Get Listing of Tables (SQLTables)   This is the same command that Crystal Reports uses to get the data source's table names to populate the Database Expert. When you select this command, the dialog box shown here is displayed.

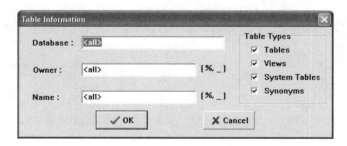

You can filter the records returned by checking or clearing the table type options and entering a specific database, or by entering a search string in the Owner or Name box. You can use wildcard characters in the search string. The percent sign (%) will match to any number of characters, and the underscore (_)will match to any single character. Clicking OK returns the matching entries, showing the database, owner, name, and type for the tables.

NOTE The Database box in these dialog boxes is used for databases like Microsoft SQL Server that store multiple databases together.

Get Fields of a Table (SQLColumns)   Selecting this command opens the dialog box shown here. You can filter the results by entering a specific database, owner, or table. Clicking OK returns the column name, type, and length. Note that when using this option, you should always enter a table name. Otherwise, you will not be able to tell which tables the returned columns belong to.

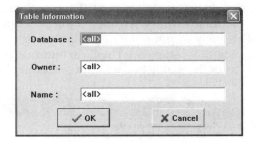

Get Listing of Procedures (SQLProcedures)   This option also displays a filtering dialog box. You can enter a specific database and a search string for owner and name. The result includes the database, owner, and procedure name.

Get Parameters of a Procedure (SQLProcedureColumns)   As with the table columns query, you should enter a specific procedure name in the filtering dialog box for this option. The query returns the parameter name, parameter type, data type, and length. The parameter types are

- **RETURN VALUE**   This parameter type indicates whether the procedure ran successfully or not. It is not part of the result set.
- **INPUT**   These are the only parameters that you must supply.
- **OUTPUT**   A procedure that returns OUTPUT parameters cannot be used by Crystal Reports.
- **RESULT COLUMN**   These are the fields of the record set that the procedure returns.

PART III

- **INPUT/OUTPUT** A procedure that returns INPUT/OUTPUT parameters cannot be used by Crystal Reports.
- **UNKNOWN** A parameter type of UNKNOWN indicates that the ODBC driver does not know what the type is.

Get Fields of a Procedure (SQLExecDirect + SQLDescribeColumn)

This procedure requires that you enter a call to a procedure using ODBC syntax, as shown here. It returns the column name, type, and length of the fields in the result set.

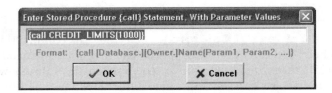

Execute a Query (SQLExecDirect) When you select this command, the Enter SQL Statement dialog box opens, as shown here. If you enter a SQL statement in the window and click OK, the results will be returned in the SQLCon32 window. You can highlight portions of the query to run separately, but this will only work if the highlighted portion is a complete SQL statement. The Clear button erases the SQL statement, and the Cancel button closes the dialog box without executing the statement.

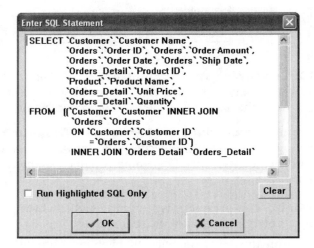

TIP You can copy a query from the Show SQL Query dialog box in Crystal Reports and run it using the Execute a Query command. You can then compare this result to the report result to see if there is processing going on in the report that is causing problems.

ODBC Trace

The ODBC Data Source Administrator has the capability to log all calls made through any ODBC driver. This logging is called *tracing*. You turn on tracing on the Tracing tab of the ODBC Administrator. You can look at the trace file to determine exactly what ODBC commands Crystal Reports is executing; this may be helpful in diagnosing problems. If you are using a connection method that requires a database client, you should first verify that the client is working correctly.

Creating the Trace File

Open the ODBC Data Source Administrator and select the Tracing tab, as shown in Figure 21-3. You will use the options on the left of the window. The options on the right are for more advanced debugging.

Log File Path   Enter or browse to the name and location of the file you want to use for logging. The default is a file named SQL.LOG in the root of the C: directory. You can empty the file before starting a new trace to limit the entries to only those you want to see, or you can create a new file. If you change the log file, click the Apply button to ensure that the change is recorded before starting the trace.

Start Tracing Now   Click the Start Tracing Now button to start logging ODBC calls. The button text will change to "Stop Tracing Now." Leave the ODBC Administrator open, and perform the action that you want to trace. If your problem is with a Crystal report, then run the report. Click it again when you want tracing to stop.

NOTE   The execution time for a report based on an ODBC data source will slow down when tracing is turned on.

Figure 21-3
Turning on
ODBC tracing

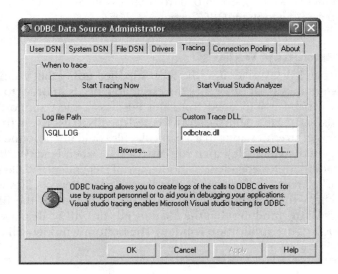

Reading the Trace File

The trace file will contain an ENTER and EXIT entry for each ODBC call. The EXIT entry will have a return code. Any return code other than zero indicates an error condition. The log file can be quite long, so if you are diagnosing an error condition, you may want to search for the word ERROR. If you want to see the query that was executed, search for the word SELECT.

The following example shows the ODBC call that executed the select statement. (The select statement has been truncated.) The calling program is listed first. For Crystal Reports, this will be crw32, as shown here. Then you see the ENTER log entry for the SQLExecDirect call. The EXIT log entry shows a return code of zero or SQL_SUCCESS, so this call was successful. If you looked further in the log, you would see the fetch calls for each record of the result set.

```
crw32   11c4-118c   ENTER SQLExecDirectW
        HSTMT                   02851FD0
        WCHAR *                 0x027C0D24 [        -3] " SELECT ...
        SDWORD                        -3

crw32   11c4-118c   EXIT  SQLExecDirectW  with return code 0 (SQL_SUCCESS)
        HSTMT                   02851FD0
        WCHAR *                 0x027C0D24 [        -3] " SELECT ...
        SDWORD                        -3
```

See Microsoft documentation for more information on the trace file entries and ODBC calls.

ODBC Test

ODBC Test is a Microsoft utility similar to SQLCon32 that allows you to test ODBC connections and calls to ODBC sources. ODBC Test is included in the Microsoft Data Access Components (MDAC) download from Microsoft. See the ODBC Test help file for information on how to use ODBC Test.

Dependency Walker

The Dependency Walker is a Microsoft-supplied utility that examines an executable file and determines what other files the executable needs in order to function. Dependency Walker can be downloaded from the Business Object support site by searching for depends20.zip. Unzip the file and execute depends20.exe to run the Dependency Walker.

If you get an error stating that a particular file could not be found (other than a report file or other user-created file), then you can use the Dependency Walker to determine the hierarchy of module dependency. Another use of Dependency Walker is to list all dependent files for reference, if you need to distribute Crystal Reports files with an application.

To check the dependencies for a particular file, open the file in the Dependency Walker. All the modules that the file depends on will be displayed in a tree view in the upper left of the application window. The bottom window will list any errors or warn-

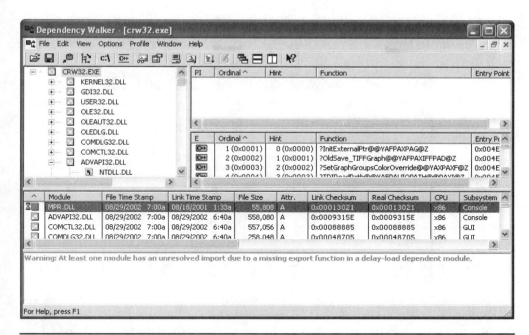

Figure 21-4   Viewing file dependencies

ings. Figure 21-4 shows the dependencies for the Crystal Reports application. See Microsoft documentation for more information on using the Dependency Walker.

Modules

You may encounter a situation where some users are experiencing problems with an application but others have no problems with the same application. You can use the Modules utility to compare the files loaded into memory by the same application on two different computers. The Modules utility can be downloaded from the Business Objects support site; search for modules.zip.

To use Modules, you must run it on a computer where the error occurs. Open Modules, and then perform the actions that cause the error. Once the error has occurred, return to Modules, and select File | New List | Memory Modules. Modules will examine the files loaded in memory and then create a tree 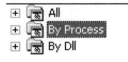 list like the one shown here. Open the By Process node and scroll to the application you are debugging. If you are debugging an error in Crystal Reports, look for CRW32.EXE. Save the listing using the File | Save As command.

Next, run Modules and then the same application on a computer that does not have any problems. Save the listing produced on that computer. Then open both listings in

Modules, and then choose Modules | Differences. The Differences dialog box will be displayed, as shown here.

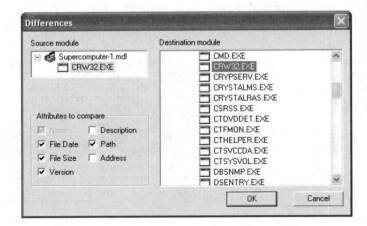

Check the file attributes that you want compared, and then click OK. A new window will open. A tree on the left will contain up to three folders: Identical, Different, or Only In. Files that were the same on both computers will be listed in the Identical node. Files that had some differences will be listed in the Different node. Files that did not exist on one computer will be listed in the Only In node. Knowing which modules are different or missing should help you correct the problem.

Exercise 21.4: Using SQLCon

1. Download and unzip SQLCon32.zip from the support site.

2. Run SQLCon32.exe.

3. Select Server | Driver Connect.

4. Select the Machine Data Source tab, and select the Xtreme Sample Database 10 entry.

5. Click OK. In the Log On dialog box, click OK again.

6. The connection should be successful, and you should see some version information for the components that were used.

7. Select SQL | Get Listing of Tables.

8. Click OK on the Table Information dialog box so that all tables will be returned.

9. Browse the returned data.

10. Leave SQLCon32 open, and open the report from Exercise 20.6 in Crystal Reports.

11. Copy the query from the Show SQL Query dialog box. If you need to supply parameter values, use a blank for the Customer parameter.

12. In SQLCon32, select SQL | Execute a Query, and paste the query into the window.

13. Click OK to run the query.

14. When the results are displayed, notice that the record count matches the Crystal Reports record count.

15. Close SQLCon32.

Exercise 21.5: Using ODBC Trace

1. Open the report from Exercise 20.6 if it is not already open.

2. Open the ODBC Data Source Administrator.

3. Select the Tracing tab.

4. Change the name of the log file to Trace206.LOG. Leave it in the root of the C: directory, or move it a location of your choice. Click Apply.

5. Click the Start Tracing Now button.

6. Go to Crystal Reports, and refresh the report using a blank Customer parameter.

7. When the report completes (this will take some time), go to the ODBC Administrator, and click Stop Tracing Now.

8. Close the ODBC Administrator.

9. Using Windows Explorer, browse to the location of the trace file and double-click it.

10. The file will open in Notepad. Select Edit | Find and search for the word **Select**.

11. You should see the select statement that Crystal Reports used for the report query.

12. Close the log file.

Chapter Review

This chapter covered how to use the Business Objects support site and several trouble-shooting utilities.

Quick Tips

- For Crystal Reports support information, go to http://support.businessobjects.com.

- There are three search engines combined in one on the support site: the knowledge base engine, the technical papers engine, and the files and updates engine.

- The knowledge base contains short articles about specific issues or problems.

- Technical papers are detailed articles explaining some feature or issue at length.

- The search engine has a basic interface or an advanced interface.

- The search string that you enter can use the asterisk as a wildcard character and is case-insensitive. The search will find articles that contain all the individual words in the search string. To search for a phrase, use quotation marks. To search for articles that contain one term or another, use the OR operator. To exclude words from the search, prefix them with a minus sign.

- When doing a basic search, you enter the search string and then choose whether to search one, two, or all three of the knowledge base, technical papers, and files and updates areas.

- When doing an advanced search, in addition to the options of the basic search, you have options for the product, sort order, file type, product version, language, category, and subject.

- Monthly hot fixes, service packs, merge modules, sample reports and applications, and critical security updates are available for download.

- The Business Objects support site contains forums for user interaction. The forums are searchable. The forums are not moderated by Business Objects employees.

- SQLCon32 is a Business Objects utility for testing ODBC connections and running queries using ODBC commands.

- Turn on ODBC tracing to have all ODBC communications logged to a text file. ODBC tracing is turned on and off from the ODBC Data Source Administrator.

- ODBC Test is a Microsoft utility for testing ODBC connections and running queries using ODBC commands. It is installed with MDAC.

- The Dependency Walker is a Microsoft utility that determines the modules that an executable needs to function properly.

- Modules is a utility that determines the currently loaded modules on a computer, can save the list, and can compare one list to another.

Questions

Questions may have more than one correct answer. Choose all answers that apply.

1. Which three areas are searched when you search the Business Objects support site?

   a. Files and updates

   b. Forums

   c. Technical papers

   d. Knowledge base

   e. Developer zone

2. You received an error message in Crystal Reports and want to find out more information. Which area would you search?

   a. Files and updates

   b. Technical papers

   c. Knowledge base

3. You want to learn more about using Crystal Reports templates. Which area would you search?

   a. Files and updates

   b. Technical papers

   c. Knowledge base

4. You need the latest database driver for your database. Which area would you search?

   a. Files and updates

   b. Technical papers

   c. Knowledge base

5. You should use the Business Objects forums to post questions to the Crystal Reports support staff.

   a. True

   b. False

6. Which two utilities can be used to test ODBC connections and run queries?

   a. SQLCon32

   b. ODBC Trace

   c. ODBC Test

   d. Dependency Walker

   e. Modules

7. Which utility would you use if your application was working for some users but not for others?

   a. SQLCon32

   b. ODBC Trace

   c. ODBC Test

   d. Dependency Walker

   e. Modules

8. Which utility would you use if you got an error indicating that a file was missing?

   a. SQLCon32

   b. ODBC Trace

   c. ODBC Test

   d. Dependency Walker

   e. Modules

9. ODBC tracing is turned on using the Tracing tab of the ODBC Data Source Administrator.

   a. True

   b. False

Answers

1. **a, c, d.** Forums have a separate search feature. The Developer Zone is not searched.

2. **c.** Search the knowledge base for short articles on specific problems.

3. **b.** Search the technical papers category for in-depth information about a feature.

4. **a.** Search the files and updates category for updated files.

5. **b.** False. Business Objects support staff do not monitor the forums.

6. **a, c.** Both SQLCon32 and ODBC Test can be used to test connections to ODBC data sources and to run SQL queries.

7. **e.** You would use the Modules utility to compare the loaded files between two different computers.

8. **d.** Use Dependency Walker to determine the files that are required to support an executable.

9. **a.** True. ODBC Trace is not a separate application; it is a feature of the ODBC Administrator.

Creating and Using SQL Commands Elective

Exam RDCR300A expects you to be able to

- Define SQL and SQL Commands
- Describe how SQL is used in Crystal Reports
- Describe server-side processing
- Compare stored procedures and SQL Commands
- Use SQL Commands
- Create and modify SQL Commands
- Save a SQL Command to the repository
- Add a command field to a report
- Create and modify parameters in SQL Commands
- Add tables to a report based on a parameter
- Report from multiple SQL Commands
- Create a dynamic Top N report
- Combine fields from multiple tables (UNION)
- Set location from multiple tables to a SQL Command

Crystal Reports can generate report queries to handle most reporting tasks. However, the queries it generates are restricted to the most basic SELECT statement features. To take full advantage of the power of your database's SQL engine, you must write the report query yourself. Crystal Reports allows you to do this with its SQL Command feature.

SQL Basics

Structured Query Language (SQL) developed in tandem with relational database management theory—a method for creating and manipulating the databases was required. SQL is a fourth-generation programming language used to create and maintain relational databases and tables. A SQL statement or program is interpreted and executed by the SQL engine of a database or database client software.

The SQL language is a standard maintained by the American National Standards Institute (ANSI). Each database vendor certifies that its version of SQL meets one of the ANSI standards to some defined degree. Most database vendors expand beyond the standard with additional features, and few meet all the requirements of the latest standard. But a solid foundation of the language is fixed and understood across vendors.

Crystal Reports generates SQL queries to obtain the required report data when working with SQL databases. It creates the SQL statement based on choices made by the report developer concerning which data sources and fields to use. Unless the report is based on a SQL Command or a stored procedure, Crystal Reports generates a SELECT statement. If the report is based on a stored procedure, Crystal Reports generates a statement that executes the stored procedure. If the report is based on a SQL Command, Crystal Reports sends the defined command to the database instead of generating one.

Data Manipulation Language (DML)

SQL includes commands to create and drop the structures of a database, such as tables, views, indexes, functions, stored procedures, constraints, and so on. However, as a report developer, you will be primarily concerned with the command that handles data retrieval—the SELECT statement. Other data manipulation commands can be run from Crystal Reports and will be mentioned briefly here. All SQL syntax shown in this chapter should be considered as a brief introduction. Full coverage of the SQL language is out of the scope of this book.

CAUTION   Crystal Reports is not intended to be a data change agent, so use data manipulation commands with care.

DELETE

The SQL DELETE statement is used to remove rows from a table. It removes entire rows; individual fields cannot be deleted. The basic syntax of a DELETE statement is

```
DELETE FROM TableName [WHERE Conditions]
```

NOTE   In this and all following syntax statements, square brackets represent optional clauses and user supplied data is shown in italics.

TableName must be the name of the table that you want records deleted from. If the table requires a qualifier (such as the owner or database) for identification, you must include it. *Conditions* are used to restrict the deletion to particular rows. Only the rows that meet the *Conditions* will be deleted. If you do not supply a WHERE clause, every row in the table will be deleted.

INSERT

The INSERT statement is used to add rows to tables. The syntax is

```
INSERT INTO TableName [ColumnList] VALUES ValueList
```

TableName is the name of the table to add rows to. *ColumnList* is a comma-delimited list of column names. If a list of column names is not given, the values will be inserted into the row in the order of the fields in the table definition. *ValueList* is the list of values that should be inserted. The simple form of the INSERT statement adds a single row to a table. Other forms can be used to add multiple rows.

UPDATE

The UPDATE statement is used to modify fields in a table. The syntax is

```
UPDATE TableName SET ColumnName = NewValue [WHERE Conditions]
```

TableName is the name of the table to be updated. *ColumnName* is the name of the field to modify. *NewValue* is an expression giving the new value for the field. The WHERE clause is optional. If it is used, only the fields that meet the *Conditions* will be updated; otherwise, every record in the table will be updated. Multiple columns can be changed by adding more instances of the *ColumnName* = *NewValue* element.

SELECT

The purpose of this section is to cover the basics of a SELECT statement as they relate to Crystal Reports. The SELECT statement was covered briefly in Chapter 20.

Basic SELECT Statement

The basic SELECT statement can take one of the following two forms. Some databases use the first, some the second, and some will accept either. Various clauses of the SELECT statement are discussed in more detail in the sections that follow.

The first form uses the WHERE clause to create the table joins:

```
SELECT [DISTINCT]<list of columns or expressions separated by commas>
  FROM <list of tables separated by commas>
[WHERE <join conditions and filtering conditions>]
[GROUP BY <optional list of columns to group by>]
[ORDER BY <optional list of columns to order by>]
```

The second form uses the JOIN keyword:

```
SELECT [DISTINCT]<list of columns or expressions separated by commas>
  FROM <tables with join expressions>
[WHERE <filtering conditions>]
[GROUP BY <optional list of columns to group by>]
[ORDER BY <optional list of columns to order by>]
```

Aliases can be created for columns, expressions, or tables simply by inserting the desired alias immediately following the column name, expression, or table name. The keyword AS may be used for clarity preceding the alias. Some databases require the AS keyword. Column or expression aliases are returned as the column name, and table aliases are used as shortcuts for the full schema-qualified table name within the query for linking or when it is otherwise necessary to distinguish which table a field belongs to.

Table, view, and column names may be defined with mixed-case characters or with internal spaces. If spaces are used in a name, references to the name must enclose the name in quotation marks. This can vary greatly per type of database and is also affected by what database driver is used for Crystal Reports.

The keyword DISTINCT can be added before the SELECT list to return only one row if there are multiple rows with the same column values. The DISTINCT keyword applies to the entire SELECT list and can cause increases in processing time due to the comparing and filtering that must be done. Avoid using DISTINCT if it is not required.

Crystal Reports constructs SELECT statements using one of the above forms, depending on the database type. It always creates aliases for tables where the alias is the table name (unless you have renamed the table using the Database Expert) and will always prefix column names with the alias it defined for the table. Crystal Reports also always encloses object names in double quotes. If you want to return distinct records, choose the Database menu item and then the Select Distinct Records option, and DISTINCT will be added to the query.

SELECT List

The SELECT list is simply a list of columns or expressions that the user wishes to return. Columns are specified by using the column name as defined in the table. A table and/or schema qualifier or alias should be added to the column name, with a dot between the qualifier and the column name, if it is needed to distinguish the correct column from other like-named columns from other tables in the query. Expressions are valid computations resulting in a single value. Expressions can be single-row or summary-level if the corresponding GROUP BY clause is included and can include functions but not procedures. For some database types, an expression can even be an entire SELECT statement as long as it returns only one value.

The asterisk can be used as a shorthand symbol that means all columns. For example if you have a command like the following, all columns from the Employee table will be selected.

```
SELECT * FROM Employee
```

The asterisk can be prefixed with a table name or table alias to indicate all columns from a particular table.

```
SELECT p.*, d."Order ID"
  FROM Product p INNER JOIN "Orders Detail" d
     ON p."Product ID"=d."Product ID"
```

SQL operators are used to create complex expressions. The available arithmetic operators are + (addition), – (subtraction), * (multiplication), and / (division). The concatenation operator varies depending on the database type. You can also use database functions in expressions. Expressions should always be given an alias.

FROM Clause

The tables listed in the FROM clause can be database tables or views or entire SELECT statements. If a SELECT statement is used, it is called an *inline view*. Some database types do not allow inline views.

Join Types

One of the most basic and valuable features of a relational database is the ability to join two tables together. As stated in Chapter 18, joins have several possible types. A join might be an inner join, a left outer join, a right outer join, or a full outer join. The link type might be equal, greater than, greater than or equal, less than, less than or equal, or not equal.

The most common joins are equal inner joins and equal left outer joins. In an equal inner join, records from both tables are returned if the values in the join columns are equal. Any records from either table that do not have exact matches in the other table are ignored. In an equal left outer join, all records from the left-hand table are returned and any records from the right hand table whose join columns match are merged into the matching row. For left-hand rows with no match, null column values are appended to the row. Equal right outer joins are identical to equal left outer joins, except that all rows from the right-hand table are returned and matching left-hand table rows are merged. In equal full outer joins, rows with identical values in the join columns from each table are merged, rows from either table that did not have matches are also returned, and the missing columns are populated with null values.

NOTE It is common to assume an equal join and omit the word *equal* when describing joins.

Nonequal joins are similar to equal joins, except that more than one row from the left-hand table may be joined to more than one row from the right-hand table. See a SQL reference for more information on nonequal joins.

WHERE Clause Joins

When linking is done in the WHERE clause, it is written in the form shown here.

```
Table1.LinkField operator Table2.LinkField
```

The operator could be =, <=, <, >, >=, <>, !=, etc. To accomplish a left outer or right outer join, some database types use the (+) symbol or the =* symbol, added to the appropriate side of the condition. A full outer join cannot be done with this notation unless you use a UNION to combine the results of a right outer join with the results of a left outer join.

EXAM TIP Understand WHERE clause joins for the exam.

FROM Clause Joins

ANSI SQL 1999–compliant join operations do the join in the FROM clause. (You need to verify that your database is SQL 1999 compliant before using these forms.) There are several forms to consider; not all are described here.

JOIN ON   The JOIN ON syntax allows you to specify join fields from the two joined tables. JOIN ON creates an inner join.

```
SELECT e."Employee ID", e."First Name", e."Last Name",
      a."City", a."Country"
  FROM Employee e INNER JOIN "Employee Addresses" a
      ON e."Employee ID" = a."Employee ID"
```

You must qualify the joined field name with a table name or alias when using it in the SELECT list. You can include anything in the ON clause that you would have previously used in a WHERE clause. However, it is beneficial to keep filtering clauses in the WHERE clause and joining clauses in the ON clause for clarity. Some databases require parentheses around the ON clause conditions. Some databases require the use of the word INNER; others consider it the default and do not require it.

OUTER   Outer joins are described earlier in the "Join Types" section. This is an example of a left outer join:

```
SELECT e."Employee ID", e."First Name", e."Last Name",
      a."City", a."Country"
  FROM Employee e LEFT OUTER JOIN "Employee Addresses" a
      ON e."Employee ID" = a."Employee ID"
```

The OUTER keyword can be omitted if desired.

This is an example of a right outer join:

```
SELECT e."Employee ID", e."First Name", e."Last Name",
      a."City", a."Country"
  FROM Employee e RIGHT OUTER JOIN "Employee Addresses" a
      ON e."Employee ID" = a."Employee ID"
```

Here is an Oracle example of a full outer join:

```
SELECT "EMPLOYEE"."EMPLOYEE_ID", "EMPLOYEE"."FIRST_NAME",
      "EMPLOYEE"."LAST_NAME", "EMPLOYEE_ADDRESSES"."CITY",
      "EMPLOYEE_ADDRESSES"."COUNTRY"
  FROM "XTREME"."EMPLOYEE" "EMPLOYEE"
      FULL OUTER JOIN
      "XTREME"."EMPLOYEE_ADDRESSES" "EMPLOYEE_ADDRESSES"
      ON ("EMPLOYEE"."EMPLOYEE_ID"=
          "EMPLOYEE_ADDRESSES"."EMPLOYEE_ID")
```

Some databases do not support full outer joins.

Filtering

Restricting the records returned based on some selection criteria is done in the WHERE clause. The Crystal Reports Select Expert translates the user's choices into expressions in the WHERE clause. For complex filtering, the selection formula can be modified manually.

Comparison conditions are used in the WHERE clause or HAVING clause to compare one expression to another. In addition to the usual =, <>, <, >, <=, >= operators, you can also use IS NULL, IS NOT NULL, LIKE, NOT LIKE, BETWEEN, NOT BETWEEN, IN, NOT IN, EXISTS, and NOT EXISTS with some database types. Comparison conditions can be joined with AND or OR and negated with NOT.

Ordering

Ordering the records returned is implemented using the ORDER BY clause. Each field is sorted in the order specified (by default, the sort order is ascending, but a descending sort order can be specified). ASC is used to indicate an ascending sort, and DESC is used to indicate a descending sort order.

Crystal Reports will generate the ORDER BY clause depending on any existing group's Change Group options and the Record Sort Order options. However, choosing the group option to sort "in original order" will have no effect, and no ORDER BY clause will be generated. If the sort "in specified order" is selected, then the sort cannot be done on the server and will be done locally by Crystal Reports.

 EXAM TIP Understand the difference between grouping and ordering (sorting).

Grouping

Grouping is accomplished using the GROUP BY clause. For some database types, the GROUP BY clause also performs a sort on the grouped fields. You must use a GROUP BY clause if you wish to use any aggregation functions such as SUM. Adding a group in Crystal Reports will not necessarily add a GROUP BY clause to the SQL query. A SELECT statement containing a GROUP BY clause will return data only at the group level; it will not return any detail rows. If a report has a group and the detail rows are suppressed, Crystal Reports will add a GROUP BY clause to the SQL query. If multiple groups exist and detail rows are suppressed, Crystal Reports will add a GROUP BY clause for the innermost unsuppressed group.

If a GROUP BY clause is specified in the query, then aggregation functions can be used. Every field in the SELECT list that is not also in the GROUP BY clause must be aggregated in some way. Common aggregation functions are SUM, COUNT, MAXIMUM, and MINIMUM.

 NOTE The SELECT statement options discussed here are only those that Crystal Reports can generate. To take full advantage of SQL Commands, you should investigate the SELECT statement options that Crystal Reports *cannot* generate for you.

PART III

Exercise 22.1: Creating a Basic Query

1. Write a query that returns the first name, last name, and birth date of each employee. (See Figure 2-3, in Chapter 2, if you need help with table and field names.)

2. A query similar to the following will meet the requirement.

```
SELECT 'First Name', 'Last Name', 'Birth Date'
FROM    Employee
```

Exercise 22.2: Creating a More Advanced Query

1. Create a query that returns the customer name, order ID, order amount, order date, and ship date for all orders. Sort the rows by Customer Name and then by Order ID, starting with the latest order.

2. The following is a query that meets the requirement.

```
SELECT C.'Customer Name', O.'Order ID', O.'Order Amount',
       O.'Order Date', O.'Ship Date'
FROM   Customer C INNER JOIN Orders O
       ON C.'Customer ID'=O.'Customer ID'
ORDER BY C.'Customer Name', O.'Order ID' DESC
```

3. Notice the use of aliases for the table names. Since the sample database is a Microsoft Access database, you must use the JOIN syntax in the FROM clause, rather than joining the tables in the WHERE clause.

Exercise 22.3: Examining a Crystal Reports–Generated Query

1. This is the Crystal Reports generated query from the Exercise 20.6 report, when "Bike" is used as the parameter.

```
SELECT 'Customer'.'Customer Name', 'Orders'.'Order ID',
       'Orders'.'Order Amount', 'Orders'.'Order Date',
       'Orders'.'Ship Date', 'Orders_Detail'.'Product ID',
       'Product'.'Product Name', 'Orders_Detail'.'Unit Price',
       'Orders_Detail'.'Quantity'
FROM   (('Customer' 'Customer' INNER JOIN 'Orders' 'Orders'
           ON 'Customer'.'Customer ID'='Orders'.'Customer ID')
         INNER JOIN 'Orders Detail' 'Orders_Detail'
           ON 'Orders'.'Order ID'='Orders_Detail'.'Order ID')
         INNER JOIN 'Product' 'Product'
           ON 'Orders_Detail'.'Product ID'='Product'.'Product ID'
WHERE  'Customer'.'Customer Name' LIKE '%Bike%'
ORDER BY 'Customer'.'Customer Name', 'Orders'.'Order ID',
         'Orders_Detail'.'Product ID'
```

2. How many fields will this query return? (9.)

3. Which tables are used? (Customer, Orders, Orders Detail, and Product.)

4. How will the rows be sorted? (By Customer Name, then Order ID, and then Product ID, all in ascending order.)

5. How is the parameter used? (It is used in the WHERE clause to filter the records.)

SQL Command Overview

SQL Commands are Crystal Reports data sources that you can create using SQL statements. After creation, a SQL Command behaves similar to a regular table that is chosen as a data source.

Benefits of Using SQL Commands

The benefits of SQL Commands make them a feature that you should learn and use whenever appropriate:

- **Leverage SQL knowledge** If you are familiar with your database's version of SQL, you can easily develop queries that will support your reporting needs. These queries can then be used directly in Crystal Reports as data sources.

- **Use advanced SQL** The report queries that Crystal Reports generates must be as generic and therefore as simple as possible. Using SQL Commands, you can take advantage of advanced SELECT options such as UNIONs, subqueries, and inline views, or any other possible processing using your database's capabilities to the fullest.

- **Server-side processing** You can design Crystal Reports such that grouping and sorting is done on the server—and you can use SQL Expressions to pass even more processing to the server. But by using a SQL Command, you can pass any valid SQL statement to the server and receive back only the result, reducing work that would have to be done locally otherwise.

Comparison of SQL Commands and Stored Procedures

In addition to an implementation of SQL, many of the large databases have their own programming language. Oracle's is called PL/SQL; SQL Server's is called Transact SQL. This language is tied closely to SQL and can execute SQL commands directly, but it also has procedural elements like other third-generation programming languages. You can create variables and execute multiple statements. There are flow control constructs and the concept of modularized code. Using this language, you can create functions and procedures that are compiled and stored in the database. These program modules can have parameters.

SQL Commands, on the other hand, are not stored on the server; they are merely sent to the server when a report is refreshed. For all SQL database types, you can create SQL Commands that consist solely of a SELECT statement. For some database types, you can write a series of statements in a SQL Command as long as the final statement results in a data set.

 EXAM TIP Understand how stored procedures differ from SQL Commands.

How SQL Commands Differ from Regular Data Sets

When you choose a table or a view as a data source, Crystal Reports constructs a query that uses that table or view. The resulting report query contains only the fields necessary for the report. When you use a SQL Command, the exact query that you create is sent to the database. If you put more fields in the SELECT list than are actually required by the report, they are not deleted from the query. They are all returned to Crystal Reports. If you use multiple tables (from the same data source) in a report, Crystal Reports generates one query with join operations. If you use a SQL Command linked to a table in a report, Crystal Reports must execute the SQL Command, retrieve the result, and then execute a separate query to return the values needed from the table. Then it must join the two results locally. This can cause a performance slowdown.

SQL Command Creation and Maintenance

SQL Commands are created using the Database Expert. They can be stored in the repository for reuse or for sharing among developers. Once a SQL Command is created, it is used exactly like a table when designing a report. The fields that are returned by the query are available in the Field Explorer as database fields, and you can join a command object to a real table, although that is not recommended.

EXAM TIP A thorough understanding of the creation and maintenance of SQL Commands is vital to passing the exam.

Creating a SQL Command

Open the Database Expert. Each connected database that allows SQL Commands will have an Add Command node under the connection name, as shown here for the sample database. Double-click the Add Command node, or select it and click the arrow button to add it to the Selected Tables list. This will cause the Add Command to Report dialog box to appear.

The Add Command to Report dialog box has only two main areas, as shown in Figure 22-1. The large list box on the left is used to enter the query. The list box and buttons on the right are used to create parameters for the SQL Command. You can enter any SQL statements that would be valid for the selected data source. Whatever you enter will be sent unaltered (except for parameter substitution) to the database. After entering the query and clicking OK, the query will be tested by executing it on the database. If it fails, you will receive an error message. If it succeeds, the dialog box will close, and you will be returned to the Database Expert.

TIP You can copy the text from a report's Show SQL Query window and paste it into the Add Command to Report dialog box as a starting point for your query.

Figure 22-1
Creating a SQL
Command

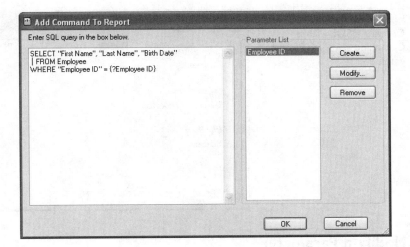

The command will appear under the Selected Tables list, as shown here. The name of the SQL Command defaults to "Command." Rename it by selecting it and clicking F2. If you select the command and click

the arrow to move it back to the Available Data Sources list box, it will be deleted.

Modifying a SQL Command

To modify a SQL Command, select it in the Database Expert, right-click, and choose Edit. The Modify Command dialog box, which is identical to the Add Command to Report dialog box, will open.

SQL Command Parameters

When using SQL Commands, you have the capability to create parameters. These parameters can be both less powerful and more powerful than regular Crystal Reports parameters. They must be simple types such as string, number, or date, and cannot be multivalue the way normal parameter fields can be. SQL Command parameters are converted to strings and added to the database query before it is sent to the server. Because of this, you can do things with these parameters that are similar to constructing the query programmatically.

Create a Parameter

To create a parameter, click the Create button in the Parameter List panel of the Add Command to Report dialog box. The Command Parameter dialog box will appear, as shown in Figure 22-2. You must enter a name for the parameter and select a data type. Prompting text and a default value are optional. Click OK to create the parameter. If you do not use the parameter in the SQL Command, it will be removed when the dialog box is closed.

PART III

Figure 22-2
Creating a SQL
Command
parameter

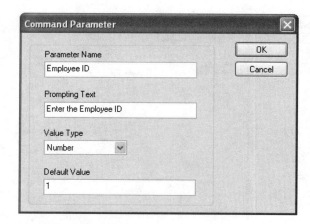

Modify a Parameter

To modify an existing parameter, select it in the Modify Command dialog box or the Add Command to Report dialog box, and click the Modify button. This reopens the Command Parameter dialog box, so you can make changes to the entries there. In addition, any command parameters that you create will also appear in the Field Explorer under the Parameters node. If you choose to edit a command parameter in the Field Explorer, the Edit Parameter Field dialog box will display, as shown in Figure 22-3. All options in the dialog box are unavailable except the Prompting text box and the Default Values button. You cannot change the data type or turn the parameter into a multivalue parameter. However, you can create a list of default values for the parameter, just as you can for regular parameters. You can also rename a command parameter in the Field Explorer by selecting the Rename option from the right-click menu.

Figure 22-3
Editing command
parameters

You can delete a command parameter in the Modify Command dialog box or the Add Command to Report dialog box by selecting it and clicking the Remove button. You cannot delete a command parameter using the Field Explorer.

Use a Parameter

Only command parameters, parameters created in the Modify Command or the Add Command to Report dialog box, can be used in SQL Commands. Parameters created in the Field Explorer cannot be used in SQL Commands. To use a parameter, type it into the SQL query, prefixing it with a question mark and enclosing it in braces ({ }). You can also double-click the parameter name to add it to the query at the cursor position.

 EXAM TIP   Only command parameters can be used in SQL Commands.

Before the command is executed, the parameter values will be substituted for the parameter placeholder in the query. The substitution will be a direct replacement of the parameter name placeholder with the value entered by the user. You can place a command parameter anywhere in a query, not just in the WHERE clause. However, you should not use a parameter for inputting field names or the entire select list. If the report is run later with different values, you will get an error. Crystal Reports retrieves the field list the first time the query is run and cannot adjust to changes made later unless you perform a database verification (Database | Verify Database). If you use a parameter for gathering a table name, or an entire clause, be sure to include whatever quotation marks are required in the query itself or in the parameter value so that they will appear in the proper places in the report query.

Storing SQL Commands in the Repository

To add a SQL Command to the repository, select it in the Database Expert, right-click, and choose Add to Repository. The Add Item dialog box will appear, as shown in Figure 22-4. You can change the name, author, and description. However, changes to the description will not be saved; the default description is the query text. You must select a folder location. Click OK to add the item to the repository.

The icon in the Select Tables list of the Database Expert will change to reflect that the command is connected to the repository. The command will also appear in the Available Data Sources list under the Repository folder. All SQL Commands appear under folders called "Query." To identify the object you want, right-click, and select Properties. The Properties dialog box will appear, and you can see the details about the object, as shown here.

In order to modify a repository SQL Command, you must disconnect it from the repository. To disconnect it,

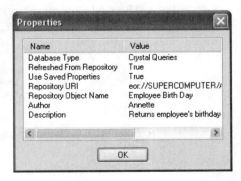

Name	Value
Database Type	Crystal Queries
Refreshed From Repository	True
Use Saved Properties	True
Repository URI	eor://SUPERCOMPUTER/
Repository Object Name	Employee Birth Day
Author	Annette
Description	Returns employee's birthday

Figure 22-4
Adding a command to the repository

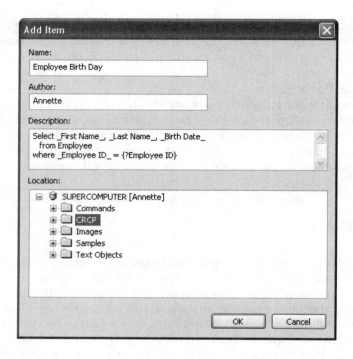

select it in the Database Expert, right-click, and choose Disconnect from Repository. To add it back to the repository after modifications, just use the Add to Repository command again, and select the old entry in the repository before clicking OK. You will be warned that you are replacing an item.

Exercise 22.4: Creating a SQL Command

1. Create a new report using the standard wizard.

2. On the Data screen, open the Favorites folder and the Xtreme CRCP data source.

3. Select the Add Command item, and click the right arrow button to move it into the Selected Tables list.

4. The Add Command to Report dialog box will open. Enter the following as the query:

```
SELECT e."First Name" & ' ' & e."Last Name" AS Name,
       e."Birth Date",
       s."First Name" & ' ' & s."Last Name" AS Supervisor
FROM Employee AS e LEFT OUTER JOIN Employee AS s
     ON e."Supervisor ID" = s."Employee ID"
```

5. Click OK.

6. Select the Command and press F2. Change the name to **EmployeeBirthday**.

7. Click the Next button.

8. Add all the fields to the report. Click Next.

9. Group on the Supervisor field. Click Finish.

10. Save the report as **Exercise 22.4**.

Exercise 22.5: Using SQL Command Parameters

1. Open the report from Exercise 22.4.

2. Open the Database Expert, select the EmployeeBirthday SQL Command, right-click, and choose Edit Command.

3. Click the Create button.

4. Create a string parameter called **Supervisor**. Click OK.

5. Add the following WHERE clause to the report:

```
WHERE s."First Name" & ' ' & s."Last Name" LIKE '%{?Supervisor}%'
```

 NOTE The string being compared to must be enclosed in quotes because it will appear to the database as a string literal. The percent signs are wildcard characters, so this clause will return any records that contain the value of the Supervisor parameter anywhere in the field.

6. Click OK.

7. You will be prompted for the Supervisor parameter. Enter **Full** and click OK.

8. Click OK to close the Database Expert.

9. Preview the report. You should see employees only for Andrew Fuller.

10. Save the report as **Exercise 22.5**.

Exercise 22.6: Adding a SQL Command to the Repository

1. Open the report from Exercise 22.5.

2. Open the Database Expert, and right-click the EmployeeBirthday command.

3. Select Add to Repository.

4. Name the item **Employee Birthdays by Supervisor**.

5. Select a repository folder, and click OK. You should now see the connected query icon.

6. Click OK to close the Database Expert.

7. Save the report as **Exercise 22.6**.

SQL Command Tips

Some particular problems arise when using SQL Commands, as described in this section. In addition, examples of using SQL Commands to solve reporting requirements that cannot otherwise be met are included. However, you should further investigate your database's version of SQL in order to exploit its unique features.

Avoid Using *

You should never return more columns in a SQL Command than will be used in the report directly or than are needed for computations. Ideally, you would embed the computations in the query too. When Crystal Reports constructs the query for you, it returns only those fields that are used in the report. If you write a SQL Command, every column in the Select list will be returned, whether or not you use it in the report.

For example, say you create a report based on this SQL Command

Item	Value
Open Document	0 ms
Run the Database Query	4 ms
Read Database Records	32 ms
Format First Page	61 ms
Number of pages formatted	1
Average time to format a page	61 ms

```
SELECT * FROM Employee
```

including the Employee ID, Supervisor ID, Last Name, First Name, Position, and Birth Date fields on the report. Then you run the report, look at Report | Performance Information, and choose Performance Timing. You would see something like the results shown at left.

Now, say you change the SQL Command:

```
SELECT "Employee ID", "Supervisor ID",
       "First Name", "Last Name", "Position", "Birth Date"
   FROM Employee
```

When you run the report and view the Performance Information again, you will see a much improved processing time, similar to that shown here.

Item	Value
Open Document	0 ms
Run the Database Query	2 ms
Read Database Records	7 ms
Format First Page	35 ms
Number of pages formatted	1
Average time to format a page	35 ms

The large performance gain this example shows is due to the large BLOB and Memo fields in the Employee table, which are returned in the first query even though they are not used.

Avoid Using Multiple SQL Commands

You should avoid using multiple SQL Commands in the same report. If you use multiple linked SQL Commands, processing time will degrade severely.

Suppose the employee listing from the previous example needs the employee's state and country added to it. You create a second SQL Command using the following SQL statement and link it to the original SQL Command using the Employee ID field.

```
SELECT "Employee ID", Region, Country
   FROM "Employee Addresses"
```

You will get the following warning message, which is always generated when using multiple data sources.

After clicking OK and running the report, you will get timing statistics similar to those shown at right.

Now remove the second SQL Command, and modify the first SQL Command to return all the needed data, as the following does:

Item	Value
Open Document	0 ms
Run the Database Query	6 ms
Read Database Records	29 ms
Format First Page	60 ms
Number of pages formatted	1
Average time to format a page	60 ms

```
SELECT e."Employee ID", e."Supervisor ID",
       e."First Name", e."Last Name", e."Position", e."Birth Date",
       a.Region, a.Country
  FROM Employee e INNER JOIN "Employee Addresses" a
       ON e."Employee ID" = a."Employee ID"
```

After running the report, the timing information will be significantly improved, as shown here.

When you use multiple SQL Commands, Crystal Reports will run the first query once, and then it will run the second query once for each record returned by the first query. When

Item	Value
Open Document	0 ms
Run the Database Query	2 ms
Read Database Records	10 ms
Format First Page	38 ms
Number of pages formatted	1
Average time to format a page	38 ms

running the second query, Crystal Reports adds no filtering; it just runs the query as is, returning the entire result set many times. You can verify this behavior by turning on ODBC tracing and examining the trace file.

EXAM TIP Know the significance and performance implications of using multiple SQL Commands on a report.

Changing a Report from Using Tables to Using a SQL Command

You may have a report that is based on more than one table that you want to convert to use a SQL Command for some efficiency reason. This is problematic. The Set Database Location dialog box is intended to directly replace one table with another, and works just as expected if you want to replace only one table with a SQL Command. However, it is not designed to allow you to replace multiple data sources with a single data source.

There are no truly good solutions to this problem. One solution uses the following steps:

1. Create a SQL Command that contains the complete query needed to supply all the fields the report requires. Save this SQL Command to the repository. (It must be saved to the repository, because you cannot create a new SQL Command while using the Set Database Location dialog box.)

2. Comment out every line of every formula to maintain the logic but avoid errors during the conversion.

3. Save a copy of the report to use as a template, so you can easily reproduce the existing formatting.

4. Remove all tables except one from the report. You will receive messages that fields from the removed tables are being removed from the report. (You cannot avoid this using this solution.)

5. Use the Set Database Location dialog box to change the location of the remaining table to the SQL Command saved in the repository.

6. Verify the database.

7. Reinsert the fields that were removed.

8. Edit each formula, removing the comment characters and making any changes required for the new location of the fields.

9. Apply the report that was saved to be used as a template to reapply the original formatting.

Another solution uses these steps:

1. Open the Show SQL Query dialog box for the report, and copy the query.

2. Use the Add Command option in the Database Expert to create a SQL Command using the saved query, and save it to the repository. Remove the SQL Command from the Selected Tables list, and close the Database Expert.

3. Open the Set Datasource Location dialog box. For each table in the report, select the table, then select the SQL Command stored in the repository, and click Update. Make no changes, and click OK on the Mapped Fields dialog box. When you are finished with this step, you will have one instance of the SQL Command for each of the original tables. Click Close to close the dialog box.

4. If you look at each table in the Field Explorer, you will now see that each is just an alias for the SQL Command. Each table contains all the fields from the SQL Command, with some fields being checked as added to the report and some not. The checked fields will differ for each table. The goal now is to change the fields used in the report so that they are accessed from only one of the aliases.

5. Decide which alias you are going to use, and then edit each formula field. Select any field references in the formula, and then double-click the field of the same name in the chosen alias. The formula should now refer to the same field names, but in the chosen alias. Do the same for any record selection formulas, formatting formulas, and section formatting formulas.

6. Perform similar replacements for the fields appearing on the report.

7. For each group, use the Group Options dialog box to change the group-by field to the field in the chosen alias.

8. At this point, no green check marks should appear next to any fields in tables that are not in the chosen alias table. Open the Database Expert and remove the unneeded tables from the report.

Choose a Table Based on a Parameter

If your database has more than one table with the same structure, you can use a parameter in a SQL Command to pick the table for a report. This situation might arise for several reasons. For example, quarterly financial results might be computed and stored in separate tables. The orders from each state might be stored in separate but identical tables. And so on.

Imagine that the Financials table in the sample database was broken up by quarter: Financials2001Q1, Financials2001Q2, Financials2001Q3, and Financials2001Q4. You could write a SQL Command query, as shown here, so that one report could be used for any of the four tables.

```
SELECT 'Company ID', 'Statement Date', 'Cash', 'Account Receivable',
       'Inventories', 'Other Current Assets', 'Land', 'Buildings',
       'Machinery etc', 'Accumulated Depreciation', 'Other Assets',
       'Accounts Payable', 'Accrued Liabilities',
       'Accrued Income Taxes', 'Notes Payable',
       'Deferred Income Taxes', 'Preferred Stock', 'Common Stock',
       'Retained Earnings', 'Net Sales', 'COGS',
       'Selling/Admin/ General Expenses', 'Depreciation',
       'Interest Expenses', 'Other Income Expenses', 'Taxes'
FROM   {?FinTable}
```

You could create the list of tables to choose from by editing the command parameter from the Field Explorer and adding Default Values. When the report is run, the user will select the table they want, and the report will use that table.

CAUTION This technique will not work for tables that are in different data sources. For that situation, you must change the table location using Crystal Reports' Set Datasource Location dialog box, or use capabilities of the database client or ODBC. If using ODBC, you can modify the DSN to point to a different database without affecting any related Crystal Reports. For Oracle, you can change the definition of the database service in the TNSNames.ora file.

Dynamic Top N

Crystal Reports' Group Sort Expert allows you to create Top N (or Bottom N) type reports, but the N value is fixed; you cannot base it on a parameter. Using SQL Commands, you can base the N value on a parameter. In addition, using a SQL Command moves the group selection to the server, whereas the Group Sort Expert does local group suppression.

A query like the following would return the country and the total order amount by country.

```
SELECT 'Customer'.'Country', SUM('Orders'.'Order Amount')
  FROM 'Customer' 'Customer' INNER JOIN 'Orders' 'Orders'
        ON 'Customer'.'Customer ID'='Orders'.'Customer ID'
GROUP BY 'Customer'.'Country'
ORDER BY 'Customer'.'Country'
```

Different databases have different ways to filter out the top or bottom of many groups. With the sample database, this query will work. A parameter called N has been created to prompt the user for the number of groups to display.

```
SELECT TOP {?N} 'Customer'.'Country', SUM('Orders'.'Order Amount')
  FROM 'Customer' 'Customer' INNER JOIN 'Orders' 'Orders'
        ON 'Customer'.'Customer ID'='Orders'.'Customer ID'
GROUP BY 'Customer'.'Country'
ORDER BY SUM('Orders'.'Order Amount') DESC
```

For Oracle 9i, the following query using a subquery will accomplish the same result.

```
SELECT * FROM
( SELECT Customer.Country, SUM(Orders.Order_Amount)
    FROM Customer INNER JOIN Orders
        ON (Customer.Customer_ID=Orders.Customer_ID)
   GROUP BY Customer.Country
   ORDER BY 2 DESC)
WHERE ROWNUM <= {?N}
```

Using UNION

The UNION operation takes the result set of one SELECT statement and appends it to the result set of another SELECT statement. This operation adds rows. Joins, on the other hand, merge rows so that you get a larger row. UNION creates more rows of the original size.

For example, a phone list is needed that contains the phone numbers for customers, employees, and suppliers together in the same report. Phone numbers for each of these entities are stored in a separate, corresponding table. A UNION operation allows us to treat them as if they were all in the same table.

```
SELECT 'Customer' AS Type,
        "Customer Name" AS Organization,
        "Contact Last Name" AS Last_Name,
        "Contact First Name" AS First_Name,
        Phone
   FROM Customer
UNION
SELECT 'Employee', Null,
        "Last Name", "First Name", "Home Phone"
  FROM Employee
UNION
SELECT 'Supplier', "Supplier Name",
        Null, Null, Phone
  FROM Supplier
ORDER BY 3, 4
```

Note that the column names or aliases from the first SELECT statement are the ones used for the entire result set. The number and types of columns in the second and third

SELECTs must match the number and types in the first SELECT, although column size can vary. If any duplicate rows are returned, UNION will eliminate them.

An ORDER BY clause is added at the end; this means that the resulting rows from all SELECT statements are sorted as one group. Only one ORDER BY clause is allowed, so individual SELECT statements cannot have their own ORDER BY clauses.

NOTE UNION ALL differs from UNION in one respect—UNION ALL will not remove duplicate rows. UNION ALL should be used if you do not want duplicates eliminated or if you are certain that there are no duplicates. UNION ALL is more efficient than UNION because it does not have to find and eliminate the duplicate rows. No sort operation is required.

WHERE Clause with Parameters

Say that you want to allow your users to add their own filtering criteria. Create a SQL Command with a string parameter:

```
SELECT "Employee ID", "Supervisor ID", "Last Name",
       "First Name", Position, "Birth Date"
FROM Employee
WHERE {?Where Clause}
```

As long as the user enters a valid WHERE clause, the query will execute and return only the rows that the user needs. Try entering **"Employee ID" IN (1, 2, 3)** in the prompt. You could also create an assortment of WHERE clauses using the Default Values option for the parameter and allow the users to choose one.

Schema-Specific Queries

Imagine that you are in an environment where each user has a copy of an application's tables. This might happen in a database that uses the schema concept, such as Oracle. In this case, the schema needs to change for each user who runs the report. This is difficult to accomplish using Crystal Reports–generated report queries because the schema qualifier is embedded in the report definition, as shown here for Joe's schema in an Oracle database.

```
SELECT  "EMPLOYEE"."EMPLOYEE_ID", "EMPLOYEE"."SUPERVISOR_ID",
        "EMPLOYEE"."LAST_NAME", "EMPLOYEE"."FIRST_NAME",
        "EMPLOYEE"."POSITION", "EMPLOYEE"."BIRTH_DATE"
FROM    "JOE"."EMPLOYEE" "EMPLOYEE"
```

If you want the same report to work for Jane, you would have to copy the report and then change the data source location—leaving you with two reports to maintain. Here is a solution for an Oracle database using a SQL Command that will work for Joe and Jane if each is logging in with their own account:

```
SELECT Employee_ID, Supervisor_ID, Last_Name, First_Name,
       Position, Birth_Date
FROM Employee
```

Because no schema qualifier is listed in the query, the database will resolve the table reference as usual, first looking in the schema of the logged-in user.

Chapter Review

This chapter covered the exam objectives for the Creating and Using SQL Commands Elective, including basic SQL statements, the creation and use of SQL Commands, and several examples of the benefits of using SQL Commands.

Quick Tips

- The SQL SELECT statement is used to return data to the calling program. Other SQL statements are used to modify the database structures and update, delete, and insert data.

- Stored procedures are programs that are stored and run on the database server. They can have parameters and return data sets.

- SQL statements generated by Crystal Reports do not necessarily take full advantage of the processing power of the database server. You can use SQL Commands to write queries of your own that are only constrained by the syntax allowed by the server.

- SQL Commands allow you to use user-defined SQL queries as the data source for a report.

- SQL Commands are created by selecting Add Command under a data source in the Database Expert.

- You can change the default name of a SQL Command using the F2 key.

- SQL Commands can be parameterized, but you can only use simple discrete parameter types.

- Command parameters must be created with the SQL Command. You cannot use regular Crystal Reports parameters in SQL Commands.

- You can modify command parameters from the Field Explorer in limited ways, particularly by adding a default pick list.

- You can save SQL Commands to the repository using the Add to Repository right-click menu item with a SQL Command selected in the Database Expert.

- SQL Commands must be disconnected from the repository to be edited.

- When using SQL Commands, you should avoid using the * operator to return all the columns of a table. Crystal Reports will return all the fields, even if they are not used in the report, causing unnecessary overhead.

- You should not use multiple SQL Commands in the same report because Crystal Reports will process them inefficiently. Combine your queries into one new query if possible.

- There is no easy way to convert a report that is based on multiple tables into a report based on a single SQL Command. Much effort and reformatting is required because the Set Datasource Location dialog box is not intended for this purpose.

- You can use a parameter to get the table name to base a query on when using a SQL Command. All tables that might be chosen must contain the fields used in the query.

- You can create a Top N–type report where the user can specify the value of N using a SQL Command if you create a parameter for determining the N value.

- The UNION operation can be used in a SQL Command to concatenate the results of two or more SELECT statements so that they will be treated as a single result set.

Questions

Questions may have more than one correct answer. Choose all answers that apply.

1. Crystal Reports generates a SELECT statement when a report uses which types of (SQL) data sources?

   a. Tables

   b. Views

   c. Stored procedures

   d. SQL Commands

   e. Business Views

2. Which of the following are true statements about stored procedures?

   a. Stored procedures can have parameters.

   b. Stored procedures are stored in the database.

   c. Stored procedures are run in the database.

   d. Stored procedures might contain variables and flow control statements.

   e. Stored procedures consist of multiple statements.

3. Which of the following SELECT statement clauses or options will never be in a report query that Crystal Reports generates?

   a. UNION

   b. Subquery

   c. Inline view

   d. INTERSECT

   e. HAVING

4. Which two Crystal Reports elements might contribute to the WHERE clause in a generated report query?

   a. Record selection formula

   b. Group selection formula

    c. Database Expert linking

    d. Group Sort Expert

    e. Record Sort Expert

5. Which elements could be in a SELECT list in the SQL Command query?

    a. `"First Name"`

    b. `"First Name" & ' ' & "Last Name"`

    c. `Employee."First Name"`

    d. `"Order Amount" * 0.15 AS Discount`

    e. `"Order Amount" * {@Discount}`

6. SQL Commands can be used to force report processing to the server.

    a. True

    b. False

7. A SQL Command is always named "Command," and you cannot change it.

    a. True

    b. False

8. To add a SQL Command to the repository, you must select the Add to Repository short-cut command in the

    a. Design window

    b. Preview window

    c. Database Expert

    d. Formula Workshop

    e. Repository Explorer

9. SQL Commands previously stored in the repository are available for use in new reports

    a. From the Repository folder of the Available Data Sources list in the Database Expert.

    b. From the Add Command node for the data source in the Available Data Sources list in the Database Expert.

    c. From the Create New Connection node in the Available Data Sources list in the Database Expert.

10. SQL Commands that you are using in your report and that are currently connected to the repository can be edited by selecting the Edit Command option from the right-click menu.

    a. True

    b. False

11. Which two methods can be used to insert a command parameter into the SQL Command text?

    a. Drag the parameter name into the query window.

    b. Select the parameter and click the Add button.

    c. Select the parameter and then click the arrow button to move it.

    d. Double-click the parameter name.

    e. Type the parameter name into the query window including its question mark and braces.

12. SQL Command parameters are created as single-value parameters, but they can be changed to multivalue ones using the Edit option of the Field Explorer.

    a. True

    b. False

13. The table that a report query uses can be based on a parameter only if the report uses a SQL Command.

    a. True

    b. False

14. Basing a report on multiple SQL Commands is not recommended because

    a. The names of the queries will be identical

    b. Linking must be performed locally

    c. It is inefficient

    d. Unless the queries use different databases, you should be able to combine the queries into one

    e. It will cause errors

15. To create a Top N report that allows the user to select the value of N, you must

    a. Use a SQL Command

    b. Use the Group Sort Expert

    c. Have groups in your report

    d. Create a command parameter

    e. Create a regular parameter field

16. You can use the Set Datasource Location dialog box to easily convert a report that uses multiple tables to a report that uses one SQL Command.

    a. True

    b. False

Answers

1. **a, b, e.** When using stored procedures an execute command is generated. When using SQL Commands the user-defined SQL statement is used. Note that when Business Views are used, a SQL statement is generated by Crystal Reports.

2. **All.** Each of the statements is true.

3. **All.** Crystal Reports–generated queries will have at most the SELECT list, FROM clause, WHERE clause, GROUP BY clause, and ORDER BY clause with no subqueries or inline views.

4. **a, c.** The WHERE clause contains the record selection criteria and may contain the table-linking directives.

5. **a, b, c, d.** Answer e is not valid because it refers to a Crystal Reports formula field. You cannot refer to formula fields in a SQL Command.

6. **a.** True, all processing defined in the SQL Command will be done on the server with only the result returned. (Further processing might still happen locally, based on formulas or other formatting.)

7. **b.** A SQL Command is named "Command" by default, but you can change the name using the F2 key.

8. **c.** SQL Commands are added to the repository from the Database Expert.

9. **a.** SQL Commands previously stored in the repository are listed under the Repository folder in the Database Expert.

10. **b.** False. You must disconnect a SQL Command before you can edit it.

11. **d, e.** You can type the parameter name into the query directly, or select the parameter and double-click to add it to the query.

12. **b.** False. You cannot change a command parameter to be multivalue. It can also not be a range or array type.

13. **a.** True. You cannot use a parameter as a placeholder for a table name unless you use a SQL Command.

14. **b, c, d.** Basing a report on multiple SQL Commands is inefficient. Linking must be performed locally. And you should be able to create one query that returns the fields you need unless the queries point to different databases.

15. **a, d.** To create a dynamic Top N report you must use a SQL Command with a command parameter for selecting the value of N.

16. **b.** False. There is no easy method to do this conversion. One method uses the Set Datasource Location dialog box, but it still requires much manual effort.

Reporting from OLAP Data Sources Elective

Exam RDCR300C expects you to be able to

- Define OLAP and OLAP terminology
- Create a basic OLAP report
- Modify the report to include a chart, multiple pages, and a parameter
- Sort, filter, and reorder members
- Show and hide members
- Add automatic totals
- Create calculations using the Calculation Expert
- Create a simple custom calculation
- Apply conditional formatting using the Highlighting Expert
- Apply conditional formatting using the Format Formula Editor

This chapter will cover the requirements for the OLAP elective of the RDCR300 exam. You will learn how to create a report based on an OLAP data source, manipulate the OLAP grid, and apply formatting to the result.

OLAP Overview

A relational database structure consisting of tables with rows and columns is very good at storing lots of detailed information and retrieving subsets of that data. Online transaction processing (OLTP) systems use relational databases to quickly store and retrieve specific bits of information. A completely different database structure is needed when you want to analyze large amounts of information, looking for trends, making projections, computing statistics, and so on. An online analytical processing (OLAP) system is structured such that aggregating large amounts of data in many different ways is fast and efficient.

OLAP cubes are data structures containing facts that can be summarized by any number of dimensions and to any level within the dimensional hierarchy. An OLAP database contains multidimensional cubes. For example, the Orders table contains a record for each order. A very simple OLAP cube might contain the sum of the order amount by customer name by product. This is a two-dimensional cube; the dimensions are Customer Name and Product. The fact that is summarized is the Order Amount. A more complex cube might contain an Order Date dimension that consists of a hierarchy including the order year, order month, and order day. Adding the Order Date dimension to the example gives you a three-dimensional cube with one dimension that supports rolling up the summary to the various date levels.

You should know the OLAP terminology that Crystal Reports uses:

- *Measures* are the facts that are being summarized. They are usually numeric values. For example, Order Amount is a measure.

- A *dimension* is a set of hierarchically related attributes. For example, a Location dimension might consist of Country, Region, and City, where the cities must belong to only one region, and each region must belong to only one country. Time is a dimension that has predefined levels in Crystal Reports.

- Dimensions consist of *levels.* In the Location example above, level 1 is the country, level 2 is the region (e.g., state), and level 3 is the city. A dimension can consist of only one level or several.

- The *members* of a level of a dimension are the values that exist for that level. For example, the Country level might consist of the members USA, Canada, and Mexico.

OLAP in Crystal Reports

Crystal Reports' OLAP grids look much like cross-tabs, but they allow the user to make modifications interactively. A report can consist only of an OLAP grid or it can have regular data in addition to one or more OLAP grids. In a report containing multiple OLAP grids, they can all be based on the same OLAP data source or on different data sources. You can create charts based on OLAP data sources.

OLAP Report Creation Wizard

You used the OLAP Report Creation wizard in Chapter 3 to create an OLAP report. This section covers the wizard in more detail. To open the OLAP Report Creation wizard, select File | New, then select OLAP from the Choose a Wizard panel of the Crystal Reports Gallery, and click OK.

OLAP Data Screen

The first screen that appears is the OLAP Data screen, shown in Figure 23-1, where the source for the OLAP data is selected. The source must be a Crystal Analysis file or a cube contained in one of the supported OLAP engines. Click the Select Cube button or Select CAR File button to find the source you want. The Cube, Type, and Server boxes will then be populated. Once you have selected a cube, the Next button becomes available.

Select Cube

Clicking the Select Cube button opens the Crystal OLAP Connection Browser dialog box, shown next. This dialog box is similar to the Database Expert, except that you use it

Figure 23-1
Selecting an
OLAP data
source

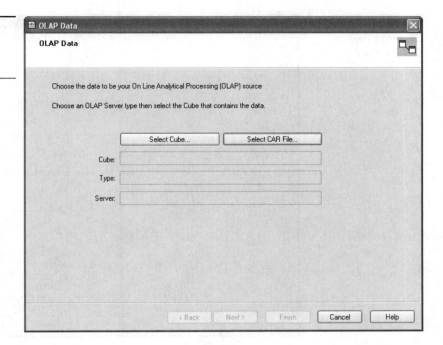

to set up OLAP rather than relational data sources. The tree list on the left of the dialog box contains all the OLAP connections that have been set up. The buttons and shortcut menu items allow you to add and manipulate the connections.

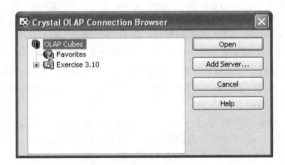

Open Button To pick a cube to use in the report, select it in the tree, and click the Open button. You will be returned to the OLAP Data screen with the Cube, Type, and Server text boxes filled in.

Add Server Button Click the Add Server button to open the New Server dialog box, shown in Figure 23-2. The New Server dialog box is used to configure connections to OLAP data sources. Its options work as follows:

- **Server Type** The supported server types are IBM DB2 OLAP Server, Hyperion Essbase, Holos HDC Cube, and Microsoft OLE DB Provider for OLAP Services 8.0.

Figure 23-2
Creating a new
OLAP connection

- **Caption** Enter a caption for the new connection. It will be used in the Crystal OLAP Connection Browser as the name of the connection.

- **Server Options** The content of the Server Options panel changes depending on the server type selected. Enter the values that are required for connection to your data source. With the Microsoft server type selected, you can choose between using an OLAP server, a local cube file, or an HTTP cube.

- **Test Connection** Click the Test Connection button to verify that the configuration is properly set up. You will receive either a connected successfully message or an error message.

- **Advanced** Clicking the Advanced button opens the Advanced Settings dialog box. You can use the Advanced Settings dialog box to set up an OLAP connection using Crystal Enterprise or Open OLAP.

Cancel Button Closes the dialog box without selecting an OLAP data source.

Help Button Opens the context-sensitive help for this dialog box.

Shortcut Menu Several commands are available when you right-click on the nodes in the OLAP data sources tree:

- **Remove Server** This command deletes the selected OLAP connection.

- **Rename** Select this command to change the caption for the OLAP connection.

- **Refresh**   Choosing Refresh causes Crystal Reports to reread the list of OLAP cubes available in the selected connection.

- **Add to Favorites**   This command adds the selected connection to the Favorites folder.

- **Remove from Favorites**   This command removes the selected connection from the Favorites folder. It does not remove the connection.

- **Add Server**   Selecting this option is the same as clicking the Add Server button.

Select CAR File

Clicking the Select CAR File button in the OLAP Data screen opens the Open dialog box, where you can search for and select a Crystal Analysis .car file to use as a data source.

Cube

The name of the cube you selected will be displayed in the Cube text box.

Type

The server type of the selected cube will be listed in the Type text box.

Server

The Server text box will display the name of the server where the selected cube is located or other location information.

Rows/Columns Screen

Once you select a cube and click Next, the Rows/Columns screen will be displayed, as shown in Figure 23-3. This screen is used to select the dimensions that will become the rows and columns of the OLAP grid, to filter the display of members, and to create parameters. Make your selections, and then click Next.

List Boxes

This screen contains three list boxes:

- **Dimensions** contains all the dimensions available in the selected cube that have not already been added to the Rows or Columns list boxes.

- **Rows** contains the dimensions that will be the rows of the OLAP grid. To add dimensions to this box, select them in the Dimensions box and click the right arrow button, or drag them from the Dimensions box to the Rows box. One dimension is added automatically and at least one dimension must be listed. You cannot delete the last dimension. The order of the dimensions can be changed using the up and down arrows.

- **Columns** contains the dimensions that will be the columns of the OLAP grid. You can perform the same actions on the Columns list box as on the Rows list box.

PART III

Figure 23-3
Setting up the
rows and
columns of the
OLAP grid

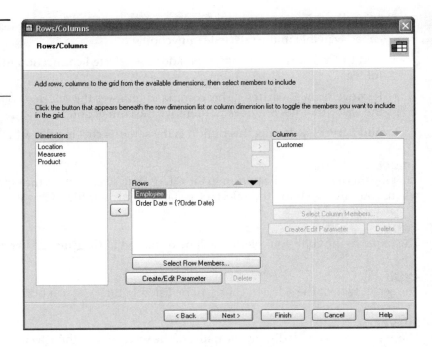

If you add more than one dimension to the Rows or Columns list boxes, it is called *stacking the dimensions.*

Select Row (Column) Members

The Select Row Members and Select Column Members buttons behave identically. If you select a dimension in the Rows or Columns list box and then click the Select Members button, the Member Selector dialog box will display, as shown here. You can check nodes to include that member in the OLAP grid and clear nodes to exclude that member from the grid.

The root of the tree is the name of the dimension selected. Under the root are two special nodes that are initially empty, Special Members and Favorites. Then there is the All node. The first level under All contains the members of the first level of the dimension. The next level contains the members of the second level, and so on. Members at a lower level are called *children,* members at a higher level are called *parents.* Check the members that you want displayed in the OLAP grid.

The Member Selector dialog box contains a toolbar and its own shortcut menu. The toolbar and menu items are described here.

 Select Button   The Select button has suboptions that check many nodes at the same time. The icon on the Select button indicates which of the following options is currently active.

- **Select All Members** checks every member at every level in the dimension.

- **Select None** clears every member.

- **Invert Selection** clears every member that is checked and checks every member that is not checked.

- **Select All Top Members** checks all the top-level members (usually just the All node). It does not clear any existing checked members.

- **Select All Members at Level x** displays the Level Selector dialog box, where you can choose from the levels that belong to this dimension. Selecting a level checks all members at that level in addition to any other currently checked members.

- **Select All Base Members** checks all the members at the lowest level in the dimension. It does not clear any existing checked members.

- **Move Selection Down One Level** looks at every checked member, clears the member, and checks all members one level down from the original member.

- **Move Selection Up One Level** looks at every checked member, clears the member, and checks the parent node of the original member.

- **Save As Favorite** saves the set of currently checked members as a favorite group with a default name.

 TIP   If you select members manually, any new members that are added to the cube will not be selected. If you use the Select button commands, any new members that would have been selected by the command will be selected.

 Select Display Mode Button   The Select Display Mode button has three options:

- **Hierarchy** displays the members of the dimension in a hierarchy based on their levels in the dimension.

- **Sort Ascending** displays all the members of the dimension in one group regardless of their level, sorted alphabetically.
- **Sort Descending** is similar to the Sort Ascending option, but it sorts in reverse order.

 Select Hierarchy Button   The Select Hierarchy button is used to select which hierarchy you want to use if the dimension has more than one hierarchy associated with it in the cube.

 New Favorite Group Button   Click the New Favorite Group button to create a new favorite group with a default name.

 Display Members Using Button   The Display Members Using button has three options:

- **Caption** displays the members' captions only.
- **Name** displays the members' names only.
- **Caption : Name** displays the members' caption and name, separated by a colon.

 Search Button   Clicking the Search button opens the Search dialog box, shown here. You can search for members by name, caption, or level. The found members are then selected in the Member Selector dialog box.

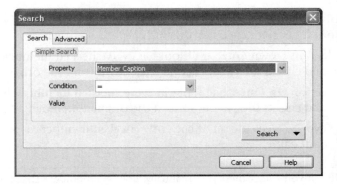

Select All Members at This Level   This right-click command selects all other members that are at the same level as the selected member.

Add Parent to Selection   This right-click command has three suboptions:

- **One Level** checks the immediate parent of the selected member.
- **All Levels** checks all the parent members of the selected member up to the root level.
- **Custom** opens the Level Selector dialog box. You can select which levels of parents should be checked.

Add Children to Selection This right-click command is similar to the Add Parents command. It also has three suboptions:

- **One Level** checks all the immediate children of the selected member.
- **All Levels** checks all children of the selected member down to the base level.
- **Custom** opens the Level Selector dialog box. You can select which levels of children should be checked.

Add To The Add To right-click command will have at least one suboption, to add the current selection to a new favorites group. If any favorite groups already exist, an option will be available to add the current selection to each of the existing favorite groups.

Delete Favorite If a favorite group is selected, you can right-click and choose Delete to remove the favorite group.

Rename Favorite If a favorite group is selected, you can right-click and choose Rename to give the group a different name. You will probably want to rename each favorite group that you create, since you cannot create a name when you create the group.

Create/Edit Parameter

Clicking the Create/Edit Parameter button displays the Create Parameter Field dialog box. If a parameter is selected before clicking the Create/Edit Parameter button, the Edit Parameter Field dialog box will be displayed. It is very similar to the Create Parameter Field dialog box. These are the same dialog boxes that were described in Chapter 6, but some differences exist for OLAP parameters.

When creating parameters for an OLAP grid, you cannot set the value type; the Value Type box is not available in the Create Parameter Field dialog box. You also cannot define parameters that contain ranges or allow editing of default values.

When setting default values for the parameter, you cannot browse the data, but clicking the Select Default Values button opens the Member Selector dialog box; you can choose the default values from there. By default, OLAP parameters display with only the description. If you manually create default values, you must create a description. The order of the default values is set to Dimension Hierarchy by default, but you can change it.

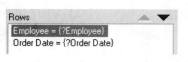

In order for regular report parameters to influence the records selected for the report, you have to add the parameter to a record selection formula. OLAP parameters are automatically used to filter the members of a dimension, as shown here; you do not need to add them to a selection formula.

Delete

The Delete button is available if a dimension with a parameter is selected. Clicking it displays the Delete Link to Parameter Field dialog box, which is similar to the Create Parameter Field dialog box but has only OK, Cancel, and Help options. Click OK to delete the parameter. You will see that the parameter reference is removed from the dimension.

Slice/Page Screen

For each dimension that you did not select for a column or row, you must select a slice or set up pages in the Slice/Page screen, shown in Figure 23-4. For example, say that you have a three-dimensional cube with Product, Customer, and Location dimensions. You chose Product for your row and Customer for your column. You must tell Crystal Reports how to treat the Location dimension in the OLAP grid. You can use the slice of the cube that contains the summaries across Product and Customer for all locations, you can pick a specific location to display, or you can create multiple OLAP grids, one for each selected member of the Location dimension.

To create one OLAP grid containing the summary for a particular location member, you use the Slice options. To create multiple OLAP grids, one for each selected member of the Locations dimension, you use the Page options. The members of Page and Slice can both be determined using parameters.

Slice   The Slice list box displays the dimensions that will be held to a particular value in the OLAP grid. By default, each dimension that is not a row or column is shown in the Slice list box with the All member selected. The Measures are shown with the first defined measure selected. You can pick a different member using the Select Slice button, or you can move a dimension into the Page list box using the arrow buttons or by dragging.

Select Slice   Clicking the Select Slice button opens the Member Selector dialog box for the selected dimension. You can select any member at any level of the dimension for the slice.

Page   The Page list box displays the dimensions that will have separate grids for each selected member. When you move a dimension into the Page list box, the Member

Figure 23-4

Configuring slices
and pages

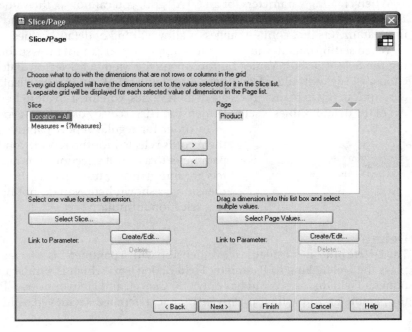

Selector dialog box will be displayed. You can select any combination of members or a group from the Favorites folder for the pages.

Select Page Values   Clicking the Select Page Values button reopens the Member Selector dialog box for the selected dimension so that you can change your member selection.

Link to Parameter   The Slice and Page areas each have Link to Parameter options. The Slice and Page parameters have the same restrictions as the Row and Column parameters. In addition, Slice parameters cannot be multivalue. Click the Create/Edit button to create a new parameter or edit an existing parameter. Click the Delete button to unlink a parameter from a dimension and delete it.

Style Screen

On the Style screen, you can select a style to apply to the OLAP grid.

Chart Screen

The Chart screen, shown in Figure 23-5, is used to create a chart based on the OLAP grid. This is the same Chart screen that is used in all the report wizards. It has the following options:

- **Chart Type**   Select a chart type. Selecting No Chart will not add a chart to the report. The other options are Bar Chart, Line Chart, and Pie Chart.

Figure 23-5
Creating an
OLAP chart

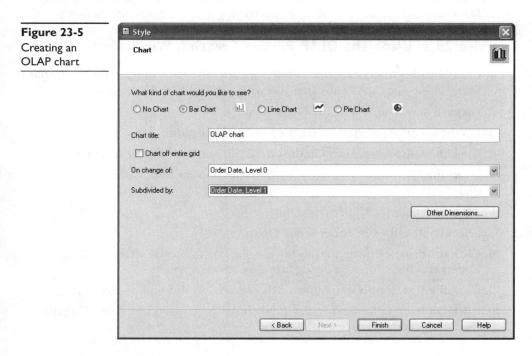

- **Chart Title** Enter the text that you want to appear as the title of the chart in the Chart title box.

- **Chart Off Entire Grid** If you check Chart Off Entire Grid, the chart will use the same options that are used in the OLAP grid and the On Change Of and Subdivided By options will be unavailable.

- **On Change Of** The On Change Of drop-down box is populated with each level of each dimension that has been used as a row or column of the OLAP grid. Select the one that you want used for the chart.

- **Subdivided By** You can select another level dimension in the Subdivided By drop-down box for a second level of the chart.

- **Other Dimensions** Clicking the Other Dimensions button opens the Format Other Dimensions dialog box. Use it to set the values for the dimensions that were not selected in the On Change Of or Subdivided By box. This is similar to selecting a slice; you must pick a member of each dimension.

After configuring the Chart options, select Finish to create the report.

Reinvoking the OLAP Report Creation Wizard

After you use the OLAP Report Creation wizard to create a new report, you can reinvoke it using the Report | OLAP Design Wizard command or by clicking the OLAP Design Wizard button on the toolbar. You will receive a warning message stating that your current report definition will be replaced, and then the wizard will display with just the OLAP Data, Rows/Columns, and Slice/Page tabs. Any charts or formatting will remain.

Exercise 23.1: Using the OLAP Report Creation Wizard

1. Copy the file Orders.cub from the accompanying CD to a location on your hard drive. This is the OLAP cube that you will use for this chapter.

2. Create a new report using the OLAP wizard.

3. On the OLAP Data screen, click the Select Cube button.

4. Click the Add Server button in the OLAP Connection Browser dialog box.

5. Select the Microsoft entry in the Server Type drop-down box of the New Server dialog box.

6. Type **Orders** in the Caption text box.

7. Select Local Cube file under Server Options.

8. Click the browse button next to the file text box to browse to the location of the Orders.cub file. Close the dialog box after selecting the file.

9. Click the Test Connection button. The connection should be successful.

10. Click OK to close the Add Server dialog box. The Orders cube should appear in the OLAP Connection Browser list box.

11. Open the folders under Orders until you can select the OCWCube, then click Open. You will be returned to the OLAP Data screen with the cube properties filled in. Click Next.

12. Place the Product dimension in the Rows list box, then select it, and click the Select Row Members button.

13. Select the All member and every member in the next level down of the hierarchy. Click OK to close the dialog box.

14. Place the Order Date and Customer dimensions in the Columns list box. Select Order Date, and click the Select Column Members button.

15. Select only the 2001 and 2002 members, and close the dialog box.

16. Select the Customer dimension, and then click the Select Column Members button.

17. Select these members: All, 7 Bikes for 7 Brothers, Alley Cat Cycles, and City Cyclist. Close the dialog box.

18. Click Next.

19. Select the Measures slice, and then click the Select Slice button.

20. Choose Sum Of UnitAmount, and close the dialog box.

21. Click Next.

22. Select the Silver Sage 1 template, and click Next.

23. Select Bar chart, and check the Chart Off Entire Grid box. Click Finish.

24. Save the report as **Exercise 23.1**.

Exercise 23.2: Creating Pages and Parameters

1. Open the Exercise 23.1 report.

2. Select the OLAP grid, and then choose OLAP Design Wizard from the Report menu.

3. Click the Yes button on the warning dialog box.

4. Select the Slice/Page tab. (You are going to create parameters here, but you create them for the row or column dimensions on the Rows/Columns tab.)

5. Move the Location dimension into the Pages list box.

6. The Member Selector dialog box will appear. Select the Canada, England, and USA dimensions, and then click OK.

7. Select the Employee dimension, and then click the Create/Edit button. In the Prompting text box, enter **Choose an Employee**.

8. Click the Default Values button, and then the Select Default Values button.

9. Check the All member and each employee's last name. Click OK.

10. Click OK three times to return to the report.

11. When prompted for an Employee parameter, select any available option.

12. Remove the chart from the Report Header section, shrink the section, and suppress it.

13. You now have a chart and a grid on each of three pages, one for each country.

14. Save the report as **Exercise 23.2**.

OLAP Expert

The OLAP wizard is used to create a new report whose primary content will be an OLAP grid. The OLAP Expert is used to edit existing OLAP grids or add new OLAP grids to an existing report. Many of the tabs used in the OLAP Expert are identical to the similarly named screens of the OLAP wizard covered in the preceding section. The OLAP Expert is invoked by selecting Insert | OLAP Grid, clicking the Insert OLAP Grid button, or by selecting OLAP Grid Expert from the right-click menu with a grid selected.

All but two of the tabs in the OLAP Grid Expert are similar or identical to the screens in the OLAP wizard:

- **OLAP Data tab**   This tab is similar to the OLAP Data screen of the wizard, except that you cannot select a .car file. You can only select a cube.

- **Rows/Columns tab**   This tab is identical to the Rows/Columns screen of the OLAP wizard.

- **Slice/Page tab**   This tab is similar to the Slice/Page screen of the wizard, but you cannot set up pages in the OLAP Expert. You must use the wizard to set up multiple grids using the Page options.

- **Style tab**   This tab is identical to the Style screen of the OLAP wizard.

See the "OLAP Report Creation Wizard" section, earlier in this chapter, for full descriptions of the use of these tabs.

Customize Style Tab

The Customize Style tab, shown in Figure 23-6, is only available in the OLAP Expert. It is used to format the rows and columns of the OLAP grid..

Columns and Rows List Boxes

The Columns and Rows list boxes contain each level of each dimension that was used in a column or row of the OLAP grid. Select one to format it using the Group Options on this tab.

Group Options

Items in the Group Options panel apply to the display of the dimension and level chosen in the Columns or Rows list box.

Figure 23-6
Formatting the
rows and
columns of an
OLAP grid

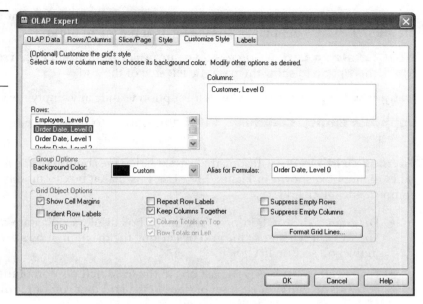

Background Color   Use this option to select a background color for the dimen-
sion/level. The color will be applied to each member of the dimension/level combination wherever it appears in the grid.

Alias for Formulas   The entries in the Rows and Columns lists are shown as the
dimension name followed by a comma and then the level number, such as "Order Date,
Level 1." You can create an alias that will be used in formatting formulas or the Highlighting Expert to make the name easier to use. For example, you could give the alias
"Order Month" to the Order Date, Level 1 dimension.

Grid Object Options
The items in the Grid Object Options panel apply to the entire OLAP grid.

Show Cell Margins   By default, a little extra space is added around the cell contents. Clear this option if you want that extra space removed.

Indent Row Labels   The members of each row dimension and level are shown in
their own cells by default. If you check this option, they will appear to all be in the same
column with lower levels indented the amount that you enter.

Repeat Row Labels   OLAP grids may spill across more than one page horizontally. Check this option to have the row labels repeat on each horizontal page.

Keep Columns Together   For grids that spill across pages, check this option to
ensure that no column splits across the page. This will force the entire column to print
on the next page if it will not fit on the first page.

Column Totals on Top   Grid column totals are usually shown at the bottom of the grid. Check this option to show the totals at the top of the grid.

Row Totals on Left   Grid row totals are usually shown at the right side of the grid. Check this option to show them on the left side of the grid.

Suppress Empty Rows   Check this option to hide any empty rows in the grid.

Suppress Empty Columns   Check this option to hide any empty columns in the grid.

Format Grid Lines   Clicking the Format Grid Lines button opens the Format Grid Lines dialog box, shown in Figure 23-7. Use this dialog box to modify the lines that compose the OLAP grid.

- **Diagram**   The top portion of the dialog box displays a diagram of the grid. You can select a part of the grid by clicking the diagram or by selecting an entry in the grid section list box.

- **Grid Section list box**   The list box in the lower-left portion of the dialog box contains an entry for each set of lines in the grid that you can format separately. Choose one to format that section.

- **Show Grid Lines**   Check this box to display grid lines. Clear it to remove all grid lines from the display.

- **Color**   Select a color to apply to the currently selected grid section.

- **Style**   Select a style to apply to the currently selected grid section.

Figure 23-7
Formatting OLAP
grid lines

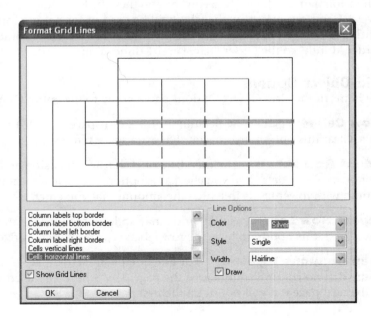

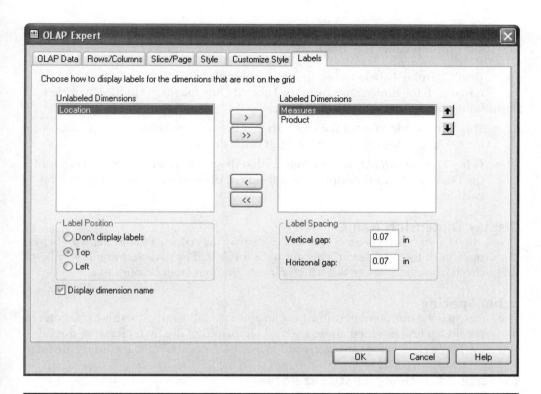

Figure 23-8   Formatting label display for unused dimensions

- **Width**   Select a width to apply to the currently selected grid section line.
- **Draw**   Clear this box to remove the currently selected grid line.

Labels Tab

By default, Crystal Reports displays a label at the top of the OLAP grid that describes which slice is being used for the dimensions that do not appear as rows or columns in the grid. You can use the Labels tab, shown in Figure 23-8, to format this display.

Unlabeled Dimensions

Move dimensions from the Labeled Dimensions list box into the Unlabeled Dimensions list box to remove that dimension's label from the grid display.

Labeled Dimensions

All dimensions not used as rows or columns are labeled by default and appear in this list. Move them to the Unlabeled Dimensions list to remove the corresponding label.

Label Position

The Label Position panel contains three choices for the location of the labels:

- **Don't Display Labels**   This option removes all labels; it is equivalent to moving all the dimensions from the Labeled Dimensions list to the Unlabeled Dimensions list.

- **Top**   This option places the labels so that they start in the upper-left corner of the OLAP grid and flow to the right. It is the default.

- **Left**   This option places the labels so that they start in the upper-left corner of the OLAP grid and flow down the left side of the grid with one dimension on each line.

Display Dimension Name

Check the Display Dimension Name box to display the name of the dimension before the slice value of the dimension. This option is turned off by default, but it is very helpful to check it so that you can tell which dimension each label belongs to.

Label Spacing

The Label Spacing options determine how far apart the labels are. The value you enter in the Vertical Gap box is added above each label, including the first. Likewise, the value you enter in the Horizontal Gap box is added to the left of each label, including the first.

Exercise 23.3: Using Customize Style

1. Open the Exercise 23.2 report. Preview it, and notice that there are several empty columns.

2. Select the grid, right-click, and choose OLAP Grid Expert.

3. Select the Customize Style tab.

4. Check Suppress Empty Rows and Suppress Empty Columns.

5. Close the OLAP Expert and preview the report.

6. Save the report as **Exercise 23.3**.

Exercise 23.4: Using the Labels Tab

1. Open the Exercise 23.3 report. Preview the report using Dodsworth as the employee. Notice the labels area in the upper-left corner of the grid area.

2. Select the grid, right-click, and open the OLAP Expert.

3. Select the Labels tab.

4. Move the Measures dimension into the Unlabeled Dimensions list box, and check the Display Dimension name box.

5. Close the OLAP Expert.

6. You will see that the text boxes containing the labels are not large enough. Select the location box, and make it wide enough to display all of "Canada." Select the employee text box and make it wide enough to display all of "Dodsworth."

7. Save the report as **Exercise 23.4**.

Customizing an OLAP Grid

You can refine the display of your OLAP grids and apply formatting to them after creation.

Manipulating the Grid

You can manipulate an OLAP grid by dragging its elements and by using drill-down and drill-up. Your users cannot manipulate the grid from Crystal Reports viewers.

Rearrange Dimensions   You can rearrange any of the dimensions displayed in the grid by dragging a dimension to a new location. To change the order of the dimensions within the row or column, drag a dimension to a new location within the row or column. A line will appear where you can drop the dimension. To change where a dimension is displayed in the grid, drag a row dimension to the column area or a column dimension to the row area. You can also drag a dimension to or from the OLAP labels area to add or remove it from the grid. A document icon will appear when you are dragging a dimension into the OLAP labels area.

Drill-Down and Drill-Up   Double-clicking a dimension will cause it to drill down or up, depending on its current state.

Resize Grid Elements   Selecting a row or column dimension or the summary value will cause a frame to display around the member. Use the resizing handles to change the size of the frame.

Grid Shortcut Menu

Use the commands on the Grid shortcut menu to access features that apply to the entire grid. Click on the grid so that the entire grid is selected, and then right-click to access the menu.

Format OLAP Grid

Select the Format OLAP Grid option to invoke the Format Editor for the grid. Alternatively, you can select Format | Format OLAP Grid or click the Format button on the toolbar. The Format Editor will appear, with the Common, Border, and Hyperlink tabs available. All the available formatting options on these tabs behave as described in Chapter 9.

OLAP Grid Expert

Select the OLAP Grid Expert option to open the OLAP Expert for the selected grid. (You can also open OLAP Expert by choosing Format | OLAP Grid Expert.) Use the OLAP Expert to modify the grid configuration as described in the preceding section.

Pivot OLAP Grid

Use the Pivot OLAP Grid command to swap the row and column dimensions of the grid. Pivot OLAP Grid is also available on the Format menu.

Set OLAP Cube Location

The Set OLAP Cube Location command opens the Set OLAP Cube Location dialog box, shown here. This dialog box is used to change the location of the OLAP cube used in the currently selected grid. This command is also available on the Database menu.

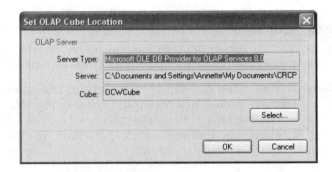

View Cube

The View Cube command opens the grid in a new window called Cube View, as shown in Figure 23-9. Cube View displays an OLAP worksheet and is highly interactive. You can move dimensions, add filtering, sorting, and formatting, and calculate new members using Cube View.

 EXAM TIP   An understanding of Cube View is not required for the exam.

Remove All Filters

Select the Remove All Filters command to remove any filters on the grid's dimensions.

Grid Elements Shortcut Menu

If you select an element of the OLAP grid and right-click, you get menu options that apply to that element rather than the entire grid.

Format Field

The Format Field command opens the Format Editor for the selected dimension and level. All unconditional formatting can be applied, as described in Chapter 9. To create conditional format formulas for grid elements, you should use the GridRowColumnValue function and the Row or Column Names functions. For example, the following formula sets the font color to red when the grid member for the fourth level of the Product dimension

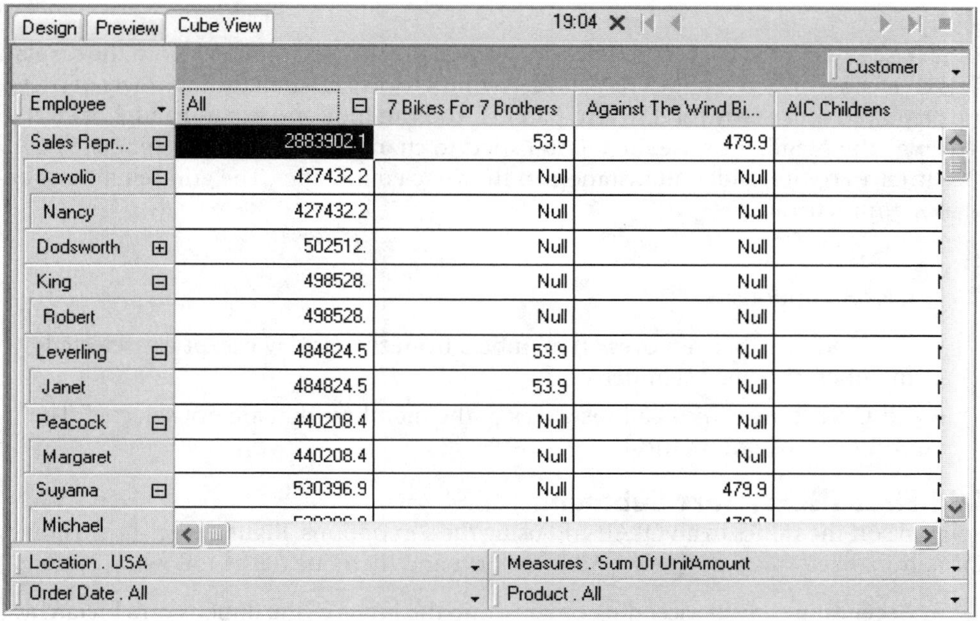

Figure 23-9   Using the Cube View

is equal to "sm." The attribute for the GridRowColumnValue function can be selected from the Row or Column Names function list.

```
If GridRowColumnValue ("Product, Level 4") = 'sm'
   then crRed else DefaultAttribute
```

See Chapter 9 for more information on conditional formatting formulas.

Highlighting Expert

If you choose the Highlighting Expert from the shortcut menu, the Highlighting Expert dialog box will appear. You can use it to conditionally format the dimensions or the summarized value, as described in Chapter 9. When highlighting a level in a dimension, you can base the formula on the current level or any higher levels of the same dimension that are used in the grid. When highlighting the summarized value, you can base the formula on any of the levels or dimensions in the grid.

Collapse Member

Selecting Collapse Member will hide all the lower levels under the selected member. The same action occurs if you double-click on an expanded member.

Expand Member

Selecting Expand Member will display the next lower level under the selected member. The same action occurs if you double-click on a collapsed member.

PART III

Hide

Hide has two options. Selected Member removes the selected member from the display. This creates asymmetry in the OLAP grid. Asymmetry exists when the members of a level are displayed differently for different parents. You can hide and expand a higher level to redisplay the member or use the OLAP Expert to change the selected members. The All Occurrences option hides all instances of the selected member. The grid remains or becomes symmetrical.

Show

Show has two options:

- **Selected Member** removes all members from the display except the selected member, creating asymmetry.
- **All Occurrences** hides all instances of the members that are not selected. The grid remains symmetrical.

Add First (Next) Sort Submenu

You can sort the values in an OLAP grid using the sort options. Right-click a dimension or the summarized value, and select Add First Sort and then one of the following options:

- **Ascending** sorts in ascending order within the limits of the dimension's hierarchy.
- **Descending** sorts in descending order within the limits of the dimension's hierarchy.
- **Ascending, Break Hierarchies** sorts in ascending order and disregards the dimension's hierarchy. Higher-level members may appear more than once in order to sort the lower-level members correctly.
- **Descending, Break Hierarchies** sorts in descending order and disregards the dimension's hierarchy. Higher-level members may appear more than once in order to sort the lower-level members correctly.

After you create one sort on the Rows or Columns dimensions, the Add Next Sort option will appear. Subsequent sorts must break the hierarchy, so only those options are listed. Only three sorts are allowed for the row dimensions or the column dimensions. After you have created three sorts, only the Add First Sort option will be available, and the next sort created removes all previous sorts.

Remove Sort

The Remove Sort option, as you might expect, removes an existing sort.

Change Direction of Sort

Change Direction of Sort changes an ascending sort to descending or a descending sort to ascending. The action is the same whether or not hierarchies are broken.

Break Hierarchies

The Break Hierarchies command appears when a sorted dimension is selected. It is checked if breaking hierarchies has been turned on and cleared if it has not. Selecting it toggles the condition.

Add Filter

Selecting the Add Filter command opens the Define Filter dialog box, shown in Figure 23-10. Use this dialog box to configure filtering for the OLAP grid dimension. You can set up a filter on the grid values using conditions that you specify, or you can filter to the top or bottom *n* or *n* percentage of values. Filtering suppresses some values but does not remove them from the OLAP cube. You can only filter on the summarized value or the innermost column or row dimension.

Filter Type   Select a dimension and then select one of the following options from the drop-down box. The option you choose determines the options available in the Filter Definition panel.

- **Actual values** sets up a filter based on the grid values. If you choose Actual values, you must select the Cell Value Is condition in the Filter Definition panel. This condition can be equal to, not equal to, less than, less than or equal to, greater than, greater than or equal to, between, outside, or missing. The missing choice requires no other inputs. Between and Outside require that you enter the start and end of the range. The other choices all require you to enter the value to use in the comparison.

- **Top / Bottom N** sets up a top or bottom N–type filter. This option requires you to choose Top or Bottom and supply an N value in the Filter Definition panel.

- **Top / Bottom N%** sets up a top or bottom percent–type filter. This option requires you to choose Top or Bottom and supply a percentage value in the Filter Definition panel.

Show Rows/Hide Rows   Select the Show Rows radio button to suppress all members that do not meet the defined condition. Select Hide Rows to suppress all members that do meet the defined condition.

Figure 23-10

Adding a filter

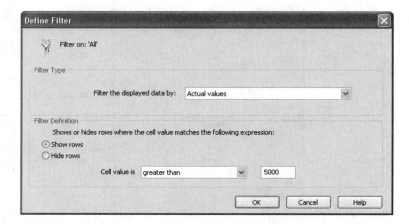

Edit Filter

To edit an existing filter, move the cursor over the dimension until the X cursor is displayed. Then right-click, and choose Edit Filter. The Define Filter dialog box will be redisplayed.

Remove Filter

To remove an existing filter, move the mouse cursor over the dimension until the X cursor is displayed. Then right-click, and choose Remove Filter. To remove all filters at once, choose the Remove All Filters command from the grid's right-click menu.

Add Calculated Member

Selecting Add Calculated Member from the shortcut menu opens the Calculated Members dialog box, shown in Figure 23-11. You can use various predefined calculation types or create your own custom calculations. The dialog box has three tabs. Use the Calculation Expert tab to create a contribution, growth, ranking, or variance calculation. Use the Data Analysis Expert tab to create a trend line, moving average, or linear regression calculation. Use the Calculation tab to create a custom calculation. Once a calculated member is created, it can be formatted, sorted, and filtered on like a regular grid member.

Calculation Expert Tab   To use this tab, you must select a calculation type and configure the calculation definition.

- **Dimension**   This text box will show the name of the dimension you selected before invoking the Add Calculated Member dialog box.

Figure 23-11
Creating a
calculated
member

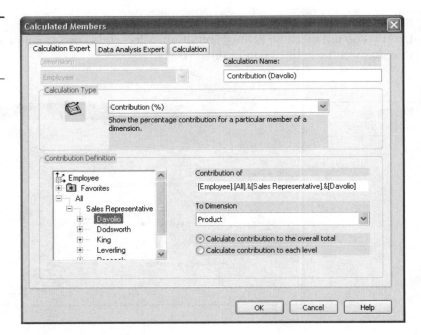

- **Calculation Name**   This text box will default to the name of the type selected in the Calculation Type drop-down box. You can change it to anything you like. As you configure the calculation, extra information will be added to the name.

- **Calculation Type**   Choose Contribution, Growth, Ranking, or Variance from this drop-down box. The items in the Calculation Definition panel will change depending on your choice. To create your own calculation, choose Custom, and then click the Calculation tab.

- **Calculation Definition**   In this panel, you set up the elements of the calculation. The left-hand list box contains the dimensions that you can use to populate some of the other boxes. Drag or double-click to move an item. The OK button will become available when enough information has been collected. See the "Calculated Member Types" section for more information about the different types.

Data Analysis Expert Tab   The Data Analysis Expert tab is similar to the Calculation Expert tab but has different Calculation Type options: Trend Line, Moving Average, Linear Regression, and Custom Data Analysis. Custom Data Analysis is the same as the Custom option on the Calculation Expert tab. If you choose it, you must create a calculation on the Calculation tab. If you select one of the other types, you can configure the computation in the lower panel of the dialog box. See the "Calculated Member Types" section for more information about the different types.

Calculation Tab   On this tab, you can create a custom computation using Crystal OLAP Syntax or MDX query language. MDX is used for cubes that are accessed via the Microsoft OLE DB Provider for OLAP Services. The calculation is written in the upper text box. You can use the dimension lists, the keypad, and the functions button to help create the calculation.

 EXAM TIP   In-depth understanding of the required syntax is not tested for in the CRCP exams.

When you close the Calculated Members dialog box, the new calculated member will display, unless an existing filter prevents it.

Edit Calculated Member
To make changes to a computation, right-click on a calculated member and select Edit Calculated Member. The Calculated Member dialog box will reopen.

Remove Calculated Member
To delete a calculated member, select it, right-click, and choose Remove Calculated Member.

Change Caption

To change the caption for a member, se-lect it, right-click, and choose Change Caption. The Change Caption dialog box will open, as shown here. You can enter a new caption in the text box or click the Default button to change the caption back to its original value.

Display Members Using

By default, the dimension members displayed in the grid are shown using their captions. (In many cases, the caption is equal to the name.) You can change the display using the suboptions of the Display Members Using command:

- **Caption** is the default option and displays members using their captions.
- **Name** displays the members by name regardless of their caption.
- **Caption : Name** displays both the caption and the name separated by a colon.
- **Unique Name** displays the member's name including the full hierarchy of the dimension down to the member level, as shown here.

[Employee].[All].&[Sales Representative].&[Peacock]

Reorder Displayed Members

To reorder the members in the grid, choose the Reorder Displayed Members command. The Reorder Displayed Members dialog box will open, as shown here. Use the arrow buttons to move members up and down in the list. You can also drag members to a new location. The Reorder Displayed Members dialog box contains only the members that are currently displayed in the grid, and it includes members from all levels of the dimension that are displayed.

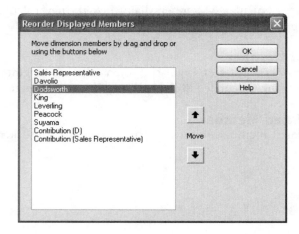

Automatic Tools

To add totals to the grid rows or columns use the Automatic Tools command. It has the following suboptions:

- **Rows (Across)**   Select Rows to create a total column at the right of the grid.
- **Columns (Down)**   Select Columns to create a total row at the bottom of the grid.
- **Both**   Select Both to create both a total row and a total column.
- **No Totals**   Select No Totals to remove both the row and column totals.

Exercise 23.5: Manipulating an OLAP Grid

1. Open the Exercise 23.4 report. Preview the report using All as the employee. Select page 3 of the report.

2. Select one of the customer members and drag it into the Labels area until the cursor becomes a page icon. Drop it in the Labels area. The Customer dimension is removed from the grid.

3. Drag Customer back into the grid.

4. Double-click on 2001. You will see the grid expand to include the months under 2001.

5. Double-click on 2001 again. You will see the dimension collapse.

6. Select the first number on the All row. It is being truncated. Resize it to show the entire number.

7. The word "All" is being truncated vertically wherever it appears. Resize the frame to accommodate the whole word.

8. Resize the Customer Name frame so that it is two lines tall. Select Center for the justification.

9. Save the report as **Exercise 23.5**.

Exercise 23.6: Working with Grid Elements

1. Open the Exercise 23.5 report. Use All for the parameter, and browse to the USA page.

2. Right-click one of the values in the green area of the grid, and select Highlighting Expert.

3. Click the New button to add a condition.

4. Change the condition to "is greater than or equal to," and enter the value **5000**.

5. Set the background color to yellow, and click OK. Notice the highlighting that has been added to the grid.

6. Select the word "All" in the first row of the grid. Right-click, choose Add First Sort, and then select Ascending.

7. Notice that the columns of the grid are now sorted such that 2002 comes before 2001 because the total for 2002 is less. In addition, the customer names are sorted according to their values within the year level.

8. Right-click the same "All" again, and choose Break Hierarchies. Notice the change in the grid.

9. Right-click the same "All" again, and choose Break Hierarchies again to clear it.

10. Save the report as **Exercise 23.6**.

Calculated Member Types

This section explains the various types of calculated members.

Calculation Expert

The Calculation Expert tab (see Figure 23-11) contains four computation types (in addition to Custom).

Contribution%

The Contribution% calculations show a member's contribution to the overall total or the total for each level of the dimension..

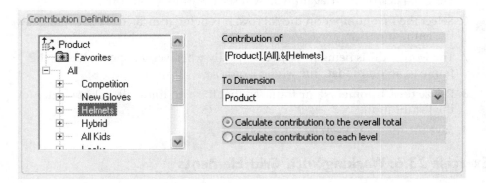

You need to set up the following properties:

- **Contribution Of** To create a contribution calculation, pick a member and add it to the Contribution Of box by double-clicking or dragging. Alternatively, you can right-click and choose Add to 'Contribution of' Field.

- **To Dimension** Select the dimension you want the contribution computed for. This should usually be left as the dimension to which the Contribution Of member belongs.

- **Calculate Contribution To** Select the Calculate Contribution to the Overall Total to compute the ratio of the selected member to the total for the selected dimension. Choose Calculate Contribution to Each Level to add a contribution calculation at each successively higher level of the dimension.

Growth

The Growth calculation computes the increase of a member from one period to the next. You can show the growth as a value or a percentage.

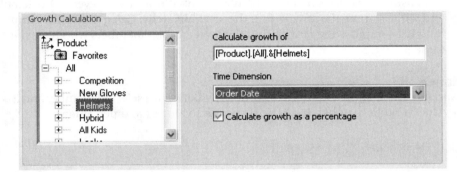

There are three Growth Calculation properties:

- **Calculate Growth Of**   Place the member whose growth you want computed in the Calculate Growth Of box.
- **Time Dimension**   Select a time dimension from the drop-down box.
- **Calculate Growth as a Percentage**   Check this option to compute the growth as a percentage. Clear it to shown the actual change in the value.

Ranking

Use a ranking function to display the rank of a member within a dimension.

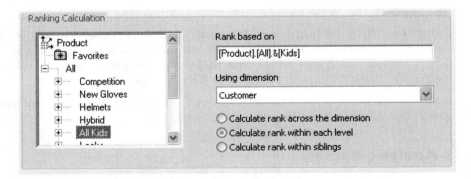

The Ranking properties are as follows:

- **Rank Based On**   Select the member to rank.

- **Using Dimension** Select the dimension to rank within. If the selected member is in a column, this would usually be a dimension that is shown in a row. Conversely, if the selected member is in a row, it should be a column dimension.

- **Calculate Rank** Choose one of the three radio buttons. Calculate Rank Across the Dimension will compute the rank using all the grid entries for the dimension, regardless of level. Calculate Rank Within Each Level is the default and will compute the rank within the level hierarchy. Calculate Rank Within Siblings computes the rank within the level, among members who have the same parent.

Variance

The Variance calculation computes the difference between a selected member and a constant value or other member. It can be shown as a value or as a percentage.

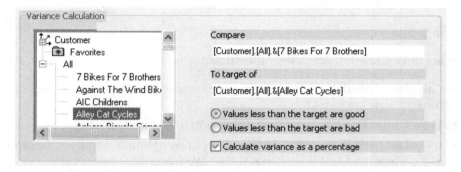

The Variance properties are as follows:

- **Compare** Select the member to use as the base of the comparison.

- **To Target Of** Select the member to compare to or enter a value.

- **Values Less Than the Target Are** Select one of the radio buttons to set the order of the subtraction. This affects which calculations will be negative and which positive. Good subtracts the compare value from the To Target Of value. Bad subtracts the To Target Of value from the Compare value.

- **Calculate Variance as a Percentage** Check this option to show the result as a percentage. Clear it to see the actual difference in values.

Data Analysis Expert

Use the options on the Data Analysis Expert tab to create trend lines, moving averages, and linear regression lines.

Trend Line

A trend line shows how the values are trending over time or another dimension.

There are only two Trend Line properties:

- **Trend Of**   Select the member to compute a trend line for.
- **Series Dimension**   Select the dimension over which to compute the trend line values.

Moving Average

Moving averages are used to smooth lines. The average is computed over the given number of periods.

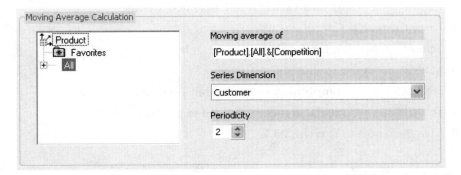

The Moving Average properties are as follows:

- **Moving Average Of**   Select the member that you want to compute a moving average for.
- **Series Dimension**   Select the dimension over which you want to compute the moving average. This is usually a time dimension.
- **Periodicity**   Select the number of periods to use in each average.

Linear Regression

A linear regression calculation computes the straight line that best fits the given set of data points.

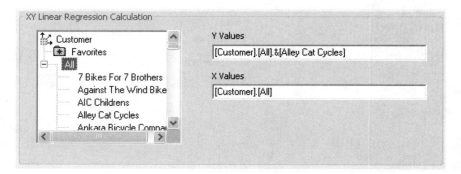

There are two required properties:

- **Y Values** Select the member to use for the Y values.
- **X Values** Select the member to use for the X values.

Exercise 23.7: Creating a Calculated Member

1. Open the Exercise 23.6 report. Use All for the parameter, and browse to the USA page.

2. Right-click a product, and select Add Calculated Member.

3. Leave the type at Contribution%.

4. Select Competition for the Contribution Of box.

5. Make Product the To dimension.

6. Select Calculate Contribution to the Overall Total, and click OK.

7. You will see the calculated member added to the grid.

8. Save the report as **Exercise 23.7**.

Chapter Review

This chapter covered the objectives for the OLAP elective.

Quick Tips

- OLAP data is data that has been presummarized and stored in a cube.
- OLAP cubes consist of measures and dimensions. The measure is the fact that is being summarized, and the dimensions are the values by which it is being summarized.

- Dimensions consist of a hierarchy of levels. Each level rolls up into the next higher level. The unique values in dimensions are called the members of the dimension.

- The OLAP Report Creation wizard consists of five screens: OLAP Data, Rows/Columns, Slice/Page, Style, and Chart.

- The OLAP Expert consists of six tabs: OLAP Data, Rows/Columns, Slice/Page, Style, Customize Style, and Labels.

- The OLAP Data screen or tab is used to configure connections to OLAP cubes. Crystal Analysis .car files can only be used as sources when you create the OLAP grid using the wizard.

- The Rows/Columns screen or tab is used to pick the dimensions for the rows and columns of the OLAP grid. You can select specific members of the dimension to display in the grid and create favorite groups of members. Parameters that are used to filter the member list are also created on this screen.

- The Slice/Page screen or tab is used to select a particular member to display for dimensions that were not used as rows or columns. If you want to display one member's values (even if this is All) you set it up as a slice. If you want to display multiple members, each in a different grid, you set it up as pages. Slices can be parameterized. Pages can only be set up in the OLAP wizard, not in the OLAP Expert.

- The OLAP Report Creation wizard can be reinvoked to modify the OLAP grid.

- The Style tab of the OLAP Expert is used to select a predefined template for an OLAP grid.

- The Customize Style tab of the OLAP Expert is used to format the grid. You can change the background color of the grid, create aliases for the level names, show or hide cell margins, use indentation instead of grid lines to demark cells in the row headers, have row labels repeat on each horizontal page, keep columns from splitting across pages, show column totals at the top instead of the bottom of the grid, show row totals at the left instead of the right of the grid, suppress empty rows or columns, and format each section of the grid lines separately.

- The Labels tab of the OLAP Expert is used to configure the display of the slice dimensions. Slices are dimensions that are held constant; they are not used in the rows or columns of an OLAP grid. The labels area is in the upper-left of the OLAP object by default and lists the constant values for the slices. You can remove labels from the display by moving them into the Unlabeled Dimensions box. You can also choose to display the dimension name with the label and change the label position and spacing.

- You can move dimensions off the grid and into the labels area to remove them from the grid. You can move dimensions from the labels area into the grid to add them to the rows or columns of the grid.

- You can rearrange dimensions in an OLAP grid by dragging them within the row or column area, from the row area to the column area and vice versa, or to the Labels area.

PART III

- Double-clicking on a dimension in an OLAP grid collapses or expands it, depending on its current state.

- You can resize grid elements by selecting them and using the resizing handles.

- You can use the Format Expert and Highlighting Expert with OLAP grid elements.

- Use the Hide and Show shortcut menu items to hide members of a dimension.

- Up to three sorts can be added to the rows or columns of an OLAP grid using the Add First Sort or Add Next Sort shortcut commands.

- OLAP grid sorts can be defined such that they break the dimensional hierarchies or maintain the hierarchy.

- You can create a filter on an OLAP dimension using comparison conditions or to the top or bottom N or N percent of the values.

- Calculated members can be added to the rows or columns of an OLAP grid.

- There are three types of calculated members: those created on the Calculation Expert tab (Contribution%, Growth, Ranking, Variance), those created on the Data Analysis Expert tab (Trend Line, Moving Average, Linear Regression), and those created using the Calculation tab (custom calculations).

- You can specify the order in which members are displayed by using the Reorder Displayed Members dialog box.

- Add totals to the grid using the Automatic Tools options. You may not need totals if you are already displaying an "All" member.

Questions

Questions may have more than one correct answer. Choose all answers that apply.

1. Which of the following elements make up an OLAP cube?

   a. Rows

   b. Columns

   c. Measures

   d. Dimensions

   e. Cells

2. Which of the following items could not be a level in the same dimension?

   a. State

   b. Country

   c. State Capital

   d. City

   e. Continent

3. Pages can be created for a grid using the OLAP Expert or the OLAP Report Design wizard.

   a. True

   b. False

4. Which screens/tabs are shared between the OLAP wizard and the OLAP Expert?

   a. OLAP Data

   b. Rows/Columns

   c. Slice/Page

   d. Chart

   e. Style

   f. Customize Style

   g. Labels

5. After you create an OLAP parameter, you must add it to the record selection formula to have it affect the report records.

   a. True

   b. False

6. What option is used to make row labels appear on each horizontal page of an OLAP grid?

   a. Repeat Row Labels on the Labels tab of the OLAP Expert.

   b. Repeat Row Labels on the Style tab of the OLAP Expert.

   c. Repeat Row Labels on the Customize Style tab of the OLAP Expert.

   d. Repeat on Horizontal Pages on the Common tab of the Format Editor.

   e. Repeat on Horizontal Pages on the OLAP tab of the Format Editor.

7. You can select one dimension for the rows, one dimension for the columns, and one measure when creating an OLAP grid.

   a. True

   b. False

8. The OLAP Report Creation wizard can be reinvoked to modify the OLAP grid.

   a. True

   b. False

9. Which tab of the OLAP Expert is used to define parameters for the grid?

   a. OLAP Data

   b. Rows/Columns

   c. Slice/Page

    d. Style

    e. Customize Style

10. What must you do to add an OLAP cube to the Favorites folder?

    a. Select the cube in the Crystal OLAP Connection Browser, right-click, and choose Add to Favorites.

    b. Select the cube in the Crystal OLAP Connection Browser, and click the Add to Favorites button.

    c. You cannot add an OLAP cube to the Favorites folder.

11. Which of the following are tasks done on the Labels tab of the OLAP Expert?

    a. Turn off the display of labels for particular dimensions.

    b. Move a dimension from a row or column to the Labels area.

    c. Change where the Labels area of the grid is displayed.

    d. Choose to display the dimension name with the fixed member in the Labels area.

    e. Change the spacing of the labels.

12. Which methods can you use to change the dimension members displayed in the grid?

    a. Click the Column Members button on the Rows/Columns tab of the OLAP Expert.

    b. Click the Row Members button on the Rows/Columns tab of the OLAP Expert.

    c. Use the Hide shortcut command for a selected grid member.

    d. Use the Show shortcut command for a selected grid member.

    e. Use the Add Filter command for a selected grid member.

13. Which two actions could be used to easily show the employees with the most orders in an OLAP grid?

    a. Use the Reorder Displayed Members dialog box to change the order of the employees.

    b. Use the Group Sort Expert.

    c. Use the Member Selector to check only the employees you want to see.

    d. Sort on the count of orders.

    e. Filter on the count of orders.

14. Which Automatic Totals option would you use to show a total column?

    a. Rows

    b. Columns

    c. Both

    d. No Totals

15. The default sort order for the Products dimension is Competition, Gloves, Helmets, Kids, and Mountain. If you want Kids to appear first in the OLAP grid, what action would you take?

   a. Apply a sort.

   b. Apply a filter.

   c. Change the caption for Kids to "All Kids," and then sort in ascending order.

   d. Use the Reorder Displayed Members dialog box.

16. Which of the following can be used to conditionally format an element of an OLAP grid?

   a. Highlighting Expert

   b. Format formula

   c. OLAP Expert Rows/Columns tab

   d. OLAP Design wizard

   e. OLAP Expert Styles tab

17. The Highlighting Expert allows you to set the font color for the Measures dimension using the values of any of the row or column dimensions.

   a. True

   b. False

18. Which of the following would you use to create a border around the entire OLAP Grid (including the slices area) but do no other formatting?

   a. The Styles tab of the OLAP Expert

   b. The Format Editor for the grid, opened via the Format OLAP Grid command

   c. The Highlighting Expert opened for the grid

   d. The Customize Styles tab of the OLAP Expert

19. Which of the following would you use to format the lines within the OLAP grid but do no other formatting?

   a. The Styles tab of the OLAP Expert

   b. The Format Editor for the grid, opened via the Format OLAP Grid command

   c. The Highlighting Expert opened for the grid

   d. The Customize Styles tab of the OLAP Expert.

20. Add Next Sort will be available for the rows or columns if how many sorts already exist?

   a. 0

   b. 1

   c. 2

    d. 3

    e. 4

21. To which OLAP grid elements can calculated members be added?

    a. Rows

    b. Columns

    c. Measures

    d. Slices

    e. Pages

22. Which of the following types of calculations can be created using the Calculation Expert tab?

    a. Contribution%

    b. Growth

    c. Ranking

    d. Variance

    e. Moving Average

23. Which of the following options would you choose when creating a ranking calculation in an OLAP grid if you want the rank computed for all members of the dimension, regardless of level?

    a. Calculate rank across the dimension

    b. Calculate rank within each level

    c. Calculate rank using All

    d. Calculate rank regardless of level

    e. Calculate rank within siblings

24. Which of the following values does a growth calculation compute?

    a. The percentage of the total for the dimension represented by the member's value

    b. The change in a member's value over time

    c. The place the member would occupy if the dimension were sorted

    d. The difference between the member's value and another value

    e. The average over three periods for each value of the member

25. Which two syntaxes can be used to create custom calculated members in an OLAP grid?

    a. Basic

    b. SQL

    c. Crystal formula syntax

d. Crystal OLAP syntax

e. MDX query language

Answers

1. **c, d.** An OLAP cube consists of measures and dimensions. A Crystal Reports OLAP grid consists of rows and columns, but the cube itself makes no distinction between dimensions. They do not become rows or columns until configured for display in a grid.

2. **c.** State Capital does not fit in the location hierarchy. It does not roll up from City.

3. **b.** False. Pages can only be added to a grid using the OLAP Report Design wizard.

4. **a, b, c, e.** The OLAP Data, Rows/Columns, Slice/Page, and Style screens are shared between the OLAP wizard and the OLAP Expert.

5. **b.** False. An OLAP parameter is automatically used to filter the members of a dimension.

6. **c.** The Repeat Row Labels option on the Customize Style tab of the OLAP Expert causes row labels to repeat on each horizontal page.

7. **b.** False. You can select multiple dimensions for the rows and columns. This is called stacking the dimensions.

8. **a.** True. You can reinvoke the OLAP Report Creation wizard.

9. **c.** Slice and Page parameters are created on the Slice/Page tab of the OLAP Expert.

10. **a.** Use the shortcut menu in the Crystal OLAP Connection Browser to add a cube to the Favorites folder.

11. **a, c, d, e.** Answer b can be done interactively in the grid or on the Rows/Columns tab of the OLAP Expert, but not on the Labels tab.

12. **All.** Any of the listed options can be used to change which members are displayed.

13. **d, e.** You could sort in descending order showing the most orders at the top of the grid, or you could use a top N filter.

14. **a.** Use Rows to create a total for each row. The totals will appear as a new column at the right side of the grid.

15. **d.** Use the Reorder Displayed Members dialog box. Sorting, filtering, or changing the caption will not work.

16. **a, b.** You can use the Highlighting Expert or create a formatting formula using the formula buttons of the Format Expert or directly in the Formula Workshop.

17. **a.** True. You can change the properties of the measures based on the value of the Measures field or any of the other dimensions used in the grid.

18. **b.** Use the Border tab of the Format Editor for the grid to draw a border around the entire grid.

19. **d.** Use the Format Grid Lines option on the Customize Style tab to format the internal lines in an OLAP grid.

20. **b, c.** If no sorts exist, only the Add First Sort option will be available. If three sorts already exist, no more can be added, so only the Add First Sort option will be available. Four sorts are not allowed.

21. **a, b.** Calculated members can be added to row or column dimensions.

22. **a, b, c, d.** Moving averages are created using the Data Analysis Expert.

23. **a.** Use Calculate Rank Across Dimension to compute a rank that includes all the members from each level.

24. **b.** A growth calculation computes the member's change in value over time.

25. **d, e.** Crystal OLAP syntax and MDX query language can be used to create custom calculated members, depending on which OLAP driver is used.

Creating Complex Formulas for Finance Elective

Exam RDCR300B expects you to be able to use

- The depreciation-related functions: DB, DDB, SYD, and VDB
- The annuity-related functions: FV, FVSchedule, PV, NPer, Pmt, PPmt, CumIPmt, and ISPmt
- The bond-related functions: AccrInt and AccrIntM
- The yield-related functions: Yield, YieldDisc, and YieldMat

This chapter covers Crystal Reports functions that are commonly used in financial reporting. You will learn about depreciation functions, compound interest functions, valuation functions, and yield functions. All the functions that are discussed in this chapter are found under the Financial folder in the Function tree of the Formula Workshop.

Depreciation

Depreciation is the measure of the amount of value that an asset loses over time. Businesses compute depreciation on their assets in order to be compliant with generally accepted accounting principles (GAAP). Depreciation is generally calculated at two levels, book depreciation (for financial statement purposes) and tax depreciation (for tax preparation). Assets that can be depreciated are usually physical items like office furniture, computers, and equipment. What can be depreciated and which depreciation method must be used is governed by (GAAP) and tax law. This section describes the most common depreciation methods.

The following terms (arguments) are used in the depreciation functions:

- **cost** is the amount that was paid for the asset. It could be substituted for the current value of the asset if you adjust other related terms accordingly.
- **salvage** is the amount that you believe the asset can be sold for at the end of the period you enter as the life of the asset.

- **life** is the number of periods that you believe the asset will be useful. (Tax codes will tell you the tax life of an item, for example, the life of computer equipment is set at 5 years.) It is the number of periods between the time that the cost value applies to and the time that the salvage value applies to. It is usually given in years.

- **period** is the time frame for which you want the depreciation computed. It is required for depreciation methods where the amount of depreciation differs from one period to another. Period and life must use the same unit of time, such as years.

- **month** is an optional argument. Use it when you want a figure for depreciation as of the end of a year. It indicates the number of months in the first period. For example, if an asset was purchased on March 31 and you want depreciation computed as of the end of the calendar year, rather than the anniversary of purchase, you would enter 9 as the month argument.

- **factor** can be used to change double declining balance computations so that they use factors other than 2.

Straight-Line Depreciation

Straight-line is the simplest type of depreciation. It computes the depreciation per period as the cost of the asset less the salvage value of the asset divided by the life of the asset. The depreciation amount for each period will be the same. If you have a piece of equipment that cost $2500 and will have to be replaced in three years, and you can sell it for $300 at the end of three years, then the straight-line depreciation per year is $733.33:

```
(2500-300)/3 = 733.33
```

Straight-line depreciation is computed using the SLN Crystal Reports function. Its syntax is

```
SLN(cost, salvage, life)
```

Exercise 24.1: Computing Straight-Line Depreciation

This exercise uses the Finance Access database, computes the periodic straight-line depreciation, and then determines the current depreciated value of each asset.

1. Copy the Finance.mdb file from the accompanying CD to your hard drive.

2. Create a new report as a blank report.

3. On the Data screen, open the Create New Connection folder, and then open the Access/Excel (ADO) folder.

4. In the Access/Excel (ADO) dialog box, browse for the location of the Finance.mdb file. When you've selected it, click Finish.

5. Select the new connection, right-click, and add it to the Favorites folder.

6. Refresh the Favorites folder so that the new connection appears. Right-click it, and rename it as **Finance** so that it will be easier to reuse in later exercises.

7. Open the Finance connection, and add the Assets and Depreciation Rules tables to the report.

8. Click OK to close the Database Expert and return to the report.

9. Place the Purchase Date, Asset Type, and Cost fields on the report.

10. Place the Print Date field in the report header.

11. Create a formula field called **SLN** to compute the periodic straight-line depreciation amount. Use the following formula.

```
SLN ({Assets.Cost},
     {Depreciation_Rules.Expected Salvage Value},
     {Depreciation_Rules.Life})
```

12. In order to compute the current depreciated value, you must determine how many full years have elapsed since the asset was purchased. Create a formula called **Full Years Since Purchase** using the following formula.

```
Local numberVar PurchaseDay := Day({Assets.PurchaseDate});
Local numberVar PurchaseMonth := Month({Assets.PurchaseDate});
Local numberVar PurchaseYear := Year({Assets.PurchaseDate});
Local numberVar CurrentYear := Year(CurrentDate);
Local DateVar PurchaseAnniversaryThisYear
                := Date(CurrentYear, PurchaseMonth, PurchaseDay);
Local numberVar YearsSincePurchase := CurrentYear-PurchaseYear;
If PurchaseAnniversaryThisYear <= CurrentDate then
  YearsSincePurchase
Else
  YearsSincePurchase - 1;
```

13. Now compute the current depreciated value. Note that an asset cannot depreciate beyond its salvage value. Create a formula called **Current Depreciated Value** using the following formula.

```
Local CurrencyVar CurValue :=
   {Assets.Cost}-({@SLN}*{@Full Years Since Purchase});
If CurValue < {Depreciation_Rules.Expected Salvage Value} then
 {Depreciation_Rules.Expected Salvage Value}
Else
 CurValue;
```

14. Place the SLN and Current Depreciated Value formulas on the report.

15. Sort the report by the Purchase Date and then by the Asset Type.

16. Insert a grand total for the Cost and Current Depreciated Value formulas.

17. In order to make the fully depreciated assets stand out, change the color of the Current Depreciated Value field when it equals the Expected Salvage Value. Invoke the Format Editor for the field by selecting it, right-clicking, and choosing Format Field.

18. On the Font tab, click the Formula button next to the Color property to open the Formula Workshop.

19. Create this formatting formula:

```
If {@Current Depreciated Value} =
        {Depreciation_Rules.Expected Salvage Value} then
   crMaroon
else
   DefaultAttribute
```

20. Close the Formula Workshop and the Format Editor and preview the report. It should look like Figure 24-1, although some of the numbers may differ depending on the print date.

21. Save the report as Exercise 24.1, and close it.

Declining Balance Depreciation

The declining balance method of depreciation determines a rate at which the asset must depreciate given its cost, salvage value, and life. The rate is then applied to each period. The rate is computed as shown here:

```
1-((Salvage / Cost) ^ (1 / Life))
```

For the first and last periods, the amount of depreciation is prorated depending on the number of months the period contains.

For example, if you have a piece of equipment that cost $2500, was purchased on November 12, will have to be replaced in three years, and has a salvage value of $300, then the declining balance depreciation is computed as follows:

```
Rate = 1-((300 / 2500) ^ (1 / 3)) = .507
Depreciation 1st Year = 2500 * .507 * 2/12 = 211.25
Depreciation 2nd Year = (2500-211.25) * .507 = 1160.40
Depreciation 3rd Year = (2500-211.25-1160.40) * .507 = 572.08
Depreciation 4th Year = (2500-211.25-1160.40-572.08) * .507 * 10/12 = 235.03
Balance Remaining = 2500-211.25-1160.40-572.08-235.03 = 321.24
```

9/14/2004

PurchaseDate	Asset Type	Cost	SLN	Current Depreciated Value
15-Mar-1999	Chair	$525.00	85.00	$100.00
15-Mar-1999	Computer	$4,000.00	1,233.33	$300.00
15-Mar-1999	Shelving	$1,250.00	150.00	$500.00
15-Mar-1999	Telephone	$125.00	27.50	$15.00
14-May-2000	Filing Cabinet	$1,500.00	208.33	$666.67
30-Jun-2000	Filing Cabinet	$1,500.00	208.33	$666.67
30-Jun-2000	Stapler	$25.00	5.00	$5.00
30-Apr-2001	Desk	$750.00	75.00	$525.00
15-Jun-2001	Printer	$1,000.00	316.67	$50.00
8-Mar-2002	Chair	$605.45	101.09	$403.27
12-Nov-2002	Computer	$2,500.00	733.33	$1,766.67
5-Mar-2003	Desk	$810.00	82.50	$727.50
		$14,590.45		**$5,725.77**

Figure 24-1   Straight-line depreciation report

The remaining balance does not exactly equal $300 due to rounding of the rate and depreciation amounts.

Declining balance depreciation is computed using the DB Crystal Reports function. Its syntax is shown here. The month argument is optional. If it is not supplied, full years will be used.

```
DB(cost, salvage, life, period[, month] )
```

Exercise 24.2: Computing Declining Balance Depreciation

This exercise will modify the first exercise replacing straight-line depreciation with declining balance depreciation. Depreciation will be computed through the most recent year end.

1. Open the Exercise 24.1 report. (If you did not close the report at the end of the last exercise, do so now, as this will avoid errors when you delete fields in later steps.)

2. Remove the SLN and Current Depreciated Value formulas and the latter's summary from the report.

3. Delete the SLN, Current Depreciated Value, and Full Years Since Purchase formula fields.

4. Create a formula field called **Period** using this formula:

   ```
   Year(CurrentDate) - Year({Assets.PurchaseDate})
   ```

5. Create a formula called **Month** using the following formula. The Month formula computes the number of months remaining in the year since the purchase date. It excludes the month if the date is the 15th or later.

   ```
   If Day({Assets.PurchaseDate}) >= 15 then
    12-Month({Assets.PurchaseDate})
   else
    12-Month({Assets.PurchaseDate})+1
   ```

6. Create a formula field called **Last Year's DB** using this formula. If the asset is already fully depreciated, there will be zero depreciation for the period.

   ```
   If {@Period} <= {Depreciation_Rules.Life} then
     DB ({Assets.Cost},
         {Depreciation_Rules.Expected Salvage Value},
         {Depreciation_Rules.Life}, {@Period}, {@Month})
   Else  0;
   ```

7. Place the Period, Month, and Last Year's DB fields on the report.

8. Insert a summary for Last Year's DB, and preview the report. It should look similar to Figure 24-2.

9. Save the report as **Exercise 24.2**, and close it.

9/14/2004

PurchaseDate	Asset Type	Cost	Period	Month	Last Year's DB
15-Mar-1999	Chair	$525.00	5.00	9.00	43.21
15-Mar-1999	Computer	$4,000.00	5.00	9.00	0.00
15-Mar-1999	Shelving	$1,250.00	5.00	9.00	93.13
15-Mar-1999	Telephone	$125.00	5.00	9.00	0.00
14-May-2000	Filing Cabinet	$1,500.00	4.00	8.00	176.42
30-Jun-2000	Filing Cabinet	$1,500.00	4.00	6.00	185.58
30-Jun-2000	Stapler	$25.00	4.00	6.00	0.00
30-Apr-2001	Desk	$750.00	3.00	8.00	98.11
15-Jun-2001	Printer	$1,000.00	3.00	6.00	159.08
8-Mar-2002	Chair	$605.45	2.00	10.00	136.83
12-Nov-2002	Computer	$2,500.00	2.00	2.00	1,160.40
5-Mar-2003	Desk	$810.00	1.00	10.00	128.25
		$14,590.45			**2,181.01**

Figure 24-2   Declining balance depreciation report

Double Declining Balance Depreciation

The double declining balance method of depreciation increases the amount of deprecia-tion in the early years. It computes a rate of depreciation that equals 2 divided by *life* and applies this rate to the cost less any previous depreciation amount until the balance is re-duced to the salvage value. You can use variations of the Double Declining Balance method by changing the 2 to another number.

If you have a piece of equipment that cost $2500, will have to be replaced in three years, and has a salvage value of $300, then the double declining balance depreciation is computed as follows:

```
Test Depreciation 1st Year = 2500 * 2/3 = 1666.67
Balance end of 1st Year = 2500-1666.67 = 833.33
  so Depreciation of 1666.67 is OK.
Test Depreciation 2nd Year = (2500-1666.67) * 2/3 = 555.55
Balance end of 2nd Year = 833.33 - 555.55 = 277.78
  which is less than the salvage value,
  so Depreciation is recomputed as 833.33-300 = 533.33
Balance end of 3rd Year = 833.33-533.33 = 300
```

The remaining balance is forced to equal $300 exactly.

Crystal Reports supplies the DDB function to compute this type of depreciation. The syntax is shown here. No adjustment is made for when the purchase date falls in the year.

```
DDB(cost, salvage, life, period[, factor])
```

The *factor* argument is optional and defaults to 2. You enter a value other than 2 to get different amounts of depreciation.

Exercise 24.3: Computing Double Declining Balance Depreciation

1. Open the report from Exercise 24.2. (If you did not close the report at the end of the last exercise, do so now, as this will avoid errors when you delete fields in later steps.)

2. Remove the Month and Last Year's DB formulas from the report. Remove the summary on Last Year's DB.

3. Delete the Last Year's DB formula field.

4. Create a formula field called **DDB** using this formula:

```
If {@Period} > {Depreciation_Rules.Life} then 0
Else
    DDB({Assets.Cost}, {Depreciation_Rules.Expected Salvage Value},
        {Depreciation_Rules.Life}, {@Period})
```

5. Place DDB on the report, and add a summary field for it. Your report should be similar to Figure 24-3.

6. Save the report as **Exercise 24.3**, and close it.

Sum-of-Years Digits Depreciation

The sum-of-years digits depreciation method, like the double declining balance method, causes more depreciation to be taken in the earlier years. For straight-line depreciation, you depreciate the same amount every year. For an asset with a life of three

9/14/2004

PurchaseDate	Asset Type	Cost	Period	DDB
15-Mar-1999	Chair	$525.00	5.00	0.00
15-Mar-1999	Computer	$4,000.00	5.00	0.00
15-Mar-1999	Shelving	$1,250.00	5.00	98.88
15-Mar-1999	Telephone	$125.00	5.00	0.00
14-May-2000	Filing Cabinet	$1,500.00	4.00	148.15
30-Jun-2000	Filing Cabinet	$1,500.00	4.00	148.15
30-Jun-2000	Stapler	$25.00	4.00	2.16
30-Apr-2001	Desk	$750.00	3.00	105.47
15-Jun-2001	Printer	$1,000.00	3.00	61.11
8-Mar-2002	Chair	$605.45	2.00	145.31
12-Nov-2002	Computer	$2,500.00	2.00	533.33
5-Mar-2003	Desk	$810.00	1.00	202.50
		$14,590.45		**1,445.05**

Figure 24-3   Double declining balance depreciation report

years, this would be one-third in each year. Using sum-of-years digits, the proportions are changed such that they are higher in the earlier years. To compute the factors for this depreciation method, you take the life of the asset and sum the sequence starting with the life and reducing by one each time until you get to zero. For a life of 3, this would be 3 + 2 + 1 = 6. The factors are then created as 3/6 for the first year, 2/6 for the second year, and 1/6 for the last year.

If you have a piece of equipment that cost $2500, will have to be replaced in three years, and has a salvage value of $300, then the sum-of-years digits depreciation is computed as follows:

```
Depreciation 1st Year = (2500-300) * 3/6 = 1100
Depreciation 2nd Year = (2500-300) * 2/6 = 733.33
Depreciation 3rd Year = (2500-300) * 1/6 = 366.67
```

The remaining balance equals $300 exactly.

Crystal Reports supplies the SYD function to compute this type of depreciation. The syntax is shown here. No adjustment is made for the purchase date of the asset.

```
SYD(cost, salvage, life, period)
```

Exercise 24.4: Computing Sum-of-Years Digits Depreciation

1. Open the report from Exercise 24.3. (If you did not close the report at the end of the last exercise, do so now, as this will avoid errors when you delete fields in later steps.)

2. Remove the DDB formula from the report. Remove the summary on DDB.

3. Delete the DDB formula field.

4. Create a formula field called **SYD** using this formula.

```
If {@Period} > {Depreciation_Rules.Life} then 0
Else
   SYD({Assets.Cost}, {Depreciation_Rules.Expected Salvage Value},
       {Depreciation_Rules.Life}, {@Period})
```

5. Place SYD on the report and add a summary field for it. Your report should be similar to Figure 24-4.

6. Save the report as **Exercise 24.4**, and close it.

Variable Depreciation

It is common practice when using the double declining balance method to switch to straight-line depreciation when the amount of depreciation using the double declining method would be less than that computed using the straight-line method on the remaining balance.

Say you have a piece of equipment that cost $1250, will have to be replaced in eight years, and has a salvage value of $50. To compute variable depreciation by initially using

9/14/2004

PurchaseDate	Asset Type	Cost	Period	SYD
15-Mar-1999	Chair	$525.00	5.00	28.33
15-Mar-1999	Computer	$4,000.00	5.00	0.00
15-Mar-1999	Shelving	$1,250.00	5.00	133.33
15-Mar-1999	Telephone	$125.00	5.00	0.00
14-May-2000	Filing Cabinet	$1,500.00	4.00	178.57
30-Jun-2000	Filing Cabinet	$1,500.00	4.00	178.57
30-Jun-2000	Stapler	$25.00	4.00	3.33
30-Apr-2001	Desk	$750.00	3.00	100.00
15-Jun-2001	Printer	$1,000.00	3.00	158.33
8-Mar-2002	Chair	$605.45	2.00	134.79
12-Nov-2002	Computer	$2,500.00	2.00	733.33
5-Mar-2003	Desk	$810.00	1.00	146.67
		$14,590.45		**1,795.26**

Figure 24-4   Sum-of-years digits depreciation report

the double declining method and then switching to straight-line, you would use the following:

```
DDB Depreciation 1st Year = 1250 * 2/8 = 312.50
Straight-line 1st Year = (1250-50)/8 = 150.00
   so use DDB, new balance is 1250-312.50 = 937.50
DDB Depreciation 2nd Year = 937.50 * 2/8 = 234.38
Straight-line 2nd Year = (937.50-50)/7 = 126.79
   so use DDB, new balance is 937.50-234.38 = 703.12
DDB Depreciation 3rd Year = 703.12 * 2/8 = 175.78
Straight-line 3rd Year = (703.12-50)/6 = 108.85
   so use DDB, new balance is 703.12-175.78 = 527.34
DDB Depreciation 4th Year = 527.34 * 2/8 = 131.84
Straight-line 4th Year = (527.34-50)/5 = 108.85
   so use DDB, new balance is 527.34-131.84 = 395.50
DDB Depreciation 5th Year = 395.50 * 2/8 = 98.88
Straight-line 5th Year = (395.50-50)/4 = 86.38
   so use DDB, new balance is 395.50-98.88 = 296.62
DDB Depreciation 6th Year = 296.62 * 2/8 = 74.16
Straight-line 6th Year = (296.62-50)/3 = 82.21
   so use straight-line, new balance is 296.62-82.21 = 214.41
```

Straight-line is then used for all remaining periods.

Crystal Reports supplies the VDB function to compute this type of depreciation. The syntax is shown here:

```
VDB(cost, salvage, life, startPeriod, endPeriod[, factor][, noSwitch])
```

The VDB function can compute the cumulative depreciation over several periods. Enter the starting period and the ending period. If you want a single period, enter the period as the end period and 1 minus the period as the start period. The optional *factor* argument defaults to 2, as in the DDB function, but you can set it to another value. The optional *noSwitch* argument defaults to False so that the switch from DDB to straight-line happens. If you do not want to switch to straight-line, set this argument to True.

Exercise 24.5: Computing Variable Depreciation

1. Open the report from Exercise 24.3.

2. Rename the DDB formula to **VDB**.

3. Edit the VDB formula, modifying it as shown here:

```
If {@Period} > {Depreciation_Rules.Life} then 0
Else
   VDB({Assets.Cost}, {Depreciation_Rules.Expected Salvage Value},
       {Depreciation_Rules.Life}, {@Period}-1, {@Period})
```

4. Remove the field heading that says DDB, and then right-click the VDB field and select Insert | Field Heading. Preview the report; it should look like Figure 24-5.

5. Save the report as **Exercise 24.5**, and close it.

Annuities

If you have purchased a home and obtained a mortgage, you probably paid some money as a down payment. Since then you have made payments each month, with part of the payment being applied directly to the original amount you borrowed (the principal) and part of it going to pay the agreed-upon interest. From your point of view, this is a loan; from the bank's point of view, this is an investment. This type of financial instru-

9/14/2004

PurchaseDate	Asset Type	Cost	Period	VDB
15-Mar-1999	Chair	$525.00	5.00	0.00
15-Mar-1999	Computer	$4,000.00	5.00	0.00
15-Mar-1999	Shelving	$1,250.00	5.00	98.88
15-Mar-1999	Telephone	$125.00	5.00	0.00
14-May-2000	Filing Cabinet	$1,500.00	4.00	148.15
30-Jun-2000	Filing Cabinet	$1,500.00	4.00	148.15
30-Jun-2000	Stapler	$25.00	4.00	2.70
30-Apr-2001	Desk	$750.00	3.00	105.47
15-Jun-2001	Printer	$1,000.00	3.00	61.11
8-Mar-2002	Chair	$605.45	2.00	145.31
12-Nov-2002	Computer	$2,500.00	2.00	533.33
5-Mar-2003	Desk	$810.00	1.00	202.50
		$14,590.45		**1,445.59**

Figure 24-5   Variable declining balance depreciation report

ment is called an *annuity*. An annuity has fixed payments in which the interest portion decreases each period and the principal portion increases by the same amount.

Several terms are used in the functions described in this section:

- **rate** is the interest rate per period.
- **nPeriods** is the number of periods.
- **payment** is the amount paid (or invested) each period. When entering a payment into the functions, use a negative amount if you are investing the money and a positive amount if you are receiving the money.
- **present value (PV)** is the value of the investment (or loan) at the beginning of the first period (or at present). When entering a present value in the functions, use a negative amount if you are investing the money and a positive amount if you are receiving the money.
- **type** indicates whether the periodic payments are made at the beginning of a period or at the end of a period; 0 is used for the end of the period, and 1 is used for the beginning of a period.
- **future value (FV)** is the value of the investment (or loan) at the end of the last period (or some other point in the future).

Future Value

The value of an investment (or loan) in the future depends on the starting balance, the interest rate, the number of periods, and the amount of any payments or withdrawals. If the rate is constant and the payment amount is constant, you can compute the future value easily using annuity formulas.

A comprehensive mathematical explanation of annuity formulas is outside the scope of this book, but here is a simple example showing how a future value is calculated using a step-by-step method. (Annuity formulas can do the computation in one step.) Suppose that you invested $10,000 in a one-year certificate of deposit that earns interest at 4 percent compounded quarterly, and you are going to add another $1000 each quarter. The value at the end of the year could be computed as shown here. Note that because of the compounding, you will earn 1 percent per quarter.

```
Balance at the end of the 1st quarter
    = 10000 + (10000*0.01) + 1000 = 11100
Balance at the end of the 2nd quarter
    = 11100 + (11100*0.01) + 1000 = 12211
Balance at the end of the 3rd quarter
    = 12211 + (12211*0.01) + 1000 = 13333.11
Balance at the end of the 4th quarter
    = 13333.11 + (13333.11*0.01) + 1000 = 14466.44
```

Crystal Reports supplies the FV function to compute the future value of an investment that has a constant interest rate and constant payment amounts. The syntax is

```
FV(rate, nPeriods, payment[, presentValue[, type]])
```

The *presentValue* argument is optional; it defaults to 0. If your investment has a starting value, such as the $10,000 in the preceding example, you would enter it as the present value. *Type* is also optional; it defaults to 0 for payments made at the end of the period. For payments made at the beginning of the period, set it to 1. The *rate* entry must be the rate per period.

Exercise 24.6: Computing the Future Value

1. Open the report from Exercise 24.1. Assume all assets are sold today for their current depreciated value and the money is invested at 5 percent compounded monthly. You want to compute the value two years from now.

2. Create a formula field called **FV1** using the following formula. The rate must be divided by 12 to get the monthly rate, and the years must be multiplied by 12 to get the period in months. The starting value is entered as a negative, since you are investing the money.

   ```
   FV (.05/12, 2*12, 0, -Sum ({@Current Depreciated Value}))
   ```

3. Add a Report Footer b section and place the FV1 field directly under the sum of the Current Depreciated Value column.

4. Place a text object in the new section and enter **Value in 2 years at 5% compounded monthly with no other deposits or withdrawals.** as the text. Use a guideline to ensure that the FV1 field and the text field are aligned horizontally.

5. Preview the report.

6. Now, assume that you will be withdrawing $100 each month from the investment. Create a second formula field called **FV2** using this formula:

   ```
   FV (.05/12, 2*12, 100, -Sum ({@Current Depreciated Value}))
   ```

7. Add a Report Footer c section, and place the FV2 field directly under the FV1 field.

8. Place a text object in the new section and enter **Value in 2 years at 5% compounded monthly with monthly withdrawals of $100.** as the text. Use a guideline to ensure that the FV2 field and the text field are aligned horizontally.

9. Preview the report.

10. Now assume that the withdrawal will happen at the beginning of the month. Create a third formula field called **FV3** using this formula:

    ```
    FV (.05/12, 2*12, 100, -Sum ({@Current Depreciated Value}), 1)
    ```

11. Add a Report Footer d section and place the FV3 field directly under the FV2 field.

12. Place a text object in the new section and enter **Value in 2 years at 5% compounded monthly with monthly withdrawals of $100 at the beginning of the month.** as the text. Use a guideline to ensure that the FV2 field and the text field are aligned horizontally. Expand the text object vertically to display all of the text.

13. Preview the report. It should look similar to Figure 24-6.

14. Save the report as **Exercise 24.6**.

Future Value with Variable Rates

Say you have an investment whose interest rate changes over time. Its future value (with
no deposits or withdrawals) is determined by taking the beginning value and multiply-
ing it by 1 plus the applicable rate for each period. For example, if you invest $10,000 for
three years where the rate for the first year is 4 percent compounded quarterly, the rate
for the second year is 5 percent compounded quarterly, and the rate for the third year is
6 percent compounded quarterly, then the value at the end of three years is determined
as shown here (numbers are rounded for display):

```
1st Quarter = 10000 + (10000*.04/4) = 10000*(1.01) = 10100
2nd Quarter = 10100*(1.01) = 10201
3rd Quarter = 10201*(1.01) = 10303.01
4th Quarter = 10303.01*(1.01) = 10406.04
5th Quarter = 10406.04*(1 + .05/4) = 10406.04*(1.0125) = 10536.12
6th Quarter = 10536.12*(1.0125) = 10667.82
7th Quarter = 10667.82*(1.0125) = 10801.16
8th Quarter = 10801.16*(1.0125) = 10936.18
9th Quarter = 10936.18*(1 + .06/4) = 10936.18*(1.015) = 11100.22
10th Quarter = 11100.22*(1.015) = 11266.73
11th Quarter = 11266.73*(1.015) = 11435.73
12th Quarter = 11435.73*(1.015) = 11607.26
```

9/15/2004

PurchaseDate	Asset Type	Cost	SLN	Current Depreciated Value
15-Mar-1999	Chair	$525.00	85.00	$100.00
15-Mar-1999	Computer	$4,000.00	1,233.33	$300.00
15-Mar-1999	Shelving	$1,250.00	150.00	$500.00
15-Mar-1999	Telephone	$125.00	27.50	$15.00
14-May-2000	Filing Cabinet	$1,500.00	208.33	$666.67
30-Jun-2000	Filing Cabinet	$1,500.00	208.33	$666.67
30-Jun-2000	Stapler	$25.00	5.00	$5.00
30-Apr-2001	Desk	$750.00	75.00	$525.00
15-Jun-2001	Printer	$1,000.00	316.67	$50.00
8-Mar-2002	Chair	$605.45	101.09	$403.27
12-Nov-2002	Computer	$2,500.00	733.33	$1,766.67
5-Mar-2003	Desk	$810.00	82.50	$727.50
		$14,590.45		**$5,725.77**

Value in 2 years at 5% compounded monthly with no other deposits or withdrawals.　6,326.64

Value in 2 years at 5% compounded monthly with monthly withdrawals of $100.　3,808.05

Value in 2 years at 5% compounded monthly with monthly withdrawals of $100　3,797.55
at the beginning of the month.

Figure 24-6　Future value report

PART III

Crystal Reports supplies the FVSchedule function to compute this type of future value. The syntax is

```
FVSchedule(PV, rates)
```

where *PV* is the present value and *rates* is an array of rates, one for each period.

 CAUTION   Be careful when using compound rates, you must enter the proper rate for each period, not the annual rate.

Exercise 24.7: Computing Future Value with Variable Rates

1. Open the report from Exercise 24.6.

2. Assume that you are going to invest the total current depreciated value in an instrument that earns 4 percent compounded quarterly for the first year and 5 percent compounded quarterly for the second year. Compute the value at the end of the two years. Create a new formula field called **FVSchedule** using the following formula:

```
Local numberVar Year1Rate := 0.04/4;
Local numberVar Year2Rate := 0.05/4;
FVSchedule (Sum ({@Current Depreciated Value}),
            [Year1Rate, Year1Rate, Year1Rate, Year1Rate,
             Year2Rate, Year2Rate, Year2Rate, Year2Rate])
```

3. Insert a Report Footer e section, and place the new formula directly under the FV3 formula.

4. Add a text field to the new section, and enter **Value in 2 years at 4% compounded quarterly then 5% compounded quarterly.** as the text. Preview the report.

5. Save the report as **Exercise 24.7.**

Present Value

The present value of an investment is its value today under the assumptions inherent in its terms. Just as you can compute the future value of an investment, you can compute the present value of an investment. For example, say that your daughter will be going to college 10 years from now and you want to put aside enough money that at an interest rate of 5 percent you will have $100,000 when she needs it. You need to know the amount that will grow to $100,000 if invested today at 5 percent. Using an annual compounding for simplicity, you could compute it as shown here:

```
X*(1.05)^10 = 100,000
X = (100,000)/(1.05^10) = 61,391.33
```

You would need to invest $61,391.33 at 5 percent to have $100,000 in 10 years.

The present value computation can also take into account payments or withdrawals as well as the timing of the payments or withdrawals.

Crystal Reports supplies the PV function for computing the present value of investments or loans. Its syntax is

```
PV(rate, nPeriods, payment[, FV[,type]])
```

Exercise 24.8: Computing Present Value

For the rest of the exercises in this section, you will create formulas that do not use any database fields. This is so that you can easily practice using the functions.

1. Create a new report as a blank report. Do not select any data sources.

2. Create a formula field called **PV** to compute the size of a mortgage that you could afford. You can make payments of $1200 per month, have a down payment of $10,000, and can get a loan at 5 percent compounded monthly for 25 years.

3. Place the formula on the report, and run the report. The formula should be as shown here:

```
PV(0.05/12, 25*12, -1200) + 10000
```

The result is $215,272.06. The down payment is added after the present value is computed, since it is already at its present value.

4. Keep the report open for the next exercise.

Number of Payments

If you know the rate, the payment amount, and the present value of an investment or loan, you can compute the number of periods. For example, say that you want to buy a house that costs $200,000, you can get a rate of 5 percent, and you can afford monthly payments of $1200. What term would your loan need to have?

Crystal Reports supplies the NPer function to compute the number of periods for a fixed rate, constant payment investment. The syntax is

```
NPer(rate, payment, PV[, FV[, type]])
```

Exercise 24.9: Computing the Number of Payments

1. Continue from Exercise 24.8 or create a new, blank report without selecting any data sources.

2. You want to buy a house that costs $200,000, you can get a rate of 5 percent, and you can afford monthly payments of $1200. What term would your loan need to have? Create a formula called **NPer** that computes the number of years needed.

3. Place the formula on the report, and preview the report. The formula should be as shown here, and the result is 24 years rounded up.

```
NPer (0.05/12, -1200, 200000) / 12
```

4. Keep the report open for the next exercise.

Payment Amount

If you know the rate, the number of payments, and the present value of an investment or loan, you can compute the required payment. For example, say that you want to buy a house that costs $200,000 and you can get a rate of 5 percent for 15 years. What monthly payment would your loan have?

Crystal Reports supplies the Pmt function to compute the payment for a fixed rate, constant payment investment. The syntax is

```
Pmt(rate, nPeriods, PV[, FV[, type]])
```

Exercise 24.10: Computing the Payment Amount

1. Continue from Exercise 24.9 or create a new, blank report without selecting any data sources.

2. You want to buy a house that costs $200,000, you can get a rate of 5 percent for 15 years. What payment would your loan have? Create a formula called **Pmt** that computes the payment.

3. Place the formula on the report, and preview the report. Assuming no down payment, the formula should be as shown here, and the result is –1,581.59. (The result is negative because it is a payment.)

```
Pmt (0.05/12, 12*15, 200000)
```

4. Keep the report open for the next exercise.

Principal Portion of a Payment

Each payment of a loan contains a portion for interest and a portion that is applied to the principal balance. Say that you take out the mortgage loan as described in the previous section. The beginning principal is $200,000 and the rate is 5 percent compounded monthly for 15 years. What portion of the payment of $1,581.59 is principal the first month? The second month?

Crystal Reports supplies the PPmt function to compute the principal portion of any payment in a fixed rate, constant payment loan. The syntax is

```
PPmt(rate, period, nPeriods, PV[, FV[, type]])
```

The *period* argument is used to indicate which period you want to know the principal portion for. The other arguments are as previously described.

Exercise 24.11: Computing the Principal Portion of a Payment

1. Continue from Exercise 24.10 or create a new, blank report without selecting any data sources.

2. You have taken out a mortgage for a house that costs $200,000, with a rate of 5 percent compounded monthly for 15 years. What portion of the first payment is principal? Create a formula called **PPmt1** that computes the principal portion.

3. Place the formula on the report, and preview the report. The formula should be as shown here, and the result is −748.25. (The result is negative because it is a payment.)

   ```
   PPmt (0.05/12, 1, 15*12, 200000)
   ```

4. Create a second formula called **PPmt2** to compute the principal portion of the second payment. Place it on the report. The principal portion of the second payment is $751.37.

5. Keep the report open for the next exercise.

Interest for a Period

In the previous section, you learned how to compute the principal portion of a payment. This section describes how to compute the interest portion of a payment. Using the previous example, with beginning principal of $200,000 and a rate of 5 percent compounded monthly for 15 years. What portion of the payment of $1,581.59 is interest the first month? The second month?

Crystal Reports supplies the IPmt function to compute the interest portion of any payment in a fixed rate, constant payment loan. The syntax is

```
IPmt(rate, period, nPeriods, PV[, FV[, type]])
```

Exercise 24.12: Computing the Interest Portion of a Payment

1. Continue from Exercise 24.11 or create a new, blank report without selecting any data sources.

2. You have taken out a mortgage for a house that costs $200,000 with a rate of 5 percent compounded monthly for 15 years. What portion of the first payment is interest? Create a formula called **IPmt1** that computes the interest portion.

3. Place the formula on the report, and preview the report. The formula should be as shown here, and the result is −$833.33. (The result is negative because it is a payment.) Note that $833.33 plus the first principal payment of $748.25 computed in Exercise 24.11 equals $1581.58, which is just one cent less than the total payment amount computed in Exercise 24.10.

   ```
   IPMT (0.05/12, 0, 15*12, 200000)
   ```

4. Create a second formula called **IPmt2** to compute the interest portion of the second payment. Place it on the report. The interest portion of the second payment is $830.22. (Add this to the principal portion of the second payment, $751.37, and you get the total payment of $1581.59.)

5. Close the report without saving changes.

Cumulative Interest

In the previous section, you learned how to compute the interest portion of a payment. This section describes how to compute the interest portion of a range of payments. Using the previous example, with beginning principal of $200,000 and a rate of 5 percent compounded monthly for 15 years, what portion of the 12 payments of $1,581.59 made over the first year would be interest?

Crystal Reports supplies the CumIPmt function to compute the interest portion of any range of payments in a fixed rate, constant payment loan. The syntax is

```
CumIPmt(rate, nPeriods, PV, startPeriod, endPeriod, type)
```

The *startPeriod* argument is used to indicate the start of the range, and the *endPeriod* argument indicates the end of the range that you want to know the interest portion for. The other arguments are as previously described.

NOTE In the functions previously discussed, you could enter a negative present value to represent an investment (as opposed to a positive present value, which represents a loan to you). In the CumIPmt function, you can only enter positive present values, so the result will always be negative.

Exercise 24.13: Computing Cumulative Interest Portions of a Range of Payments

1. Continue from Exercise 24.12 or create a new, blank report without selecting any data sources.

2. You have taken out a mortgage for a house that costs $200,000, with a rate of 5 percent compounded monthly for 15 years. What portion of the first two payments is interest? Create a formula called **CumIPmt** that computes the total interest.

3. Place the formula on the report and preview the report. The formula should be as shown here, and the result is –$1663.55. (The result is negative because it is a payment.) Note that interest for the first period was $833.33, and the interest for the second period was $830.22, as computed in the previous exercise. The total is $1663.55.

```
CumIPMT (0.05/12, 15*12, 200000, 1, 2, 0)
```

4. Edit the CumIPmt formula to compute the total interest for the first year (from period 1 to period 12). You should get $9791.35.

5. Close the report without saving changes.

Interest Portion of Payments with Constant Principal Amount

In the previous sections, you learned how to compute the principal or interest portion of a payment for an investment with constant total payments. This section describes how to compute the interest portion of a payment if the principal portion is constant. The principal payment each period will be the beginning principal divided by the total number of periods. Since the principal portion is constant and the interest portion will decrease each period due to the declining principal balance, the total payment will also be decreasing. Using the previous example, with beginning principal of $200,000 and a rate of 5 percent compounded monthly for 15 years, what portion of the payment is interest the first month? The second month?

Crystal Reports supplies the ISPmt function to compute the interest portion of any payment in a fixed-rate, constant principal payment loan. The syntax is

```
ISPmt(rate, period, nPeriods, PV)
```

The *period* argument is used to indicate which period you want to know the interest portion for. Here, unlike with the previously discussed functions, you should enter a 0 for the first period, 1 for the second period, and so on. The other arguments are used as previously described.

ISPmt returns $833.33 for the first period, the same as the IPmt function. The result is the same because no principal payment has yet been made. ISPmt returns $828.70 for the second period. This differs from the $830.22 returned by the IPmt function for the second period. The lower value is expected because more principal will be paid in the first period for a constant principal payment investment than for a constant total payment investment.

Interest on Bonds

Bonds generally pay interest coupons, with the total principal amount returned at maturity. This is different from the investments and loans discussed in the previous section, which paid some principal at each payment date. In addition, the interest payments or coupons are paid out at intervals and do not accrue interest themselves; that is, there is no compounding.

This section will explore the Crystal Reports functions that are used to compute interest that has accrued as of the purchase date or at the maturity of a bond. *Accrued interest* is usually defined as the portion of interest that has been earned but not yet paid, which is the interest earned since the last payment was made. However, its use in this section

PART III

refers to all interest, including both paid and earned. Several new terms will be used with the functions in this section:

- **issueDate** is the date that a bond was issued.
- **maturityDate** is the date that a bond matures.
- **firstInterestDate** is the date that a bond makes its first interest payment.
- **settlementDate** is the purchase date of the bond. A bond could be purchased immediately after issue or many years after issue.
- **parValue** is the face value of a bond.
- **frequency** is the number of coupons (interest payments) that a bond makes in a year. The options are
  - 1 Annual
  - 2 Semiannual
  - 4 Quarterly
- **rate** is the annual interest rate, not the periodic interest rate.
- **basis** is an indicator of the assumption used for the number of days in a month and number of days in a year when computing interest for a security. The options are
  - 0 American 30/360 (30 days in a month, 360 days in a year)
  - 1 actual/actual (actual number of days in the month and year)
  - 2 actual/360 (actual number of days in the month, 360 days in a year)
  - 3 actual/365 (actual number of days in the month, 365 days in a year)
  - 4 European 30/360 (30 days in a month, 360 days in a year)

Accrued Interest from Issue to Purchase

When you purchase a bond, unless you purchase it on a coupon payment date, it will have some interest accrued. For example, suppose that you purchased a bond with a face value of $1000 on July 1 that was issued on January 1 and pays interest of 10 percent annually. The annual coupon payment of $100 will be paid to you as the holder of the bond next January 1st, but you are not entitled to the entire amount because you only held the bond for six months of the year. The amount of interest that has accrued as of July 1 is $50, half the annual payment, and you will have to pay this amount along with the purchase price to the seller of the bond.

Crystal Reports supplies the AccrInt function to compute the interest accrued from issue to purchase. The syntax is

```
AccrInt(issueDate, firstInterestDate, settlementDate,
        rate, parValue, frequency[, basis])
```

FirstInterestDate is required, in case the bond makes its first payment at a time that is not exactly one frequency period after the issue date. All subsequent payments use *firstInterestDate* as the starting point. *Basis* is optional; the default value is 0 or American (30/360).

Exercise 24.14: Computing Accrued Interest

For the rest of the exercises in this section, you will create formulas that do not use any database fields. This is so that you can easily practice using the functions.

1. Create a new report as a blank report. Do not select any data sources.

2. Create a formula field called **AccrInt** to compute the accrued interest discussed in the preceding example (*parValue* = 1000, *issueDate* = January 1, 2005, *settlementDate* = July 1, 2005, *rate* = 10%).

3. Place the formula on the report and run the report. The formula should be as shown here:

   ```
   ACCRINT (Date(2005,1,1), Date(2006,1,1), Date(2005,7,1), .1, 1000, 1)
   ```

   The result is $50, as expected. Since no first interest payment date was given, it was assumed to be one year after issue on January 1, 2006.

4. Now suppose that the first payment date was September 15, 2005. What would the accrued interest be? Change the AccrInt formula to find out. The result is still $50 because the total interest earned (whether paid out or not) between January 1 and July 1, 2005, is what is being computed, and no full interest periods exist.

5. Now suppose that the security was issued on January 1, 2004. Change the formula and see what the result is. It is $150, since if the security was issued one year earlier, it would earn one more year's interest of $100.

6. Keep the report open for the next exercise.

Accrued Interest from Issue to Maturity

Some bonds pay interest only at maturity. These are generally shorter term bonds. For example, suppose that you purchased a bond with a face value of $1000 that was issued on January 1, pays interest of 10 percent annually, and matures in six months. The amount of interest that will accrue as of the July 1 maturity date is $50, computed as $1000 \times 0.10 \times 6/12$.

Crystal Reports supplies the AccrIntM function to compute the interest accrued from issue to maturity. The syntax is.

```
AccrIntM(issueDate, maturityDate, rate, parValue[, basis])
```

The basis is optional; the default value is 0 or American (30/360).

Exercise 24.15: Computing Accrued Interest at Maturity

1. Continue from the previous exercise or create a new, blank report without selecting any data sources.

2. Create a formula field called **AccrIntM** to compute the accrued interest discussed in the previous example (*parValue* = 1000, *issueDate* = January 1, 2005, *settlementDate* = July 1, 2005, *rate* = 10%).

3. Place the formula on the report and run the report. The formula should be as shown here:

```
ACCRINTM (Date(2005,1,1), Date(2005,7,1), .1, 1000)
```

The result is $50, as expected.

4. Now suppose that the bond was issued on February 15, 2005. Change the formula and see what the result is. It is $37.78.

5. Close the report without saving it.

Yields

It often desirable to compare different investments, but how does a bond with a cost of $24,500, a face value of $25,000, a maturity in 10 years, and semiannual coupons of 6.5 percent compare to a bond with a cost of $25,500, face value of $25,000, a maturity in 8 years, and quarterly coupons of 7 percent? The yields of the two bonds can be computed and used as a comparison. The *yield* is defined as the rate of interest at which the present value of returns from an investment is equal to the present value of the contributions into the investment. It is often called the internal rate of return (IRR).

Several terms are used with the yield functions:

- **settlementDate** is the date the bond was purchased.
- **maturityDate** is the date the bond matures.
- **couponRate** is the rate that is used to compute coupon payments entered as an annual rate.
- **price** is the current cost of the bond computed as the amount per $100 of face value.
- **redemptionValue** is the value for which the bond can be redeemed at maturity, computed as the amount per $100 of face value. This is usually $100.
- **frequency** is the number of coupon payments per year.
- **basis** is a code determining which basis system to use.

See the "Interest on Bonds" section for more details.

Simple Yield

How does the yield on a bond with a cost of $24,500, a face value of $25,000, a maturity in 10 years, and semiannual coupons of 6.5 percent compare to the yield on a bond with a cost of $25,500, face value of $25,000, a maturity in 8 years, and quarterly coupons of 7 percent?

Crystal Reports supplies the Yield function to compute yields on bonds that pay periodic coupons. The syntax is

```
Yield( settlementDate, maturityDate, couponRate, price,
       redemptionValue, frequency[, basis])
```

Exercise 24.16: Computing Yield

For the rest of the exercises in this section, you will create formulas that do not use any database fields. This is so that you can easily practice using the functions.

1. Create a new report as a blank report. Do not select any data sources.

2. Create a formula called **Yield1** that computes the yield on a bond with a cost of $24,500, a face value of $25,000, maturity in 10 years, and semiannual coupons of 6.5 percent, if you purchased it on July 1, 2005. Assume that it is redeemed at par (face value) and uses the default basis.

3. Place the formula on the report and preview the report. In order to better see the rate, edit the formula and multiply it by 100. Format the rate to show with three decimal places. The formula should be as shown here, and the result is 6.779 percent.

```
100* Yield (Date(2005, 7, 1), Date(2015, 7, 1),
            0.065, 24500/250, 100, 2)
```

4. Create a formula called **Yield2** that computes the yield on a bond with a cost of $25,500, a face value of $25,000, a maturity in 8 years, and quarterly coupons of 7 percent, if you purchased it on July 1, 2005. Assume that it is redeemed at par and uses the default basis.

5. Place the formula on the report and preview the report. Format the field so that three decimal places show. The result is 6.675 percent using the following formula.

```
100* Yield (Date(2005, 7, 1), Date(2013, 7, 1),
            0.07, 25500/250, 100, 4)
```

6. Keep the report open for the next exercise.

Yield with a Discount

Bonds purchased at a price that is less than $100 are said to be *discounted*. Regular bonds that pay coupons may be purchased at a discount. It is also common for short-term bonds to be sold at a discount and pay no coupons. In this case, the yield or the return on the bond is entirely due to the difference between the purchase price and the redemption price.

Crystal Report supplies the YieldDisc function to compute yields on bonds purchased at a discount that do not pay periodic coupons. The syntax is

```
YieldDisc(settlementDate, maturityDate, price, redemptionValue[, basis])
```

Exercise 24.17: Computing Yield on a Discounted Bond

1. Continue from the previous exercise or create a new, blank report without selecting any data sources.

2. Create a formula called **YieldDisc** that computes the yield on a bond with a cost of $24,500, a face value of $25,000, and maturity in 4 months, if you purchased it on July 1, 2005. Assume that it is redeemed at par and uses the default basis.

3. Place the formula on the report and preview the report. In order to see the rate better, edit the formula and multiply it by 100. Format the rate to show with three decimal places. The formula should be as shown here, and the result is 6.122 percent.

   ```
   100*YieldDisc ( Date(2005, 7, 1), Date(2005, 11, 1), 24500/250, 100)
   ```

4. Keep the report open for the next exercise.

Yield When Interest Is Paid at Maturity

Some bonds pay all their interest at maturity along with the redemption value. These are usually short-term investments.

Crystal Report supplies the YieldMat function to compute yields on bonds that pay interest at maturity. The syntax is

```
YieldMat(settlementDate, maturityDate, issueDate, couponRate, price[, basis])
```

Exercise 24.18: Computing Yield on a Bond That Pays Interest at Maturity

1. Continue from the previous exercise or create a new, blank report without selecting any data sources.

2. Create a formula called **YieldMat** that computes the yield on a bond with a cost of $25,500, a face value of $25,000, maturity in one year, which was issued on June 1, 2005, and pays 6.5 percent interest, if you purchased it on July 1, 2005. Assume that it uses the default basis.

3. Place the formula on the report and preview the report. In order to see the rate better, edit the formula and multiply it by 100. Format the rate to show with

three decimal places. The formula should be as shown here, and the result is 4.388 percent.

```
100*YieldMat (Date(2005, 7, 1), Date(2006, 7, 1),
            Date(2005, 6, 1), 0.065, 25500/250)
```

4. Close the report without saving changes.

Chapter Review

This chapter covered the objectives for the Complex Formulas for Finance elective.

Quick Tips

- The attributes used with the depreciation functions include *cost,* the amount that was paid for the asset; *salvage,* the amount the asset can be sold for at the end of its life; *life,* the number of periods that the asset will be used; *period,* the time frame that you want the depreciation for; *month,* the number of months the asset was held in the first period; and *factor,* which defaults to 2 for double declining balance but can be changed to another value.

- Use the SLN function to compute straight-line depreciation. Straight-line depreciation computes a fixed amount of depreciation per period. The syntax is

  `SLN(cost, salvage, life)`

- Use the DB function to compute declining balance depreciation. Declining balance depreciation computes depreciation at a constant rate based on the remaining balance. The syntax is

  `DB(cost, salvage, life, period[, month] )`

- Use the DDB function to compute double (or other factor) declining balance depreciation. The syntax is

  `DDB(cost, salvage, life, period[, factor])`

- Use the SYD function to compute sum-of-years digits depreciation. The syntax is

  `SYD(cost, salvage, life, period)`

- Use the VDB function to compute depreciation that starts as double declining balance and then switches to straight-line. The syntax is

  `VDB(cost, salvage, life, startPeriod, endPeriod[, factor][, noSwitch])`

- The interest compounding functions use the same arguments. They are *rate,* the interest rate per period; *nPeriods,* the number of periods; *payment,* the amount paid each period; *present value (PV),* the value of the investment at the beginning of the first period; *future value (FV),* the value of the investment at the end of the last period; and *type,* an indicator of whether payments are made at the beginning of a period or at the end of a period.

PART III

- To compute the future value of an investment with a constant interest rate and fixed payments, use the FV function. The syntax is

```
FV(rate, nPeriods, payment[, presentValue[, type]])
```

- To compute the future value of an investment with variable interest rates and no payments, use the FVSchedule function. The syntax is shown here; *rates* is an array of interest rates.

```
FVSchedule(PV, rates)
```

- To compute the present value of an investment with a constant interest rate and fixed payments, use the PV function. The syntax is

```
PV(rate, nPeriods, payment[, FV[, type]])
```

- To determine the amount of the payment for an investment with a constant interest rate and fixed payments, use the Pmt function. The syntax is

```
Pmt(rate, nPeriods, PV[, FV[, type]])
```

- To determine the number of payments for an investment with a constant interest rate and fixed payments, use the NPer function. The syntax is

```
NPer(rate, payment, PV[, FV[, type]])
```

- To determine the principal portion of a payment for an investment with a constant interest rate and fixed payments, use the PPmt function. The syntax is

```
PPmt(rate, period, nPeriods, PV[, FV[, type]])
```

- To determine the interest portion of a payment for an investment with a constant interest rate and fixed payments, use the IPmt function. The syntax is

```
IPmt(rate, period, nPeriods, PV[, FV[, type]])
```

- To determine the total interest amount of a range of payments for an investment with a constant interest rate and fixed payments, use the CumIPmt function. The syntax is

```
CumIPmt(rate, nPeriods, PV, startPeriod, endPeriod, type)
```

- Terms used with the accrued interest functions include i*ssueDate*, the date that a bond was issued; *maturityDate*, the date that a bond matures; *firstInterestDate*, the date that a bond makes its first interest payment; *settlementDate*, the purchase date of the bond; *parValue*, the face value of a bond; *frequency*, the number of interest payments that a bond makes in a year; *rate*, the annual interest rate; *basis*, an indicator of the assumption used for the number of days in a month and number of days in a year when computing interest for a bond.

- To determine the amount of interest accrued between the issue date and the settlement date of a bond, use the AccrInt function. The syntax is

```
AccrInt(issueDate, firstInterestDate, settlementDate,
        rate, parValue, frequency[, basis])
```

- To determine the amount of interest accrued between the issue date and the maturity date of a bond, use the AccrIntM function. The syntax is

```
AccrIntM(issueDate, maturityDate, rate, parValue[, basis])
```

- The yield functions use several arguments: *settlementDate,* the date the bond was purchased; *maturityDate,* the date the bond matures; *couponRate,* the rate that is used to compute coupon payments; *price,* the current cost of the bond computed as a price per $100 of face value; *redemptionValue,* the value for which the bond can be redeemed at maturity, computed as a price per $100 of face value; *frequency,* the number of coupon payments per year; and *basis,* a code determining which basis system to use.

- To compute the yield on a bond that makes periodic coupon payments, use the Yield function. The syntax is

```
Yield(settlementDate, maturityDate, couponRate, price,
      redemptionValue, frequency[, basis])
```

- To compute the yield on bonds purchased at a discount that do not pay periodic coupons, use the YieldDisc function. The syntax is

```
YieldDisc(settlementDate, maturityDate, price,
      redemptionValue[,basis])
```

- To compute the yield on a bond that pays interest at maturity, use the YieldMat function. The syntax is

```
YieldMat(settlementDate, maturityDate, issueDate, couponRate,
      price[, basis])
```

Questions

Questions may have more than one correct answer. Choose all answers that apply.

1. Match the terms to their definitions.

   a. Cost

   b. Salvage

   c. Life

   d. Period

   e. Factor

   f. Month

   g. The interval that you want the depreciation for

   h. The multiplier that defaults to 2 for double declining balance

   i. The amount that was paid for the asset

   j. The amount the asset can be sold for when it is no longer useful

   k. The number of months the asset was held in the first period

   l. The number of periods that the asset will be used

2. Which depreciation method will result in the same amount of depreciation for each period?

   a. Straight-line

   b. Declining balance

   c. Double declining balance

   d. Sum-of-years digits

3. Which depreciation methods use the new balance to compute the next period's depreciation?

   a. Straight-line

   b. Declining balance

   c. Double declining balance

   d. Sum-of-years digits

4. You must supply a rate of depreciation for the double declining method.

   a. True

   b. False

5. Which depreciation methods result in more depreciation in the early years than the later years?

   a. Straight-line

   b. Declining balance

   c. Double declining balance

   d. Sum-of-years digits

6. Which argument would you use to cause VDB to result in the same values as DDB?

   a. *startPeriod*

   b. life

   c. noSwitch

   d. factor

   e. *month*

7. What would the sum-of-years digits be if *life* is 4?

   a. 4

   b. 5

   c. 6

   d. 8

   e. 10

8. What is the third argument for the SYD function?

   a. *cost*

   b. *salvage*

   c. *life*

   d. *period*

    e. *factor*

    f. *month*

9. Which depreciation function can be used to return the depreciation for more than one period?

    a. SLN

    b. DB

    c. DDB

    d. SYD

    e. VDB

10. If you want to use the same method as double declining balance, but you want to triple the speed of depreciation, what would you do?

    a. Use DB with the *factor* argument set to 3.

    b. Use DDB with the *factor* argument set to 3.

    c. Use VDB with the *factor* argument set to 3.

    d. Use DDB with *life* divided by 3.

    e. Use VDB with *life* divided by 3.

11. Match the terms to their definitions.

    a. *rate*

    b. *present value (PV)*

    c. *future value (FV)*

    d. *nPeriods*

    e. *Payment*

    f. The interest rate per period

    g. The value of the investment at the end of the last period

    h. The number of periods

    i. The amount paid each period

    j. The value of the investment at the beginning of the first period

12. Which function would you use to determine the amount that will be due to you on an investment of $100 a month at 4 percent, for two years, at the end of the second year?

    a. FV

    b. FVSchedule

    c. PV

    d. NPer

    e. Pmt

     f. PPmt

     g. IPmt

     h. CumIPmt

13. Which function would you use to compute the total amount of interest that you paid on your mortgage last year?

     a. FV

     b. FVSchedule

     c. PV

     d. NPer

     e. Pmt

     f. PPmt

     g. IPmt

     h. CumIPmt

14. Which function would you use to determine the amount that you will need to invest each month at 4 percent for two years to have $10,000 end of the second year?

     a. FV

     b. FVSchedule

     c. PV

     d. NPer

     e. Pmt

     f. PPmt

     g. IPmt

     h. CumIPmt

15. Which function would you use to determine the number of monthly payments of $500 that you need to make at 4 percent to pay off a loan of $10,000?

     a. FV

     b. FVSchedule

     c. PV

     d. NPer

     e. Pmt

     f. PPmt

     g. IPmt

     h. CumIPmt

16. You would like to know how much of your current monthly mortgage payment is principal. Which function would you use?

    a. FV

    b. FVSchedule

    c. PV

    d. NPer

    e. Pmt

    f. PPmt

    g. IPmt

    h. CumIPmt

17. You make an investment that returns 4 percent the first year, 4.5 percent the second year, and 5 percent the third year. Which function would you use to determine the value of the investment at the end of the third year?

    a. FV

    b. FVSchedule

    c. PV

    d. NPer

    e. Pmt

    f. PPmt

    g. IPmt

    h. CumIPmt

18. Which answer will return the principal portion of a payment for the third month of a 20-year loan of 250,000, at 6 percent?

    a. `PPmt(6, 20, 3, 250000)`

    b. `Pmt(0.06/12, 3, 20*12, 250000)`

    c. `PPmt(0.06/12, 20*12, 3, 250000)`

    d. `PPmt(0.06/12, 3, 20*12, 250000)`

    e. `Pmt(0.06/12, 20*12, 3, 250000)`

19. Which answer will return the interest portion of a payment for the third month of a 20-year loan of 250,000, at 6 percent?

    a. `IPmt(6, 20, 3, 250000)`

    b. `CumIPmt(0.06/12, 3, 20*12, 250000)`

    c. `IPmt(0.06/12, 3, 20*12, 250000)`

    d. `IPmt(0.06/12, 20*12, 3, 250000)`

    e. `CumIPmt(0.06/12, 20*12, 3, 250000)`

20. Which answer will return the value at the end of the last period for an initial investment of $10,000, with withdrawals of $200 a month, invested in an account that pays 5 percent compounded monthly for three years?

   a. `FV(0.05/12, 3*12, 200, -10000)`

   b. `FV(0.05/12, 3*12, -200, -10000)`

   c. `PV(0.05/12, 3*12, 200, -10000)`

   d. `PV(0.05/12, 3*12, -200, -10000)`

   e. `FV(0.05/12, 3*12, -200, 10000)`

21. How would you compute the mortgage amount that you could afford if you want to pay $1500 a month for 15 years at 4 percent?

   a. `FV(0.04/12, 15*12, -1500)`

   b. There is not enough information to compute the mortgage amount.

   c. `PV(0.04/12, 15*12, 1500)`

   d. `Pmt(0.04/12, 15*12, -1500)`

   e. `PV(0.04/12, 15*12, -1500)`

22. Which answer will return how long it would take you to pay off a loan of $5000 at 5 percent if you were making payments of $250 a month?

   a. `Pmt(0.05/12, -250, 5000)`

   b. `Pmt(0.05/12, 250, 5000)`

   c. `Pmt(0.05/12, 250, -5000)`

   d. `NPer(0.05/12, -250, 5000)`

   e. `NPer(0.05/12, 250, 5000)`

23. The rate argument used in the AccrInt and AccrIntM functions must be converted to the proper periodic value.

   a. True

   b. False

24. Which function call will return the amount of interest accrued between the issue date of April 15, 2005, and the purchase date of May 1, 2005, for a bond with a par value of $1000, a rate of 8 percent, a first coupon payment on June 30, 2005, and semiannual payments, using the default basis?

   a. `AccrInt( Date(2005, 6, 30), Date(2005, 4, 15),`
   `     Date(2005, 5, 1), 0.08/2, 1000, 2)`

   b. `AccrInt( Date(2005, 6, 30), Date(2005, 4, 15),`
   `     Date(2005, 5, 1), 0.08, 1000, 2)`

c. AccrInt(Date(2005, 4, 15), Date(2005, 6, 30),
   Date(2005, 5, 1), 0.08, 1000, 2)

d. AccrInt(Date(2005, 4, 15), Date(2005, 6, 30),
   Date(2005, 5, 1), 0.08/2, 1000, 2)

e. AccrInt(Date(2005, 4, 15), Date(2005, 6, 30),
   Date(2005, 5, 1), 0.08/2, 1000, 2, 0)

25. Which function call will return the amount of interest accrued between the issue date of April 15, 2005, and the maturity date of May 1, 2005, for a bond with a par value of $1000, a rate of 8 percent, and using the default basis?

   a. AccrIntM(Date(2005, 4, 15), Date(2005, 5, 1), 0.08, 1000)

   b. AccrIntM(Date(2005, 4, 15), Date(2005, 5, 1), 0.08, 1000, 1)

   c. AccrIntM(Date(2005, 5, 1), Date(2005, 4, 15), 0.08, 1000)

   d. AccrIntM(Date(2005, 5, 1), Date(2005, 4, 15), 0.08, 1000, 1)

   e. Not enough information is given to compute the accrued interest.

26. The yield is the internal rate of return of an investment.

   a. True

   b. False

27. Which yield function would you use to compute the yield on a bond that was purchased at a discount and pays semiannual coupons?

   a. Yield

   b. YieldDisc

   c. YieldMat

28. Which yield function would you use to compute the yield on a bond that was purchased at a discount and pays no coupons?

   a. Yield

   b. YieldDisc

   c. YieldMat

29. Which yield function would you use to compute the yield on a bond that pays interest at maturity?

   a. Yield

   b. YieldDisc

   c. YieldMat

30. Which two yield arguments must be expressed per $100 of face value?

   a. *settlementDate*

   b. *maturityDate*

c. *couponRate*

d. *price*

e. *redemptionValue*

Answers

1. (a, i), (b, j), (c, l), (d, g), (e, h), (f, k)

2. **a.** Straight-line depreciation is the same for every period.

3. **b, c.** Declining balance and double declining balance use the new balance to compute the next period's depreciation.

4. **b.** The double declining method computes the rate that will depreciate the asset from its cost to its salvage value over its lifetime.

5. **b, c, d.** Straight-line depreciation is the only type that does not result in more depreciation in the early years.

6. **c.** Setting *noSwitch* to True will cause the computation to be double declining balance for the life of the asset.

7. **e.** 4 + 3 + 2 + 1 = 10

8. **c.** The third argument is *life*.

9. **e.** VDB takes a *startPeriod* and an *endPeriod* argument and returns the depreciation between the two periods.

10. **b, c.** You can use either DDB or VDB and set the factor to 3.

11. (a, f), (b, j), (c, g), (d, h), (e, i)

12. **a.** Use the FV (future value) function.

13. **h.** Use the CumIPmt function to compute the total interest paid over a range of payments.

14. **e.** Use the Pmt function to determine the required payment amount.

15. **d.** Use the NPer function to compute the number of payments required.

16. **f.** Use the PPmt function to determine the principal portion of a payment.

17. **b.** Use the FVSchedule function to compute the future value of an investment with varying interest rates.

18. **d.** The proper function is PPmt, the syntax is `PPmt(rate, period, nPeriods, PV[, FV[, type]])`, and you must convert the rate and the term to monthly.

19. **c.** The proper function is IPmt, the syntax is `IPmt(rate, period, nPeriods, PV[, FV[, type]])`, and you must convert the rate and the term to monthly.

20. a. The proper function is FV, the syntax is FV(*rate, nPeriods, payment, presentValue*), withdrawals are entered as positives, and deposits are entered as negatives.

21. e. The proper function is PV, the syntax is PV(*rate, nPeriods, payment*), and the payment should be entered as a negative.

22. d. The proper function is NPer, the syntax is NPer(*rate, payment, PV*), the payment should be entered as a negative, and the loan amount should be entered as a positive.

23. b. Unlike the compound interest functions, the rate for the accrued interest functions is always given as an annual rate.

24. c. Use the AccrInt function whose syntax is AccrInt(*issueDate, firstInterestDate, settlementDate, rate, parValue, frequency[, basis]*). The rate should not be converted, and the basis is not required since you are using the default.

25. a. Use the AccrIntM function whose syntax is AccrIntM(*issueDate, maturityDate, rate, parValue[, basis]*).

26. a. The yield is the internal rate of return of an investment.

 EXAM TIP The exam may equate the yield with the interest earned on an investment.

27. a. Use Yield because the bond pays coupons.

28. b. Use YieldDisc since no coupons are paid.

29. c. Use YieldMat for bonds that pay interest at maturity.

30. d, e. Price and redemption value must be expressed per $100 of face value.

PART IV

Exam RDCR400,
Report Methodology
and Business Views

Report Development Methodology and Documentation

Exam RDCR400 expects you to be able to

- Describe the advantages of using a methodology
- Define the seven steps in report development
- Describe the importance of completing all seven steps
- Define business needs
- Define technical and user requirements
- Define and build a specification document
- Document reports
- Define the report definition file
- Get additional support

This chapter introduces report design methodology and then further defines the requirements-gathering process and the creation of a specification document. It also covers the maintenance phase of the report-development methodology. This phase includes creating documentation for the report, if it was not created during earlier phases, and supporting the report.

NOTE Finding additional support is an objective of the RDCR400 exam. Business Objects support options are fully covered in Chapter 21. Be sure to review that chapter when preparing for this exam.

Basic Methodology

Most software produced today, whether for commercial purposes or enterprise use, is developed using a specific methodology or a mixture of several methodologies. All methodologies consist of a set of processes that are executed in a defined order. Report development should also follow a methodology.

The *waterfall model* is the traditional methodology used by software developers. It usually consists of steps for requirements gathering, analysis, design, implementation, testing, deployment, and maintenance. In this model, the steps are completed one after the other, with each step feeding into the next step. Strict linear models like this are no longer considered adequate for most application development processes, and many other models are now used.

Most problems with the waterfall model arise because it does not mirror reality. It is rarely possible to *completely* define requirements up front. Users change their minds over time or based on what they see developing. The design may not adequately address the problems discovered during the coding phase. And so on. To address these issues, other models have been created that allow for iterative development, including RAD (Rapid Application Development), JAD (Joint Application Development), XP (Extreme Programming), Agile, and the Microsoft development framework.

The simple waterfall model can still be applied to the much smaller scope of developing a single simple report. However, if requirements change during the process, be sure to document the change and repeat all the subsequent phases.

Report Development Phases

The following topics describe the waterfall method as applied to report development.

Requirements Phase

The requirements-gathering step kicks off the process. This is the step where you determine the needs of the user. Understanding the report requirements is essential to the successful completion of the rest of the steps.

Report requirements are generally gathered by having discussions with the users, but might also be obtained via forms or questionnaires. Having checklists of questions to ask is helpful. Drawing a mock-up of the report can be useful in determining the placement of report objects. If the report requestor has an earlier version of the report or the code used to generate their previous request, these can be quite helpful. They can assist with report layout as well as assist in determining data elements (from a technical point of view).

Your requirements gathering should include more than the content and look of the report. You also need to know the manner in which the report will be accessed, the data sources for the report, the audience for the report, how often the report needs to be run, whether other similar reports exist, and so on. (See "Report Requirements" later in the chapter for more detail on the requirements-gathering step.) The output of this step will be informal and might include filled-in forms or questionnaires, notes taken during user interviews, notes taken during discussions with systems support staff (such as a DBA or business analyst), and your memory of the entire process.

Analysis Phase

During the analysis phase, you must analyze the requirements and verify several things. This phase could be very short for a simple report or very long for a complex report. There are two main parts of the analysis: data and report formatting.

You must determine whether the data required by the report can be obtained and how best to obtain it. This determination is vital to the process and may involve the choice of database drivers and the decision on whether to use views or stored procedures, as well as the implementation of any required middleware. For SQL databases, you should create a query that returns the data required by the report. This data must include not only fields that will be displayed on the report but also any fields required for formulas, grouping, or sorting. Even if it is not used in the report directly as a SQL Command, this query can be used for testing the report output later and can be shown to the user to verify that the correct data is being obtained before report development begins. Output from this part should include a test query for SQL data sources, as well as the drivers, client software, and configuration required to create a connection to the data sources.

NOTE   This step is often done as the first step in the report development phase, using Crystal Reports itself to generate the report query. This may be appropriate for simple reports or reports against non-SQL databases, but separating the data-determination step from the report-creation step helps clarify issues inherent in the data collection versus issues involved in formatting.

If the requirements-gathering phase resulted in any unusual or difficult formatting needs, they should be prototyped to determine the best method of implementation. For example, if the user needs to be able to choose a field at run time and have that field used as a group-by field, then you would need to investigate methods of accomplishing this, since the ordinary practice is to group by static database fields. (If you have done this before and already know a technique that will accomplish it, then no further analysis is required.) The output of this step should be an understanding of how to implement all the report display requirements.

The analysis phase should also include research into the reuse of existing components or the creation of components that have the potential for reuse. There may be formulas that have been used in previous reports that could be converted into custom functions for use in the new report. An existing report may be appropriate for use as a formatting template for the new report, or the creation of a generic template might be called for. A repository SQL Command may exist that returns the data required by the new report or that could be modified slightly for use with the new report. The addition of parameters to an existing report may allow one report to meet the requirements of multiple original report requests. All opportunities for reuse or standardization should be researched in this phase.

Design Phase

Once the requirements have been gathered and analyzed, they need to be documented. The design phase should result in a specification document that can be used as a blueprint for the development of the report. It should also be understandable to the end user. The specification document should contain all the information required to create the report. It serves as the official understanding of the report requirements and analysis, and as such it should be signed by the report requester to verify that their needs have been addressed. If the report developer is not the same person as the analyst or designer, it could also be signed by the developer to indicate that he or she understands the specifications. The output of this step is the signed specification document. Report development can then begin.

Development Phase

The implementation or development phase is the stage when the report is created. The report should be built according to the contents of the specification document. This step should include testing by the developer. The output of this step is a report file.

Testing Phase

Systematic testing of the report for adherence to the specification document and for display of the correct information is done in this step. Testing may be done by several groups, including the developers and analysts, but must also include end-user testing. Since most reports simply extract data and do not change it, the report can and should be tested against production data. All facets of the report should be tested, including all possible parameter values, drill-down, group trees, and formatting. The report should be viewed using all methods that are in the requirements, such as via the Web, an application, or Crystal Enterprise. Exporting to the destinations and with the formats listed in the requirements should be validated. Once testing is complete, the end user should be required to sign off on the report file.

Deployment Phase

In the deployment phase, the report is put into production use. This may involve publishing it to Crystal Enterprise and setting the proper access privileges, or incorporating it into a desktop or web application. Part of deployment should include verification that the right set of users has access to the report and that any other security features are working as required. A sign-off can be required at this point.

Maintenance Phase

The maintenance phase includes any changes required after deployment—whether initiated by the user or caused by changes to the underlying systems—and any assistance that users might require when running the report. This phase may include the creation of report documentation, but documentation should ideally consist of the documents already generated during the previous processes.

Phase Dependencies

When you use a waterfall methodology, you must ensure that each phase is complete and accurate before moving on to the next phase. Each phase is dependent on the previous phases. If a vital requirement is missed in the requirements-gathering phase, each of the subsequent phases will have to be either partially—or completely—redone. If the analysis phase is incomplete, it may or may not lead to an erroneous design, but will certainly cause more time to be spent in the design phase than necessary. If the design phase produces an inadequate specification document, the development phase will be extended. And so on. Not completing all phases accurately can lead to more development hours and therefore higher expenses. In addition, the developer no doubt has other commitments, so other projects or reports will also be affected. You will look bad to your customers—particularly if you must ask the same questions repeatedly because you failed to document requirements properly.

EXAM TIP   Business Objects defines the steps of report development as (1) requirements gathering, (2) creating the specification document, (3) creating a connection to the data source, (4) building the report, (5) testing, (6) deployment and distribution, and (7) support and maintenance.

Advantages of Using a Methodology

Having a defined framework for the development process has many benefits, both for the developer and for the client or user.

Successful Reports   If all steps of the methodology are followed, the likelihood of creating a report that meets the requirements is increased.

Project Planning   Breaking report development into phases allows for improved project planning, tracking, and reporting.

Documentation   A methodology includes the steps required for documentation. Documentation is an integral part of the process since it is required for sign-off at various points. The existence of high-quality documentation makes the developer's job easier (even if developers change during the course of development), improves the user's understanding of the report, and simplifies any subsequent maintenance that is required.

Process Improvement   Comparisons between the development of one report and another can be made more readily if each phase of the methodology is adequately tracked. Asking questions like "Why was *this* report in the development phase so much longer than *that* report?" may lead to improvements overall. The methodology itself can be improved. It may be discovered that more phases are required, that some phases can be better defined, and so on.

Client-Developer Relations   Obtaining client sign-off at the various stages is vital to a common understanding of the report. If the client signs off on the specification document and later requests changes, they should not be scolded for supplying incomplete specifications, but everyone involved should understand that requirements *changed* and consequently rework was required. Changes are inevitable, even for something as small in scope as a report. Using a methodology helps pinpoint the effect of changes and minimizes the tendency to place blame.

Report Requirements

Report requirements can be grouped into three categories: business, technical, and user. Business requirements express the reason for creating the report: Why is this report needed? Technical requirements detail the exact data and formatting required for the report, as well as the requirements of the distribution mechanism. User requirements are concerned with how the users interact with the report. How will they access it? Will they need to export it?

Report requirements can be gathered in various ways, but you should standardize your methods as much as possible. You might use an interview or supplement a questionnaire or form with verbal questioning. You should probably not rely solely on a form due to the lack of flexibility and possible misunderstandings by users. You should also not rely solely on an ad hoc verbal exchange. When conducting a requirements-gathering interview, you should have a standard set of questions prepared and make sure that all relevant topics are covered. If you are thorough, you may gain information that will help with the development of other reports; it should also foster the user's confidence in the process.

Business Needs

Clearly stating the business need for a report can help both the client and the developer. The user often has a clear, straightforward reason for requesting a report and little refinement is required. However, it is also true that many times the user has a more vague and hard-to-describe goal in mind. Agreement on the business need early in the process will facilitate the later phases.

The business need for a report is not just a description of the report; it is a description of the problem that the report will solve. The problem might be a direct need for information to run the business, or it might be a need for information concerning quality assurance, customer relations, or competitive advantage. For example, say a report showing current cash on hand is requested. The business need for this report might be to allow for proper short term investing, for accounting or auditing requirements, or for cash forecasting needs. Each of these business needs might indicate a slightly different report output or format.

Technical Requirements

The technical requirements for a report include the design of the report from both the developer's and the user's perspective and details about how the report will be delivered. What fields should be shown? Are any calculations required? What type of grouping should be done? How should records be filtered? Are parameters required? And so on. In addition, you must determine how the report will be delivered to the users. Is the report to be run on demand or scheduled? Is it going to be part of an application, Crystal Enterprise, or some other distribution channel? Are there security requirements? The user requesting the report may not be able to answer all these questions. Systems staff such as the DBA, network administrator, or Crystal Enterprise administrator may be needed.

User Requirements

User requirements involve the users' interaction with the report. Will they export the data? Do they desire an interactive experience, or hard copy? How sophisticated are they in using software tools? Is there more than one group of users with different needs?

Exercise 25.1: Compiling Report Requirements Questions

List the questions that you would ask when gathering report requirements. Classify them according to type.

The following are sample lists of questions in the business, technical, and user categories. However, note that the categorization is flexible; some questions could go in more than one category.

Business Needs Questions These questions address the business purpose of the report:

- What is the purpose of this report?
- How will the output of this report improve business processes, lead to better business decisions, or meet regulatory requirements?

Technical Requirements Questions These questions address the user's desired content and format, as well as any required back-end analysis or support:

- What is the name of this report?
- Is this a modification of an existing report?
- What is the source of the data for this report?
- What database drivers are required? Which Crystal Reports database drivers should be used?
- Should tables be accessed directly, or should SQL Commands, views, or stored procedures be used?
- What is the general format of the report (standard, cross-tab, OLAP, mail labels, standard plus other objects, summary with drill-down, etc.)?
- Is there a standard format or template that should be applied?
- What page size and orientation should be used?
- Which fields should appear on the report?
- What should the field headers be?
- Are calculated fields required?

- Do the fields require conditional formatting?
- How should the report be grouped?
- Does the report require page breaks for some groups?
- How should the report be sorted?
- What record filtering should be done?
- Should any group filtering be done?
- Are parameters required?
- Should charts be added to the report?
- Should there be alerts or flags for particular conditions?
- Are subreports required?
- How will the report be deployed (Crystal Enterprise, application, other)?
- Does the report need to be scheduled?
- Who is allowed to run this report? View the output?
- How can the output of the report be validated?
- Is there a need for column- and row-level security?

User Requirements Questions   These questions should address how the users will interact with the report.

- Will this report be viewed interactively? On hard copy?
- Who will use this report?
- Will this report be exported to another application?
- Which viewer will be used?
- Should a group tree be used?
- Does the user need search capabilities?
- What types of printers might be used to print the report?
- Should the report be optimized for color viewing or black-and-white printing?

Report Specifications

Once report requirements have been gathered and analyzed, they must be organized into a report-specification document. This document should clearly define the report. The report requestor should sign this document to signify that their requirements were understood. The report developer should be able to use this document as a blueprint for building the report. A prototype showing the desired layout of the report may be included for visual documentation.

Report Specification Template

You will probably want to create a template and use it for all your report-specification documents. The template could be created in a word processing or spreadsheet program, a project-planning utility, or any other appropriate application. Creating a template will ensure that your report-specification documents are similar and include all the necessary items. If you use a formlike structure, be sure to allow the input of free-form comments in each section.

Identification   This section should include items like the name of the report or another unique identifier. It might also include the request date, requestor, and the audience. If you use keywords to classify reports, they could go in this section.

Security   Note any security that should be applied to the report. Most security is implemented via constraints on the data sources or the application or via Crystal Enterprise, but you need to understand the security requirements.

Delivery Methods   This section should include the details about how the report will be delivered. If printed, what printer will be used? Who should receive the output? Will it be exported? If so, to what formats? Should it be e-mailed? If so, to whom? Will it be available on Crystal Enterprise? What folder will it be located in? Will it be part of an application?

Page Setup   This section should describe the page layout. What margins should be used? What size of paper should be used? What orientation will be used? It might also include a description of the page headers and footers and the report headers and footers. What should display in the page header? Page footer? Report header? Report footer? Should a logo be included? What about the print date or total page count?

Templates or Formatting Standards   If specific templates or formatting standards should be applied, describe them in this section. Note that multiple templates can be applied to the same report, and may even be required.

Data Sources   Each data source should be listed in this section, including the database or location where it resides and whether it is a table, view, stored procedure, Business View, or other source. You should include linking information where required, as well as any special notes about the specific data source.

Parameters   Describe the required parameters. List their names, what the prompt should be, and the data type, and indicate whether they are discrete, multivalue, or range value. Indicate whether default values should be created and what they should be.

Record Selection   Define the record selection that should be used. Include the use of parameters where indicated.

Test Query   If a test query is available that is known to return the correct data, include it here.

Fields   List the fields that will be used in the report. Indicate the type of field, whether it is a database field, formula field, running total field, and so on. For fields that will display on the report, state which section they fall in and their order within the section, as well as the desired field heading. For computed fields, describe the required calculation. Indicate whether summaries should be computed and on what groups and with what type of summary operation.

Groups   Indicate which fields should be grouped by, including the ordering of the groups and the sort order within the group. If the group should be kept together or have headers repeat, note that requirement.

Group Sorting   This section should describe any desired Top N or Bottom N type group sorting that is required.

Group Selection   This section should describe any group selection that is not accomplished via the group sorting section.

Special Formatting   Describe any special formatting requirements that are not covered by the templates section here. This might include conditional formatting for flagging certain values.

Section Formatting   For each section of the report, indicate any special formatting. For example, if the Details section should be hidden, indicate that here. If underlay should be used, describe it here.

Alerts   Describe any conditions that should trigger an alert.

Lines and Boxes   Describe any lines or boxes that should be drawn on the report.

Charts   Describe any charts that should be added to the report. Include the section where the charts should be located and whether drill-down should be allowed.

OLAP Grids   If any OLAP grids should be added to the report, describe them in this section.

Maps   If maps should be included in the report, describe them here.

Subreports   Describe the positioning and linking of subreports, and include a separate specification document for the details of each subreport.

Comments   Each section should include its own space for free-form commenting. Use this section for comments that apply to the report as a whole.

Signatures   This section should include space for the signature of the report requestor indicating that they believe the report specification is accurate. You may want to include other signatures here as well.

Exercise 25.2: Creating a Report-Specification Template

Use Microsoft Word or some other application to create a report specification template. A sample template that uses Microsoft InfoPath is included on the accompanying CD.

NOTE A trial version of InfoPath can be downloaded from http:// www.microsoft.com/office/infopath/prodinfo/trial.mspx.

Exercise 25.3: Creating a Report-Specification Document

In this exercise you will create a report to be run on an ad hoc basis that shows orders that have not yet been shipped. This report will be used by the order pickers to create the shipments. Use the template created in Exercise 25.2 or the InfoPath template supplied to create a specification document given the following report requirements:

- Group by the Required Date and then by the Order ID.

- Use 1-inch margins on all sides, and apply the Xtreme template that was created in Exercise 9.11. Use the same typeface for all report items and a 10-point font size except as noted. (MS Comic Sans is used in the examples.)

- In the header for the required date show "Required Date: 55/55/5555." Format the date in bold, and apply a font size of 14 points.

- In the header for the Order ID group, show the order ID such that it appears as "Order ID: 5555," with the order number only in bold. Also show the shipping address, including the customer name. Put the title to the left and use "Ship To:". Use a 12-point font size for the order ID text object.

- In the Details section, show the Quantity, Product ID, Product Name, Color, Size, and M/F fields. Draw a box around the details, and show the field headers for each detail section. Do not show the field headers in the Page Header section. Use a font size of 8 for the field headers.

- Separate each order with a dashed line.

- As a footnote for each order, create a text object that says **Contact *Jane Doe* at 444 to resolve any questions about the order**" where *Jane Doe* is the employee associated with the order and *444* is the employee's extension. Make the note italic.

- Use Can Grow wherever needed to ensure that no items are truncated.

- Call the report specification document **Exercise 25.3**.

A specification document using the InfoPath template is shown in Figure 25-1. Some assumptions were made for missing requirements.

Exercise 25.4: Creating a Report from a Specification Document

Use the specification document created in Exercise 25.3 to create a report. Figure 25-2 shows a sample page of the resulting report.

Report Requirements 1

Exercise 25.3

This report displays unshipped orders for use by the shipping derks for order fulfillment.

| Requestor | Joe Shipping | Request Date | 9/29/2004 |

Documenter | Annette Harper

| Keywords | • Sample | Audience | • Shipping Clerks |

Subject | Orders

Comments

Report Delivery Methods

Printer | HP CP 1160

Recipients | 1. Shipping clerks
2. Shipping supervisor

Page Setup

Template <u>Xtreme</u>

Printer Driver for <u>Select...</u>
the report design

| Right Margin | 1" | Left Margin | 1" | Top Margin | 1" | Bottom Margin | 1" |

Paper Size | ⦿ Letter   ○ Legal

Orientation | ⦿ Portrait   ○ Landscape

Page Header	☑ Logo ☐ Print Date ☐ Page Number ☐ Total Pages	
Page Footer	☐ Logo ☑ Print Date ☑ Page Number ☑ Total Pages	

Data Sources

Database	Schema	Source Type	Source Name
Xtreme		Table	Customer
Xtreme		Table	Employee
Xtreme		Table	Orders
Xtreme		Table	Orders Detail
Xtreme		Table	Product

Link Notes | Link using default linking.

Record Selection

not {Orders.Shipped}

Groups

Group Number	Group On	Sort	Keep Together	Repeat Header
1	Required Date	Ascending	☐	☑
2	Order ID	Ascending	☑	☐

Page 1 of 3

Figure 25-1   Sample specification document

Fields

Field 1   Type <u>Text</u>

Name Group 1 Header

Title No title

Notes

"Required Date: {Required Date}", 14 point font, bold the embedded field.

Field 2   Type <u>Text</u>

Name Group 2 Header

Title No title

Notes

"Order ID: {Order ID}", 12 point font, bold the embedded field.

Field 3   Type <u>Text</u>

Name Ship To Header

Title No title

Notes

"Ship To:", place in Group 2 Header in the middle of the section horizontally.

Field 4   Type <u>Text</u>

Name Ship To Content

Title No title

Notes

"{Customer Name}[line break]{Address1}[line break]{Address2}[line break]{City}, {Region} {Postal Code}[line break]{Country}", suppress embedded blank fields.

Field 5   Type <u>Database</u>

Name Quantity

Title Quantity

Notes

Create a new Group Header 2 section and place the field header in it. Use 8 points for the field header.

Field 6   Type <u>Database</u>

Name Product ID

Title Product ID

Notes

Treat field header as described for Field 5.

Field 7   Type <u>Database</u>

Name Product Name

Title Product Name

Notes

Treat field header as described for Field 5.

Field 8   Type <u>Database</u>

Name Color

Title Color

Notes

Treat field header as described for Field 5.

Field 9   Type <u>Database</u>

Name Size

Title Size

Notes

Treat field header as described for Field 5.

Field 10   Type <u>Database</u>

Name M/F

Notes

Treat field header as described for Field 5.

PART IV

Page 2 of 3

Figure 25-1   Sample specification document *(continued)*

Field 11	Title	M/F	Notes
	Type	Text	"Contact {First Name} {Last Name} at {Extension} to resolve any questions about the order.", place in a new Group Footer 2 section and set to italic.
	Name	Footnote	
	Title	No title	

Lines   Draw a dashed line above the Order ID.

Boxes   Draw a box around the details, including the field headers.

Figure 25-1   Sample specification document *(continued)*

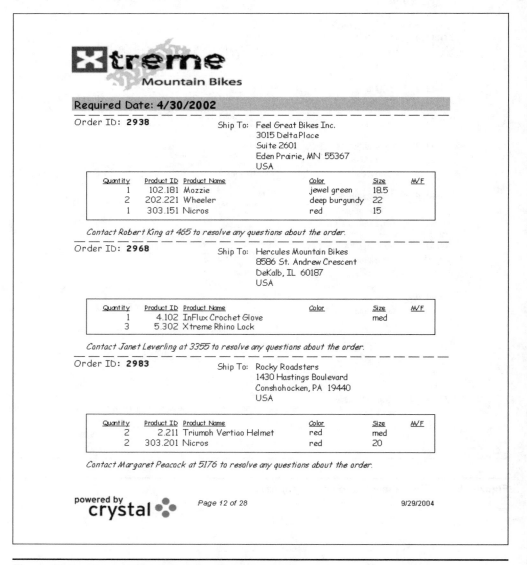

Figure 25-2   Report created from specification document

Documenting Reports

Most report documentation should be created while the report is being created. It should be an integral part of the development process. You'll want to create and follow standard procedures and naming conventions for the various report parts, as outlined in the following sections.

Documenting the Report File

The report file itself should adhere to your standards in several ways. The name and location of the report should be such that other developers or administrators understand which report it is. You should embed as much documentation in the report file as possible. You can use the document properties to attach some values to the file, and you can add commentary to a section that is suppressed to augment that.

Naming Conventions

It is important to adhere to a naming convention for your reports. How strict the convention is depends on the environment. Where there are few reports and they are significantly different, the names can be simple descriptions of the report. In an environment where there are hundreds of reports and many of them are similar, you may have to assign them numbers to uniquely identify each one. In that case, the description of the report should be entered in the document properties for the report file or be otherwise available.

Report filenames can be quite long, but you will usually want to abbreviate some common words that may be used in many reports. For example, you may have several reports that contain quarterly data, so you need to put the word "Quarterly" in their names. You should define a convention for how to abbreviate it: Qtrly, Qtr, or just Q. The overriding concern should be consistency. Each report name needs to use the same abbreviation so that everyone can quickly understand what the report name means.

If you have a well-defined file folder structure, you must decide whether to depend on the file location to help identify the report or whether the report name should be unique independent of its location. For example, if you have a folder structure that contains folders for each line of business, and each line of business has a sales report, you must decide if the name of the sales report needs to include the line of business to which it applies, or if the location of the report file in a particular line of business folder is sufficient.

Summary Information

You should use the Summary tab of the Document Properties dialog box (select File | Summary Info) to enter identifying information for the report file. Figure 25-3 shows properties for the report created in Exercise 25.4.

If the report file is closed and you are browsing using Windows Explorer, you can select a file, right-click, and choose Properties to display the values that were entered for the file in Crystal Reports. Figure 25-4 shows the Summary tab of the Windows Properties box for the same report that Figure 25-3 summarizes.

PART IV

Figure 25-3
Entering
summary
information

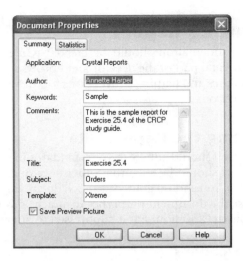

In addition to the values that can be entered in Crystal Reports, you can add more information using the latter Properties dialog box. Referring to Figure 25-4, you can see that the Category is empty. You can fill in a category on the Summary tab. To enter other types of information, use the Custom tab. You can select a name for the data element from the Name drop-down list or enter a new name. Or you can select a data type from the Type drop-down list, then enter a value in the Value box, and click Add. To remove a data element, select it, and then click the Remove button. See Figure 25-5 for a Custom tab that has a new entry for the Request Date.

Figure 25-4
Viewing summary
information in
Windows
Explorer

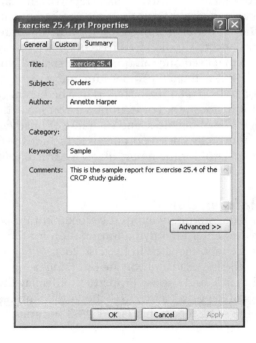

Figure 25-5
Entering custom
document
properties

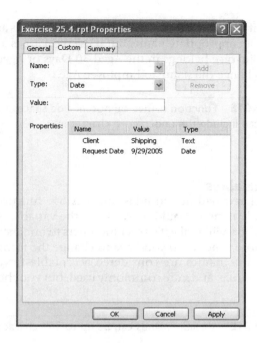

Any document properties that you enter or create are stored with the report file. They can be viewed by other users or used in file searches. You should determine which entries are useful in your environment and set up a standard so that they are consistently applied.

Using a Suppressed Section for Comments

You can create a new report section such as a Report Footer section, place text objects in it for documentation, and then suppress it. This will make it visible only to report developers. You may want to suppress it conditionally based on a parameter so that it can be displayed and printed for reference. For example, you could institute a process whereby the developer enters comments in a text object in the suppressed section each time the report is modified. This will then contain a history of changes that is maintained with the report. Of course, this will increase the size of the report file, but not significantly.

Documenting Formulas and Custom Functions

It is important to document formulas and custom functions so that future changes, whether made by you or by another developer, will be easier.

Naming Formulas and Custom Functions

Just as it is important to develop a naming convention for your report files, it is also important to have a naming convention for formulas and custom functions. The names of formulas and custom functions should describe what the formula or function returns.

For example, if you have a formula that returns a person's age given their birth date, then Age might be an appropriate name. But if the term *age* is also applied to invoices to determine if an invoice belongs in the Aged 30 Days or Aged 90 Days category, then you may need to change the name to Employee Age.

NOTE Function names cannot include spaces or start with a number. They can include the underscore character.

Naming Variables

Variables declared within formulas and custom functions should have meaningful names. Variable names should reflect what the variable is intended to contain. Using names like x and y will make it harder for others to understand your code; they may even cause *you* to lose time when you have to change the formula a year from now. Single-character variable names are considered acceptable for counter variables in looping structures where *n*, *i*, and *x* are commonly used, but you should avoid them in other situations.

NOTE Variable names can be up to 254 characters long.

Using Comments

You should add comments to formulas for documentation, but don't comment things that are clear from reading the code. Add comments where explanation of the logic or the situation is required, and comment for purely documentary reasons, such as adding a comment for each major modification of a formula to explain the changes.

NOTE The comment character is // for Crystal syntax and a single quote (') for Basic syntax.

Here is an example of comments that might be placed at the start of every formula:

```
//Dated Created: 10/11/2004
//Author: Annette Harper
//Purpose: To calculate quarterly commissions.
//Placement: Group Footer
//Dependent formulas: Filtering formula {@Top sales reps for Q1}
//Notes: Requires the commission rate.
```

Exercise 25.5: Entering Summary Information

1. Open the report from Exercise 25.4.

2. Choose File | Summary Info to display the document properties.

3. Using the report specification document from Exercise 25.3, fill in the Summary tab.

4. Close the report.

5. Browse to the report using Windows Explorer. Right-click and choose Properties.

6. Select the Summary tab, and enter **CRCP** as the Category.

7. Select the Custom tab. Select Client from the Name drop-down box, and enter **Shipping** as the value. Click the Add button.

8. Type **Request Date** in the Name box, select Date in the Type drop-down box, and enter the request date from the report specification document as the value. Click Add.

9. Click Close.

Report-Definition Files

A report-definition file is a text file containing a description of a report. The report-definition file can act as a "readable" version of the report file and might be used to search for the use of a particular field or as a last ditch resource if a report has to be re-created (but since many parts of a report are not documented in the file, a reliable backup would be a better choice).

A report-definition file is created by selecting Report Definition as the Format option in the Export dialog box. The name of the file defaults to the name of the report file with a .txt extension, but you can change it if you like.

Sections

The output of the report-definition export is a text file with several numbered sections. These sections can be empty.

1.0 File Information

The File Information section lists the report title from the file's summary information and the .rpt version number.

```
Report File: Exercise 25.4
Version: 10.2
```

2.0 Record Sort Fields

The Record Sort Fields section contains one line for each record sort in the report. An A indicates an ascending sort; D indicates a descending sort.

```
A - {Employee.Employee ID}
D - {Orders.Ship Date}
```

3.0 Group Sort Fields

The Group Sort Fields section displays a line for each group in the report and shows the field that is being grouped on and the sort order.

```
D - Sum ({Orders.Order Amount}, {Customer.Country})
D - Sum ({Orders.Order Amount}, {Customer.Customer Name})
```

4.0 Formulas

The Formulas section will have subsections if any formulas exist in the report.

4.1 Record Selection Formula
This section will contain the record selection formula for the report, if one exists.

```
{Orders.PO#} <> {?PO Param} and
{Orders.Order Date} = {?Order Date Param} and
{Orders.Ship Via} = {?Ship Via Param}
```

4.2 Group Selection Formula
This section will contain the group selection formula for the report, if one exists.

```
Minimum ({Orders.Ship Date}, {Orders.Order Date}, "quarterly")
      >= DateTime (2002, 01, 01, 00, 00, 00)
```

4.3 Other Formulas
This section lists the Formula Fields defined in the report. SQL Expression fields are not shown here.

```
Name: {@Percent Of Total Salary}
Formula: 100*{Employee.Salary}/Sum ({Employee.Salary})

Name: {@21 At Hire}
Formula: {@AgeAtHire} >= 21
```

5.0 Sectional Information

This area will contain a child area for each section in the report, numbered 5.1, 5.2, and so on. If a report section has subsections, they are shown as Subsection.1, Subsection.2, and so on. The name of the section will follow the 5.n number, as shown in the following example for Group Header Section #2. Next will be any section formatting that applies to the entire section. In the example, you see only the Visible indicator. The Subsection listings then follow, showing any section formatting for any existing subsections. Subsection.1 will always exist. Following the Subsection format listings will be a list of all the objects that reside in the entire section (including all subsections). This example shows a text field (Order ID:) and a database field ({Orders.Order ID}).

```
5.7 Group Header Section #2
     Visible

     Subsection.1
          Visible, Keep Together

     Subsection.2
          Visible, Keep Together

     Subsection.3
          Visible, Keep Together

     Order ID:
          String, Visible, Left Alignment, Top Alignment,
          Keep Together

     {Orders.Order ID}
          Numeric, Visible, Left Alignment, Top Alignment,
          Keep Together,
          Bracketed, No Thousands Separators, 0 Decimal Places,
          Rounding: 1, Thousands Symbol: ',', Decimal Symbol: '.'
```

If a section has conditional formatting associated with it, the format formula will follow the Subsection.*n* heading. If a report field has conditional formatting associated with it, the format formula will follow the object in section 5.*n*.

Notes

The report-definition file contains information about subreports, but it does not contain a complete description of a report file. Some of the missing items or formatting information is noted here.

- **Subreports**   If a subreport exists in a section, the report-definition file will contain a complete embedded report-definition file for the subreport in the 5.*n* section where the subreport exists.

- **Object placement**   Information on the exact placement of objects in the report is not available in the definition file. This portion of the file tells you which section the object is placed in but not where it is located in that section.

- **Lines and boxes**   Lines and boxes drawn on the report are not documented in the report-definition file.

- **Data Sources and Linking**   Data source and linking information is not given directly in the report definition file. However, since field names are given, you might be able to reconstruct some of this information.

- **Charts and maps**   Charts and maps are not documented in the report-definition file.

- **Cross-tabs and OLAP grids**   Cross-tabs and OLAP grids are not documented in the report definition file.

- **Highlighting Expert formatting**   Conditional formatting created with the Highlighting Expert is not documented in the report definition file.

Exercise 25.6: Creating a Report-Definition File

1. Open the report from Exercise 25.4.
2. Select File | Export, and choose Report Definition as the format and Disk as the location. Click OK.
3. When the Choose Export File dialog box appears, accept the default filename, and select the folder where you saved the Exercise 25.4 report.
4. Click Save.
5. Use Windows Explorer to find the exported file. Click it to open it in Notepad.
6. Examine the report-definition file.
7. Close the files.

Chapter Review

This chapter introduced the concept of a report development methodology, explained the phases in a waterfall method, and described the benefits of using a methodology. It also covered the requirements-gathering and design phases of the report development methodology in greater detail. A report specification document is the result of the design phase and should be the first point of sign-off by the user or requestor. Finally, this chapter described techniques that you can use to document reports and defined and explained the sections of a report-definition file.

Quick Tips

- Report development, like other software development, should adhere to a methodology.
- The traditional waterfall methodology consists of phases for requirements gathering, analysis, design, development, testing, deployment, and maintenance.
- Incomplete or inaccurate phases lead to rework and affect subsequent phases, resulting in increased development time, higher expenses, increased use of resources, and delays to other projects.
- User sign-off should be obtained for the specification document, after testing, and possibly after deployment.
- Using a methodology has several benefits including the production of successful reports, facilitation of project planning and tracking, production of

documentation (which eases maintenance), generation of process improvements, and an improved relationship between developer and client.

- There are three types of report requirements: business, technical, and user.

- Business requirements state the business purpose of the report.

- Technical requirements describe the report content, design, format, and environment.

- User requirements explain how the user will interact with the report.

- Report requirements are gathered via forms, questionnaires, interviews, and research.

- A report-specification document is created by analyzing and organizing the information collected during the requirements-gathering phase. It has two primary purposes. The first is to serve as the official document that the requestor will sign to indicate that the report requirements are correct. The second is to act as a blueprint for the report developer.

- The report-specification document will contain all the information needed to create the report, including any special notes or comments. It will have sections for describing the data sources, fields, grouping, formatting, computations, and so on.

- Report documentation can include file-naming conventions, the file's document properties, and the use of suppressed sections.

- The primary goal of a naming convention should be the generation of consistent, meaningful names.

- Formulas and custom functions should be documented using comments and a naming convention for the formula name and variable names.

- A report-definition file is a text file that contains a description of a report.

- A report-definition file has sections containing information on the report file, record sort fields, group sort fields, formulas (record selection, group selection, and other), and sections.

- The Sectional Information portion of a report-definition file contains information about each section of a report. It includes formatting information for the section, lists the field objects in the section and their formatting, and includes a report definition for any subreports in the section.

- The report-definition file does not tell you the exact placement of field objects, nor does it document lines, boxes, charts, maps, cross-tabs, OLAP grids, formatting created with the Highlighting Expert, or the exact data sources for the report.

PART IV

Questions

Questions may have more than one correct answer. Choose all answers that apply.

1. In which phase is the report created?

   a. Requirements

   b. Analysis

   c. Design

   d. Development

   e. Testing

2. A failure in which phase will have (potentially) the greatest effect on the entire process?

   a. Requirements

   b. Analysis

   c. Design

   d. Development

   e. Testing

3. Which phases might require user sign-off ?

   a. Requirements

   b. Analysis

   c. Design

   d. Development

   e. Testing

   f. Deployment

4. Which phase might include the creation of documentation if the documents created in the other phases are inadequate?

   a. Analysis

   b. Design

   c. Development

   d. Deployment

   e. Maintenance

5. Which of the following is not an advantage of using a methodology?

   a. Faster report production

   b. Successful reports

   c. Better project planning and tracking

    d. Documentation

    e. Process improvement

6. Using a methodology increases the probability of being able to reuse certain components, such as custom functions and templates.

    a. True

    b. False

7. What are the three types of report requirements?

    a. Environmental

    b. Display

    c. Business

    d. Technical

    e. User

8. Which type of report requirement defines the look of the report?

    a. Environmental

    b. Display

    c. Business

    d. Technical

    e. User

9. Which type of report requirement defines the way that the users will interact with the report?

    a. Environmental

    b. Display

    c. Business

    d. Technical

    e. User

10. Which type of report requirement defines the purpose of the report?

    a. Environmental

    b. Display

    c. Business

    d. Technical

    e. User

11. Which of the following are recommended methods that might be used to gather report requirements?

    a. Forms

    b. Informal e-mail messages

    c. Questionnaires

    d. Interviews

    e. Ad hoc conversations

12. Whose signature is vital on the report specification document?

    a. Analyst

    b. Requirements gatherer

    c. Report requestor or client

    d. Report developer

    e. User

13. A report-specification document is used when interviewing the report requestor to gather requirements.

    a. True

    b. False

14. Which of the following will not be in a report-specification document?

    a. Data sources

    b. Fields

    c. Record selection

    d. A complete description of each subreport

    e. Special formatting

15. A template is commonly used to create a report-specification document to promote consistency and completeness.

    a. True

    b. False

16. A report-specification document need not contain information about how the users will export data because that will not affect the design.

    a. True

    b. False

17. What is the main goal when implementing a naming convention?

    a. Long, meaningful names

    b. Consistent, meaningful names

    c. Short, meaningful names

    d. Names that depend on their location in the file structure

    e. Names that do not depend on their location in the file structure

18. A naming convention should be used for report filenames.

    a. True

    b. False

19. A naming convention should be used for formula names but is not important for variable names.

    a. True

    b. False

20. When adding comments to a formula, you should

    a. Comment every line

    b. Comment to explain complex logic

    c. Comment each major modification

    d. Comment to explain a single-character variable name

    e. Never comment

21. You have a formula that returns the discount percentage to be applied to an order. The discount is dependent on the total order amount. Which of the following are good names for this formula?

    a. Discount

    b. Order Amount Discount

    c. Order Amount Percent Discount

    d. Discount Percent for Total Order Amount

    e. Tot Ord Amt Discount %

22. Which file extension does a report-definition file use by default?

    a. .rpt

    b. .pdf

    c. .doc

    d. .rtf

    e. .txt

23. A report-definition file can be opened in Crystal Reports.

    a. True

    b. False

24. Which of the following is documented in a report-definition file?

    a. The report filename

    b. The title associated with the report file

    c. The version of Crystal Reports that created the report file

      d. The Crystal Reports version that the report file was saved to

      e. The author of the report file

25. Formatting formulas are displayed in the Formulas section of a report-definition file.

      a. True

      b. False

26. Which of the following are documented in a report-definition file?

      a. Subreports

      b. Lines

      c. Linking information

      d. Charts

      e. Conditional formatting created with the Highlighting Expert

Answers

1. **d.** The report is created during the development, implementation, or build phase.

2. **a.** A failure in any phase affects all subsequent phases, so a failure in the requirements-gathering phase would potentially have the greatest impact.

3. **c, e, f.** The user should sign off on the specifications document, which is the result of the design phase, and after testing and deployment.

4. **e.** Additional documentation may be created in the maintenance phase.

5. **a.** Reports might be produced faster using a methodology, but this is not necessarily the case.

6. **a.** True. Using a methodology improves the chance that you may find opportunities for reusing some components.

7. **c, d, e.** The three types are business, technical, and user.

8. **d.** The technical requirements describe the report.

9. **e.** The user requirements describe how the users will interact with the report.

10. **c.** The business requirements define the purpose of the report.

11. **a, c, d.** It is not recommended to gather report requirements via informal conversations or e-mail.

12. **c.** The report requestor's signature should be required. Others may sign off as well.

13. **b.** The report-specification document uses the results of the requirements-gathering process as input to produce an organized design document.

14. **d.** Each subreport must be fully described in its own report-specification document.

15. **a.** A template ensures that all topics are covered and produces similar report-specification documents from one project to the next.

16. **b.** False. Understanding how the report will be used may affect the design.

17. **b.** The main goal of a naming convention should be the generation of consistent names.

18. **a.** True. Report filenames should follow a naming convention.

19. **b.** False. A naming convention should be used for both formula names and variable names.

20. **b, c.** You should comment to explain complex logic or to add documentation about formula modifications.

21. **d, e.** Answers a, b, and c do not fully describe the formula, although they might be OK under some circumstances. Answer d fully describes the formula, as does Answer e, even though it uses abbreviations.

22. **e.** A report-definition file uses the .txt extension by default.

23. **b.** False. A report-definition file is a text file; it cannot be opened in Crystal Reports.

24. **b, d.** The title associated with the report and the Crystal Reports version that the file was saved as are listed in the File Information section of the report-definition file.

25. **b.** False. Formatting formulas are displayed in the Sectional Information section of the report-definition file.

26. **a.** Subreports are documented in a report-definition file.

Applying Report Design Concepts and Methodology

Exam RDCR400 expects you to be able to
- Apply various report design concepts
- Apply seven steps to a report project

This chapter will enable you to apply what you have learned about report methodologies. You will be given report requirements to use to create a report-specification document and then develop the report. These reports will contain some common situations that arise in everyday reporting. Full solutions are given so that you can learn techniques you may not have seen before. Solutions to common report-development problems may be tested on the exam.

NOTE Because this chapter focuses on the application of knowledge gained previously it contains no Quick Tips or Questions. It consists entirely of creating practice reports.

Group Suppression Based on Detail Values

This example will show you how to suppress an entire group depending on the value of the detail records it contains.

Requirements

Your client wants to add a gift to orders that contain a certain product. The product that qualifies for a gift will vary over time. The report should look like the report that was developed in Exercise 25.4. However, it should show only orders that contain a specific product type, and the product type must be user selectable. The report title should be "Orders with Gifts," and the product type that qualifies an order for a gift should be displayed in the page header.

Analysis

Looking at the Exercise 25.4 report, note the following:

- It contains two groups, the outer group is Required Date, and the inner group is Order ID.

- It does not use the Product Type table where the Product Type Name is stored.
- It could happen that no orders for a required date contain the gift product.

You determine that you must do the following things to create the new report starting from the Exercise 25.4 report.

- Add the Product Type table.
- Create a Gift Product Type parameter and populate its default values with all Product Type values.
- Create a record-level formula that returns True if the Product Type equals the value of the new parameter. Call the formula **Record Contains Gift Product Type**.
- Create a group selection formula that selects only groups where the maximum of the Record Contains Gift Product Type formula is True computed across an Order ID. (True is considered greater than False, so the maximum of a group that contains any Trues will be True.)
- Add a text object for the title, **Orders with Gifts**. Use a font size of 20 points.
- Add a text object under the title containing **Qualifying Product Type is {?Gift Product Type}**.

Exercise 26.1: Creating the Orders with Gifts Report

1. Create the report specification document using the preceding requirements and analysis. Use the template that you created in Chapter 25 or the InfoPath template supplied on the accompanying CD.

2. Develop the report. Figure 26-1 shows the first record of the report when Helmets is selected as the gift qualifying product type.

3. Test the report using different values for the parameter.

Figure 26-1
Running Orders with Gifts report for Helmets

Orders with Gifts
Qualifying Product Type is Helmets

Required Date: 4/21/2002

Order ID: **2955**

Ship To: Deals on Wheels
6073 Cambie Court
Suite 1214
DeKalb, IL 60153
USA

Quantity	Product ID	Product Name	Color	Size	M/F
3	2,215	Triumph Vertigo Helmet	white	lrg	

Contact Anne Dodsworth at 452 to resolve any questions about the order.

Alternative Solutions
Alternative solutions include the following:

- You could use section suppression instead of a group selection formula. In that case, you would need to suppress all sections between and including Group Header 2 and Group Footer 2 if the maximum across Order ID of Contains Gift Product Type is False. In addition, you would have to suppress all Group Header 1 and Group Footer 1 sections if the maximum across Required Date of Contains Gift Product Type is False.

- You could do the group selection on the server if you used a SQL Command, as shown here. The bulk of the command is identical to the report query created by Crystal Reports. The addition of the subquery at the end will filter to orders that contain the product type that qualifies for a gift.

```
SELECT 'Orders'.'Shipped', 'Orders'.'Order ID', 'Orders'.'Required Date',
       'Orders_Detail'.'Product ID', 'Orders_Detail'.'Quantity',
       'Product'.'Product Name', 'Product'.'Color', 'Product'.'Size',
       'Product'.'M/F', 'Employee'.'Last Name', 'Employee'.'First Name',
       'Employee'.'Extension', 'Customer'.'Customer Name',
       'Customer'.'Address1', 'Customer'.'Address2', 'Customer'.'City',
       'Customer'.'Region', 'Customer'.'Country', 'Customer'.'Postal Code',
       'Product_Type'.'Product Type Name'
  FROM
   (((('Orders' 'Orders'
       INNER JOIN 'Orders Detail' 'Orders_Detail'
       ON 'Orders'.'Order ID'='Orders_Detail'.'Order ID')
       INNER JOIN 'Customer' 'Customer'
       ON 'Orders'.'Customer ID'='Customer'.'Customer ID')
       INNER JOIN 'Employee' 'Employee'
       ON 'Orders'.'Employee ID'='Employee'.'Employee ID')
       INNER JOIN 'Product' 'Product'
       ON 'Orders_Detail'.'Product ID'='Product'.'Product ID')
       INNER JOIN 'Product Type' 'Product_Type'
       ON 'Product'.'Product Type ID'='Product_Type'.'Product Type ID'
  WHERE  'Orders'.'Shipped'=FALSE
AND 'Orders'.'Order ID' IN
  (Select DISTINCT 'Orders'.'Order ID'
   FROM
   (('Orders'
    INNER JOIN 'Orders Detail'
      ON 'Orders'.'Order ID'='Orders Detail'.'Order ID')
    INNER JOIN 'Product'
      ON 'Orders Detail'.'Product ID'='Product'.'Product ID')
    INNER JOIN 'Product Type'
      ON 'Product'.'Product Type ID'='Product Type'.'Product Type ID'
   WHERE 'Product Type'.'Product Type Name' = '{?Gift Product Type}')
```

Forcing Group Headings When No Details Exist
In a report that contains groups, if no detail records exist for a particular group value, there will be no corresponding group section (since Crystal Reports cannot group on a value that it knows nothing about). Any charts or cross-tabs that are based on the data

will have the same problem. In some cases, this is the desired result; in others, the report requirements may include displaying all groups whether or not they are empty.

Requirements

Your client wants a report developed that displays the total order amount by customer by month for a user-selected country and year. The client wants to see all customers, whether or not they had any orders. A chart should be added to the report that displays one stacked bar for each customer in which the components of the bar are the months for the selected year. All customers should display on the chart even if they made no orders. Use the Xtreme template you developed in Chapter 9.

Analysis

You understand immediately that this would be a very simple report request except for the requirement to show all customers even if they had no orders. Doing an inner join of the Customer and Orders tables will eliminate any customers that had no orders. You consider a left outer join from the Customer table to the Orders table. You know that the database will first construct the joined records and then apply any filtering. You devise a sample using the following data to determine what will happen.

Customer Table

Customer ID	Country	Customer Name
1	USA	Bikes Galore
2	USA	Yikes! Bikes
3	USA	All Bikes
4	Canada	Bikes Are Us
5	USA	New Bike Co.

Orders Table

Order ID	Customer ID	Order Date	Order Amount
100	1	8/15/2001	20000
101	1	5/20/2002	1500
102	2	6/30/2001	3500
103	2	9/25/2001	600
104	4	3/18/2001	6500
105	5	11/25/2000	4200
106	5	4/28/2002	650

A left outer join of the Customer and Orders tables will result in the following records.

Customer ID	Country	Customer Name	Order ID	Order Date	Order Amount
1	USA	Bikes Galore	100	8/15/2001	20000
1	USA	Bikes Galore	101	5/20/2002	1500
2	USA	Yikes! Bikes	102	6/30/2001	3500
2	USA	Yikes! Bikes	103	9/25/2001	600
3	USA	All Bikes			
4	Canada	Bikes Are Us	104	3/18/2001	6500
5	USA	New Bike Co.	105	11/25/2000	4200
5	USA	New Bike Co.	106	4/28/2002	650

If the user selected USA and chose order dates in 2001, the result would be filtered to the following.

Customer ID	Country	Customer Name	Order ID	Order Date	Order Amount
1	USA	Bikes Galore	100	8/15/2001	20000
2	USA	Yikes! Bikes	102	6/30/2001	3500
2	USA	Yikes! Bikes	103	9/25/2001	600

You have now lost All Bikes and New Bike Co., which should appear as customers for the selected country. Looking back at the original join result, you see that if you modified the filter to include NULL order dates, you could retain All Bikes, but would still not retain New Bike Co. You realize that the problem is arising because you are doing the left outer join *before* the filtering.

If you filter the Customer table, filter the Orders table, and then do a left outer join, the result will be what you need, as shown here.

Filtered Customer Table

Customer ID	Country	Customer Name
1	USA	Bikes Galore
2	USA	Yikes! Bikes
3	USA	All Bikes
5	USA	New Bike Co.

Filtered Orders Table

Order ID	Customer ID	Order Date	Order Amount
100	1	8/15/2001	20000
102	2	6/30/2001	3500
103	2	9/25/2001	600
104	4	3/18/2001	6500

Result of Left Outer Join

Customer ID	Country	Customer Name	Order ID	Order Date	Order Amount
1	USA	Bikes Galore	100	8/15/2001	20000
2	USA	Yikes! Bikes	102	6/30/2001	3500
2	USA	Yikes! Bikes	103	9/25/2001	600
3	USA	All Bikes			
5	USA	New Bike Co.			

To implement your solution, you know that you must write the report query yourself in a SQL Command because Crystal Reports cannot generate such a query. Your analysis includes the following directives.

- Create a SQL Command with two parameters, Country and Year, and the following text:

```
SELECT "Customer Name", "Order Amount", "Order Date"
  FROM
    (SELECT "Customer ID", "Customer Name", Country
        FROM    Customer
       WHERE  Country='{?Country}') A
    LEFT JOIN
      (SELECT "Customer ID", "Order Date", "Order Amount"
          FROM    Orders
         WHERE   ("Order Date">={ts '{?Year}-01-01 00:00:00'}
                 AND "Order Date"<{ts '{?Year}-12-31 00:00:01'})) B
  ON (A."Customer ID"=B."Customer ID")
```

- Group by Customer Name and Order Date, with Order Date in monthly groups.

- Add summaries of Order Amount for both groups and the grand total.

- Add a chart to the report header with a bar for each customer and layers within each bar for the monthly amounts.

Exercise 26.2: Creating the Order Amount by Customer Report

1. Create the report specification document using the preceding requirements and analysis. Use the template that you created in Chapter 25 or the InfoPath template supplied on the accompanying CD.

2. Develop the report. Figure 26-2 shows the first page of the report when Canada and 2002 are selected for the parameters.

3. Test the report using different values for the parameters.

Alternative Solutions

Alternative solutions include the following:

- You can create a main report showing all customers for the selected country and then add a subreport (filtered to the correct dates) with the orders that belong to each customer, linking it on the Customer ID field. In order to get a grand total of the order amount, you would have to create formulas using shared variables. The chart would also be more difficult to construct.

- You can use a different method for your SQL statement. Union a select statement that returns all the customers to the statement that returns customers with orders. Then group by Customer Name and Order Date to get a result set that includes both customers with orders and customers without orders, like so:

```
SELECT  "Customer Name", "Order Date",
        SUM("Order Amount")  AS "Total Order Amount"
```

```
  FROM
(SELECT   "Customer Name", "Order Amount", "Order Date"
    FROM    Customer INNER JOIN Orders
      ON (Customer."Customer ID"=Orders."Customer ID")
   WHERE   Country='{?Country}'
    AND   "Order Date">={ts '{?Year}-01-01 00:00:00'}
    AND   "Order Date"<{ts '{?Year}-12-31 00:00:01'}
UNION
  SELECT  "Customer Name", NULL, NULL
    FROM    Customer
   WHERE   Country='{?Country}')
GROUP BY "Customer Name",   "Order Date"
```

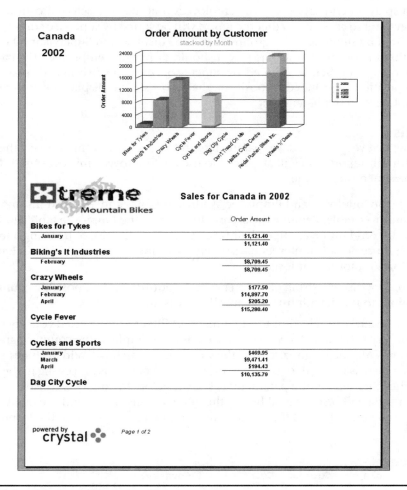

Figure 26-2   Running order amounts by customer report

Using Parameters in Complex Record Selection and Grouping

Real-life reports often require complex record selection that is driven by parameter choices. The addition of an "All" option to multivalue parameter default lists is a common request. You may occasionally be asked to create a report whose group-by field is user selectable. This example demonstrates such a situation.

Requirements

Your client is requesting a report that displays employee information. The client would like to display all employees or only employees that live in a selected country. At run time, they want to choose whether the report will be sorted by supervisor or by position. When sorted by supervisor, the groups should be displayed in Supervisor ID order but display the supervisor's name. The report should display the employee's ID, name, and Social Security number. If grouped by supervisor, the report should display the employee's position. If grouped by position, the report should display the employee's supervisor. Use the Xtreme template.

Analysis

You know that you will need two parameters and a couple of formulas to get the desired output for this report. You will also need to use the Employee table twice in order to retrieve the supervisor's name.

- Use the Employee and Employee_Addresses tables and a second instance of the Employee table. Rename the second instance of the Employee table **Supervisor**. Link from Employee.Supervisor ID to Supervisor.Employee ID using a left outer join since not all employees have supervisors. Link Employee_Addresses.Employee ID to Employee.Employee ID.

- Create a discrete string parameter called **Country**. Add all possible country values to the default list. Add an **All** entry to the default list.

- Create a record selection formula that will filter to the selected country or do no country filtering if All is selected. Here is an example: If the country parameter equals All, the formula returns the value True, which will add no filtering. Note that there is no need to use a SQL Expression to push this processing to the server. Since the value of the parameter is known before the query is constructed, this formula will be evaluated before the query is constructed and the query will contain only the WHERE clause that is implied by the *result* of the formula.

```
If {?Country} = 'All' then
  True
Else
  {Employee_Addresses.Country} = {?Country}
```

- Create a discrete string parameter called **Group By** whose default values are Supervisor and Position, used for determining the field that should be grouped by. Clear the Allow Editing of Default Values When There Is More Than One

Value check box to eliminate the possibility that the user will type in some unsupported group value.

- Create a formula called **Group** to use for grouping that returns either the supervisor ID or the position, depending on the value of the Group By parameter. Since the supervisor ID is a number it must be converted to a string that will maintain the proper sort order, for example:

```
If {?Group by} = 'Position' then
  {Employee.Position}
Else
  ToText({Employee.Supervisor ID},'0000')
```

- Insert a group on the Group formula field.

- Since the user wants to see the supervisor's name instead of the ID, use a formula for the group name, as shown here:

```
If {?Group by} = 'Position' then
  {Employee.Position}
Else
  (If IsNull({Employee.Supervisor ID}) then
     'No Supervisor'
  Else
    {Supervisor.First Name}&' '&{Supervisor.Last Name})
```

- Create a formula called Display to show whichever field was not selected for grouping, as shown here:

```
If {?Group by} = 'Position' then
  {Supervisor.First Name}&' '&{Supervisor.Last Name}
Else
  {Employee.Position}
```

- Create a formula called **Display Header** to use as the field heading for the display field.

```
If {?Group by} = 'Position' then
  'Supervisor'
Else
  'Position'
```

- Create a formula called **Name** that concatenates the employee's first and last names (or use a text object with the fields embedded).

- Place the Employee ID, Name, Display, and SSN fields on the report. Remove the default field heading for the Display field, and replace it with the Display Header formula field.

- Add a title using a text field with the content **Employees by {1?Group by}**.

- Add a subtitle using a text field with the content **For {?Country}**. Suppress the subtitle if the country is All using this formula:

```
{?Country} = 'All'
```

Figure 26-3
Employee report
by supervisor for
all employees

Mountain Bikes

Employees by Supervisor

Employee ID	Name	Position	SSN
No Supervisor			
2	Andrew Fuller	Vice President, Sales	751513641
Andrew Fuller			
5	Steven Buchanan	Sales Manager	954421324
10	Albert Hellstern	Business Manager	644564135
13	Justin Brid	Marketing Director	322412002

Exercise 26.3: Creating the Employee Report

1. Create the report specification document using the preceding requirements and analysis. Use the template that you created in Chapter 25 or the InfoPath template supplied on the accompanying CD.

2. Develop the report. Figure 26-3 shows part of the first page of the report when Supervisor and All are selected for the parameters. Figure 26-4 shows the first page of the report when Position and France are selected for the parameters.

3. Run the report using various combinations of the parameters to verify that it is working correctly.

Customizing Date Groups

Crystal Reports' date grouping options—days, weeks, two weeks, half months, months, quarters, half years, and years—are convenient when you need to group by these intervals, assuming that your days end at midnight, your weeks start on Sunday, you use calendar quarters, and so on. If you need to group by intervals that do not follow the rules, you must create them yourself.

Requirements

Your client wants a chart that shows the top three products, determined using the order quantity, as a stacked bar for various intervals. The intervals should be calendar quarters for the current year and full years for all previous years.

Figure 26-4
Employee report
by position for
employees from
France

Mountain Bikes

Employees by Position
For France

Employee ID	Name	Supervisor	SSN
Advertising Specialist			
15	Laurent Pereira	Justin Brid	322698901
Marketing Associate			
14	Xavier Martin	Justin Brid	640055400
Marketing Director			
13	Justin Brid	Andrew Fuller	322412002

Analysis

You determine the following:

- The report requires the Orders, Orders_Detail, and Product tables.

- You will create an Interval formula using the following code to group on:

```
If Year({Orders.Order Date}) = Year(CurrentDate) then
  ToText(DatePart('yyyy',{Orders.Order Date}),'0000')
    &' Q '
    &ToText(DatePart ('q', {Orders.Order Date}),'0')
Else
  ToText(DatePart('yyyy',{Orders.Order Date}),'0000')
```

- The chart will be a stacked bar chart, and you must use the Advanced layout. In that layout you will use the Interval formula field and the Product Name field for the On Change Of fields. You will use the sum of the Quantity field for the Show Values list. For the Product Name field, you will invoke the Group Sort Expert using the Top N button and set the properties so that only the top three products are displayed. The chart will be placed in the report header.

- All other sections can be suppressed.

Exercise 26.4: Creating the Top 3 Products Report

1. Create the report specification document using the preceding requirements and analysis. Use the template that you created in Chapter 25 or the InfoPath template supplied on the accompanying CD.

2. Develop the report. Use Report | Set Print Date and Time to set the date to any date in 2002, which is the last year for which sample data exists. Figure 26-5 shows the chart.

3. Test the report.

Figure 26-5
Top 3 Products
chart

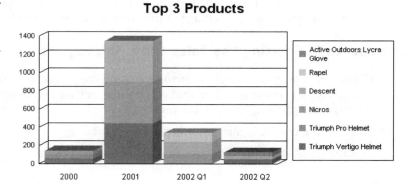

PART IV

Alternative Solutions

Alternative solutions for this report include the following:

- Instead of creating a formula to group on, you could use the Named Group options to create the groups you need. However, this approach would be time-consuming and would have to be redone when the current year changes.
- Since only summary-level values are needed for the report, a SQL Expression could be created for the interval computation in order to push the grouping to the server.

Using Multiple Summaries in Cross-Tabs

Cross-tabs usually contain only one summarized value in their cells, but you may be required to show multiple summaries for some reports.

Requirements

Your client would like a cross-tab report that shows the total order amount by customer by order year across each employee, for customers in Canada. The cross-tab should also show the percentage that the order amount in the cell contributed to the year's total. The cross-tab should be formatted to fit on one page. No subtotal for the customer is required.

Analysis

After analyzing the report requirements, you determine the following:

- The Orders, Customer, and Employee tables are required.
- The report is a cross-tab only, with no other sections.
- The columns will be the employees; the rows will be the order years by customer. You will use Order Date with the For Each Year option to obtain the order year.
- The summarized fields will be the Order Amount summed and the Order Amount summed as a percentage of the column values.

Exercise 26.5: Creating the Sales Cross-Tab Report

1. Create the report specification document using the preceding requirements and analysis. Use the template that you created in Chapter 25 or the InfoPath template supplied on the accompanying CD.

2. Develop the report. Figure 26-6 shows the report.

3. Test the report to verify that your result is correct.

Canadian Sales by Customer across Employee

Customer	Year	Davolio	Dodsworth	King	Leverling	Peacock	Suyama	Total
Bikes for Tykes	2000	$0.00 0.00 %	$0.00 0.00 %	$296.62 16.24 %	$0.00 0.00 %	$0.00 0.00 %	$1,530.42 83.76 %	**$1,827.04** 100.00 %
	2001	$16,975.05 51.19 %	$16.50 0.05 %	$11,337.45 34.19 %	$1,752.64 5.29 %	$785.40 2.37 %	$2,294.55 6.92 %	**$33,161.59** 100.00 %
	2002	$0.00 0.00 %	$1,121.40 100.00 %	$0.00 0.00 %	$0.00 0.00 %	$0.00 0.00 %	$0.00 0.00 %	**$1,121.40** 100.00 %
Biking's It Industries	2000	$0.00 0.00 %	$1,391.08 59.25 %	$33.00 1.41 %	$923.61 39.34 %	$0.00 0.00 %	$0.00 0.00 %	**$2,347.69** 100.00 %
	2001	$14,434.56 35.90 %	$983.65 2.45 %	$4,062.57 10.11 %	$4,624.10 11.50 %	$3,010.35 7.49 %	$13,087.35 32.55 %	**$40,202.58** 100.00 %
	2002	$2,699.55 31.00 %	$0.00 0.00 %	$130.20 1.49 %	$0.00 0.00 %	$0.00 0.00 %	$5,879.70 67.51 %	**$8,709.45** 100.00 %
Crazy Wheels	2000	$0.00 0.00 %	$0.00 0.00 %	$0.00 0.00 %	$1,529.70 100.00 %	$0.00 0.00 %	$0.00 0.00 %	**$1,529.70** 100.00 %
	2001	$3,814.67 13.27 %	$11,281.09 39.24 %	$7,840.81 27.28 %	$871.33 3.03 %	$1,114.71 3.88 %	$3,824.45 13.30 %	**$28,747.06** 100.00 %
	2002	$0.00 0.00 %	$7,616.75 49.85 %	$1,565.25 10.24 %	$161.70 1.06 %	$0.00 0.00 %	$5,936.70 38.85 %	**$15,280.40** 100.00 %
Cycle Fever	2001	$0.00 0.00 %	$0.00 0.00 %	$0.00 0.00 %	$0.00 0.00 %	$8,819.55 100.00 %	$0.00 0.00 %	**$8,819.55** 100.00 %
Cycles and Sports	2000	$548.70 100.00 %	$0.00 0.00 %	$0.00 0.00 %	$0.00 0.00 %	$0.00 0.00 %	$0.00 0.00 %	**$548.70** 100.00 %
	2001	$5,218.45 13.75 %	$5,040.40 13.28 %	$7,936.07 20.90 %	$7,544.40 19.87 %	$371.75 0.98 %	$11,854.65 31.22 %	**$37,965.72** 100.00 %
	2002	$0.00 0.00 %	$563.70 5.56 %	$161.70 1.60 %	$0.00 0.00 %	$8,907.71 87.88 %	$502.68 4.96 %	**$10,135.79** 100.00 %
Dag City Cycle	2001	$0.00 0.00 %	$0.00 0.00 %	$0.00 0.00 %	$863.74 100.00 %	$0.00 0.00 %	$0.00 0.00 %	**$863.74** 100.00 %
Don't Tread On Me	2001	$0.00 0.00 %	$0.00 0.00 %	$0.00 0.00 %	$0.00 0.00 %	$0.00 0.00 %	$274.35 100.00 %	**$274.35** 100.00 %
Halifax Cycle	2001	$0.00 0.00 %	$0.00 0.00 %	$959.70 100.00 %	$0.00 0.00 %	$0.00 0.00 %	$0.00 0.00 %	**$959.70** 100.00 %
Pedal Pusher Bikes Inc.	2000	$5,811.96 100.00 %	$0.00 0.00 %	$0.00 0.00 %	$0.00 0.00 %	$0.00 0.00 %	$0.00 0.00 %	**$5,811.96** 100.00 %
	2001	$6,184.69 17.09 %	$2,489.40 6.88 %	$1,682.15 4.65 %	$10,886.79 30.08 %	$11,935.90 32.98 %	$3,010.95 8.32 %	**$36,189.88** 100.00 %
	2002	$5,312.04 22.92 %	$0.00 0.00 %	$17,743.12 76.55 %	$83.30 0.36 %	$0.00 0.00 %	$40.50 0.17 %	**$23,178.96** 100.00 %
Wheels 'n' Deals	2001	$0.00 0.00 %	$0.00 0.00 %	$0.00 0.00 %	$0.00 0.00 %	$1,799.70 100.00 %	$0.00 0.00 %	**$1,799.70** 100.00 %
Total		**$60,999.67** 23.51 %	**$30,503.97** 11.76 %	**$53,748.64** 20.71 %	**$29,241.31** 11.27 %	**$36,745.07** 14.16 %	**$48,236.30** 18.59 %	**$259,474.96** 100.00 %

Figure 26-6   Canadian Sales by Customer across Employee report

Averaging Time Data

Time data cannot be correctly averaged with the Average summary function. In order to average time data, you must convert to a number of hours, minutes, seconds, or fraction of seconds; compute the average; and then convert back to a time type or otherwise format the result for display.

Requirements

Your client has requested a report that shows the average time between the date an order was placed and the date that it shipped, computed across the order month. The result should show the average in days, hours, minutes, and seconds. The order month should display as March 1999.

Analysis

After analyzing the requirements, you determine the following must be done to create this report:

- The Orders table is required.
- You need to group by Order Date with the monthly option, and customize the formatting to show the full month name followed by the year.
- The order detail can be hidden.
- You must create a formula called **SecondsBetweenOrderAndShip** that computes the difference between the order date and the ship date in seconds, as shown here:

```
DateDiff ('s', {Orders.Order Date}, {Orders.Ship Date})
```

- This formula field will be averaged.
- A second formula must be created that converts the average number of seconds back to days, hours, minutes, and seconds, as shown here:

```
Local numberVar Days;
Local numberVar Hours;
Local numberVar Minutes;
Local numberVar Seconds;
//Store the average time in seconds for use later in the formula;
Local numberVar AverageTimeInSeconds:=
    Average ({@SecondsBetweenOrderAndShip}, {Orders.Order Date}, "monthly");
Local numberVar SecondsInAMinute:= 60;
Local numberVar SecondsInAnHour:= 60*60;
Local numberVar SecondsInADay:= 60*60*24;
Local numberVar SecondsRemaining;

Days := Int (AverageTimeInSeconds/SecondsInADay);
SecondsRemaining:= AverageTimeInSeconds-(Days*SecondsInADay);
Hours := Int (SecondsRemaining/SecondsInAnHour);
SecondsRemaining:= SecondsRemaining - (Hours*SecondsInAnHour);
Minutes := Int (SecondsRemaining/SecondsInAMinute);
SecondsRemaining:= SecondsRemaining - (Minutes*SecondsInAMinute);
Seconds := SecondsRemaining;
//Format the result for display;
'Days: '&ToText(Days,0)&' Hours: '&ToText(Hours,0)
  &' Minutes: '&ToText(Minutes,0)&' Seconds: '&ToText(Seconds,2);
```

Exercise 26.6: Creating the Average Time report

1. Create the report specification document using the preceding requirements and analysis. Use the template that you created in Chapter 25 or the InfoPath template supplied on the accompanying CD.

2. Develop the report. Figure 26-7 shows the report.

3. Test the report to verify that your result is correct.

Alternative Solutions

The TimeSerial function could be used to format the time portion of the result into a string like hh:mm:ss, eliminating the need for separate Hour, Minutes, and Seconds variables and the statements that compute them.

```
//TimeSerial (0, 0, AverageTimeInSeconds-(Days*SecondsInADay))
```

Figure 26-7
Average Time
report

Average Time Between Ordering and Shipping

February 2000	Days: 4 Hours: 13 Minutes: 13 Seconds: 28.16
December 2000	Days: 2 Hours: 21 Minutes: 33 Seconds: 48.66
January 2001	Days: 3 Hours: 15 Minutes: 5 Seconds: 52.53
February 2001	Days: 2 Hours: 15 Minutes: 24 Seconds: 40.76
March 2001	Days: 2 Hours: 20 Minutes: 34 Seconds: 17.14
April 2001	Days: 2 Hours: 12 Minutes: 49 Seconds: 39.31
May 2001	Days: 2 Hours: 15 Minutes: 32 Seconds: 22.45
June 2001	Days: 2 Hours: 19 Minutes: 58 Seconds: 4.80
July 2001	Days: 2 Hours: 16 Minutes: 58 Seconds: 32.20
August 2001	Days: 2 Hours: 14 Minutes: 21 Seconds: 49.09
September 2001	Days: 2 Hours: 22 Minutes: 34 Seconds: 34.58
October 2001	Days: 3 Hours: 4 Minutes: 48 Seconds: 0.00
November 2001	Days: 2 Hours: 20 Minutes: 53 Seconds: 31.51
December 2001	Days: 2 Hours: 14 Minutes: 47 Seconds: 8.57
January 2002	Days: 2 Hours: 17 Minutes: 34 Seconds: 17.14
February 2002	Days: 2 Hours: 14 Minutes: 0 Seconds: 0.00
March 2002	Days: 2 Hours: 19 Minutes: 44 Seconds: 17.94
April 2002	Days: 3 Hours: 6 Minutes: 40 Seconds: 0.00
May 2002	Days: 2 Hours: 20 Minutes: 18 Seconds: 27.69

PART IV

Using Weeks That Do Not Start with Sunday

Some businesses do not use a normal week that starts with Sunday and ends with Saturday. Crystal Reports' date functions default to the normal week, although many of them have an optional parameter for specifying the first day of the week.

Requirements

Your client requires a report that displays the number of orders and the total order amount by order week with the week starting on Thursday. The group title for the order week should display the last day of the week in each group.

Analysis

After analyzing the report requirements, you determine the following::

- The Orders table is required.
- You must compute the week, since the group options for dates do not allow you to input an alternative starting day. The week of the year when the week starts on Thursday can be computed using the following formula. (Note that a week may cross the year-end boundary and be week 52 or 53 of one year as well as week 1 of the next year. You have verified that the client wants to split the week, showing part of it in both years.) Call this formula **Week**.

```
DatePart ('ww', {Orders.Order Date}, crThursday)
```

- You must group by the order date with the Yearly option and the computed week formula.

- You must create summaries showing the count of orders and the sum of the order amounts for the two groups.

- You must use a formula to create the group names for the week groups to display the last day of the week. (Since the weeks start on Thursday, the weeks should all end on Wednesdays except the last week of the year, which will end on December 31st.)

```
//Determine the date of the first day of the order year.
Local DateVar Jan1 := Date(Year({Orders.Order Date}),1,1);
//Determine the day of the week of the first day of the order year.
Local numberVar Jan1DayOfWeek := DayOfWeek (Jan1);
//If the first week of year is also the last week of the previous year,
// (the year did not end on a Wednesday)
// an adjustment must be made when computing the end date of the week.
Local numberVar WeekAdj;
If Jan1DayOfWeek <> 4 then WeekAdj:=1 Else WeekAdj:=0;
//Temporary ending date contingent on the last day of the year.
Local DateTimeVar EndingDate;
//Use DateAdd to add the computed number of weeks to the
// last Thursday of the previous year. Thursday is the fourth
// day of the week.
//Use DateSerial to determine the last Thursday of the previous
// year by starting with January 1 of the order year and then
// subtracting the number of days between the day of the week of
// January 1st and Thursday.
EndingDate:= DateAdd ('ww', {@Week}-WeekAdj,
   DateSerial(Year({Orders.Order Date}),1,1-(Jan1DayOfWeek-4)));
//If the ending date is in the next year, set it back to 12/31.
If EndingDate > Date(Year({Orders.Order Date}),12,31) then
   EndingDate := Date(Year({Orders.Order Date}),12,31);
//Format the date for display.
ToText(EndingDate,'dddd MM/dd/yyyy');
```

Exercise 26.7: Creating the Order by Week Report

1. Create the report specification document using the preceding requirements and analysis. Use the template that you created in Chapter 25 or the InfoPath template supplied on the accompanying CD.

2. Develop the report. Figure 26-8 shows the report.

3. Test the report to verify that your result is correct.

Alternative Solutions

As with any date computation, there are numerous other ways to obtain the desired result. You may also be able to take advantage of date processing functions available via SQL for your database type.

Creating a Dashboard Report

A dashboard report commonly shows a small amount of very current information in an easy-to-understand graphical format. In many instances, this type of report will consist of subreports containing charts.

Figure 26-8
Orders by Week
report

Orders by Week

Week Ending	Orders	Order Amount
Wednesday 02/16/2000	19	$49,715.21
Wednesday 02/23/2000	30	$42,415.15
Wednesday 11/29/2000	21	$40,974.52
Wednesday 12/06/2000	56	$69,188.26
Wednesday 12/13/2000	19	$17,898.47
Wednesday 12/20/2000	24	$29,058.00
Wednesday 12/27/2000	12	$10,141.03
2000	**181**	**$259,390.64**
Wednesday 01/03/2001	11	$15,038.60
Wednesday 01/10/2001	28	$46,091.63
Wednesday 01/17/2001	37	$57,560.78
Wednesday 01/24/2001	31	$52,419.06

Requirements

Your client has requested a report that shows yesterday's total order amount in a gauge and yesterday's top three products by order amount in a bar graph. The gauge should show bands for these ranges: 0 to 10000, 10000 to 15000, and 15000 to 20000.

Analysis

After analyzing the report requirements, you determine the following must be done to create this report:

- There will be a main report containing two subreports.

- The gauge subreport needs only the Orders table. A gauge chart should be placed in the report header and all other sections can be suppressed. Quality bands should be created for the ranges mentioned in the requirements. In addition, each band should be assigned a different color using the Chart Options menu.

- The top products subreport will require the Orders, Orders Detail, and Products tables. A formula must be created to compute the order amount for each product.

```
{Orders_Detail.Unit Price}*{Orders_Detail.Quantity}
```

- A group on the Product Name is required so that the Group Sort Expert can be used to filter to the top three products, based on the sum of the preceding formula.

- A bar chart based on the report data should be created and placed in the report header section. All other sections can be suppressed.

- Both subreports should use the following record selection formula to return only yesterday's orders. (Hint: Set the print date in the main report to 4/10/2002 since the last data available is for 4/9/2002. The print date setting will pass through to the subreports.)

```
{Orders.Order Date} in [CurrentDate-1 to DateAdd ('s', -1, CurrentDate)]
```

PART IV

Figure 26-9
Yesterday's Order
report

- The subreports should be placed side by side in the report header section of the main report. They are unlinked. Any format changes needed to fit the reports should be made. Any text that is too small to read should be changed.

Exercise 26.8: Creating the Yesterday's Orders Report

1. Create the report specification document using the preceding requirements and analysis. Use the template that you created in Chapter 25 or the InfoPath template supplied on the accompanying CD.

2. Develop the report. Figure 26-9 shows the report.

3. Test the report to verify that your result is correct. You can change the print date to see different results. Verify that each subreport's SQL query is passing the date filter to the server.

Alternative Solutions

Other methods could be used to obtain yesterday's date, and you could compute yesterday's date in the main report and link to the subreports that use it, rather than putting a record selection formula in each subreport.

Accounting for NULLs

NULL values can cause many problems in reports. Many of these problems are not immediately noticeable because no error messages are generated.

Requirements

Your client has requested a report that shows the order amount and discounted order amount by customer for customers from Canada in 2002. The discount that an order receives is based on its purchase order number according to the table shown here. In addition to displaying the customer totals for the order amount and discounted order amount, a customer's total discount percentage should be calculated.

Starting PO#	Ending PO#	Discount Factor
0	1000	0.00
1001	2000	0.01
2001	3000	0.02
3001	4000	0.04
4001	5000	0.05
5001	6000	0.07
6001	7000	0.09
7001	8000	0.15
8001	9000	0.20
9001	9999	0.25

Analysis

Your analysis of the requirements results in the following points:

- The report requires the Customers and Orders tables.
- The record selection formula should be as shown here:.

  ```
  {Customer.Country} = "Canada" and Year({Orders.Order Date}) = 2002
  ```

- The report should be grouped by Customer Name.
- The report should display the order ID, order date, and order amount.
- A formula to compute the discount factor is required:

  ```
  select ToNumber({Orders.PO#})
     case      UpTo 1000: 0.00
     case 1000 _To 2000: 0.01
     case 2000 _To 3000: 0.02
     case 3000 _To 4000: 0.04
     case 4000 _To 5000: 0.05
     case 5000 _To 6000: 0.07
     case 6000 _To 7000: 0.09
     case 7000 _To 8000: 0.15
     case 8000 _To 9000: 0.20
     case  UpFrom_ 9000: 0.25;
  ```

- A formula to compute the discounted order amount is also required:

  ```
  {Orders.Order Amount}*(1-{@DiscountFactor})
  ```

- Summaries of the order amount and discounted order amount by customer should be added.
- A summary formula to compute the customer's total discount percentage is required:

  ```
  100*(1-Sum ({@Discounted Order Amount},{Customer.Customer Name})
          /Sum ({Orders.Order Amount}, {Customer.Customer Name}))
  ```

- The customer's total discount percentage should be placed in the group footer to the right of the other summaries.
- The report should be sorted by the order date.

Exercise 26.9: Creating the Overall Discount Report

1. Create the report specification document using the preceding requirements and analysis. Use the template that you created in Chapter 25 or the InfoPath template supplied on the accompanying CD.

2. Develop the report. Figure 26-10 shows the report for the first three customers.

3. Test the report. Does the report seem correct? Are the total discounts reasonable given the discount table? It should be obvious that there is a problem. This report is returning incorrect data.

Second Analysis

Upon investigation, you notice that the purchase order number is often missing. NULL purchase orders are returning NULL discount factors, and NULL discount factors are

Figure 26-10
Overall Discount
report

Overall Discount for Canadian Customers
for 2002

ID	Order Date	Order Amount	Discounted Order Amount	Total Discount
Bikes for Tykes				
2,646	28-Jan-2002	$1,121.40		
		$1,121.40		
Biking's It Industries				
2,672	01-Feb-2002	$16.50	$15.02	
2,695	06-Feb-2002	$5,879.70	$5,820.90	
2,724	15-Feb-2002	$113.70	$108.02	
2,742	20-Feb-2002	$2,699.55	$2,294.62	
		$8,709.45	**$8,238.55**	5 %
Crazy Wheels				
2,580	10-Jan-2002	$101.70		
2,625	22-Jan-2002	$75.80		
2,677	01-Feb-2002	$1,565.25	$1,502.64	
2,688	04-Feb-2002	$3,479.70		
2,722	14-Feb-2002	$5,893.20		
2,731	18-Feb-2002	$3,959.55		
2,886	03-Apr-2002	$43.50	$40.46	
2,925	15-Apr-2002	$161.70	$137.45	
		$15,280.40	**$1,680.54**	89 %

causing NULL discounted amounts to be computed. To correct the problem, the discount factor computation should be changed as shown here. Note that the addition of a default case to the select statement will not correct the problem.

```
If IsNull({Orders.PO#}) then 0.00 Else
select ToNumber({Orders.PO#})
  case      UpTo 1000: 0.00
  case 1000 _To 2000: 0.01
  case 2000 _To 3000: 0.02
  case 3000 _To 4000: 0.04
  case 4000 _To 5000: 0.05
  case 5000 _To 6000: 0.07
  case 6000 _To 7000: 0.09
  case 7000 _To 8000: 0.15
  case 8000 _To 9000: 0.20
  case  UpFrom_ 9000: 0.25;
```

Exercise 26.10: Correcting the Overall Discount Report

Correct the report as indicated by the second analysis. The report should now match Figure 26-11.

Creating Cross-Tabs Manually

Crystal Report's cross-tab feature is very powerful; however, situations arise that require creation of a cross-tab style report manually because it is too complex to use the Cross-Tab Expert.

Requirements

For each product type, show the amount ordered for the three months of the selected quarter, the amount ordered for the same three months in the previous year, and the growth for each month over the same month in the previous year.

Analysis

A cross-tab object cannot be used to create this report. You cannot obtain the difference in two columns of a cross-tab. You determine that you must mimic the style of a cross-tab using formulas.

Overall Discount for Canadian Customers
for 2002

ID	Order Date	Order Amount	Discounted Order Amount	Total Discount
Bikes for Tykes				
2,646	28-Jan-2002	$1,121.40	$1,121.40	
		$1,121.40	$1,121.40	0.00 %
Biking's It Industries				
2,672	01-Feb-2002	$16.50	$15.02	
2,695	06-Feb-2002	$5,879.70	$5,820.90	
2,724	15-Feb-2002	$113.70	$108.02	
2,742	20-Feb-2002	$2,699.55	$2,294.62	
		$8,709.45	$8,238.55	5.41 %
Crazy Wheels				
2,580	10-Jan-2002	$101.70	$101.70	
2,625	22-Jan-2002	$75.80	$75.80	
2,677	01-Feb-2002	$1,565.25	$1,502.64	
2,688	04-Feb-2002	$3,479.70	$3,479.70	
2,722	14-Feb-2002	$5,893.20	$5,893.20	
2,731	18-Feb-2002	$3,959.55	$3,959.55	
2,886	03-Apr-2002	$43.50	$40.46	
2,925	15-Apr-2002	$161.70	$137.45	
		$15,280.40	$15,190.49	0.59 %
Cycles and Sports				
2,620	21-Jan-2002	$469.95	$469.95	
2,786	03-Mar-2002	$8,907.71	$8,907.71	
2,803	08-Mar-2002	$563.70	$563.70	
2,894	06-Apr-2002	$32.73	$32.73	
2,940	18-Apr-2002	$161.70	$150.38	
		$10,135.79	$10,124.47	0.11 %
Pedal Pusher Bikes Inc.				
2,619	20-Jan-2002	$83.30	$79.97	
2,661	30-Jan-2002	$8,819.55	$8,819.55	
2,718	13-Feb-2002	$8,837.46	$8,837.46	
2,765	28-Feb-2002	$86.11	$86.11	
2,826	18-Mar-2002	$5,312.04	$5,312.04	
2,986	29-Apr-2002	$40.50	$38.88	
		$23,178.96	$23,174.01	0.02 %

Figure 26-11   Corrected Overall Discount report

The general method involves creating one formula for each column of report. Each formula is a conditional formula that results in the value that needs to be summarized if the record's value belongs in that column; otherwise, it is zero. For example, if you wanted to show the order quantity by customer across 2000, 2001, and 2002, you would create three formulas. The formula for 2000 would equal the order quantity when the order date is in 2000 and zero otherwise. The formulas for 2001 and 2002 would do the same for those years. Each of these formulas could then be placed in the detail section and summed at the customer group level to give the desired result.

For this report, you have decided to use the method described in the following points:

- The Orders, Orders Detail, Product, and Product Type tables are required.

- The extended price should be calculated using the following formula:

```
{Orders_Detail.Unit Price}*{Orders_Detail.Quantity}
```

- The user must select a quarter, so you must create a Quarter parameter. To make the selection easy on the user, you will populate the defaults for the parameter as **1 Q 2000, 2 Q 2000, 3 Q 2000, 4 Q 2000**, and so on through **2 Q 2002**.

- To filter the data to the proper dates, you must determine the current year, previous year, and the starting and ending month of the selected quarter. You will create several formulas for this purpose, as shown in the following table. (Month2 is not required for record filtering, but will be used in other ways.)

Formula Name	Formula
CurrentYear	ToNumber(Right({?Quarter},4))
PreviousYear	ToNumber(Right({?Quarter},4))-1

Month1	Local numberVar Quarter:= ToNumber(Left({?Quarter},1));
	Select Quarter
	  case 1: 1
	  case 2: 4
	  case 3: 7
	  case 4: 10;

Month2	Local numberVar Quarter:= ToNumber(Left({?Quarter},1));
	Select Quarter
	  case 1: 2
	  case 2: 5
	  case 3: 8
	  case 4: 11;

Month3	Local numberVar Quarter:= ToNumber(Left({?Quarter},1));
	Select Quarter
	  case 1: 3
	  case 2: 6
	  case 3: 9
	  case 4: 12;

- The record selection formula should be as shown here:

```
({Orders.Order Date}>=DateTime({@PreviousYear},{@Month1},1,0,0,0) and
 {Orders.Order Date}< DateTime({@PreviousYear},{@Month3}+1,1,0,0,0))
Or
({Orders.Order Date}>=DateTime({@CurrentYear},{@Month1},1,0,0,0) and
 {Orders.Order Date}< DateTime({@CurrentYear},{@Month3}+1,1,0,0,0))
```

- Each month's amount for the months from this year's quarter and last year's quarter will be computed using the formulas in the following table.

Formula Name	Formula

CurrentMonth1Amount	If (Year({Orders.Order Date})={@CurrentYear} and
	  Month({Orders.Order Date})={@Month1}) then
	  {@Extended Price} Else 0

CurrentMonth2Amount	If (Year({Orders.Order Date})={@CurrentYear} and
	  Month({Orders.Order Date})={@Month2}) then
	  {@Extended Price} Else 0

CurrentMonth3Amount	If (Year({Orders.Order Date})={@CurrentYear} and
	  Month({Orders.Order Date})={@Month3}) then
	  {@Extended Price} Else 0

Formula Name	Formula
PreviousMonth1Amount	If (Year({Orders.Order Date})={@PreviousYear} and Month({Orders.Order Date})={@Month1}) then {@Extended Price} Else 0
PreviousMonth2Amount	If (Year({Orders.Order Date})={@PreviousYear} and Month({Orders.Order Date})={@Month2}) then {@Extended Price} Else 0
PreviousMonth3Amount	If (Year({Orders.Order Date})={@PreviousYear} and Month({Orders.Order Date})={@Month3}) then {@Extended Price} Else 0

- The growth for each month will be computed using the following formulas.

Formula Name	Formula
Month1Growth	{@CurrentMonth1Amount}-{@PreviousMonth1Amount}
Month2Growth	{@CurrentMonth2Amount}-{@PreviousMonth2Amount}
Month3Growth	{@CurrentMonth3Amount}-{@PreviousMonth3Amount}

- To show the correct month names in the headings, you will use the following formulas.

Formula Name	Formula
Month1Header	MonthName ({@Month1})
Month2Header	MonthName ({@Month2})
Month3Header	MonthName ({@Month3})

- Place CurrentMonth1Amount, CurrentMonth2Amount, CurrentMonth3Amount, PreviousMonth1Amount, PreviousMonth2Amount, PreviousMonth3Amount, Month1Growth, Month2Growth, and Month3Growth in the Details section.

- Create a group on Product Type Name, and sum each of the fields in the Details section at that level.

- Suppress the Details section.

- Place the month name headers above the month column that they belong to in the current year, previous year, and growth columns. Center the CurrentYear formula over the three month columns for the current year, center the PreviousYear formula over the three month columns for the previous year, and center a text object containing the word **Growth** over the three growth columns.

- Place lines on the report to mimic a cross-tab's grid.

- Title the report **Growth by Product Type**.

- Give the report a subtitle consisting of **For** plus a space and the selected parameter value.

- Format the values such that all columns are visible easily. Guidelines will be used to fine-tune the column placement.

Growth by Product Type
For 2 Q 2002

	2002			2001			Growth		
	April	May	June	April	May	June	April	May	June
Competition	123,015	24,158	0	139,193	152,594	333,991	(16,177)	(128,437)	(333,991)
Gloves	1,405	171	0	1,184	909	1,695	221	(738)	(1,695)
Helmets	3,915	594	0	5,680	4,292	6,057	(1,765)	(3,698)	(6,057)
Hybrid	27,158	1,620	0	5,779	23,961	24,119	21,379	(22,342)	(24,119)
Kids	1,379	0	0	2,716	2,492	8,050	(1,337)	(2,492)	(8,050)
Locks	608	147	0	229	825	1,197	379	(678)	(1,197)
Mountain	25,998	1,290	0	46,937	32,202	69,569	(20,939)	(30,912)	(69,569)
Saddles	359	102	0	469	375	1,520	(110)	(273)	(1,520)

Figure 26-12   Growth by Product Type report

Exercise 26.11: Creating the Growth Report

1. Create the report specification document using the preceding requirements and analysis. Use the template that you created in Chapter 25 or the InfoPath template supplied on the accompanying CD.

2. Develop the report. Figure 26-12 shows the report when 2 Q 2002 is chosen for the parameter.

3. Test the report. Try other parameter values.

Chapter Review

This chapter has presented some typical report development problems. You practiced solving those problems while using the report development methodology described in Chapter 25.

Business Views

Exam RDCR400 expects you to be able to
- Define metadata and Business Views
- Define the Business Views components
- Define the Business Views security model

This chapter describes Business Views, the components that make up a Business View, and how Business Views fit into the Crystal Reports and Crystal Enterprise architecture.

Metadata is broadly defined as data about the data. The structure of your database, including its definitions for tables, views, stored procedures, columns, and constraints, is metadata. Metadata in its original form is often considered too complex, confusing, or non-user-friendly to be used by end users or even report writers. Business Views can provide an easier-to-understand and more user-friendly way to access the underlying data. For example, columns can be given more user-friendly names, joins can be predefined, and summaries can be created. Business Views can also add a layer of security on columns as well as rows of data. Since Business Views can be based on many different data sources, a Business View administrator can manage all the reporting-related data sources from the same application.

Using Business Views inserts a layer between the data sources and the Business Objects applications that use the data sources, as shown in Figure 27-1. The client layer can be any Business Objects application that can access Business Views. The Business View layer repackages or translates the metadata of the data sources and can add detailed security constraints to the data. The Data layer is made up of the underlying data sources.

Business View Components

As you can see in Figure 27-1, a Business View is built from lower-level components. The use of these building block components allows the recombination of the components in order to build other Business Views. Components that may be used in a Business View include Data Connections, Dynamic Data Connections, Data Foundations, and Business Elements. Business Views are created using the Business View Manager, which is an application contained in Crystal Enterprise. Business Views can be used as data sources by Crystal Reports and Crystal Analysis. Business View components are stored in the Crystal Repository within the Crystal Enterprise framework.

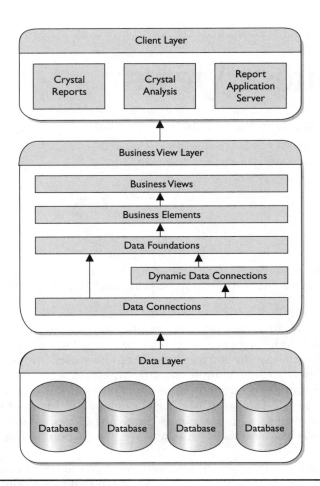

Figure 27-1   Business View architecture

Data Connections

Data Connections are similar to regular Crystal Reports data sources. Data Connections contain all the settings necessary to connect to a particular database. In addition, a Crystal Enterprise administrator can restrict access to the Data Connection.

Logon credentials can be stored with the Data Connection so that users are not prompted for logon information. In this case, every report user is logged on to the data source using the stored credentials (as the same user), and any desired security must be implemented in Crystal Enterprise. If logon credentials are not stored, users will be prompted to log on when running reports based on the Data Connection. Prompting is controlled by the Runtime Prompt Mode setting.

Dynamic Data Connections

Dynamic Data Connection objects contain a list of Data Connection objects. When a report is run, the user is prompted to choose which Data Connection to use. In this way, a report can be run against the test database or the production database without requiring the developer to change the data source location in the report itself. All the Data Connections used in a Dynamic Data Connection must have the same structure (so that switching between them does not affect the report), and they must not prompt the user for logon information. When using a Dynamic Data Connection, make sure that the Data Connection objects it contains have user-friendly names.

 TIP If you need to use data sources that have similar but not identical structures, you can create a view in one database to convert any necessary names or data types so that they match the names and data types in the other database.

Data Foundations

A Data Foundation is logically similar to a regular data source in Crystal Reports. It acts as the source of data for the Business View. However, though it appears as a single source, it may be constructed from more than one Data Connection and/or Dynamic Data Connection. Any table-like objects from the underlying Data Connections, including tables, views, stored procedures, or SQL Commands, can be added to the Data Foundation. If multiple tables are used, the joins are defined in the Data Foundation.

Within the Data Foundation object, you can create other objects, as described here.

Formula Fields   You can create formula fields in the Data Foundation. This is very useful when many report developers need to create the same computations. The computation need not be redefined in every report that uses it, and developers see the formula as just another available field. If the business rules change for a formula it can be modified in the Data Foundation, and the changes will apply to any report that uses it. You have access to repository custom functions for use in your formulas.

SQL Expression Fields   As with formula fields, you can create SQL Expression fields in the Data Foundation for databases that are accessed using SQL. SQL Expression fields will be evaluated on the server.

Parameters   Parameters created in the Data Foundation will be prompted for in any reports that are based on the Data Foundation. If certain parameter values are always required, creating the parameters in the Data Foundation will mean less work for each report.

Filters   Security can be applied to Data Foundation objects. Any security that you apply to a Data Foundation will apply to the Business Elements and therefore the Business Views that are constructed from the Data Foundation. You can limit the records that users can access by creating *filters*. Filters are similar to record selection formulas, but you can have multiple filters and apply them to different Crystal Enterprise users or groups. Filters can reference other filters.

Business Elements

Business Elements are logically similar to fields in a regular data source, but they appear as tables in Crystal Reports. In addition, a Business Element can consist of multiple related fields, such as First Name and Last Name, or fields that are related hierarchically like an OLAP dimension, such as Country, Region (State), and City. The fields in a Business Element are called Business Fields whether the source object is a database field, formula, or SQL Expression. The creator of the Business Element can supply names for the fields that differ from the names in the source database. Security can be applied at the Business Element level, including column-level security. If a user does not have access to a column, NULL values will be returned for it.

Business Views

A Business View is logically similar to a database view, but is not stored in the database. Business Views are made up of Business Elements. All Business Elements used in a Business View must come from the same Data Foundation. Only one Business View can be used as the data source for a report. When a Business View is used as the data source, the Business Elements that it contains appear as tables, and the fields in the Business Elements appear as fields. Security can be applied to a Business View. Figure 27-2 illustrates possible relationships between Business View components. Table 27-1 describes the constraints that apply to Business View construction.

 EXAM TIP A Data Foundation can be made up of multiple Data Connections or Dynamic Data Connections and can spawn multiple Business Elements, which in turn can spawn multiple Business Views. But a specific Business View can only contain Business Elements that came from the same Data Foundation. In effect, a Business View can be based on only one Data Foundation.

Data Source	Data Connection	Dynamic Data Connection	Data Foundation	Business Element	Business View
One data source can be used by multiple Data Connection objects.	Can be based on only one actual data source.	Can be based on multiple Data Connections.	Can be based on any number of Data Connections or Dynamic Data Connections.	Can be based on only one Data Foundation.	Can be based on multiple Business Elements if all are based on same Data Foundation.
If a report uses a Business View as a data source, it cannot use any other data sources.	Can be used by more than one Data Foundation.	Can be used by more than one Data Foundation.	Can be the source of many Business Elements.	Can be part of many Business Views.	Can be used in multiple reports.

Table 27-1 Business View Construction Rules

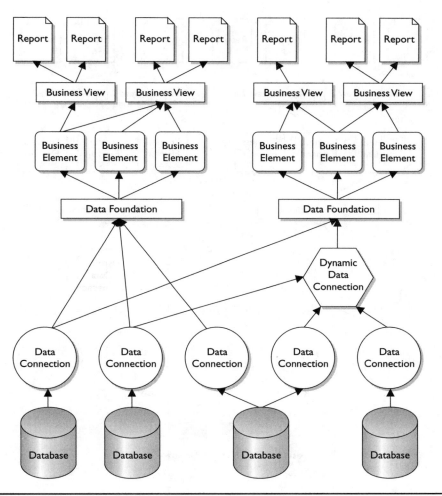

Figure 27-2 Connections among Business View components

Exercise 27.1: Identifying Structural Problems in Business Views

Looking at Figure 27-3, identify the errors in the structure. The errors include the following:

- Data Connection 2 is being derived from both Database 1 and Database 2. A Data Connection can be built from only one actual data source.

- Business View 2 is being derived from both Data Foundation 1 (via Business Elements 1 and 2) and Data Foundation 2 (via Business Element 3). A Business View can be based on only one Data Foundation.

- Report 5 is being created using Business Views 3 and 4. A report can be based on only one Business View.

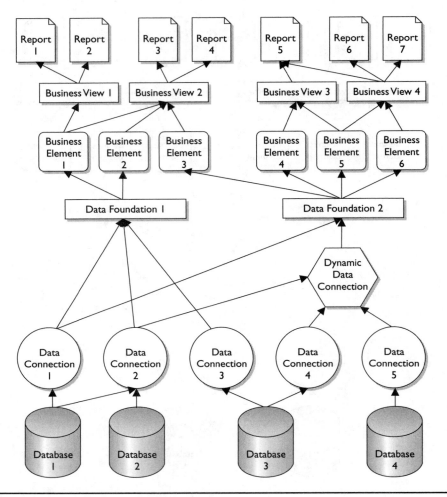

Figure 27-3 Finding errors in a Business View structure

Business View Security Model

Security on Business View components follows the general Crystal Enterprise security model. Security is applied to the Business View components stored in the Crystal repository. It affects how those objects can be manipulated in the Business View Manager; how Business Views, Business Elements, and Business Fields can be used by report designers; and what records and fields can be viewed by end users.

 EXAM TIP Understanding Business View security is important to passing the exam.

Privileges

Security is controlled by privileges. Three categories of privileges are used by Business Views: object privileges, data access privileges, and report data viewing privileges. To implement a security scheme, you must grant privileges on objects to Crystal Enterprise users or groups. However, privileges can also be inherited, and in some cases this will affect users' working privileges. It is important to understand how the different privilege values interact.

An object's privileges will be set to one of the three following values:

- **Granted** means that the right is explicitly given to the user or group selected. Note that a privilege can be explicitly granted and yet still be denied in practice due to an inherited denial.

- **Denied** means that the right is explicitly taken away from the user or group selected. If a privilege is explicitly denied, it will be denied in practice regardless of inheritance.

- **Inherited** means that privileges to the current object for the user or group selected have been neither explicitly granted nor denied and so will be inherited from the security for the object's folder or the user's group settings. An inherited denial overrides an explicit grant. If the privilege is not set to Granted or Denied at any parent level, or if the privilege does not exist at the parent level, Inherited will be treated the same as Denied.

Inheritance of Privileges

Privileges that apply to an object can be inherited from the folder structure where the object is saved. Privileges that apply to a group can be inherited by the users who belong to the group.

Inheritance from Folders   If a user or group is granted privileges to a folder, then they receive the same privileges to any object or subfolders that are contained within the folder (or added to the folder later) unless the user or group is explicitly granted different rights to the child objects. The only exception is that an inherited denial overrides an explicit grant.

The View privilege on the root folder of the Crystal Enterprise system is set to Granted for the Everyone group by default. If you do not want every Crystal Enterprise user to have the View right to every object, then you can set this privilege to Inherited. Inherited will result in Denied, since the root folder has no parent. You should not set the privilege to Denied for the Everyone group because a denial cannot be overridden by a lower-level grant.

Inheritance from Groups   Users can inherit privileges from groups to which they belong. If a group is granted a privilege to an object, then every user who belongs to that group will have the same privilege unless a specific user is denied the privilege directly, via another group to which he or she belongs or via folder inheritance. If a user is granted a privilege directly via a group membership, but is specifically denied the privilege either directly or via a group, the privilege will be denied.

Object Privileges

Three privileges apply to all Business View components: View, Edit, or Set Security. These same privileges can be granted to Crystal Enterprise folders.

 NOTE Regardless of an object's privilege setting, the actual security status that is assigned depends on properties set (or inherited) for the folder where the object resides or from settings for a group to which the user belongs.

View The View privilege controls whether the object is visible to the logged-in user in the Business View Manager. For Business Views, it also controls whether the object is visible to the user in Crystal Reports. In addition, users who have View rights to a Business View will be able to view the components that make up the Business View (Business Elements, Data Connections, and so on) no matter what their explicit privileges to the component objects are.

 CAUTION The View right does not control access to data, so, for example, a user may be able to access data that is provided by a Data Connection object that they cannot see.

Edit The Edit privilege controls whether the logged-in user can modify the object (exclusive of its security settings) in the Business View Manager.

Set Security The Set Security privilege controls whether the logged-in user can modify the security settings of the object in the Business View Manager.

 NOTE When a new object is created, the View, Edit, and Set Security rights are set to Inherited by default.

Data Access Privileges

The Data Access object privilege applies to Data Connections and Dynamic Data Connections only. It controls whether a user can access the data source defined in the object. The Data Access right does not exist at the folder level, so it cannot really be inherited. In this case, if the privilege is set to Inherited, it will always mean Denied.

 NOTE When a new Data Connection or Dynamic Data Connection object is created, the Data Access right is granted to the Everyone group by default.

Report Data Viewing Privileges

You can limit the data in a report that will be seen by a user by setting record filters or restricting the View Field Data privilege on specific fields.

Apply Filter   Filters can be created for Data Foundations and Business Elements. Filters act like selection formulas and restrict the rows that the user can see. Multiple filters can be created and applied to different users or groups. Every Data Foundation is created with a Full Data Access filter and a No Data Access filter, but these are not applied to any user or group.

The Apply Filter option can be set to Applied or Not Applied. If a filter is applied for a user or group, then the filter will be active. If the filter is not applied, the row restrictions that it defines will not be used for that user or group. A new filter defaults to Not Applied.

You cannot set the Apply Filter option unless you have the Set Security privilege for the Data Foundation or Business Element that contains the filter. Filters set at the Data Foundation level flow through to the Business Elements that are created from the Data Foundation. If filters are created in a Business Element as well as the Data Foundation, the effect is cumulative. Filter creation is covered in depth in Chapter 28.

 NOTE   A report based on a Business View that applies filters cannot do grouping on the server because the detail records are required for the filter evaluation, and this is done in Crystal Enterprise and not on the back-end database.

View Field Data   The View Field Data privilege can be set for Data Foundation fields, Data Foundation formulas, Data Foundation SQL Expressions, and Business Element fields. You cannot set the View Field Data privilege unless you have the Set Security privilege for the Data Foundation or Business Element that contains the field. The privilege can be set to Granted, Inherited, or Denied. The View Field Data right is granted to the Everyone group by default. A report designer can design a report that uses a particular field even if he does not have the right to view the data in the field.

Common Security Settings

Security settings that are appropriate for each user's needs should be created. There are several groups of users whose security needs can be discussed in general terms.

Business View Administrators   Users who are acting as Business View administrators should be given all object rights to all Business View components. The object rights are required so that the administrator can manage all Business View objects via the Business View Manager. In addition, they should be given the Data Access right for Data Connections and Dynamic Data Connections because the creation of the other components depends on reading the database structure of the data source.

Business View Designers   Users who are responsible for creating Business Views will need the Data Access right to Data Connections and Dynamic Data Connections, the View right to all objects, and the Edit right for the object types that they create. Business View designers may or may not create Data Connections, Dynamic Data Connections, or Data Foundations, but they usually create Business Elements and Business Views. Business View designers may or may not require the Set Security privilege, depending on their responsibilities. If Business View designers need to set the Apply Filter option or the View Field Data privilege, then they need the Set Security privilege for Data Foundations and/or Business Elements.

Report Designers   Report designers need the Data Access right to Data Connections and Dynamic Data Connections and the View right to Business Views. No other privileges are specifically required in order to create reports based on Business Views. Users with View rights to a Business View will be able to see the components that make up the Business View.

Report Users   Report users need the Data Access right to Data Connections and Dynamic Data Connections and the View right to Business Views.

Other Security Issues

Security settings that are enforced by Crystal Enterprise can be circumvented in several ways. You need to understand the possible loopholes and your overall environment to ensure that all necessary security is maintained.

Access to Data That Does Not Use Crystal Enterprise   Be aware that any access to data that does not require a login to Crystal Enterprise will not use Crystal Enterprise security. If applications exist that connect directly to data sources or if ad hoc querying from other applications is allowed, Crystal Enterprise security will be bypassed. You need to consider the proper combination of database security and Crystal Enterprise security.

Exported Reports   If a user exports a report or data from a report, then that data is no longer protected by Crystal Enterprise security.

Disconnect View Security   A report designer can use the Disconnect View Security check box in the Save As dialog box to save a report based on a Business View and disconnect it from Crystal Enterprise. The saved report can then be opened without logging in to Crystal Enterprise, and any Crystal Enterprise security is disabled. However, the report cannot be refreshed or reconnected to Crystal Enterprise.

File Location   Report files can be opened by anyone who has access to the file location where they are stored. If files contain saved data, it can be viewed without restriction. In general, report files should be saved to secure locations.

Edit Rights Dialog Box

Privileges are granted using the Edit Rights dialog box in the Business View Manager. To set privileges for an object you must have the Set Security right to the object. The Edit Rights dialog box is used for all privilege setting. It is invoked by selecting an object and then selecting Edit Rights from the right-click menu, selecting Edit | Edit Rights from the menu, clicking the Edit Rights button on the toolbar, or for open objects by clicking the ellipsis next to the Rights field of the Property Browser, as shown here. If an object has been modified, it must be saved before the Edit Rights dialog box will display.

In the Edit Rights dialog box, users and groups are listed alongside the rights that can be set for them. Clicking a right repeatedly scrolls through the available options for that right. The Edit Rights dialog box for a Data Foundation object is shown here. The toolbar buttons of the dialog box are the same no matter what type of privilege is being set.

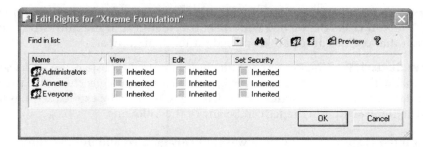

Find in List and Search Groups and Users   If your list of users and groups is long, you can use the Find in List options to find the one you want quickly. Enter a name in the Find in List box and then click the Search Groups and Users button (the binoculars) to find that name.

Delete   To remove a user or group from the list box, select it and then click the Delete button.

Add Groups   To add a group so that you can set privileges for it, click the Add Groups button. The Add Groups dialog box will open, as shown here. It has the following options:

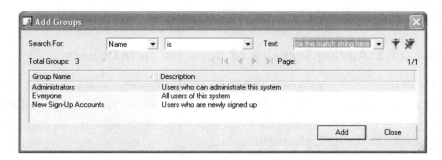

- **Add button**   Select a group and then click the Add button to add it to the Edit Rights dialog box.

- **Close button**   When you are finished adding groups, click the Close button.

- **Page navigation buttons**   Use the page navigation buttons to scroll from page to page of the list. These buttons will be active if you have many groups.

- **Search For options**   If you have a long list of groups, you can filter the list using the Search For options. In the first drop-down box, select Name or Description to select which property will be searched. In the second drop-down box, select the condition to use in the search. In the Text box, enter the text that should be searched for. Click the Search button to filter the list. Click the Clear Search button to return to the original display.

Add Users   To add a user so that you can set privileges for it, click the Add Users button. The Add Users dialog box will open. It is identical to the Add Groups dialog box except that user accounts are displayed rather than groups.

Preview Security   The Preview Security button is used to display the actual security settings that will be enforced considering inheritance. It is a toggle: click once to display the cumulative rights with inheritance; click again to display the explicit settings for the object. The rights with inheritance can be any of the following:

- **Granted (Explicit)**   The right was explicitly granted and not overridden by any inherited denial.

- **Granted (Inherited)**   The right was granted to some higher-level folder or group and was inherited by the current object, group, or user because no denial was inherited.

- **Denied (Explicit)**   The right was explicitly denied for the object for the user or group listed.

- **Denied (Inherited)**   The right was denied at some higher-level folder or group and was inherited by the current object, group, or user.

- **Denied (Never Specified)**   The right was never explicitly granted or denied to the current object or any objects from which it inherits rights.

Help   Clicking the Help button opens the Business View Manager help file.

Exercise 27.2: Adding Security to Business View Objects

1. Open the Business View Manager and log on as Administrator.

2. In the Repository Explorer, open the Samples\Business Views\Xtreme folder.

3. Right-click the Xtreme Sample Connection object, and select Edit Rights. The Edit Rights dialog box will open.

4. Set the Set Security right to Denied for your user ID, as shown here for Annette.

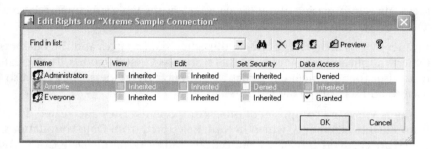

5. Click the Preview button and examine what the resulting privileges will be, as shown here.

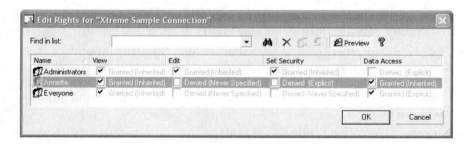

6. Click OK to close the Edit Rights dialog box.

7. Open the Xtreme Foundation object by double-clicking it.

8. In the Object Explorer, expand the Tables folder until you can select the Customer.Customer Name field.

9. In the Edit Rights dialog box, click the Preview button. The cumulative right for your user ID should be Granted (Inherited).

10. Set the View Field Data right for the Everyone group to Inherited.

11. Click the Preview button. The right for your ID is now Denied (Never Specified).

12. Click OK to close the Edit Rights dialog box.

13. Close the Business View Manager.

Chapter Review

This chapter introduced the component model for Business Views and described the dependencies between Business View components. It also covered Business View security concepts and how to set rights on Business View objects.

Quick Tips

- Metadata is information about the data such as the table structures, relationships, and security.
- Business Views are a layer between the actual data sources and the Business Objects applications that can use them, such as Crystal Reports. They create a more user-friendly metadata structure for report developers. They can also be used to add security to data.
- Business Views are composed of other components. They are created directly from Business Elements, which in turn are created from Data Foundations, which are created from Data Connections and/or Dynamic Data Connections.
- Data Connections are components that encapsulate and possibly add security to an actual data source.
- A Dynamic Data Connection is a collection of similarly structured Data Connection components. It gives the user the option of choosing the actual data source at run time from the collection.
- Data Foundations are components that are built from any number of Data Connections or Dynamic Data Connections. Joins and filters, as well as added security can be defined at the Data Foundation layer. Formula fields, SQL Expression fields, and parameters can be created for a Data Foundation component.
- Business Elements are constructed from groups of related fields, such as Last Name and First Name. They can also include hierarchies like Country, Region (State), and City.
- A Business View must be created from Business Elements that come from the same Data Foundation.
- A report can be based on only one Business View.
- Business View components are secured using the Crystal Enterprise model via the Business View Manager application.
- Business View components inherit the security set for the Crystal Enterprise folder to which they belong.
- Crystal Enterprise users and groups are assigned privileges to Business View components. Users inherit the privileges that are assigned to groups they are members of.
- All Business View components have View, Edit, and Set Security rights.
- Data Connections and Dynamic Data Connections have the additional Data Access right.
- View, Edit, Set Security, and Data Access rights can be set to Granted, Denied, or Inherited using the Edit Rights dialog box. A denial, whether explicitly set or inherited, overrides any grants, even explicit grants.

- Report records (rows) that are visible to a user (at either design time or view time) can be controlled using filters. Filters can be created in Data Foundation objects or Business Element objects. Filters can be applied to users or groups using the Edit Rights dialog box.

- Report field (column) data that is visible to a user (at either design time or when viewing) can be controlled using the View Field Data right for fields in Data Foundations or Business Elements.

- The Preview button in the Edit Rights dialog box displays the cumulative rights, including inheritance.

- A report developer needs Data Access rights to Data Connections and Dynamic Data Connections and View rights to Business View objects to create reports based on Business Views.

Questions

Questions may have more than one correct answer. Choose all answers that apply.

1. Business Views are created in the source database.

   a. True

   b. False

2. The Business View Manager is

   a. A web-based application included in Crystal Enterprise

   b. A Windows application included in Crystal Reports

   c. A Windows application included in Crystal Enterprise

   d. A web-based application included in Crystal Reports

   e. A web-based application included in eportfolio

3. A Data Connection cannot be based on

   a. An Oracle database

   b. A stored procedure

   c. A SQL Server database

   d. An Excel spreadsheet

   e. A DB2 database and an Informix database

4. A Dynamic Data Connection is

   a. A collection of similarly structured Data Connections

   b. A collection of similarly structured data sources

   c. A Data Connection that can be given a data source at run time

   d. A Data Connection that will disconnect automatically when it is not in use

   e. A Data Connection that will automatically update when the underlying data source changes

5. The Data Connections used in a Dynamic Data Connection must have logon credentials stored with the component.

   a. True

   b. False

6. A Data Foundation can be based on

   a. A single Data Connection

   b. A single Dynamic Data Connection

   c. More than one Data Connection

   d. More than one Dynamic Data Connection

   e. A Data Connection and a Dynamic Data Connection

7. Which of the following might be defined in a Data Foundation

   a. Table joins

   b. Formula fields

   c. SQL Expression fields

   d. Parameter fields

   e. Filters

8. A Data Foundation can spawn multiple Business Elements.

   a. True

   b. False

9. A Data Foundation cannot include

   a. Tables

   b. Views (database)

   c. Business Views

   d. SQL Commands

   e. Stored procedures

10. A Data Foundation can have only one filter, but the filter can be given different security settings for different users.

    a. True

    b. False

11. Match the Business View component to the Crystal Reports object that it will appear as in the Database Expert or Field Explorer.

    a. Business Field

    b. Business Element

    c. Business View

    d. Data source

    e. Table

    f. Field

12. Business Elements cannot contain

    a. Related database fields

    b. Hierarchically related database fields

    c. Formula fields

    d. SQL Expression fields

    e. SQL Commands

13. Business Elements can be created from more than one Data Foundation.

    a. True

    b. False

14. More than one Business Element can be created from the same Data Foundation.

    a. True

    b. False

15. Business Views cannot be based on Business Elements that

    a. Contain hierarchically related fields

    b. Contain more than one field

    c. Rename the underlying fields

    d. Are based on different Data Foundations

    e. Are based on the same Data Foundation

16. If a user does not have access to a Business Field used in a report, what will happen?

    a. The report will fail.

    b. A security violation alert will be triggered.

    c. NULLs will be returned for the Business Field.

    d. The user will be disconnected from Crystal Enterprise.

    e. The report will run, but no data will be returned.

17. Business View security is not dependent on folder security in Crystal Enterprise.

    a. True

    b. False

PART IV

18. For a user to successfully use a Business View based on a Data Connection, they must have which of the following rights on the Data Connection object?

    a. View

    b. Edit

    c. Set Security

    d. Data Access

    e. Connect

19. For a user to successfully use a Business View based on a Dynamic Data Connection, they must have which of the following rights?

    a. View rights to the Business View

    b. Data Access rights to the Dynamic Data Connection

    c. Data Access rights to each Data Connection in the Dynamic Data Connection

    d. View rights to the Business Elements used in the Business View

    e. View rights to the Dynamic Data Connection

20. Filters are applied only when a report is viewed by a user but not when a report is viewed by a report developer.

    a. True

    b. False

21. View Field Data restrictions are applied only when a report is viewed by a user but not when a report is viewed by a report developer.

    a. True

    b. False

22. What is the resulting privilege in the following situation: a user is granted the View right to a Data Foundation, and the Everyone group is denied the View right to the Data Foundation?

    a. The user will have the View right because it was explicitly granted.

    b. The user will not have the View right because the denial was inherited from the Everyone group.

    c. The user will have the View right because the denial cannot be inherited from the Everyone group.

    d. The user will have the View right because denials are not inherited from groups.

    e. There is not enough information to determine the resulting privileges.

23. If a right is never explicitly granted or denied to a particular object or to any objects from which the object inherits privileges, the right will be denied.

    a. True

    b. False

24. Which of the following will not invoke the Edit Rights dialog box?

    a. Edit Rights toolbar button

    b. Edit | Edit Rights menu command

    c. Edit | Rights menu command

    d. Edit Rights shortcut menu command

    e. Rights ellipsis in the Property Browser

25. Which Business View components have the Data Access privilege?

    a. Business Views

    b. Business Elements

    c. Data Foundations

    d. Dynamic Data Connections

    e. Data Connections

26. You must have the Set Security right in order to set the Apply Filter option.

    a. True

    b. False

27. You do not need the Set Security right in order to set the View Field Data privilege.

    a. True

    b. False

28. Business View administrators should usually be granted which of the following rights?

    a. Data Access rights to Dynamic Data Connections and Data Connections

    b. View rights to Dynamic Data Connections and Data Connections

    c. View rights to Business Elements

    d. Edit rights to Business Elements

    e. View rights to Data Foundations

29. Exported data is subject to the same security as the report from which it was exported.

    a. True

    b. False

30. Applying Business View security protects the data, no matter how it is accessed.

   a. True

   b. False

Answers

1. **b.** Business Views are created in the Crystal Repository using the Business View Manager.

2. **c.** The Business View Manager is a Windows application included with Crystal Enterprise.

3. **b, e.** A Data Connection represents the connection to a data source, not any specific object in the data source, so a stored procedure (b) cannot be a Data Connection. A Data Connection can be based on only one data source, so Answer e is not valid.

4. **a.** A Dynamic Data Connection is a collection of similarly structured Data Connections.

5. **a.** The Data Connections used in a Dynamic Data Connection must not prompt the user for logon information.

6. **All.** A Data Foundation can be based on any number of Data Connections and/or Dynamic Data Connections.

7. **All.** A Data Foundation can contain any of the listed items.

8. **a.** A Data Foundation can be the basis for many Business Elements.

9. **c.** A Data Foundation cannot use a Business View as a source.

10. **b.** A Data Foundation can have multiple filters.

11. (a, f), (b, e), (c, d)

12. **e.** Business Elements are composed of field-type items. They cannot contain SQL Commands.

13. **b.** A Business Element must draw all of its fields from the same Data Foundation.

14. **a.** Many Business Elements can be created from the same Data Foundation.

15. **d.** A Business View must be created from Business Elements that are all based on the same Data Foundation.

16. **c.** If the user does not have access to a field, NULLs will be returned.

17. **b.** Business View component objects inherent the privileges set for the folders in which they reside.

18. **d.** The user needs the Data Access privilege. They do not need any other right on the Data Connection to use a Business View based on the Data Connection.

19. **a, b.** The user needs View rights to the Business View and Data Access rights to the Dynamic Data Connection.

20. **b.** The filter is applied in both cases.

21. **b.** The filter is applied in both cases.

22. **b.** The inherited denial will override the explicit grant.

23. **a.** This is the Never Specified case, and the right will be denied.

24. **c.** There is no Edit | Rights menu item.

25. **d, e.** Data Connections and Dynamic Data Connections have the Data Access right.

26. **a.** You must have the Set Security right for the Data Foundation or Business Element in order to set the Apply Filter option for filters they contain.

27. **b.** You must have the Set Security right for the Data Foundation or Business Element in order to set the View Field Data privilege for fields they contain.

28. **All.** Business View administrators should have all the listed rights.

29. **b.** Exported data is not covered by any security settings.

30. **b.** Business View security only protects data that is accessed via Crystal Enterprise (including the repository).

Managing Business Views and Business Elements

Exam RDCR400 expects you to be able to
- Work with the Business View Manager
- Modify Business View objects
- Modify Business Elements
- Plan your Business View
- Create a Business View

This chapter will acquaint you with the Business View Manager application. You have used this application previously, but this chapter will describe its features in depth. In addition, Using the Business View Manager to plan, create, and modify Business Views and Business Elements will be covered.

Business View Manager

The Business View Manager is a Windows application available with Crystal Enterprise that is used to create and manage all Business View components. It can also be used to manage the Crystal Repository.

Welcome Dialog Box

If it has not been turned off, the first thing you will see after launching the Business View Manager and logging into Crystal Enterprise is the welcome dialog box, shown in Figure 28-1. If you do not want this dialog box to be displayed, clear the Show This Dialog After Crystal Enterprise Logon check box.

The welcome dialog box has three tabs:

- **New** The New tab contains a display of icons representing Business View components. Select an icon and then click the Create button to create an object of that type. In addition, it has an icon titled Business Element Wizard. You can use the Business Element Wizard to create multiple Business Elements from a Data Foundation.

- **Open** The Open tab displays the Repository Explorer, where you can browse to an object and open it. You can also filter the objects that are displayed, delete objects, and create new folders. See the "Repository Explorer" section for more details.

- **Recent** The Recent tab displays a list of recently opened objects. You can select one and click the Open button to reopen it.

Main Window

The main window of the Business View Manager displays open objects, as shown in Figure 28-2. The display changes depending on the object type. A tab for each open object is created at the top of the window along with buttons that scroll through the tabs and a button that closes the active object. For some object types there are also tabs at the bottom to display different parts of the object.

Object Explorer and Property Browser

The Object Explorer and Property Browser windows can be docked or free-floating. The Object Explorer displays a tree view of the items contained within the selected object. The Property Browser displays the attributes of the item selected in the Object Explorer. The content of these windows depends on the object type.

Exploring the Menus

The Business View Manager consists of several menus, a toolbar, and several dockable windows. Many of the menu items are familiar, but some are unique to the Business View Manager.

Figure 28-1
Exploring
the welcome
dialog box

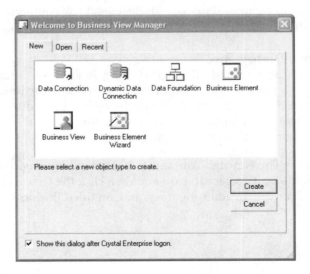

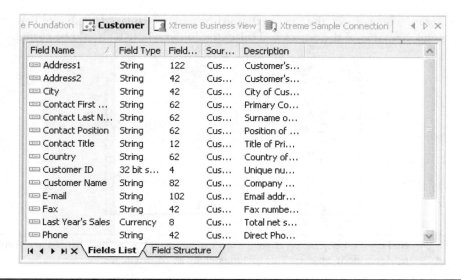

Field Name	Field Type	Field...	Sour...	Description
⊞ Address1	String	122	Cus...	Customer's...
⊞ Address2	String	42	Cus...	Customer's...
⊞ City	String	42	Cus...	City of Cus...
⊞ Contact First ...	String	62	Cus...	Primary Co...
⊞ Contact Last N...	String	62	Cus...	Surname o...
⊞ Contact Position	String	62	Cus...	Position of ...
⊞ Contact Title	String	12	Cus...	Title of Pri...
⊞ Country	String	62	Cus...	Country of...
⊞ Customer ID	32 bit s...	4	Cus...	Unique nu...
⊞ Customer Name	String	82	Cus...	Company ...
⊞ E-mail	String	102	Cus...	Email addr...
⊞ Fax	String	42	Cus...	Fax numbe...
⊞ Last Year's Sales	Currency	8	Cus...	Total net s...
⊞ Phone	String	42	Cus...	Direct Pho...

Figure 28-2   Viewing open objects in the Business View Manager

File Menu

Some File menu commands apply to the currently selected open object in the main window. The title of the Business View Manager will include the name of the current object in square brackets.

New   The New command contains a submenu listing the types of Business View components that can be created as well as a link that launches the Business Element wizard. These choices are identical to their equivalents on the New tab of the welcome dialog box, described in the preceding section.

Open   Selecting the Open command displays the welcome dialog box with the Open tab active. Select an object to open it.

Close   Selecting the Close command closes the current object.

Save   Selecting Save saves the current object. If other open objects are dependent on the current object, a dialog box similar to the one shown here will be displayed. Click Yes to save and reload the dependent objects.

If you save a new object, the Save As dialog box will be displayed, as shown here. You can change the name of the object and select the folder where it should be stored.

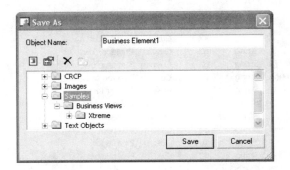

 NOTE If an object has changed, it must be saved before the changes are visible to dependent objects. This includes changes to privileges.

Save All   Selecting Save All saves all open objects.

Recently Opened Objects List   This section of the File menu displays recently opened objects. You can select one to reopen it.

Exit   Selecting Exit closes the Business View Manager. If any objects have been modified but not saved, you will be requested to save them.

Edit Menu
Items appear on the Edit menu depending on the currently selected object or the most recent action.

Undo   The Undo command reverses the most recent action that can be undone.

Redo   The Redo command redoes the last action that was undone.

Delete   The Delete command will appear if the selected object can be deleted. For example, it will appear for a Business View object if a Business Element field is selected, for a Data Foundation object if a table is selected, and for a Business Element object if a field is selected.

Reset Field Structure   The Reset Field Structure command will be available for Business Elements. If the structure of the fields in the Business Element has been modified by creating hierarchies, selecting the Reset Field Structure command will return the fields to their original structure.

Set Table Location   The Set Table Location command will be available for Data Foundation objects when the Tables folder or an item in Tables folder is selected. See Chapter 29 for information on changing a table's location.

Edit Connection   The Edit Connection command will be available for Data Connection objects. You can use it to change the underlying data source for the object. See Chapter 29 for more information.

Edit Password   The Edit Password command will be available for Data Connection objects. You can use it to change the user ID and password stored with the object. See Chapter 29 for more information.

Add Data Connection   The Add Data Connection command will be available for Dynamic Data Connection objects. Use it to add connections to the object. See Chapter 29 for more information.

Delete Data Connection   The Delete Data Connection command will be available for Dynamic Data Connection objects. Use it to remove connections from the object. See Chapter 29 for more information.

Edit Rights   The Edit Rights command will be available when any Business View component object is selected. It will also be available for filters and fields. Selecting it opens the Edit Rights dialog box, which is used to set the privileges that users or groups have to the object. See Chapter 27 for information on using the Edit Rights dialog box.

View Menu

Use options on the View menu to determine which Business View Manager elements are currently visible. Each item is a toggle: if an item is selected, a check mark will appear beside it and the corresponding element will be displayed.

Toolbar   Select this option to toggle the display of the toolbar. The toolbar contains speed buttons for various actions. The toolbar is displayed by default.

Status Bar   Select this option to toggle the display of the status bar at the bottom of the Business View Manager window. The status bar is displayed by default.

Repository Explorer   Select this option to toggle the display of the Repository Explorer window. The Repository Explorer displays all items in the repository and allows you to manage them. See the "Repository Explorer" section later in the chapter for more information. The Repository Explorer is displayed and docked to the right by default.

Object Explorer   Select this option to toggle the display of the Object Explorer window. It contains a tree view showing the structure of the currently selected object. See the "Object Explorer" section later in the chapter for more information. The Object Explorer is displayed and docked to the upper left by default.

Property Browser   Select this option to toggle the display of the Property Browser window. It displays the properties of the item selected in the Object Explorer. See the

PART IV

"Property Browser" section later in the chapter for more information. The Property Browser is displayed and docked to the lower left by default.

Referenced Data Connections/Referenced Data Foundation   Select this option to toggle the display of the Referenced Data Connections/Referenced Data Foundation window. This window is not displayed by default. If the current object is a Business Element, the Referenced Data Foundation window will display. It shows information about the Data Foundation object that the Business Element uses. If the current object is a Data Foundation, the Referenced Data Connections window will display. It shows information about the Data Connection objects that the Data Foundation uses.

Insert Menu

The options available on the Insert menu depend on the type of the selected object.

Data Foundations   For Data Foundation objects, the following commands are available. See Chapter 29 for how to use these commands.

- Insert Data Tables
- Insert Formula
- Insert SQL Expression
- Insert Filter
- Insert Parameter
- Import Custom Function

Business Views   For Business View objects, the Insert Business Elements command is available. See the "Working with Business Views" section for more information.

Business Elements   For Business Element objects, the following commands are available. See the "Working with Business Elements" section later in the chapter for more information.

- Insert Business Fields
- Insert Filter
- Insert Parameter

Linking Diagram Menu

The commands on the Linking Diagram menu pertain only to Data Foundations—or to Business Views whose underlying Data Foundation allows the links to be overridden—and are similar to commands available on the Linking tab of the Database Expert in Crystal Reports. See Chapter 29 for more information about Data Foundations and the Linking Diagram options.

Tools Menu

The Tools menu contains items that are always available and items appropriate to the active object.

Export   The Export command opens the Export dialog box, where you can extract Business Views, text objects, bitmap objects, SQL Commands, and Custom Functions from the repository. The export is saved in an XML file and can be imported into other repositories. When a Business View is exported, all its dependent objects are also exported.

Import   The Import command opens the Import dialog box, where you can import objects stored in XML files into the repository.

Install Repository Samples   Select Install Repository Samples to load sample repository objects into the repository. Exercise 1.6 (in Chapter 1) steps you through the process.

Show Dependent Objects   This option opens the Dependent Object dialog box, shown in Figure 28-3. The Dependency Graph window displays all objects that are dependent on the active object in a tree view. Dependent objects are objects that are based on the active object. Items that are directly dependent are shown as the first-level nodes. Objects that are dependent on those objects are shown as lower-level nodes. In the Display Type panel, you can choose to display only the name of objects or their complete folder path. You can save the dependency information to a text file using the Save To File button.

Show Referenced Objects   This option opens the Referenced Object dialog box. It is identical to the Dependent Object dialog box except that it displays the objects upon which the active object depends.

Verify Database   The Verify Database command is available for Data Foundation objects. It is identical to the Verify Database command available on the Database menu of Crystal Reports, which is covered in Chapter 19.

Check Dependent Integrity   If you modify a Business View component object, it could create problems for any object that is dependent on it. The Check Dependent Integrity command will check the dependent objects to verify that they are not adversely

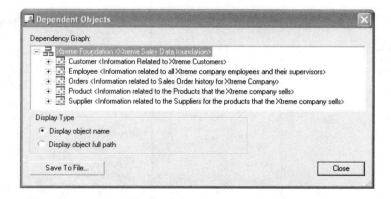

Figure 28-3   Checking dependent objects

affected. This command is available for all object types except Business View objects because no other type is dependent on a Business View. If a Data Foundation changes, it may trigger a request for remapping for dependent Business Elements.

Rights Test View The Rights Test View option will be available for Business View objects. It opens the Rights Test View dialog box, shown in Figure 28-4. This dialog box is used to check a user's (not a group's) rights to a Business View and the Business Elements and Business Fields contained in the view.

The Rights Test View dialog box has the following elements:

- **User Name** Select a user from the User Name drop-down box.
- **Select User** If the name you want to check is not listed, click the Select User button to add the desired name.
- **Business View Visible** This item will be labeled "True" if the Business View is visible to the selected user and "False" if it is not.
- **Visible Business Elements and Business Fields** This list box displays the Business Elements and Business Fields used in the Business View that are visible to the selected user. If the selected user does not have access to view the data in a given field, there will be a red × over its icon.
- **Apply** To check what filter will be applied for the user, check the boxes next to all of the items that you want included, and then click the Apply button. All selected items will be checked for the existence and applicability of a filter.
- **Final Filter Text** The cumulative resulting filter for the user will be displayed in this box.

Test Connectivity This command is available for Data Connection objects. It verifies that the connection is valid by attempting to connect using the current properties of the Data Connection object. If the connection was successful, you will receive a message indicating that. If it wasn't, you will see a list of error messages.

Figure 28-4
Checking a
user's rights to
a Business View

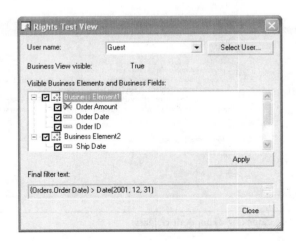

Window Menu

Commands available in the Window menu are used to close open object windows or to set the active window. These commands apply only to the open objects that appear in the main window, not to the Repository Explorer, Object Explorer, Property Browser, or Referenced Data Connections windows.

Close This command closes the active window. It is the same as the File | Close command.

Close All This command closes all open object windows.

Open Objects List A list of the open object windows is displayed after the Close All command. You can select one to make it the active window.

Windows Selecting the Windows command opens the Windows dialog box, shown here. You can select a window from the Select Window list and then make it active by clicking the Activate button. You can also select one or more windows and save or close them by clicking the Save or Close Window(s) button. The OK button closes the dialog box.

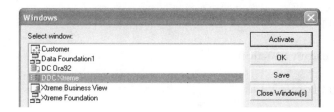

Help Menu

The Help menu contains the usual entries for opening the help file, the help file index, the welcome dialog box, the about box, and links to relevant web sites.

Exploring the Toolbar

Every toolbar button is a shortcut to a menu command. The buttons and their menu equivalents are listed here.

Help | Welcome Dialog

File | Open

File | Save

Edit | Undo
Clicking the down arrow displays a list of the recent actions that can be undone.

Edit | Redo
Clicking the down arrow displays a list of the recent actions that can be redone.

Edit | Delete

Edit | Set Table Location

Tools | Verify Database

Insert | Insert Data Tables

Insert | Insert Formula

Insert | Insert SQL Expression

Insert | Insert Filter

Insert | Insert Parameter

Insert | Import Custom Function

Linking Diagram | Locate Table

Linking Diagram | Select Visible Tables

Linking Diagram | Rearrange Tables

Linking Diagram | Change Linking View

Edit | Add Data Connection

Edit | Delete Data Connection

Insert | Insert Business Fields

Edit | Reset Field Structure

Edit | Edit Rights

Tools | Rights Test View

Tools | Check Dependent Integrity

Tools | Show Dependent Objects

Tools | Show Referenced Objects

Help | About Business View Manager

Repository Explorer

The Repository Explorer is a tree view of items stored in folders in the repository. It includes all object types that can be held in the repository, not just Business View components. It can be docked or free-floating, as shown here. Double-clicking an object in the Repository Explorer opens it in the Business View Manager main window.

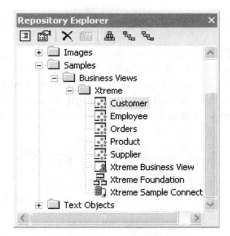

The Repository Explorer has a toolbar and shortcut menus, but no main menu. Objects and folders can be dragged to new locations within the tree.

CAUTION Moving an object or folder may change the security applied to it, or to the items it contains, due to inheritance of different settings from the new parent folder.

Toolbar

The Repository Explorer toolbar contains the following seven buttons.

 Change View Settings   Clicking this button opens the View Settings dialog box, shown here. You can configure the display of items in the Repository Explorer using this dialog box. Check the types of objects that you want displayed, and then choose the sort order for the tree.

 Advanced Filtering   The Advanced Filtering button is a toggle. When it is clicked, the Repository Explorer window layout changes to include two search text boxes and an Apply button, as shown here. To display only items with certain text in their names or created by a certain author, enter the search text in the appropriate box, and click the Apply button. The filter is removed once the Advanced Filtering button is clicked again.

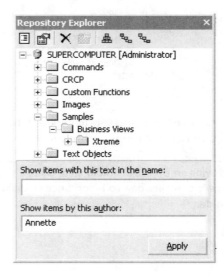

Delete the Item/Folder   The Delete button deletes the currently selected object or folder.

Insert a New Folder   This button allows you to create new folders in the repository. New folders are created under the current folder with a name of "New Folder." You can change the name immediately after creation.

Object Buttons   The three object buttons—Check Dependent Integrity, Show Dependent Objects, and Show Referenced Objects—work exactly like their counterparts on the main toolbar, except that the object that each works on is the selected object in the Repository Explorer rather than the active object in the main window.

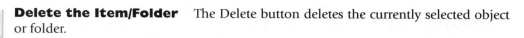

Shortcut Menu

Commands available on the Repository Explorer shortcut menu apply to both folders and objects, except for the Properties command, which applies only to objects.

Edit Rights   Selecting Edit Rights opens the Edit Rights dialog box for the selected object. If the object is already open in the main window, you must use the Edit Rights button on the main toolbar. The Edit Rights dialog box for objects is covered in Chapter 27. Folders have the same object rights as the Business View objects: View, Edit, and Set Security. Items in folders inherit the rights set for the folder.

Rename   Select Rename to rename the folder or object. You cannot rename open objects.

Delete   Use Delete to delete the selected folder or object. You cannot delete open objects. If you delete a folder or an object that has dependents, you will be warned that dependent objects will also be deleted.

New Folder   This command is the same as the New Folder button.

Refresh   The Refresh command rereads the repository content.

Expand All   Select Expand All to open all the folders beneath the selected folder.

Advanced Filtering   This command is the same as the Advanced Filtering toolbar button.

Change View Settings   This command is the same as the Change View Settings toolbar button.

Properties   Selecting the Properties command opens the Properties window for the selected object. The Properties window displays the name, type, last modification date, and description of the repository object.

Working with Business Views

An overview of Business Views and their architecture is given in Chapter 27. The process of creating Business Views and maintaining them is covered in this chapter. Business Views appear as data sources in Crystal Reports.

Creating a Business View

Use the welcome dialog box, the File | New | Business View command, or the New toolbar button to create a Business View.

Adding Business Elements

Any of the methods will cause the Insert Business Elements dialog box to be displayed, as shown here. It contains a tree list of all the Business Elements in the repository. Select a Business Element, and click the Add button to add it to the Business View. Click Close when you are finished adding elements. You are then returned to the main window with the new Business View open.

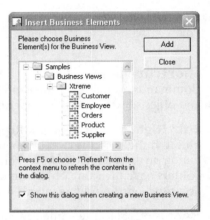

 TIP If you do not want the Insert Business Elements dialog box to display in the future, clear the Show This Dialog When Creating a New Business View check box. Some of the shortcut menu items available for the objects in the Repository Explorer (as described in the preceding section) are available for objects in this dialog box.

Saving the Business View

Save the Business View using the File | Save command or the Save toolbar button. The Save As dialog box will appear; there you can change the name of the Business View and select the folder where you want to store it. A Business View is created with a default name of "Business View" plus a number. You can either change the name of the Business View in the Save As dialog box or select the root node in the Object Explorer and then edit the Name attribute in the Property Browser before saving it.

Changing a Business View

Once a Business View is created, you can modify many of its properties, add more Business Elements, and override the linking used in the underlying Data Foundation.

Object Explorer

The Object Explorer for a Business View displays the name of the Business View as the root node and all of the Business Elements that it uses under a node called Business Elements, as shown here.

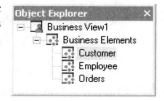

The shortcut menu for the Object Explorer differs depending on what type of item is selected.

- **Edit Rights**   This option appears for the Business View node. It opens the Edit Rights dialog box, where you can set security options for the Business View.

- **Rights Test View**   This option appears for the Business View node. It opens the Rights Test View dialog box, where you can test a user's rights to the Business View.

- **Insert Business Elements**   This option appears for the Business Elements node and reopens the Insert Business Elements dialog box so that you can add new Business Elements.

TIP   You can drag Business Elements from the Repository Explorer to the Business Elements node of the Object Explorer to add them to the Business View.

- **Show Business Element Detail**   This option appears when a Business Element is selected. It opens another tab for the Business View that displays the Business Fields contained in the Business Element.

- **Delete**   This option appears when a Business Element is selected. It removes the Business Element from the Business View.

Property Browser

The attributes displayed in the Property Browser depend on the type of item selected in the Object Explorer. The name of the attribute is shown in the left column and its value is displayed in the right column. If you cannot edit the attribute it is grayed out.

Business View Attributes   A Business View has the following attributes, some of which can be modified in the Property Browser:

- **Name**   You can change the name of the Business View. If you save the Business View with a new name, it replaces the old object in the repository.

- **Description**   Enter a description for the Business View. This description is used as a tooltip in the Repository Explorer.

Property Browser	
Name	Business View1
Description	
Author	Administrators
Parent Folder	/CRCP/Test/
Business Element Filter Combination	OR
Rights	...

PART IV

- **Author**   This defaults to the name of the Crystal Enterprise user who created the Business View. However, you can change it to anything. It appears with the description as a tooltip in the Repository Explorer.

- **Parent Folder**   The folder location for the Business View is displayed in this attribute. You cannot change it here. To change the location you must save the Business View to a new location.

- **Business Element Filter Combination**   The default for this setting is OR. You can change it to AND. The Business Elements that are used in the Business View may have filters. This attribute determines how the filters will be joined if there are filters in more than one of the Business Elements. AND will select a record for display only if it meets the conditions specified in all the filters. OR will select a record if it meets the conditions in any of the filters.

- **Rights**   Selecting the Rights attribute will display a button in the Value column. Click the button to open the Edit Rights dialog box for the Business Element.

Business Element Attributes   If you select a Business Element in the Object Explorer, the Property Browser will display information about the Business Element. You cannot modify the attributes here; instead, you must open the Business Element and modify them there.

Overriding the Data Foundation's Linking

If the Data Foundation used by the Business View allows its links to be overridden, two menu items will be available in the Linking Diagram menu:

- **Override Linking**   Selecting this option will open a Linking Override tab for the Business View. This tab displays the links used in the Data Foundation. You can modify them, and the changes will apply only to this Business View.

- **Revert Linking**   Select the Revert Linking command to close the Linking Override tab and return the links to their original configuration.

 NOTE   Changes to a Business View are not reflected in Crystal Reports until the user logs out of Crystal Enterprise and logs in again.

Exercise 28.1: Creating a Business View

1. Open the Business View Manager (Start | Programs | Crystal Enterprise 10 | Business View Manager), and log on as Administrator.

2. Select File | New | Business View, or select the Business View icon from the welcome dialog box.

3. In the Insert Business Elements dialog box, open the Samples\Business Views\ Xtreme folder.

4. Select the Customer Business Element, and click Add. Select Employee, and click Add. Select Orders, and click Add.

5. Click Close. Your Business View will appear as the active object.

6. Click the Save button on the toolbar.

7. In the Save As dialog box, set the Object Name to Business View **28.1**, and select the CRCP folder. Click Save.

8. Leave the Business View Manager open for the next exercise.

Exercise 28.2: Modifying a Business View

1. If it is not already open, open the Business View Manager and log on as Administrator.

2. Open the Business View 28.1 object.

3. In the Property Browser for the Business View, change the Author attribute to your name.

4. Give the Business View a description.

5. Select the Rights attribute, and then click the ellipsis button.

6. In the Edit Rights dialog box, grant your user ID the right to view and edit the object. Close the dialog box.

7. Click the Rights Test View button on the toolbar. Select different users, and see what their rights to the Business View are.

8. Drag the Product Business Element from the Repository Explorer to the Business Elements node to add it to the Business View.

9. Save the Business View.

10. Hold the cursor over the Business View in the Repository Explorer and note the text of the tooltip.

Working with Business Elements

Business Elements are collections of fields derived from the same Data Foundation. They appear as tables in Crystal Reports.

Creating a Business Element

Use the welcome dialog box, the File | New | Business Element command, or the New toolbar button to create a Business Element.

Choose a Data Foundation Dialog Box

The Choose a Data Foundation dialog box will be displayed, as shown here. It contains a tree list of all the Data Foundations in the repository. Select a Data Foundation and click the OK button.

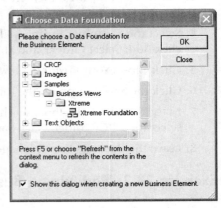

The Insert Business Fields dialog box will then appear. Select the fields you want to include in the Business Element and click the Add button. Continue to select and add until you have added all the fields you need. You can add regular database fields, formula fields, and SQL Expression fields. All field types will be treated as Business Fields once they are added to the Business Element. Click Close to return to the Business View Manager.

If you do not want the Choose a Data Foundation dialog box to display, clear the Show This Dialog When Creating a New Business Element check box. The Insert Business Fields dialog box will also not display. Some of the same shortcut menu items are available for the objects in these two dialog boxes as in the Repository Explorer.

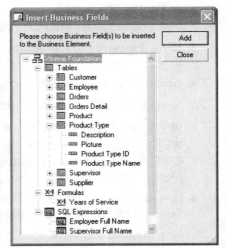

Saving a Business Element

Save the Business Element using the File | Save command or the Save toolbar button. The Save As dialog box will appear, where you can change the name of the Business Element and select a folder to store it in. A Business Element is created with a default name of "Business Element" plus a number. You can change the name of the Business Element in the Save As dialog box or select the root node in the Object Explorer and then edit the Name attribute in the Property Browser before saving it.

Modifying a Business Element

Once a Business Element has been created, you can modify several of its properties.

Changing the Field Structure

The main window for a Business Element initially contains two tabs: Fields List and Field Structure, as shown next. The Fields List tab shows all the fields that were selected for inclusion in the Business Element in a grid-type display.

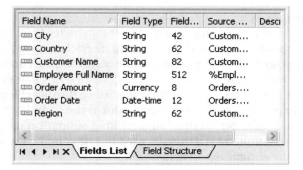

The Field Structure tab shows the fields in a tree view, and you can rearrange the fields into a hierarchy by dragging them to new locations, as shown here.

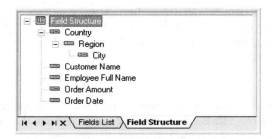

To return the fields to their original structure, click the Reset Field Structure toolbar button; select Edit | Reset Field Structure; or select the Business Element node in the Object Explorer, right-click, and choose Reset Field Structure.

Viewing the Referenced Data Foundation

When a Business Element is open, you can open the Referenced Data Foundation window shown here. Select the Referenced Data Foundation command from the View menu to open it. This window displays the Data Foundation used by the Business Element in a tree view. You can drag items from the Referenced Data Foundation window to the Business Element to add them to the Business Element.

Adding Additional Fields

After creating a Business Element, you can add fields to it in several ways. You can drag them from the Referenced Data Foundation window, or you can use the Insert Business Fields toolbar button, the Insert Business Fields shortcut menu item in the Object Explorer, or the Insert | Insert Business Fields menu command to reopen the Insert Business Fields dialog box.

Creating Parameters

Create a new parameter by selecting Insert | Insert Parameter from the menu, clicking the Insert Parameter toolbar button, or by selecting Insert Parameter from the right-click menu for the Parameter node in the Object Explorer. The Create Parameter Field dialog box will open, and you can create parameters as described in Chapter 6.

Note that a report based on a Business View that uses a Business Element containing a parameter will only prompt for the parameter value if the parameter is used in a filter that will be applied. Parameters defined in the Data Foundation used by the Business Element will also be prompted for if they are used in a filter in the Data Foundation that will be applied for the current report generation.

Changing Field Names

To change the name used for a Business Field, select the field in the Object Explorer and modify the Name attribute in the Property Browser, as shown here. The name you enter will be the name that developers see in Crystal Reports when using a Business View based on this Business Element.

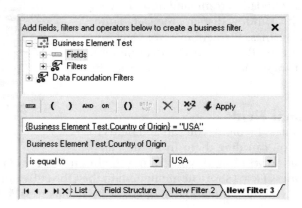

TIP Rename fields so that their content is easily understood by users. You can create multiple Business Elements with different names for the same field if different sets of users are familiar with different names.

Creating Filters

Filters act like the record selection formula in Crystal Reports. They limit the report records that will be visible for the users to whom they apply.

To create a new filter, click the Insert Filter toolbar button, select Insert | Insert Filter from the menu, or right-click the Filters node of the Object Explorer and select Insert Filter. The Filter will open in its own tab in the main window, as shown here.

The filter window has a tree list at the top. You can select fields, other filters in this Business Element, or other filters in the underlying Data Foundation from the list to add to this filter. You can drag items or double-click them to move them into the filter text window. Between the tree list and the filter text window is a toolbar. The buttons on the toolbar are described here.

Adds the item selected in the tree to the filter

(Inserts an opening parenthesis into the filter

) Inserts a closing parenthesis into the filter

AND Inserts the word AND into the filter

OR Inserts the word OR into the filter

() Encloses the selected text in the filter with parentheses

and→ Changes a selected AND to an OR, or a selected OR to an AND
↳or

✕ Deletes the selected portion of the filter

x·2 Checks the filter and displays any errors in its construction

⚡ Apply Saves any changes made to the filter

The area beneath the filter text box is used to define individual expressions within the filter, as shown here. The display changes depending on the portion of the filter that is selected.

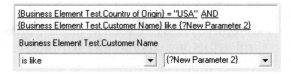

In order to make a filter active, you must use the Edit Rights dialog box to select the users or groups to which it should apply. The Edit Rights dialog box can be opened by clicking the Edit Rights toolbar button, selecting Edit | Edit Rights from the menu, right-clicking

the filter in the Object Explorer and choosing Edit Rights, or by using the Rights property in the Property Browser. A filter can be set to Applied or Not Applied.

 NOTE   Filters created for the underlying Data Foundation may be applied in addition to the filters at the Business Element level.

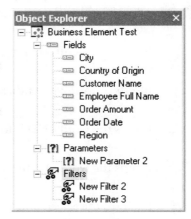

Object Explorer

The Object Explorer for a Business Element displays the fields, parameters, and filters contained in the object, as shown here.

The shortcut menu items differ depending on the node selected.

- **Edit Rights**   This command appears for the Business Element node, the field nodes, and the filter nodes. It opens the Edit Rights dialog box for the selected item. Edit the rights of field nodes to set the View Field Data right.

- **Reset Field Structure**   This command appears only for the Business Element node.

- **Insert Business Fields**   This command appears only for the Fields node.

- **Browse Field**   This command appears only for the field nodes. It opens a dialog box that shows a sample of the data contained in the field.

- **Delete**   This command appears for field nodes, parameter nodes, and filter nodes. It deletes the selected item.

- **Insert Parameter**   This command appears only for the Parameters node.

- **Edit Parameter**   This command appears only for parameter nodes.

- **Insert Filter**   This command appears only for the Filters node.

- **Edit Filter**   This command appears only for filter nodes.

Property Browser

The various items that make up a Business Element have different properties. As each item is selected in the Object Explorer, its properties are shown in the Property Browser. Items that are not grayed out can be changed.

Business Element Attributes   The properties for the Business Element are

- **Name**   The name of the Business Element. You can change it.
- **Description**   A text description of the Business Element.

- **Author**   Defaults to the name of the Crystal Enterprise user who created the Business Element, but you can change it.
- **Parent Folder**   The Crystal Enterprise folder where the object is stored.
- **Data Foundation**   The name of the Data Foundation used by the Business Element.
- **Rights**   Click the button in the Rights value column to open the Edit Rights dialog box for the Business Element.

Business Field Attributes   The properties for a Business Field are

- **Name**   The name of the Business Field. Change it to give the field a user-friendly name.
- **Description**   A text description of the field.
- **Field Type**   The data type of the field. You cannot modify it.
- **Source Data Field**   The name of the field in the source database. You cannot modify it.
- **Rights**   Click the button in the Rights value column to open the Edit Rights dialog box for the Business Field. This is where you can set rights for viewing the data in the field.

Filter Attributes   The properties for filters are

- **Name**   The name of the filter.
- **Description**   A text description of the filter.
- **Rights**   Click the button in the Rights value column to open the Edit Rights dialog box for the filter. This is where you set the users or groups the filter applies to.

Parameter Attributes   The properties for parameters are

- **Name**   The name of the parameter. You can change it.
- **Prompting Text**   The text used for prompting for the parameter. You can change it.
- **Field Type**   The data type of the parameter.
- **Allow Multiple Values**   A Boolean indicating whether the parameter is multivalue or discrete.
- **Allow NULL Value**   A Boolean indicating whether NULLs are allowed as a parameter value.
- **Parameter Type**   The type of the parameter.
- **Default Value**   The default value set for the parameter.

Business Element Wizard

You can create multiple Business Elements from the same Data Foundation simultaneously using the Business Element wizard. Start the wizard from the welcome dialog box, the New toolbar button, or the File | New | Business Element Wizard command. The Choose a Data Foundation dialog box will open as it does when you create a single Business Element. Select the Data Foundation you want to use, and then click Next.

Create Business Elements Screen

The Create Business Elements screen will appear, as shown in Figure 28-5.

From Data Foundation   This list box displays the fields, formulas, and SQL Expressions in the Data Foundation that can be used to create Business Elements.

Business Elements   Initially, this box contains one Business Element with a default name. You can add more Business Elements and rename them using the buttons to the upper right of the box. Fields, formulas, and SQL Expressions are added to the Business Elements from the Data Foundation list box.

Arrow Buttons   Use the arrow buttons to move one or many fields between the Data Foundation and Business Elements list boxes. Items can also be dragged.

New Business Element   This button is used to create a new Business Element. Create as many as you need.

Figure 28-5
Creating multiple
Business Elements

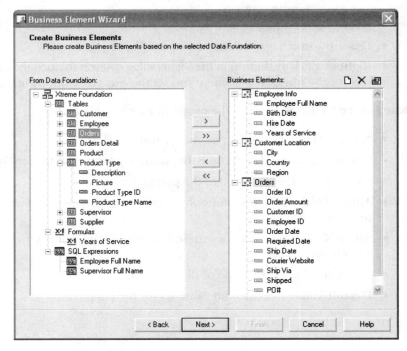

Figure 28-6
Selecting a finish
option

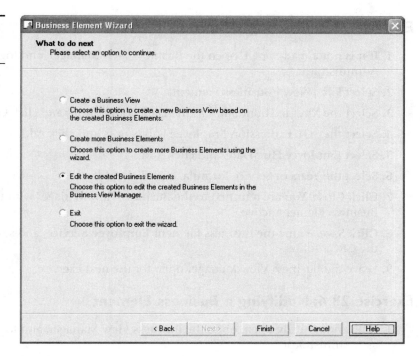

 Delete Selected Objects   Use this button to delete items selected in the Business Elements list box. Deleting a field is the same as moving it back to the Data Foundation list box.

 **Rename Selected Object**   This button is used to rename Business Elements and Business Fields.

Saving the Business Elements
When you have finished populating your Business Elements, click Next. The Save to Repository screen will appear. Select the repository folder where you want the Business Elements saved, and click Next. The What to Do Next screen appears, as shown in Figure 28-6. You have four options.

Create a Business View   This option creates a Business View using all the Business Elements and opens it in the Business View Manager.

Create More Business Elements   This option saves the Business Elements and restarts the wizard.

Edit the Created Business Elements   This option opens the Business Elements in the Business View Manager so that you can make further changes to them.

Exit   This option closes the wizard without saving the Business Elements. It is the same as Cancel.

PART IV

Exercise 28.3: Creating a Business Element

1. If it is not already open, open the Business View Manager, and log on as Administrator.

2. Select File | New | Business Element.

3. Select the Xtreme Foundation as the Data Foundation, and click OK.

4. Select the SQL Expression Employee Full Name, and click Add.

5. Select Employee.Hire Date, and click Add.

6. Select the Years of Service formula, and click Add.

7. Click Close. You are returned to the Business View Manager with the new Business Element active.

8. Click Save. Name the Business Element **Employee Service**, and save it to the CRCP folder.

9. Leave the Business View Manager open for the next exercise.

Exercise 28.4: Modifying a Business Element

1. If it is not already open, open the Business View Manager, and log on as Administrator.

2. Open the Employee Service Business Element.

3. Open the Referenced Data Foundation window.

4. Drag the Supervisor Full Name field from the Referenced Data Foundation window to the Fields node.

5. Right-click the Parameters node, and select Insert Parameter.

6. Call the parameter **Employee Name**, and use **Enter an employee name or part of an employee name** as the prompting text. Click OK.

7. Right-click the Filters node, and select Insert Filter.

8. Use the options on the filter tab so that the filter text is this:

   ```
   {Employee Service.Supervisor Full Name} = CurrentCEUserName
   ```

   Note that this is just an example. Since Supervisor Full Name does not match any Crystal Enterprise user name, all records will be filtered out.)

9. In the Property Browser, change the name of the filter to **Supervisor Filter**.

10. Click the button in the Rights row for the filter. Select Yes when prompted to save the object.

11. In the Edit Rights dialog box, apply the filter to the Everyone group. Close the Edit Rights dialog box.

12. Save the Business Element.

Chapter Review

This chapter introduced you to the Business View Manager and described the creation of Business Views and Business Elements.

Quick Tips

- The Business View Manager consists of a main window that displays open objects, a menu, a toolbar, and other dockable windows.

- When a Business View component object is created and saved, it inherits the rights set for the folder where it is saved.

- The Repository Explorer window is used to browse the repository, open objects, drag objects into Business View components, and manage repository folders. All repository objects are displayed, not just Business View objects. Some actions available for open objects can also be performed on closed objects in the repository tree.

- The Object Explorer displays the structure of the active open object in a tree view.

- The Property Browser displays the attributes of the item selected in the Object Explorer.

- The Show Dependent Objects toolbar button or Tools menu command displays all objects that are dependent on the active object.

- The Show Referenced Objects toolbar button or Tools menu command displays all objects that the active object refers to or depends on.

- The Check Dependent Integrity toolbar button or Tools menu command verifies that changes made to the active object do not invalidate any of its dependent objects.

- Business Views are created using the welcome dialog, the File | New command, or the New toolbar button.

- Business Views are composed of Business Elements, and the selection of Business Elements is the only required step in creation of a Business View. Business Elements are added to a Business View using the Insert Business Elements dialog box.

- The Insert Business Elements dialog box can be invoked at any time to add Business Elements to a Business View.

- A Business View has several properties that can be modified using the Property Browser: Name, Description, Author, Business Element Filter Combination, and Rights. The Property Browser also displays the folder location of the Business View.

- The Business Element Filter Combination property is used to control how filters from the Business Elements contained in the Business View are combined. The choices are AND or OR. If AND is selected, a record must satisfy every filter to be included in the report. If OR is selected, a record must satisfy one of the filters to be included in the report.

PART IV

- The Rights Test View tool displays the access that the selected user has to a Business View. It shows whether the user can view the Business View, its Business Elements, and Business Fields.

- The Export function can be used to export repository objects to XML files. The Import function can import XML files into the repository. Privileges on imported files depend on the security set for the objects in the file and the security set for the folder to which the object is imported.

- Business Elements are created by selecting fields, formulas, and SQL Expressions from a Data Foundation object.

- The fields in a Business Element can be arranged in a hierarchy using the Fields Structure tab of the main window.

- Additional fields can be added to a Business Element at any time by invoking the Insert Business Fields dialog box.

- Parameters can be added to Business Elements. They will only be prompted for in a report if they are used in a filter that applies when the report is run.

- Filters can be created for Business Elements. Filters are similar to record selection formulas but apply only to the users or groups who have the Apply right for them. Filters are set to Not Applied by default.

- You can modify the name of a Business Field in a Business Element by changing its name in the Property Browser.

- The Business Element Wizard can be used to create many Business Elements at the same time.

- The Referenced Data Foundation window can be opened when a Business Element is active. It displays a tree view of the Data Foundation used by the Business Elements. Items, including filters, can be dragged from the tree view into the Business Element.

Questions

Questions may have more than one correct answer. Choose all answers that apply.

1. Business View components can be saved to a file location or to the Crystal Repository.

   a. True

   b. False

2. Users automatically have all rights to any object they create in the Business View Manager.

   a. True

   b. False

3. If a Business View contains two Business Elements with filters and the Guest user would have both filters applied, what are the possible results?

    a. Denial, any denial overrides any grant.

    b. If the Business Element Filter Combination property for the Business View is set to AND, a record would have to pass both filters to be visible.

    c. If the Business Element Filter Combination property for the Business View is set to AND, a record would have to pass one filter or the other to be visible.

    d. If the Business Element Filter Combination property for the Business View is set to OR, a record would have to pass both filters to be visible.

    e. If the Business Element Filter Combination property for the Business View is set to OR, a record would have to pass one filter or the other to be visible.

4. For which of the following Business View components is the Rights Test View tool available?

    a. Business Views

    b. Business Elements

    c. Business Fields

    d. Data Foundations

    e. Data Connections

5. How will a Business Field be displayed in the Rights Test View tool if the selected user has been denied the View Field Data right for it?

    a. It will not be listed.

    b. It will be grayed out in the list.

    c. It will be listed with its name in red.

    d. It will be listed with an × over its icon.

    e. It will be listed with no indication that it is not available.

6. The Rights Test View tool works on both users and groups.

    a. True

    b. False

7. For which object types can you set security using the Business View Manager?

    a. Business Views

    b. Business Elements

    c. Text objects stored in the repository

    d. Bitmap objects stored in the repository

    e. Repository Custom Functions

    f. SQL Commands stored in the repository

8. To which file types can you export repository objects?

    a. Text

    b. XML

    c. HTML

    d. Rich text format

    e. Crystal Reports (.rpt)

9. Which of the following object types are selected to create Business Views?

    a. Business Fields

    b. Business Elements

    c. Data Foundations

    d. Data Connections

    e. Dynamic Data Connections

10. The table linking in the underlying Data Foundation for a Business View can be changed for just the Business View.

    a. True

    b. False

11. What are the two steps required to create a Business Element?

    a. Select a Data Connection.

    b. Create filters.

    c. Create parameters.

    d. Select a Data Foundation.

    e. Insert Business Fields.

12. The Fields Structure tab of a Business Element is used to

    a. Create a hierarchical structure.

    b. Define the data types of the fields.

    c. Define record selection related to the fields.

    d. Pick the fields to include in the Business Element.

    e. There is no such tab.

13. If a parameter exists in the Data Foundation used to construct a Business Element, it will not be prompted for in a report that uses a Business View based on the Business Element unless it is specifically redefined in the Business Element.

    a. True

    b. False

14. A parameter defined in a Business Element will not be prompted for if it is not used in an applied filter at run time.

    a. True

    b. False

15. Where can field names for Business Fields in a Business Element be modified?

    a. Main window for the component.

    b. Object Explorer.

    c. Property Browser.

    d. They cannot be modified.

    e. Referenced Data Foundation window.

16. Which Business View Manager tool can you use to create multiple Business Elements at the same time?

    a. Business Elements Wizard

    b. Business View Wizard

    c. Referenced Data Foundation Tool

    d. Element Creation Tool

    e. Business Element Extractor

17. What does the Referenced Data Foundation display?

    a. The name of the Data Foundation referenced in a Business View

    b. The name of the Data Foundation referenced in a Business Element

    c. A tree view of the Data Foundation referenced in a Business View

    d. A tree view of the Data Foundation referenced in a Business Element

    e. The names of the Business Elements that refer to a particular Data Foundation

18. A Business Element filter must be applied to a user or group using what dialog box before it becomes active?

    a. Insert Business Filters

    b. Set Filters

    c. Edit Rights

    d. User Properties

    e. Group Properties

19. Which of the following field types in a Data Foundation can be added to a Business Element?

    a. Database fields

    b. Special fields

    c. Formula fields

    d. SQL Expression fields

    e. Parameter fields

20. There is no distinction between database fields and formula fields in a Business Element.

    a. True

    b. False

Answers

1. **b.** Business View component objects are always saved to folders in the repository.

2. **b.** An object initially inherits its rights from the folder where it is saved. The user may not have all privileges on that folder.

3. **b, e.** Using AND requires the record to pass both filters; using OR requires it to pass one of the filters.

4. **a.** The Rights Test View tool is used only on Business View components.

5. **d.** Business Fields that are not available to the selected user will be shown with an × over the field icon.

6. **b.** The Rights Test View tool works only on users.

7. **All.** You can set security for any object that is stored in the repository using the Repository Explorer window in the Business View Manager.

8. **b.** Objects can be exported to XML.

9. **b.** Business Elements are selected to create Business Views.

10. **a.** If the Data Foundation allows its linking to be overridden, it can be overridden in the Business View.

11. **d, e.** To create a Business Element, you must select a Data Foundation and then insert Business Fields.

12. **a.** The Fields Structure tab is used to create a hierarchical relationship among the fields.

13. **b.** The parameter will be prompted for if it is required by a filter even if it was defined in the Data Foundation and not mentioned in the Business Element.

14. **a.** Parameters that are not used in applied filters are not prompted for.

15. **c.** Field names are modified in the Property Browser.

16. **a.** Use the Business Elements Wizard to create multiple Business Elements from the same Data Foundation.

17. **d.** The Referenced Data Foundation windows displays a tree view of the Data Foundation used by a Business Element.

18. **c.** Use the Edit Rights dialog box to apply a filter to a user or group.

19. **a, c, d.** Database fields, formula fields, and SQL Expression fields can all be added to Business Elements as Business Fields.

20. **a.** All field types are shown and treated identically in Business Elements.

Data Foundations and Data Connections

Exam RDCR400 expects you to be able to
- Modify Data Foundations
- Modify Data Connections and Dynamic Data Connections

This chapter continues the Business View topic by covering the creation and maintenance of Data Foundation, Data Connection, and Dynamic Data Connection components.

Working with Data Foundations

Data Foundations are the workhorses of the Business View component family, even though they do not appear in Crystal Reports directly. Data Foundations are used to select tables, views, or stored procedures from one or more Data Connection or Dynamic Data Connection objects; to define SQL Commands; and to define the links between the selected objects or SQL Commands. Users of the Data Foundation do not need to understand the underlying data sources.

In addition, Data Foundations can simplify report development by allowing you to create formula fields, SQL Expression fields, and parameters that will be available in the Business Elements created from the Data Foundation. Security can be applied at the Data Foundation level to database fields, formulas, SQL Expressions, and filters, ensuring that any Business Views created from the Data Foundation inherit those settings. You do not need any privileges to the Data Foundation in order to create a report based on a Business View that uses the Data Foundation.

 EXAM TIP You must have the View privilege for the underlying Data Foundation to be able to view the SQL query for a report based on a Business View.

Creating a Data Foundation

Use the welcome dialog box, the File | New | Data Foundation command, or the New toolbar button to create a Data Foundation.

Choose a Data Connection

Any of those methods will cause the Choose a Data Connection dialog box to be displayed, as shown here. It contains a tree list of all the Data Connections and Dynamic Data Connections in the repository. Select one or more, and click the OK button. If you select a Dynamic Data Connection, you will be asked to select one of the Data Connections that make up the Dynamic Data Connection, because the Business View Manager must read the database structure information from an actual database connection.

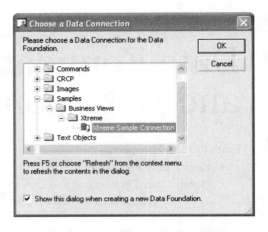

The Insert Data Tables dialog box will then appear, as shown here. Select the tables you want to include in the Data Foundation, and click the Add button. Continue to select and add until you have added all the fields you need. You can select more than one table at a time. You can select regular database tables, views, and stored procedures. You can create SQL Commands using the Add Command option. You can select tables from more than one Data Connection. Click Close to close the dialog box and return to the Business View Manager.

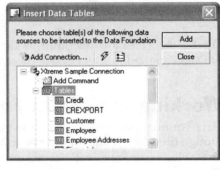

Click the Options button or select the Options command from the shortcut menu of the Insert Data Tables dialog box to display the Database Explorer Options dialog box, shown here. Use this dialog box to filter or sort the data source listings. All the items in this dialog box duplicate options in the Database Expert, and are described in Chapter 18 (see the "Options—Database Tab" section in that chapter).

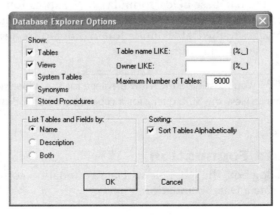

If you do not want the Choose a Data Connection dialog box to display when you create a new Data Foundation, clear the Show This Dialog When Creating a New Data Foundation check box. The Insert Data Tables dialog box will also not display. Some of the same shortcut menu items that are available for the objects in these two dialog boxes are available in the Repository Explorer.

Saving a Data Foundation

Save the Data Foundation using the File | Save command or the Save toolbar button. The Save As dialog box will appear, where you can change the name of the Data Foundation and select the folder where you want to store it. A Data Foundation is created with a default name of "Data Foundation" plus a number. You can change the name of the Data Foundation in the Save As dialog box as described or select the root node in the Object Explorer and then edit the Name attribute in the Property Browser before saving it.

Modifying a Data Foundation

Once you have created a Data Foundation, you will need to modify it in various ways to make it useful.

Creating Links

The main window for a Business Element initially contains one tab, the Linking Diagram, as shown here. The Linking Diagram tab shows all of the tables or other objects that were selected for inclusion in the Data Foundation similar to the Link tab of the Database Expert in Crystal Reports. No links are created by default.

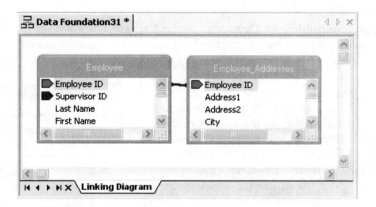

When you use a Business View to create a report in Crystal Reports, the linking set up in the Data Foundation (or overridden in any Business Elements) will be displayed in the Database Expert, but you will not be able to change it in the report.

The process of creating links and a discussion of the various link types and other link options can be found in Chapter 18. The Link Diagram menu options are as follows; many of them are also available as shortcut commands:

- **Smart Linking by Key** Creates table links using primary and foreign key information.

- **Smart Linking by Name** Links tables by matching field names in pairs of tables.

- **Clear Links** Removes all links.

- **Order Links** If there is more than one link, you can use this command to specify the order in which the links should be created.

- **Locate Table** Use this command to pick a specific table from a list and make that table active. This command is useful if you have many tables and need to find a particular one on the Linking Diagram.

- **Rearrange Tables** This command will move tables so that they are not overlapping and the links go from left to right.

- **Select Visible Tables** Use this command to select which tables are displayed on the Linking Diagram and which are hidden. Hidden tables are not removed from the Data Foundation, just from the display.

- **Fetch Table Indexes** This command causes the Business View Manager to read information about the table indexes from the data sources. Index flags will appear if they were not already displayed.

- **Index Legend** Use this command to display a dialog box that maps the index flag color to an index.

- **Change Linking View** This command is a toggle. Click it once to display only the table names and hide the table field names; click it again to redisplay the field names.

Set Table Location

The Business View Manager Set Table Location command differs slightly from the version in the Crystal Reports Database Expert. In the Database Expert, you can change the source for a table or an entire database. In the Business View Manager, you can change the source for a table or an entire Data Connection.

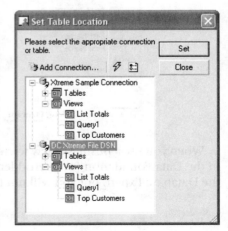

When you select Set Table Location from the Edit menu, the Object Explorer shortcut menu, or click the Set Table Location toolbar button, the Set Table Location dialog box appears, as shown here. If the Tables node of the Object Explorer was selected when the Set Table Location command was invoked and you select a new Data Connection in the Set Table Location dialog box, all tables will be converted to use the new Data Connection. If one or more tables are selected when the Set Table Location command is invoked, only those tables will be converted to use the new Data Connection or table location.

When changing the Data Connection, the table names must match between the original source and the new source. When changing an individual table, the table names need not match. If field names or types do not match, you will be presented with the Map Fields dialog box described in Chapter 19, where you can map individual fields to new locations.

Referenced Data Connections

When a Data Foundation is open, you can open the Referenced Data Connections window, shown here. Select View | Referenced Data Connections to open it. This window displays the Data Connections used by the Data Foundation in a tree view. It is very similar to the Insert Data Tables dialog box. You can drag tables from the Referenced Data Connections window to the Data Foundation to add them to the Data Foundation. You can also create new connections.

Adding Additional Tables

After creating a new Data Foundation, you can add tables to it in several ways. You can drag them from the Referenced Data Connections; or you can use the Insert Data Tables shortcut menu item in the Object Explorer, the Insert Data Tables toolbar button, or the Insert | Insert Data Tables menu command to reopen the Insert Data Tables dialog box.

Creating Formulas

You can create formula fields in a Data Foundation object. Any formula fields that you create are available on the Insert Business Fields dialog box when you create a Business Element from the Data Foundation. Once a formula field is added to a Business Element, it is treated the same as any other field type. Using this method, you can create complex computations and make the result seamlessly available to report developers or Business View designers.

To create a formula field, right-click the Formulas node of the Object Explorer, and select Insert Formula, select Insert | Insert Formula from the menu, or click the Insert Formula button on the toolbar. The Formula Workshop will open in a new tab in the main window, and the formula will be given a default name. You can change the name using the Property Browser for the formula. (Creating formula fields is described in Chapters 8 and 17.)

TIP The View Field Data privilege can be set for formula fields in the way that it is for regular database fields.

Data Foundation formula fields cannot reference a custom function unless it has been imported into the Data Foundation. See the "Importing Custom Functions" section for more information. Once a Custom Function has been imported, it will appear in the Custom Function folder of the Function tree in the Formula Workshop and will be available for use.

Creating SQL Expressions

You can also create SQL Expression fields in a Data Foundation object. They are treated similarly to formula fields and appear in the Insert Business Fields dialog box when you create a Business Element from the Data Foundation. You should use SQL Expression fields instead of formula fields when possible, to push processing to the server.

To create a SQL Expression field, right-click the SQL Expressions node of the Object Explorer, and select Insert SQL Expression, select Insert | Insert SQL Expression from the menu, or click the Insert SQL Expression button on the toolbar. The Formula Workshop will open in a new tab in the main window, and the SQL Expression will be given a default name. You can change the name using the Property Browser. SQL Expression fields are created as described in Chapter 20.

The Formula Workshop tab for the new SQL Expression has one extra item not seen when it is used in a Crystal report. The Data Connection being used is displayed at the top, as shown here. You can select a different connection using the ellipsis button to the right of the connection name.

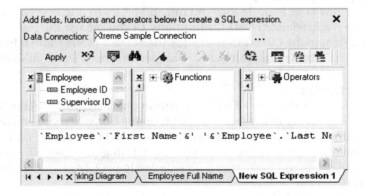

TIP The View Field Data privilege can be set for SQL Expression fields in the same way that it is for regular database fields.

Importing Custom Functions

A repository custom function can be used in a formula field of a Data Foundation after it has been imported into the Data Foundation. After the import, it appears in the Formula Workshop for use in formulas. A custom function contained in a Data Foundation is not directly available for use in Business Elements.

To import a custom function, right-click the Custom Functions folder of the Object Explorer, and select Import Custom Function, select Insert | Import Custom Function, or click the Import Custom Function button on the toolbar. The Choose Custom Functions dialog box will display, as shown here. Select a function and click Add to have it imported. Continue to select and click Add until you have added all the functions you need. Click Close to close the dialog box and return to the Business View Manager.

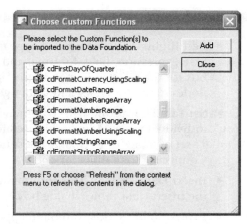

Creating Parameters

Parameters for a Data Foundation are created exactly as they are for a Business Element. See Chapter 28.

Note that a report based on a Business View that uses a Data Foundation containing a parameter will only prompt for the parameter value if the parameter is used in a filter that will be applied. Parameters defined in any Business Elements based on the Data Foundation will also be prompted for if they are used in a filter in the Business Element that will be applied for the current report generation.

Creating Filters

Filters for Data Foundation objects are created and applied exactly as they are for Business Elements (see Chapter 28). Filters created in Data Foundations flow through to the Business Elements that are based on the Data Foundation, and hence to the Business View. It is better to create filters at the Data Foundation level rather than the Business Element level if they are needed for all the Business Elements based on the Data Foundation. That way, the filters can be created just once, so creation and maintenance is easier. Security is also enhanced, since any restrictions are applied at a lower level and there is no possibility of forgetting to apply it to the Business Elements.

Data Foundations are created with two default filters: Full Data Access and No Data Access. These filters cannot be modified or deleted, but you can apply them to users or groups using the Edit Rights dialog box.

Object Explorer

The Object Explorer for a Data Foundation displays the tables, fields, formulas, SQL Expressions, parameters, filters, and custom functions contained in the object, as shown here.

NOTE All data source types appear under the Tables node whether they are actual tables or not.

The shortcut menu items differ depending on the node selected.

- **Edit Rights**   This command appears for the Data Foundation node and the SQL Expression, field, formula, and filter nodes. It opens the Edit Rights dialog box for the selected item. Edit the rights of field, formula, and SQL Expression nodes to set the View Field Data right.

- **Set Table Location**   This command appears only for the Tables node and the individual table nodes and is used to change the Data Connection for a table or set of tables or to change the source to a different table in the same Data Connection or a different one.

- **Insert Data Tables**   This command appears only for the Tables node. It opens the Insert Data Tables dialog box.

- **Browse Table**   This command appears only for table nodes. It opens the Browse dialog box, shown in Figure 29-1.

- **Browse Field**   This command appears for the field, formula, and SQL Expression nodes. It opens a dialog box that shows a sample of the data contained in the field.

- **Delete**   This command appears for table, parameter, formula, SQL Expression, custom function, and filter nodes. It deletes the selected item.

- **Insert Parameter**   This command appears only for the Parameters node. It creates a new parameter.

- **Edit Parameter**   This command appears for parameter nodes. It opens the Edit Parameter Field dialog box.

- **Insert Filter**   This command appears only for the Filters node. It creates a new filter.

- **Edit Filter**   This command appears for filter nodes. It makes the selected filter tab active.

- **Insert Formula**   This command appears only for the Formulas node. It creates a new formula.

- **Edit Formula**   This command appears only for formula nodes. It makes the selected formula tab active.

- **Insert SQL Expression**   This command appears only for the SQL Expressions node. It creates a new SQL Expression.

- **Edit SQL Expression**   This command appears only for SQL Expression nodes. It makes the selected SQL Expression node active.

- **Import Custom Function**   This command appears only for the Custom Functions node. It opens the Choose Custom Functions dialog box.

Figure 29-1
Browsing table
data

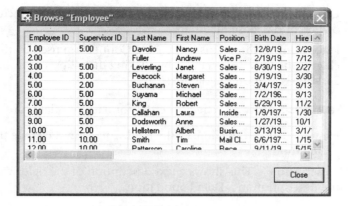

Property Browser

The various items that make up a Data Foundation have different properties. As each item is selected in the Object Explorer, its properties are shown in the Property Browser. Items that are not grayed out can be changed.

For the Data Foundation   The properties for the Data Foundation object are

- **Name**   This is the name of the Data Foundation. You can change it.

- **Description**   This is a text description of the Data Foundation.

- **Author**   This property defaults to the name of the Crystal Enterprise user who created the Data Foundation, but you can change it.

- **Parent Folder**   This shows the Crystal Enterprise folder where the object is stored.

- **Allow Table Joins Override**   This property controls whether Business Elements created from the Data Foundation can change the table linking set up in the Data Foundation. It is set to False by default, meaning that the linking cannot be overridden. Change this attribute to True if you want to allow the linking to be changed in Business Elements based on the Data Foundation.

- **Rights**   Click the button in the Rights value column to open the Edit Rights dialog box for the Data Foundation.

For Tables   The properties for a table are

- **Table Alias**   This is an alternate name for the table. You can change the table alias to anything you desire. The alias will flow through to Business Elements created from the Data Foundation.

- **Physical Table Name**   This is the actual name of the table in the underlying database.

- **Description**   This shows a text description of the table. You can modify the description.

PART IV

- **Qualified Table Name** This is the actual table name, including any schema, owner, or database qualifiers.

- **Data Connection** This is the Data Connection used by the table. You can change the Data Connection by clicking the ellipsis button, which opens the Set Table Location dialog box.

For Database Fields The properties for database fields are

- **Name** This is the name of the field. You cannot change the name in a Data Foundation.

- **Description** This shows a text description of the field. You cannot modify the description in a Data Foundation.

- **Field Type** This is the data type of the field. You cannot modify it.

- **Field Length** This is the length of the field. You cannot modify it.

- **Rights** Click the button in the Rights value column to open the Edit Rights dialog box for the field. This is where you can set rights for viewing the data in the field. These settings flow through to the Business Elements created from this Data Foundation.

For Formula Fields The properties for formula fields are

- **Name** This is the name of the formula. You can change the name.

- **Description** This shows a text description of the formula field. You can change the description.

- **Field Type** This is the data type of the result of the formula. You cannot modify it in the Property Browser. Modify it by changing the formula.

- **Formula Syntax** This is the syntax used in the formula. It can be Crystal or Basic. You can change the syntax in the tab for the formula.

- **Formula Text** This is the text of the formula. You can change it in the tab for the formula.

- **Rights** Click the button in the Rights value column to open the Edit Rights dialog box for the formula. This is where you can set rights for viewing the data in the formula. These settings flow through to the Business Elements created from this Data Foundation.

For SQL Expression Fields The properties for a SQL Expression are

- **Name** This is the name of the SQL Expression. You can change the name.

- **Description** This shows a text description of the SQL Expression field. You can change the description.

- **Field Type** This is the data type of the result of the SQL Expression. You cannot modify it in the Property Browser. Modify it by changing the result of the SQL Expression.

- **Formula Syntax**   This property will always be "SQL Expression."
- **Formula Text**   This is the text of the SQL Expression. You can change it in the tab for the SQL Expression.
- **Data Connection**   This is the Data Connection used by the SQL Expression. You can change it in the tab for the SQL Expression.
- **Show in Linking Diagram**   You can set this property to True or False. If set to True, the SQL Expression field will appear in the Linking Diagram and can be used to link tables. If set to False, the field will not appear and cannot be used for linking.
- **Rights**   Click the button in the Rights value column to open the Edit Rights dialog box for the SQL Expression. This is where you can set rights for viewing the data in the SQL Expression. These settings flow through to the Business Elements created from this Data Foundation.

For Custom Functions   The properties for a Custom Function are shown here. They are obtained from the repository and are read-only.

- **Name**   This is the name of the Custom Function.
- **Description**   This shows a text description of the Custom Function.
- **Author**   This is the author of the Custom Function.
- **Formula Text**   This is the text of the Custom Function.
- **Category**   This shows the folder hierarchy where the Custom Function resides in the repository.
- **Return Type**   This is the data type of the result of the Custom Function.

For Filters   The properties for filters in Data Foundations are the same as for filters in Business Elements; see Chapter 28 for details.

For Parameters   The properties for parameters in Data Foundations are the same as for parameters in Business Elements; see Chapter 28 for details.

Exercise 29.1: Creating a Data Foundation

1. Open the Business View Manager and log on as the Administrator.
2. Select File | New | Data Foundation, or select Data Foundation from the welcome dialog box.
3. In the Choose a Data Connection dialog box, select the Xtreme Sample Connection from the Samples/Business Views/Xtreme folder, and click OK.
4. From the Insert Data Tables dialog box, add the Employee, Customer, and Orders tables, and then close the dialog box.

5. The Data Foundation is created and you are returned to the Business View Manager. On the Linking Diagram tab, right-click to display the shortcut menu, and select Smart Linking by Name to create table links.

6. Click the Save button on the toolbar. Enter **Exercise 29.1 Data Foundation** as the name of the Data Foundation, and save it to the CRCP folder.

7. Leave the Business View Manager open for the next exercise.

Exercise 29.2: Modifying a Data Foundation

1. Continue from the previous exercise, or log in to the Business View Manager as Administrator, and open the Exercise 29.1 Data Foundation object.

2. Select View | Referenced Data Connections to open the Referenced Data Connections window.

3. Drag the Orders Detail table from the Referenced Data Connections window on to the Linking Diagram.

4. Manually create a link between the Orders table and the Orders Detail table using the Order ID field.

5. Right-click the Formulas node of the Object Explorer, and select Insert Formula. Use this as the text of the formula:

```
{Employee.First Name}&' '&{Employee.Last Name}
```

6. In the Property Browser for the formula, change the formula name to **Employee Full Name**.

7. Select the Employee.Salary field in the Object Explorer.

8. Right-click, and select Edit Rights from the shortcut menu.

9. In the Edit Rights dialog box, change the View Field Data privilege to Inherited for the Everyone group. Change the privilege to Granted for your user ID. Click the Preview button to see what the resulting rights will be. Click OK to close the dialog box.

10. Select the Orders_Detail table in the Object Explorer. In the Property Browser, change the name to **Order_Details**. (Note that table names in the Data Foundation cannot contain spaces.)

11. Create a SQL Expression called **Extended Price** using the following formula:

```
'Order_Details'.'Unit Price'*'Order_Details'.'Quantity'
```

12. Create a parameter called **Customer** using **Select Customer to display.** as the prompting text. Populate the default values for the parameter using the Customer Name field.

13. Create a filter called **Customer** such that the Customer Name field must match the Customer parameter:

```
{Customer.Customer Name}={?Customer}
```

14. Apply this filter to the Everyone group so that it will always be used.

15. Save the Data Foundation.

Working with Data Connections

Data Connection objects define all the properties necessary to connect to a particular database or data source.

Creating a Data Connection

Use the welcome dialog box, the File | New | Data Connection command, or the New toolbar button to create a Data Connection.

Choose a Data Source Dialog Box

Any of those methods will display the Choose a Data Source dialog box, as shown here. It is similar to the Database Expert's list of data sources, but displays only the Create New Connection node. All data types for which drivers are installed are available. Select a node to create a new connection of that type or see a list of current connections for that type.

If you do not want the Choose a Data Source dialog box displayed when you create a new Data Connection in the future, clear the Display This Dialog When Creating a Data Connection check box.

Set Data Connection Password Dialog Box

The next step in creating a new Data Connection is to optionally select a password. When the Set Data Connection Password dialog box appears, as shown here, you can enter a user name and password. You may also click Cancel if no password is required or you do not wish to store credentials with the Data Connection. In addition, the Runtime Prompt Mode drop-down box can be set to Always Prompt or Never Prompt. If it is set to Always Prompt, the credentials stored in the Data Connection will not be used, and the user will be prompted to log in. If it is set to Never Prompt, the user will never be prompted to log in. In this case, if the data source requires credentials, you must enter them and store them with the Data Connection.

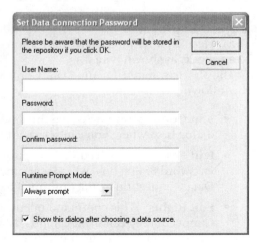

If you do not want the Set Data Connection Password dialog box displayed in the future, clear the Show This Dialog After Choosing a Data Source check box.

Main Window

After creating a connection, you will be returned to the main window of the Business View Manager. The contents of the main window vary depending on the type of connection. Here are examples of an ODBC connection and an Oracle connection.

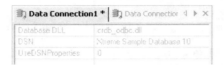

Test Connectivity

To verify that your connection settings work, click the Test Connectivity button on the toolbar or select Tools | Test Connectivity. You will receive either a message that the connection was successful or a list of errors.

Saving a Data Connection

Save the Data Connection using the File | Save command or the Save toolbar button. The Save As dialog box will appear. You can change the name of the Data Connection there and select the folder where you want to store it. A Data Connection is created with a default name of "Data Connection" plus a number. You can change the name of the Data Connection in the Save As dialog box or select the root node in the Object Explorer and then edit the Name attribute in the Property Browser before saving it.

Modifying a Data Connection

You can modify a Data Connection after creation in several ways.

Object Explorer

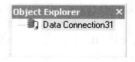

The Object Explorer for a Data Connection object contains only a root node, as shown here.

The shortcut menu for the Data Connection item contains the following commands:

- **Edit Connection**   Selecting this option reopens the Choose a Data Source dialog box, where you can select a different connection.

- **Edit Password**   Selecting this option reopens the Set Data Connection Password dialog box, where you can change the credentials stored with the Data Connection or the Runtime Prompt Mode.

- **Edit Rights**   This command opens the Edit Rights dialog box for the Data Connection. Recall from Chapter 27 that Data Connection and Dynamic Data Connection objects are the only ones that have the Data Access privilege. It is granted to the Everyone group by default, and it cannot be inherited. Users and report developers must have the Data Access privilege to create or run reports based on any dependent Business Views.

Property Browser

The properties for a Data Connection object are shown here. You can modify any of the properties except the Parent Folder.

- **Name**   This is the name of the Data Connection. You can change it.

- **Description**   This shows a text description of the Data Connection.

- **Author**   This property defaults to the name of the Crystal Enterprise user who created the Data Connection, but you can change it.

- **Parent Folder**   This is the Crystal Enterprise folder where the object is stored.

- **User Name**   This is the user name stored in the Data Connection.

- **Password**   This is the password stored in the Data Connection. Change it by clicking the ellipsis button, which reopens the Set Data Connection Password dialog box.

- **Connection**   This is the data source used by the Data Connection object. Change it by clicking the ellipsis button, which reopens the Choose a Data Source dialog box.

- **Runtime Prompt Mode**   Set this property to True or False using the drop-down box.

- **Use Owner**   This property defaults to True. Set it to False to exclude the "dbo" part of a qualified table name in the report query for SQL Server and other databases that use it.

- **Use Catalog**   This property defaults to True. Set it to False to exclude the owner or schema part of a qualified table name in the report query for databases that use it.

- **Rights**   Click the button in the Rights value column to open the Edit Rights dialog box for the Data Connection.

Exercise 29.3: Creating a Data Connection

1. Open the Business View Manager, and log on as the Administrator.

2. Select File | New | Data Connection or select Data Connection from the welcome dialog box.

3. In the Choose a Data Source dialog box, select the Xtreme Sample Database 10 connection under the ODBC folder. If the connection does not appear, click the Make New Connection node, and set up a connection to the ODBC DSN for the sample database. Click OK.

PART IV

4. In the Set Data Connection Password, leave the user ID and password boxes empty, since none are required, and set Runtime Prompt Mode to Never Prompt. Click OK to close the dialog box and return to the Business View Manager.

5. Click the Test Connectivity button on the toolbar to verify your connection. You should receive a success message. Click OK to close the message box.

6. Set the name of the Data Connection to **Exercise 29.3 Data Connection** in the Property Browser.

7. Click the Save button on the toolbar. Save the Data Connection to the CRCP folder.

8. Leave the Business View Manager open for the next exercise.

Exercise 29.4: Modifying a Data Connection

1. Continue from the previous exercise, or log in to the Business View Manager as Administrator and open the Exercise 29.3 Data Connection object.

2. Enter a description for the Data Connection using the Property Browser.

3. Set the Use Owner and Use Catalog properties to False.

4. Open the Edit Rights dialog box, and set the Data Access privilege to Inherited for the Everyone group and to Granted for your user ID.

5. Click the Preview button to see the final security that will be applied. Click OK to close the dialog box.

6. Save the Data Connection.

Working with Dynamic Data Connections

Dynamic Data Connections contain a list of Data Connection objects. The specific Data Connection to use when running a report is selected via a parameter. All of the Data Connections used must contain the same structure or else errors will occur. In addition, they must have their Runtime Prompt mode set to Never Prompt

Creating a Dynamic Data Connection

Use the welcome dialog box, the File | New | Dynamic Data Connection command, or the New toolbar button to create a Dynamic Data Connection.

Choose a Data Connection Dialog Box

Any of those methods will cause the Choose a Data Connection dialog box to be displayed, as shown here. It displays all Data Connection objects that currently exist in the repository. Select a Data Connection object and click Add to add it

to your Dynamic Data Connection. Continue to add objects until you are finished. Then click Close to close the dialog box.

If you do not want the Choose a Data Connection dialog box displayed when you create a new Dynamic Data Connection in the future, clear the Display This Dialog When Creating a Dynamic Data Connection check box.

Main Window

After closing the Choose a Data Connection dialog box, you will be returned to the Business View Manager. The main window for a Dynamic Data Connection is shown here. It lists the Data Connections that were added.

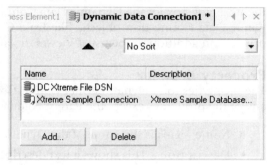

Saving a
Dynamic Data Connection

Save the Dynamic Data Connection using the File | Save command or the Save toolbar button. The Save As dialog box will appear. You can change the name of the Dynamic Data Connection there and select the folder where you want to store it. A Dynamic Data Connection is created with a default name of "Dynamic Data Connection" plus a number. You can change the name of the Dynamic Data Connection in the Save As dialog box or select the root node in the Object Explorer and then edit the Name attribute in the Property Browser before saving it.

Modifying a Dynamic Data Connection

You can modify a Dynamic Data Connection after creation in several ways.

Adding Data Connections

To add additional Data Connections to a Dynamic Data Connection, you can drag them from the Repository Explorer, click the Add button in the main window or the Add Data Connection button on the toolbar, or select Edit | Add Data Connection to reopen the Choose a Data Connection dialog box.

Deleting Data Connections

To remove Data Connections from a Dynamic Data Connection, you can select the Data Connection and then click the Delete button in the main window or the Delete Data Connection button on the toolbar. Or you can select Edit | Delete Data Connection. The Data Connection will be removed from the Dynamic Data Connection.

Sort Data Connections

You can sort the list of Data Connections using the drop-down box in the upper right corner of the main window. The options are No Sort, Alphabetical Ascending, and Alphabetical Descending. In addition, you can move the selected Data Connection up or down using the arrow buttons above the list box.

PART IV

Object Explorer

The Object Explorer for a Dynamic Data Connection object contains only a root node, as shown here. The shortcut menu for the Data Connection item contains only the Edit Rights command. This command opens the Edit Rights dialog box for the Dynamic Data Connection. Dy-

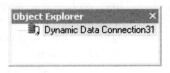

namic Data Connection objects, like Data Connection objects, have the Data Access privilege in addition to the usual View, Edit, and Set Security options.

Property Browser

The properties for a Dynamic Data Connection object are listed here. You can modify any of the properties except the Parent Folder.

- **Name** This is the name of the Dynamic Data Connection. You can change it.

- **Description** This shows a text description of the Dynamic Data Connection.

- **Author** This property defaults to the name of the Crystal Enterprise user who created the Dynamic Data Connection, but you can change it.

- **Parent Folder** This is the Crystal Enterprise folder where the object is stored.

- **Prompt Text** This property contains the prompt that will be displayed when users are queried for which Data Connection to activate for the current report run.

- **Rights** Click the button in the Rights value column to open the Edit Rights dialog box for the Dynamic Data Connection.

Exercise 29.5: Creating a Dynamic Data Connection

1. Open the Business View Manager, and log on as the Administrator.

2. Select File | New | Dynamic Data Connection, or select Dynamic Data Connection from the welcome dialog box.

3. In the Choose a Data Connection dialog box, select the Xtreme Sample Connection under the Samples\Business Views\Xtreme folder. Click Add.

4. Select the Exercise 29.3 Data Connection under the CRCP folder. Click Add.

5. Click Close to close the dialog box.

6. Set the name of the Dynamic Data Connection to **Exercise 29.5 Dynamic Data Connection** in the Property Browser.

7. Click the Save button on the toolbar. Save the Dynamic Data Connection to the CRCP folder.

8. Leave the Business View Manager open for the next exercise.

Exercise 29.6: Modifying a Dynamic Data Connection

1. Continue from the previous exercise, or log in to the Business View Manager as Administrator and open the Exercise 29.5 Dynamic Data Connection object.

2. Enter a description for the Dynamic Data Connection using the Property Browser.

3. Select the Exercise 29.3 Data Connection in the Dynamic Data Connection window, and click the Delete button.

4. Drag the Exercise 29.3 Data Connection from the Repository Explorer into the Dynamic Data Connection.

5. Sort the Data Connections in alphabetical order.

6. Enter prompting text for the Dynamic Data Connection in the Property Browser.

7. Save the Dynamic Data Connection.

Chapter Review

This chapter covered the creation and modification of Data Foundation, Data Connection, and Dynamic Data Connection objects.

Quick Tips

- Data Foundations are created by selecting tables, views, stored procedures, and SQL Commands from one or more Data Connection or Dynamic Data Connection objects.

- The tables, views, stored procedures, and SQL Commands in a Data Foundation can be given aliases.

- Additional tables can be added to a Data Foundation at any time by invoking the Insert Data Tables dialog box.

- Links for the tables in a Data Foundation are created on the Linking Diagram tab.

- Parameters can be added to Data Foundations. They will only be prompted for in a report if they are used in a filter that applies when the report is run.

- Formula fields and SQL Expression fields can be added to Data Foundations. They will appear as regular Business Fields in any Business Elements based on the Data Foundation.

- To use Repository Custom Functions in the formula fields of a Data Foundation, you must first import the Custom Functions.

- Filters can be created for Data Foundations. They flow through to the Business Elements based on the Data Foundation.

- You can modify the alias of a database field, formula field, or SQL Expression field in a Data Foundation by changing its name in the Property Browser.

- The Referenced Data Connections window can be opened when a Data Foundation is active. It displays a window similar to the Insert Data Tables dialog box. Tables can be dragged from the window into the Data Foundation.

- You can use the Set Table Location command to change the Data Connection for a table or set of tables or to change the source of a table to a different table.

- The View Field Data privilege can be denied to database fields, formula fields, and SQL Expression fields in Data Foundation objects to restrict access to the field data.

- Data Connections are created by configuring connections to data sources. One data source is accessed via one Data Connection.

- The configuration settings for a Data Connection can be modified after it is created. You can change the data source or the logon credentials.

- Use the Runtime Prompt Mode property of a Data Connection to control whether users are required to enter logon credentials. If you set this property to Never Prompt and the data source requires credentials, you must save them with the Data Connection.

- You can test a Data Connection with the Test Connectivity command.

- Data Connections and Dynamic Data Connections have the Data Access privilege. It is granted to Everyone by default and cannot be inherited from any parent object or folder. (Setting it to inherited results in denial.)

- Dynamic Data Connections are composed of lists of regular Data Connection objects. When a Dynamic Data Connection object is used in a Business View, the user is prompted to select which Data Connection should be used for the current run.

- All the Data Connections used in a Dynamic Data Connection must have the same structure, and their Runtime Prompt Mode property must be set to Never Prompt.

- After creation, you can add, delete, or sort the Data Connections contained in a Dynamic Data Connection.

Questions

Questions may have more than one correct answer. Choose all answers that apply.

1. A Data Foundation can contain only one Dynamic Data Connection, but it can use multiple Data Connections.

   a. True

   b. False

2. Which of the following can you use to add tables to a Data Foundation?

   a. Referenced Data Connections window

   b. Insert Data Tables shortcut menu item in the Linking Diagram tab

   c. Insert Data Tables shortcut menu item in the Object Explorer

   d. Insert | Insert Data Tables menu command

   e. Insert Data Tables toolbar button

3. In which of the following places can you override the table linking set up in a Data Foundation that has the Allow Table Joins Override property set to True?

   a. Crystal Reports

   b. Business View object

   c. Business Element object

   d. Crystal Enterprise

   e. Nowhere

4. In which object should a filter be created if it is required for every Business Element based on a particular Data Foundation?

   a. Business View

   b. Business Element

   c. Data Foundation

   d. Data Connection

   e. Dynamic Data Connection

5. The Set Table Location command allows you to change the source for a table in a Data Foundation, but only to another table in the same Data Connection.

   a. True

   b. False

6. For which objects must a report developer have the View privilege to create reports from a Business View and display the SQL query?

   a. Business View

   b. Business Element

   c. Data Foundation

   d. Data Connection

   e. Dynamic Data Connection

7. Formula fields created in a Data Foundation object can refer to database fields.

   a. True

   b. False

8. Custom Functions added to Data Foundations can be used as Business Fields in Business Elements based on the Data Foundation.

a. True

b. False

9. A SQL Expression field created in a Data Foundation is tied to a particular Data Connection.

a. True

b. False

10. For which of the following properties or components of a Data Foundation can you change the name or create an alias?

a. The Data Foundation object itself

b. Tables

c. Database fields

d. Formula fields

e. SQL Expression fields

11. Which of the following are true of the Data Access privilege?

a. Data Connection objects have it.

b. Dynamic Data Connection objects have it.

c. It is set to Inherited for the Everyone group by default.

d. It is set to Denied for the Everyone group by default.

e. It is set to Granted for the Everyone group by default.

12. You can configure a Data Connection such that report users do not need to log on to the data sources it uses, even if the data sources require a logon.

a. True

b. False

13. A single Data Connection object can be configured to access more than one data source.

a. True

b. False

14. Which of the following are properties of a Data Connection object?

a. User Name

b. Password

c. Runtime Prompt Mode

d. Use Owner

e. Rights

15. The structures of the underlying data sources used by a Dynamic Data Connection must be the same.

   a. True

   b. False

Answers

1. **b.** You can use any number of Dynamic Data Connections or Data Connections in a Data Foundation.

2. **a, c, d, e.** There is no Insert Data Tables shortcut command on the Linking Diagram tab's shortcut menu.

3. **c.** Setting the Allow Table Joins Override property for a Data Foundation to True allows you to override the linking in any Business Elements that are created from the Business View. You can never override the linking in Crystal Reports.

4. **c.** Filters can only be created for Business Elements and Data Foundations. It is best to create filters in the Data Foundation if they are required for all Business Elements based on the Data Foundation.

5. **b.** Set Table Location allows you to change the location for a table to another table in the same Data Connection or a different Data Connection.

6. **a, c.** The developer must have the View privilege on the Business View to create a report based on the Business View. In addition, in order to view the SQL query, he or she must have the View privilege for the Data Foundation object. Note that the developer must also have the Data Access privilege for any Data Connections used in the Data Foundation.

7. **a.** Formulas created in Data Foundations are identical to formulas created in Crystal Reports. (Custom functions cannot refer to database fields.)

8. **b.** Custom functions can only be used in formula fields in the Data Foundation. They are not accessible to Business Elements based on the Data Foundation.

9. **a.** Since a SQL Expression is written in the database's SQL syntax, it must be tied to a particular Data Connection. You can change the Data Connection if necessary, but you might have to rewrite the SQL Expression in that case.

10. **a, b, d, e.** You cannot change the name or create an alias for database fields in a Data Foundation. You must do that in the Business Element.

11. **a, b, e.** Both Data Connections and Dynamic Data Connections have the Data Access privilege, and it is set to Granted for the Everyone group by default.

12. **a.** You can store a user ID and password with the Data Connection and set its Runtime Prompt Mode property to Never Prompt to use the stored credentials for everyone.

13. **b.** There is a one-to-one relationship between data sources and Data Connection objects.

14. **All.** These are all properties of a Data Connection object.

15. **a.** If the database structures are not the same, errors will occur when the different Data Connections are selected for report executions.

About the CD-ROM

The CD included with this book comes complete with the MasterExam software and the electronic version of the book. You can browse the electronic book directly from the CD without installing the software. To take the practice exams, you will need to install MasterExam.

System Requirements

The software requires Windows 98 or later, Internet Explorer 5.0 or above, and 20MB of hard disk space for full installation. The electronic book requires Adobe Acrobat Reader, which is included on the CD.

Installing and Running MasterExam

If your computer's CD-ROM drive is configured to auto run, the CD will automatically start up when you insert the disc. From the opening screen, you can install MasterExam by selecting the MasterExam link. This will begin the installation process and create a program group named LearnKey. To run MasterExam, use Start | Programs | LearnKey. If the auto run feature does not launch your CD, browse to the CD, and click the LaunchTraining.exe icon.

MasterExam provides you with a simulation of the actual exam. The number and type of questions and the time allowed are intended to be an accurate representation of the exam environment. You have the option to take an open book exam, including hints, references, and answers; a closed book exam; or the timed MasterExam simulation. When you launch MasterExam, a digital clock display will appear in the upper left-hand corner of your screen. The clock will continue to count down to zero unless you choose to end the exam before the time expires.

NOTE   To register for a second bonus MasterExam, simply click the Online Training link on the CD's main page and then follow the directions to the free online registration.

Electronic Book

The entire contents of this book are provided in portable document format (PDF). (Adobe Acrobat Reader is included on the CD.) Additional files needed to complete some of the exercises can also be found on the CD.

Help

A help file is provided through the Help button on the main page in the lower left-hand corner. Individual help features are also available through MasterExam.

Removing Installation(s)

MasterExam is installed to your hard drive. For best results when removing the program, use the Start | Programs | LearnKey | Uninstall option to remove MasterExam.

LearnKey Technical Support

For technical problems with the software (installation, operation, removing installations), and for questions regarding the online bonus exam registration, please visit http://www.learnkey.com or e-mail techsupport@learnkey.com.

Content Support

For questions regarding the technical content of the electronic book or MasterExam, please visit http://www.osborne.com or e-mail customer.service@mcgraw-hill.com. For customers outside the 50 United States, e-mail international_cs@mcgraw-hill.com.

INDEX

INTERNATIONAL CONTACT INFORMATION

AUSTRALIA
McGraw-Hill Book Company
Australia Pty. Ltd.
TEL +61-2-9900-1800
FAX +61-2-9878-8881
http://www.mcgraw-hill.com.au
books-it_sydney@mcgraw-hill.com

CANADA
McGraw-Hill Ryerson Ltd.
TEL +905-430-5000
FAX +905-430-5020
http://www.mcgraw-hill.ca

**GREECE, MIDDLE EAST, & AFRICA
(Excluding South Africa)**
McGraw-Hill Hellas
TEL +30-210-6560-990
TEL +30-210-6560-993
TEL +30-210-6560-994
FAX +30-210-6545-525

MEXICO (Also serving Latin America)
McGraw-Hill Interamericana Editores
S.A. de C.V.
TEL +525-1500-5108
FAX +525-117-1589
http://www.mcgraw-hill.com.mx
carlos_ruiz@mcgraw-hill.com

SINGAPORE (Serving Asia)
McGraw-Hill Book Company
TEL +65-6863-1580
FAX +65-6862-3354
http://www.mcgraw-hill.com.sg
mghasia@mcgraw-hill.com

SOUTH AFRICA
McGraw-Hill South Africa
TEL +27-11-622-7512
FAX +27-11-622-9045
robyn_swanepoel@mcgraw-hill.com

SPAIN
McGraw-Hill/
Interamericana de España, S.A.U.
TEL +34-91-180-3000
FAX +34-91-372-8513
http://www.mcgraw-hill.es
professional@mcgraw-hill.es

**UNITED KINGDOM, NORTHERN,
EASTERN, & CENTRAL EUROPE**
McGraw-Hill Education Europe
TEL +44-1-628-502500
FAX +44-1-628-770224
http://www.mcgraw-hill.co.uk
emea_queries@mcgraw-hill.com

ALL OTHER INQUIRIES Contact:
McGraw-Hill/Osborne
TEL +1-510-420-7700
FAX +1-510-420-7703
http://www.osborne.com
omg_international@mcgraw-hill.com

Sound Off!

Visit us at **www.osborne.com/bookregistration** and let us know what you thought of this book. While you're online you'll have the opportunity to register for newsletters and special offers from McGraw-Hill/Osborne.

We want to hear from you!

Sneak Peek

Visit us today at **www.betabooks.com** and see what's coming from McGraw-Hill/Osborne tomorrow!

Based on the successful software paradigm, Bet@Books™ allows computing professionals to view partial and sometimes complete text versions of selected titles online. Bet@Books™ viewing is free, invites comments and feedback, and allows you to "test drive" books in progress on the subjects that interest you the most.